The Diary of George Templeton Strong

THE TURBULENT FIFTIES
1850–1859

The DIARY of
George Templeton Strong

★ ★

THE TURBULENT FIFTIES

1850—1859

EDITED BY

ALLAN NEVINS

AND

MILTON HALSEY THOMAS

THE MACMILLAN COMPANY

New York : 1952

CONTENTS

[*v*]

ILLUSTRATIONS

DRAMATIS PERSONAE

HENRY JAMES ANDERSON. Spending much time in European travel after his retirement as professor of mathematics in Columbia College in 1843, Anderson was converted to Catholicism in Italy. A trustee of Columbia from 1851, he and Strong constantly met at board sessions. "Cautious, rational, and judgmatical," wrote Strong; "clear-headed, money-making, real-estate-buying, demonstrating." He was the "incarnation of a right angle," but he could also refine tiny points and torture arguments like a medieval scholastic.

GEORGE C. ANTHON. The intimacy between Strong and the nephew of his awesome old Latin and Greek professor deepened in the 1850's. Anthon, still unmarried, was one of the most frequent diners at the Strong home and often accompanied the young couple to the opera, concerts, and art exhibitions. When his brief tenure of the professorship of Greek at New York University ended with a summary dismissal in 1851, Strong defended him stoutly, even composing his answer to the Council's charges, though he privately considered him not entirely equal to filling the chair. In the fall of 1853 Anthon began teaching in the Columbia Grammar School under the supervision of his uncle, Professor Charles ("Bull") Anthon.

WILLIAM B. ASTOR. When John Jacob Astor died in 1848, his son (who had previously inherited a large fortune from his uncle, Henry Astor) became the richest man in America. Strong admired him as a "liberal, unostentatious, and intelligent man," and records that he was "always very kind and polite to me." Indeed, Strong was at some of his notable entertainments—including a dinner in 1857 for William L. Marcy, just retired as Secretary of State.

EDWARD KNIGHT COLLINS. One of the tragic figures of this record. The most enterprising of American shipowners, this formidable rival of the Cunard interests lost his liner *Arctic* in 1854 with nearly all on board—including his wife and two children; and a year and a half

[ix]

later another of his best vessels, the *Pacific*, disappeared with all aboard. Strong describes the blow these catastrophes dealt New York.

GEORGE WILLIAM CURTIS. Strong thought the very tame *Nile Notes of a Howadji* indecent, and was a bit shocked when the brilliant and handsome essayist broke his engagement with Eliza Winthrop. But he saw a good deal of George and his brother Burrill, liked them, and admired *Putnam's Magazine*, which George helped edit during part of this decade.

CHARLES PATRICK DALY. As Recorder Daly was both a good judge and a great social favorite, Strong mentions him repeatedly. The marriage of this one-time sailor and carpenter to Miss Maria Lydig, of an aristocratic and wealthy family, was a temporary sensation in New York. Strong hoped that Daly, so wont to "preach and prose," would not "desolate his own fireside as he lays waste foreign fields."

JOHN A. and MORGAN DIX. Despite a distinguished early career as soldier in the War of 1812, member of the "Albany Regency," New York's secretary of state, and United States Senator, and despite great abilities, John A. Dix was in political exile during this period. The Southern slavery men hated him. He was forced to turn to law practice and railroad management. Meanwhile, his gifted son Morgan was advancing in the Episcopal Church, becoming assistant minister of Trinity in 1855 and assistant rector four years later. Strong greatly esteemed and liked both men.

JOHN WHETTEN EHNINGER. Strong's faithful friend "Jack," a young bachelor who had studied painting with Leutze in Düsseldorf and Couture in Paris, was busy illustrating books and exhibiting genre paintings that could be called good but not excellent. He was a Columbia man (1847), and became a National Academician in 1860.

HAMILTON FISH. First governor, then United States Senator, Fish was already counted among the most eminent of Columbia's alumni, and became chairman of the board of trustees in 1859. He united ability, character, wealth, and family prestige. But in the Gibbs controversy his ingrained caution made him play a wobbling part, and Strong was justly critical of his wishy-washy course: "O Piscicule, Piscium minimicule!"

WOLCOTT GIBBS. Just two years younger than Strong, this grandson of Oliver Wolcott had come through Columbia College on the diarist's heels. Then he had given himself the finest possible training in chemistry, studying three years under the best German and French masters. In this decade he was teaching in New York, first at the College of Physicians and Surgeons, and then at the Free Academy (which became City College). He was just the man for the chair of natural and experimental philosophy and chemistry vacated by James Renwick. Strong writes: "Gibbs is a cast-iron man who would take little trouble for me, or any one else, *I think*. But his transcendent abilities and energy must be secured for Col: Coll: if any exertion of mine can put him there." They became warm friends.

FRANCIS GRIFFIN. Son of a law-partner of Strong's father, Yale graduate, and one-time pupil and clerk in the Strong law office, this irascible man behaved badly when the building operations of S. B. Ruggles threatened to involve him in financial loss. Strong calls him "menacing, unjust, merciless, insolent, and cruel"; and he was all that.

ADAM GUROWSKI. A Polish refugee with black mustache, blue spectacles, bearish manners, and a rough tongue. Strong was interested in him at first because he had known Heine and other great Europeans, and cultivated "the men who have ideas." In time, however, the diarist decided that he was intolerably pushing, rude, and boorish.

WILLIAM HENRY HARISON. Lawyer, trustee of Columbia, vestryman of Trinity Church, and for a time comptroller of Trinity Corporation. When he died on May 1, 1860, at Saratoga, Strong—who had seen much of him—wrote that he had been a dominant power in Trinity affairs, and that his churchly zeal, acute mind, retentive memory, and fluent speech had made him useful; but that he showed "a certain arrogance, self-sufficiency, waspishness, a Daniel-Lord-ishness," that rendered him intensely unpopular.

EDWARD YOUNG HIGBEE. Assistant minister of Trinity Church in New York from 1836 until his death in 1871, the Reverend Mr. Higbee was, Strong wrote, "by far the most eloquent and impressive preacher I ever listened to." The name appears almost uniformly as "Higby" in the diary, and the editors finally tired of correcting it.

OGDEN HOFFMAN. When Strong came to the bar, this scion of an old Federalist family, a brother of the Matilda Hoffman beloved by Irving, was a member of Congress from New York City. For two years, 1853–1855, he was attorney-general of the state, and Strong gives a vignette of him as seen at the St. Denis Hotel. "Very loaferish looked the

Attorney-General, with the chewed-up stump of an extinguished cigar in his mouth, a shirt in which he must have loafed for three days and slept two nights, a used-up shooting jacket, blue pantaloons, slippers that were twins only in dirtiness, a wisp of a cravat and no stockings." A chronic basker in the sun, Hoffman lived "like the lilies of the field." But he was a man of brilliance, power, and sincerity, whom Strong greatly valued. When he died the diarist was deeply grieved: "Where will one look for anything like his genial, courteous manner, his mellifluous, brilliant, persuasive talk?"

FRANCIS LIEBER. At the beginning of this decade Lieber filled the chair of history and political economy at the South Carolina College. Strong pronounced him in 1850 "a clever man, but not quite so clever as he thinks himself." In 1853 Lieber produced two learned volumes called *On Civil Liberty and Self-Government;* three years later, having failed of election to the presidency of his college, he resigned and came north; and in 1857, with the backing of Strong and Ruggles, he was made professor at Columbia.

CLEMENT CLARKE MOORE. Oldest member of the Columbia board of trustees. A man of wealth, learning, and exalted character, he filled a long life with good works, but is remembered for a bit of Christmas verse. A staunch Episcopalian and the son of a bishop, he had the courage to vote for giving the Unitarian Wolcott Gibbs a chair at Columbia.

NAPOLEON III. Strong watched his rise to power in France with ironic eye, for he recalled (1855) that the Emperor had once been "a shabby, loafing 'French Count,' an unknown, dirty, *soi-disant* prince," who had frequented disreputable places in New York and left bills unpaid.

GOUVERNEUR MORRIS OGDEN. Lawyer, Trinity vestryman, graduate and trustee of Columbia, and arch-reactionary, this "simple-hearted, sincere, thick-headed, addlebrained son of Adam" led the battle against Wolcott Gibbs, and wrote a pamphlet on the controversy which Strong characterized as "feeble and flat, verbose, wooden, and stupid."

HORATIO POTTER. A dignified, tactful, moderate Episcopal churchman who was made provisional bishop of New York in 1854, and who did much to pour oil on waters ruffled by the Onderdonk controversy (see the first volume of this diary). He became full bishop in 1861. Not to be confused with his more eminent nephew and successor Henry Codman Potter.

SAMUEL B. RUGGLES. Strong's father-in-law, Yale graduate at fourteen, one of the ablest and most public-spirited citizens of New York during a long generation, and the best member of the Columbia board of trustees, labored hard throughout this decade to make Columbia College efficient and progressive. In this endeavor he had the diarist's ardent cooperation. The two bore the brunt of the fight for Wolcott Gibbs. This decade also witnessed the tragic collapse and painful rebuilding of Ruggles's financial fortunes.

WINFIELD SCOTT. At West Point and elsewhere Strong saw a good deal of the hero of the Mexican War. The diary comments on his many foibles—his "bad French and flat jokes, his tedious egotisms, his agonizing pedantries of connoisseurship in wine and cookery, his insipid, inflated gallantries, and his painful exhibitions of suspicious, sensitive conceit." Nevertheless, Strong had high respect for the man.

CHARLES E. STRONG. Cousin, law-partner, and highly congenial companion of the diarist. They had many qualities in common: modesty, interest in literature, industry, and conscientious devotion to duty. Charles's marriage to Eleanor Burrill Fearing in 1850 pleased both George and Ellen Strong. The two young couples saw much of each other.

ELLEN RUGGLES STRONG. Memories of his wife's nearly fatal illness and loss of her first baby in the spring of 1849 haunted the diarist during her second pregnancy in 1851. His relief and joy at the birth of John Ruggles Strong in the autumn of that year were unbounded. The birth of a second son, George Templeton Strong, Jr., in May, 1856, caused less anxiety and brought great happiness. Mrs. Strong, with her keen interest in music, theatre, art, literature, and friends, made their home a gay, stimulating place.

WILLIAM MAKEPEACE THACKERAY. The great novelist made two visits to America during the decade, and impressed Strong as favorably as he did everyone else. As a lecturer, he seemed to the diarist "very effective, clear, and truthful," delivering ideas which had a "plain-spoken, masculine tone," and showing complete "freedom from humbug." At the Century Club and in other social circles he was a very good fellow.

JONATHAN MAYHEW WAINWRIGHT. This English-born churchman, who had taught at Harvard, became provisional bishop of New York in 1852 and died in 1854. At first Strong disliked him. The diarist speaks of his "oleaginous urbanity"; when Wainwright comes back from an English visit with an Oxford D.C.L., we are told that he is "more urbane, more inflated, and much more genteel, like a male turkey polished by travel." But Strong learned to respect the bishop, and in the end paid tribute to his administration as "laborious and earnest" and to the man as "deservedly regretted."

FERNANDO WOOD. Though the Tammany leader was defeated for mayor in 1850 after a former business associate charged him with flagrant frauds, he was elected in 1854, and two years later, with many of the best merchants and professional men behind him, re-elected. Strong thought his initial measures excellent, hailing him in 1855 as "our Civic Hero—inquiring, reforming, redressing, laboring hard with ample result of good." It was not long, however, before he saw Wood as the meretricious demagogue that he was.

1850

The year opened with Strong's law business in Wall Street flourishing, with his health excellent except for a touch of dyspepsia, and with himself and Ellen immersed in a busy social life. He was soon to argue an important civil case against that redoubtable champion of the New York bar, Charles O'Conor. To get rid of the dyspepsia he was beginning to diet, and we find him writing under date of March 20: "I've turned an entirely new leaf—cut Delmonico's, and put myself on a yet shorter allowance of food, the prelude to an entire abstinence therefrom." Among the friends who came most frequently to his house was John Whetten ("Jack") Ehninger, the artist and illustrator, who was just back from study at Düsseldorf under Leutze, and who was to score his first popular success this year with a spirited engraving of Peter Stuyvesant, widely distributed by the American Art Union. The Strongs also began to see something of that eccentric Pole, Baron Gurowski, a man of voluble tongue, fierce prejudices, and irascible temper, destined to attain a certain fame through his cantankerous Civil War diaries. With "society" in the narrow sense, the diarist still had little to do, and he was frankly contemptuous of it. When a wealthy young acquaintance, caught in a scandalous intrigue with a married woman, fled to Havana, Strong moralized (January 21) on the temptations to which the idle rich were subjected. "Words cannot express the destitution and nakedness moral and mental, the threadbare and ragged state of intellectual dilapidation into which, in this country, so barren of excitements and occupations for an idle man, people like Langdon, of vast wealth, weak minds, and no resources within themselves, sooner or later sink."

In Washington the fierce sectional struggle over the spoils of the Mexican War was now well under way. On January 21, 1850, President Taylor in a special message stated his plan for meeting the situation. Eight days later, Henry Clay proposed in the Senate his comprehensive scheme which eventually gave the country the Compromise of this year. However interested in the great conflict between North and South, Strong was more directly concerned with two events nearer home. One was the engagement of Charles E. Strong, after a feverish courtship, to a charming and much-sought-after young woman of fine family, Miss Eleanor B. Fearing. The other was the sudden death of the diarist's brother-in-law John Ruggles. He had gone to California; he wrote that he was about to open a mercantile business in Marysville with $3,000 capital; and then came news of his end.

January 5, SATURDAY.   Another New Year, and the beginning of a new decade. Thus far I have found it a dreary period enough. Were I possessed of a reasonable, average good sense, I should be of good courage, dismiss all my forebodings, and look forward to the happiness which more or less is mixed up with the other ingredients in twelve months of every man's life, and not to the inevitable cares and the possible sorrows that are only made heavier and more bitter by anticipating them—and I should think more of the things to be *done* than of the things to be enjoyed or to be suffered. But I'm not commonly very rational on the subject of borrowing trouble, and for the past week I've been in a particularly uncomfortable and unreasonable state of mind.

However, let that pass while I narrate the events of the week. The soirée of Monday night was very pleasant. . . . Next morning I got up with the sick headache that had been budding for a week fully blown. Couldn't breakfast, dressed at eleven, turned out and made seven or eight calls, and had to go home. Spent the next day moping miserably. Ehninger and Charley [Strong] dined with us, and divers people looked in in the evening. Many calls were made here, people generally expressed vast admiration of the house, and to be sure it's a very handsome house, quite free, I think, from the epidemic of humbug and sham finery and gin-palace decoration.

The two Miss Maurans abandoned us the next day. Thursday evening we had Henry Dorr here, Granby Colcroft, and one *Baron Gurowski*, a remarkable foreigner in a black moustache and blue spectacles, a Russian-ized Pole, much detested by his compatriots as a traitor, and professing an admiration for "liberal" political principles. He may be a Russian spy for aught I know, but he's about the most entertaining man going.[1] At least, despite the difficulties of his jargon of French and German and villainous English, I talked with him from eight till twelve about various matters and people, and especially of Henry Heine and Görres of Munich, *both* of whom he has known intimately. That conjunction of friends is sufficient to shew him a man of catholic and comprehensive taste in choosing his acquaintances, but he says that his chief object in life has been to know those men "die haben Ideas."

Other memoranda of the week: The increasing prosperity of Charley's operations—his next summons, I think, will bring a surrender. Mrs. Woodbury Langdon's party—the Party of the Age—last Thursday; must have cost $4000. Abraham Schermerhorn seriously ill—one lung hepatized, so that he can never recover, though he may live on indefinitely. . . .[2]

January 9, WEDNESDAY. The third day of persevering drizzle and every prospect of a fourth tomorrow. Nothing very new. Invitation to slight musical soirée at the Stevens's last night. Ellie wanted to go sadly, but the weather and I were inexorable. . . .

There's no longer any doubt about the subject of my last ten days' anxiety and wretchedness. God preserve my poor little wife or *take me*, that is all I can write about it.

January 16. *Gratias Deo*. I'm so relieved by finding that we've been mistaken about Ellie's state of health in one particular that I feel as if all the rest were nothing. She has caught a little cold and coughs or "scrapes" more than I care to hear, but I trust it's nothing of moment. She can return to her cod-liver oil now. It has been omitted for the last eight days, and she has rather felt the want of it; and on Friday she proposes, for safety's sake, to try a little counter-irritation. So much for that subject.

---

[1] Adam Gurowski (1805–1866) had come to the United States in 1849. Eccentric, ugly, and ill-tempered, he attracted attention by his fund of European experiences, pushing ways, and genuine ability. For a time he was a translator in the State Department. He poured out books on Russia, Poland, Belgium, Pan-Slavism, and the Turkish question, and in due course published a most untrustworthy series of diaries of Civil War observations.

[2] The Schermerhorns were a numerous family who grew wealthy by mercantile pursuits and prudent marriages. Abraham is listed in Moses Beach's *Wealthy Citizens of New York* (1845) as worth $500,000. J. J. von Görres (1776–1848), mentioned above, was a German publicist.

Charley has had his "consult" with Curtis, who is solemn and sensible and diplomatic.[3]

If it be true that two young people who like each other can't marry on $5,000 a year, then has snobbishness made greater strides towards universal empire in New York than I had deemed possible. Curtis doesn't say so *totidem verbis*, but merely hints a doubt. If such be the fact, I'll come out as the apostle of sumptuary laws and progressive taxation. Better that a sans-culotte mob should invade the Fifth Avenue, better that Wm. B. Astor's estate be subjected to a "benevolence" of fifty per cent, better that vested rights and the sanctity of property be all trodden down into the mire of democracy and Fourierism, than that we should all become snobs together. . . .

January 21, MONDAY. Very rampant Northeaster. Day opened with a deposit of half a foot of sleet and snow which the rain that followed has washed utterly away. Yesterday was pleasant and bright. Went to Trinity Church. Miss Eleanor [Fearing] went with us and dined here. After dinner I walked down to Leonard Street to see after Charley [Strong]. He has erysipelas in his arm. The scissors' scratch (to which were attributed at first the swelling and inflammation) probably brought it out, but any other little accident would have done the same, they say. Bad business, for it has attacked him "not lightly and after the manner of dissemblers," but in very rough earnest, with the usual accessories of fever, restlessness, acute pain and so forth. . . . There are not many people for whose sickness or health I care a very great deal, and Charley is among the more precious of those few. . . .

January 26. . . . Ellen pretty well. Charley improving. Have been calling daily in Leonard Street to see him so that I've had more intercourse with his household—my cousins according to the flesh—in the last week than in all my life before. Doubtless very nice people, but on the whole I "desire we may be better strangers." Very amiable to myself, but their purr always seems to hide a half-suppressed snarl. Charley received his billets from the New York Hotel as regularly as his poultices and his homeopathic belladonna, and I dare say the notes are as emollient and soothing to his sensibilities as the slops and the slippery elm to his inflamed cellular tissues. Certainly those daily despatches and their very decided expression of interest and anxiety and sympathy and so on are conclusive as an implied *assumpsit*.

[3] Probably George Curtis (1796–1856), New York banker, acting as Miss Fearing's guardian.

Arthur and George Jones sail for Havana Monday. Arthur's health is a good deal damaged, probably by suppers, late hours, and the other trials incident to a New York season of soirées. . . . Mr. Ruggles back from Washington. He reports the South very rampant and a good deal in earnest. Probably they will go into convention, and there will be much fuss and many speeches more or less eloquent, and that will produce a panic and United States fives will fall like lead. But I think the convention will be a safety valve that will save us from an explosion, though things are not in a comfortable state, and it is not easy to see our way out of the complication we're in very distinctly. No doubt a small party at the South wants dissolution for its own sake, because they prefer being first in a Southern confederacy to being second-rate and insignificant in the Union. And the great body of slaveholders certainly have troubles and trials, grievances, perhaps, that may well make them restless and uneasy and may account for their being unreasonable, though it's not easy to see what they would gain by dissolution. All the slaves in the frontier states of the new confederation would run away the first night. Mr. Garrison and Abby Folsom would set up agencies for the seduction and reception of fugitive niggers all along the line.[4] The bitterest feeling of hatred would arise between the two rival nations and the North would become enthusiastic in abolition—and frontier disputes would be followed by servile wars in the *outside* states that would compel them to abolish slavery for their own peace and quiet and to save their property and their lives, and so anti-slavery would gradually march towards the South. Nothing but rigid non-intercourse could save them. . . .

February 1, FRIDAY. Delicious weather for a day or two past. Just looked over *Pendennis* No. 12, ending Vol. 1. Clever, decidedly. Stopped as I came uptown at the Huntington Exhibition—a blunder in Mr. Huntington, though there are some nice things in the lot.[5] But his mind is not fertile and he repeats himself and a collection of his works forces his mannerism and his tautologies on everybody's notice. *Don Giovanni* Tuesday night; a glorious composition, but much damaged and defaced in the performance. The Don is a gentleman (in the George the Fourth sense), whereas Beneventano enacts a rank and unmitigated brute Bowery

[4] Abigail H. Folsom was a worthy but deranged abolitionist whom Emerson called "that flea of conventions"; she had been nearly as prominent as William Lloyd Garrison in various New England gatherings.

[5] Daniel Huntington (1816–1906), who had studied painting under Morse and Inman and had spent some time in Italy, was already well known for landscapes and historical subjects, but above all as a portrait painter.

roué, and suggests no ideas but those of adultery and fornication and all manner of uncleanness. Bertucca is but a mechanical sort of Zerlina, and Donna Anna gives Truffi nothing to do that allows of her showing her strong points. . . .

Ellen still doing well. Charley downtown today. Abraham Schermerhorn worse and sinking fast.

February 2.   Ellen has put on blister No. 2 today, by way of precaution. Thank Heaven winter is half gone. I say *half*, for March is the fourth winter month. Take out the Diurnal chiefly to chronicle the fact that Charley is probably now—8 P.M.—in a state of nervous irritability, for he was to go, by appointment, to the New York Hotel tonight, and expected to bring about a crisis. I've no doubt at all that the crisis will terminate favorably, but I suppose he may be going upstairs just at this moment, and if he is, his philosophy is doubtless leaving him at the rate of a pound for each step.

February 4.   March weather of the most malignant sort. Ellen pretty well today. . . . Came home early and walked down with her to look at Huntington's pictures. Second visit affirms the decision of the first. It's an inferior assortment. Alarm of fire this morning as I was walking downtown. Crossed the Park to look for it and found that a fearfully destructive accident had just happened. The boiler of a steam engine in some kind of factory in Hague Street (one of the complicated alleys that constitute the "Swamp") had exploded, knocking the building to flinders. The whole structure collapsed and settled down into a heap of ruins, in one moment, they say, and with about 120 operatives *in it*. A few had been taken out of the burning pile of rubbish, dead or dying; many more were alive beneath it. The loss of life is not certainly known, but probably fifty people are killed or desperately hurt.[6]

Poor Charley! More bedevilment and bewilderment of the insanest kind, which I won't write down here. I trust matters are coming out right, and I'm sure I devoutly hope so, for he's now involved so far that failure would be a calamity to him. But that can hardly happen, from present appearances. Abraham Schermerhorn died yesterday, in spite of his half million.

February 10, SUNDAY. . . . The past week has been a week to remember, entirely delightful and happy. I walked downtown on the Tuesday morn-

[6] A large boiler in A. B. Taylor's machine-shop at 5 Hague Street, exploding at eight o'clock in the morning, had brought down the six-story building. During the week sixty-three dead bodies were taken from the ruins.

ing, as I well remember, feeling some little misgivings about Charley's fortunes, but on the whole, of good courage. He marched radiant into the office ten minutes after I got there, and announced the result, and we did *not* apply ourselves very diligently to our professional engagements for the rest of that day. To tell the truth, the week has been a lazy one. I've been luxuriating on the spectacle of Charley's beatitude, and only not quite as delighted as he.

Tuesday night I took Ellie to the opera. Suydam's box transferred to us for a few nights; *Don Giovanni*. Mrs. Ruggles went with us. Wednesday evening we called at the New York Hotel and carried Miss Eleanor off, and after a while Charley joined us, and the public opened eyes and adjusted opera glasses. Thursday, the little lady dined with us, also Miss Ellen Rogers, Charley, and Jack Ehninger, and very nice it was. Friday as I was walking uptown, dirty and deliquescent, I saw Miss Eleanor making signals from a carriage window, and assuming it to be her own private particular hack, I bolted in without ceremony, and found myself making the fourth to a trio of Ellen, Miss Eleanor, and her mamma. Yesterday our little cousin-elect spent the day here, and Charley came to dine, and they went home at eight to be quiet and happy together. So it has happened that I've seen Miss Eleanor almost every day since her engagement. . . .

February 11, MONDAY. . . . To church yesterday. Heard a remarkable sermon from Wainwright . . . and Higby in the afternoon. Listened to John Ruggles's very interesting letter to his father, bringing his wanderings down to October 28th and Vancouver, and then settled into a malignant sick headache. . . .

February 17, SUNDAY. Charley is still in a very sunshiny condition indeed. His engagement is slowly breaking from behind the clouds upon the astounded public. Laight and Hoffman and all the fellowship of her disgusted admirers look blank and black. The rest of the world are loud in their felicitations. I'm specially anxious that they should set up their tabernacle in this neighborhood, for if they don't I foresee that the difficulty of keeping our two households as intimate as they ought to be will prove fatal in the long run.

It is delicious to be in the society of so happy a man as Charley, so happy and so hopeful and so outrageously in love. Schiller is right—to have "lived and loved" is to know the length and breadth of the happiness this earth can give. That happiness can endure for a longer or a shorter time, but all the treasures and resources of the world cannot increase it.

He who possesses it has but one piece of good fortune more to wish—
that he may die *before* it is taken from him. It's hard to realize how much
there is in the world besides what comes under our own eyes—how many
thousands there are tonight in gay capitals and secluded little towns, in
stately old ancestral homes, and around humble firesides, everywhere,
from the long resounding fjords of the North to the bright shores of the
Mediterranean, watched over by the still white summits of Alpine peaks,
listening to the winds sighing through miles of Russian pine forest,
lulled to happy sleep tonight by the distant sounds of English fog, or of
the Baltic surf upon its sandhills, dreaming of making love in every
language, tongue, speech, and dialect. How many thousands of capital
fellows as happy as Charley, and each with the same sufficient reason,
and all with the same blue sky and bright stars looking quietly down on
their happiness. Think of the thousands of beautiful girls, too, blonde and
brunette of every shade, simple-hearted little rusticities not dressed in
the best taste, and radiant, highbred beauties of every degree, whose
little hands are trembling and whose little heads are swimming *tonight*,
as they think of the mighty event of the last week and of the announcements and congratulations of tomorrow.

A man who could fairly and fully get hold of that idea could write a
"Song of Joy" that would rival Schiller's and could arrange a choral
symphony for it that should bang Beethoven's.

And then, if he will—as I won't—let him reverse the picture, and try
to realize the tears that are flowing and the hearts that are breaking, or
worse, withering away in slow sorrow all over the earth, at this moment.

February 21, THURSDAY. . . . Trinity Church vestry meeting Tuesday
night. Alienation of the endowment of St. George's (including the Beekman Street Church) agreed to on certain conditions. Not clear that they
can be carried out by St. George's. Voted against the whole proposition,
having a weakness for the inviolability of all endowments in real estate. . . .

February 26. Half-past eleven P.M. Tired and jaded and fagged out
with several days of quite hard work, sitting up till one or two every
night. Charley and Miss Eleanor spent this evening here, and I couldn't
devote it to Ray *v.* Van Hook or Furniss *v.* Brown. These two litigations
are my chief incubi at present. The latter especially looks squally and unpromising. Cutting and Nat Blunt and Prescott Hall are all mixed up in
it. Cutting's for Brown, and I think he's a little alarmed at Brown's
prospects.[7] I'm not less so at Furniss's and we both want to settle, but

[7] Francis B. Cutting (1804–1870), who later entered Congress.

can't tell how to do it. . . . Charley's going on with the buying of furniture in great activity, and has all but concluded his purchase of a lot on the other side of Gramercy Square. Shan't feel easy until the lot's bought, the house built, and they've moved in.

March 4, MONDAY. . . . Saturday night was charming. Took Ellie to the Philharmonic. First I've attended for two years. It was that well-remembered dark A Symphony, the most essentially Beethovenish production extant so far as I know, and selections from Mendelssohn's lovely *Midsummer Night's Dream* music. . . .

As to the Symphony in A, I hold it to be an immoral composition—immoral just as *Childe Harold* is immoral, from the absence of good rather than the presence of evil. Don't that sound like *puppyism?*

The debate in the Senate on Clay's compromise plan rose to a climax this month. On March 4, Calhoun, his life almost done, tottered into the chamber to hear Mason of Virginia read the last great speech that the South Carolinian wrote. It contained an eloquent plea for the South and her institutions. Calhoun opposed both Clay's and President Taylor's schemes for meeting the current crisis. He wished the North to give the South equal rights in the new Western territories; to enforce faithfully the Fugitive Slave Act; to stop the anti-slavery agitation; and to consent to constitutional changes which would give the South full rights of self-protection. "If you of the North will not do this," Calhoun warned, "then let our Southern states separate and depart in peace." Webster followed on March 7th with one of the most famous and most courageous of all his public utterances. Pleading for the Union and the Constitution, and pronouncing peaceable secession an impossibility, he gave emphatic approval to Clay's proposals. While abolitionists and radical free-soil men denounced Webster violently, many moderate Northern Whigs rallied behind him.

March 9. Notabilities of the day. Calhoun's speech and Webster's are both clear, strong, and statesmanlike efforts. Calhoun's grand fallacy is the notion of an "equilibrium between North and South." Why should the Potomac be a recognized landmark rather than the Mississippi, and why should not Arkansas lift up her voice and lament that there is a want of equilibrium between the states east of the Father of Waters and those west thereof? California gold is coming in—I hate California and its gold. N.B. Little Ogden Hoffman is going there, in hope that his one talent of multitudinous words, his one faculty of unlimited gab, may be made auriferous at San Francisco. It has not proved pecuniary here. . . . I get bluer and more blue as I write of anything connected with California. I don't see how any of its gold is to get in to my pockets, and I'm thinking of the possibility—a probability according to T. Butler King and other intelligent people—of such an influx of money into the world as shall make the article cheap and those who have it poor.

March 20. Charley is in a jolly state. He was here with Miss Eleanor last night. That little lady has been quite ill with influenza. Ante-nuptial settlements in process of construction.

Trial of Dr. Webster has begun.[8] Jury will probably disagree. Don't think they will acquit, unless the defense has some new matter to set up in avoidance of what the prosecution say they'll prove. Improbable as it seems, I fear Webster is guilty.

I stopped at Ehninger's atelier this afternoon. His "Peter Stuyvesant" is very creditable indeed for so young a beginner. Saw two lovely little cabinet-size landscapes there, by Saal and Weber; the former I did covet most criminally. I am tempted to the sin of covetous longing and "inordinate desire" by nothing more strongly than by a really lovely landscape. Even a *natural* landscape inspires me with the feeling. I never can see, for example, a beautiful summer sunset with its soft horizontal light streaming among the trees, or poured over green fields, or blended with cool shadow as it falls among the slopes and swellings of any commonplace tract of uneven ground, without coveting what I see, wishing to go to somebody's shop and buy that very thing. And the consciousness that I *can't* always dashes a little subdued annoyance into the pleasure of the sight. Lucky that people can't buy such things. How some of our Fifth Avenue people would monopolize the brightness of the earth if they could, to add splendor to their soirées and to decorate their supper tables. . . .

March 26. . . . Webster's trial advancing slowly, but making a decided advance every day. Very black lookout for poor Prof. Webster at present. The defense has not yet shewn its hand and it's impossible to tell what they mean to set up. Public opinion has settled down against the accused. Scarcely a voice is raised in his favor now. If he is innocent, this is the

---

[8] The trial of Professor John White Webster of Harvard for the murder of Dr. George Parkman, which attracted universal interest, lasted eleven days. John H. Clifford defended Webster, after Rufus Choate had (it is said) refused to take the case. When 116 witnesses had been examined, and Dr. Parkman's dentist had identified the teeth of the corpse which Webster had tried to burn, the jury found the defendant guilty.

cruelest case on record of circumstantial evidence leading to false conclusions.

March 31. . . . Easter Sunday. Wainwright at Calvary this morning. That parish, by the by, is in huge agitation. New ticket got up for vestry, omitting Comstock and Carpenter and Mr. D. H. Hoyt. If it succeeds, the church may be saved. If it fails, Dr. Comstock will probably be speedily relieved from all cares of office by the intervention of the mortgagers, the sheriff, and the power of the county (if necessary). .

Dr. Webster convicted of murder! He hurt himself much by a preposterous speech after the summing up was closed—petulant in manner and improbable in its statements, and such as only a mean, cowardly, shabby, treacherous man could have made, for he seems to have accused his counsel, by implication, of mismanaging his case and keeping back testimony he could have given—insinuated pretty distinctly that if he were convicted, it would be their fault. A most cruel thing to say in a capital case. Only a scoundrel at heart would have sought to better his chance with a jury by such a miserable device. Poor man, his choice now is between strychnine and strangulation, for he ought not to hope for a commutation of punishment. The executive must assume him to be guilty, and if guilty, to spare him would be a sin against God and man, against civil society, and against the thousands of men hanged for less atrocious crimes, because ignorant, illiterate, and friendless. Apropos of the gallows, we have Carlyle's Latter Day Tract No. 2, *Model Prisons and Capital Punishment*. May it prove tonic as moral quinine to the weakly sentiments and paralyzed moral sense of the philanthropists and humbugs whom he seeks to convert; Mrs. Kirkland, Judge Edmonds, and John Jay and that tribe of soft-brained, nerveless sufferers from the lack of moral virility. . . .

April 2, TUESDAY.   Charley just left and Ellen and little Miss Eleanor [Fearing] are upstairs together. It's charming to have that little lady here and Charley coming up to see her and to spend some of those most precious hours of every man's existence—the time spent with his fiancée —under this roof. A house gains a kind of domestic consecration from goings-on of that sort. Births and deaths and marriages and all the events of social life, pleasant meetings, nice visits, sorrowful partings, household troubles escaped or endured—of such things is made up the Life, as it were, of every Dwelling Place of Men—and the neat new house that has had no time to be the theatre of human action and sorrow and joy, and has no *past* to be remembered or imagined by those who sojourn in it, is like a western prairie, or an unexplored tropical forest when thought of in connection with the richly storied towns and cities of the Old World, where generation has followed generation of our brethren in faith linked to each other and to us by community of thought and hope and aim and interest—and motive, and every human passion and principle.

I never pass the old Fourth Avenue house of last year and look up at those windows through which the sun shone in upon the nameless horrors of that 16th of April last, without thinking how much every common-place abode in this city has to tell of the tragedy and comedy of life that has passed within it—how little there is in a world of men that is not far from commonplace or insignificant in itself or its associations. How serious a thing is in any row of monotonous twenty-five-foot brick fronts, if one considers what each of them has witnessed or will witness. . . .

April 10, WEDNESDAY. . . . At a Trinity Church vestry meeting Monday evening. Annexation of Calvary Church brought forward by Philip Hone.[9] The proposition scared up young Harison and others to oppose, and if it's ever acted on favorably, it will be after a hard struggle. Referred at last to the Standing Committee. Then followed a discussion about making the appointments of Haight and Hobart during pleasure, instead of from year to year, and that change was made. . . .

Charley's wedding day draws near. Don't find that he's much afflicted by the prospect of its coming. Went over his house with him this morning. Nearly furnished, and looking very bright and very snug. . . .

April 19, FRIDAY. . . . Charley was married yesterday. We went early, calling on our way to pick up Miss Josephine Mauran, and were first on the ground. The ceremony was badly performed by [the Rev. Orville] Dewey. Both parties a good deal agitated—a parlour is far more trying to the nerves than a church. Eleanor saved herself from tears and hysterics and so forth only by a strong and visible effort, for she was evidently in great nervousness and excitement and left the room immediately after the ceremony. I was surprised that Charley felt it so strongly, for I well remember how nonchalant I felt when undergoing the same process, and I was much more likely to have been embarrassed than he. But he was infected, I suppose, by the tremors of his pretty little bride and sympathized in the struggle she was making to control herself. They were married exactly at twelve. I stayed an hour or so, talked to Dr. Johnston,

[9] The former mayor and diarist (1780–1851), whose appointment by Taylor as naval officer in the New York custom-house had given him a respite from poverty, was now in rapidly failing health.

Mr. and Mrs. Paige, Miss Schmidt, Miss Annie Jaudon, Hamilton
Hoppin, Jem Strong, and so on. Cut a variety of cousins intentionally
and accidentally. Came downtown at one, and Mr. and Mrs. Charley
took flight at four by the New Haven Railroad, en route for Boston. . . .

April 22.   Just from hearing the *Favorita* by the Havana Company at
Niblo's. Tremendous house, immense enthusiasm, and an undeniably
admirable performance. Steffanone falls a little short of my expectations,
but the power and expression and cultivation of the tenor (Salvi) triumphed
over all deficiencies in the rest—and gave a tone and character to the
whole performance quite beyond anything in the way of opera I've ever
heard. Of course I speak merely of the execution, not of the music executed, for the *Favorita*, though more to my taste than anything of Donizetti's I've heard, and full of passages that actually mean something
beyond mere vocalization (not a great deal, to be sure) is but a weak and
watery treatment to sit under for three hours. . . .

April 24. . . . At the Academy of Design with Ellen this afternoon. A
few nice pictures there. Influence of the Düsseldorf exhibition very manifest. Long interview Tuesday with Higby, Parks, and Wainwright about
the proposed annexation of Calvary Church. They are very zealous in
the cause. Perhaps endangering their object by pushing it too hard.
Berrian has come out dead against it. Dunscomb and Harison and probably the Chief Justice will back him, so there's no chance of putting it
through just now. I shall advise a masterly inactivity, for if the measure
be pressed it must fail. . . .

April 28, sunday. . . . Went to Niblo's Friday night with Ellie,
Charley *et ux.*, and her cousin Miss Watson of Providence. *Macbeth*,
almost scene-for-scene with the tragedy, and absurd enough is the attempt
to marry Northern legend to modern Italian music, even were the legend
not canonized and beatified by Shakespeare, and the music not that of
Verdi. The music is Verdiesque. Screaming unisons everywhere, and all
the melodies of that peculiar style the parallel whereof is rope-dancing;
first a swing and flourish, hanging on by the hands, then a somerset, and
then another swing to an erect position on the rope, a few shines cut
there, and then down again. The unfortunate man is incapable of real
melody—his airs are such as a man born deaf would compose by calculation of the distances of musical notes and the intervals between them.
His *supernatural* music in this opera is especially comical. Like very many
of his brethren of this day, the deluded author has no means whatever of
expressing *feeling* in music except by a coarse daubing of *color*. Passion

is typified and portrayed by a musical phrase instrumented with the brass; softer emotion by the same phrase written for the oboes and flutes; terror by ditto through the medium of the brasses judiciously heightened with the big drums and the ophicleide; and so of every other subject of musical expression. . . .

May 26, SUNDAY. . . . Sad news from the Pacific—John Ruggles died at sea on the 6th.

I have been occupied Friday and yesterday from morning till night examining Turnbull *de bene esse*, and last night I took tea at Mr. Ruggles's, where Ellen had been spending the day. At about nine o'clock, Mr. Ruggles was called out into the hall, and a few minutes after he sent for me, and I found him with a young man named Moore, who had left San Francisco with John, in the *Tennessee*, April 19th, and reached here (via the Isthmus) yesterday in the *Crescent City*. There was also a letter from Dr. Pattison of Goshen, one of John's business connections at Marysville, who left with him and took care of him, and on the arrival of the *Crescent City*, went straight to Goshen.

The news was broken to his mother and sister last night, and a cruel time it was.

John left about the end of April last year, during poor Ellen's terrible illness, and with George Gibbs joined the Rifle Regiment and proceeded overland to the mouth of the Columbia, and thence by sea to San Francisco, leaving Gibbs in Oregon. He reached San Francisco the 9th February, with health fully restored, and there formed a partnership with this Dr. Pattison and one Browne, late of this city, and as I suspect, a very questionable kind of person. Alfred Seton was also a partner, or in some way connected with the concern. They were to carry on their business at Yubaville (or Marysville), the head of navigation on the Feather River, and thither they went with goods purchased at San Francisco. There seems to have been much fatigue and exposure in the shipment of their goods and landing them at this place. It was done in a season of pouring rain, by John and his associates personally. Their store and dwelling place was some kind of canvas house, probably an insufficient defense from the weather. All this brought on an attack of diarrhoea, and this was followed by another. Then he was affected with a swelling (probably scrofulous, for he had that disease in his system, I fear) of the glands of the neck, and Pattison advised him that he must return home or die. But he could not come back with nothing accomplished; he said he would succeed in California, or die there, and probably postponed his departure till it was too late.

He seems to have had every attention and help that the place could furnish, but labor and exposure and the climate of the country were steadily undermining his constitution. Meanwhile, Browne's movements were unsatisfactory to his associates. The purchase of lots in Marysville and of the two iron houses appears to have been made with partnership funds, but on his private account, and Pattison determined to abandon the concern and return home. He prevailed on John to accompany him. They left San Francisco April 19th. John's health was then improving, and a few days at sea so far restored him that he probably thought care and prudence no longer necessary. The *Tennessee* put in at Acapulco and was there three days. Pattison made an expedition into the country, and John went ashore and exposed himself in the sun. When Pattison rejoined the steamer John had had a violent relapse; his disorder had become dysentery, very possibly of a malignant type; he was delirious, and I suppose past help. This was on the 5th, the day the steamer left Acapulco. On the 6th, he was insensible and sinking. Pattison stayed by him, exhibiting stimulants every hour, but that night he died, and the next morning at eleven the engines of the steamer were stopped, passengers and crew assembled on the quarter deck, the burial service was read, and poor John was consigned to his grave in the ocean.

I never knew John *intimately*. In fact, I doubt whether anyone but his mother had his full confidence, such was the reserve and independence and shyness of his character. He was social and gay and popular, but he was confiding with but few, and shrunk from the sympathy of a stranger, and even of his own family, in his troubles and distresses, of which he had enough. But though I never knew him very well, I could appreciate the manliness and honesty and force of his character, his sincerity and freedom from humbug and cant, the genuineness and reality and earnestness of everything he thought and said and did, right or wrong. He was fast working himself free of all the eccentricities and errors that at one time made him pass with his friends for much less than he was worth, and a year or two longer would have shewn him to every one to be the sterling kind of person I always upheld him for. . . .

June 16, SUNDAY. . . . Memorabilia of the past week, few—except the "Rochester knockings," which enlightened performances I've attended twice, and about which I'm mystified.[10] The production of the sounds is hard to explain, and still stranger is the accuracy with which the ghosts guess of whom one is thinking—his age, his residence, vocation, and the like. They do this correctly nine times out of ten at least, where the inquirer is a stranger to the Exhibitors, where he is asking about people of whom they can know nothing, and where he asks the question by pointing to a series of words and figures, some right and some wrong, from which the ghost picks the right one as infallibly as the learned pig did the letters of the alphabet.

The chances are a thousand to one that this is produced by some sleight of hand, and skill in the indications, furnished by the face and the voice of the inquirer. But may there not possibly be some magnetic or electrical or mesmeric agency at work which is employed by these (very commonplace) women, perhaps without their being able to explain or describe it themselves? A systematic trick and deliberate legerdemain producing these results is about as incomprehensible and as difficult to believe.

As to the supernatural theory which so many people are swallowing whole, I can't quite take it down. Not because I see any impossibility in ghostly communications, nor because I think the trifling and undignified demeanor of these ghosts conclusive evidence against their genuineness, for we know absolutely nothing of the laws of spiritual existence, and for aught we can tell "there may be as great fools out of the flesh as there are in it"; but because, all things considered, it seems much more likely to me that some obscure, occult, mysterious, but *natural* agency should be concerned, *if* anything but adroit humbug is concerned in the matter.

July 9, TUESDAY. . . . Very busy today. Tonight to Mr. Ruggles's and thence to Mr. Ray's, where I spent a couple of hours. The President very ill—the indomitable Zachary is all but succumbing to cholera morbus with typhoid symptoms, and one telegraphic despatch announced that he was not likely to get through the day. I hope he may be spared, for his death would be a calamity at this time. . . .

[10] The Rochester rappings were the work of Margaret and Kate Fox, daughters of a farmer of Hydesville, Wayne County, New York. Their prankish tappings were accepted by their mother as the work of spirits; and when an elder married sister living in Rochester took the girls to that city, the mysterious sounds attracted wider attention. In the summer of 1850 the sister brought the pair to New York for seances which proved highly remunerative. Horace Greeley gave them publicity in the *Tribune*, and they helped to make spiritualism a potent cult. Margaret ultimately confessed that the rappings had been produced by toe movements.

July 11.   At home again. The President died at half-past ten Tuesday evening. A very unhappy event, not only because he was a good and upright man, such as is uncommon in high office, but because everybody North and South had a vague sort of implicit confidence in him, which would have enabled him to guide us through our present complications much better than his "accidental" successor, of whom nobody knows much, and in whom no party puts any very special trust or faith.[11]

Went to West Point last evening; returned this morning by the *Columbus.* The boat is not of the first class by any means, but a decent sloop would be better than that filthy railroad. It is aggravating, though, to see the trains come squealing and stinking after us as we lounge up the river and rush past and out of sight as if our meek little steamboat were at anchor. . . .

July 29, MONDAY. . . . Horrid, hot day, the severest of the season. Came to town this morning. Went up Saturday afternoon with Miss Rosalie, who's to spend a fortnight with us, also Mr. Ruggles, Jem, and Professor Lieber. Lieber is a clever man, but not quite so clever as he thinks himself. He regards himself as a drilled and disciplined Coleridge, but he's no such thing.[12] Nothing new at the Point, except Spencer, Lord Bishop of Jamaica, who officiated at church yesterday and with whom I've had some long talks, a very intelligent, courteous, dignified, agreeable person—and except Charley and Mrs. Charley, who returned from Niagara and Trenton Saturday.

September 2, MONDAY. . . . Jenny Lind has arrived, and was received with such a spontaneous outbreak of rushing, and crowding, and hurrahing, and serenading as this city has never seen before. The streets round the Irving House blocked up with a mob night and day; horses hardly permitted to carry her through the streets, so vehemently did the mob thirst for the honor of drawing her carriage, and so on. Really it's very

[11] The death of President Taylor, who was taking a stubborn position in favor of his own plan for ending the sectional dispute, and whose quarrel with such Southern leaders as Robert Toombs threatened to end in war, opened the way to a peaceable settlement. Millard Fillmore, succeeding to the White House, threw the Administration influence behind Clay's compromise plan.

[12] Francis Lieber (1800–1872), professor in South Carolina College, had just attracted much attention by a series of letters on the problems of slavery addressed to Calhoun, arguing the unsoundness of the institution and declaring the position of the South untenable. Though not published, they were seen by many. Nationally famous as teacher, lecturer, and writer on history, government, and politics, Lieber kept in touch with numerous influential Northerners. Aubrey George Spencer (1795–1872), Bishop of Jamaica, was an authority on Negro life in his island.

strange—Miss Jenny is a young lady of very great musical taste, and possessed of a larynx so delicately organized that she can go up to A *in alto* with brilliancy and precision, and sing with more effect than any other living performer. Furthermore, she is a good, amiable, benevolent woman, fully equal, I dare say, to the average of our New York girls; and having in her vocal apparatus a fortune of millions, she devotes a liberal share of it to works of charity. But if the greatest man that has lived for the last ten centuries were here in her place, the uproar and excitement could not be much greater and would probably be much less. . . .

Jenny Lind, brought to America by P. T. Barnum, arrived in New York on the steamship Atlantic *on Sunday, September 1st, and was greeted with the wildest enthusiasm. Shipping, piers, and wharves were covered with thousands of spectators who roared their delight as she passed through two triumphal arches, one inscribed "Welcome, Jenny Lind!" and the other "Welcome to America!" Within ten minutes after she reached the Irving House, no fewer than twenty thousand persons had massed about the entrance. At midnight that night she was serenaded by the New York Musical Fund Society; and other displays of popular enthusiasm, adroitly stimulated by Barnum, marked the ensuing days.*

Strong had taken his family to West Point for the summer, and paid frequent visits to that place by steamboat or rail. He saw much of all the teachers there, including Dennis Hart Mahan, professor of civil and military engineering; William H. C. Bartlett, professor of natural and experimental philosophy; and Jacob W. Bailey, professor of chemistry, mineralogy, and geology. The superintendent of the institution was Henry Brewerton, who, two years later, would give way to Robert E. Lee. Strong became especially intimate with Professor Bailey, who interested him in Infusoria; for Bailey was adept with the microscope and made some important improvements in it. There was a pleasant social life at the post, with dances, dinners, and teas. One of Strong's casual jottings reads: "Some of the officers got up a series of Shakespeare readings last winter by way of varying the routine of mess life. One of their readings was new and remarkable. Ophelia replies to a question of Hamlet's by asking another, 'Honest, my lord?' Alexander (I think) who knows more of artillery practice and topographical engineering than of polite literature, read it with great emphasis and expression, thus: 'Honest?!! My Lord!!' "

Other brief items concern Charles Astor Bristed, who had published a letter castigating "a Lord Somebody whom he fêted here and who cut him in London"; a fashionable young man, Jerry Van Rensselaer, "who ought to be whipped, if only for his ostentatious parade of retail adultery and uncleanness on a cash basis, not only in this iniquitous city, but even among the staid and sharp-sighted moral philosophers of Boston"; and Professor Webster, who was duly hanged "and seems to have conducted himself with much gravity and decorum on that very trying occasion." On September 4th he noted: "Jenny Lind mania undiminished."

September 9. . . . . Dined with George Anthon, who's just about entering on his academic duties in that white marble building that calls itself a university, on Washington Square.[13] Honorable post—hope it won't be a barren one. Will he marry his last love? By his account he can if he will, but I fear he's a very *fainéant* kind of wooer, and will never bring his case to a crisis, though he seems in love to the full extent of his faculties. . . .

Jenny Lind mania continues violent and uncontrolled. Auction of seats for her first concert Saturday; Genin the hatter took seat No. 1 at $225, Moffat and Brandreth bidding against him—a rare conjunction of asses.

Congress has acted at last on the great Southern problem; passed the Texas and California bills, checked the Southern chivalry in the generation of gas, and blighted the hopes of Billy Seward and his gang of incendiaries, who wanted to set the country on fire with civil war that they might fill themselves with place and profit in the confusion. Extreme people on both sides much disgusted with the result, but the great majority satisfied and relieved. For there was some cause for anxiety. Texas and little South Carolina would probably have run into their holes when they found the general government was going to maintain its rights, and was prepared to substitute light artillery and mounted riflemen for proclamations and Congressional eloquence; but there might have been some sort of armed resistance got up among the lank loafers of the Texan frontier, and if a single horse-stealer had been knocked in the head by Uncle Sam's regulars, a serious breeze might have sprung up. I'm glad it's settled, though it would have been refreshing to see Texas snubbed

[13] It was natural for a Columbia College man to speak somewhat slightingly of New York University, now but twenty years old; although Albert Gallatin had helped found it, and S. F. B. Morse, a faculty member, had conducted there his experiments with the telegraph.

and South Carolina spanked. That preposterous little state is utterly below the city of New York or Boston or Philadelphia in resources, civilization, importance, and everything else; but Goliath of Gath with all his war paint on was not a more obstreperous, intolerable braggart and bully. . . .

David Hubbell Hoyt has made a shocking bad break, swindling the *Churchman*, it's said, for which he was some sort of agent. Did Kearny out of $500. . . . Apropos of Hoyt, one of the pillars of the Calvary Church and the great man of its present vestry, Hawks is said to have accepted its call; conditionally, that is, on its being made very loud—$6,000 a year and some provision for that insolvent shepherd's arrears of debt. He's the Jenny Lind of the Church.[14]

September 17, TUESDAY. . . . Strolled the Battery for an hour after sunset very pleasantly, and watched the shoals of people pouring into the Garden to hear Jenny. She is like the good little girl in the fairy story who spat pearls and diamonds out of her mouth whenever she opened it to speak; only Jane's expectorations are five-dollar bills each syllable, a variation that suits the more prosaic imagery of the nineteenth century. The house at her first concert holding $36,000 worth, how much did each semi-quaver realize to the parties interested? . . .

Call from Comstock this morning to discuss Calvary Church and frighten me into a surrender of my pew for the consideration of scrip payable at the Greek Calends, to help carry out the arrangement with Hawks. Was not frightened much. Shall write him word that I may be induced to surrender on receiving exactly what I paid, not otherwise.

[14] The Rev. Francis Lister Hawks (1798–1866) was a smooth-tongued North Carolinian who had been a lawyer, legislator, and supreme court reporter in his native state prior to his ordination in the Episcopal church in 1827. While rector of St. Thomas's Church in New York he was made historiographer of his denomination and spent several months in 1836 working in English church archives; the first two volumes of his Episcopal church history met with such unfavorable reception that he abandoned the project. When his church school in Flushing failed for $30,000 in 1843, Hawks removed to Holly Springs, Mississippi. Elected bishop there, he encountered opposition in the General Convention of 1844, and though he was cleared after his "great Apologetic oration" which Strong reported (Oct. 14), he declined the post and various other bishoprics offered to him. He was rector in New Orleans for five years and also first president of the University of Louisiana. He returned to New York in 1849 and became rector of Calvary Church, remaining until his Southern sympathies compelled his resignation in 1862 (see the entry for Oct. 15). Living in Baltimore during the remainder of the war, he was back in New York with plans for a new church in 1865, but after the cornerstone laying in September, 1866, his health broke down and he died the same month. Strong never esteemed him more highly than these entries would suggest, and one looks in vain in his biography for any traces of spirituality.

Hawks is a humbug. He says he admires the character of St. Paul mainly because when that apostle's field of usefulness was exhausted in one place, he invariably emigrated in the most disinterested way to another, regardless of perils in the great deep or elsewhere; and leaves his hearers to observe for themselves the apostolic precedent for his own nomadic propensities. I say he's more like a medieval leech, traveling through the country to bleed and shave his customers. . . .

September 24. . . . Dined at Cozzens's with General Scott on Sunday; [Henry Augustus] Wise and his wife (daughter of Boston Everetts), both intensely ugly and decidedly clever, especially *he*.[15] "I ain't handsome, but I don't have fits," is his portrait of his own physique. . . . The General is the George Griffin of the army, as strong in great things and as weak in little things. Any man who should listen for half an hour to the general's bad French and flat jokes, his tedious egotisms, his agonizing pedantries of connoisseurship in wine and cookery, his insipid, inflated gallantries, and his painful exhibitions of suspicious sensitive conceit would pronounce him the smallest and feeblest of created men. A silly giant, a euphuistic Goliath, if we did not know that he had proved himself a brave, prudent, skillful, brilliant, and humane commander, and a warmhearted and excellent man. His faults, I suppose, are chiefly vanity, arbitrary disposition, and an uncertain temper. . . .

October 5, SATURDAY. . . . News of the day. Ellen has commenced a new course of musical education under Bonzanini. Mrs. Ruiz and Wolcott Gibbs and Miss Laura took tea here the other night. Judge Oakley and John Griswold came in and discoursed [about] Calvary Church. I have nearly concluded to give in at last, and let them deal with my unlucky pew as they like. Lindomania unabated; instead of an epidemic *lycanthropy* like that of the Middle Ages, it's a prevalent morbid passion for assuming the form of an ass and paying six dollars and so on for the privilege of drinking in her most sweet voice through the preternaturally prolonged ears of the deluded victims of this terrible new disorder. *Fugitive Slave Bill* much discussed in the city. Still more out of it. Sewarddom in great excitement, of course, and as for Garrison and Gerrit Smith and their tail, black and white, they exhausted the vocabulary of Billingsgate so thoroughly long ago that they can find no adequate

---

[15] Henry Augustus Wise (1819–1869), a naval officer best remembered for his book *Los Gringos, or, an Inside View of Mexico and California* (1849), had married a daughter of Edward Everett. He was a cousin of the more explosive and more famous Henry A. Wise who became governor of Virginia.

expression of their wrath in that or any other dialect. They deserve to be scourged and pilloried for sedition or hanged for treason, but as the execution of justice upon them would do more harm than good and draw attention to their impotent efforts for evil, it is better to let them alone.[16] The state must temper justice not only with mercy (which these people cannot claim), but with due regard to expediency, and must sometimes wink at projects of crime because they are despicable, and might be made dangerous if their authors were consecrated into martyrs by the gallows they deserve.

My creed on that question is: That slave-holding is no sin.

That the slaves of the Southern States are happier and better off than the niggers of the North, and are more kindly dealt with by their owners than servants are by Northern masters.

That the reasoning, the tone of feeling, the first principles, the practices, and the designs of Northern Abolitionists are very particularly false, foolish, wicked, and unchristian.

N.B. The question of the expediency of slave-holding, and of the policy of upholding the institution, is a very different affair.

October 10, THURSDAY. . . . Auction sale of pews in Calvary Church yesterday. Very successful as I hear. Certainly I've no fault to find with the result from present appearances. William Kent bought my pew; and as I was *not* deluded into any concern with the scrip operation, he must pay me back my $550 before he gets it. I no more expected ever to see that long-lost sum back again than I now expect to see last year's snow; and I am grateful to Hawks—the rather because putting money into anybody's pocket (but his own) is a thing he is not used to, and this is a very marked exception to all his habits in my favor. Catch me buying another pew anywhere! I was always willing enough to subscribe what I could to get that church out of its scrape, whenever a decent and reputable set of people should be put in charge of its affairs, and its vestry could be trusted with a five-dollar bill; but paying heavy premiums for pews to raise

[16] The principal measures of Clay's compromise scheme had been carried through Congress piecemeal, with Stephen A. Douglas prominent in managing their passage. As part of the general arrangement, the Fugitive Slave Act was signed by President Fillmore on September 18. Setting up a machinery of recapture under Federal commissioners and Federal marshals, it provoked much Northern antagonism. While Negroes domiciled in the North fled in large numbers to Canada, angry protest meetings were held in various cities. Josiah Quincy presided over one in Boston. Steps were taken to counteract these gatherings by calling large Union meetings in support of the Compromise.

funds to compromise the private debts of a clever quack is a different
business altogether. . . .

October 16. . . . Up late every night trying to understand the [John
Jacob] Astor will, a document of which [Daniel] Lord must be ashamed.
Few papers of importance have I ever seen so full of ambiguities and so
bunglingly put together. . . .

October 18. . . . Mr. Ruggles was here after dinner, with Jem, just
returned from his tour through the carboniferous counties of Pennsylvania. Long talk of the Dauphin Mining Company, wherein I would
invest if I had the indispensable surplus; also of California and its possible
influence on things here. He's shivering in the wind now, and coming
round to the notions he laughed at me for suggesting a year ago. Probably it's that part of our conference that left a stamp of indigo blue on
me. Rate of interest falling, and prices rising—pleasant prospect. Well,
I should be thankful that I've no reason to expect what so many better
men contrive to exist and be tolerably happy in, *absolute* dependence on
my own work and labor. The worst that can reasonably be expected
would be surrendering our big house, lowering our "style" of living, and
a refuge in some cheap little country town; nothing that a rational man
need shudder at or shrink from.

Hear that Farish, who was to have married Miss Serena Jones yesterday, wrote her a civil note the evening before, declining the honor.
Reason, his scruples about her marriage settlement, drawn by G. W.
S[trong]. Cram told me there had been a hitch about it, but that the
marriage was to go on. He advised him not to sign it; rather odd, as the
settlement was unusually favorable to the husband. The lady has had a
lucky escape. I trust she may act as she should, and treat his probable
penitence as it deserves to be treated. He ought to be ostracized from the
company of decent men.

Last night went with Ellen to Mr. Bishop's concert. Opening of
Tripler Hall. Room ornate and spacious; well suited for its purposes, and
its decorations on the whole tasteful. Concert rather a failure. Orchestra
a multitudinous, undisciplined mob, with Bochs to lead it; chorus little
better. The C minor Symphony badly played, of course (except the
andante), but human bungling can't much interfere with its splendors.
Chorus *Meeres-stille*, called Beethoven's; never heard it, or of it, before,
and it was as dead and flat as its subject. Overture of *Euryanthe*; air from
Marriage of Figaro deliciously sung by Mrs. Bochsa; and for finale the
Hallelujah Chorus, which they triumphed over completely and killed

dead, by singing it to the time of a dead-march. But for the symphony
and overture, the performance would have been a bore, but two bars of
either intelligibly rendered can leaven and redeem two hours of trash.

The idea of people being worried and anxious about a little more or
less of income, when there are such things to make one happy on earth!

October 27, SUNDAY. . . . Ellen considerably uncomfortable and lying
down all day. Stayed at home with her until five, when she began to get
rid of her headache, etc., and then I walked up to Houghton's little bit of
a church (styled "of the Transfiguration") in Twenty-seventh Street,
where I engaged a pew for our afternoon occupation, Trinity being too
far off for more than one visit per Sunday. This church is an unpretending
little wooden affair, but its interior and arrangements "do please me," as
my prototype Pepys would say. Rain stopped; wind came out sharp from
the northwest; setting sun made the ragged fringes and frayed-out seams
of the curtain of clouds overhead burn with beautiful orange and crimson,
and cast a faint warm glow on brown sandstone fronts innumerable
around Madison Square. . . .

How this city marches northward! The progress of 1835 and 1836
was nothing to the luxuriant, rank growth of this year. Streets are spring-
ing up, whole strata of sandstone have transferred themselves from their
ancient resting-places to look down on bustling thoroughfares for long
years to come. Wealth is rushing in upon us like a freshet.

October 31. . . . Last few days don't furnish a great deal for this Diurnal.
Went last night to the "Union" meeting at Castle Garden. Better attended
than I hoped; much howling and hurrahing and other demonstrations of
patriotic furor, and a large quantity of vapid spouting. On the whole, I
am prepared to hurrah for the Castle Garden platform. The Northern
Nullifiers of the Fugitive Slave Law are opening a crevasse for anarchy.
They denounce and repudiate and resist this law because it enforces the
rights of the owner in a kind of property which they consider it sinful to
possess. Twenty years hence, when the new Gospel of Fourier shall have
been watered and increased by Horace Greeley and the Devil into more
vigorous existence than has yet been vouchsafed it, there will be an equally
respectable minority to maintain that the possession of superfluous real
estate and the ownership of an excess of chattels is a sin and a crime and
an injustice and a fraud upon all our brethren who have less than what
they regard as enough of either. Then the sins of the fathers will be
visited on their children: the offspring of Horace Mann and William Jay
and Arthur Tappan will seek to reclaim their debts from some red re-

publican debtor, and will be met by the "power above the law" which
their foolish fathers helped to conjure up. They will sue amid the frowns
of an indignant community; they will recover judgment from a reluctant
court; they will cause the resignation of one or two conscientious deputy
sheriffs, and be finally put down and snubbed into a compromise at ten
per cent by the menacing attitude of an enlightened populace looking
sternly on while the deputy tries in vain to make a levy. Truths are often
forgotten because they are truisms, disbelieved because they are self-
evident, just as we look at familiar objects without seeing them and
cease to hear the noise of a waterfall or an engine factory after we have
lived near it long enough. And we need in these days to be reminded of
the truism that if people don't obey laws because they are laws, anarchy
can only be warded off by despotism.

But according to the popular philosophy of government these people
are right enough. If a state is a mere aggregation of units like sand on
the seashore, without a common life and growth and unity; if society is
founded only on the surrender by each man of some of his rights for the
sake of mutual comfort and quiet, there is no sanctity or virtue in the word
Law that can entitle any Act of Congress, or of any other law-making
power, to one particle of respect when the conscience judgment or private
opinion of any man tells him it is unjust or inequitable. . . .

Vestry of Trinity Church: more committee meetings. . . . Convention
called for November 27th to elect a "provisional" Bishop—a most
revolutionary style for him to bear. Strong feeling in favor of Seabury;
Harison, Samuel Jones, Verplanck, and many others all look that way,
and among the clergy of the dominant party he will run well. . . .

*Strong High-Church and Low-Church antagonism was bound up in the
contest over the provisional bishopric of New York. Samuel Seabury (1801–1872)
was a grandson of the eminent Loyalist divine, Samuel Seabury, the first
Episcopal bishop in America. He also had title to consideration in his own
achievements. He had helped found the Church of the Annunciation in New York
(1838), had taught in the General Theological Seminary, and since 1833 had
been editor of* The Churchman, *the principal weekly organ of the denomination.
A fervent adherent of High-Church doctrine, he greeted the Oxford Movement
with enthusiasm, and used* The Churchman *to defend Tractarian principles
so zealously that the Low-Church element in 1846 established a rival journal,*
The Protestant Churchman. *As Strong indicates, the High-Church party*

was in control of the diocesan convention; and Seabury in 1848–50 was the most influential member of the diocesan committee which administered the affairs of the New York churches. As his duties on this body and in his Church of the Annunciation grew, he resigned his editorship early in 1849. Other candidates for the bishopric included the Rev. Henry J. Whitehouse and the Rev. Jonathan Mayhew Wainwright, who had been rector of Grace Church and was now assistant minister of Trinity, in charge of St. John's Chapel. Wainwright, a handsome, affable man who combined learning with strong social inclinations, had published various sermons and books. We shall hear more of him. Strong's first inclination was to support measures of conciliation with the Low-Church element; but as the contest wore on he became convinced that this was useless. His own High-Church sentiment never abated.

Ellen went to visit friends in Boston, leaving her husband in a "state of desolation."

November 3. Disagreeable cloudy Sunday. Haven't been to church today. I confess with humiliation that I overslept myself this morning and finished my breakfast too late for Trinity. George Anthon dined here. Discussed his professorship and his mutinous Junior class; his enforcement of discipline against Cutting's nephew, [William Cutting] Wilson, who has been expelled; Miss Jane M., whom he ought to marry; Seabury's chance of the Episcopate; etc. Tea at my father's and then took a loafing walk in the region of Tompkins Square. Letter from Ellie, bless her. She writes in good health and spirits, and seems to be welcomed by an army of old friends—Mr. Agassiz, Robert Winthrop, and Appletons and Carys without end; not to speak of the inevitable Mrs. Paige, who seems to be as hospitable as ever. I shall try to get off Wednesday night or Thursday morning. One cause of detention is Woodbury Langdon's last folly. He knows no more of business than a cow does of conic sections, but he has a taste for speculation and goes into it blindfold. He spoke to me yesterday about an operation of his where he was afraid he should lose the sum he'd advanced, and specially dismayed was he on learning that he'd made himself liable as a *partner* for the debts, present and future, of a parcel of vagabond Italians. I shall have to work hard and very warily to save him from a most unpleasant scrape.

"Union meeting" has put forth a ticket, substantially such as I had resolved to vote—Seymour and Cornell. It will run well here, badly in the western counties, which are copiously pustulated with the Seward eruption. It is no doubt a fact that many sober-minded people at the South anticipate a dissolution of the Union within five years. The North laughs at them and proceeds to prove that the South would lose by the separation by way of shewing that it's not supposable that the South will separate. But people will do foolish things when they're in a passion, and the damage to the South won't lessen the damage to the North. And the South has reason *now* for getting into a state of indignant exaltation, for the law-loving citizens of Massachusetts have been nullifying law and treading on the verge of treason, and they have made it evident that legislation is inoperative, and that the South can look for no redress from anything Congress can do. . . .

November 5, TUESDAY. . . . Result of today's election not known. Wish Sewardism might encounter a rebuke, even at the sacrifice of some pretty good men, as Hunt, but the Whigs have doubtless carried the state. Hunt's friends stand up for him stoutly, but he has not quite cleared his skirts of the charges against him. Anyhow, I trust this city won't send Isaiah Rynders to the Legislature.

November 8. To Boston Wednesday night, leaving 27th Street at 3:30 P.M. Edward Jones and Redfield in the cars. Night cloudy and dark. Springfield and supper at 8; Boston at 12. Haskey [Hasket Derby] on the lookout at the depot, and Boylston Street vigilant for my arrival. Yesterday, Mrs. Paige, the Athenaeum, and in the evening slow tea-drinking at G. B. Emerson's, where were the Curtises, who confirmed my judgment of them as nice people. This morning up at 6, off at 7:30, dined in a fragmentary way at New Haven at one, and was at 27th Street (in a hard rain) at 4 P.M. . . .

Nothing new in Boston met my observation. Derby found time to expound to me the growth of Boston, and to demonstrate its enormous commercial and other advantages, as usual. . . . Much talk of the Fugitive Slave Law; they all say it will be executed whenever a case shall occur. Doubt it. The law will be nullified, not by violence but by strict construction and legal impediments, and the slave-owner will lose his remedy as Shylock claimed his—"Since that the trade and profit of this city consisteth of all nations," South Carolina included, and the law must be administered. . . .

November 9. . . . Result of election continues doubtful. James Gordon Bennett got a kicking and castigation from little Graham this morning. Graham has lost his election as district attorney, and Bennett, I dare say, contributed to defeat him by his abuse of the last fortnight.

November 13, WEDNESDAY. . . . Busy times; last new botheration a
sharp transaction of the Griswolds, for which they are in trouble, and I'm
fagging at an answer to help them. . . . I'm beginning to feel a desire to
make money, and I avow and asseverate that it's a new feeling with me.
In this city the feeling is necessary to enable one to sympathize with the
rest of mankind and be sure of his common humanity with the people
about him. . . . Jenny Lind's last and greatest triumph came off yesterday;
my father and mother of their own free will went to hear her! Amphion
never achieved anything more marvelous. I must hear her myself. Vestry
meeting of Trinity Church Monday night; walk with Dayton Hobart.
Seabury's prospects as they were; his chances good, but if he's elected it
will be after a rough and tumble fight of the wildest sort. Hobart and the
Ogdens and all that set are against him strong; an important indication
as to the lay vote. Per contra, the wires and levers that originate in
Trinity Parish will work in his favor. Convention is called for the 27th
inst. Hobart surprised me a little by some notions of his about Roman
Catholicism. *I* often feel a wish obtruding itself that I'd been originated
in that form of faith. . . .

Went over Mr. Astor's new hotel at the corner of Eighteenth Street
and Fourth Avenue, now nearly finished—the Clarendon. Very nice
affair, *bating its mortgages.* . . .

November 19, TUESDAY. . . . Still much talk about the election of provisional bishop. Whitehouse [is] the Low-Church candidate; very low
and very slow and not like to run well. Seabury's lookout *not* good at all.
Rather a tendency towards Wainwright in some quarters, but he's always
talked of for everything and never elected.

Mr. Ruggles [is] president of the Dauphin Company. Its coal is said
to be the very thing wanted for steamboat consumption, and Collins's
Line wants 50,000 tons on the spot. Very favorable indication for dividends. Hideously overworked in Wall Street of late. . . .

November 22. . . . Parks of Trinity, and Bartlett, called here yesterday
afternoon. Parks's candidate for the Episcopate is *Wheaton*, in whose favor
he makes out a strong case. Bartlett tells me this morning that he may
be sent to the Convention from Weir's Church, and that he shall vote for
Parks. Were I a delegate I should vote with him, for I hold Parks in
higher respect than any clergyman I know. Seabury will have a plurality
on the first ballot, no doubt, but it's an even chance if he get a majority
at last.

After their visit, went to the Clarendon, Mr. Ruggles having invited two or three hundred Whigs there to receive Washington Hunt and have a *gaudeamus* over the election. Very pleasant evening; various nice people there, politicians and others, clean and unclean; a speech from [Washington] Hunt and from Cornell, and much champagne. . . .

As this entry indicates, the Whigs, despite a serious split between the followers of the radical Senator Seward and the moderate President Millard Fillmore, had triumphed in the fall elections of 1850. They had nominated Washington Hunt for governor and George J. Cornell for lieutenant-governor, while the Democrats had named Horatio Seymour and Sanford E. Church. Both the leading candidates were popular and able. For some weeks after the election its result remained in doubt. Finally the official count gave Hunt the narrow plurality of 262 votes in a total of nearly 430,000 cast! The Whigs also gained a safe majority in the legislature, and elected a majority of the Congressmen from the state.

Meanwhile Strong was much troubled by a lawsuit involving some property of Woodbury Langdon, John Jacob Astor's son-in-law. "I have long conferences daily with Langdon," he writes on November 22. "He is not the natural idiot I thought him at first. With decent advantages and a respectable education he might have made a man of ordinary sense. Had he not been cursed by the prospect of a vast inheritancy, his faculties would have had a chance to develop and he would not have wanted a certain amount of common sense."

The last week of November witnessed an utterly abortive meeting of the Episcopal Convention called to elect a provisional bishop. Balloting began on November 28th with Seabury ahead and Williams next; "everybody very acrimonious, ill-tempered, and excited." On the 29th Strong noted: "Seabury thrown overboard and Southgate taken up, on trial, by the High-Church men; today he was dropped and Creighton was the candidate at the last advices." But the Low-Church party stuck manfully to Williams, and a deadlock ensued. On the night of the 29th "both parties concluded that any more balloting would be a waste of time and temper, and an adjournment was carried."

November 25, MONDAY. . . . South still clamorous, querulous, and absurd, *Quattlebum Rampans,* preventing people from seeing their just grounds of complaint by the preposterous vaporing, bombast, and brag wherewith they make themselves and their concerns ridiculous. They want their 50,000 runaway niggers back, after their six months or six years respectively of independence and citizenship at the North!! That is, they want 50,000 centres of resistance and insurrection scattered over their plantations to preach the rights of man and make their black brudders restless, discontented, ambitious, and dangerous. They want 50,000 scabby sheep introduced into their flocks, 50,000 sparks disseminated among their powder barrels. And their row about their cotton! —Were man definable as a being that exists by cotton alone and were their poverty-stricken coasts the sole region that could produce it, that privilege would no more render them arbiters of the destiny of nations than the exclusive possession of the tea-plant has made China the mistress of mankind. I'm beginning to think that Southern Ultraism may be let alone to cut its own throat and punish its own lunatics, without let or interference. Where will they divide the Mississippi? . . .

December 9, MONDAY. . . . But little news current. Lots of gold pouring in from California. Prospect of war between Austria and Prussia diminishing, though the weather in Central Europe is squally. The great nation of South Carolina still restless and vituperative, and full of the most horrible anticipations of its own future triumphal career. Wolcott Gibbs and Mr. Ruggles here Friday night. Gibbs's "polytechnic" project headed off and merged in a plan for the regeneration of the whole department of physical science in Columbia College, from which somnolent seat of learning, or easy chair of science, Renwick, it seems, is about to upheave one-half his bulk and to withdraw one-half the sluggish droppings of his stagnating course of lectures, leaving chemistry vacant, and one or two kindred subjects, which it is proposed that Gibbs shall take. But he stipulates for a good deal in the way of apparatus, accommodations, etc., and I doubt whether the plan ever bears fruit.

December 12. (Thanksgiving Day.) To church this morning at the Church of the Transfiguration. . . .

Heard the *Creation* last night at the Tabernacle, with Ellen, her mother, and Jem. Choruses admirably well done, solo parts middling or tolerable, all but a tenor with a scrannel pipe of a larynx. . . .

The year closed uneventfully. Strong was called down on December 15 to the bedside of Woodbury Langdon, who had been stabbed in Broadway. This was not an attempted assassination, but "nothing more than a casual jostling of Mr. Langdon by two or three loafers, the knocking down of one or two of them by him, and a scuffle, in which the loafers used their knives." Governor Hunt had offered to make S. B. Ruggles's son Jem his private secretary, and Strong thought that the young man should accept. It would give him good training. It would also "bring him into contact with people whom the New York Club call snobs, and cause him to become aware that there is something in this world, not to speak of the other, beyond white gloves" and gentility. The Art Union had held a "distribution" or raffle of paintings, in which the chief prizes were canvases by Leutze and Church; but for his five dollars Strong won neither. Leutze was exhibiting another picture, his "John Huss," which Strong thought finished but not great. Christmas seemed to the diarist "an inferior article of the kind," for he was almost prostrated with a sick headache.

December 27, FRIDAY. . . . Today chiefly at the [City] Hall. Young Ethiopia was out in great force, filling up corridors and offices, for there's another fugitive slave case in progress, and Jay was chattering and scratching and fluttering at chambers, like one of his blue namesakes when its nest is beleaguered by a copperhead. They (the volunteer champions of the blackey) took out a habeas corpus before the Supreme Court addressed to the commissioner, who, of course, returned very promptly that he had no nigger in his custody; whereupon they issued another writ to the marshal returnable in the Superior Court before Campbell; and while I was getting myself appointed guardian for George Jones's children, in came marshal and fugitive and a posse of police and Jay with his tail on.[17] The tail, however, prudently stayed outside the door, not caring to venture itself in too dangerous propinquity to judges and United States marshals and the agents of Southern slaveholders. Campbell, I suspect, will uphold the law. But from some talk I had with Mitchell, I should be a little apprehensive of his decision in such a case; though he would always do his duty, or try to do it, and administer the law as he found it written, whatever his notions might be of natural equity and partial legislation.

The *Tribune* quotes Daniel Webster as quoting Hooker's description of LAW in some recent speech or letter of his, and asks Daniel solemnly whether he can in his heart believe that this Fugitive Act is within the meaning of that grand eulogium. If the *Tribune* should ask me, I should tell it most undoubtingly that such was *my* belief. But the school of the *Tribune* can see no justice or right in laws that recognize or enforce

[17] John Jay (1817–1894), grandson of the famous Chief Justice and a graduate of Columbia College in the class of 1836, had become head of the New York Young Men's Anti-Slavery Society, and since the signing of the Fugitive Slave Act, was serving as counsel for many fugitive Negroes.

inequalities in men. Lucky for the universe it is that Greeley cannot raise his voice with the smallest prospect of success in any great comprehensive scheme for the reformation of its numerous inequalities and the amelioration of its thousand inequitable diversities of condition and other crying abuses that must strike his philosophic eye every time he opens it. . . .

1851

MR. RUGGLES'S FINANCIAL TROUBLES · CASTLE GARDEN
OPERA · CUBAN FILIBUSTERS · KOSSUTH'S VISIT

Though the nation was prosperous, and the political quiet following the passage of the Compromise Bill was broken only by continued opposition to the Fugitive Slave Act, the year 1851 was destined to have its share of interesting occurrences. It witnessed the formal opening of the Erie Railroad, with a triumphal excursion by President Fillmore, Daniel Webster, and other notables all the way from Piermont on the Hudson to Dunkirk on Lake Erie. It saw the practical initiation by Mayor Ambrose Kingsland of steps which shortly led to the creation of Central Park in New York; an enterprise in which Strong's friend Frederick Law Olmsted was to play the principal part. The novelist Fenimore Cooper died late in the summer; Henry J. Raymond launched the New York Times *upon its great career; and Louis Kossuth arrived to find a greeting of tumultuous enthusiasm, but very little cash or other material aid in his plans for renewing the struggle of Hungary against Austria. Strong began the year very busy professionally, and in good health. Much was hoped by his father-in-law, S. B. Ruggles, from the governorship of Washington Hunt; but that chieftain was deficient in tact, and soon embroiled himself with the legislature over the Erie Canal. James F. Ruggles had accepted the post of secretary to the governor. "Jem and I," said Hunt, "will administer the state in a spirit that is mild but firm." But Strong was never much concerned with state politics. He was more interested in affairs at home—in Columbia College, Trinity Church, the Philharmonic, and such matters as the dispute of his friend George Anthon with the authorities at New York University.*

January 2, THURSDAY. . . . Am threatening to become a Patron of Art. First, there's my father's portrait; second, Mr. Ruggles's; third, the pictures by Saal and Weber of Düsseldorf that I'm negotiating about with Ehninger; and fourth, the grand Camphausen that's to come along some time next spring or summer; all which makes up rather a bad look-out for the savings bank account.

January 6. The desk tonight has a savor of Wall Street; it is covered with big papers and little and veined with straggling ends of red tape. Another visit tonight from my bull-headed friend [James] Such, and per-suaded him with some trouble to cease indulging the insane hope that Valentine G. Hall would pay him back five hundred dollars because he had to surrender his contract to buy the Degraw Street property. . . .[1]

January 8. . . . Henry Long, the interesting black representative of the Rights of Man, adjudged this morning to be lawfully held to service and delivered up to the Philistines of Virginia, notwithstanding the rhetoric of John Jay. . . .

January 16, THURSDAY. . . . Bad accident in this street between Fifth and Sixth Avenues yesterday. The houses Tom Emmet and Ferris Pell (or rather his widow) were putting up and on which the Bank has a rather large loan, tumbled down spontaneously, killing or mangling and muti-lating some two dozen people. Cause, the criminal economy of the con-tractor. Saw some of the *mortar*, a greasy, pulverulent earth or clay, apparently far less tenacious than an average specimen of Broadway mud. The contractor, who certified to the sufficiency of his work three hours before the crash, has discreetly run away.

News from Albany: the canal policy announced by Hunt in his mes-sage, and backed by Mr. Ruggles in his powerful letter of last year, now just reprinted for the expected contest, is to be squashed and abandoned. Seward can't afford to have any more great men in the state of New York. Fish is to be Senator. Anything beyond a large minnow would naturally bore the Triton.[2] Ehninger to dinner, afterwards George Anthon with a

[1] James Such, a teacher, had involved himself in some unfortunate real estate speculations.

[2] A successor had to be elected to Senator Daniel S. Dickinson, whose term expired March 4, and the Whigs controlled the choice. Although James Watson Webb, the explosive Apollo of the press, aspired to the place, Hamilton Fish, who had just completed a successful term as governor, had larger claims. The Fillmore or moderate Whigs rallied behind Webb, and the Seward Whigs behind Fish. A bitter contest of two months ensued before Fish won—and he was a much abler man than Webb. Meanwhile, the question whether the Erie Canal should be enlarged had aroused strong feeling. On the earnest recommendation of Governor Hunt and S. B.

narrative of grievances at the hands of the faculty of the New York University. They are trying to treat him very meanly and oppressively, but he has met them fairly and is not disposed to be sacrificed in compliance with their very cool proposition. Charley here this evening on his way to the Bristed party. Haight's big ball the other night, the town talk, nine rooms open, "wintergarden," "moonlight illumination,"— birds and butterflies, and a hose company privately entertained in the cellar to interfere in case of a conflagration.[3]

January 21, TUESDAY. . . . The *Atlantic* still missing.

Certain grizzly bears in the London Zoological Gardens, having become afflicted with cataract, and their usefulness thereby impaired, have been operated upon successfully, while under the influence of chloroform.

January 23. No news of the *Atlantic* yet, and consignees are insuring at twenty-five per cent.[4]

January 28, TUESDAY.

Died, Monday night, 27th inst., Benjamin Strong. . . .

Received the melancholy intelligence above chronicled this morning as soon as I was up, and received it almost incredulously, for Uncle Benjamin was in my office yesterday at noon, and encountering poor old tremulous John Bowen there, the two octogenarians began sallying each other on their respective degrees of vigor and youthfulness; and Uncle Benjamin talked with rather more than his usual liveliness about his anticipa-

---

Ruggles, the Assembly empowered the state government to borrow nine millions to begin immediate work. Most of the Whigs supported the enlargement policy and most Democrats opposed it. A prolonged struggle took place in the Senate, but in the end it approved the nine-million bill. Ruggles was triumphant—until the Court of Appeals held the measure unconstitutional.

[3] Charles Astor Bristed (1820–1874), son of "Oxonian Bristed" and grandson of John Jacob Astor, was educated at Yale (1839) and Trinity College, Cambridge, returning to write a valuable two-volume memoir, *Five Years in an English University* (1852). He married the daughter of Henry Brevoort, traveled extensively, and wrote voluminously, somewhat cynically, and with wide culture and much scholarship on a variety of topics. His book *The Upper Ten Thousand* (1852) sketched New York society life. The Rev. Benjamin Isaacs Haight (Columbia 1828), also a prominent figure in New York society, was assistant minister of Trinity, professor in the General Theological Seminary, and trustee of Columbia. In 1873 he declined the bishopric of Massachusetts; his later years were clouded with mental illness.

[4] The transatlantic line of steamers built by E. K. Collins to compete with the Cunard line was now achieving its swift rise, a prelude to an even swifter fall. Its first vessel, the *Atlantic*, had sailed from New York to Liverpool on April 27, 1850; three other fine ships, the *Pacific*, *Arctic*, and *Baltic*, were soon in service. New Yorkers took a proud interest in them, and anxiety over a delayed passage was keenly felt.

tions of sport on Love Island next summer, and so forth. He had just got over a sharp attack of influenza, and seemed uncommonly well, energetic, and cheerful. He left the Seamen's Bank at one, feeling quite ill, oppressed, and exhausted; went home; Dr. Peters was sent for, gave him some medicine, and said there was nothing the matter but a little over-fatigue encountered too soon after the influenza. He continued to grow more comfortable all the afternoon, and at about eleven went to bed as usual, and requested Oliver Strong to read to him a chapter in the New Testament. Before more than a dozen verses had been read, Oliver noticed a peculiarity in his breathing, laid down his book, and found his father insensible. He was unable to swallow, and within ten minutes was dead. Dr. Hobart was instantly brought in from next door, but it was over, and there was nothing to be done. . . .[5]

Have been going on for the past few days as usual; tolerably full of work, and of the same old prosaic work. The mill goes round as it has gone, the horse-boat travels along, and I, the blind horse, continue to keep it moving, by the same monotonous trot performed within my box in Wall Street. George Anthon came to see me today. Old Myndert Van Schaick seems to be a party to the rather disreputable manoeuvring by which Anthon is to be got rid of for the pecuniary benefit of his brother professors,[6] which intrigue seems to be still going on. But George feels no call to martyrdom in that cause. If he's eliminated, it will be by the *vis major contra invitum*, and if he is got out by harsh means, I suspect that like Samson he'll bring the rotten old structure about the ears of Bill McMurray and John Johnston and Company. Mr. Ruggles here tonight. There's no doubt that a little exertion would get him the Senatorship. He's not willing to make it, and professes to doubt whether he would take the place. I know he would, and have advised him frankly against taking it on many grounds: his health, his private affairs, the canal policy, his various undertakings that would have to be abandoned, and so on. Webster, Fillmore, and all the Silver Greys are very anxious that he should prevail against Fish. I trust they may be disappointed.

[5] Benjamin Strong had been president of the North River Sugar Refining Company early in the century, and later was a director of the Merchants' Bank and the North River Insurance Company. He was a Presbyterian, a businessman of unimpeachable integrity, and an active participant in various public charities. "There are not many *good* specimens now left in the city of the simplicity of taste and manners which he carried with him unchanged from the primitive years in which his career began," wrote Strong.

[6] That is, in the not yet well-established New York University.

Theodore Winthrop dined with us Friday; Porter, Sunday.[7] The major's prolixity has not grown less during the past three months. Alexander has got married to a daughter of Curtis Bolton's. . . . Ehninger sails for Europe tomorrow. *Atlantic* still missing. Collins's *blue* is settling into black, and I don't dare to ask after her any more. . . .

February 1, SATURDAY. Looking into *David Copperfield* lately; can't read it through and won't; too delicate an organization, I suppose, and sensibilities too exquisite; at least I found myself blowing my nose and sniveling in the most touching way over the sixteenth part (*poor little Dora*) and gave it up. I don't particularly need to be reminded of the hard times of May, 1849.

February 4. . . . Wolcott Gibbs's Columbia College plan was too much for the faculties of the Board of Incurables which dozes periodically over the affairs of that institution, and has been laid aside for the present; its magnitude not admitting of its being thought about all at once. So Gibbs is going forward with the Polytechnic project, in which, with his energy, he is not unlikely to succeed.[8]

No *Atlantic* yet, and no news of her, though the *Canada* is in. Proceedings at Albany as to the United States Senatorship going on. Fish nominated in the House, but wants *one* of nomination in the Senate; James W. Beekman recalcitrates.[9] S. B. Ruggles wrote some days ago, refusing to be the candidate of a section of the party. . . .

It's quite terrific to see the strides extravagance and luxury are making in these days. Langdon's arrangements for his ball tonight remind me of the fact. Though I thought a few years ago that I was or might be hereafter tolerably well off, I'm satisfied from the way the style of living grows and amplifies that I am to be always poor, relatively speaking,

[7] Theodore Winthrop (1820–1861), just back from Europe, was employed by the Pacific Mail Steamship Company; his fame as an author lay a decade in the future. Major Porter was probably Fitz-John Porter (1822–1901), now instructor and adjutant at West Point.

[8] Oliver Wolcott Gibbs (1822–1908) was now fully launched on his distinguished scientific career. Full of ambitious plans for the improvement of scientific instruction in the United States, he was destined to find a field for them not at Columbia, but at Harvard.

[9] The state Senate held fifteen Democrats and seventeen Whigs. Hamilton Fish's election to the national Senate should have been easy enough. But his views on slavery and the Fugitive Slave Act were too stern to suit conservative men, and a moderate Whig senator from New York City, James W. Beekman, deserted his party to bring about a tie, sixteen to sixteen. The Whigs had to wait for the absence of some Democratic senators from Albany to get their chance to send Fish to Washington.

and perhaps some day an absolute pauper, unable to live in New York. But I don't know that I need be very wretched if I have to subside into some economical retreat in the wilds of Suffolk, or among the spurs of the Catskills. . . .

February 5. Working hard for the last four hours; Ellen sitting by and reading *David Copperfield.* Morning papers (Whig) rave at James W. Beekman. Saw Fish, who didn't allude to the subject of his thoughts, but looked as if he felt there was nothing true but Heaven. Fidgeted about the Hall to find Mitchell, and then went to Wall Street. . . . Paid two big bills, received one or two more. Saw William Schermerhorn, who's abetting Mrs. Stevens in her tableaux that are to be, provided human diplomacy and the bribe of a supper can prevail on any of the people one knows to take the second-rate parts. . . .

February 14. Cold weather has given place to fog and drizzle. Past few days present no very prominent features. Busy as usual, and now eupeptic. Much shocked at discovering my bank account to be in a state of depletion, threatening speedy insolvency. . . . Great excitement in Wall Street this morning occasioned by a sudden vociferous outbreak of newsboys with "Arrival of the *Atlantic.*" It meant merely that she has been *spoken* when four days out. Am beginning to consider her case doubtful. An accident to her machinery accounts for her delay, to be sure, for she would make but slow progress with only her canvas. But if such an accident had happened in a heavy gale, she would stand a bad chance of broaching to and foundering in the trough of the sea before her head could be got round. At meeting of Trinity Church committee on the new chapel this afternoon. Very embarrassing state of things, but the problem we have to solve is as old as architecture, viz.: to produce a building of the dimensions and dignity we want, and not to pay as much as such a building will cost. With near $500,000 debt, we ought not to be lavish, and I cannot get some of the parochial fathers to understand that size, good proportions, genuineness, and solidity will make the proposed chapel respectable without elaborate detail, decoration, costly curly-wurlies, paneling, pinnacles, and other appendages. . . .

February 17, MONDAY. *Atlantic's* safety announced Saturday night; news brought by the *Africa,* and communicated to Gramercy Square at about 11:30 by a herd of highly excited newsboys. Tumbled out of bed, and downstairs in an ethereal costume, and got an extra. I did not get the rheumatism, though the winds of heaven visited my legs roughly as I bellowed for a paper at the front door. . . .

February 26. . . . George Anthon and Wolcott Gibbs dined here today. . . . Anthon still in some trouble with his brethren at the New York University. That institution is a rotten humbug, which I trust the beneficent operation of the laws of nature will soon bring to an end.

March 1, SATURDAY. . . . Went to hear *St. Paul* with Ellen and the Miss Maurans in the evening at the Tabernacle. Excellent performance —choruses quite perfect. It may have been a pair of over-tight boots, but I did not enjoy the music very intensely, or discover much force or freshness in any of it, except the grand and glorious "Sleepers, Awake," the "O, Be Gracious, Ye Immortals," and one or two things beside. The air "Jerusalem, Jerusalem" is a lovely composition, but it smacks of "Comfort Ye My People." Indeed a great deal of the music seems a straining after Handel, and half the choruses might have been written by Handel dyspeptic or grown senile and stupid. Except, however, "How Lovely Are the Messengers," which is a very genuine and original affair. Mendelssohn mistook his vocation when he wrote oratorios. He's the Shelley of composers, not to be matched in exuberance of delicate fancies —spiritual and exquisite in his conceptions to the utmost limit of intelligibleness to mortal ears, but cramped by heroics, and incapable of any approach to sublimity. The *Midsummer Night's Dream* music—the overture especially—is his characteristic production; there the peculiarity of his mind shews itself unmistakably. . . .

March 7. . . . George William Curtis's book of eastern travels [*Nile Notes of a Howadji*]; don't esteem him the more for what I've read in it, though too little perhaps to found a fair judgment. There are elaborate affectations and conceits in every other paragraph that obscure the man's meaning and make one sigh for Mandeville's *Travels* or Benjamin of Tudela's *Itinerary* or any book, however stupid, which speaks its meaning simply and sensibly. I notice in various passages also, occurring with remarkable frequency, a kind of euphuistic obscenity or puppy-lewdness, indicating a habit of mind common in boys of fourteen but unusual in later life, that of regarding all animals, brute or human, first and chiefly in their sexual relations. . . .

March 11. . . . My criticism on "Howadji" Curtis agrees with the judgment of everybody who has read or tried to read his very disreputable and indecent book, so far as I've yet heard. Even Mrs. Fearing has committed herself against him, and as for Mrs. Eleanor [Strong], I hear that a chapter or so read aloud threw her into a state of indignant excitement which might have injured her in her present delicate condition. For my part I can't read the book through. *The Transcendental Erotics*, which give the book so high a mark as a contribution to the phallic literature of America, I finished, sustained by the stimulus of curiosity to see what could possibly be coming next, and partly I fear by the natural depravity of the thought of the flesh, whereby licentious silliness is rendered easier to read than mere ordinary, decorous silliness. But the rest of the Howadji's lucubrations I have found impenetrable and impracticable; no thoroughfare. The Howadji never says what he means, but always expresses himself in a symbolical way by some conceit, or far-away allusion, or hints at the fact by some sudden jumping interjection or apostrophe, from which the reader has to find out his meaning by a careful study of the context, and is not commonly repaid by any very valuable result. It should have been published with an interlinear version into the vulgar tongue for the benefit of plain people, and notes critical and explanatory like an edition of Lycophron. . . .

March 17, MONDAY. . . . Much vexed on Saturday afternoon by being suddenly called on to extricate Collins from a very threatening scrape, in which there was nothing to be done but to take possession, by help of the *vis major*, of the subject matter of dispute, viz., the steamer *Pacific*— and to do so with the very questionable title of mortgagee *before* default. I was sufficiently uneasy on the subject till today, when it turned out that Brown's audacity had failed him, and that he had surrendered at discretion and paid up his $30,000 like a lamb. But it might have been a bad business for all parties. . . .[10]

Mr. Ruggles came here in the evening with Martin Farquhar Tupper, the Proverbial Philosopher, who seems a nice sort of man. . . .

March 18. . . . Curtis said to be excessively vexed and disgusted at the reception the Howadji has met from a good many of his personal friends. Burrill [his brother] has written him in great affliction on the subject.

March 21. Most notable recent event within my knowledge is my rising early enough yesterday morning to be at the Brooklyn City Hall at nine o'clock. George C. Anthon came to see me twice last evening, and again today, in much tribulation. Those sons of Belial, his brother professors, are pushing him hard, and the Council [of New York University]

---

[10] Collins had the financial backing of James and Stewart Brown, New York partners of the Anglo-American banking house of Brown Brothers; and this entry refers to a quickly adjusted dispute between the Browns and the organizer of the Collins Line.

at their instigation are threatening his removal without assigning any reason or making any charge; a serious injury to his future prospects. [Luther] Bradish alone seems disposed to insist that there shall be some order and show of decorum and fair dealing observed. But he will be defeated and Anthon will be displaced. What can be expected from such a lot of men but vulgar pride in power and abuse of authority and absolute ignorance of courtesy as well as scholarship? Their president is John C. Green, a prosperous and wealthy tea dealer, who has spent all his life in China and has not an idea beyond that of a successful trading voyage. Young John Johnston, their vice-president, is a mean little Scotchman. Tommy Suffern commenced active life behind a wheelbarrow, and all the money he has made since can't buy him a knowledge of English orthography. The majority of them are rich merchants, illiterate and purse-proud, with a slight infusion of Presbyterian Divines. If Anthon goes out I think it likely that this seat of learning will suffer as the Temple of Dagon did when Samson brought his career to an ending.

Hamilton Fish Senator. . . .

March 27, THURSDAY. . . . Last night I had [George] Anthon here and concocted plans upstairs while the Schermerhorns were singing with Ellen in the music room. The squabble in the New York University is drawing towards a crisis. If Anthon attempted his proposed movement at the meeting of the faculty today, and carried it through with tact and decision, he has the Cabal on the hip. If he tried it and failed, he's gone. If he didn't try it, he is in a tight place, but there is a chance things may be smoothed over, though a very remote one. At all events it's certain he won't be got out but after much scratching and biting on his part; and he'll probably rend the body to which he belongs like an unclean spirit routed out of a demoniac by a drastic exorcism.

Huntington's lecture on Christian art at the "Hope Chapel" Tuesday evening was very well. It was not very original, loosely hung together, and injured by unseasonable jokes, but in general character, substance, and sentiment excellent, and especially in its forcible and almost fierce denunciations of those who profane art by debasing it into the vehicle of refined sensuality. I did not suppose that Huntington had the mettle requisite for that portion of the lecture. . . .

April 2. Very specially pressed with work for the past three or four days. [George] Anthon was served with a copy of the *Resolution* of the Council on Friday night and since then I've been devoting every spare minute to drawing his answer. Got through at twelve last night. Not at all satisfied with the paper, though John Anthon and Bradish are pleased to approve of it. It may have some effect as a bold piece of brag, but if they do give us the investigation we demand so pathetically in the name of all laws human and divine, I fear we shall have trouble in proving our case. There are two peculiar difficulties in managing his affairs for him and advising him as to his course: one his tendency to take things for granted, the other his want of tact and *savoir faire*. The latter has got him into one scrape, and I fear the former will get him into another. This morning I went down to the University through a filthy drizzle to attend Anthon's examination of his classes. As far as scholarship went, it was fair enough and showed that the cubs had been faithfully belabored with instruction and doctrine. But the deportment of the classes—especially the Sophomore —was bad, indifferent, and disrespectful. I saw a part of [Elias] Loomis's examination of another class—the Junior—and though the comparison was not strictly fair, it left an unfavorable impression on me as to Anthon's position. Though I've denied the fact so stoutly on paper, I'm afraid Anthon is incapable of managing the boys, not from any fault of his own, but because they are used to turbulence and have been set against him. Thereafter I went to see Professor [Caleb Sprague] Henry and talked the matter over with him for an hour. I see the game the faculty are playing very clearly from Henry's talk, for he's impulsive and incontinent in his speech, and I see that there is nothing behind their movements of any importance. They're in a scrape, as well as the Greek Professor, and it will be a cut-throat business on both sides. But that don't help Anthon.

Came downtown. Harison called, and we discussed our church build-ing project. The proposed chapel must be razed. We can't spare $100,000 just now.

The Council of the University meets tonight to pass on the question of Anthon's removal. They may remove him summarily or direct an in-vestigation, or, what's most likely, postpone the subject to another meeting. . . .

April 3. They turned the Greek Professor [Anthon] out last night, without ceremony. Kent, Bradish, Spring, McMurray and James Brown urged an enquiry, but the majority had made up their minds to ampu-tation, and did their surgery in a summary way. . . .

April 16, WEDNESDAY. Northeast storm howling savagely without. This is the anniversary of the *noche triste*, the dark and perilous night of two years ago. God deliver me from such another. Very diligent of late. Finished revising Anthon's malignant manifesto this evening. It goes into the printer's hands forthwith, and will not be thought overloaded with compliments by the New York University, its faculty, council, or undergraduates. Have worked on it *con amore*; for that institution is a hurt and a scandal to the cause of good manners and sound learning, and any assault on the nuisance is a good work. . . . Have allowed a formidable arrearage of work to pile itself up against me in Wall Street. A great, dirty alluvial deposit from the last week's flow of the River of Time, and the stream will not run clear again till the channel's dug out. I must work like several horses for ten days to come. Ellen continues preternaturally well and bright. Ruskin's *Stones of Venice* to be read. Fear that his vein is worked out; his pamphlet on church government is flimsy—pert, declamatory denunciation, founded on what seems a very superficial acquaintance with the subject he writes on. . . .

April 21.   Pacific in after a miraculous passage of nine days. E. K. Collins looks like the Man of Ross, or the Vicar of Wakefield, or any other embodiment of beaming benevolence and good will towards men.

The principal event of the spring in Strong's circle was the terrible crisis in S. B. Ruggles's financial affairs. He had invested heavily in an anthracite company and real estate enterprises which did not turn out well. In particular, he had borrowed rashly to build some large warehouses on the Atlantic Docks in Brooklyn; and when his creditors pressed him he did not have enough fluid capital to meet their demands. Strong recorded on April 24: "Some talk with Mr. Ruggles last night. Certain affairs of his have taken a more hopeful turn than we'd a right to expect; but he is blue and despondent as to the result, and not without reason, I think." The next day he added: "The barometer runs very low about these times, and points to cloudy weather. It's such a serious business that I wonder that I can write or think about it except in the gravest tone of regret. But after the gorgeous visions of last December, and the glowing prophecies I listened to then with my eyes and mouth wide open, it seems like a piece of stern, caustic comedy. There may be salvation yet, but it is likely to come from no source at present visible." As events showed, Ruggles could not escape disaster.

But the troubles of his father-in-law did not wholly darken Strong's life. He saw much of George Anthon, George William Curtis, Charles Curtis, Wolcott Gibbs, and others. One evening when Charles and Eleanor Strong brought in a friend named Richard Willis, they all sang German songs—Heine and Uhland. He went to see a melodrama called The School for Reform, *which had a preposterous plot but was made tolerable by the performance of the actor W. E. Burton. George Anthon's pamphlet in denunciation of the faculty of New York University occupied part of his time, for Anthon kept revising it. Under date of April 25th, the diarist tells us that Anthon had inserted a note making an exception of John W. Draper. "He is not so great a sneak as his brethren."*

April 26, SATURDAY NIGHT.   Philharmonic with Ellen this evening. Beethoven's Symphony in C minor, the great feature of the concert. Perfectly played, only the andante rather slow. It is music that I should think an orchestra of angels, such as one sees in old pictures before Raphael, might love to play. No mortal instruments can do justice to the andante and finale. Some poetry can't be thoroughly felt when it's read out of a book—far less when it's listened to—it must be recited mentally. And those two movements, the second so magically sweet, so glowing with serene strength and beauty, and the fourth so full of fire and majesty and many-voiced triumph, both when best played fall far below the adequate expression of the ideas they embody. They must be thought about to be understood. The rest of the concert was commonplace. It ended with an overture entitled "Robespierre" by one Litorff. Very rampant and vociferous music, seemingly elaborate and careful, but of which I understood nothing but a highly decorated, aggravated, and eloquent reproduction of the "Marseillaise"; much enforced by cymbals and triangles, and quite dashing and agreeable.

Nothing very new today. The "Geary" lot, corner Union Square and Seventeenth Street, sold by Bleecker. Bought it in myself for $12,000. The Union Club are to build there.

April 29.   Conference with Mr. Ruggles Monday afternoon on Chegaray property, Clarendon Hotel, and so forth. . . . Looked in at Academy of Design on the way uptown. As usual, everybody says it's the worst exhibition yet, but some things struck me favorably in the course of a quick walk through the rooms. . . . Anthon's pamphlet seems destined to turn out flat; too many counselors at work on it. There may be safety in their counseling—certainly there is stupidity and tameness. Anthon's blown about by every wind of doctrine, and after everything is settled, consults some new critic who objects to one passage, and then another who thinks something else too strong, and so he goes on snipping out, and coming to me to sew up the hiatuses, till I'm sick of the subject, and shall leave it to appear as tattered and torn as the critical scratching of Bradford and Jonathan Nathan and Anthon may make it.

Hear that I've been, or am to be, nominated to a vacant trusteeship in Columbia College. Perhaps so; but there are other alumni with prior claims to mine, and I doubt whether I'm put in and don't much care, though I'd rather like the position.

May 5. Philip Hone (senior) died this morning; a short illness, but he has been very sadly broken down for some months.[11] Anthon's pamphlet is approved by such as have read it, so far as I've heard. It might have been very much better. . . .

Half the city is being pulled down. The north corner of Wall and Broadway, an old landmark, is falling amid the execrations of pedestrians whom its ruins and rubbish drive off the sidewalk. The building on the north side of Trinity churchyard is to follow.

May 6, TUESDAY. Had a very sombre evening with the Archivarius. Prospect black for Mr. Ruggles; he thinks a speedy finale certain. I'm disposed to agree with him. The ruinous infatuation has borne its fruits. We *have* seen a darker outlook than this followed by sunshine, but such unhoped-for changes don't occur twice in one lifetime. Still, there's matchless strength, fertility of resources, energy of purpose, and an abundance of friends to be counted on; and with the help of Heaven, there may yet be a rally. I devoutly trust there may. The person most directly affected by the calamity would feel it in his inmost soul. I fear the blow would be crushing—that he would not long survive it.

May 8. Today I had several conferences with Mr. Ruggles, who is disposed to confide in me and act on my counsels to an extent that I think imprudent, for in affairs of this magnitude and complexity I doubt the safety and value of my judgment. The crash seems to be inevitable. Is it desirable to put it off for a week or a year? Edward Curtis is behaving very badly. People who are gentle and generous in every other relation of life are converted into harpies and devils when their dealings relate to debtor and creditor accounts. God preserve me from owing money! The person chiefly concerned in this matter suffers fearfully from hour to hour in the struggle. I trust he may not break down under it. . . .

What a lesson this miserable business is against speculation! Talents, genius, that could have gained a fortune in ten years' steady legitimate

[11] Ex-Mayor Philip Hone had closed his great diary on April 30, 1851, by writing part of his own epitaph, with some religious verses appended.

labor, bearing no fruit but insolvency, bitter self-reproach, and the memory of a life's unavailing struggle, of a long series of harrowing cares and sickening uncertainty—and ruin at last.

May 11, SUNDAY.   Nothing new in the Ruggles perplexity, except that F. Griffin has been enlightened as to the facts and as to his own position and prospects, and I understand "behaved very well"—as was to have been expected of him. It may be that the interview has opened some rat-hole of hope, but I don't believe escape possible, and I doubt whether it is desirable. Far better to wind up the affair at a time like this of prosperity, abundant capital, and high prices, than to wait for a crisis, and be obliged to settle in the midst of a panic at an inevitable sacrifice.

Berrian preached this morning at Trinity. What an unhappy usage it is that compels thousands of able, exemplary, and efficient clergymen throughout the country to become weekly bores and nuisances! In the common opinion of men, to *preach* is their primary duty, and to preach their own compositions is the only reputable way of fulfilling it. By their oratorical faculty do they practically stand or fall. They may have the intellect of Samuel Seabury, or the business faculty of Haight, or the self-denying piety of poor little Houghton, but if they cannot write clever essays and read them effectively it is naught; they are "slow." . . . And therefore men like Haight and Berrian are compelled to afflict congregations with hebdomadal doses of platitudes and commonplaces.

May 12.   Spent an hour trying to get myself phototyped for the benefit of my mother, but without success. . . . To No. 24 for Ellen, and a long talk with Mr. Ruggles. Things look worse; the only thing to be hoped for is euthanasia—a noiseless finale, without scandal. Life cannot be sustained—the stimulants have ceased to work—indeed, I could have predicted the result years ago if I had known the workings of the system. I don't think it desirable that it should go on.

May 13.   For the last two hours with Mr. Ruggles. Worse and worse. He will bring down others, I fear, in his fall. H. & H. are likely to be heavy losers. It will be well if they're not ruined. F. Griffin can survive his loss, but these men and some others of the same sort will have hard work to stagger under theirs, and I fear will fall. It's a cruel business on both sides. The trust estate of Mrs. Ruggles is in a bad position, but with promptitude and good luck, I hope it may be saved from serious loss.

May 16, FRIDAY NIGHT.   I have not been very fruitful of good works for the past three days. Mr. Ruggles's perplexities and troubles have occupied my mind a good deal and made me listless and inefficient. It is sad to see the ruinous wreck of the plans and operations that have been going on so long, the total loss of years of labor, the sacrifice of property acquired by so much energy and talent. It is sad, too, to see its effect on the domesticities of No. 24; for this will be an honest failure, to be followed up by retrenchment and close economy, and the surrender of everything but Mrs. Ruggles's private estate, or what is left of it. I could not but think of it yesterday—the change from the old, happy day of which it was the anniversary; the brightness and gaiety of the house then, and its condition now with the black shadow of insolvency at the door; the "Let us depart hence" of all its household gods; the gloom and despondency and stillness that have taken their abode in every room; John dead, Jem away, Ellie no longer there, all who remain busy in the sad work of saving the poor fragments of sudden and sickening ruin, and preparing to remove to some humbler lodging. . . .

A note will lie over at the Chemical Bank tomorrow, so the case is a pretty clear one. Mr. Ruggles tells me tonight of a matter that I'm glad of, for it breaks the fall a little; a movement on the part of W. B. Astor, the Kings, and others to raise a fund to purchase the Clarendon at its full value and a little over, and so enable him to wind up his affairs and make at least a fair settlement with his creditors. But it won't be done— it's a mere flicker of hope burning out in the socket. The case is at present perfectly remediless. May I be delivered from the lunacy of debt!

Heard Jenny Lind Wednesday night with Ellen. As much pleased as I expected to be, and no more. All that I heard her sing was overloaded with *fiorituri* and foolery, marvelously executed, but I always find that sort of thing a bore. The low and middle notes of her voice are superb, and the high notes as good as such notes can be, but she runs too much on music written for the altitudes. No doubt she does it with perfect ease, but that don't make it the pleasanter to hear. A man who could walk on his head as comfortably as on his feet would be a fatiguing person to look at, if he abused his faculty of locomotion and was habitually upside down. The lady's personal appearance took me much by surprise. None of her portraits do her any justice. She is not pretty nor handsome, nor exactly fine-looking, but there's an air about her of dignity, self-possession, modesty, and goodness that is extremely attractive.

Anthon's pamphlet is favorably noticed in two or three papers. Students of the New York University have had a meeting and passed some silly resolutions.

May 19. Today a good deal with Mr. Ruggles. His affairs not flourishing. Minturn and others active in the Clarendon plan, with some reason to hope for success, but that infatuated Scotchman Robert Henry is cutting his own throat and his debtor's at once, by such fantastic folly as none but the most wrong-headed of angry creditors would dream of. With Mr. Ruggles tonight to Bidwell's, and thence to my father's. . . .

I'm beginning to be uneasy about F. Griffin. If he should not stand this shock, there would be a specially miserable complication.

May 27.   Tremendous row at Hoboken yesterday; a battle of the peoples, like Leipzig. German loaferism warring with the Aaron Burrs of New York, the gutterhorn soaplocks and shortboys of the wharves and their Irish allies. Some lives lost, and strong possibility that the fight may be renewed here.

Mr. Ruggles's affairs worse and worse and worse and worse, and as he falls he will propagate ruin and spread desolation and devastation around him. The two Harriots, [Francis] Griffin—the black catalogue may develop itself. I'll not forestall time in its miserable work. I wish some new nineteenth century saint would arise and preach a curse upon all credit systems, a crusade against negotiable paper, and proclaim all the woes of the Apocalyptic Babylon against that complex work of devilish ingenuity whereby ruin, bankruptcy, and dishonor are made so fearfully familiar to this enlightened age; the system that makes the utmost fruit of steady industry vulgar and cheap when compared with the glittering results that form exceptions only to its legitimate and usual result, but yet occur often enough to lure the multitude and make us a nation of gamblers, easily classified as a minority of millionaires sprinkled through a majority of bankrupt beggars.

God deliver me from *debt*! Yet the insolvent debtor, I suppose, cares but little for the incubus, as a general rule, after he has become resigned to the conviction that it can't be thrown off, and that he must live under it as he best may. That is the worst of our wretched "financial" system. It degrades, debases, demoralizes its victims. They look men in the face whom they have ruined by breaking their promises, and have nothing to say but that it was a "business transaction." It dissolves out all the sterling integrity there may be in the great mass of people, and leaves the dross and dirt behind. The practical question for the merchant and the financier becomes, "For how much is my credit good in Wall Street?"— *not*, "Shall I be able to keep my promise and pay this debt I'm contracting?" And when the operator is cornered, he will, in nine cases out of ten, borrow to the extent of his faculty, for the chance of getting through, in full consciousness that the chance of his failing to pay what he borrows is threefold as good. The sanctity and religious force of a promise to pay money or do anything else is lost sight of. People who fail, get a discharge, and pay their creditors when they have made money are paragraphed in the papers as prodigies, commented on as interesting martyrs to a nice sense of honor, praiseworthy, though perhaps a little over-trained, and glorified as if they had sacrificed all their earthly possessions in endowing hospitals and founding churches.

Mr. Ruggles suffers from the system into which brilliant and sanguine men, possessed of energy, fertility, and ambition, must inevitably be led in this age and country. It was not in his nature to keep out of the vortex. His mental constitution, talents, temperament, all combined to control his destiny and carry him into operations like those in which others engage, only without his range of view and his power of combination. I attach no shadow of blame to him for working on the basis of his ample credit, nor for the particular undertakings that have brought this calamity upon him. Nor has he a trace of the callousness to unpaid debt, the insensibility to broken engagements, which this fatal system engenders in common men. For his sake, I wish he could acquire a little of it. It is with him remorse, bitter self-reproach, the sense of defeat, of indignation at himself for projects which seemed demonstrably certain of success six months ago, all preying on him so fiercely that, were it not for the incessant exertion his affairs demand just now and the constant strain on his mind to devise help for those whom his fall is like to shatter, I should fear much for the effect of this on his physical frame. I look forward with much anxiety to the next four or five months. . . .

June 3, TUESDAY.   Mr. Ruggles's affairs growing tense: I trust they won't get much lower, if indeed they can. [Francis] Griffin has shifted his ground and become menacing, unjust, merciless, insolent, and cruel, and in a long interview on Sunday afternoon dealt in the gravest charges and the bitterest denunciations. He accused his unhappy debtor of fraud, deliberate dishonesty, of systematically abusing his confidence to his ruin, and the like. And I fear he is spreading these slanders recklessly through Wall Street, though without an atom of credence for them and without anything on which he has a right to found a suspicion of the truth. Much is to be pardoned to a man in his position; but the invention of injurious falsehoods and the deliberate assertion of them is not to be pardoned to any man in any position. I tell Mr. Ruggles that he ought not to see Griffin again. No conceivable relation of debtor and creditor justifies such treatment, or makes it proper or becoming to incur its in-fliction more than once. One such interview cancels everything but the pecuniary obligation, wipes out everything but the legal liability for so many dollars. All regret for the injury the creditor has sustained, all self-reproach, all sense of humiliation, all that can make an honorable man suffer when he has become the involuntary means of injuring another, ought to vanish before this atrocious and malignant broadside of insult and untruth. The unintentional *injury* is repaid with interest; on that score the parties are at least equal.

Today things look still bluer, for the Street is ringing with the report that Griffin has stopped. No wonder. The last few months have been fruitful of calamities for him. His $25,000 in Dauphin [anthracite] stock has gone down to zero. Some $70,000 comes upon him from Mr. Ruggles's embarrassments and he has been endorsing to the amount of $45,000 for Sam Ward (Ward & Price). He is reputed worth $200,000 and upwards, but he is engaged in extensive building operations with E. Davis and involved in contracts and engagements of great extent and complexity. He can't wind up his affairs on a sudden, or raise $100,000 except at murderous sacrifice. How he is secured on the Ward & Price indorsements I don't know. "Property in California" is talked of—probably as available for the emergency as property in the planet Jupiter. But against Mr. Ruggles's paper he has the Atlantic Dock stores, with their mortgages, an ample security *if* he can hold it till the rents pay off the incumbrances. On the whole, he'll have to make an assignment.

June 4. Griffin is horribly savage, and what I dread most is that in the vindictive heat and fervor of his wrath he may go blindly to work and seek to avenge himself by persecution, under the Sulwell act or *otherwise*. He has thrown out vague threats that sound ominous, but he has no ground to stand on and such measures would inevitably recoil on himself —and they might well kill his victim first.

June 6, FRIDAY. Lost another day yesterday by the fiend of headache. . . . Very limp today, but some work has been done. Mr. Ruggles in better spirits, or rather, not quite so deep in despair. Griffin seems to be subsiding a little—as he has reason, when Mr. Ruggles is proposing to get his wife's assent to the surrender of some of her separate property. But I give up Mr. Griffin for a cruel and cowardly bully, and trust that I may never have the ill luck to fall into his hands.

June 7. Rainy day, and a reasonably industrious one. More confer-ring with Mr. Ruggles. He is broken in spirit, but I hope his courage

HOME OF GEORGE TEMPLETON STRONG
EAST TWENTY-FIRST STREET AT GRAMERCY PARK
CALVARY CHURCH AND FOURTH AVENUE IN THE DISTANCE

JENNY LIND

JENNY LIND'S FIRST APPEARANCE IN AMERICA
CASTLE GARDEN, 11 SEPTEMBER 1850

will revive before long. F. Griffin is spreading slanderous untruth with a bountiful hand; the substance of his statements being, first, that he always supposed himself to be an endorser for $20,000 instead of $70,000, and was by some unexplained means made to be ignorant of the notes he put his name on, and secondly, that there is property secreted and that the failure is a dishonest one. As to the first, this gentleman signed a receipt some two months ago for $80,000 worth of mortgages lodged with him as security for these very endorsements. If it is his way to sign his name *ad libitum* for the asking, in utter ignorance of the extent of the liabilities, agreeing to receive securities and give receipts for them without knowing what he is about, or looking at the papers that are put into his hands, it is very proper that he should say so, and whoever believes the story will acquit him of intentional slander and malicious mischief, and concede to him all the imbecility and all the recklessness for which he claims credit. However, he says nothing about his receipt dated April 1st for the Atlantic Dock mortgages—probably he has forgotten them in his wrath. His charge as to the endorsements is merely that he signed whatever he was asked to sign, and never knew what or how much; a most probable and plausible story for a shrewd business man to tell of himself. I wish Mr. Ruggles saw the matter as it strikes me. I can't get him to feel, or at least to express, an atom of bitterness or a trace of irritation against this man, who is deliberately exerting himself to the utmost to blast his character and to make the wreck of his fortunes hopeless. He says that allowances are to be made for excitement, that Griffin may lose heavily, and so forth. Out on the unwholesome softheartedness of this emasculated age!

June 10, TUESDAY.   Ellie has made another out-break into the country —viz., to Mrs. James Strong's—whither I can't follow her, for I'm working now in a frenzy of hurry to get up my brief and so forth in H. *v.* N. . . . Mr. Ruggles's affairs seem to have got down to the nadir of utter, notorious, avowed bankruptcy, believed by half the public to be discreditable if not dishonest. I don't see that they can grow a great deal worse. It is a very uncommonly miserable business.

It's a selfish feeling perhaps, but I'm specially grateful that I'm nowise mixed up with it, either in fact or in enlightened opinion of the public. To be sure, I may be wrong as to the latter, for I should be the last person to hear any reports that I was the secret depositary of a few hundred thousand dollars. . . .

Webb *v.* Willis and vice versa. Very nasty position is Webb's—he's trying to bluster it through, like a genuine Front de *Brass* as he is—but it won't do.[12] Warm and lovely evening. Cholera at Cincinnati, and virulent in the West generally. May it not travel hitherwards! Warm weather is developing the stench of our filthy streets—the "kakodyle" of civic chemistry. They were very *"noisy"* (query, corruption of *noisome* or a bold figure of speech?) tonight; strong as the notable fragrance I encountered in Beaumont's *Psyche*; a queer place to find it, and the most pungently aromatic passage I know in English poetry:

> She waked the Stink,
> A Stink which might disdain what Araby
> And all her odors could against it do—
> An *aged stink*—which in that sordid sty
> Had *mellowing lain*.

June 13. Day of tearing hurry. Commenced testimony in *Higgins* case; to be a long job—having postponed to July term—probably lies over till fall—so I've no need to be as much over-worked for the next week as I expected. . . .

Called at Mr. Ruggles's for Ellen this evening. Napoleon in better spirits—don't know why. This would seem to be his *Waterloo*, but probably his destiny is not yet accomplished. Hear that he's reported to have made immense settlements on his children, which as far as Ellen is concerned he certainly hasn't. She was a "tocherless" bride, God bless her; I love her the more for it. There is something unpleasant in getting money with one's wife, though "money is a noble thing." It's said that he built *this* house, which is a figment. But I know how the story originated; the title to all four lots passed through him. He bought up all and then conveyed to my father, Aunt Olivia, and me. It was done for the greater convenience of the parties. My father paid for the land.

June 16, MONDAY. Church yesterday as usual. Cram dined with us. Evening at home. Today a good deal occupied. Went to Bidwell's at five to meet my father and Mr. Ruggles for a consultation on certain doubtful points connected with the proposed transfer by Mr. Ruggles of certain securities to Griffin. Had a conference with Griffin, at *his request*, Saturday afternoon, and took the opportunity to tell him that if he had originated

---

[12] An ancient feud had existed between the quarrelsome James Watson Webb and N. P. Willis. During the Forrest divorce case Willis, with Parke Godwin and others, warmly espoused the cause of Mrs. Forrest, and were repaid by the actor with abusive accusations. Webb seized the opportunity to circulate charges that Willis was a Lothario, and so got into trouble; for the charges had no substantial basis.

any stories about my being depositary of any funds, or about *settlements* on Mrs. George Templeton Strong, he had become an author of fiction. Griffin in reply immensely polite and panegyrical. Disclaimed any such thing; had never entertained a suspicion that I could be party to any irregular or questionable transaction, etc., etc. He wanted to see me to make some enquiries about Mrs. Ruggles's separate estate, which I answered to my ability. He suspected clearly that Mr. Ruggles had *created* some trust in favor of his wife, which is not the case. First impression as to the interview satisfactory, but I strongly suspect from some remarks that within a little while he will open a campaign of some sort—against the trust property, perhaps—of much energy. Meanwhile Mr. Ruggles dies hard, and fights grimly with fate, thus far with good success. One creditor after another is arranged with. . . .

June 20, FRIDAY. Opera has commenced at Castle Garden and I've given three evenings this week to it. Very pleasant hearing the Havana Company (first among the second-rates, if not entitled to rank among the first) in a room so big that it can't be crowded, with that lovely outside gallery to walk on when one's tired of listening, and without the baneful necessity of any preliminary toilette. Tuesday was *Marino Faliero*, a threadbare reproduction of Donizetti's commonplaces—the same shabby old subjects worked over again for the fiftieth time—but well sung. Wednesday was *Lucrezia Borgia*, which is a trumpery affair enough, but its intelligible plot, its abundant dramatic situations, and its scraps of lively melody make it pleasant to hear when rendered by a good company. Tonight we had *Don Giovanni*. Bosio was perfect as Zerlina, her "Batti, batti" and "Vedrai, Carino" were sung as they deserve to be, without fault or failure, according to the letter of Mozart and with full expression of their feeling. Donna Anna (Truffi) D. Elvira (Virginia Whiting), and Don Ottavio (Forti) were satisfactory. . . . But the music is celestial. I can't commence criticizing so transcendent a subject at a quarter-past twelve. Ellen has gone with me, and without fatigue or apparent harm. She continues well and bright, thank Heaven.

Some progress has been made in Mr. Ruggles's affairs. Some assignment is made by Mr. Ruggles's trustees to Griffin and Harriot. Saw Griffin on Tuesday or Wednesday. Curious conversation, in which he *admitted* that he didn't know whether the injurious charges he has been spreading were true or false. . . .

Prodigious fire at San Francisco—half the city burnt up. Loss probably much exaggerated. Deducting the gold dust, I don't suppose that

$20,000,000 of property and buildings existed in the place, and gold dust is incombustible.

June 24. Today has been hot and burning. Had full experience of its intensity from one to three in toiling through the streets of Brooklyn to look after H. *v.* N. Reference did not come off. Vanderbilt *sick*, or probably too inert to come out of doors in this weather, for he is the unwieldiest lump of laziness and premature obesity I know.

City somewhat stagnant; news but little. Mr. Ruggles back from Albany —saw him a moment today. Griffin, I hear, is "somewhat pacified." I'm sluggish in making up my mind about new things, but I'm now quite clear on that subject. The slanders he has spread so widely were not strictly malicious, perhaps, because they were flung about in reckless, vindictive excitement and passion. They were not deliberate, for a very little calm reflection would have shewn that they could easily be refuted, and that if they were believed, they would make any future exertions of the debtor to make provision for these liabilities hopeless; and while they gave him the character of a knave, they stamped his creditor as the most verdant of dupes—proclaimed him unfit for the care of his property, entitled him to a place by the side of the softest rustic that ever figured in the police reports as the victim of a watch-snatcher on the Five Points. But they were none the less flagitious, and the injury they have done is none the less irreparable. They were gross, sweeping, wholesale charges of dishonesty in concealing the amount of liability a confidential friend was blindly incurring; yet he had written evidence of the amount, and mortgages to secure him against it in his hands for months, which he says *he never looked at.* But people listen to the disgraceful charge and remember it, who will never hear, or change their minds with, its easy refutation. The mischief can never be wholly cured. A man publicly accused of swindling today may demonstrate himself innocent tomorrow, but he no longer stands where he stood before. People hear his name twenty years after and say—"Mr. A? Wasn't there once something said against him?"

Mr. Ruggles has two grave faults, a sanguine disposition that has led him into this scrape, and an excessive, ultra-deluded hyper-charitable amiability that prevented his taking strong ground when these falsehoods were first emitted against him, and meeting them with decision and energetic denial.

June 25. At Castle Garden tonight with Ellie. *Ernani:* Bettini far the best Ernani I've seen. The music is vile, and no living or possible company of performers can make it other than vile. But it's pleasant to listen to it. It brings back so keenly the spring of 1848. Those well-remembered unisons in the finale of the third act, that used to keep ringing in my ears as I walked downtown, half-delirious, from Astor Place—the fragrance of that time comes again whenever I think of them! So with Truffi's aria in the first act; the very extravagance and slangwhanging absurdity of the music gives it character, and identifies the memory with which it's associated.

June 28, SATURDAY.   Opera still patronized by Ellen and me; last night *Don Giovanni*, tonight Donizetti's *Favorita*, both well sung and rather listlessly performed. . . . G. C. Anthon's pamphlet subject of discussion in legislature. Townsend moved to strike out appropriation to New York University, and there was some rather highly flavored discussion of the deserts of that learned corporation. As this is not a new gift, but rather the fulfilment of an old promise, the University will probably get its $1500.

June 30.   A little cooler this evening, thanks to the sea breeze that so rarely fails to come with sunset. It brings needed refreshment tonight, for the city has been fizzing and frying all day long with fervent heat. Last night we were without it—a severe dispensation. Rose languid, sore, flaccid, and exhausted, after an hour or so of disagreeable doze in which I was keenly conscious of flies lighting on my damp forehead.

July 2, WEDNESDAY NIGHT.   Spent yesterday driving about Queens Co. with my little Cornwall protégé investigating transactions connected with his grandfather's death in 1838 and inquiring especially into the extent to which that venerable man's brain had become addled before he died, by a fanaticism for bad brandy. Result highly favorable; think I can shew the old fellow's acquiescence to have been that of imbecility. Little Higgins, or Cornwall, as he is now particular to call himself, spite of his illegitimacy, is a very fine, intelligent little fellow, and I shall work the harder, if possible, in this case, for a client who promises so well, without having had any but bad associations about him and without advantages of any sort.

July 7, MONDAY NIGHT.   To West Point Thursday morning in the *New World*. Overcast, but cool and pleasant, and after we reached the Point, bright enough and quite comfortable. Eleanor came to meet us, and we found our friends of the past two summers, Clitz, Maury, Porter, and so forth, all in good preservation; and were in our old rooms, completely domesticated and arranged and enjoying their lovely outlook up the river, within half an hour after our arrival. Our establishment this year consists of the invaluable grandmother, whose company I made an indispensable condition precedent to our going out of town anywhere *this* summer—for special and sufficient reasons—and Ellen's *Marie*, who promises to be a very useful and comfortable handmaiden.

The Fourth was a pleasant and cool day. Went to the chapel; heard the Declaration of Independence read, of course, and then listened to a highly appropriate Fourth of July oration from a cadet, name forgotten, made up of the regulation commonplaces of the subject, enlivened by copious bombast and abundant tropes after the manner of the best authorities and examples. The orator was belligerent, of course, and reveled in the raw-head and bloody-bones branch of his subject. . . .

Read at the Point Curzon's *Monasteries of the Levant*, and *Alton Locke*; began *Yeast*, by the author of *Alton Locke*, one Kingsley. The first is the best book of Oriental travel I've met, very healthy, lively, and pleasant, without pretence, magniloquence, monkeyism, or affectation of any kind. The two novels are strong books, and according to my first impression, *true* ones.

Talk of the ennobling pursuits of literature, historic research, art, music, the elevating influence of investigations into natural science, the noble object of reviving a fit and reverent style of church architecture, and the other subjects which the better class of cultivated men select as their business or their relaxation—they are all good. But what is there for an Englishman, with more or less of surplus time and faculties, after making due provision for himself and his household, to *do* in the year of grace 1851 *before* he has done something to help the thousands and tens of thousands that are perishing hopelessly in profligacy, drunkenness, and starvation in the cellars and workshops of every city in England? It strikes me that most "liberal pursuits," no matter how purifying to the tastes and invigorating to the intellect, are something like a wretched waste of time and perversion of talent and an insane misapplication of energy and industry, while men and women and children in multiplying thousands lie rotting alive, body and soul at once, in those awful catacombs of disease and crime, and even the question how to save them is yet unsolved.

And the same question is to be asked, and must be answered, here in New York; though, Heaven be praised, it does not *yet* stand out with such terrible prominence before all other questions of duty to society here as in London and Manchester.

Yet we have our Five Points, our emigrant quarters, our swarms of seamstresses to whom their utmost toil in monotonous daily drudgery gives only bare subsistence, a life barren of hope and of enjoyment; our hordes of dock thieves, and of children who live in the streets and by them. No one can walk the length of Broadway without meeting some hideous troop of ragged girls, from twelve years old down, brutalized already almost beyond redemption by premature vice, clad in the filthy refuse of the rag-picker's collections, obscene of speech, the stamp of childhood gone from their faces, hurrying along with harsh laughter and foulness on their lips that some of them have learned by rote, yet too young to understand it; with thief written in their cunning eyes and whore on their depraved faces, though so unnatural, foul, and repulsive in every look and gesture, that that last profession seems utterly beyond their aspirations. On a rainy day such crews may be seen by dozens. They haunt every other crossing and skulk away together, when the sun comes out and the mud is dry again. And such a group I think the most revolting object that the social diseases of a great city can produce. A gang of blackguard boys is lovely by the side of it.[13]

Meantime, philanthropists are scolding about the fugitive slave law, or shedding tears over the wretched niggers of the Carolinas who have to work and to eat their victuals on principles inconsistent with the rights of man, or agitating because the unhanged scoundrels in the City Prison occupy cells imperfectly ventilated. "Scholars" are laboriously writing dissertations for the Historical Society on the First Settlement of the Township of Squankum, and consuming the midnight oil in elucidating and illustrating the highly interesting MS collection of letters in the possession of the Smith family supposed to have been written by Petrus Smith who died somewhere about 1690, to the great weariness and dreariness of the patient men who attend the meetings of that association. Clergymen are compiling treatises on Ancient Egypt, or evolving windiness that they imbibed "under the shadow of Mont Blanc."

And what am I doing, I wonder? I'm neither scholar nor philanthropist nor clergyman, nor in any capacity a guide or ruler of the people, to be sure—there is that shadow of an apology for my sitting still. But if Heaven will permit and enable me, I'll do something in the matter before I die— to have helped one dirty vagabond child out of such a pestilential sink would be a thing one would not regret when one came to march out of this world—and if one looks at FACTS, would be rather more of an achievement than the writing another *Iliad*.

July 8.   In town tonight, to my disappointment, and to E's likewise,

[13] Charles Loring Brace's book on *Our Pauper and Vagrant Children* (1859) proves that Strong's statements are not exaggerated.

I fear. Spent an active day, smiting beastly blows at the accumulated hosts of *agenda*, enlivening myself by cashing the Langdon order on the Trust Company for $2,000. Talked with Kearny about Ruggles's scrapes and Griffin's slanders; K. spoke with much feeling on the subject. Mr. Ruggles, by the by, is not by any means killed by his fall. His feline tenacity of life and elasticity of frame don't desert him; a cat thrown from a three-story window don't find her feet again sooner than he finds work and purpose and hope. He has taken an office and got a tin sign, a suit, an advertisement in the papers, and has "resumed the practice of his profession."

As Strong wrote, the resilient Ruggles, though now in his fifty-second year, made a rapid and complete recovery in his financial and professional fortunes. He prospered at the bar and in his business activities; within a few years he was again comfortably wealthy. His prestige in the community was not impaired, and before long he was to lead the liberal element in the Columbia College Board of Trustees in a vigorous contest for the exclusion of all sectarian tests in the selection of professors. Strong and his wife were now expecting a baby. They went for a short time to West Point, where they renewed their friendships with such familiar figures as the hotel-keeper, William B. Cozzens; the professor of natural and experimental philosophy, William H. C. Bartlett; and the professor of mathematics, Albert E. Church. But it was soon concluded that Mrs. Strong would be safer and more comfortable in the immediate vicinity of New York.

July 15, TUESDAY. Pete Strong has returned after a three years' absence. Judge King's opinion in Alston *v.* Jones sensible and creditable. . . . Prospects of the "uptown park" growing bright. The Schermerhorns don't like it a bit, or pretend they don't, notwithstanding the $1,500,000 of which they'll get their share. Financial horizon overcast. I expect to bust by the middle of September next. Shuffled out tonight. Called at Mr. Ruggles's, lounged back, watched a little with the microscope over some Infusoria from the Bronx, obtained when I was at Mr. Lydig's.

July 21. Mr. Ruggles's affairs making no progress in particular. Prospect that there will be a judgment recovered in two or three days, and an assignment therefore is becoming indispensable. Griffin has not seen fit as yet to recant any of his slanderous misstatements. I've gone as far as was fitting in my suggestions to Mr. Ruggles as to his proper course in the premises, and as he don't choose to do anything, I suppose these charges against him must be considered as taken *pro confesso. I* would make a very grim kind of fight before a *la stoccata* should so "carry it away," but every man must judge of his own affairs. He is timid to a fault. It is no part of Christian meekness to be silent and passive when one is belied; and though we are bidden to live peaceably with all men, so far as may be, we are not called on to acquiesce in all the virulent falsehoods an angry man can invent and circulate, because he would wax more wroth and might be obstreperous if they were contradicted. Mr. Ruggles "expects" that Griffin will see his error and voluntarily proclaim it; a kind of "waiting on Providence" likely to be without results. . . .

His true course would be, or would have been, for the time is past now, to address a letter to Griffin: "You have stated this and that, all which is untrue: the following facts are conceded to be true. Now please to state how you reconcile your charges with these. If you cannot, have the kindness to say so in writing. If you do neither, I'll publish your refusal in every known newspaper, and sue you for slander besides."

I always grow unphilosophically excited when I think of Griffin, so intolerably mean, cowardly, and cruel has been his part in this miserable tragi-comedy.

July 29, TUESDAY. Cuban Insurrection, *pronunciamento*, etc., falling generally into disrepute: thought to be manufactured for this market. But sooner or later the area of freedom will be enlarged by the absorption of the island. It's too tempting and too accessible to be long left unstolen.

Heard one act of *Sonnambula* at Castle Garden tonight, and the first chorus of the second. Immense crowd. The opera has created quite a furor. Everybody goes, and nob and snob, Fifth Avenue and Chatham Street, sit side by side fraternally on the hard benches. Perhaps there is hardly so attractive a summer theatre in the world as Castle Garden when so good a company is performing as we have there now. Ample room; cool sea breeze on the balcony, where one can sit and smoke and listen and look out on the bay studded with the lights of anchored vessels, and white sails gleaming. . . . I don't wonder that the people are *Sonnambula*-mad. The plot of the opera is pretty for an opera plot; the music is pretty and shallow and taking and is sung by Bosio and Salvi. It's not very reasonable, to be sure, to prefer "Ah, non giunge" to "Vedrai, Carino," but that delusion is less debasing than the superstitious belief in Donizetti and Verdi that prevails so lamentably.

August 4, MONDAY NIGHT. News by telegraph in tonight's paper of another calamitous fire in San Francisco. Scarcely credible, when the ashes and ruin of the last are hardly cold yet. It may very well have been invented by the bull operators of the Exchange, for the money market here is suddenly growing painfully tight and tense; lenders "wait in fear and dread," and borrowers go perspiring through the streets in vain, though it's cool weather for August. If this story finds credit, tomorrow stocks will go down "like the full sail when the mast is broken"—to quote Dante. More Lynch law reported in operation upon the sinful citizens of the modern Ophir. The last case that we heard of was curious, as showing the existence and effective actions of a secret tribunal of criminal law in San Francisco, self-constituted, and seemingly composed of "respectable" people in the midst of a populous and wealthy community. What was the *Vehmgericht* more than a medieval Judge Lynch, with some picturesque accessories? Where there is an established social system with institutions consecrated to the determination of right and the execution of justice, which prove so tardy or insufficient or incumbered with forms that their office is unfulfilled and the guilty go unpunished, the true remedy, of course, is to reform the system by lawful ways, and lawfully to remove whatever impairs its vigor. Any other course is wrong. But it may be a question whether the crime ought to pass unvisited by vengeance where the machinery of law has shewn itself by repeated instances too weak to inflict it; whether those who deliberately, solemnly, and on due enquiry execute on a notorious criminal the just will of a whole community, and assume the functions of the judge, because the courts of law have been found unable to use them with energy, are guilty of murder. . . .

To West Point in *Henry Clay* Saturday afternoon, somewhat of a crowd. Talked to Cozzens, and that snob of snobs Horace Clark.[14] Did not go to church yesterday, feeling somewhat headachy and out of spirits. After dinner started with C. for the top of Cro' Nest in hope of exorcising the headache. Did not succeed and had to resort to another suicidal dose of physic when I got home. But had a very delightful, inspiring, and perspiring walk. The rugged plateau at the top, with its thick underbrush, its stunted oaks spreading their low distorted branches here and there among the rocks, its black, peaty morass stretching far back to the west, and its occasional lovely views up the river to the Catskills, and southwest over still secluded valleys among wooded hills, and across to the bold and broken ranges of the highlands on the east shore, is a very fascinating place to me.

[14] Horace F. Clark married Marie Louise Vanderbilt, one of the nine daughters of the Commodore.

August 12, TUESDAY. In town for the season, rather unexpectedly. Found Ellie not quite well when I reached the Point Saturday night; cold, face-ache, etc. However, we got along very comfortably that evening walking the piazza and listening to the band playing in Camp. . . .

I have taken possession of Mrs. Ruggles, the invaluable grandmother, and intend that she shall abide with us till Ellie's troubles are over. Without her I should not feel easy for an hour.

Principal topic discussed at the Point for the past few days the outrage at Cozzens's hotel on Friday afternoon by an excursion party of volunteers, Jersey City Riflemen, "short boys," and other scum, who were refused the privileges of the bar and the run of the house by Mr. Cozzens, having landed at his dock without licence, and who thereupon proceeded to break windows, pull up the planks of the piazza, smash chairs, etc., broke Cozzens's head, and hurt his two sons badly. It was a melée of the fiercest sort for a few minutes; the three Cozzenses, five workers and Mrs. Connolly (*vide* last Academy of Design) against some sixty blackguards, the latter finally beaten off.

August 15. Autumnal day, refreshingly cool and clear. Ellen's cough better, but not well yet. Left home intending to go to Rockaway this afternoon to look for quarters, but hearing that the place is filled full, stayed away and went with Ellen to *Don Pasquale* instead. Good house and enthusiastic. Opera performed twice as well as it deserves, though there's much in it that's lively and piquant for Donizetti. Clarendon foreclosure arrested to abide the decision of the Law Committee of the Bank. I'm a good deal uneasy about that matter.

Half inclined to take Ellen back to West Point, for it seems impossible to find any suitable or tolerable marine locality. But she don't favor the proposition. Pity the metropolis should taint the country as it does for a circle of at least thirty miles radius around it. Within that distance the civic scum ebbs and flows on Sundays and holidays—gent, snob, blackleg, fast-man, whore, and Bowery gal, some or all of them radiate from New York in every direction, to infest Long Island and Richmond County; and all conveniently accessible hotels and boarding houses are overrun by the vermin that hot weather roasts out of its homes in town. Coney Island, for instance, seems to be nothing more than Church Street transported bodily a few miles out of town.

August 18. Rockaway being full, we have half determined to make an experiment on Edwin Powell's at Whitestone, where my mother has rooms engaged and unoccupied. I shall try to make a reconnaissance on Wednesday. Hitch in this Clarendon matter yet unsettled. Probably it will be settled the wrong way and perhaps it's as well it should.

August 24, SUNDAY.   Last night we were at Castle Garden again. Sat on the terrace and inhaled the sea-breeze, listening only at distant intervals to the not heavy music of *Ernani*, and looked out on the bay and the stars above and the stars below—for the night was dark and nothing was to be seen an hundred yards off except the multitudinous lights great and small, near and distant, scattered over the surface of the bay, like another series of constellations below us. Now and then the white sail of a sloop drifting along glimmered faintly through the night and then dissolved out of sight again, in a ghostly manner; but at other times one seemed to be at the edge of the world—the jumping off place—looking up and down at the stars of both hemispheres.

News of the second Cuban expedition, the raid or foray of the moss-troopers of Mississippi upon the Southerners. It has been a woeful hunting thus far. The intelligence of the execution of some fifty of the marauders has made a commotion here, the end of which is not yet. If these unfortunate loafers were clearly identified as part of the gang, they fully deserved their fate. The Captain General was justified by the law of nations in shooting them on the spot, and though he might have remembered mercy, we've no right to quarrel with him or his government because he executed justice vigorously on people taken red-hand in piracy and unable to offer ignorance or anything else in mitigation of their offense. But my first feeling on reading the intelligence at Delmonico's the other morning was to make reprisal by the instant assassination of a little whiskered monkey of a Spaniard who was innocently swallowing his chocolate at the next table. And from my own case I infer that the South and West, not remarkable for conservatism or a disposition to forgive anything they consider a national affront, will ferment into fury, and that we shall have another and a stronger expedition before long. If Lopez could keep himself and the graceless ragamuffins that back him in a whole skin for a month longer, he's a *made man*. . . . But Lopez is probably shot or garroted long before this. Anyhow, Cuba will be annexed—or independent of Spain within ten years.

August 28, THURSDAY.   Weather cool and autumnal as it has been since Monday night, when the northwest wind visited us in mercy and scattered the dense vapors that two or three days of sultry heat had raised. That evening Ellen and I and Miss Rosalie had to leave Castle Garden in the midst of the *Barbiere*, so oppressive was even that coolest of all summer theatres. . . . We heard *Lucia* that night. Sad stuff it is. Badiali, the Ashton (the Figaro of the night before), is certainly a great actor—far the best I have ever seen in opera. . . .

No certain news yet about Lopez and his gang. There has been a row at New Orleans, and Rynders tried to raise one here, but without success. The Spanish government will probably set up its back on learning that its consul at New Orleans has been mobbed and that the authorities made little or no effort to protect him. Additional squads of filibusters have sailed to look after Lopez. If news should come of the shooting of another batch of fifty or thereabouts, the fury of the people will be likely to know no bounds. We might expect to see even in this city a strong demonstration against Spanish residents. At the South such a thing would be more than probable. Suppose the mob of Havana proceed to make reprisals on the Yankee consul and some of his countrymen? It's a hotbed from which a *casus belli* is very like to germinate. If the filibusters get a firm foot hold in the island and are able to prosecute the war for a few months on anything like terms of equality, it will be a most savage and fiendish warfare on both sides; no quarter given on either.

September 1. Have just heard two acts of *Norma* at Castle Garden, with one Rose de Vries as the heroine. Plenty of voice and little music— lots of action and no go, as sporting people say. The house was crowded and enthusiastic; the louder this lady screamed, the more uproariously they applauded, and her solitary windpipe was a fair match for the vociferous bravos of her 5,000 admirers. In the grand explosion scene of the second act, where that unhappy man Pollione has to be bullied and repudiated by the two ladies together, Norma holloed so and fell foul of her recreant lover in such desperate earnest, and so made the fur fly, that the exaltation of the audience knew no bounds—and the triumph of the Signora became a fixed fact. . . .

Spent an hour at Delmonico's with Wolcott Gibbs today, just returned in the *Atlantic.*

September 4. Edward Curtis and his wife here tonight. Talked about Cuba with Mr. Curtis, who is a confidant of [Sidney] Webster's, and knows or ought to know a good deal on the subject. He thinks it will end in nothing—that the invasion of this Robert Guiscard of the nineteenth century is killed, and that the invaders stay where they are for the simple reason that a rat stays in a trap. Probably true—but our telegraph and other reports, since the intelligence that reached here on the 23d or thereabouts, have been merciless lies and are entitled to no weight at all. And we should have had authentic despatches from the Governor General by this time, if there had been news of a victory to communicate. It would have been natural that such news be sent here as soon as possible, as a dash of cold water on supplementary expeditions. It is not too clear to me, therefore, that this crew of rugged blackguards may not be holding its own, even against the tremendous odds it has to encounter.

In the revolutionary year 1848 Narciso Lopez, a Venezuelan by birth who had lived in both Spain and Cuba, had attempted to launch an uprising among the Cuban people. He met but a feeble response, and had to flee to the United States. Finding among the Southerners a keen desire for the acquisition of the island, and meeting with encouragement from Senator John C. Calhoun, he planned a filibustering invasion. In the spring of 1850 he landed a small force at Cárdenas and seized some Spanish officials; but learning to his great disappointment that the Cubans would not join his standard, he returned to Key West, and was shortly arrested by the American authorities in New Orleans. The prosecution was half-hearted and broke down. Meanwhile, Lopez had planned a larger and better-equipped expedition, and had raised funds by selling bonds in the South. Many enthusiastic young Southerners, encouraged by politicians and the press, flocked to his colors.

The miscarriage of this second expedition was not painful to Strong and other sober New Yorkers, who thought it both illegal and outrageous. Nevertheless, it had its very tragic aspects. On the night of August 11, 1851, Lopez brought a mixed body of Cubans and Americans ashore sixteen miles from Havana. Fifty recruits under a brave young Southerner named Crittenden were captured, hurried to Havana, and after military trial executed. Lopez himself, fighting hard in the jungle, was seized and garroted. News of the defeat of the filibusters and the death of many American volunteers reached New Orleans on August 21, creating such excitement that a mob immediately wrecked the Spanish consulate and a Spanish newspaper office. Riotous demonstrations took place in other Southern cities. While the Northern press for the most part warmly condemned the plots that had outraged American neutrality laws and cost so many reckless youths their lives, sentiment in the South treated "the gallant fifty-one" as martyrs. The American government had to pay $25,000 in damages for the work of the New Orleans mob and to proffer its apologies to Madrid; and it also had to put up with the appearance of French and British warships in the Gulf under orders to help protect Cuba against new assaults. The South, however, *remained as anxious as ever to see the rich slave-holding island added to the American domain, and Southern pressure soon brought about the issuance of the notorious "Ostend Manifesto."*

September 5, FRIDAY.   Warm. Rumor seemingly authentic that Lopez has been caught and garroted, and certain of his following with him. Summary justice; creditable to the promptitude and decision of the Cuban criminal judiciary. If this little band of militant philanthropists and self-consecrated missionaries of Republican scum has been exterminated, it will be long before filibusterism recovers from the shock. For the failure of the expedition proves either that the Creoles are not desirous of a revolution, or that if desirous, they are afraid to take arms even when a nucleus of fire-eating Mississippians volunteer to strike the first blow and give the natives something to rally around. And in either case filibuster oratory has lost its most important theme, the only pretext for invasion that can decently be avowed, the oppression of a high-minded race, etc., etc. The real motive remains, of course, viz.: a lust after other people's productive coffee-estates, a thirst for personal property, specie, jewelry, and the like, owned by somebody else, the desire of being on the winning side in a grand period of confiscation, and larceny on a large scale. But that won't do for the groundwork of manifestos and can't be made publicly available to influence opinion and win recruits. The only chance left for the agents in this intrigue is to embroil our government with Spain, which won't be accomplished while this administration is in power, unless Moses Y. Beach and General Quitman have extraordinary luck.[15]

September 12, FRIDAY.   No news. The letters, etc., from the Cuba volunteers indicate that they have been wickedly deceived as to the state of feeling among the Creoles, and are not unnaturally somewhat indignant at finding that they have been cheated into the hands of Spanish courts-martial. But the effort to manufacture public opinion continues. The solution probably is that a few wealthy Creoles want to effect a change and furnish money and lies to their agents here. Newspapers crowing over the victory of [John Cox] Stevens's yacht [America], which has beat everything in the British seas; quite creditable to Yankee ship-building certainly, but not worthy the intolerable, vainglorious vaporings

[15] Moses Y. Beach, owner of the New York *Sun*, and John A. Quitman, Mexican War hero and former governor of Mississippi, had helped Lopez promote his enterprises.

that make every newspaper I take up now ridiculous. One would think yacht-building were the end of man's existence on earth.

September 18. Committee meeting (Trinity Chapel) this morning. Little progress; my duties as secretary are not onerous. Much gossip and conjecture about the Assistant Bishop that's to be elected by the Convention. . . . Prominent names are Creighton, Kip, Vinton, and Wainwright. The first has the best chance. Miss Camilla Scott engaged to Goold Hoyt. There is the material of a very noble kind of woman in the young lady, impulsive and ill-regulated as she is. But she has made a fatal blunder. Hoyt has the look and manner of a Spaniel puppy, and I never discovered a trait in his character but pettiness, meanness, selfishness, and conceit. But he has lots of money.

September 24, WEDNESDAY. Diocesan Convention meets today for the Episcopal election. The Low-Church Party has nominated Taylor, whose chance is as good as mine may be of a Comanche chieftainship. As they've put forward a man they certainly won't elect, I suppose they mean to let their opponents have their own way, unless they see danger of too strong a man being elected, and will then resort to their old tricks of last session. Probably they'll be guided by the nominations that are made. If Creighton's put up, they will cast their votes for Taylor; if Seabury or any man like him, they will unite with some other section of the Convention.

September 26. Just from Convention at St. John's, which I suppose will adjourn tonight. Balloting began yesterday. Taylor nominated by the Low-Church men, Vinton by the other side; Creighton[16] declining the nomination (in caucus). Last night I looked on awhile, and the vote taken before I left gave Vinton 75 clerical and 77 lay votes, Taylor 32 and 49, Wainwright 40 and 37, the rest of the 185 and 184 scattering— and no election. They kept at it till near midnight, and on the fourth ballot Wainwright had 81 lay votes, a majority of 3, and 90 clerical—91 necessary to a choice; Vinton was 72 and 78. Taylor nowhere; his friends had transferred their votes to Wainwright. This morning Vinton was withdrawn and Creighton put forward, and at the last ballot this afternoon he was *elected* by a pretty close vote, to the confusion and wrath of his opponents, who are very bitter without being able to say why; for

[16] William Creighton (1793–1865), Columbia 1812, had been rector of St. Mark's Church, New York, from 1816 to 1836, and was at this time rector of Christ Church, Tarrytown. Though elected Provisional Bishop, he declined the office and remained at Christ Church until his death.

Creighton is a very amiable and inoffensive man, and his faults are exactly the same with Wainwright's, only not so prominent.

Tonight's proceedings opened with the prayer for the Church Militant, etc.; but first the Convention was invited to unite in the *Te Deum*, which was thereupon sung *con spirito* by enough of its members fairly to balance the full power of St. John's big organ. And though the chant was not the most effective that could have been selected, being one of the dreary, old-fashioned country church compositions that everybody has winced under of hot Sunday mornings for the last thirty years at least, the great body of voices made it a very stirring performance. I doubt whether every member of the convention contributed. The Rev. Henry Anthon's expression was probably rueful if he did, and his voice must have died away at times into a snarl. Tyng must have sung it as a "reconciled" Jew may have sung under Philip II, with a mental undercurrent of fluent and various malediction.

Vinton would have made a better bishop. The diocese needs his iron will and energy, as France needed Napoleon in 1796. Creighton will be inert and perhaps timid, but his friends and advisors will, I think, be the right set. His disposition will be to conciliate and avoid extremities; I fear, to avoid responsibility, too. Vinton would have bred an earthquake in the diocese within three months after his consecration. He would have operated on it like a ten-grain dose of calomel and with salutary results, I suspect. He would have invaded the next meeting of the Pastoral Aid Society in person, kicked out the members if necessary with his own episcopal foot energetically applied, locked the door, and carried off the key; would have silenced Tyng and bullied down Anthon, and ruled the flock committed to his keeping with a thick rod of red-hot iron. . . .

Money market desperately tight. Two or three New Jersey banks have collapsed, and people are talking ominously today about possible explosions among our own, and prophesying a panic and a run. Don't believe it will happen. If it does happen, it is a consolatory reflection that my own bank account is particularly small. I'm sadly vulgarized and degraded of late by the itching for money that has come over me. Oh, for $100,000—well invested! A skilful operation resulting in an enormous profit with no risk has all the charm for me now of poetry or romance.

Poor Wainwright—to come so close to the long-coveted mitre and to fail! The diocese had a narrow escape. He would have ornamented the office, adorned it by a venerable aspect and oleaginous urbanity. But gentleman-bishops have been and are the bane of the Anglican Churches—

venerable prelates of cultivated tastes and elegant scholarship. Better that a bishop should be a very little of a blackguard, a novice in the use of silver forks, and practically ignorant of the blessings of clean linen frequently renewed, than err on the other side. Harison has had a narrow escape, too. If Wainwright had been elected, Harison would have burst a blood vessel instantly, and if he had survived the shock, would have fled to the caves and rocks of St. Lawrence County and spent the rest of his days there, an eremitical lunatic, like him of Engaddi in *The Talisman*. I never could learn why he hates Wainwright so cordially, nor why Wainwright's generally emollient views of men and things always become a little acid and acrid whenever Harison is distantly alluded to. Wainwright electioneered indefatigably, they say, to get Harison the comptrollership.

October 1, WEDNESDAY. Today has been busy, and remarkably blue. Find that I enter on this quarter with every reason to expect a state of hopeless insolvency before it's half over, having anticipated a large slice of its proper income, and the dividend of this morning being below the average. Never mind—I console myself by the reflection that since October 1, 1850, when I began my saving-system, I've bottled up $5,660.85. If I could hope to do half as well for the next ten years, I'd retire from practice at the end of them. But there have been one or two specially lucky coincidences this year that have run up the balance beyond what I'd any right to expect.

October 2. Went to Dr. Berrian's tonight: invited to meet the provisional Bishop-elect and the Bishop of Fredericton (who didn't come) —also the Bishop of the Black Sheep at Cape Palmas, or somewhere else.[17] Creighton was no less imperturbable than usual. Talked with Higby, Muhlenberg, Hawks, and Seabury. Gave Higby a poke in his most sensitive spot with an idea from *Alton Locke*, which set him off instantly, as I intended, in a very dashing declamation on one of his hobbies. He's a very showy and splendid talker. Hawks was funny and Seabury demure. Muhlenberg came out strong on the St. Luke's Hospital that is to be. He looks forward to the establishment of some sort of Beguinage or female "sodality" to do the work of the hired nurses in other hospitals, under the training, perhaps, of "professional nurses" but

[17] Dr. William Berrian, rector of Trinity 1832–1862, who has been frequently mentioned before, would naturally be host on such an occasion. The other churchmen here named are also familiar figures. William Augustus Muhlenberg (1796–1877) was at this time rector of the Church of the Holy Communion in Sixth Avenue, and was chief promoter of St. Luke's Hospital.

doing the great mass of the work as amateurs. He says he shall "despair of the Church" if, when the object is fairly presented, women can't be found for this duty.

I'm glad the experiment is to be tried. The Founder of Christianity went about doing good to both the bodies and souls of men. His example and His command both indicate the office of His Church to be the same, and so the church has in almost every age interpreted its mission. But here, at the present time, one half of this duty—perhaps the *first* half in *point of time* in the true theory or idea of the church—is tacitly abandoned. The church does nothing to relieve temporal sorrow and calamity; it only recommends individuals to do it when the opportunity comes in their way. The church upholds the creeds and doctrines of the Catholic Faith, but *as a church,* I see no works in its history since the sixteenth century.

October 6.   Money market easing up a little as the stream of California gold sets in. Another California has come to light in New Holland [Australia]. All very propitious for the development of the Anglo-Saxon race, language, and institutions, but not favorable to the future prosperity of any but real estate holders. Money is to fall in value—*property* to rise. And as I'm not an extensive freeholder, my financial future is much darkened by these auriferous discoveries. Moreover, my financial *present* is gloomy; my bank account slender and my liabilities numerous.

October 15.   Douglas Robinson, who married Miss Fanny Monroe, has gone to smash financially. The money market is easier, a remark that don't apply to my private monetary concerns. Kossuth is coming here, and there is to be a pow-wow and reception. I've never been able to sift out the truth from among the legion of conflicting lies about that personage, and about the Hungarian struggle, and shall not commit myself by hurrahing for him.

October 18.   Stocks have rizzen. My Bank of Commerce, bought at $2\frac{7}{8}$ is at 5, whereby I have (constructively) made twenty-two dollars and fifty cents. James G. King renominated for Supreme Court; him I shall vote for. In the Supreme Court the Whigs run C. P. Kirkland and Murray Hoffman, the Locos Oakley and Bosworth; my ticket is Oakley and Kirkland. Hoffman is a very estimable person, honest man, and sound lawyer, but I've far too much respect and regard for him to contribute my vote towards putting him on the bench of that court, for he's about as competent to sit at *nisi prius* as a horse. Bradford is an excellent surrogate and must be re-elected, though Isaac Fowler is a very respectable nomination on the other side. John J. Townsend I shall vote against for the Common Pleas, whoever runs against him. In Kings County I see that my wretched little pettifogging friend Cady is nominated for the County Court. Had he been nominated to the office of sweeping the courtroom, I could have guessed at his qualifications, though I should have thought honester men might have been found for the place.

Apropos of the judiciary, our treason prosecutions in Pennsylvania and at Syracuse seem to be in flourishing progress—an interesting contribution to some future scene of American State Trials.[18] I've no sympathy for this gang of maudlin philanthropists and Quaker bravos, and consider that it would probably be with advantage to themselves and to society that they be sent out of the world before they've done more sin and mischief in it; but it is making the awful name of treason very cheap, especially as two-thirds of the traitors are run-away niggers themselves —keepers of oyster shops, black barbers, "hands" on the farm.

October 20, MONDAY. Half-past twelve P.M. Thank God, we are happily at the end of today—the first great peril is over. Ellie was very bright through the morning; played a game of chequers with me, read aloud, and so forth, her pains occurring every ten minutes or thereabouts. She dined here in the library, and by six o'clock the pains were much more frequent and began to be severe. At about 7:30, she went to bed in a good deal of suffering, and from that time till the finale, suffered terribly, though I suppose no more than is the common lot of women. She bore up bravely, only begging sometimes for chloroform, which Johnston most stoically and imperturbably declined giving. My nerves tingle yet at the remembrance of her cries and struggles of pain. But at ten minutes after ten her baby was born, a boy, and they say a very fine one; certainly vociferous—his ululations first informed me that he had come into the world.

October 21. Downtown early this morning, after a night in my chair. Knocked off a good deal of pressing work. Raced about through the streets of Brooklyn and nearly suffered a sun-stroke in my hurry to get through and home again, for it was a morning of fervent heat, most unwonted in the latter days of October, and a most beaming and radiant day besides,

[18] Strong refers to cases involving runaway Negroes and mob resistance to the Fugitive Slave Act. In Pennsylvania a Maryland slaveholder, trying to reclaim two fugitives, had been killed in September, 1850; in Syracuse the next month the slave Jerry, pursued by an agent from the South, was liberated by a mob and hurried into Canada. Indictments followed these interferences with the law, and like most conservative men, Strong believed the law should be upheld.

with the loveliness whereof I sympathized. Congratulated by a great variety of people, for everyone remembers the terrible time she had two years ago, and it was a matter of quite general interest how she would get through with this trial.

This has been a very happy day. *Te Deum Laudamus.*

October 30. That baby is making the house vocal from the garret to the cellar, filling it with an atmosphere of ululation; inarticulate expostulations with Destiny, about as rational as those of most adults—perhaps more so, for the infant is nowise to blame for the stomach-ache that Providence visits him with.

But I hope there's nothing the matter with this sucking Byron. As it is, it frets and worries his mama sadly.

November 4, TUESDAY. Election today. Spent an hour in the densest possible crowd, very dirty but good-natured, at the Bull's Head, and succeeded in getting in my vote at last. The Whigs not sanguine, but their chance is the best, I think. The Democrats have borrowed a little of their thunder by pretending to take up Hunt's Canal policy, and may diminish a little thereby the Whig majority in the canal counties, which would otherwise be overwhelming. But their conversion to the enlargement comes late and is suspicious. The "Union Party Ticket" will not take off many votes from either side. I see that a good many of the jobbers in Broadway are decorating their shop-doors with the big handbills of that party, a manifest advertisement for Southern custom.

November 8, SATURDAY. Whigs were beat in this city very badly, losing the charter officers—register, recorder, judiciary, and so on. Bradford keeps the surrogateship by a tight vote. Result in the state still unknown. It is claimed that Ullman is attorney general, and thought that the rest of the Whig ticket is lost. Except Foot, who stays in the Court of Appeals by virtue of the Anti-Rent vote, I'm better pleased with the result in this city than if the Whigs had carried their ticket clean through. Though James J. Roosevelt and Bosworth are not particularly calculated to adorn the bench, either is better than little Townsend, and if Murray Hoffman had been elected to the Supreme Court, he would have made wild work at *nisi prius.* But I hoped that there were enough sensible people in the city to retain the existing incumbents without regard to party.

So much for the Political Department. Domestic affairs are unhappily disturbed and squally. Ellie's well, thank Heaven, but the baby's existence for the last two days has been one prolonged howl. "Wind," of course. Last night, after everybody in the house had run in every direction for a few hours, Peters was sent after and he administered infinitesimals. Then there was a great calm for a little while, the patient being, in fact, rather tired with the shindy he had been making; but this morning he awoke much refreshed, and began again where he'd left off the night before and has continued the same Vocal Entertainment throughout the day, with an occasional intermission of half an hour for refreshments.

November 17, MONDAY.　Past week one of nasty weather. Today is fine, but unsettled still. Ellie famously well; went downstairs yesterday and looks charming. The young boy of Basan well and vigorous. Grows like a fungus and is said to have laughed, and to have begun to "take notice," and is a fat, moon-faced, "flabby dobby hobby." Its only troubles have been an occasional turn of colic, evidenced by a more than usual persistence in screaming. Election in the state decided at last. The Democrats carry the day by a slender majority; sore discomfiture to Seward. The state was lost by Ontario County, where the Whigs could count on 3,500 majority heretofore, but Seward deliberately presented them with little Sam Blatchford, a small copy of himself, as nominee for the Supreme Court, and bade them swallow the dose on their allegiance to the party. But they recalcitrated—it was drawing the reins a little too tight; the unhappy man was snubbed down by a Democratic majority of 1,000, and the state ticket lost in that county the 300 or 400 votes that were wanted to save it. . . .

November 23, SUNDAY AFTERNOON.　A very anxious and painful time since my last entry. I was called up at half-past four Friday morning with the report that the baby was out of order; some sort of cold, so that he couldn't take any nourishment. Found him in a half-stifled state, breathing badly and in great distress and discomfort. Didn't suppose anything serious the matter, but the mamma being in such trouble, I started for the doctor. It was a savage southeaster, pouring rain and wind that soon blasted my umbrella into the form of a wine glass. Knowing that Johnston wouldn't come out on any such demand on such a night, I invoked Peters, who said he didn't suppose it was anything of moment, but volunteered to go up with me. He at once said it was a grave affair, and that he wanted help. Off again, called for [Dr. J. Augustus] McVickar, who couldn't come; then routed up Johnston, who refused point-blank to do anything in the premises.

Back again, and again went off to find McVickar, who came up this time, and agreed with Dr. Peters that the case was nearly desperate.

They called it "thymus asthma" or "Millar's asthma." It was marked by spasm of the throat, inability to swallow, blueness of the face, etc.

At about 8:30 I went for Hawks, and the poor little insensible thing was baptized by the name of *John Ruggles*. Then as things grew still worse, I went for Dr. Gray, and after waiting for a long while, succeeded in obtaining an interview with that great man—and home again, not expecting to find the child alive. But I was met by Ellie at the nursery door with the news that *he was better*—the spasm had terminated. During the day he slept heavily and an unusual degree of drowsiness continued till last night; Peters had some little misgiving about a possible affection of the *brain*. But that has passed off and today there has been wakefulness enough and noise more than enough. . . .

Fearful calamity at a public school in Ninth Ward Thursday afternoon, a false alarm of fire, a panic, a stampede downstairs of 1,800 children, and near fifty killed on the spot and many more wounded—a massacre of the innocents. The stair banisters gave way, and the children fell into the square well round which the stairs wound, where the heap of killed and wounded lay for hours before help could reach them. The doors opened inwards. The bodies were piled up to the top of the doors; they did not dare to burst them open and had to cut them slowly away with knives.

Among the notable events of the autumn of 1851 were the founding of the New York Times, *which, under Henry J. Raymond, began publication September 18th; the death that same month of Fenimore Cooper, who had filled his later years with controversy, but who was genuinely mourned, as a memorial meeting in New York, with Daniel Webster in the chair and William Cullen Bryant and Washington Irving as the principal speakers, showed; the opening of the Hudson River Railroad (chartered nearly half a dozen years earlier) to Albany; and the first appearance on the New York stage of the child-singer Adelina Patti and the danseuse Lola Montez. Strong showed no special interest in these events. But he was greatly concerned with the suit which the coarse and irascible Edwin Forrest had brought for divorce from his wife, the former Catherine Norton Sinclair. This case, which came to trial in December and ran for six weeks, received a prodigious amount of newspaper attention; and Forrest behaved so badly that nearly everybody agreed with Strong in condemning him. Strong was interested also in the founding of St. Luke's Hospital, a general institution for the sick poor without distinction of race or creed. This Episcopal philanthropy was first proposed by the rector of the Church of the Holy Communion,*

Dr. William Augustus Muhlenberg, whose enthusiasm kindled a response in many members of the church. The hospital was incorporated in 1850, money was diligently collected, and the cornerstone was finally laid by Bishop Wainwright in the spring of 1854. Another subject which received earnest attention from Strong, as from nearly all other Americans, was the visit of the Hungarian patriot Kossuth. He crossed on the Humboldt, *having left the* U.S.S. *Mississippi, sent to Constantinople to fetch him, at Gibralter to visit England. He was received here with enthusiasm, but his tour, as the skeptical Strong predicted, did very little for the cause of Hungarian independence, and its results sorely disappointed the ardent visitor.*

November 25, TUESDAY. The baby has had no recurrence of its troubles of Friday. . . .

Meeting of St. Luke's Hospital last night. The city corporation have passed the ordinance for a grant of the land in Fifth Avenue; and we must now go to work to conspire to get money to build on it. Dr. Muhlenberg spoke to me about the motto for our corporate seal, and wanted me to hunt up something. Have explored several cartloads of charters in Dugdale, dipped into St. Bernard, pumped *Mores Catholici*, and so on, thus far without much results.

November 27. Thanksgiving Day. "Thanks-gave" at Trinity Church. Heard a very drastic sermon on almsgiving from Weston the Deacon, a man who carries raw material in his head enough to produce considerable results and who seems to have the energy and industry necessary to work it up. It's not very often that a clergyman goes on steadily improving in vigor of thought as well as of diction. The development of a clergyman's mind is apt to stop after his professional education and course of study is ended. Took little George Derby with me. Spent an hour or so in Wall Street. Talked New Chapel with Verplanck; walked uptown with George Derby, stopping at the Art Union, where I met General Dix and talked pictures. He's a man whom I greatly affect.

December 1, MONDAY NIGHT. Another cantankerous headache yesterday, brought on, I think, by the slowest and woodenest of all *Te Deums* at Trinity, written either by Hodges himself or by some austere English composer of the reign of Edward VI, in the simplest of severe styles. Went to bed with both my ears stuffed full of *cotton*, a precaution against the turmoil of that baby, which has got into one of the habits of the *Noctivagous Mammalia*, that, namely, of howling at night like the felinae, the great apes, jackals, hyenas, and wild dogs picturesquely described by travelers in tropical parts.

The Psalmist speaks of the young lions roaring by night; he was a bachelor when he wrote that psalm, or he would have cited young babies as the better instance of habitual nocturnal ululation.

December 4. Everybody looking out for Mr. Kossuth, now hourly expected. A flag will be displayed in the Merchants' Exchange when the *Humboldt* is telegraphed at Sandy Hook. Mr. Kossuth is to be dropped temporarily at Staten Island, where there are to be demonstrations and orations addressed to Mr. K., and answers to be returned by him. Then a steamboat chartered for the purpose is to bring him to the city, where the firemen and the militia and the volunteer companies and a miscellaneous assortment of associations and societies are to receive him and escort him up Broadway, and down the Bowery, and under one or two painted prize triumphal arches that look like frames for fireworks, to the City Hall, where there will be more speeches, of a superior quality, and then there is to be a banquet and what follows in the programme I don't remember.

Kossuth is a man of genius—so much is clear from his speeches; but he may be a humbug nevertheless. Only a great man can be a great humbug. He is master of the art of stump oratory, and is gifted with much tact, presence of mind, and appreciation of national character. But I recollect no instances in history where a great work has been done by platform and dinner-table oratory, or much farthered thereby; no instance of a truly great man working much with tools of that kind. But this 19*th* century is a peculiar period, and if great men live in it they must do their work under the conditions they find around them. So, being in doubt on the subject, I shall not commit myself by hurrahing for Mr. Kossuth, but shall patiently wait for more light. Meantime, it's absurd to witness the enthusiasm of his admirers. At least nine-tenths of those who are sounding the glories of this martyr in the cause of free institutions and denouncing all who hint at the possibility of there being any question as to his title to the homage of the American people would be dreadfully puzzled to find Hungary on a map of Europe without names, and have as little notion of the institutions that Kossuth contended for, as the institutions that Austria established in spite of him, as they have of the habits of *Entomostracous* fossils.

Can't fathom the *Golden Legend* altogether. The first act or subdivision, in which he has drunk of the magic fluid "called Alcohol in the

Arab speech" results so disastrously (it is left rather uncertain why and
how), seems like a contribution to the Poetical Literature of Total Abstinence—a warning against the use of ardent spirits even as a medicine.
But the finale points to another moral—viz.: that the Devil is not so bad
as people think and will come out all right some of these days—

> . . . is God's Minister
> And labors for some good
> By us not understood. . . .

Cornell has become mesmeric, and more than half a believer in the
polter-geister of Rochester. He has conferred with Edmonds and Dr.
Gray, and his talk abounds in marvels and prodigies. Edmonds is actually
going to publish a book on knockers, detailing his own personal experiences.

I fear I shall get the reputation of keeping company with the Rochester
Ghosts, for when that subject or mesmerism is talked of, I commonly
find myself stoutly insisting that the grounds on which they are assailed
and ridiculed are unphilosophical and absurd: as indeed they are, leading
logically to a disbelief in everything but objects of sense. . . .

Kossuth has come, and is to be received at Castle Garden tomorrow,
with artillery and complimentary ovations. Painful to consider what
murderous outrages will be committed on the canons of rhetoric and the
rules of good taste, modesty, and moderation before tomorrow is over.

December 6, SATURDAY.   Cram came in; he'd been to Staten Island
and returned in the steamboat that brought the illustrious Magyar to the
city. The reception at Castle Garden seems to have been badly managed.
There was some little noise and confusion, and the hero, after commencing
an oration, stopped abruptly and withdrew from the platform. Cram is
Kossuth-mad. There's a strong undercurrent of No-Popery feeling mixed
up with the legitimate Hungary enthusiasm. The *Freeman's Journal* has
thrown cold water on the reception to the utmost of its ability, the Irish
Catholics generally keep aloof from it, and people talk bitterly about
Bishop Hughes, and accuse him of intriguing and manoeuvring to embarrass the "Kossuth movement."

December 12.   Magyar-mania epidemic; with my proclivity to hero-
worship, it is hard to escape the contagion, but it has attacked me thus
far only in a very mild type. The hero is a man of talent, certainly; possibly of genius, but I'm able as yet to think of him and of the political
movement of which he's the Peter the Hermit with some sort of coolness

and sobriety. "Municipal Banquet" last night, i.e., dinner at the Irving House. Kossuth's speech prodigiously able, and very plain-spoken and honest as to his ultimate views and designs. Col. Webb tried to make a speech in *reply* and to confute the orator, the most impudent act—the occasion considered—of the Colonel's impudent life. But he was coughed down.

December 16, TUESDAY. At Mr. Cottenet's Saturday night, where William Schermerhorn and his wife are staying. Nice people and a lovely house, its decorations all elegant; costly enough, I dare say, but they don't obtrude an impertinent intimation of costliness. . . .

Kossuth mania still rages. The bar committee failed to secure the hero for a dinner, and there's to be a "reception" at Tripler Hall Friday night. They expect to raise $15,000 for the "Hungarian fund," and some of them are suddenly waking up to a sense of their position as a *revolutionary committee*—raising funds towards an insurrection in a friendly state. If the approaching French election should raise a tempest in Italy and Germany, which is possible, these funds may do service, otherwise they will not. An isolated rising in Hungary would be overwhelmed by Russia and Austria, if half the wealth of the United States went to supply the sinews of war to the insurgents.

For myself, I don't think I've a call to give money to promote the cause of freedom among the Magyars. I believe they're a fine race of men, though rather given to a roystering, hard-drinking, cock-fighting kind of life, unless fame belie them. But I think other "causes" have a prior claim on a New Yorker. Dr. Muhlenberg's hospital, for instance, calls louder, and though the appeal of this and other distressed nationalities be powerful, there are distressed individuals around us, to the number of around 50,000 at least in this city and county, whose appeal is stronger.

December 20, SATURDAY NIGHT. Reception to Kossuth by the bar last night, subsequent dinner speech of John Duer's, much out of place, disputing the soundness of the new Hunnish views of our proper national policy. Shindy in consequence. Cram was conspicuous in it; *he* says he was trying to preserve order and decency, but the newspapers generally name him as foremost among those who clamored Duer down. The *Mirror* speaks of "Cram, Sickles and Co., and the other young filibusters of the bar"; pleasant for Cram, Sickles belonging to the filthy sediment of the profession, and lying somewhere in its lower strata. Perhaps better to say that he's one of the bigger bubbles of the scum of the profession, swollen and windy, and puffed out with fetid gas. Anyhow, Cram's name is everywhere coupled with his.

Cram goes the Intervention Policy to its full length, but admits that when he gets cool he may very well think differently. If such a policy is to be adopted, it will be hard to define it exactly. . . .

At the opera with Ellen last night. *Robert le Diable* (in Italian) very fairly sung. Know but little of Meyerbeer's music, and can't form an opinion of his style from hearing this very elaborate work but once. It seems a mixture of French, Italian, and German, the first and last predominant. Not very rich in melody, but copious in "effects"—complex, finished, ingenious, and brilliant. . . .

December 22, MONDAY. Snowstorm. Great news from France: Louis Napoleon has pricked the bladder and it has collapsed. The sublime structure of civil liberty and social order, so often and so touchingly appealed to as evidence that at least one of the lands of the Old World was capable of self-government, has crumbled quietly down and vanished into nonentity at the first kick given it by the first ambitious man of moderate abilities who had a popular name and the army to back him. And it seems to be regarded by Paris as rather a good joke. The well-intentioned endeavor of the rump of the Assembly to get itself together and vindicate its own vitality, and the prompt descent of a company or two of grenadiers upon it, seems to have been a subject of "much derision" to these enlightened pioneers of Europe in the science of constitutional republicanism. It's all very well for Horace Greeley to howl at Louis Napoleon for doing it, but it was the heroic French people who let him do it. Suppose Washington Hunt were to march the Sixth Division of New York State Infantry up to the Capitol at Albany, arrest the Democratic majority of the Assembly, and send off Azariah C. Flagg, Dr. Brandreth, and Billy McMurray to the Auburn State Prison, and then appeal to the people and order an election to be held next Tuesday to decide who should be Governor for the next ten years!!!

And if this is the faculty of France for self-government, what kind of prospects for a quiet life would be those of republican Hungary and democratic Wallachia?

It's said that this will hurry off Kossuth; that he'll start for Europe next week. Probably it's an event of not unmixed misfortune for his cause. It's the extinguishment of the last glimmer of constitutionalism on the Continent, the retrogression of France to absolutism and the sovereignty of a standing army.

December 24, CHRISTMAS EVE.   Cold snow clouds overhead, but it's too cold to do more than keep up an intermitted "spitting." Further news from France. Louis Napoleon as yet firm in his new position; the army and the people thus far acquiescent. Letter from Jack Ehninger at Paris. He seems to think there is a latent feeling of general disgust at the usurpation, but the newspaper correspondents don't. The Capitol, Washington, on fire; library burned up, rest of the building hardly escaped. Kossuth inflammation subsiding a little. Perhaps a reform in the hats of America will flow from the preaching of the illustrious Magyar. It's to be hoped it may, for the Hungarian hat has the advantage in grace and comfort both of our American stove-pipe sections. I doubt the likelihood of any other lasting result from his mission. Cram publishes a very proper note in the *Tribune* explaining his share in the disturbance at the bar "banquet" caused by Duer's speech. He dined here yesterday with Mr. Ruggles and Rosalie, who's sojourning here for a few days. Forrest case slowly dragging its dirty length along in the Supreme Court, like a wounded skunk. I'm strongly prejudiced against that king of blackguards, Edwin F., or I dare say I should think the evidence was beginning to pinch Mrs. Forrest pretty closely. Talked about it with Oakley yesterday, who was very funny. He has ruled out the "Consuelo" letter. Found, he supposed, that Consuelo was a naughty woman, and he was astonished when I told him she was a superhuman and doubly-refined extract of all kinds of sublime virtue and purity.

December 29. . . . At a St. Luke's Hospital meeting tonight, and Heaven help me, was put in the Finance Committee, the main duties whereof are those of mendicancy; a new office, and a most thankless and disgusting one. But some one must undertake the work, and I don't suppose I ought to decline it, in so important a cause, though I shall make a bad beggar. . . .

Kossuth at Baltimore. Says the Louis Napoleon coup d'état is the very thing he most wished for; also, that he had confidently predicted it for some time, and has made all his arrangements accordingly.

Financial horizon, lead-colored.

1852

FORREST DIVORCE CASE · THE CRAZE OVER SPIRITUALISM · DEATHS OF CLAY AND WEBSTER · FRANKLIN PIERCE TRIUMPHS OVER SCOTT · THACKERAY'S VISIT

Strong's domestic horizon was unclouded as the year 1852 opened; for his wife was in better health and his baby son, usually referred to as the Dauphin, the Czarevitch, or the Prince of Wales, remained well and strong. He was busier than ever in the practice of law, as he had need to be. His family expenses were increasing, and gold production in California and Australia had inaugurated an era of rising prices. In foreign affairs, all eyes were bent upon France. Louis Napoleon, president of the Second French Republic since 1848, had seized upon the anniversary of Austerlitz (December 2, 1851) for a coup d'état; proclaiming the dissolution of the Assembly and a temporary dictatorship, pending a plebiscite upon a proposal to entrust himself with the revision of the constitution. The bulk of the French population acquiesced; a few riots were easily suppressed; and such dissenters as Victor Hugo were hustled out of the country. Strong had an opportunity, in 1852, to chronicle the transformation of France from a republic to an empire, with Louis Napoleon, before the year ended, taking the title of Napoleon III. Naturally this disgusted the diarist.

In New York the chief event early in the year was the conclusion of the dramatic Forrest trial. Amid general rejoicing, the actor lost his case and was compelled to pay alimony and costs. Bitterly convinced that his wife was guilty of all he had charged against her, he appealed the case again and again. As Strong records, both principals in the suit made brazen public appearances. Forrest acted for more than two months at the Broadway Theatre as Damon;

his divorced spouse made her debut at Brougham's Lyceum as Lady Teazle.
Meanwhile, Kossuth continued a tour that was rich in applause but poor in
more material rewards.

January 3, SATURDAY. The year came in pleasantly with sunshine
and mild air. Did my duty to society by making twenty-five to thirty
calls, some of them quite agreeable ones, as for example at Mr. William
Schermerhorn's and Mrs. Richard Ray's and the Lydigs', and so on. . . .
The Stevenses of Bleecker Street were lively and cordial, but there's a
painful sense of arduous exertion that I feel whenever I meet them. They
are always in a state of effort, like the statue of an athlete with every
muscle in its anatomy straining and turgid, gasping to maintain or to
establish the exalted social and intellectual position of the family and all
its members; that unparalleled brute Master Austin included, in a prophetic
vision of whom Shakespeare must have conceived Cloten in *Cymbeline.*

January 6. The Forrest trial is still trailing along. O'Conor has at
last got hold of some she-keeper of an assignation house, whose reluctant
testimony punches the great tragedian much harder than any of evidence
singled out in the opening. Chances now are decidedly in favor of a verdict
for Mrs. Forrest, in case the jury agrees at all.

January 8. Ellie saw poor Mrs. Griffin today for the first time since
her husband's death.[1] The stately, imperious, and rather cold-hearted
Miss Kean of three years ago is crushed prostrate by the weight of sorrow
—humbled, softened, and utterly changed. I believe she and her husband
were devoted to each other, and that she loved him and feels his loss very
much more than I supposed she could love or feel for anything. He was
a brilliant, attractive, and agreeable person, a very likely man to bring
out whatever faculty of loving there might be in any woman. His wife
nursed him most faithfully through long months of illness. I have always
thought hardly of her [for I] judged her to be cold, selfish, conceited, and
artificial. But it's rarely worth while to pass sweeping condemnation on
any man, still more rarely on any woman. Good blossoms out where one
least expects to see it. Very likely the Daughter of Herodias had her
amiable traits that might have been developed by a more judicious mother.
Perhaps they were afterwards, nobody knows. . . .

O'Conor seems to be carrying all before him in the Forrest case.
Van Buren, with all his progression and audacity, is utterly over-matched,

---

[1] Commander William Preston Griffin, U.S.N., had died in December; in 1849 he
had married Miss Christine A. W. Kean, sister of Mrs. Hamilton Fish.

and the testimony O'Conor brings up in rebutting seems to be over-whelming.[2]

January 9.   Captain Granby Colcraft was on the stand today in the Forrest case, and much vexed and obstinate by Van Buren's cross examination, which, for the mere purpose of annoying a hostile witness, brought up all that ugly mystery of the Captain's marriage some twenty years ago. Colcraft is an absurd person enough, but Van Buren is a brute and a blackguard, I fear, and seems to be losing ground daily as this case goes on. . . .

Reading Carlyle's *Life of Sterling.* I like it much, mainly for the feeling that has evidently prompted it. Haunted by a scrap of Tennyson's poetry I've stumbled over—"The Bugle-Song" in *The Princess,* it's called. But there's not a word of it in my copy of that poem. Don't certainly know whether I understand it, but its lovely, melodious cadences are floating about me all the time. Meaning or unmeaning, the mere movement and rhythm of poetry has immense power with me, and always had as long as I remember. It always decided my first judgment of verse and has much to do with the last. It's the same pleasure, I suppose, that's given by one of Rossini's melodies, perfectly without significance, but delicious in sound. However, this song is something more than mere word jingle.

January 13, TUESDAY.   Pinching cold again. St. Luke's Hospital gains ground a little. Spent some time on Saturday with Bleecker, Curtiss, Moore, and Dr. Hobart in conference with Harison, and finally agreed on resolutions expressing the assent of the Trinity Church vestry to the transfer from the city to the hospital, on certain nominal conditions to be complied with by the latter. The conditions are a farce. Nobody ever supposed we should do otherwise than they require, and must always be dictating terms to everybody. He's a little piqued at not being made Chief Manager and General Committee of everything of St. Luke's. These resolutions were passed *sub silentio* at the Trinity Church vestry meeting last night. Then Weston's affair came up. Livingston and I were added to the committee on diocese arrangement of Trinity Church, which has been virtually abolished for three years and ought to be now done away with formally, so as to remove a technical difficulty in the way of Weston's advancement. Bleecker *read* a very vehement and absurd

[2] "Prince John" Van Buren, son of the ex-President, was representing Forrest in this case, and lost stature by it; the redoubtable Charles O'Conor represented Mrs. Forrest more successfully.

GENERAL WINFIELD SCOTT

GEORGE TEMPLETON STRONG, 1857

oration on the subject, which stirred up Moore, who is instinct with red pepper, to a high degree of excitement. I think we shall carry Mr. Weston through. . . .

Saturday night I went to the Philharmonic Concert with Ellie and Miss Rosalie. The first part was the *Eroica*, played with much fire and accuracy. The first three parts gained on me, the fourth did not. Nobody but Beethoven could have written it, but it's hardly worthy to be the finale to such a work. Then came an overture of Bennett's, *Die Wald-nymphe*—a charming production, full of feeling, and abounding in fine effects. Mendelssohn's copied from, though—almost larcenously; the Mendelssohn's lovely piano concerto in G minor. Then a trumpery quintette for stringed instruments, and finally Weber's *Oberon*, magnificently rendered. So the concert was very fitting at the price.

Francis Griffin was quite seriously ill all through last week, with some kind of malignant sore throat, and died Sunday night. *A most unhappy event* in many points of view. He was just coming round after his fit of fright and frenzy last spring to acknowledge and certify that he was wrong and unjust in all he'd said to Mr. Ruggles at that time, and now the chance of Mr. Ruggles's obtaining that important result is gone forever. I had urged on him to demand it again and again, but it was always postponed till a more convenient time. Griffin leaves his affairs in a tolerably compact and manageable state, considering. He made a will soon after his disorder began to look ominous. No one dreamed of its ending fatally so soon. . . . Forrest case in slow progress. O'Conor still thought to be gaining ground daily.

January 19, MONDAY.   Griffin's affairs said to be less in a prosperous state. Went to his funeral Wednesday morning. Large attendance. But for the awful framework of coffin lid and white silk, I should have thought he was asleep, so natural was the expression of his face. . . . Evidence in Jones *v.* Forrest nearly closed. Result doubtful, but if the jury agree, I think it will be on a verdict for Mrs. Forrest.

January 20.   Heard *Favorita* last night, well sung. Richard Grant White sat near us, a person it's agreeable to hear talk. Saw Mrs. Camilla [Hoyt], who used to be the most cordial and exuberant of people at West Point and she always rushed to meet me and shake hands when I came there and condescended to be decidedly a friend of mine. But the young lady was out of humor, or has heard that I don't appreciate her husband's merits, for she distinctly avoided my well-intentioned and modest attempt to pay my respects—in fact it was a tolerably clear cut.

January 24. A few damp spots appeared on the sidewalks where the sun was brightest, a refreshing sight. I was tending rapidly to crystallize under this long frost. Forrest trial ended today. O'Conor summed up with great force and dexterity, giving Forrest a due dose of vitriol and caustic. Oakley charged in a noncommittal way, and the verdict, if there is any, has not yet reached Twenty-sixth Street. The chance is, there will be none. According to gossip, eleven jurors are clear for the defendant, the twelfth dubious; and by the same authority, the defendant says these proceedings have cost him $80,000—doubtless a magnificent lie. I hope O'Conor has succeeded.

January 26. Verdict in Forrest case: for defendant on all the issues, with $3,000 alimony. The verdict will stand, I think, beyond question, all but the alimony, which is doubtful. The mob hurrahed for O'Conor all the way from the Hall to his office in Nassau Street. I should have hurrahed, too, had I been there. . . . St. Luke's Hospital meeting tonight. Another hitch in obtaining the assent of Trinity Church, but this time it's not clear on which side the error is.

January 28, WEDNESDAY. Movement of members of the bar to get up some "testimonial" for O'Conor, wherein I cheerfully concur. His course in the Forrest case does him vast credit personally, and over and above the professional glory of his success. He has made all other business give way to the cause of a woman who had no claim on him but that she was helpless and oppressed by a powerful, unscrupulous, and popular man. Has himself borne all the heavy outlay, five or six thousand at least, given up as much more in value of his time, and declined business worth at least as much beside. He's an honor to the bar of New York. Few of the Cuttings and Sandfords and Woods would consider themselves in such a case the King of Heaven's Attorney General and bound, ex officio, to prosecute.

I don't suppose his client utterly blameless, and she is certainly a lady of little distinction and questionable taste, but that it was sought to crush her by the worst means I've no doubt. . . .

February 2, MONDAY. . . . Mrs. Forrest appears at Brougham's Lyceum tonight, a most absurd step. Very probably there'll be a row, for the chivalry of the Bowery is said to be in fierce wrath at the verdict against her husband. If the chivalry undertake to interfere as they did with Macready, it's to be hoped a few of them may be shot, and if the great Tragedian were to be picked off among them, I don't know that the "good time coming" would be postponed much in consequence.

Ellie and I are going off extemporaneously to Niblo's to hear *Don Giovanni* (not my baby—we can hear him enough at home—but Mozart's). Badiali is the Don, a different creature from Beneventano.

Heard *Don Giovanni* accordingly. House crowded, but cold and interested in nothing, unless perhaps by some of Zerlina's irresistible music. It would be strange if a miscellaneous mob of operatic New Yorkers should appreciate Mozart. They have taken it for granted that Verdi's sustaining unisons and Donizetti's stilted commonplaces of languid sentiment are good, and *Don Giovanni* must, therefore, be to them something far from good. I should as soon expect people whose reading has been chiefly in Eugene Sue to become excited over the *Vicar of Wakefield*.

February 3. No row of consequence at Mrs. Forrest's debut last night, the police being on the ground in force, and a detachment of militia (the veterans of the Astor Place riot) strongly posted in an adjacent groggery as a *corps de reserve*. So the Cossacks of the Bowery contented themselves with distant expressions of their disapprobation and broke no windows. . . .

February 13. Miss Josephine Mauran staying here. Great times in the evenings with Mozart's symphonies, four-handed. I appreciate Mozart now, which I did not of old. I can see that he stands on the same plateau as Beethoven, and possibly above him. I don't know and don't care to decide. One appreciates Mozart later than Beethoven. Met [President Charles] King of Columbia College, [Arnold H.] Guyot, the Swiss geologist, and [Francis L.] Hawks at dinner at Mr. Ruggles's Wednesday. Thence to the opera with the ladies to hear *Robert le Diable*, and had the privilege of hearing *Norma* instead. Very well done, but I've read up that opera; after about the twelfth performance, it is utterly threadbare and shabby.

Quite excited about the stereoscope. Spent an hour at Pike's examining one, and have sent through Livingston & Wills for one of Soleil's. Its effects are very startling and beautiful.

February 24, TUESDAY EVENING. Mr. Ruggles back from Albany. Matters improving a little. Noyes has talked with Thomas E. Davis, and got him committed to a narrative of the Griffin affair, *quorum pars magna fuit*, a provident step. T. E. Davis bland and urbane, of course, but his narrative is accurate and may be important. The securities that Griffin "couldn't find" Mr. Davis knows he did find, which may save me the disagreeable duty of certifying that Griffin admitted to me that he'd found them. And in other particulars his statement is of importance. He speaks highly of Mr. Ruggles's conduct in the matter. Whereupon Mr. Ruggles, of course, thinks that Mr. Davis is not so bad after all, that he shows much good feeling, and that probably he didn't stir up and instigate Griffin to the explosion of last spring. Whereas I believe that Davis's policy while Griffin was alive was to drive him to an assignment and to manoeuvre their joint property into his individual pockets, and that he frightened and irritated Griffin from his habitual inert good nature with that view. But that now Griffin's dead, and it's apparent that his children will make money out of his connection with Mr. Ruggles, and that there's not likely to be any property to pick up cheap, and that the tide is rather turning in Mr. Ruggles's favor in the public judgment, he's disposed to lament Griffin's errors and most conscientiously to repair them.

February 27, FRIDAY. Bishop Doane is in great trouble and has printed a very fierce "protest" against Bishop Lee and two of his brethren, who have recommended him to call his convention together and to submit to that body whether it had not better prosecute him canonically for trial for divers offenses, of which I believe lying and swindling are the chief.[3] Much discussion about the Maine Liquor Law, now before the legislature. It won't pass, though the demented fanatics who back it will spare no effort. If it should pass, and were enforced in this city (which it never could be), I'm not sure but that its effect would be wholesome. Charles Augustus Davis wants to toady Irving by getting the name of Gramercy Park changed to Irving Place and sticking a statue of Irving, or Cooper— I don't know which—in the centre of it.

March 2, TUESDAY EVENING. March rampant in a new form. The streets this morning vanished with a thin glaze of sleet, slippery as butter. Weather went through various phases of sulkiness till this noon, when the sun came out bright with the most rumbustious of north winds. Horribly savage all day; spent a good deal of it in hunting lost papers, an occupation that tends not to the development of Christian graces. Bored frantic by old Beers, an inveterate, pertinacious, chronic Don Quixote of punctuality and accuracy, who considers himself injured if all other business is not made to give way to his trumpery collection suits and quite aggrieved if he has to pay five dollars, dearly earned by the

[3] George Washington Doane, Episcopal bishop of New Jersey, had been thrown into bankruptcy three years earlier by financial indiscretions, including generous but ill-judged expenditures for educational institutions at Burlington; see page 89.

man who has to undergo the bore of half an hour of his society. Well, let it pass with the others of the profession. I'm sometimes tempted to let this house, retire to a shanty on top of the Palisades, walk to and from Wall Street daily, live on bread and water, and hoard every cent I can scrape together for ten years, and then on the pelf I have accumulated, cut the law finally. The bench is becoming a beer garden, Roosevelt and Edmonds overruling each other and nullifying each other's orders and ruling, [hurling] opinions at each other about usurpation and interference and so forth, all which comes naturally of our delectable new judiciary system.

March 8.   N. P. Willis is stricken with deadly disease, epilepsy and consumption together. The idea of death and of the man who writes editorials for the *Home Journal* are an unnatural combination. Death seems too solemn a matter for him to have any business with it.[4]

March 13, SATURDAY.   The city seems dull at present. The Maine Liquor Law is the principal subject of late, and it's a very dull one. . . .

I have been reading Hawthorne's *Twice-Told Tales* and don't like them. Great power, much imagination, fertility and felicity of thought and diction, and occasional passages of real beauty. But such a dismal series of ghostly, ghastly charnel-house conceptions I never met with, unless in the author of *Villona Corrombona* perhaps. . . .

Poor David Graham has sailed for Europe, alone, on a subscription raised by a few of his professional brethren, probably to die. A sad end of a rather brilliant career. He has been desperately ill with some very painful, harassing disease that required repeated surgical aid and that has worn him into consumption. A handsome, negligent, extravagant, heartless harridan of a wife has aggravated the case sadly. She has the bad blood of the female Hyslops in her veins, has spent her husband's property, run him into debt, and left him in his suffering to the care of hirelings.

March 18. . . . Peter Schermerhorn is said to be failing rapidly, his constitution undermined by a chronic disease—enlargement of the bank account—which has shattered his nervous system by sleepless nights and hypochondriacal anxiety. He is said to be threatened with dropsy now. . . .

March 27. . . . If our baby grows and prospers, I must be careful to avoid becoming what some of my friends have become, an habitual bore.

---

[4] The gay, airy, and gracefully inconsequential Willis (Yale 1827), author of *Pencillings by the Way* and other forgotten books, and one of the founders of the *Home Journal*, which survived into the twentieth century, fought off death for fifteen years longer.

It is bad to be nothing more than the Boswell of a baby, and to have no available subject to talk of but the baby's precocious articulations and signs of future sagacity. . . .

March 28, SUNDAY. . . . Looked into Heine's *Romanzero*—much of it filthy and flagitious, but the book, on the whole, a moral lesson of the grim and ghastly sort. The author is broken down with paralysis or some such thing, and several of these poems—the "Lamentationem"—are written in view of coming death, and shew what are the consolations of philosophy for the witty, sensual, enlightened author of the *Reisebilder*. Instead of writing apocryphal stories about the death beds of Hume, Voltaire, and Tom Paine, the Tract Society should republish the *Romanzero*, omitting a little of its blasphemous bawdry. It's a dismal picture that is made up from the hints of this book. Poverty, bedridden in a Parisian garret, without friends, except it seems "Mathilde," who comes up sometimes, and is not probably, it strikes me, a very fascinating personage. She is evidently fat and finds the ascent fatiguing.[5]

There is little comfort in solitary meditation, to judge from the specimens he gives of his reveries. He dreams that he is young again and is running "with Ottilie hand in hand" down the path from the old country house, boy and girl together, and then he awakes to the night and the sick woman. Then he dreams of the deserted theatre, the audience gone, nothing left but silence and rats and the smell of rancid oil; a violin string breaks with a clang in the orchestra; the last forgotten lamp flickers and goes out, and all is dark. He tells how he was young once and friends swarmed around him and everything was glowing and glorious. Now care watches at his bedside through the winter night with a snuffbox and a dirty nightcap, and when he dreams that he is young and that the old days have returned, the snuffbox creaks and the old woman blows her nose and he is awake again.

It is a bitter story, told with power, and with only so much reserve as makes it more effective. It reminds one of Richter's *New Year's Eve Dream of an Unhappy Man*.

March 31. A very disgusting rainy day, which I have spent in taking a bilious view of the future; stimulated thereto chiefly by discovering an error in my check book, and overdrawing my account in the Bank of America a trifle before I discovered it. . . .

[5] In 1848 Heine had been relegated to a "mattress grave" in Paris by a painful spinal ailment, from which he suffered until his death in 1856. He was married to a Frenchwoman, Eugénie Mirat, who survived him.

St. Luke's Hospital flourishing; meeting last Monday night brilliantly successful. Anonymous subscription of $10,000 (probably Minturn); another of $5,000, another of $2,000, and lots of $1,000. I found myself representing the pauper interest.

April 4, SUNDAY.   Higby this morning at Trinity. Jury disagreed and was discharged in O'Sullivan's case. Jay's last nigger case decided against him, after a very stormy session, in which Jay's head was punched by Busteed, of counsel for the claimant, who appears to very little advantage in the reports of the proceedings. . . .[6] Eisfeld's quartette soirée last night at the Apollo—Beethoven's No. 74 in E-flat, Spolia's 130, with piano, and Haydn's 63 in D; exquisite compositions, rendered with spotless accuracy.

St. Luke's Hospital is in something like a scrape with the Church of "St. George the Martyr." Interview with Charles Edwards Thursday that shed a new light on the relations of the two bodies, and as Murray Hoffman is off to Albany to attend the Court of Appeals, I've a sufficiently troublesome job before me to negotiate with the comptroller, and that miserable H. E. Davies, about straightening the title of the hospital to the Fifth Avenue lots. . . . Mr. Ruggles here tonight. His "examination" nearly finished. He proposes to print it, as a statement of the facts that were so talked of and so distorted last spring. A very proper step, but at best an imperfect remedy of the mischief then done him—mischief that Griffin's death has made remediless. . . .

People say that Doane will certainly be "presented" for trial, and convicted, and that in that event his diocese will stand by him and secede from our present organization. Doubtful. It looks like a calamity at first, but such an event might *possibly* lead to much good.

George Washington Doane, the second Episcopal Bishop of New Jersey, leader of the High-Church party in the American Episcopal Church—the party to which Strong belonged—had for some years been a center of controversy. He was a vigorous, handsome, learned churchman, incessantly active in charitable work, but lacking in business system. His support of the Tractarian Movement brought sharp criticism upon his head. Highly benevolent, he gave so freely to the support of educational institutions at Burlington that in 1849 he was thrown into a discreditable bankruptcy. His diocese stood loyally behind him, and in convention exonerated him from any shadow of wrongdoing.

[6] The philanthropic-minded William Jay and his son John had made themselves legal champions of Negroes in New York.

Nevertheless, persistent efforts were made to bring him to trial before the House of Bishops, an ordeal from which—as a man of great pride and dignity —he shrank. In the end, as we shall see, he successfully blocked all proceedings. But temporarily he was under a heavy cloud. The possibility of a trial kept the bishops at home for a time, with the result that Jonathan Mayhew Wainwright of Trinity Church was sent to London as American delegate to the third jubilee anniversary of the Society for the Propagation of the Gospel. Among the other events of the spring which interested Strong was an attempt, initiated by President Charles King and warmly supported by S. B. Ruggles, to convert Columbia College into a university. It was not the first such attempt, and like its predecessors, it met spirited opposition from the conservative trustees. Yet the movement, thanks to President King, and to a little group of progressive trustees—Ruggles and Hamilton Fish the most prominent—did in the end bring about some much-needed improvements. Columbia College now had funds for expansion; New York was becoming a great metropolitan city; and the time had obviously arrived to adopt a bolder policy. The first projected step, shortly recommended by a committee which comprised Fish, William Betts, and H. J. Anderson, was the removal of the College from its old site in Park Place to a more advantageous situation uptown.

April 13, TUESDAY. This is a very foul and grimy spring: two days of cloudy weather and drizzle followed by one of sunshine and *da capo.* Easter Sunday was decently bright. . . . Heard a novelty at Trinity Church this afternoon, an experimental service, at which the "Church Choral Society" assisted. The whole service was *"intoned."* Effect infinitely better than I expected, though the performance was rough and faulty.

Much scandal afloat here touching our New York Society in Paris— how [William R.] Morgan *licked* his wife, that lovely little décolletée Miss Louise Selden, whom I remember to have seen at Miss Christine's party Heaven knows how long ago, and her father's apoplexy was brought on by his wrath thereat. How [Charles Astor] Bristed keeps a grisette, and how Mrs. Bristed met the couple somewhere and the two ladies clapper-clawed.

Doane very like to be "presented," and a great row anticipated.

Mr. Ruggles in a great state of excitement about his university project.

April 15. William Moore here tonight, investigating the stereoscope just received. Also Mr. Ruggles, in great affliction over the rash undertaking Columbia College has just plunged into, the improvement of their up-town lots at the cost of $160,000 of additional debt—a sudden reckless outburst of that board of fogies. No one is so dangerous as an enraged coward and no speculator so foolhardy as a timid old conservative once bitten with the gambling mania.

Special vestry meeting at Trinity Church last night. Tried to get some encouragement for the Church Choral Society and could have carried my resolution, but Dunscomb was so frightened at the bare idea of a No–Popery excitement that I did not press it.

April 21. Very blue today; in a great rage with myself on various sufficient grounds, and much exercised by a conversation with Harison and Moore and Verplanck about California and Australia, price of consols, rate of discount, and so on. Never mind. Perhaps when the great monetary revolution comes I shall be dead and buried, so there can be no use in grumbling and fretting over the prospect till I learn whether I'm really to be affected by it.

April 25, SUNDAY. One or two exceptional days of sunshine. Higby at Trinity this morning, decidedly strong on his favorite subject, which will earn him the name of the resurrection-man if he's not careful. . . . Dr. [Horatio] Potter of Albany here last night. Very valuable person. Projected movement for the rejuvenation of Columbia College may end in gas and clack. I hope not.

May 1. Fine weather has returned. State of the streets defies description. You can hardly get into an omnibus without going ankle deep in juicy black mud. . . . The baby continues to make night hideous. When Marie begins out-screaming him with a bravura lullaby (able of itself to give me a cramp in the stomach), and two cats commence a duet, andante, from the top of some adjacent house, all at once, it is a fearful combination of noises. . . .

Sent for to K's Tuesday night about his will. He was very sick and much excited by fever, and his verbal faculty impaired so that he constantly mistook words. But I think unquestionably *compos mentis.* It's not very material whether he was or not, this will being little more than a re-engrossment of the former one, omitting some provisions that had become inoperative. He had been much concerned about the will, and to quiet him they had told him I had been seen on the subject and would call there two or three days ago. He was in great wrath because I had not called. I thought it best not to undeceive him, and changed the subject and parried his enquiries with tolerable dexterity.

May 5, WEDNESDAY NIGHT.   Quite indefatigable in the affairs of St. Luke's Hospital. I'm getting to be an Aminadab Sleek. Astor, by the by, has (unsolicited) raised his $3,000 to $13,000. This is very creditable. If he and Whitney and the other twenty or thirty millionaires of the city would do such things a little oftener, they would never feel the difference, and in ten years could control the course of things in New York by the public confidence and gratitude they would gain. Property is the ruling element in our society. Wealthy men are meant to have supreme influence in the long run; they do not possess it because they will not use the power wealth gives them.

To Strong's great pleasure, the spring of 1852 found Theodore Eisfeld and a company of German musicians giving a series of concerts at the Apollo Rooms, No. 410 Broadway. In May, Jenny Lind, who had become Mme. Otto Goldschmidt, made her last appearances in America, assisted by Sr. Cesare Badiali, Mr. Joseph Burke, Mr. Henry Appy, Mr. Otto Goldschmidt, "and a grand orchestra of eighty performers, under the direction of Mr. Theodore Eisfeld." Two of these farewell appearances took place at Metropolitan Hall, and the third at Castle Garden. Tickets were snapped up at the low prices of $1 to $3.

Like nearly everybody else, Strong was meanwhile interested in the spiritualist mania which had developed since the "Rochester knockings" of 1848–49 and the subsequent public exhibitions of the two Fox sisters who had produced the uncanny sounds. We have noted that in 1850 the sisters had come to New York, where they demonstrated their powers in a house at Nineteenth Street and Eighth Avenue. "Spirit Circles" sprang up, famous men came to watch and hear, new media emerged by scores, and believers commenced the publication of spiritualist magazines. Of these periodicals the Spiritual Telegraph, *issued in New York from 1853 to the outbreak of the Civil War, was the chief. Many adherents of mesmerism, Fourierism, and Swedenborgianism became ready devotees of spiritualism. Important political figures, as Strong notes below, were converted, and one member of Congress even proposed an appropriation for a government investigation into the subject. James Russell Lowell, scoffing at the movement, remarked of a certain Judge Wells that he "is such a powerful medium that he has to drive back the furniture from following him when he goes out, as one might a pack of too affectionate dogs."*

May 9, SUNDAY.   At Eisfeld's concert last night. Beethoven's *Leonore* was its great feature, a most magnificent composition. It was played at the third Philharmonic of the first season and I then thought it a very abstruse and rather tedious piece of profundity. Glad to find that my faculty for the highest kind of music has improved since then. I could follow and enjoy the whole of it, except parts of the finale last night. Considering the scanty material to which Beethoven has limited himself, it may stand by the side of any of his orchestral music.

May 15, SATURDAY.   Thursday evening, Charles and Eleanor and James Lydig and Lydig Suydam, Walter Cutting and Ellie and I went off to 78 Twenty-sixth Street and had a private interview with Mrs. Fish and her knocking spirits, and then came back here and had some supper. The knockers are much talked of now, from Edmonds' extraordinary publications in the *Shekinah*. One of his two articles is a mere rhapsody or parable, very obscure and ill-written, but the other is meant to be a statement of facts, a vision of Heaven and Hell in which Benjamin Franklin and William Penn and Sir Isaac Newton and the late Mrs. Edmonds appear and express their views. Sir Isaac informs the Judge that he made a great mistake about the Law of Gravitation and the Judge adds a note stating that he had been convinced that it was so for a great many years.

I suppose the vision is a tolerably faithful record of a vivid waking dream produced by opium, drink, and mental excitement. The developments of this spiritual school have become very extraordinary and extensive. Beside their quarterly periodical printed at Bridgeport, they have one or two newspapers in this city, and I believe others published elsewhere. There is a stout little duodecimo volume consisting of "communications" from George Washington, Jefferson, Andrew Jackson, Margaret Fuller, and a great many other people, all of them writing very remarkably alike, and most of them very questionable grammar. People publish statements of extraordinary visitations made them by six individuals "in ancient costume," who promenade about for a long while and finally disappear, leaving Hebrew and Sanscrit MSS behind them, not specially relevant to anything. Edgar A. Poe spells out bad imitations of the poetry he wrote while in the flesh. Tables loaded with heavy weights are made to dance vigorously. . . . It is a strange chapter in the history of human credulity at all events, and as such worth investigating.

May 21, FRIDAY NIGHT.   Have been strangely bilious and blue for the past week, a most unaccountable and unreasonable state of vapidity, reluctance to work, disgust at myself, gloomy thoughts of the future, bitter annoyance at every trifle. . . . In the midst of it all the baby has been howling for the last hour or two like a wagon-load of lunatics. Pleasant and soothing is the peevish squall of a colicky child to a man out of temper. After a brief calm he is recommencing now with the staccato yelps that presage another storm coming. Don't know whether it's wind or teething that is the exciting cause; probably the former.

There have not been many very tangible troubles to give me this fit of the blues. Only one indeed of much moment, a complication arising from a blunder of the commissioners in the last Remsen partition suit, or rather a blunder of Bayard & Clarke's whereby some of his Twelfth Street lots and James Henry Strong's have got strangely mixed up, and I fear I shall have a deal of trouble before I can get matters straight again. . . .

At Jenny Lind's concert Tuesday night. She sings marvelously, but I would rather hear the overture to *Egmont* played by the orchestra that Eisfeld leads than even the scene from *Freischütz* and the lovely air from the *Nozze di Figaro* sung by any possible woman. Weber's *"Konzertstück"* I was rather disappointed in.

May 23, SUNDAY. Dickens's *Bleak House*, Nos. 1, 2, and 3. It promises to be better than anything he has written. I suspect that Esther will learn with surprise that she is the daughter of the law-copyist in the garret, by Lady Dedlock. Mr. Boythorn must once have been in love with the lady. Harold Skimpole is going to be the villain of the crowd, or at least its Evil Principle and agent of mischief, perhaps without malice aforethought.

May 27. . . . Prospect of a domestic revolution, a coup d'état on the part of Mrs. Strong, who is conspiring against her Marie, the nurse—an excellent woman in many respects, but a Tartar of the deepest dye, who keeps the household in hot water and has got to be displaced at all risks. . . . At Niblo's with Ellie night before last—some of that idiotic foolery called ballet, and part of the *Bayadère* badly sung.

May 31. Just from a meeting of St. Luke's Hospital. The subscription list becalmed in the latitude of $50,000. Very busy of late as a member of the Obstetrical Committee, that is the committee appointed to make arrangements with an ancient Lying-in Asylum Society incorporated in 1799, which has been in a state of suspended vitality for a long time, and now exists only to hold on to some $30,000 of assets. Had a meeting here Saturday night.

The baby has suddenly become quiet. The change was so sudden as

to be quite alarming. It occurred before Marie left, or I should have concluded she had been in the habit of pinching him to produce ululation.
Eleanor Curtis is still without sign of improvement. Spent last evening
with her, and had never seen her looking more worn and feeble. . . .

Doane's trial postponed, perhaps so as to vitiate all the proceedings
and make another presentment necessary. If so, he'll meet it by setting
up the action of his convention as a bar. McCoskry and DeLancey thus
enabled to go to England; sailed Saturday with Jenny Lind Goldschmidt.
Wainwright will be a disgusted man when he hears of their arrival. He
will have been fêted and feasted by the aristocracy and the bishops, will
have had his portrait in the *Illustrated News*, possibly in *Punch*, will be
expecting a royal command to dine at Windsor, and the degrees of LL.D.
and D.C.L. from Oxford as the representative of the Anglo-American
Church, when the real representatives will most unexpectedly appear and
he will collapse and be extinguished—like the false Lord Foppington in
the play.

Anyhow, he has done Trinity Church out of leave of absence and
$1,000 for his expenses. He ought to come straight back and pay over all
the money except the cost of the two voyages.

June 4, FRIDAY EVENING. . . . Walked the Hospital this morning with
J. F. De Peyster. Long as I have lived in New York I was never within
its gates before. Want to get some ideas that might bear on St. Luke's.
The establishment seems to be managed with much system and efficiency,
and it's far more extensive than I supposed. . . .

Democratic Convention in session at Baltimore, no result yet known.
Cass stood best on the first ballot, next Buchanan, next Douglas, but far
behind. By the twenty-sixth Cass had fallen off to the third place. Buchanan
had gained largely and was at the top of the list. Douglas had gained still
more and was No. 2. I'd bet on Douglas, though the Buchanan men may
be impracticable and render it necessary to unite on somebody no one
thinks of now. The quadrennial Walpurgis Night of the Whigs comes in
a fortnight. They'll no doubt nominate Scott on the first ballot. There is
no chance for Fillmore and little for Webster. Scott bids fair to be President, but I fear the contest will be sectional and fraught with mischief.

Gold pouring in from California, and my anticipation of insolvency
continues lively. After all, worse things may happen to a man. . . . Another
vacancy in Trinity Church vestry that it will not be easy to fill. . . .

The baby has squalled rather less of late, and the expression and
sentiment of his ululations has rather changed. Instead of a querulous

wailing, his expostulations with destiny have assumed a tone of super-passion and are now generally a shrill squeal of fury, like that of an indignant cat in circumstances of desperation.

June 7. After some forty-odd labor pains in the shape of balloting, the Democratic Convention has brought forth its candidate: Franklin Pierce of New Hampshire, with William Rufus King for Vice-President. Nobody knows much of Franklin Pierce, except that he is a decent sort of man in private life. Very possibly he may run all the better, as Polk did, for his insignificance. Democracies are not over-partial to heroes and great men. A statesman who is too much glorified becomes a bore to them. Aristides was held a nuisance because he was called just, a typical fact in history not regarded as it ought to be. Democracy is secretly jealous of individual eminence of every sort, not merely of that which grows out of wealth or station. Daniel Webster's chance for the presidency was gone forever when his friends dubbed him the Great Expounder of the Constitution. So that it is not impossible that the Locos will *pierce* their enemies in 1852 as they *poked* them in 1844, which joke is not original. Scott's foibles are so many that he's vulnerable and can be made ridiculous, and this galvanized cypher, of whom nothing can be said but that he is a cypher, may very well beat him. . . .

June 10, THURSDAY EVENING. General Laight died Wednesday morning very suddenly, though there had been no thought of his complete recovery for a long while. Strange that he and Adam Newell should have passed away so close together. Both were splendid old men, among the finest specimens I have known of the ancient race now nearly extinct. . . .

Very poor; bank account running frightfully near low-water mark. I don't wish I were rich that I might live better, or buy pictures or anything else, but I do groan in spirit to be rid of these never-ending sordid cares about money.

Mrs. Sam Ward, who's living in Paris while her husband's in California, said to be the mistress of a Russian prince.

Webster's prospects of nomination frightening a little. Pierce ratified by the whole Democratic family, John Van Buren and the Barn-Burners included, and promises to run the race that is set before him with credit to his backers.

June 17, THURSDAY AFTERNOON. The great Whig palaver at Baltimore in full activity over its nominations, the three great sections of the party—Scott, Webster, and Fillmore—intriguing, caucusing, bragging, and betting in an excitement that must be very trying with the thermometer at 90°. Scott on the whole seems to stand the best chance, but the result of the incubation is mere matter of guess. . . . The baby don't seem to suffer much from the hot weather so far, but I suppose he'll soon feel it if it lasts much longer—nobody but must. Think of the agony of having one's lower end muffled and swathed in the barbarous trappings for which the nineteenth century has invented no humane substitute! I should go mad in two hours under the infliction. An extra thick neckcloth on one of these hot mornings would be fearful, but words can't express the misery a perpetual state of diaper must produce. No wonder the unhappy infant remonstrates with Fate sometimes, as he's remonstrating now.

June 19. Had to come uptown at twelve with a splitting headache. Such a ride uptown! Such scalding dashes of sunshine coming in on both sides of the choky, hot railroad car, and drawing stale, sickly odors from sweaty Irishmen in their shirt sleeves; German Jew shop-boys in white coats, pink faces, and waistcoats that looked like virulent prickly heat; fat old women, with dirty-nosed babies; one sporting man with black whiskers, miraculously crisp and curly, and a shirt collar insultingly stiff, who contributed a reminiscence of tobacco smoke—the spiritual body of ten thousand bad cigars. Then the feast of fat things that came reeking under one's nose at each special puddle of festering filth that Center Street provided in its reeking, fermenting, putrefying, pestilential gutter! I thought I should have died of the stink, rage, and headache before I got to Twenty-first Street. But luckily this headache was one of the sort that goeth off with profound, impenetrable, apoplectic sleep, and at five o'clock I awoke in the library chair after four hours of it, refreshed and free.

No news from Baltimore of any result. Thus far between twenty and thirty ballotings, all obstinately alike; about 130 for Fillmore, the same for Scott, and some 30 for Webster; 140-odd necessary for a choice. It's a trial of endurance between the Websterites and the Fillmoreites, and it is like to end by the faction that's soonest worn out going over to the other side and uniting against Scott, the common enemy. I am only surprised that they stand out so long in this sultry weather. But there are many chances that may bring out Scott ahead. *Tribune* greatly disgruntled by the platform. The black philanthropists of Ohio, New York, and Massachusetts will look coldly on the nominee, whoever he may be.

June 22. Scott is the nominee at last: the fact was made known to the crowd that beset the *Courier's* office and half blocked the street, at twelve yesterday, and was received with a quartette or quintette of cheers, the mob being somewhat apathetic, and a few performers being left to do what enthusiasm was done.

His chance of election, I think, is small. Ike Fowler, Vanderpoel, Van Schaick, and John Van Buren say he'll be an easy man to beat. That may be mere brag. But his friends forget that in neither Taylor nor Jackson nor Harrison was there any trace of that conceit and absurdity which have gained Scott the epithet of Fuss and Feathers, and that the enthusiasm which was got up for them will be hard to get up for the Hero of Mexico. The Whigs here receive the nomination coolly. Several have said they won't vote at all. Scott has endorsed "The Platform," and so may do better than was expected in the Southern States, but he won't be helped by Horace Greeley's editorial of this morning, wherein he repudiates and spits upon the plank of the platform which affirms the Fugitive Slave Law. The General's old alliance with Native Americanism will tell against him with the immense foreign vote.

June 27, SUNDAY. Peter Schermerhorn was reduced to destitution, deprived of all his property and estate real and personal, last Wednesday —having been so recklessly extravagant as to die on that day. He must be sadly bored in a world where there are no rents to collect and no investments to be made. . . .

Scott is going to run better than I thought at first. The struggle will be close enough to be interesting. The latest indication is Kossuth's advice to his countrymen and the Germans to take the Democratic side, which most of them would have done without being told to do it. Cornell, who's clear-headed and sagacious on such subjects, thinks the Whig prospect very fair.

July 2, FRIDAY NIGHT. Dinnerless and disconsolate, having been bedeviled with sick headache most of the day, though not so badly handled but that I could attend to my avocation till about four o'clock. Since which time I've been spelling over some of Haydn's Mass, No. 2, which "do please me," and reading *Redgauntlet*, *The Antiquary*, and *The Talisman*, with selections from *Old Mortality* and *The Black Dwarf*.

Charles Curtis has gone to West Point. We propose following Wednesday next. . . . Henry Clay died; eulogy and regret very general in both parties.[7] Sold out Soule yesterday; a very beggarly return will

[7] Henry Clay had been ailing for more than a year, but had determined to die in the national service, and had returned in the fall of 1851 to his senatorial chair in Washington. He passed away June 29 in the National Hotel, and was given a thousand-mile funeral procession to Lexington, Kentucky.

Langdon get for his $7,000 investment. Letters from Wainwright, who's having a grand time among the pleasant places of the Establishment. And he was *so* agreeably surprised when the two Bishops came after all! Prospects of the political campaign more and more beyond calculation. Scott will make an available candidate, if he don't write letters, and don't strut himself to death before November. . . .

We shall have to get up a volunteer force in this city before long, a sort of Holy Vehm or Vigilance Committee, if rowdyism continues to grow on us at its present rate. The Common Council is notoriously profligate and corrupt; the police force partly awed by the blackguards of the brothel and groggery, partly intimate with them. And if some drunken ruffian is arrested, he's sure to be discharged by some justice or alderman, who feels that it won't do to lose the support of the particular gang to which he belongs. An organized amateur society of supporters of law would be wholesome, an association that should employ agents to prosecute violence and corruption vigorously, and to follow up with the penalties of the law those of its ministers who are too timid or dishonest to enforce it. It might not effect a cure, though, unless it went further and took the law into its own hands. . . .

July 5, MONDAY EVENING.   Have been at home all day writing. Tonight went on the roof awhile. It's a beautiful sight the city presents. In every direction one incessant sparkle of fire balls, rockets, roman candles, and stars of all colors shooting thick into the air and disappearing for miles around, with now and then a glare of colored light coming out in some neighborhood where fireworks on a large scale are going off. A foreigner would put it in his book of travels as one of the marvels of New York, and compare it to a swarm of tropical fireflies gleaming in and out through a Brazilian forest.

July 8.   Left for West Point in the *Francis Skiddy* yesterday morning. Mr. and Mrs. Noyes on board, going to the same place. Very comfortable voyage, the Dauphin having been in a state of repose till he was transported to the omnibus, when he squealed lustily. . . . West Point don't much like General Scott's nomination. The General seems to have lost popularity of late with the younger officers. They laugh at his weaknesses more than formerly.

Strong and his wife, always fond of West Point, Highland Falls, and the surrounding country, took rooms again for the summer at Cozzens's Hotel; placing Baby John in a corner apartment "where half his nocturnal

*ululations will diffuse themselves over the Plain instead of making the whole
second floor of the hotel uninhabitable."* Some interesting people visited the
Point. Among them were Jerome Bonaparte and his wife; their son, Jerome,
Jr., had completed his course as cadet, showed to advantage in his undress
uniform, *"and seems a decidedly favorable specimen of the West Point graduate, which is saying much for him."* General Winfield Scott's wife and
daughter Ella were also there; and Strong gives us some gossip about the other
daughter, Camilla. *"Mrs. Scott hasn't got over her disgust at her daughter's
sacrifice of herself to that silky mongrel of spaniel and baboon, Goold Hoyt.
The story at the Point is that Mrs. Scott gives the credit of the calamity to the
tyrannous caprices and petty inflictions whereby the General made his household wretched, and that she speaks of little Goold without stopping to choose
epithets."* Still interested in microscopy, Strong hastened to renew his friendship with the congenial professor of chemistry, mineralogy, and geology,
Jacob W. Bailey.

In common with everyone else in the Hudson Valley, Strong was shocked
this summer by two terrible steamboat disasters. On July 28, the vessel Henry
Clay left Albany to make her usual run to New York City. Near Kingston
she fell in with the rival ship Armenia, the two began racing, and the Henry
Clay, in order to make the Kingston landing first, actually ran into her competitor and crowded her toward shore. Below Kingston the contest was resumed; heavy fires were built and every ounce of steam crowded on. Various
passengers expostulated with the crew of the Henry Clay, but to no avail.
Near Yonkers the steamboat caught fire amidships. By some blunder most of
the passengers were herded aft, and by another the vessel was run ashore, just
below Yonkers, head on instead of diagonally. An east wind swept the flames
toward the stern, with the result that more than ninety passengers were either
burned to death or drowned. The captain and part-owner, John F. Tallman,
with others of the crew, were condemned by the coroner's jury for culpable
negligence and criminal recklessness, and were arrested on federal warrants.
Among those who perished were Stephen Allen, ex-mayor of New York, and
the landscape architect and horticulturist A. J. Downing; while Strong, as he
records below, lost some of his close friends at West Point.

Another horrible accident took place only a few weeks later when the
boiler of the steamboat Reindeer exploded. This vessel was carrying 169
passengers from New York to Albany and way points, and had just left

Malden. Fifty or sixty passengers were seated at dinner in the lower cabin, which was instantly filled with live steam. Some were killed outright, and others so dreadfully scalded that within a few days the death-list rose to thirty-three. These two calamities, with a disastrous collision in August on Lake Erie in which many lives were lost on the ship Atlantic, *had much to do with the early passage by Congress of an efficient steamboat inspection law.*

Meanwhile the presidential canvass of 1852 dragged on without much incident, for no sharply defined issues were at stake. The New York Herald *complained that it was the most uninteresting presidential campaign in history. After the Free Soil wing of the Whig Party in August rejected Scott, nominating Senator Hale of New Hampshire for President, it was generally assumed that the election of Franklin Pierce was certain.*

July 17, SATURDAY.   The money-article man of the London *Times*, and rising prices everywhere, point in the same direction—to depreciation of money and the ruin of everyone who holds anything but real estate. I've been exacerbated on this subject from time to time for the last four years and have been a Cassandra to all my friends who hold bonds and mortgages or favor bank stock. But a talk with a financier (G. C. A.) and one or two signs and tokens of change within the last three days have given me a special season of dismayed anticipation, and now I see the revolution as inevitable and am beginning for the first time to take a practical view of things to be *done*, as well as evils to be expected.

July 22. . . . Considerable talk about cholera. Henry Clay's sham funeral Tuesday very imposing. Streets very generally draped in mourning, specially Broadway. The Astor House shrouded in black bombazine from cornice to sidewalk. Only the windows left unveiled.

July 29, THURSDAY, AT WEST POINT. . . . Yesterday morning came the news that Captain Marcy's command, some eighty men exploring in the Red River country, had been cut off to a man by a horde of Comanches. With them was Captain McClellan of the Engineers, a very fine fellow whom we all liked extremely, and John Suydam, brother of Jem and Lydig Suydam, who accompanied the party as an amateur.

Judge [Lewis Halsey] Sandford dead of cholera at Toledo.

Charles Curtis and I walked over to Bailey's at about ten o'clock to talk over a little chemistry in connection with possible poisoning by lead or copper at the Hotel. He was just leaving for Greenport, taking his family with him, and was in the best of spirits. . . . Home. Took a nap after dinner, and went to parade with Ellie. Returned. Heard that the *Henry Clay* had been burnt, and as Bailey and his family were understood to have gone to New York in that boat, Ellie and I went straight to his house after tea, with misgivings.

At the door was old Lipsey, the ferryman, with a scrawled note addressed to one of the children, and old Aunt Nancy, poor Mrs. Bailey's colored servant and prime minister and confidant for thirty years. "Mr. Bailey would be home on Tuesday, and Missus and Miss Kitty week after." Lipsey said, "*They were on board the Clay, Sir*, and this note has been sent up and I don't want to give it to the children." Mahan came along, and it was handed to him. He walked into the house to read it, and came back to tell us that Mrs. Bailey and poor, pretty, bright, graceful Miss Kitty were lost. The Professor and his youngest son were saved.

Poor Ellie cried bitterly, and it was the saddest night I ever spent at West Point. Mrs. Bailey, with all her faults of manner, was so hospitable and generous, so warm in her friendships, and so full of kindly impulses, that Ellie had become attached to her without knowing it. She had almost oppressed us with her little thoughtful attentions to Ellie's comfort and the baby's welfare. Little Miss Maria, "Miss Kitty" as everybody called her, inherited her father's brightness and his special delicacy of thought and character, and sympathized with him in all his great pursuits; had her little albums of colored seaweeds and her little feminine collections of shells and minerals. The last time I saw her she was full of her projects for the fall. She was to go on with her German under her father, and her French under Agnel, and her music with Apelles, and had seen at Burlington what was the right way to study and was sure she should make great progress. She must have been fifteen or sixteen, and poor Bailey was wrapped up in her. It is a sickening business—such things make this seem a cruel world to live in.

The loss of life seems to have been fearful, and the transaction a case of wholesale murder. Reckless racing leading to mischief, and then panic and frenzy among the passengers, imbecility in the officers, and murderous absence even of *boats* to save a dozen or two.

July 30. Went up by railroad last night. The funeral took place this morning, attended by nearly every one on the Point; a melancholy business it was. I shall never forget poor Bailey's figure, and look of apathy—almost of stupor; and the three little boys clinging round him and crying, unnoticed; the still sunlight on the cemetery, the burial service, the multitude of sad faces, the two coffins with which we all felt that all the life and hope and heart of one man were sinking into the earth to wither into dust. And all this and so much beside, *that the Henry Clay might beat the Armenia.*

It is time that this drowning and burning to death of babies and young girls and old men to gratify the vanity of steamboat captains were stopped. I would thank God for the privilege of pulling the cap over the eyes of the captain and owners of this boat, and feel as I completed my hangman's office that I had not lived utterly in vain.

The boat had been run on shore at right angles so that her bow nearly tore up the railroad track. Boiler and engines are high and dry, while the stern is in fifteen feet of water. Had she been run in *diagonally*, probably not a life need have been lost.

The scene at the wreck yesterday morning was hideous: near thirty bodies exposed along the shore—many children among them.

And some enterprising undertakers from Yonkers and New York had sent up their stock of coffins on speculation.

"Looking for deceased friend, sir?" "Buying a coffin, sir?" "Only five dollars, sir, and warranted."

Public feeling is very strong now. But it will die out within the week. These scoundrels will never be punished, not even indicted. *Damn them!* No, I retract that, for God knows we all stand in need of something less than the rigor of justice. But a thousand years or so of fire and brimstone after hanging in this world, would be a moderate award of retribution. . . .

August 12, THURSDAY MORNING. . . . At West Point Tuesday night. Mrs. Georgiana Peters there. How she has been improved by matrimony! As a young lady she was my aversion. Went to Cozzens's with an omnibus load of ladies, including Ellie and Mrs. Peters and her mother and so forth, to a tableau. Rode home sitting behind on the omnibus in a military cloak and a pelting rain through a night as dark as Erebus. The tableaux were well enough. Talked with Governor [Washington] Hunt and his wife. The Governor is a pleasant person, and his close relations with Mr. Ruggles make him very gracious to me. . . .

August 16. . . . Some talk with Peirce and Mr. Ruggles about the proposed plan for putting new life into Columbia College. Peirce holds that professors may be prevented from degenerating into drones, like Renwick, by requiring of them to accomplish something every year or every six months, making it a condition of holding office that at certain periods they produce some essay, memoir, or investigation in their respective departments. . . .

August 23, MONDAY NIGHT. . . . Mrs. Colonel Henry Scott at the Hotel has developed into a haystack of a woman, with the face and bearing of a chambermaid. Miss Ella is with her, an undeniably lovely lady, and seemingly very willing to be gracious, but as cold and impenetrable and unexcitable as a fish. Also the juvenile Winfield Scott—of whose baptism by Bishop Hughes Mrs. General Scott gave me a moving account the other night. How first they put oil on him and then put salt on him and she really thought they'd make a salad of the poor little creature and end by cutting it up. . . .

Ellie is well, thank Heaven. Baby ditto, with its mouth as full of teeth as a shark's. It claws and scratches me playfully in the enthusiasm of its filial tenderness. Don't know when I shall bring them to town. Not soon, I think, for the city is pestilential; the streets smell like a solution of bad eggs in hartshorn.

August 31, TUESDAY NIGHT.   Was at the Point Thursday evening. Chief event, stag dance of cadets on the plain surrounded by a parallelogram of candles, which were finally kicked out. It was followed by songs in chorus—"Benny Havens," of course. . . .

September 6, MONDAY NIGHT.   Yesterday at the Point was a day to be had in grateful remembrance for its sunshine and clear sky and delicious fall atmosphere. Such days amid woods and hills are not cheap things, of course, to a Cockney. . . .

Another murderous "accident," coming close on the *noyades* of the *Henry Clay* and the *Atlantic*, and varying their monotony by a new mode of execution at least equally piquant. The instrument in this case was a flue emitting red-hot steam into a cabin full of men and women, scalding and skinning alive some twenty or thirty; a couple of young Southern girls of seventeen and nineteen among the rest—dead at last, poor things, after only a few hours of agony. Pleasant memories must be those of old experienced captains and engineers! The Basia of Joannes Secundus are commonplace beside *theirs*—charring white necks, blistering rounded arms and bosoms, making the flesh to drop from slender waists with their fervent embraces, unloosing the zone of beauty with a vengeance, and drawing off dainty kid gloves with the skin *in* them. Of course, there was no officer of the *Reindeer* at all to blame. What a sagacious people we are with our "reverence for human life" and our increasing scruples about the lawfulness of capital punishment! . . .

Governor Hunt and General Scott are at Cozzens's, with a swarm of smaller politicians round them. The General tries to look as wise as the Sphinx, but accomplishes only a puzzled, dubious gaze into vacancy, which says, "I'm in a scrape and a bad one. I may come out all right, but I can't help thinking sometimes I shall come out wrong, and then it's as if cold water was poured down my back, and all the blood in my body gets into my face. And what's very bad, I'm afloat at sea, don't understand this sort of campaigning near as well as the other, and don't see that I can do anything, unless I write letters, and my friends make such a row if I hint at such a thing that I daren't to do it." And all this time the poor General is being discussed *and* analyzed and pulled to pieces in newspapers and speeches and pamphlets through all the land. His dignity would be shocked and outraged by the presumption and impertinence of an eulogy not *exactly* in good taste. What must be his sensations when he's called Fuss and Feathers in half the village newspapers of the United States?

I fear the General's chance is none of the best. He is said to talk confidently of the result; if he is confident his looks belie him.

September 27. I appreciate West Point more and more fully as our departure there draws near. The place is very lovely now, with the sunshine and clear air and gold and ruby-tinted foliage of fall. The leaf begins to change early this season, and the woods wear their coat of many colors already. Maples in great glory, sumachs blazing in scarlet, and every now and then a drapery of wild creeper that makes a sunshine in this shady place or rather lights up the woods as crimson fireworks might. But we're to return to brick walls on Thursday. . . .

Count Sartiges is married to a Miss Thorndike of Boston, or rather a minister plenipotentiary is married to $100,000.[8] He's a beast, and proposed "an intrigue" to Mrs. H., at Newport, pending this engagement, and apologized on being called to account, and pleaded ignorance of the usages of the country. Call on Mrs. Abraham Schermerhorn tonight. . . .

All well in town, and no special news stirring. The [Diocesan] Convention is trying to elect a bishop, thus far unsuccessfully. Vinton, Seabury, and Wainwright are prominent candidates. They say Vinton can't secure a majority; if so, there will not be any election, probably. Hawks has been elected to the vacant episcopate in Rhode Island. Very likely he'll accept for the sake of a change. The Rt. Rev. Philander Chase is dead at last. No doubt to him to die is gain. It's clearly no loss to the Church; he'd become an Episcopal mountebank. . . .

October 2, SATURDAY EVENING. Rather dyspeptic and headachy. Wainwright is Bishop after all!!—elected by a small majority at last. People were

[8] Eugène de Sartiges, the French minister in Washington.

worn out with waiting and balloting, and resolved to elect some one, and
only a compromise candidate could be elected. Nobody is quite satisfied
and a good many are quite savage, but I suppose that it's the best thing
that could have been done. Perhaps a milk poultice is better for the diocese
than such a mustard plaster as Vinton. But the Bishop-elect should insure
his life at once, for it would be consistent with all his former fortunes to die
the day before consecration. Where's the Episcopal income to be got?
It won't be decent for the Bishop to continue an active minister of the
church, and it is not clear that if he resigns the vestry will consent to fill
up the deficiencies in the Episcopal fund. . . .

It is a shocking bad choice, no doubt. There are twenty men, at least,
in the diocese altogether better fitted for the office. But probably not one
of them could have been elected, at this Convention at least, and another
adjournment, *re infecta*, would have been scandalous. The period of this
administration, I suppose, is to be an "Era of Good Feeling."

October 11. Scott is brightening daily, I think. But this series of
stump speeches is a lamentable anti-climax, a sad falling off from the
Triumphal Entry into Mexico. The general electioneers as badly as
Coriolanus would have done if he had condescended to try.

October 15. Cold news for Scott from Ohio and Pennsylvania, though
Greeley accounts for it all very much to his own satisfaction and proves that
the state elections don't afford the least indication of the vote for President.
Perhaps they don't. John L. Stephens is dead; also Frederick R. Griffing,
Master Tom's wealthy bachelor uncle.

October 20. Very little to write about this evening. The three chief
ingredients of common talk are: 1st, Cuba and the shindy about the *Crescent
City's* expulsion from the harbor of Havana; 2d, the Broadway Railroad;
3d, Scott and his chances. I pronounce Scott to be in a bad way. No election
ever drew near so quietly, no two candidates ever developed so little
enthusiasm. Scott's stumping tour may have done good among the masses,
but I'm sure it has lost him respect with sensible people everywhere.
His speeches are awkward, strained, vapid, and egotistical. Pierce has a
talent for silence that will serve far better than his antagonist's electioneering. As to Cuba, I'm rapidly being demoralized into a filibuster. My
appreciation of our manifest destiny is increasing—my disgust at the
filthy imbecility of the worn-out Spanish breed has become intense. If
Spain and France and England had a right to invade the New World and
take its control from those who couldn't make it useful to mankind, I don't
see why the "Saxon race" isn't justified in routing out the black-muzzled

breed that monopolizes Cuba without developing its resources, or allowing better men to help them do so.

October 22, FRIDAY NIGHT.   To Brougham's (or Wallack's) Lyceum with Ellie and Mr. and Mrs. Ruggles. *Much Ado About Nothing*; Beatrice, Miss Laura Keene. On the whole very satisfactory. . . .

Daniel Webster is reported *in extremis*. A sad hole his death will leave, and one not easy to fill. From the old heroic race to which Webster and Clay and Calhoun belonged down to the rising race of Sewards and Douglases and Fishes is a dismal descent.

October 25.   Webster died early yesterday morning, and seems from the brief notices that have come here by telegraph to have made a stately exit, to have died self-possessed, thoughtful, and resigned, in style fitting his great career and his lofty place in the eyes of Europe and America. It is the ending of one of the greatest men of this time; one of the greatest intellectually, not morally.[9] His position in the North would have been far more commanding if there had been moral weight in his character. But love of office and improvidence in his private affairs sometimes made him do things unheroic to gain place or money. There was undue love of brandy and water, too.

Still, everyone felt confidence in his ability to do all he undertook. All complications foreign or domestic were felt to be in a fair way towards settlement when Daniel had once laid hands on them. Everybody of all parties, except a few phrenetic abolitionists and ismatizens like John Jay, feels this, and the sense of loss is more general and deeper than in any like case I have known. Horace Greeley is resigned and submissive, to be sure.

Jay was "on the point of leaving church" yesterday, being greatly outraged and lacerated by some remarks in poor little Bedell's sermon about the calamity the country had sustained.

Nothing else for the Journal, of much account. Mr. Ruggles spent the evening here yesterday talking rivers and harbors, the hobby he is riding for the present. He might ride it to much purpose. The issue is one which will surely be decided in favor of the federal power by the next generation, if not by this.

November 1, MONDAY.   Prospects of the Whigs very bad for tomorrow, specially so in this city, if this foul weather lasts. The last notable event

---

[9] It is noteworthy that Strong makes much more of the death of Webster than of Clay. All members of the bar realized that the majestic Daniel was one of the greatest constitutional lawyers the country had yet known. He had been ill for some time with cirrhosis of the liver, and had returned to his beloved Marshfield to die.

of the campaign is the *Tribune*'s ferocious onslaught on poor little Belmont, the agent of the Rothschilds!—the successor of Hulsemann!!!—for interfering in the election of a Free People and putting his name to some Democratic committee notice or other. It seems a very silly business, but they say it will tell effectively on the Kossuthite foreigners of this city and the Pennsylvania Germans.

I don't care much about the general result. I shall vote a hybrid ticket. It's commonly said that Pierce's success will be followed by some more filibustering on a national scale, and the appropriation of Cuba. I want to see the Whigs carry this state. Also, I shouldn't object to F. B. Cutting's being beat (but he won't be), and there may be some choice between the tickets for charter officers, but who shall be President for the next four years, I care surprisingly little. If I ever bet I'd bet three to two on Pierce. The only consideration that makes me feel less than certain of his success is that some very clear-headed and cool-blooded Whigs are pretty well satisfied that Scott will run far ahead of all state tickets and bring out a vote that hasn't been called on to show itself yet.

November 2. The game is decided by this time, and the polls are closed, for it's half-past six P.M., and they've begun counting votes in all the Eastern and Atlantic states. In California and perhaps in the Far West the battle is still raging, but the sun has set in states enough to settle the result, and tomorrow morning's paper will tell it, by grace of the telegraph (which this storm may have deranged, by the by), unless it's a much closer business than I expect.

It rained all last night; the morning was lowering and damp. The sun shone out at noon and by about 3 o'clock the rain set in again, hard. I voted, and nearly had my coat pulled off my back in a desperate struggle to reach the polls.

Votes in the city will turn out very light, I think. Many were kept off by the weather, and many were specially indifferent. The Webster people seemed more vicious and obstinate in inaction than I expected. There will be some votes for a Webster electoral ticket here and in Massachusetts; probably these votes, if they're elected, will be cast for Fillmore.

November 3. Till the day when Babylon the Great shall be cast down into the sea as a millstone, there will not be such another smash and collapse and catastrophe as yesterday befell the Whig party. This morning's *Courier* began its revelations of calamity by avowing that it was certain that Pierce was yesterday elected by the largest vote ever given any candidate for the office, and the returns coming in during the day only certify the truth of this frank confession. It's a cataclysm of Democracy flooding the whole country and overwhelming the tallest Whig strongholds as the deluge of old covered the tops of the high mountains. The victory in this city, in the state, and in the Union is beyond all shadow of question.

If Webster's ghost don't sing a comic song at Mrs. Fish's spiritual soirée tonight, or rap out a Hallelujah chorus under the table, I'm mistaken. Pity he couldn't have lived to see this day.[10]

Poor Scott!!! Whether he'll rend his own garments is questionable, but he must be furious, and very like to rend somebody else's. I'd give a dollar to see the first interview between him and little Seward. To have tried so hard and traveled so far and condescended to so many speeches, and shaken hands with every sort and condition of snob so liberally, and all for this—to run behind his ticket everywhere and to go down to posterity as the worst beaten candidate yet.

November 6, SATURDAY NIGHT.   General opinion seems to be that the Whig party is dead and will soon be decomposed into its original elements. Shouldn't wonder. Where is its leader or leaders? No man commands the confidence or respect of the whole party. Even the Democracy is likely to be disintegrated by the election. The Whigs have long been nothing but a hoop to keep northern and southern democracy more or less bound together by fear of the common enemy; a charge of negative electricity developing positive on the other side of a thin dividing wall. If one party dies the other must perish of inaction, for there's no principle to give either an independent life.

Every good political analyst had expected Pierce's victory; but his triumph over Winfield Scott was even more crushing than had been anticipated. The Democrats carried twenty-seven states, the Whigs only four; Scott had the 42 electoral votes of Kentucky and Tennessee on the border, and Massachusetts and Vermont in New England, while Pierce had the 254 electoral votes of the rest of the Union. Indeed, it seemed clear that the Whig Party had received its death blow. Schuyler Colfax of Indiana wrote his friend Tom Corwin in Ohio that it seemed "almost annihilated"; and Thurlow Weed remarked, "There may be no political future for us." The New York Tribune, for ten years one of the great Whig organs, declared that the party could hardly be revived.

[10] Webster, greatly disappointed that his own presidential ambitions received so little support in 1852 among the Whigs, and convinced that Winfield Scott had no qualifications whatever for the White House, had repudiated Scott's candidacy.

Radical free-soilers seized hope from the election that a new party would now emerge, dedicated to the principles of the Wilmot Proviso. The way lay open in the North for a strong free-soil party, and a host of voters only awaited a new proslavery blow—which came as they thought, in Douglas's Kansas-Nebraska bill of 1854, with its repeal of the Missouri Compromise—to undertake its organization. Before another presidential election, the Republican Party would be in the field, strong enough to have high hopes of success. The Southern Whigs, meanwhile, felt that they could no longer ally themselves with the hated Seward-Weed-Greeley Whigs of the North. They too tended to gravitate into a new party, the Know-Nothings, though not a few of them joined the Democrats. The old-time party alignment, in short, was henceforth completely broken up. The slavery question had begun to wreck it, and its demolition was to be completed in 1854–1855. Strong was among the former Whigs who would vote for Frémont in 1856, and still more ardently for Lincoln in 1860.

This November found Harper's issuing in book form Thackeray's new novel Henry Esmond; *and on the 16th the novelist arrived in New York, just in time to hear George Bancroft deliver an address before the New-York Historical Society. On November 19th Thackeray lectured in Dr. Bellows's church on Broadway to the most distinguished audience that New York could muster, leaving them, wrote Bryant, "perfectly united in the opinion that they never remembered to have spent an hour more delightfully in their lives"; and of that audience Strong was one.*

November 14. Wainwright was consecrated Wednesday the 1st, in very great state. There was a vast crowd, and though poor little Ellie went down early in the morning, she had to take one of the lowest seats and saw little of the performances except the unrolling of the long parchment scroll inscribed with the testimonials. . . . I don't see very clearly the future probable course of things under this administration. Many of the churchmen of this city are as yet far from cordial towards the Provisional Shepherd. Harison, for instance, don't care to conceal the fact that he's quite hostile and spiteful.

Have been meditating over a plan for the benefit of George Anthon and to help along the projected infusion of a little velocity into Columbia College. Suggested it to him in the course of a long walk up the east side of the town Monday afternoon, and he took it at once, and thinks it feasible, but I've my doubts. It is to raise $20,000 among the alumni and endow a professorship of archaeology or some such thing. I don't want to make the attempt unless with reasonable prospect of success, for a failure would injure him. But the present indications are on the whole encouraging.

Everybody talking about a rather queer subject, *moving tables*. Not by any Rochester ghosts nor by an ordinary means, but by some alleged unknown motive power. George Bancroft was talking of such a performance having taken place at his house, when he and some of his family sat down by a table and went through the motions with no expectation of any such result. . . .

November 21, SUNDAY AFTERNOON. At Thackeray's first lecture Friday night, with Ellie. Subject, Swift. Lecture very effective, clear, and truthful. Specially pleased with the plain-spoken, masculine tone of its criticism on Swift and his books. He handled him without regard to conventionalities, spoke of the man as he deserved, were he ten times as great in intellect. Freedom from humbug is the central point of Thackeray's constitution. . . . I've come to the conclusion that my professorship plan for George Anthon is not feasible. Pity.

November 28. This has been quite a dissipated week in a small way. Monday night, Thackeray's lecture on Congreve and Addison. Very judicious view of the drama of the reign of Charles II; the sterling old English drama discussed with plainness of speech. Tuesday, Miss Margaret Lydig dined here and George Anthon. . . .

My respect for Thackeray increases with each successive lecture. It's not merely their manner that's attractive—their substance is sound and true, and often original.

December 4. Two more lectures by Thackeray, spirited and original, though not so striking as the first two. They are still crowded. . . .

Lamentable commentary on the Vanity of Human Greatness in Thackeray's inquiry of Bancroft, "Who is a Mr. Astor who has left a card for me?"[11]

December 9, THURSDAY. Thackeray's final lecture Monday night was one of his very best. I came near a disagreeable scrape. The crowd and heat were such that Ellie came pretty near fainting, and only saved herself by concentrated exertion of *will*. If she *had* succumbed, getting her out through the close-packed aisle and into a carriage would have been no comfortable task. . . .

Last night at Putnam's (G.P.'s), where were Hawks, and George

[11] This was William B. Astor, counted the richest man in America.

Curtis (how the deuce did he get self-control enough to sacrifice so many evenings to absence?), Bigelow, Dr. Bethune (a great, pig-headed fat man), Miss Bacon, and various other literary and aesthetic notabilities. With them, Jesse Spencer (called Sponge)[12] whom I've not seen to speak to for two years, and whose last communication from me was a notice that I didn't think it incumbent on me to adopt his suggestions about a little *loan*, but who was *so* glad to see me this time, and thought it such a funny coincidence that he should have put a note to me into the post office that very morning, asking a little assistance.

December 17, FRIDAY NIGHT.   Thackeray says Miss Sally Baxter is Beatrix in *Henry Esmond.* Haven't read it yet.

Terrible looking forward into insolvency and big bills, about this time. The baby is pretty well. "Teething cough," which very nearly started me out of bed for Dr. Peters night before last. . . .

December 19, SUNDAY NIGHT.   The Columbia College reformation projects are simmering. I doubt whether much will ever be developed from them. Charles King, on whom the heat of the battle necessarily falls, is too impulsive, unsteady, and unsubstantial.

December 26.   Two or three squashy wet days, among which was Christmas. Today is clear and mild. At church yesterday. Higby preached. Dined at No. 24 Union Square and came home soon after dinner with a slight migraine for a Christmas gift, but able to begin *Henry Esmond,* which I pronounce to be Mr. Thackeray's *opus maximum.* Next come the *Snob Papers. Esmond* is the only novel I ever read which fairly takes one back to its own time. *Waverley* and *Peveril* might have been written as books of the nineteenth century and then been *trimmed* with the phrases and decorations of the period chosen for them. Mr. Francis Osbaldistone thinks and talks much like a subject of George Fourth, only with an embroidery of allusions and expressions that mark the time. But this book smells of Jacobite and Hanoverian, of the era of powder and hoops. Diction,

---

[12] John Bigelow (1817–1911), Union 1835, was at this time a partner with William Cullen Bryant in the ownership and editorship of the New York *Evening Post.* Rev. George Washington Bethune (1805–1862), Dickinson 1823, son of the eminent New York merchant Divie Bethune, was pastor of a Dutch Reformed church in Brooklyn. Delia Bacon (1811–1859), daughter of a bankrupt missionary to the Indians and sister of the theologian Leonard Bacon, was about to go to England in pursuit of her monomania: the theory that Lord Bacon and others wrote the Shakespearian plays. Hawthorne befriended her there and wrote a preface to her book, *Philosophy of the Plays of Shakespeare Unfolded* (1857). He also wrote his recollections of her in *Our Old Home* (1863). Rev. Jesse Ames Spencer had been in college with Strong and was an Episcopal parson and compiler of textbooks.

and ideas (with few exceptions), allusions, everything else are characteristic. The author must have great industry and patience, great power of
realizing what he reads and of transporting himself back to the date of his
story and living *pro tempore* in other times. The book makes me feel exactly
as when I look at the portraits of Queen Anne's lords and ladies in *Lodge*. . . .

It is proposed by a number of afflicted taxpayers to engage Mr.
Ruggles as counsel or general agent to put down this corrupt and devilish
common council of ours that is swindling away five millions of dollars
per annum. It's high time something were done, and he can go out against
the Dragon of Wantley with as good prospect of success as any one I know.

December 31, FRIDAY NIGHT. . . . Monday night, a Noah's ark of a party
at Judge Campbell's. All sorts and conditions of men and women assisting,
from Mrs. William B. Astor to Dick Willis and his pretty wife. . . . Tuesday evening at the John C. Hamiltons'.[13] Pleasant enough. Mrs. Camilla
Hoyt was there, looking queenly and resplendent. I kept out of the lady's
way. We were great friends at West Point a couple of summers ago, but
she snubbed me once when I was going out of my way to be civil to her,
and I don't mean she shall again. . . .

Last night at a small male gathering, cleric and lay, at Provisional
Bishop Wainwright's, the model of ecclesiastical deportment—vide *Bleak
House*. Respectable and slow. Harison was not on hand. He carries his
animosity too far. It seems the Bishop intends (knowing when he's well
off) to stand by Trinity Parish, feeling that his usefulness will be much
enlarged and increased by a continuance of his connection with that corporation. I didn't understand the exact meaning of the appointment of a
committee on Harison's motion at the last vestry to devise a new system,
or new regulations, or some such thing, for our clerical organization; but
the object, it seems, is to legislate Wainwright out in some way. That
won't do, and if Harison commits himself to such a measure, he'll be
beat down, and his own throat cut from ear to ear. It would be becoming in
Wainwright to resign an office the duties of which he can no longer perform, but if he thinks differently, it will never do for us to proceed *in invitum*
and kick him out. It would be an ungracious act in our rich corporation, would
do us much harm, and would save nothing after all, for somehow or other
we should have to make up the deficit in the Provisional Episcopal salary.

[13] John Church Hamilton, son of Alexander Hamilton, had published a seven-
volume edition of the *Works* of his father in 1850–1851, and was doubtless now
engaged on the six-volume *History of the Republic . . . as Traced in the Writings of
Alexander Hamilton*, a large-scale documentary biography, which he issued in 1857–
1860.

1853

MUNICIPAL CORRUPTION · DEATH OF STRONG'S MOTHER · CRYSTAL PALACE EXPOSITION · THE KNOW-NOTHINGS

New York State had a new governor in Horatio Seymour, an industrious and conscientious Democrat who detested all three of the main types of extremists then rampant—prohibitionists, abolitionists, and nativists. The metropolis had a new mayor of fine quality in Jacob A. Westervelt, whom everyone trusted, but who could do little to control the corruption in the Board of Aldermen and the city departments. Press and public began the year 1853 with much talk of municipal reform, and action was badly needed. The "Forty Thieves" who made up the two-chambered city legislature had gained an unhappy facility in voting away transportation, dock, ferry, and other franchises in return for bribes. One of the aldermen was William M. Tweed, shortly to grow notorious. In Washington, meanwhile, where the Senate was debating the Clayton-Bulwer Treaty, everybody was expectant of the new Democratic Administration. But on January 7, the nation was shocked to learn that on the previous day President-elect Pierce, his wife, and his only son had been involved in a train accident on the Boston & Maine near Andover, the boy being instantly killed.

The events of the early weeks of the year included the appearance of Putnam's Monthly, *the best general literary magazine the country had yet seen, edited by Charles F. Briggs with the assistance of Parke Godwin and George William Curtis; and the opening of the splendid new St. Nicholas Hotel, a six-story, marble-fronted edifice on Broadway between Spring and Broome Streets. Strong frequently saw George William Curtis, whom he found charming but not impressive. "He's a nice, pleasant, amiable, superficial, genial*

[114]

Epicurean," declared the diarist. On January 11, Captain Ericsson demon-
strated his new "caloric engine" by means of a trial trip of the ship bearing his
own name. While crowds watched intently from the Battery, the vessel moved
gaily up and down the bay at an average speed of about ten knots, bearing an
enthusiastic bevy of journalists and friends. Before the month ended, the Five
Points Mission, which had taken possession of an old brewery, laid the corner-
stone of its new center on the site of this demolished building.

Strong's own circle prospered, though he was distressed by occasional
slight illnesses of his infant son and by his own dyspepsia and headaches. His
law office was busy with important cases, one of them under Judge Roosevelt.
February found him rejoicing over the engagement of Peter Strong to Miss
Mary Stevens, daughter of the wealthy and stuffily dignified John Austin
Stevens. The girl he pronounced sweet, sensible, and pretty; the parents a most
stately and forbidding pair.

January 4, TUESDAY. I hereby wish myself a happy New Year. The
First of January was rainy and filthy; walked a little way and made a
dozen calls or less round the square, and as far as Mr. Ruggles's.

January 10. The *Commercial*, of all papers in the world, endorses
table moving, certifies to its successful performance by "a party of young
people," and says it is "manifestly an effect of magnetism," which shews
that the editor is not up in physical science. If there be anything in this
very queer business but humbug and lust for the marvelous, it is neither
magnetism nor electricity in any of their known manifestations, or acting
under any of their known laws. Some new imponderable, some "vital
dynamic force," it must be.

January 12. Ericsson engine understood to be established as a great
fact by successful trial trip. I hope it may prove so. The *Henry Clay* case
on. Hall, whom I saw last night, speaks hopefully of the result.

January 31, MONDAY. Weather has been frosty for the past ten days,
but the streets are sloppy again at last, and the snow vanishing very fast.
I have been, on the whole, blue and uncomfortable—cause: anticipated
financial vacuity. Memoranda of the last week not new or important.
. . . Heard [Mme. Henrietta] Sontag in *Fille du Régiment*. Marvelously
preserved for a woman of fifty, in face and figure and the power of putting
on girlish buoyancy and spirit. I like the lady much. . . .[1]

[1] A season of opera was being given at Niblo's Garden by Signor Cesare Badiali's
Company, with Carl Eckert as conductor. Mme. Henrietta Sontag was the prima
donna and Donizetti's piece her most popular part.

Rather clever and quite just article in last *Putnam's* on "Our Best Society," manifestly by George William Curtis, exposing the supper-room and the German cotillion and the unutterable vapidity and folly of the whole system, with some spirit. I think he's inspired thereto by Miss Eliza Winthrop's preference of saltation to aesthetics.

Bishop 〔Levi Silliman〕 Ives seems indubitably to have enlisted under the Pope. Dayton Hobart shewed me a letter from his sister, Mrs. Verplanck (who's traveling with the Bishop), dated at Rome, in which she says that their visit there is not pleasant "for reasons you'll know soon enough.' This, followed by the French newspaper paragraph, with some other matters, makes me feel little doubt about the story. Hawks, to whom I paid a visit the other night, says that Ives is crazy, and gave instances of total failure of memory and delusions about trifling matters that looked like it.[2]

February 6. There was a slight gathering of people at Mr. Ruggles's to meet Governor Hunt. Two lions, both of whom I tackled, Thackeray and Louis XVII or Eleazar I, King of France, the great topic of conversation since the curious article in *Putnam's* last number. The Bourbon is a plain, homespun personage enough, with no sign of Indian blood and with a profile like his alleged illustrious father's. His diction is tolerably good; he speaks with considerable accent, not French, but caught from the Caughnawaga or Cock-in-the-Water Indians. His story, as published by Hawks & Hanson, attracts great attention, and I think is generally *half* believed. It is plausible and curious, but there's a good deal that might be said on the other side.[3]

Thackeray is a pleasant person, with much to say and a great ease of manner, and a faculty of constantly saying things that are clever and

[2] Ives, who had once been assistant minister of Trinity in New York, had been a bishop of the Episcopal Church since 1831, and had published a number of theological works. He had married a daughter of Bishop J. H. Hobart. The Oxford movement in England had attracted him, and journeying to Rome in 1852, he made his submission to Pope Pius IX on Christmas Day. His career in the Catholic Church was not destined to be distinguished.

[3] Eleazar Williams (1789–1858), son of a mixed-breed St. Regis Indian, for a time declared himself the lost Dauphin. A handsome man of great vanity and vagrant tastes, he had hoped to create an Indian commonwealth in what is now Wisconsin. As early as 1839, he had begun talking of himself as heir to the French throne. In February, 1853, a romantic-minded minister named J. H. Hanson published in *Putnam's* an article entitled "Have We a Bourbon Among Us?" which brought Williams into general notoriety. For a time, controversy raged about him, William Gilmore Simms attacking his claims. He soon relapsed into obscurity and poverty, holding a small pastorate among the St. Regis Indians at Hogansburg, New York.

pointed. *The Lady of Lyons* at Wallack's the night before; Wallack and Miss Laura Keene. Very effective play for the stage; I caught myself snivelling more than once. . . . David Kennedy dead, of typhus fever. Louis Napoleon has made a love match, a subject for future dramatists, perhaps tragedians. He's not a commonplace man.

February 16. Visit from Edward A. Strong this morning, discussing the drunkenness, whoremongering, insubordination, and total worthlessness of poor Bob [Strong], and with much feeling and distress. Poor Bob!—and poor young America generally, from Jem Pendleton and the "Pup-Club" down. Was there ever among the boys of any city so much gross dissipation redeemed by so little culture and so little manliness and audacity even of the watchman-fighting sort? It has grown to be very bad, the tone of morals and manners has, even among the better class of young men about town. Sam Whitlock was telling me of his being driven out of the Club the other night (the New York Club, the resort of older and graver men) by the talk of Jem Strong, LeRoy, Lupp, and so forth, about various women against whom he had never heard anything. Mrs. A. was going to have a baby—was B. or C. its father? and the like. Sam cleared out in haste, fearing the next person he heard criticized might be Mrs. Whitlock. And this was in the presence of a roomful of men for attentive listeners.

Apropos of "our best society," [George William] Curtis's engagement with Miss Eliza Winthrop is ruptured and bust; cause, "uncongeniality," particulars unknown. The young lady seems to suffer no special affliction or depression in consequence, and Curtis is said to be deeply "mortified." So everybody was probably right and it was a match agreed on without real attachment on either side and from a brief mutual fancy.

February 18. The Winthropidae [are] behaving foolishly about this ruptured engagement of Curtis's with Miss Eliza, putting it on the ground of Curtis's "socialism and infidelity," so says Sandy Bliss (George Bancroft's stepson), who was in the office today; the same whom Longfellow exquisitely and ingeniously calls "Arabia Felix." Sufficiently absurd, for Bob Winthrop cares little about Fourier and Strauss, and the young lady's objections to marrying any but a professor will get little credit. . . .

I maintain the cause of the French Empress sturdily in these times, with no very tangible reason except that she has auburn hair and Eugénie is a very pretty name. I rather like the notion of Napoleon III, who, ten or twelve years ago, was a disreputable, dirty, drinking, penniless, foreign prince prowling about these streets and ordered out of the bar room of the old Washington Hall (where Stewart's shop is now) because he was too great a loafer to be allowed to hang about even those disreputable premises, who had so long been wriggling in the gutters and Cloaca of the social system, being now on terms of equality with kings and czars, and making something his friends call a *mésalliance* with the beautiful representative of one of the first among the haughtiest nobility in Europe. There's a romance about it that's altogether refreshing. It will be a curious chapter for readers of history in 1953. As to the attacks on the young Empress's fair fame, I utterly renounce them. *Vivat* Donna Eugenia. . . .

March 2. Wolcott Gibbs's engagement with Miss Josephine [Mauran] promulgated in form; a very sensible and judicious transaction in many respects. . . .

Chief subject of talk the. Aldermen, the presentment of the Grand Jury, the indictment of two City Fathers, the proceedings in the Superior Court, the general profligacy of the city government, the necessity of speedy change, and the difficulty of making it. No one doubts that that little black-muzzled, obese scoundrel Sturtevant is a scoundrel, but most people are resigned in the conviction that Sturtevant will always reign over us. I trust not. It is a memorable struggle (in the Supreme Court) between the judiciary and the civic legislature. Fortunate that the question of supremacy is to be decided in a case in which all public sympathy is with the judges. Henry Erben, with whom I had the privilege of an interview today, declares that there was moral evidence enough before his Grand Jury and that legal evidence enough exists to found indictment against the late mayor, Davies, and at least nine out of ten of both boards. . . .[4]

Miss Laura Belden here night before last, with the most stupendous stories of "table-moving." These stories are a phenomenon, true or false. For if it be all a delusion, as I suspect, they establish the fact of

[4] The Grand Jury presented to the Court of Sessions on February 26 evidence showing that three prominent aldermen named Sturtevant, Smith, and Bard, with certain associates, had been guilty of gross corruption. According to the Grand Jury, one unnamed alderman had asked for $2,000 as the price of his services in obtaining a grant of water rights. The body reported that "enormous sums," so large as to seem incredible to most citizens, had been offered and taken in connection with street railway franchises. Unfortunately, a majority of the judges in the Court of Sessions were aldermen! While the *Times*, *Tribune*, and *Evening Post* vigorously agitated the subject, decent citizens appealed to the Supreme Court for action.

mortal fallibility even on subjects within the range of sense, and tend more or less to illustrate the value of our "rational" judgment, on various subjects. If true, they point to the existence of something in physical science that upsets many of our received notions.

March 3. Edward Laight said to be most positively and publicly engaged to Miss Caroline Nevins; some say privately married to her since last summer. The mighty are fallen, the light of the ballroom is darkened. Edward Laight, irresistible in flirtation, who might have run away with half the pretty debutantes of the last ten years, for whom a dozen heiresses have been ready to scratch out each other's eyes, is to marry Miss Caroline Nevins. Well, she is clever and bright, and will make him a good wife, I dare say.

March 4. New administration has an unlucky day for its beginning. But I think it will work in spite of that disadvantage. Pierce seems to me a respectable person. . . .

Curtis says he broke off his engagement, or rather guided the young lady to break it off, not so much because he felt that she cared little for him as because he felt from time to time that he should be ashamed of her. That's rather bad. Curtis is not such a combination of sage and saint that he has a right to feel ashamed of any good-hearted, pure-minded girl who may do him the honor to let him love her, merely because she's unlearned in aesthetics. Of course, Curtis doesn't say this publicly. Various cards and letters appearing in the papers denying various facts stated in the last presentment of the city government. None of them much attended to.

March 7. At the Lydigs' Saturday night. Met William Schermerhorn and wife there, and *moved tables*. Miss Maggie is a "medium." Her table answers questions by the alphabet. It was a brilliant performance, not obviously explicable on any theory. Very queer, indeed; no deliberate mystification, unquestionably. Could the effects have been produced by unconscious muscular effort of any person assisting? Hardly. I'm satisfied that if both subjects be not wholly humbug or the effect of an excitable imagination, both this and the Rochester ghost business depend on quite other than supernatural causes.

March 9. Mr. Ruggles here talking over his affairs a couple of hours tonight. He has shown great tact and energy in retrieving himself, and had Frank Griffin lived, I think it likely that everything would be cleared up by this time. As it is, he has arranged, or is just on the verge of finally arranging, with Harriot & Henry, which will leave against him only the very disputable balance of $20,000 in favor of the Griffin estate, over and above the $50,000 consideration-money named in the deed by which he conveyed the Atlantic Dock property to Francis Griffin. Very probably some attack will be made on that conveyance by the general assignee as on an inadequate consideration.

Strong prospect of the final elimination of Professor James Renwick from Columbia College. We must make a grand effort for Wolcott Gibbs if that happens. . . .[5]

March 11. Stocks down. Wonder whether I'd better invest some loose savings in another Erie bond at present prices, or wait for a farther depression? Alas, alas, alas, for all the dreams of former times, the dreams to which this journal bears witness! Is it the doom of all men in this nineteenth century to be weighed down with the incumbrance of a desire to make money and save money, all their days? I suppose if my career is prosperous, it will be spent in the thoughtful, diligent accumulation of dollars, till I suddenly wake up to the sense that the career is ended and the dollars dross. So are we gradually carried into the social currents that belong to our time, whether it be the tenth century, or this cold-blooded, interest-calculating age of our own. . . .

March 19, SATURDAY. At Mr. Ruggles's last night for an hour or so. He's deep in a complicated negotiation that promises to set him on his legs again, financially, and extricate him from his present entanglements by the substitution of new promises to pay, at a long day, for the old ones that are cracked, and through the help of William B. Astor, Brooks, James G. King, and others of his enthusiastic admirers, and by his own indomitable, fitful energy that happens to be exerted on this particular transaction, I think he'll carry it through. But his accumulating property and becoming a wealthy citizen is an extravagant conception, should he have fifty years longer lease of life to do it in. Went tonight with Ellie and George Anthon to look at Abbott's exhibition of Egyptian antiquities. Very curious and interesting; especially the little vases with Chinese characters, the jewelry, and so on. But I feel no lively interest in ancient Egypt; it is so remote and so unlike ourselves that it is hard to recognize a common humanity.

[5] The versatile James Renwick (1792–1863), still busy with engineering projects, had now been professor of natural and experimental philosophy and chemistry for thirty-three years.

Dr. Henry Abbott, who had resided more than twenty years in the Middle East, was exhibiting at the Stuyvesant Institute, 659 Broadway, a collection of what he called "Prahonic and Ptolemaic remains"; admission fifty cents. A group of citizens purchased the collection and presented it to the New-York Historical Society in 1860.

March 22.   Heard with very great regret this morning of Dr. Robeson's death, after a short illness.[6] He was rather seriously ill last night, threatened, it was said, with congestion of the lungs, but nobody supposed his case serious. His family are probably left with scanty provision. . . .

Poor Robeson! I owe his memory deep gratitude for the service he did us in that awful time four years ago, when he was so diligent and so devoted. How I can recall, this minute, his figure as he and Johnston came together into the room that fearful 16th of April, how well I remember his vigilance and anxiety during that day, and his readiness to stay in the house every night for a fortnight after. Though he was only Johnston's aid-de-camp, I felt more confidence in him and talked of the matter more with him than with Johnston, and I know he took as much interest in the fluctuations of hope and fear and despair as any physician could. How we used to sit at twelve or one at night in the back parlor of the Fourth Avenue house over cold beef and port wine, and talk of pathology, and then he would go upstairs for a nap, while I walked the piazza for an hour or two and wished I had never been born, and then lay down on a sofa and dozed wretchedly. . . .

March 29.   Walked uptown today with Sam Whitlock, whom I find to be a convert to the Dauphin, and to table-moving.

The temporary spasm of the money-market is relaxed and California and Australia are felt again. Mr. Maunsell Field, Webb, and the *Journal of Commerce* in vigorous warfare—skunk and rattlesnake—but the conflict damages the prospect of city reform. Hodges told me this morning that he'd been looking through Haydn's and Mozart's Masses to see if there was anything he could "adapt"!!! Called on by Evarts today, about a subscription for poor Robeson's widow, and conscience would not let me put myself down for less than a hundred, though I can ill afford it

[6] Dr. Abel Bellows Robeson (Yale 1837) was in his thirty-sixth year; his wife was the daughter of Professor Nathaniel W. Taylor of New Haven.

just now. But that lady is left penniless, and common gratitude to poor Robeson forebade my declining to do what I could. . . .

April 10, SUNDAY.   Charles Curtis had Thackeray to dine with him Friday. Cram and wife and Whitlock here this morning. At Wallack's Theatre Friday night; *The Road to Ruin* very well put on the stage.

April 21.   Took Ellie to hear Alboni in *La Sonnambula* Monday night.[7] She makes a robust Amina. It certainly is a pretty and captivating opera, very respectable of its kind. Bellini is no great light in the musical firmament, but when the bills announce one of his operas, I go. I prefer hearing his music to hearing Mrs. Marietta Alboni's, so Wednesday night, I cut the *Gazza Ladra* and turned over my ticket to Mr. Ruggles. George Anthon spent the evening here. Last night at Mr. Willis's; small party, some nice music. . . . A very pleasant evening. Great respect for Richard Willis, his only drawback his brother, N. P. Willis, author of the Blidgims story and (according to common report) of other things only not quite so flagitious. Wish *he* would go to Australia.

April 25. . . . Can't get the Beekman matter *on*, which impairs my felicity. So does California's gold. Every casual observation I hear about rising prices makes the blood tingle in my face. Very strange; I am sure I'm not such a slave to the enjoyments money buys as that would indicate. One would think I held diminished wealth to be absolute, infinite ruin. Yet if I know myself, I could be personally as comfortable on $500 a year as $5,000. The intensest moments of pleasure I've ever had have come from the memory of a musical phrase, the sight of a clear sky, or a book and sometimes a silly one. (And I am not a puppy, though the last sentence looks fearfully like it; at least, I hope I am not. I never say such things.) Why then should I be so sensitive to suggestions of diminished fortune? I believe it depends on horror of change, which seems a deep-seated element in my character.

April 30.   Academy of Design. Very creditable, especially in landscape. Ehninger has two nice little cabinet pictures there. Not very strong, but giving promise of a marketable and available talent, and very creditable beside. Durand is as prolific as a shad or herring; has turned over an entirely new leaf and abandoned his old, conventional big tree. Church has produced some most covetable landscapes. So has Inness, though his pictures look to me like servile copies of the "old masters." The "Washington Gallery" at the Art Union rooms [offers] a far better collection,

---

[7] A second opera company was now active in New York, with Mme. Marietta Alboni (1823–1894), the Italian singer, as prima donna.

but I was a little disappointed in it. Went to Mr. Tighe's tonight for Ellie and made a call there of respectable duration. Mr. Ruggles is fighting hard in his restoration campaign, with promise of success, but time must tell the result. His genius and power of combination are marvelous. Had they been concentrated on any one subject, political or financial, they might have produced great results.

The spring was one of great despondence for Strong, who writes repeatedly that he had never been bluer in his life. He was overworked in Wall Street, some of his cases giving him great anxiety; and he was worried over his finances, recording at the end of March that he had overspent his budget for the quarter by some $400, and that "the financial prospects for the coming three months are thick darkness." Doubtless because the baby needed cool sea air, he planned to send his family this summer to Nahant instead of to West Point, and made an exploratory trip to the Massachusetts coast. His father-in-law was still laboring hard to retrieve his financial position, and greatly impressed Strong by his tremendous vigor and skill in getting half a dozen refractory interests to combine in restoring the value of the Atlantic Dock property. Peter Strong's marriage to Miss Stevens, which took place the middle of May, was a happy event. The diarist writes that the "sweet little bride, in the fresh, bright graciousness of her youth and loveliness, moving through the crowd and shaking hands with everyone, was surely never much surpassed by any form of mortality."

To deal with the flagrant municipal corruption, the legislature had passed a new charter for New York, which was submitted to popular vote on June 7, and carried by a heavy majority. It abolished the Board of Assistant Aldermen, and put an end to the practice by which aldermen had sat in the Court of Sessions and the Court of Oyer and Terminer. Strong heartily approved of the change. He was still laboring valiantly to give St. Luke's Hospital a good start. In July he began spending week-ends with his family at Nahant, loafing on the rocks and studying marine life. But the journey by the Fall River steamboats and the Fall River Railroad was a grim ordeal. "Which is the greater bore, thither or back?" he writes. Among the books he read was the second volume of Ruskin's Stones of Venice, which he found informative and beautiful.

May 2. Mr. Ruggles is fighting the sons of Belial vigorously. Brooks has backed out of the proposed arrangement, not handsomely as it strikes me, but he has already done so much that Mr. Ruggles won't hear a word against him. The baby a little perturbed today by the progress of dentition. I have seen clearly for the last three months that Master John R. Strong, if he lives and prospers, is to be a hard boy to manage. Very great obstinacy, high temper, and sensitiveness will be traits of his, I predict.

May 7. . . . Another murderous *noyade* on the New Haven Railroad yesterday. More than fifty lives lost; a car full of people pitched over an open draw into the Norwalk River, as a trap with its rats is soused into a wash-tub, by the brute stolidity of the engineer, who didn't see the appointed signal that told him to pull up. Or quite as truly by the guilty negligence of the directors who reappointed this man after he'd been dismissed two years ago for causing an accident by some piece of gross recklessness. What is to be done? Think of the *Henry Clay* last summer, and her indicted owners and officers not yet brought to trial! Think of the carnage recorded from month to month in newspaper paragraphs of another frightful calamity and so many lives lost by collision or fire or explosion, almost in every case so narrated as to raise a presumption that the evil has been caused by negligence or defective equipment; always followed by an "investigation," often by a finding that captain or owners or conductors are responsible, never by anything more. What one man has yet been hanged for any one of these flagrant outrages? Ordinary legal means are manifestly inadequate to do justice in the premises. I should have thought the surviving passengers and the good people of Norwalk far from clearly unjustifiable in this case had they administered Lynch Law to the criminal on the spot. . . .

This morning I "assisted," chiefly as spectator, at Mr. Ruggles's final adjustment with the Griffin estate. Its result: the settlement of that account in full and the reconveyance of the Atlantic Dock stores—in many respects a most fortunate event. N.B. I've turned over a new leaf, or half-turned it at least. I contributed $5,000 on a second mortgage behind $20 of Sedgwick's, and may probably take the fee. I don't like coming in for the management of such a thing, though by the end of the year, when it falls due, I might well be able to pay it down to ($2.+ 1.+ 1 +2) 14,000 when it would be an investment no one need be timid about holding; the government rent being $3,400 on a lease with ten years yet to run. It's hardly to be called speculating, there being no liability incurred, or risk of loss. And as far as it goes, it's an anchor to windward against California.

May 13, FRIDAY.   Evenings not fruitful of work this week. Monday night at a Trinity Church vestry meeting. Tuesday at Wallack's: *Merchant of Venice*, well played—Wallack, Lester, and Miss Laura Keene.[8] Wednesday, Hippodrome; very big and brilliant. Much idiotic trumpery and foolery; "pageantry," the handbills call it. Some surprising feats of strength and some lively racing, quadrigae, young ladies on horseback, and monkeys on ponies. Yesterday, George Jones, Miss Laura Belden, and others dined here comfortably. Miss Rosalie [Ruggles] is staying with us. Tonight I'm dyspeptic; couldn't work, talked finance with Mr. Ruggles, read Kingsley's *Hypatia*, rather a forcible book, and Reichenbach's *Odische Briefe*, lent by Wolcott Gibbs, who's an anxious inquirer into Odyle.

May 22.   Went Monday night to Wallack's Theatre; Lester's benefit. (Mr. Ruggles had taken thirty seats.) *Don Caesar de Bazan*, and *Used Up*. Very reputable performance and most frightful heat. "What won't people do for pleasure? Suffer like dogs," as Mrs. Chancellor Kent said when she was traveling in crowded stage coaches to the White Mountains. It was a *noche triste*, that. But the womankind stood it decently well, though I had to *walk* up with Ellie and Miss Rosalie, and though all the ice cream shops were closed.

May 28.   Table-moving has got into France and Germany, and it is to be hoped that men of science there will do what ours have been too dignified and conservative to attempt: investigate its alleged phenomena and either prove them humbug, or study out their connection with the other facts of the visible world. If it be all delusion, the fact is perhaps even more important than the discovery of a new imponderable or motive agency would be. It throws new light on man's faculty of self-deception in relation even to subjects of sense. Rochester knocking needs inquiry in the same scientific spirit and for exactly the same reason.

June 13.   Not many events to be noted during the past fortnight. Very tragical interview (believe that was a little earlier) with my "woman taken in adultery" at her much-injured husband's request.[9] Much syncope, tears, ululation, protestation, and supplication, the last addressed to me

---

[8] James W. Wallack (1795–1864), of the famous Anglo-American family of actors, was now—as the diary indicates—at the height of his activity. He had leased Brougham's Lyceum Theatre on Broadway, and with his sons John Lester and Charles was managing an excellent stock company; playing many parts himself with talent and vigor.

[9] One of Strong's legal cases; he suppresses the names involved.

as "holding her destiny in my hands." Her rôle somewhat that of Mrs.
Frankford in Heywood's play, only without the confession. Don't think
the lady's destiny is where she supposes it, for her husband is manifestly
impressed by her relatives' threats of recrimination. Trinity Church
vestry Thursday night, preliminary to Dr. Berrian's voyage to Europe.
. . . Woodbury Langdon back from Europe. Kane engaged to Miss
Edith Brevoort, and one of the junior Astors to Miss Caroline Schermerhorn. Trust the young couple will be able to live on their little incomes
together. . . . George Anthon has half settled on an arrangement with
"Bull" Anthon to connect him with the Grammar School, as a sort of sub
rector *de jure*, though without the title; the professor's leading motive
being, as I suppose, the humiliation of his rebellious jackal Drisler by
putting a new man over his head. . . . City Reform ticket carried triumphantly June 7th, ten to one. Will any good result? Doubtful. Reading
certain lectures on chemistry by Faraday. They include one great step
in advance of most modern science: the expression here and there of
certain moral feelings, truths rather, connected with their subject.

June 30. We start for Nahant tomorrow afternoon. . . . Fear that
Ellie will be disappointed in Nahant. There are drawbacks there. This is
John R. Strong's "second summer" and I suppose critical, so people say.
He was a little out of order this morning, but certain molars that caused
the trouble have emerged, and he has undeniably stood the warm weather
well thus far. I'm beginning to be attached to the cub, with his sunshiny
curls and earnest eyes, his broken words and little wicked wilfulnesses.
He's fond of me, too, and when I came out to West Farms after a couple
of days' absence, was quite demonstrative.

July 12. Adsum qui feci. I'm the man that went and did it, that
carried off my small family to Nahant and subjected myself to the bore
of a weekly journey there and back that's undermining my constitution.
But I'm too tired for philosophical history: chronicle is all I'm equal to.

Went off in *Empire State* Friday afternoon, 1st inst. Vast crowd. At
Nahant by twelve. Bother about baggage, set at rest by its arrival. To
Mrs. Paige's that evening. Mrs. Hatty, wife of Abbott Lawrence (Lauren-
tius Abbott, Jr.), and Miss Kitty Lawrence, whom I pronounce a very
specially promising young lady; clever, intelligent, rational, accomplished, musical, unaffected, and unostentatious, notwithstanding her
experience of nobility and royalty abroad. Engaged to one Lowell. Pro-

fessor Peirce of Harvard called, and Mrs. Lodge.[10] Monday, the 4th, dinner at Mrs. Paige's. Came off Tuesday and into town Wednesday morning, fagged out. . . .

Find Verplanck hostile to Collier's Shakespeare emendations, and inclined to think the annotated folio a forgery. This desolate house is getting to be like Robinson Crusoe's island; the brute creation has no longer any fear of man. Cockroaches and "croton bugs" roam fearless and free through the dining room. They looked like little black pigs when I went downstairs last night, and trotted frankly up to me, so big and so many that I fear they'll treat me as the mice served Bishop Hatto before the summer's over.

August 9.   Friday, 15th July, to Nahant; Monday 18th, back again. Friday, 22d July, ditto; Monday 25th, ditto. Friday, 29th July, ditto; stayed over a week, and back to the sweltering city this morning. All per Fall River line. Which is the greater bore, thither or back? On the whole, I think the latter. Either way there's a gap between conveyances to be spent at Boston, too short to go anywhere or do anything and much too long to be agreeable, when it has to be survived in a depot, or in lounging through the complex arrangement of dingy rat-holes that are the thoroughfares of those unhappy little people who live in Boston. And there's a small boy on the Eastern Railroad ferryboat whom I fear I shall be driven to slay solely for the accent and intonation of his " 'Ere's the *Times*, *Herald*, and *Journal*." . . .

Other notabilia of the past three weeks, not many. Two fishing scrapes at Nahant, one very successful, the other, after tataug on the rocks, much less so. Visit to Crystal Palace; promising establishment.

August 17.   Last week was terrific in its persevering, concentrated cruel heat, sixty deaths and upwards daily by *coup de soleil!* So say the papers. As I sat at my desk, the perspiration *rained* off my face more than once, not slowly and sparsely, but in big drops, fast and frequent. Going up the Sound Friday night, the current of air we made was tepid and sickly. Since I've got back to town it has been less fiercely hot, for the sun has forborn to shine much, and it has been foggy and muggy and deadly

[10] Katharine Lawrence was the daughter of Abbott Lawrence, who had been our minister to England in 1851. She married Augustus Lowell; and from the union sprang the poet Amy Lowell, the astronomer Percival Lowell, and the Harvard president A. Lawrence Lowell. Benjamin Peirce of Harvard (1809–1880) was the noted mathematician and astronomer. Mrs. Lodge was doubtless Mrs. John Ellerton Lodge, mother of Henry Cabot Lodge.

damp, with much heavy rain. How if a spark of the yellow fever that's depopulating New Orleans should *catch* in our crowded colony-houses, and be fanned by the malaria of our stinking streets? . . .

Prospect of war in Europe increasing. Hurrah for the Czar! His *casus belli* is nonsense and he knows it, but any quarrel's good enough that will rid Europe of the olive-colored infidels and aliens that have squatted in Constantinople for 400 years.

August 24, WEDNESDAY. To Nahant Friday afternoon as usual; Ellie well, and the Third Estate also. . . .

Read Ruskin's *Stones of Venice*, Volume II. Valuable and beautiful. Mr. Ruskin is not worked out yet, though this wants his primal freshness and there's now and then a trace of effort after fine writing. Most notable ideas of the book are, first, the relative claims of color and form in art (a very new and striking view, at least to *me*); and second, the effect on our social system of exchanging the mechanic and operative for the rude artist (I mean, vice versa); gaining finish, completeness, and money-profit by the change and losing vitality and value in the work done, and making a class of men wretched because they feel themselves degraded into fractions of men by "division of labor."

August 25. Am much concerned about my mother, not with my usual fidgetiness about small ailments, but with a grave and deep anxiety that I fear rests on reality. For a year she has had "a cold," a cough cured today and recurring tomorrow, and I think had been slowly losing strength all the time. This summer it has been more troublesome than ever, and perhaps from my seeing her daily, I have not noticed signs of failing strength manifest to others. . . .

September 1. The first day of fall, with its promise of cool weather, is welcome after such a summer as this has been. . . . Question of war in Europe not yet fully settled. Chinese revolution progressing. Great results in the world's history may depend on its fortunes. California and Australia continue auriferous to an absurd extent.

September 7. George Anthon has commenced the performance of his new duties at the Grammar School. He and his venerable Uncle Bull are allies and friends just now, but how long that state of feeling will last is doubtful. I am liberal with advice to him to watch and be wary, for the temperament of both and the experience of the last fifteen years point to a quarrel as likely within six months. Trust he may have the tact to avoid a rupture, but ten to one he won't. It's a grand opening for him, potentially, and might be made worth any two professorships in the country.

The first days of September were enlivened by two conventions of radical-minded folk: a World's Temperance Convention which met in Metropolitan Hall on the 6th, and a Women's Rights Convention which gathered at The Tabernacle on the same day. The temperance advocates were manifestly anxious to keep their cause unembarrassed by association with other movements. Some of the women's rights enthusiasts were equally eager to effect an alliance with the temperance forces. Supported by Horace Greeley and the Tribune, *various women leaders—Susan B. Anthony, the valiant and attractive Lucy Stone, garbed in trousers, the pioneer woman preacher Antoinette Brown, the elderly Negro crusader Sojourner Truth, and others—adopted a militant attitude. They tried to place Lucy Stone on the platform of the World's Temperance Convention and to gain a hearing for her. The foes of liquor resolutely excluded her—and also denied a seat as delegate to a Negro minister of New York. While the* Tribune *indignantly denounced the conservative temperance men, the* Times *castigated the "female pests." Meanwhile, New Yorkers were flocking in numbers to the Crystal Palace just completed in Reservoir Square, now Bryant Park, with its creditable exhibitions of varied American products, and were attending the concerts of the violinist Ole Bull in Niblo's Garden. Good citizens were pleased by the initial steps which five city commissioners were taking to lay out Central Park. Every steamer arriving from Europe brought news of the crisis over Turkish affairs, which threatened to end in a war between Russia on one side, and Britain, France, and Turkey on the other. People and politicians at home were busy discussing the Koszta affair, with much praise for the intrepid American naval officer who had forced an Austrian warship in Smyrna harbor to release a former Hungarian who was now becoming an American citizen.*

September 8, THURSDAY. Steamer *Bay State* in trouble last night; something or other connected with her crank or her walking-beam knocked in the head of her cylinder, and that long saloon was filled with scalding steam. Great shindy between Bloomers and anti-Bloomers, at the Temperance Convention in session here. As for the "Rev." Antoinette Brown & Co., I should be glad to see them respectfully pumped upon by a crowd of self-appointed conservators of manners and morals, though perhaps they have womanhood enough left in spite of themselves to be worthy of better usage. The strumpets of Leonard and Church streets are not *much* further below the ideal of womanhood than these loathsome dealers in clack, who seek to change women into garrulous men without virility. I'm glad I'm too stolid tonight for full realization of their folly. It would lead surely to a sick headache tomorrow. Womanhood is still reverenced in this irreverent age and country, as every omnibus and railroad car can testify. Destroy its claim to concession and protection and courtesy by putting it on an equality in everything but physical strength with manhood, and manhood is gone, too. . . .

William Morgan (Matthew Morgan's son) is ill-treating his wife, Dudley Selden's sweet little daughter, most flagitiously. I'd be glad to help ride him on a rail. The poor little lady was confined only a month ago, and this hound is beating and kicking her so that she has had to call on the civil authority for help.

September 9. Two or three of the sufferers by the accident to the *Bay State* died today. William Morgan's villainy has found its way into the papers.

September 13. I've a bad report to make of mamma, whom I found this morning very unwell. She seems to have lost much of the ground gained during last week.

Astounded by the report, general and looking authentic, that O'Conor is engaged to Mrs. McCrackan, whose husband died six months ago. He of all men, with his austere, unsocial disposition and jealous temper, should make no such alliance. It's somewhat on the Dombey model.[11]

September 15. William Morgan (after beating his wife a good deal) has been cowhiding Isaac S. Hone for interfering. Hone's old enough to be his grandfather.

September 17. O'Conor is to be married before October first, they say. As McCrackan's dear remains are on their way from the Coast of Africa, O'Conor may probably have a chance to officiate as chief mourner. The lady says, I hear, that she has long loved that eminent man in secret. Poor O'Conor! It's a disagreeable thing to jot down such a notion in reference to any lady of whom one knows (of his own knowledge) nothing whatever, but I'm afraid he is done most uncommonly brown, and that the elder Weller's caution against widows will be remembered by him too late. Unpromising enough the transaction seems when judged according to gossip and rumor. However, this lady is not quite so bad as the wealthy and brilliant Mrs. Diaconus of Boston, who travels with a

[11] Strong's forebodings proved well founded. The eminent attorney did indeed marry Cornelia Livingston McCrackan, widow of John L. H. McCrackan. But their life together proved unhappy and they separated.

pair of the sainted Diaconus's old boots and puts them outside her room door at Newport and Saratoga "that it may seem as if she were not entirely unprotected."

September 24.   Two nights this week to the Crystal Palace with Ellie and others. The interior lit up is undeniably very imposing and splendid, and there is much to be seen. Show of statuary very good; the picture gallery rather a failure. Last night to Jullien's concert at Castle Garden. Much clap-trap, perfect of its kind, and some real music most effectively played; especially the overture to *Fidelio* and the "Scherzo" of Beethoven's F Symphony.[12]

September 30.   Last night at Jullien's in Tripler Hall. Overture to *Leonore*; long-laboured, peculiar, and not clear, on a first hearing; "Scherzo" from F Symphony, most lovely and Haydnish; the C minor Symphony played through with some mutilation of the third and fourth movements. Lights and shadows come out grandly in so massive an orchestra. That noblest of compositions was never so played in this city before. Ellie was cured of a cold by it.

Another Revolution. John Jay's annual motion carried at last, and the nigger delegation admitted into the Diocesan Convention. John Jay must be an unhappy, aching void, as when one's stomach, liver, and other innards have been dexterously taken out.[13] Luther Bradish, Creighton, and Hoffman delegates to General Convention; this is an era of good feeling with a vengeance. Think I see the policy that dictates that move.

October 4.   James G. King died suddenly last night at Highwood. Great loss for Wall Street; geniality and high principle do not abound there.[14]

Read last numbers of *Bleak House* this evening, a better and more subdued finale than usual with Mr. Dickens. But his art is that of a minor theatre, his groupings just such as would tell with the pit of the Bowery. Crystal Palace losing money fast according to Dupont, who ought to

[12] The Crystal Palace was open daily except Sundays from ten in the morning till ten at night, and was universally regarded as a splendid spectacle. Louis Antoine Jullien, the Franco-English composer (1812–1860), was giving a series of twenty-four concerts in Castle Garden.

[13] John Jay, the grandson of the great Chief Justice, had waged a seven years' battle to obtain representation for St. Philip's Church, a Negro congregation in New York, to the Episcopal Convention.

[14] James Gore King was a son of the eminent Rufus King, Senator and minister to England. The younger King had gone into business, had lived for some years in Liverpool as partner in King & Gracie, and had later become a member of the firm of Prime, Ward & King. He had a country seat at Weehawken.

know. It will prove a bad speculation, unless they make P. T. Barnum chief director. . . .

October 10, MONDAY. Sunday at church as usual. The altar screen (reredos, rather) at Trinity now unveiled, with its new coat of gilding and colors—effect very good. Evening at Mr. Ruggles's awhile, where I met some people I didn't count on meeting, and got much out of temper and am only just getting in again.

October 11. At the Crystal Palace tonight with Ellie and George Anthon. More impressed at each visit by the variety and beauty of the collection. But it won't pay; the stock's at 55 with a downward impetus, and those holders who bought at 175 will be badly bit. The picture gallery is a humbug, however. The most notable things there are a very sweet picture of Hubner's and an admirably painted atrocity by Biard, depicting a pile of very naked rather than nude shipwrecked Europeans about to be devoured by a horde of grotesque, hideous African savages, who are performing a dance around their dinner.[15] But there are many most covetable things scattered through the building—furniture, jewelry, bronze, and so forth, not to speak of various appetizing nuggets and bars and chunks from California. The minerals, however, are not very striking as a whole.

October 12. Sim Draper has stopped! His big "bust" followed instantly by two little ones, and by a general collapse in the stock market; possibly premonitory of revulsion, but I rather guess not.[16] James G. King's estate comes out a million and upwards. . . .

On the whole, I shan't be surprised if this failure of Draper's *should* prove the beginning of the smash that must come some day. Hope I may be able to press several matters into a comfortable position before it comes; so selfish and abominable are the thoughts that this servitude to money-making inspires. Rents, prices, luxury, extravagance, and so on all indicate a smash that would have come long ago but for California.

October 13. News from Europe imperfectly reported, but looking blue. The Allied fleets seem to have left Benka Bay and come to anchor before Constantinople; whether to help the peace in that city, and prevent an outbreak of the fanatical mob of misbelievers against their pacific Sultan, or as a demonstration against Russia, don't appear yet.

October 16. Friday night at a meeting to organize a Reform Asso-

[15] A. F. Biard, French painter, 1798–1882; R. J. B. Hubner, German painter, 1806–1882.

[16] Simeon Draper, Jr., was an auctioneer.

ciation for the Eighteenth Ward; tolerably promising. Peter Cooper presided; very worthy man, but rather prosy and egotistical. But much may be forgiven a man who has given much, three or four hundred thousand, to public education, though perhaps not on the wisest plan. Yesterday Ellie spent at William Schermerhorn's. I drove out there with him to dine, and brought her home. Never went through "Jones's Woods" before. The grounds are very beautiful, and strangely intact for the latitude of Sixty-first Street. . . .

Judge Edmonds's book on "Spiritualism" out. Have looked through it; to read it is not possible. It's a phenomenon about which there's much to say. The school to which it's a contribution is one of the most astounding facts of this age. No doubt he does not overestimate its numbers, and no doubt very many conscientious, educated, intelligent people belong to it. I can't adopt at once the imposture and delusion theory. It may be the explanation, probably it is, but if it is, the existence of the delusion is a most significant and important fact.[17]

October 22.   Bad weather for a day or two, warm and rainy. Such weather as in the fall of 1848, which prepared the way for cholera. Went to Jullien's Thursday night. Heard the *Jupiter Symphony* and an admirable arrangement from *Don Giovanni*, which did fuller justice to parts of the opera (for example, the finale of the first act) and expressed Mozart's ideas more clearly than any performance on the stage within my experience.

October 25.   Looked in at the Hall on the trial of Collyer and the other *Henry Clay* people for manslaughter. Jordan was damaging an important witness for the prosecution a good deal by his usual ferocious cross-examination; and I didn't like the looks of two or three of the jury. They'll doubtless disagree.

October 26.   My mother passed a very bad night, unable to lie down, worse than anything yet. Went downtown early to expedite Peters, and hoped when I came up at 4:30 that she might be better. Find no improvement; so far as I can judge, a falling off. . . . I am nearly driven wild by memories of all sorts of pleasant scenes and times, when I was a child at Greenwich Street and at Whitestone, that come on me in crowds, vaguely remembered, but most bitter.

[17] John Worth Edmonds (1799–1874), a jurist of note, resigned from the New York Court of Appeals this year. He was an earnest believer in spiritualism, and in collaboration with Dr. George T. Dexter brought out the book which Strong mentions —which attracted wide attention.

October 27. What promise there was last night is not fulfilled. Sent for at six this morning; find she had passed a yet worse night, and begged for morphine.

October 28. Twelve o'clock. Not downtown at all today. No better, no relief except by morphine, and this morning stimulants required. But at Peters' last visit he thought there was some little sign of improvement and spoke of having "some hope," pulse was stronger and slower. Probably from the wine. . . .

October 29. Two P.M. Weather sadly bright and clear. What small hope there was last night—gone or going. Two severe turns of oppression since last evening. . . .

November 2. Today the pulse is good, mind quite clear at intervals, aspect and voice natural. She knew me, and spoke as usual.

November 3. Still a little hope, not much. Strength holds out wonderfully.

November 8. I fear my poor mother is not doing well. There is pneumonia again today and more than there was a week ago, and the delirium and wakefulness and restlessness wholly unrestrained. . . .

Election today. Result very uncertain. Voted a split.

November 9. Election returns. Whigs seem to have swept the state, but Charles H. Ruggles and Denio probably elected to the Court of Appeals. In the city the "Reform ticket" has done pretty well. The notorious O. W. Sturtevant and one or two more like him who had the courage to stand and fight are badly beat. Whether little D. D. Lord is alderman of the Eighteenth Ward seems still a little dubious. I voted against him, as did many others well disposed toward the reform movement.

November 11. *Very bad.* Called up at two this morning, and on going in next door found her in a spasm that they thought she could not get through. It has been a terrible day.

November 14. This is a very blue, bad, hard, dismal time. Seems like an ugly dream. I'm beginning to feel sore from sleeping in my clothes on a sofa that's like a slab of porphyry.

November 15. I slept very soundly last night, contrary to my expectations, for I came uptown from a Trinity Church vestry meeting which it was necessary to attend, late, with a headache. At the meeting in question, I withdrew my name and nominated R. H. Ogden for clerk; and there were two ballotings, and no election, nine to nine. A good deal of business got through. Report that hostilities have commenced on the

Danube. Another spasm in Columbia College from the Galvanism that
Fish and Ruggles are putting into that venerable cadaver. Report from a
committee in favor of moving uptown, which will be slept over for two
years. Anthony Bleecker has got back from abroad. Got our additional
$42,000 voted for the Chapel last night after some grumbling. There is
quite a little flare-up of excitement about the clerkship. R. H. Ogden
wants it very bad and it is quite an object, pecuniarily, to him as well as
to G.M.O. By Ehninger's account, Paris is even a more degraded and
sodomized puddle of iniquity than I thought, judging from the morals of
the artists' quarters. He (J. W. Ehninger) is better than I expected; has
traveled and studied to good purpose, and if he holds out, will do well.
Glad to find that he looks on the Wilkie or Mount school, to which he
has devoted himself hitherto, as only a transition to something more
heroic, historical and religious art. . . .

There is John R. Strong upstairs, squalling and chattering by turns
just now. I like to think of him as a grown man, or of his children, turning over these memoranda, as a queer old journal in the family that
nobody could read through, but which contains curious illustrations of
old times. . . .

Mr. Ruggles here tonight. Renwick has resigned, and by nine to
seven the trustees of Columbia College have resolved to move uptown.
There are three vacancies in that board and I'd give a good deal to fill
one of them, for I'd like to work hard in pushing the College, and believe
I might do so to some purpose. . . .[18]

November 16.   Mr. Ruggles and Miss Rosalie looked in and dined
with us. Haight and one or two more are trying quite hard to get me in
for one of the vacancies in the Board of Columbia College. They won't
succeed, for there are several more prominent and useful men in nomination and all the Presbyterian element in the Board object to any more
Trinity Church influence. I don't care much how it goes. . . .

The music of the Seventh Symphony has been running in my head for
a fortnight (the A major). Carefully kept out of my thoughts for four
years as uncanny and perilous. That looks absurd, I dare say, but few
facts are more real to me than the deadliness of that composition. I've

[18] A momentous step in Columbia history. King's College, later Columbia College, had occupied a tract west of Broadway between Murray and Barclay Streets,
extending down to Greenwich Street, which was at first the shoreline of the Hudson.
The original building, its cornerstone laid in 1756, had been used during the Revolution
as barracks and hospital. The College was now—that is, within a few years—to
move uptown to Madison Avenue at Forty-ninth and Fiftieth Streets.

scrupulously tried to forget it since the time of Ellen's illness, when it kept ringing in my ears. Always, when I've thought of it, sorrow or sickness of heart, a dread of coming evil, have been with me and have grown darker under its shadow. It cannot be a mere vagary of my own; that unwholesome, unearthly mark is stamped on it from opening to finale. It depicts despair and atmosphere in darkness; the vivid memory and realization of its melodies are an omen of ill.

November 17. Mamma very materially and unmistakably better for the time. Indeed, Gray thinks she will get through! And her firm pulse, clear mind, and ample remnants of vigor induce me sometimes to admit the possibility. Last night she passed without much serious trouble. I did not enjoy the night particularly. First, I had such a headache, and secondly, at about two o'clock there was what seemed a great fire to the northeast of us, probably in some shipyard, for it was as light as day and the cloudy sky was covered with the most beautiful and threatening glow of crimson. The Second Avenue firebell kept tolling the alarm and every stroke was like the discharge of a six-pounder under my sofa pillow.

November 18. I fear my mother's life cannot be very much prolonged. . . .

Have been in Wall Street working with decent energy. Progressing *in re* Beekman, and so on. Saw Dayton Hobart and Henry Youngs, severally much in earnest on different sides of the Trinity Church vestry clerkship controversy. All hands very complimentary to my distinguished self and telling me I could be unanimously elected; urging me to serve, and R. H. Ogden's friends grateful for my "magnanimity and generosity." Save their wits! I've no fitness for the place and no magnanimity in this or any other connection.

November 21. Mr. Ruggles is much exercised at present about a very difficult problem:—viz., the exact part that physical science should play in education.

November 22, TUESDAY. Not encouraging. She slept comfortably last night, except for two bad turns of nervous excitement or delirium, and is much the same this morning, only weaker.

At Columbia College last night they hinted Jem Renwick's resignation and appointed a committee to look up a successor. Now we must decide what is to be done about Wolcott Gibbs. Draper will put in for a chance, and then George Anthon will come down on him for his share in putting Anthon out of the University on the ground of his being an alumnus of Columbia College. The election of trustees was postponed.

It seems that the two parties, fogy and progressive, are so nearly tied that my election is quite an important matter, and King, Ruggles, Hoffman, and others are straining hard to carry me in; Van Wagenen, Wells, Morris, and the other fossils opposing ponderous inertia to keep me out. I would not have consented to stand if I'd thought I should be battled over in this way like the body of Patroclus. I don't care sixpence how it goes.[19]

Thursday, November the twenty-fourth, at half-past two in the morning, my mother, Eliza Catharine Strong, departed this life, in peace, by a quiet and gentle death in the sure and certain hope of eternal rest, and of the resurrection that awaits those who have lived in faith and charity.

Yesterday, November the twenty-fifth, at four o'clock, my mother was laid in her grave, in Trinity Churchyard. Pall bearers: Mr. Bidwell, Mr. George Griffin, John A. Stevens, Anthony J. Bleecker, Peletiah Perit, James Suydam, Benjamin L. Swan, and David Codwise. She lies in the old Brownjohn vault, with two generations of her ancestors, where I just remember to have seen her mother's coffin going down, twenty-five years ago.

I thank God for her good example, her life of charity, and her death in peace after thirty days of agony, and for having given me forever the memory of so much love, self-denial, and gentleness.

As November ended, the Irish leader John Mitchel, who had escaped from his exile in Van Diemen's Land, arrived in New York, where he received an enthusiastic reception. He at once made preparations to issue a newspaper, the New York Citizen. *Oliver Wendell Holmes completed early in December a series of six lectures on the English poets, including Tennyson and Browning; but Strong's preoccupation with his mother's illness prevented him from attending any of them. Decent citizens of New York were aroused during*

[19] The Columbia board, when filled up this year, consisted of twenty-four members, and election to it was a high distinction. It included Senator Hamilton Fish; President Charles King of the College; Clement C. Moore; S. B. Ruggles, a man of wide affairs; and others of note. Eleven were lawyers, six were clergymen, and three doctors. With respect to the violent controversy now about to begin over the nomination of Wolcott Gibbs to Renwick's vacant chair, it was an important fact that nineteen of the trustees were Episcopalians, and one a Catholic. Three were members of the Dutch Reformed Church and one was a Presbyterian; none was a Unitarian, as Wolcott Gibbs happened to be. The movement to give the professorship to Wolcott Gibbs, who was certainly one of the best-equipped men in the country for it, was energetically headed by Ruggles and supported by Charles King. But it was certain to encounter the opposition of those whom Strong calls the fogies.

December to a high pitch of indignation by an effort of the notorious Jacob Sharp and others to railroad through the city legislature a bill granting them a valuable street-railway franchise in Broadway. But the mayor interposed his veto, and the grab was stopped. Cholera was raging in New Orleans, and sporadic cases of it appeared in New York. War had broken out between Russia and Turkey, with some early Turkish victories; and as it was understood that France, Prussia, Austria, and Britain insisted that the existing territorial position should not be changed, much apprehension was felt that the conflict would widen. Meanwhile, President Pierce had sent his first annual message to Congress. It was a rather colorless document, but Senator Stephen A. Douglas was preparing to explode a bombshell in the shape of his Kansas-Nebraska bill.

Strong included in his diary, as the year ended, many nostalgic memories of happy boyhood days by his mother's side.

December 2.   This has been a kind of blank period, about which there is much to write, but not just at present. George C. Anthon was here to-night. I've been downtown as usual through the week, not doing a great deal of work. Next Monday I must try to get myself into system and diligence.

So our life saddens as its path winds downward. At each stopping place we look back and wonder to see how bright it was, how much brighter than it ever can be again.

She died before daylight of the 24th. Her Thanksgiving Day was not kept with us. It was not my dear mother that lay in the silent room with its windows opened wide to let in the cold clear air, and no doctors and nurses to watch and help any more, and looking younger and calmer and more like herself than she had seemed for so long. *She* was *elsewhere*, thanking God for freedom from that prolonged misery of the last month.

December 5.   Meeting of the Trustees of Columbia College this after-noon, at which I was elected to one of the three vacancies in the Board, Dr. Wainwright and a certain Presbyterian or Dutch Reformed Dr. Beadle being put into the other two. So I was certified by Ruggles and Ogden Hoffman as I walked uptown this afternoon, and by Professor Anderson tonight at a St. Luke's Hospital meeting. On many accounts much gratified by the result.[20]

[20] It may be noted here that Strong was destined to remain a trustee until his death, and to do a great and progressive-spirited work in helping convert the College into an institution plainly destined to become a University.

Quite a shindy in St. Luke's Hospital growing out of the notice given by R. B. Muhlenberg in a great hurry of our claim to the funds collected in England. Have seen Minturn (laid up with a sore leg) once or twice at his house, have written divers letters, and anticipate a very lively breeze before the controversy is ended. Whether we have a legal claim to the fund or not, we can make out a moral right, by Minturn's letters from England, that will silence Barclay & Busch and compel them to give us a large slice of it. Other topics of the last ten days: Burrill Curtis engaged to a tall Scotch lady of thirty-five, granddaughter of Tytler the historian, and intending to take a degree at Oxford or Cambridge, and a charge in an English rural district. Query: if it will hold out? He's a friend of Maurice and belongs to the High-Church wing of the Broad-Church party. R. H. Nevins dead of cancer in the stomach.[21]

December 7.   Mr. Ruggles has gone or is going to Lockport where Washington Hunt lies very ill. Wainwright has got to be manoeuvred with a little. He called at 68 Wall Street yesterday and we had a conference. He is going to identify himself with the Low-Church party, so far, that is, as his nature will allow him to get off a fence.

Knox has written to Gibbs, in a candid and fair way, to know whether he holds the "Divine Plenary Inspiration" of the Bible *quoad* physical science, of course, in reference to the Columbia College professorship. Gibbs's reply, which I saw tonight and which will be sent in without change or addition, is excellent in condensation of thought and language and in honesty and clearness. The position he takes is impregnable, viz.: that the material world is itself a Revelation, and that where it seems in conflict with the other, the necessary inference is that *one* is misunderstood.

December 10.   Great fire today. Saw the smoke swelling out in great masses against the clear sky at two o'clock, and put for the scene. The "devouring element" was occupied with Harpers' premises (Cliff Street through to Pearl) and the Walton House (I believe) on the opposite side of Pearl. Very fierce and obstinate, and more than commonly dramatic and splendid was the conflagration. From the corner of Peck Slip and Pearl Street you looked up a little ascent to Franklin Square, crowded and busy, with three or four great double-banked engines rising above the crowd and working slowly. Fire on both sides, sometimes arching the street, more generally kept down by the columns of water that *stood*, like bars, penetrating the smoke and ruin. Walls thundering down at intervals, each fall followed by a rush upwards of tawny, ropy, blinding smoke and

[21] R. H. Nevins was a broker in the important firm of Nevins & Townsend.

a rain of powdered mortar. Across Pearl Street there stood in beautiful contrast with the lurid masses of flame and smoke, an arch of rainbow, brightening and fading as the northwest wind fell, formed on the spray of the engines. The Walton House saved; I think only the roof destroyed. The loss to the Harpers must be immense and they are probably able to bear it.[22]

December 11, SUNDAY.   At Trinity; Higby preached, and very feebly. People are beginning to talk cholera a little. Nine deaths last week, including John R. Stuyvesant, who may well have died with great resignation, considering the ridiculous mess he'd got himself into.

December 15.   Prospect of a No-Popery riot here. Very numerous and bitter indignation meeting in the Park yesterday, growing out of the arrest of a loafer who undertook to preach Native Americanism and anti-priestcraft in the streets last Sunday and was taken in custody to prevent a riot. He sets up for a Protestant martyr on the strength of his detention, and swears that he will preach in the same place next Sunday; in which case there will be a mob originating with the Irish and German Papishes if he's not arrested, and with the Order of United Americans and the godly butcher boys of the Hook and the First Avenue if he is.[23]

If Roman Catholicism as transplanted here shall retain all its aggressive and exclusive features, in other words, its identity, I don't see but that a great religious war is a probable event in the history of the next hundred years; notwithstanding all our national indifference to religious forms.

[22] Harper & Brothers was the largest publishing house in America and one of the largest in the world. A plumber had carelessly ignited a basin of camphene, the fluid used to clean ink off the press-room rollers; and the tall buildings on Cliff and Pearl near Franklin Square, stored with combustibles, were soon wrapped in flames. In all, property worth a million and a half was destroyed, of which Harper & Brothers lost nearly if not quite a million, their insurance amounting to less than $200,000. The printing work in hand was at once distributed among other cities, twenty new presses were immediately ordered, and plans were drawn for a better plant. The current issue of *Harper's Magazine,* which was in press at the time, was wholly destroyed, but it was reproduced and distributed with only a few days' delay.

[23] The arrival in America of a Papal Nuncio, Msgr. Bedini, to settle a church dispute and visit the episcopal sees, had aroused much popular antagonism. Anti-Catholic demonstrations took place in Cincinnati, Baltimore, Boston, Philadelphia, and other cities. The Native American or Know-Nothing movement was becoming vigorous, and in New York it helped to foment anti-Papal gatherings. On the Sunday previous to Strong's entry, the police had silenced an inflammatory street preacher, and on the 14th a noisy indignation meeting, nominally in behalf of freedom of speech, was held in City Hall Park.

Much concerned about Gibbs's prospects for Renwick's vacated chair. He will be attacked on the ground of Unitarianism, and certainly with some force. *But* (1) his duties will not carry him into contact with *transcendental* physics. And I cannot think that talking to boys about NO_3 and CHO_2 and Fer Cy Ka has any connection (for practical purposes) with theological truck. (2) He has, in fact, no theological position at all. He is a Unitarian from the accident of education. It is not suggested that we should require a truly religious and devout man for the place, and Gibbs is nothing more than nine-tenths of those who are not so described, nothing less or worse, I should have said. (3) A Unitarian is not much if at all farther from right than a blue Calvinist, and from his belief being simply negative and his mind blank on religious subjects, is much more likely to come out *right* and to react into the church, if at any time the religious instinct be developed within him.

Meantime, Russia and Turkey have come to blows and the misbelievers have crossed the Danube, and there have been one or two serious "affairs" in the Principalities. As it comes from time to time, the news is obscure and vague and often contradictory. But it seems clear that the Czar has not done much to brag of yet.

December 19. Spent the morning chiefly *in re* Wolcott Gibbs. N.B. My efforts for him are strictly disinterested. Personal feeling influences me but little. Gibbs is a cast-iron man who would take little trouble for me, or any one else, *I think*. But his transcendent abilities and energy must be secured for Columbia College if any exertion of mine can put him there.

Took my seat in the board at two this afternoon. Session of two hours. Not much done, save to discuss the arrangements with John C. Stevens about the lots most improvidently leased to him on the northwest corner of the Green, where his house is, and to illustrate the dominion of fogyism in the board, and the necessity of concert among the progressive people to meet the organized inertia of Betts and his set, who control the Standing Committee and, through it, everything.[24]

Walked up with Mr. Ruggles. Vestry meeting at the house of that interesting invalid, Dunscomb, 29 Bleecker Street. Dick Ogden, clerk; James I. Jones to fill one vacancy, and then after two or three ballotings, G. M. Ogden beat James G. King 11 to 9 for the other. . . .

[24] William Betts, a conservative corporation attorney and professor of law, had been a trustee of Columbia College since 1842, and was now clerk of the board. He was an Episcopalian.

Wainwright, with whom I had some talk today, will, I think, come out right on the Gibbs question. Couldn't help overhearing some remarks of Knox's that pointed the same way. On the other hand, Berrian is dubious, though clearly open to conviction.[25] I sounded him tonight. Haight will probably go as he does. Much depends on the alumni signatures, to secure which I've set to work.

December 23, FRIDAY.   Leading feature of the week, Gibbs. About ten names now down on the alumni "recommendation," and there may be as many more on other lists I know not of. Russel has several *out*, and W. Romaine, Richard Tucker, and that fat Pennell are all working in various directions. George Anthon hasn't reported himself for several days. Charles King and Professor Bache here last night, and this evening F. H. Wolcott (who's a cousin of Wolcott Gibbs), more efficient and energetic than I expected; has been engaged with the medical faculty and brings in emphatic letters from Dr. Stevens, Dr. Ludlow, and Dr. Frank Johnston. Saw Berrian yesterday, and have strong hopes of his going in the right path at last.

I can't even get fairly in the harness for my legitimate business, and am glad to go blindly into this. . . .

Eleven or twelve o'clock; I've been busy for the past two hours pasting and repairing her "album" or commonplace book of poetry that begins with her name, "Eliza C. Templeton, August 27, 1797"—full of M. G. Lewis and Walter Scott and Southey and Langhorne and Beattie. So much since the time when that dingy volume came into her hands, probably a great acquisition, and she began to write her poor little copies of the Erl King and "Ollie the Lion" and "Mary the Maid of the Inn"! Everything so changed since then, since the time when the proud, handsome girl of eighteen began her manuscript collection of poetry, so deeply felt through all her life on earth; when the city did not exist north of Chambers Street, and was a pleasant country town instead of the roaring chaos of corruption it is now.

December 24.   Christmas eve. Very appropriate bitter frosty night. Evening has been quite lively; Ellie receiving and sending out presents, and enthusiastic over the black lace I got her. Sophie has dressed up a little table with all Johnny's presents (including hers and Louisa's) and

[25] Dr. William Berrian, the rector of Trinity, had been a trustee of Columbia since 1832. Bishop Wainwright, whom Strong at this time regarded as vain, shallow, and timid, had just been elected to the board. The Rev. John Knox, who presided over the Middle Dutch Church, had been a trustee since 1836.

candles and Christmas greens, and everybody that came into the house has been trotted up to the nursery to see. Sophie's laugh and ecstacy over each new present that arrived was worth the ascent of two flights of stairs. . . . Saw Charles King. Very nice letters from Peirce and Agassiz on Gibbs. . . .

December 27.   Severely cold. News from Europe that the Czar has had some luck at last, naval victory in the Black Sea. Prospect increasing of intervention of France and England in the war. No-Popery riot and attempt to lynch Monsignor Bedini at Cincinnati. Another bad fire last night and this morning; Water & Front Streets near Dover, and sparks and cinders flew over one intervening block sufficient to set fire to the immense *Great Republic* lying at the wharf, the biggest merchant vessel extant. She was used up, with two other ships. Walked to the locality this morning; sinister stink, loafers, mud, slush, muddy water, and a cross fire of squirts from leaky hose.

Miss Emily Fowler is married to one Ford.[26] St. Luke's Hospital last night, not much done. Anderson tells me that Knox concedes Gibbs's superiority to Schaeffer, but can't understand his views about "divine plenary inspiration of the Scriptures" and means, therefore, to vote against him. If so, it's a bad business as he'll probably carry three votes at least with him. Gibbs's friends must do their uttermost. I shall despair of the college being ever redeemed from fogyism if Schaeffer is elected. . . .

About 120 alumni now registered as Gibbsites. Doubt whether they will produce much impression on Clement Moore and G. W. Morris. . . .[27]

Legend of the anaconda is old, but too delightful not to be commemorated, especially as it is literally true. After McCrackan burst,[28] he departed for the Coast of Africa, as agent for the purchase of palm-oil, ivory and pigments, and there purchased from the natives a magnificent boa, which he put into a box and sent on board ship as a present to Mrs. McCrackan, from which she could make a little money. And after he had put it on board, the coast fever attacked him and he sank and died and his remains

[26] Emily Ellsworth Fowler was the daughter of Professor William Chauncey Fowler of Amherst and the granddaughter of Noah Webster, whose lexicographical labors were continued by Professor Fowler; her husband was Gordon Lester Ford of Brooklyn, lawyer and railroad executive. They became the parents of Worthington Chauncey Ford (Columbia 1879), editor and historian, and Paul Leicester Ford, historian and novelist, who was tragically slain by a disinherited brother in 1902.

[27] Gerard Walton Morris, grandson of the Signer Lewis Morris, a lawyer, an Episcopalian, and a conservative, had been a trustee since 1851.

[28] That is, after John L. H. McCrackan failed in business.

were boxed up, or barreled up in spirits, and put on board the same craft to which he had entrusted this delicate testimonial of his affection. After O'Conor's wedding, arrived the remains of his predecessor and the separate property and estate of his wife. The former were conveyed to Greenwood, O'Conor declining to assist at the ceremonial, which was wrong of him. The latter, viz., the snake, was offered to Barnum, but he would give only $200, insisting that anacondas are *down* at present. Thereupon, the gift of the deceased McCrackan was (rather heartlessly) put up at auction and brought $250, and is now exhibiting at the corner of Broadway and Walker Streets.

The current story that the anaconda was found to have *swallowed* the defunct McCrackan during the voyage home, is without foundation. . . .

December 31, SATURDAY. The Broadway Railroad ordinance in its contemplated form broke down in the Common Council last night, contrary to general expectation. A very innocent resolution was adopted instead. So the grand row that was to have come off between an indignant public and the three thousand Irishmen who were to have commenced pulling up the pavement and laying the rails by torchlight is postponed. Not impossible a riot might have occurred, which would have been bad and would have associated New York with the semi-barbarous town of Erie.

I was told as I came uptown in one of those vast omnibus sleighs, in company with some seventy other people as uncomfortable as myself, that the Court of Appeals had affirmed the orders of the Superior Court in the matter of the attachment against Sturtevant and his brethren. Very good. May they be locked up one and all! . . .

Snowing again now. I expected rain. The city enters on its New Year in a stainless robe of innocent white, like a baptismal garment, soon to be polluted.

Rather less row and firing audible from the great German settlements to the southeast than is common on New Year's Eve. . . .

This year goes out sadly. God save us from another New Year's eve of like sorrow, and carry those we love safe through the year that has now begun!

And God grant that the years that are coming, be they few or many, may be more fruitful in good works than those this volume records.

And that those I love, and especially my poor little Johnny, may not have to suffer for my unworthiness. Amen.

Finis—Finis—Finis.

1854

THE BATTLE OVER WOLCOTT GIBBS · VICTORY OF COLUMBIA COLLEGE MOSSBACKS · THE KANSAS-NEBRASKA BILL · CRIMEAN WAR

*T*he early weeks of 1854 found attention in Washington riveted upon Stephen A. Douglas's unexpected and audacious bill to organize the Territories of Kansas and Nebraska, repealing the Missouri Compromise restriction on the entry of slavery into the new area. In Europe, meanwhile, the focus of interest was the Russo-Turkish War, with the four Western Powers still trying to bring about a peaceable settlement. Rioting at Erie, Pennsylvania, furnished many headlines; for the little city had long profited from a break in railroad gauge which compelled the transfer of passengers and freight at that point, and offered violent obstruction to the laying of a new standard-width track. Strong was little concerned with any of these subjects. His feelings were intensely enlisted in the movement to make Wolcott Gibbs the new professor of chemistry at Columbia, and against the clerical party who opposed that brilliant scientist, wishing instead to elect a mediocre but orthodox man named George C. Schaeffer. Late in December he had secured the signatures of a large number of alumni to a petition requesting the trustees to name Gibbs. It was an undisputed fact that the charter of King's College had provided that it should never make any religious test; it was also an undisputed fact that Gibbs would be the last man in the world to use his academic position to press any religious argument or tenet. No divines in the country had a higher reputation for learning and piety than that to which the Unitarian William Ellery Channing had attained—or that which Henry W. Bellows of All Souls' Church in New York was attaining. But the conservative members of the Columbia Board of Trustees were singularly narrow and obstinate.

[145]

January 8, SUNDAY. . . . Went last evening with Mr. Ruggles and George Anthon to Professor Charles Anthon's for a council over the affairs of the College, and particularly Gibbs. First time I've spoken to "Bull" since 1838, for some six years before which time he was the object of my reverent admiration and dread, an awful, unaccountable divinity, most frequently malevolent. Spent a couple of hours with him very pleasantly, then to Charles King's awhile, and then home. Was reading in this library at one or thereabouts, when an alarm of fire and the sight of a fine rich column of smoke lit up with a very angry red light rolling off toward the southwest, seemingly not far off, sent me on a brisk trot down the Fourth Avenue and Broadway, through the frosty air and along the silent streets of a January midnight. No one was stirring anywhere, but now and then a pedestrian on the same errand as mine. Fire was in Tripler Hall and Laffarge's Hotel, very showy and splendid. . . . When I came off at a little before four, the fire was rampant and volant throughout all the building, and this morning it appears badly burnt up and burnt out. Fires are epidemic this season, three bad ones within a month: Harpers', the *Great Republic,* and this half-million hotel. . . .

Of course, the leading idea of the past ten days has been Gibbs. No time to go into particulars, but there will be "a murder grim and great" before his defeat and all the chain of consequences are disposed of. Result of election uncertain and unpromising. We meet tomorrow at two; the committee will report simply the papers in its hands, without recommending anything. And it may be that the *Fossil* party, having a majority (Hoffman can't come down from Albany), will insist on an election at once. If so, we must talk against time or use any other lawless weapon chance may provide. But I don't think they'll be disposed to take that course—and that Schaeffer won't be elected is far less uncertain than that Gibbs will.

Certain resolutions will be offered that will make the fur fly a little, the ayes and noes being called for, and an intimation made of a committee of inquiry from the legislature if they are voted down. . . .

January 9. . . . Now for Columbia College. We met at two P.M. Mr. Ruggles offered his resolutions, and a storm followed such as was foreseen. All the six clerical members of the board pronounced distinctly and expressly against them and *against Gibbs* on the sole ground of his religious belief, and the resolutions were "indefinitely postponed" on motion of Dr. Spring. Election postponed to a week from Tuesday. Gibbs's election no longer to be hoped, but I think Schaeffer may be defeated, who

UNION SQUARE, 1859

LOOKING NORTH ON FOURTH AVENUE

THEODORE W. DWIGHT

SAMUEL BULKLEY RUGGLES

is utterly unfit for the place. Wainwright, Haight, and one or two men of Gibbs's opponents won't vote for Schaeffer, if they can help it.

Vestry meeting tonight. Very ill-tempered and vicious, a mere series of squabbles without result.

I am most thoroughly disgusted with the action and language of the clerical members of the board of Columbia College, including the three members of the clerical staff of Trinity. The resolutions offered and objected to by them were, in substance, that inasmuch as the original charter and the subsequent acts of the legislature since the Revolution prohibited any religious qualification for office in the College, members of the board cannot rightfully or lawfully object to any candidate for the vacant professorship on account of his religious creed. One would think it a truism, a mere formal assertion, that men with the enlightened conscience of a professed theologian cannot lawfully do that indirectly by ballot and *sub silentio* which the law of the land and this special contract with the state forbids them to do directly and avowedly; that if it was conceded to be wrong, unlawful, and a breach of trust to adopt a resolution that Unitarianism or Deism or Roman Catholicism should debar a man from office in the College, it was quite as wrong to debar him from that office on that avowed ground without that resolution.

Yet these gentlemen, churchmen and dissenters, all avowed distinctly that they would not vote for any Unitarian candidate, whatever might be his qualifications for the place.

I asked Haight and Wainwright: Suppose Gibbs went to Trinity Church, would you not vote for him? Their answer was *"Yes, most gladly"* —or if he went to the Presbyterian Church. But they say this is *not* establishing a religious test, or violating the provisions under which they hold office. . . .

Wainwright, Spring, and Knox during the meeting of the board, and Haight in talk after the adjournment, were *explicit* on this subject.[1] And the unutterable illogicality of their talk! Confusion of practical immorality with the soundness or error of the tenets in matters of religion to which the enactments in question refer. Confusion between what one *can* do and what one can *lawfully* do. Ignoring of any responsibility except to the Supreme Court on a *quo warranto*. These are thy *priests*, O, Israel!

[1] The Rev. Jonathan M. Wainwright, Provisional Bishop of New York; the Rev. Gardiner Spring, minister of the Brick Presbyterian Church; the Rev. John Knox, pastor of the Middle Dutch Church; and the Rev. Benjamin Isaacs Haight, assistant minister of Trinity Church; all conservative trustees.

My feeling is very strong just now in favor of resigning from Trinity Church vestry.

January 10. . . . Have had Wolcott Gibbs's testimonials copied today for the printer. There is going to be some fight yet, and success not *absolutely* impossible.

If this ground is definitely taken, viz.: the right to make religious belief a test, one good may follow that Knox, Spring, and Fisher don't anticipate. It is competent for us to draw the line at one point as well as another. If we can exclude a man for unsoundness as to the Divine Nature, we can exclude him for denying the existence, supremacy, and organization of the Visible Catholic Church. We can make the College Anglican and Catholic, root and branch.

The reasoning of my astute clerical colleagues is that, although the law forbids a resolution that the act shall be done, it does not forbid the act itself. Very honest casuistry. There are Jesuits outside the pale of Rome and "blacksnakes" unclassified in herpetology.

January 12. . . . The first shot in the Gibbs campaign outside the frontier was fired today in this afternoon's *Post*. I cut out the paragraph and pasted it on a flyleaf of this book for preservation. It is very unfortunate anything of the kind should have appeared just now, and this will do incalculable harm; probably destroys the last chance by putting C. C. Moore and Edward Jones on their dignity,[2] and strengthening the repugnance of this very stately board to a candidate sought to be forced into office by "outside pressure."

Had a conference with Betts and Van Wagenen this morning; Betts urbane but spiteful; Van Wagenen uncommonly ill-tempered and inclined to be vituperative.[3]

January 14. . . . Have been turning over *Hot Corn Stories*,[4] a book that has sold more abundantly than any since *Uncle Tom's Cabin*. Not meritorious as a work of art; melodramatic, and I think appealing to depraved curiosity in its details about assignation houses and kept women. But (at least as to the former fault) it must be remembered that the book seems

[2] Clement C. Moore, the oldest member of the board, to which he had been elected in 1813, is best remembered for his verses on a visit of St. Nicholas. Edward Jones, a physician and a member of the board since 1849, may be recalled as uncle of the novelist Edith Wharton.

[3] Gerrit G. Van Wagenen, a lawyer, had been a trustee since 1845. Like Betts, he was an Episcopalian of staunch conviction.

[4] By Solon Robinson, agricultural editor of the New York *Tribune*; the book sold 50,000 copies in six months.

honestly meant to promote a certain end, for the sake of which artistic errors, violations of artistic truth, may well be pardoned. If perfectly correct in form and taste, it would have made less impression on an un-aesthetic community.

The cleverest thing about it is its choice of a title. *Hot Corn* suggests so many reminiscences of sultry nights in August or early September, when one has walked through close, unfragant air and flooding moonlight and crowds, in Broadway or the Bowery, and heard the cry rising at every corner, or has been lulled to sleep by its mournful cadence in the distance as he lay under only a sheet and wondered if tomorrow would be cooler. Alas for some far-off times when I remember so to have heard it!

Have got the Gibbs papers printed and sent them off this afternoon. . . . Probably my elder brethren of the board will snub me for presuming to print. Be it so. I'm right—and entitled to call myself on terms of equality with Betts and Gouverneur Ogden.

The *San Francisco* last news arrived this morning. Disease and drowning swept off some two hundred of her crew and passengers. Five hundred safe. Terrible story of suffering and tragedy in the water–logged steamer, with something like cholera raging among the crowd of survivors. . . .[5]

Miss Josepha Bleecker dead. An old reminiscence (in name at least) departed. Robert B. Minturn's wife's mother also dead. Have discoursed with him latterly somewhat. He is too good, *too much* merchant prince and liberal Christian, and glorified donor to charitable uses. Fatuous and fat-headed, I think, and puffed up, I fear.[6]

Hot Corn has stirred me up, for the present; God grant not merely for the present. Reverend Hoyt is acting vigorously, I believe, in the same direction, with the philanthropists of the *Tribune*, and I shall put myself *en rapport* with them.

January 15, SUNDAY.   John R. Strong has a rather emphatic cold. . . . Wonder if he'll live to turn over these memoranda and the preceding volumes of the series, after my funeral, and look sadly back to January, 1854. Or will his children own the old MS Journal, and sometimes look through it and back to the distant time when it was scribbled?

[5] The Pacific Mail liner *San Francisco*, fresh from the builder's yard, had left New York late in 1853 with a body of regular troops and many passengers. A heavy gale shortly crippled her and washed nearly a hundred persons overboard. Disease took an additional toll. Sailing ships finally rescued most of the survivors.

[6] Robert B. Minturn (1805–1866), merchant and shipowner, was a partner in Grinnell, Minturn & Co., which at one time owned more than fifty ocean-going vessels, including some of the most notable American clippers.

I think of that often in reference to my poor mother that is gone, when I look at those sorrowful memorials that date back to 1798. It's an indefinable feeling, though so strong and keen, the thought of the old, departed, perished days, of sunshine and sultry moonlight nights that passed over her long ago. It can't be written down and defined on paper, the sad retrovision to which I refer. Surely they have not perished utterly, in some sense they live and shall live. In Dickens's last book, *Bleak House*, he speaks of another world, "where the old times are." Those old times of hers, when she was full of youth and joy, and sank to sleep on moonlight nights listening to the wind stirring the trees, and dreamed of pleasant memories, and woke to the kindly salutations of home, and her walk in the sunshiny garden and her work and books at mid-day and the quiet and peace of the evening again—all that is not past utterly away and gone, like the sounds waked by the wind from harp strings. It is and shall be. For our weal or woe, all we do and all we feel abides for ever.

January 16, MONDAY.   G. J. Cornell returned.[7] Enlisted him instantly to operate on Spring, with whom he professes a certain intimacy. John Mason Knox was to have tackled his papa yesterday. The Reverend James H. M. Knox has written a letter of eight pages to the same venerable casuist in favor of Gibbs, his classmate. Probably quite unavailing; both gentlemen are too strongly committed. . . .

Gibbs must be beat tomorrow, I think. Perhaps the election will be postponed and perhaps indefinitely postponed, by appointing some scrub of a tutor to perform the duties of professor. That will be equivalent to defeat, and then Russel and Cornell and J. W. Beekman may fire away if they like.[8] Dana of the *Tribune* and Bryant will be only too happy to raise a storm. I had hard work to persuade Bryant to make no farther row as yet, to hold back his thunders for a few days. . . .

January 17, TUESDAY.   At Columbia College at two; long meeting without definite result. Mr. Ruggles dined here and at eight Ellie and I went to Gibbs's rooms, where was some nice music with Mrs. Gibbs and Miss Teresa Mauran and Mrs. Isaac Wright.

[7] George James Cornell (Columbia 1839), New York lawyer and sometime member of the state assembly. The Knoxes were sons of the Rev. John Knox, frequently acting chairman of the trustees at this time in the absence of Beverley Robinson; he was elected to the post in February.

[8] William Channing Russel (1814–1896), Columbia 1832, a Unitarian and an attorney in New York; he was later a professor and acting president of Cornell University. James William Beekman (Columbia 1834), wealthy New York lawyer descended from the earliest Dutch settlers, was a leader in many public causes.

Columbia College meeting ill tempered and not of good omen. The Schaeffer papers were read and, though they do not in truth amount to much, they will weigh with the two or three undecided men who want a pretext for voting against Gibbs by reason of his Unitarianism, the "outside pressure" generally, and the *Evening Post* article in particular. The outside pressure argument means that whenever any course is so manifestly wise and prudent that all mankind is unanimous in favor of the trustees adopting it, they cannot properly adopt it, and must do the precise opposite, in order to maintain their independence and dignity. . . .

As to the *Evening Post*, I shall see Russel tomorrow and tell him that I withdraw my special request that he do no publishing for the present, that I can be privy to no newspaper war and no petitioner to the legislature, but that the case cannot now be injured thereby, and that if he sees fit to adopt that or any other treatment, to let slip the dogs of war in any form, he may do as he pleases.

John C. Spencer is furious, ditto Erastus Brooks. If Russel or Beekman sees fit to commence a campaign at Albany, there will be facilities therefor.

January 18.   The Gibbs conflict is spreading a little. John C. Spencer's letter received today commits him beyond all recall. Mr. S. B. Ruggles has written a letter to Fish that will tell—exceedingly able, compact, plain-spoken, and Saxon. Russel came here after dinner. He proposes to cross the Danube and commence hostilities, and I can't help it if he does.

The more I see of the way public opinion is shaping, the more plain it is that the Church has made a serious blunder in this matter, a misstep that may lead to very bad results. . . .

Now, waiving all the most weighty considerations of their [the trustees'] duty under their contract with the state to apply no religious test to this case; assuming it to be a church institution, as it is called by Minturn; passing over the presence in the board of Knox and Spring and Fisher and Beadle, brought in avowedly as Dissenters to secure dissenting patronage; taking the highest ground a churchman can take as to its proper management and government, what is it? What is "a church college"?

Not, as I suppose, a hospital for decayed churchmen, an institution created to provide salaries and situations for weak-minded, inefficient presbyters with bronchial afflictions that forbid their venturing on a parochial charge, or most estimable and high-minded laymen who can't take care of themselves and must be provided for somewhere; but an institution in which (1) whatever is done or attempted is done as honestly and thoroughly as its means and opportunities will permit . . . and (2) in which whatever direct or indirect teaching there may be on matters of religion coincides with and enforces the truths held by the Church. . . .

January 19. Walked up with Mr. Ruggles at four and found the "New City Hall," alias the old Almshouse, on fire. It had caught in the third story under the roof, probably from furnaces, and was enveloped in smoke, with a few bright tongues of flame rolling out under its wooden cornice just above the Central Park Commissioners' office. It was plainly going to be a serious combustion. We went into the library at the west end on the first floor, and after some debate with Cowdrey and Gouverneur Ogden, Russel, and others, succeeded in getting out the books and furniture. When I left at 6:30 the fire had not got into that room, but it was flooded with water.

January 24. News from Europe menacing and martial. A general war conceded by everyone now to be altogether probable. . . . As to Gibbs, there is strange indecision and inertia among his alumni friends after all their brag. It will end in smoke. Saw Bartlett of West Point today, church-loving but law-loving, and he views the question as I do. Columbia College is destined to be a sleepy, third-rate high school for one or two generations more. . . .

I am thoroughly disgusted with Wainwright. The further I trace him in this business the clearer are the signs of double-dealing, want of principle, cowardice, meanness, and humbug.

January 27. There is scarce a possibility of electing Wolcott Gibbs as the case stands now. Knox has come out against him after much wavering.

January 28, SATURDAY. "Snapping cold"; this is a hard winter. . . . Tonight I called on (Professor) Anderson, and talked of St. Luke's Hospital and Columbia College. Confound that subtlest and most ingenious of reasoners! I brought forward the question of ethics connected with the doings of that venerable prelate J. M. Wainwright and his abettors, and Anderson talked and talked, slowly, deliberately, clearly, compactly, and well, and talked on, till the room seemed to be whirling gravely round and round. I saw nothing but the fire in the grate, and *him* sitting, twiddling his thumbs and calmly grinding out logic and casuistry, and knew nothing except that I did *not know* anything, and that it was perfectly conceivable that two and two might be five. . . .

January 29, SUNDAY. George Anthon took tea here, and Mr. Ruggles looked in. We must get up an expression of opinion from parents and guardians of the present undergraduates. That will tell even more emphatically than the alumni petition, and help to corner Wainwright & Co. The difficulty is to get the work done before the next meeting of the trustees. As to Wainwright, I don't think the Church of God ever had a much feebler and shallower shepherd among her chief governors, since her reign on earth began. . . .

January 30, MONDAY. Had some talk tonight at Muhlenberg's with William Hobart. Wainwright has been asserting at Sidney Brooks's dinner table that he is *not* committed against Wolcott Gibbs on the ideological ground. If the game were worth the chase, and if I had not other work to do, I should begin to agitate the presentment and trial of that Rt. Rev. gentleman for lying. I can pardon W. H. Harison's violence against him now. In view of his cowardice, meanness, and manifold tergiversation, the impulse is strong to identify oneself with the opposition party and to use every legitimate weapon against the present incumbent of the dishonored Episcopate. But it would not be right, and must not be done. . . .

I fear we shall feel very flat if Gibbs is elected after all. And as Bidwell and Jonas Miller tell me that Van Wagenen declares himself uncommitted and Hobart thinks (probably not correctly) that Edward Jones will vote right, that calamity is not physically impossible.

February 2. Wainwright called on Richard Grant White yesterday at the *Courier* office to deplore and condemn the very decorous and sensible leader that appeared in that paper a day or two since, and to inquire if Mr. King or Mr. Ruggles had not written it? White discussed the question of its deplorability and the justice of its condemnation, and seems to have dodged and chased his Rt. Rev. opponent all round the board (like a king in the last stage of a close game of chess); and by his own account cornered him at last to admit that the dealings of this corporation were legitimate subjects of comment by the newspaper press, and that he, the Rt. Rev. J. M. W[ainwright], Provisional Bishop, "had opposed and should oppose" Wolcott Gibbs *on the Unitarian ground*. Wainwright was relieved to learn that the editorial was White's own. "It would have been his duty to have administered a severe rebuke to King" were he an accessory to it.

I think I see him a-doing it! Probably a trustee is entitled to confer with his trust; and for whom are we "Trustees of Columbia College" if not for the community? There is going to be a "general war" before this matter is disposed of; and I think Wainwright will find himself more and more in the wrong place as the conflict thickens and deepens. Probably he wants to get the presidency as a convenient sinecure after two or three years of an overworked episcopate. Our friend R. B. Minturn seems to back him in this swindle, and I know of no other outsider who does so, lay or cleric. Higby won't, probably, for he has got excited about the Trinity Chapel business, and says "I made that man bishop, and now he wants to grasp everything," or words to that effect. . . .

February 4.   The *Herald* has defined its position on the Gibbs question against that gentleman, on the ground that Unitarianism is a stepping-stone to infidelity, and that Spinoza, Socinus, and other unchristian philosophers "of the last century" are shrewdly suspected to have held the same opinion; and because Voltaire had a strong leaning toward it. It regrets the advance of religious dissension from the Five Points to the shades of the College, and is so exactly what I should have wished it that I half suspect some friend of Gibbs's to have smuggled it in surreptitiously in the guise of an editorial. . . . Drafted and sent to Albany a special act which, if we can get it through at this session, will secure us Fish's and Hoffman's vote. It authorizes *proxies* by trustees absent as holding political office. The "parents and guardians" document not as generally signed as I hoped, only some twenty names in at four today.

I think Monday's meeting must be followed by well-marked schism and open war. If so, our clerical brethren will find, perhaps with surprise, that this is not a question of liberality or illiberality, bigotry or enlightenment, but one of good faith or bad faith, honesty or fraud, to which the ordinary truisms of conservative and vigorous theologians are entirely inapplicable. If it were proposed to procure a law excluding Unitarians from all civil rights, and banishing or burning them, their reasoning would be pertinent. But they propose to go further, and to make the enormity of their error a justification for breaking a contract with the state in reference to Unitarianism (or indirectly *with* Unitarians as individuals of the state), and all their statements and arguments are impertinent to that controversy. Unless they are prepared to maintain the proposition that no faith is to be kept with heretics; that the maker of a promissory note endorsed to Peter Cooper or Moses H. Grinnell may lawfully and rightly evade its payment if he believes that the amount there is on it will be applied by the endorsee to the publication of Unitarian tracts or the building of an Unitarian Church; and that it is morally right to do moral wrong for the maintenance of truth or the repression of error—then Wainwright and Berrian and Spring have no logical position at all. They must justify the violation of safe-conduct for the sake of executing justice on a heretic, or admit themselves guilty of dishonesty and immorality for the sake of religious truth, truth which demands many sacrifices but condemns *that*. It's not often that a layman is entitled to the luxury of "sassing" a bishop, that a vestryman of Trinity Church stands on moral ground from which he can look down on Rev. William Berrian, D.D., Rector. But I think I'm so privileged at this time.

Hoffman is ill, his confounded larynx being the subject of venous congestion, and his unprincipled uvula morbidly enlarged.[9] Fish writes that he can't come, some caucus having decided that something about the Nebraska bill is to be pushed or to be opposed. So we can't elect Wolcott Gibbs next Monday under any circumstances. . . .

February 6, MONDAY. Columbia College meeting at two o'clock. General attendance (bating Fish and Hoffman and Beverley Robinson). Even poor, gouty Morris had been dragooned out. Fisher was the only absentee without manifest apology, the only member not present or accounted for. We began by a discussion of the proposition whether the premises north of the new street (continuing Park Place to the west) had best be leased to the United States or to the city authorities pursuant to certain applications that had come in. On that there was a trace of discord and belligerency in the call for ayes and noes on the question of a reference to the standing (or sleeping) committee, and the matter was referred to the Bishop, Van Wagenen, and myself (happily *not* with power) to report at a meeting next Tuesday week. Then I was moving a resolution about financial policy and the plan for creating a $300,000 debt, when Gouverneur Ogden asked me to give way to him, and I did so, and the fun began. Gouverneur M. Ogden wanted to move, and did move, a preamble and long string of resolutions about the newspaper publications of the last few days, and supported them by a long speech; read the articles in question (carefully cut out and pasted on sheets of foolscap) and commented on them—"Hamadryads" and "Jesuitry" and all—in the gravest good faith and with all earnestness, giving due emphasis to their most stringent and vituperative paragraphs (Wainwright and the others sitting still and looking disgusted beyond measure and occasionally intervening with an inef-

[9] Ogden Hoffman, of the class of 1812 at Columbia, had been Congressman and was now Attorney-General of the state. One of the ablest criminal lawyers of his day and one of the most popular men in New York, he was in poor health, with little more than two years to live.

fectual call to order), and enforcing on the board, with the sagacity of Mr. Bumble in *Oliver Twist*, everything disrespectful, scurrilous, and contumelious to be found in them. His resolutions were utter bosh: that we had not violated our charter, and didn't mean to, that we had done our duty and should do it, that the publications were all wrong because we had not yet elected or decided to elect, that the trustees had been diligent and efficient, that they were to act independently of outside pressure, and the like.

Spring seconded them (without any pledge to vote for them), and made a most dignified and able speech on the whole subject, which seemed (and perhaps was) strong, candid, and clear, without touching the essence of the controversy. Tom Wells said a word or two of not much to the purpose, and Edward Jones more briefly and more to the point. Then Mr. Ruggles began, but gave way at 5:30 to a motion to adjourn, after having said some very pungent and emphatic things, that will *tell*, and after the foreshadowing of some other things that will tell still more.

When I came uptown, dined with Jack Ehninger and pretty little graceful Miss Lily Snelling, who has the freshness of a school girl with the dignity of a woman, modest and self-possessed at once. . . .

February 8. There will be a continuation of the academic perform-ances at Columbia College tomorrow, and I look to its result with no little anxiety. I am still, A.D. 1854, criminally timid about assaults even from such a blockhead as Ogden, even if absolutely without foundation in fact or in reason. I have no moral doubt that some of my friends have published, though I don't *know* it. If they have done so, I am not responsible even to this exalted board. And if I myself had, over my own name or other-wise (as I have not, though I have come very near it or argued myself nearly into conviction that I lawfully might and justly might), I could defend the act on grounds both of principle and of policy. But I am nervous at the thought of attack, in a board of grave and respectable gentlemen, to whose presence I am not yet used.

February 9, THURSDAY. Another Columbia College meeting at two P.M. Opened with a continuation of the order on G. M. Ogden's resolu-tions, which after a shindy in which my honest friend Thomas L. Wells shewed himself a little wrong-headed, were laid on the table. Then there was council and debate over financial measures; then additional testi-monials as to new candidates were read; R. O. Doremus, McCulloh of Princeton, Lieutenant Peck of West Point and one Henry Onderdonk of St. Timothy's Hall, Maryland, and one or two more having been brought in by our advertisement for proposals for a professorship.[10] Then some debate on the relative merits of candidates, Schaeffer and Gibbs especially, in which Mr. Ruggles spoke very effectively, though holding back much that he had prepared on the theological branch of his subject; and then we balloted thrice, each time with the same result, viz.: Gibbs 9, Schaeffer 8, Doremus 2, and then adjourned to Tuesday.

If our men are staunch and if Fish and Hoffman can attend, and G. W. Morris have the gout rather severely, we may succeed. But of that there is little likelihood. Anyway the act is done; our clerical friends have voted in violation of their duty, and I don't see why Cornell and his friends should not act at once if so advised. . . .

Seabury, Tyng, Henry Anthon, John A. Dix, and John C. Spencer are strong backers [of Gibbs]. Wainwright and poor old senile Berrian will find it hard to stand against the whole current of popular prejudice, with such men to enforce its pressure on them and condemnation of them.

February 11, SATURDAY.   Conference with Mr. Ruggles from ten to twelve. Fish has been written to by him, G. J. Cornell, and King; if this wretched Nebraska bill don't prevent, he will surely come on. If Dix were in town, he might be seen and possessed of all this case, with its contingencies of disaster to the Church, and could talk to Wainwright and Berrian with effect. But I fear he is spending this week and next in Westchester County. I saw him a few days ago, and found that his view was that of . . . all who act on any principle of right and wrong, from Tyng, Anthon, Seabury, and John C. Spencer to Moses Grinnell. . . .

I've been brought up in an accursed feminine reverence for the White Cravat. Alas, that it should be shaken, for I can afford to spare no safeguards. But this clerical dishonesty is driving me into sympathy with Red Republican Socialist Greeleyan talk about "priests" and ecclesiastical tyranny.

February 14.   Prolongation of drizzle and fog. Today's special matter another step in the Columbia College campaign. . . . First ballot Gibbs 10; Schaeffer, 8; McCulloh, 1; Blank, 1. Second ballot, exactly the same. (Hoffman was present.) Then Dr. Fisher offered a resolution that we strike out the names of the two highest candidates, Gibbs and Schaeffer, and exclude all votes for them; the absurd proposition was seconded by Gouver-

---

[10] Only Richard S. McCulloh (1818–1894) requires comment. He was a graduate of Princeton, where he had sometimes served as assistant to Joseph Henry, the eminent scientist. Publishing some scientific monographs of minor value, he was made professor of natural philosophy at Princeton (then the College of New Jersey) in 1849. A Marylander by birth, he sympathized strongly with the South.

neur Ogden and sustained in a small speech, and opposed by him as inadmissible five minutes after in another small speech. (Ogden is the most stolid man I know. Dunscomb is a Machiavelli to him.) Then more debate opens, and at last Fisher withdraws his motion. Then ballot number four: Gibbs 8, Schaeffer 3, McCulloh 4, Porter 3, Peck 1, Doremus 1. Number five: Gibbs 9, Schaeffer 3, McCulloh 7, Porter 1. Then a most judicious motion to adjourn carried by a skillful move of Hoffman's. Dined here with Ruggles and George Anthon.

Schaeffer is killed, I think. McCulloh is a strong man; he is likely to be Gibbs's most formidable competitor, and he will do his work well, if elected. Wainwright is likely to have certain episcopal duties early in March that will keep him from our next meeting. But if there's a word said about it to anybody, Jonathan will countermand his appointments. Coward and traitor, without principle or courage to avoid a want of principle, is the Rt. Rev. Provisional Bishop, I fear.

February 15, WEDNESDAY.   Met the Columbia College committee at two. . . .

Fish writes that he'll probably be able to attend our next meeting, and also that the Nebraska bill may perhaps fail in the Senate, which people generally don't expect. He is confidential and mysterious about the matter, and there seems to be some mechanism working on the subject that I know not of.

Should Fish and Hoffman both attend and Wainwright be missing, there would be (including Morris, who would be lugged out if his health permitted him to be present) 21 votes: eleven, a majority. And if Ray and Edward Jones, who are weak brethren and probably the men who fell off from the Gibbs ticket yesterday, return to their former faith, we shall have eleven votes and carry in our man. . . .

February 16.   Trinity Churchyard war goes vigorously on, and I think we shall maintain it intact. From Columbia College there is not a syllable of news. Our policy, I think, is inactivity; there may be a chance of success in abandoning agitation and allowing ill-temper to die out. There's clearly nothing to be done by increasing the pressure *ab-extra*.

Canal enlargement undoubtedly triumphant, ten to one, though the vote is very light.

February 17.   Pleasant weather. This week's *Churchman* is out on the Gibbs controversy, with a small article that combines the wisdom of the *Epistola Obscurorum Virorum* with the elevated tone of the New York *Herald;* equally vile in logic, in taste, and in temper. "We take it that the trustees have a right to vote as they judge best without giving their reasons first." Consolatory doctrine to many a guardian and executor timidly meditating a disposition of the trust fund that will further his own little private financial operations, and who will gladly and properly draw the inference that he may use his discretion and invest as he pleases, without giving his reasons. And so on for half a column of bosh and insolence!

February 21. Clear day. Streets blockaded with snow; prospect of a long period of deliquescence and nastiness before we are rid of it. But on this first day of its fall, the snowdrifts and banks, though very inconvenient and uncomfortable, are beautiful objects. But the lovely whiteness and purity of their soft, complex curves of surface will soon be polluted and will degenerate into mire and gutterwater and mud broth. . . .

(Extracts from a letter dated Columbia, S.C., 15 Feby., 1854, to S. B. Ruggles, the joint composition in alternate lines of Francis Lieber and the Astronomical Gould):

> What an unchristian white-cravat is Wainwright
>   To spend his calumnies against Wool Gibbs:
> And can the reverend Knox be in the main right
>   To circulate such anti-Christian fibs?
>
> Do tell us, who in earth can be Doremus:
>   And who the tenebrists that vote for him?
> Eight votes for Schaeffer too:—O Nicodemus!
>   Against such men poor Wolcott's chance is slim.
>
> Haste, haste to Washington and fish the Fish up,
>   And snake out Hoffman from his lurking hole,
> To countervail that execrable Bishop
>   And Knox, that reverend benighted soul.
>
> Hang all the blockheads, fogies, and the Bonzes!
>   They make nine-tenths the mischief that's about,
> And from your College, if there only once is
>   A chance, O thou dear Ruggles, smoke them out. . . .

And so on for a full letter-sheet of fun and doggerel. Held council with Mr. Ruggles tonight when he handed me the letter from which I've extracted as above. The only thing now legitimately to be done is to put the argument into some tangible form, and bring it before members of the board and hereafter before the people generally. (Hereafter meaning after the special controversy now before us has been decided by Wolcott Gibbs's defeat.) Two or three of our co-trustees may possibly feel the effect of an irresistible argument. If they don't, outsiders will.

February 23. Encountered Frederick Wolcott, who told me what I've suspected for some time, that Wolcott Gibbs, if elected by a bare majority, won't take the professorship. On the whole, relieved and comforted by the intelligence. It's scarce to be hoped that by the utmost exertions we could carry him in, even by a majority of one, and if we are beat we stand in a far better position for further reformatory and *vivificant* operations. But, of course, I don't know that he will refuse the plan if offered to him, and must go on in good faith to use all lawful means for his election.

March 2. . . . Have been a busy man since Saturday, working tolerably in Wall Street, and drudging by night till two and three and four in the morning over the Gibbs manifesto. Mr. Ruggles arranged the collocation of ideas very ably and strongly. My office has been to re-write, working in one or two additional notions, and he again has compacted and clarified any crude suggestions and emendations and interpolations, and I think it will make a strong paper, not quite unworthy the strength of the case. There are a couple of Schiller's scriveners at No. 24 Union Place tonight working on the copies. It probably takes the form of a letter to Betts, to be delivered Saturday morning, and to be printed after our Monday meeting. It can hardly change a single vote. Will they act on it or be affected by it in any way? Will they favor a postponement of the question to give time for a counterplea? Will they offer a resolution that the board deprecates public discussion of any question before it (for the intention to print will be naturally inferred from the length and elaboration of this document)? If so, they are delivered into our hands. Any answer to the allegation of our manifesto, any argumentation of the questions it raises, will be conclusive. . . .

Schermerhorn fancy ball; costume of *Louis Quinze.* The present nine days' wonder. It was quite successful. No fancy ball can approximate to common sense that does not adopt some single period. The chaos of nuns and devils, Ivanhoe and Harlequin, Loyola, Paul Pry, the cavalier and the Swiss peasant, presented by a ball on any other principle, or rather without principle of any sort, is so incoherent and insane that a thoughtful spectator would certainly be qualified for the Bloomingdale Asylum after some assignable period of inspection. . . .

Nebraska or Nebrascal controversy raging in the *Post* and *Tribune.* My difficulty is to see how the old act of legislation called "the Missouri Compromise" acquires the attributes of a contract. That point conceded, the question before the principalities and powers at Washington seems plain enough. Our contract with the United States for the lease of Columbia College buildings at $70,000 seems to have flattened out and failed. Uncle Sam won't take the premises at the price, and no wonder.

March 3. Friday night, or rather about 3 A.M. of Saturday. Have been drudging since about half-past two (with an interval for dinner and for a call from Rev. Piggy Bedell) on the Columbia College manifesto. At Mr. Ruggles's till eleven, and since then Mr. Ruggles and Schiller and one of his "engrossers," a most downtrodden, seedy, and suffering individual, who wished he was back in the h'old country or else hout West, have been energizing on these premises. Finished now, I believe, though a fortnight's thought and labor might have been added with advantage. . . .

March 5, SUNDAY. . . . We meet tomorrow. Not one of the enemy will strike to logic. Not one is capable of conversion, except it may possibly be Van Wagenen, and except the Bishop, who might cave in because he dreads public opinion most horribly and has wit enough to see that considerations which should logically lead him to a certain course may make the public think ill of him if he take any other.

Ogden and Tom Wells are exceptions to the rule that when the brains are out the man must die. Betts himself has had barely time to see the scope and force of this document and the magnitude of the questions it raises clearly enough to shake his convictions perceptibly. His clique, to whom he may shew it a few hours before the meeting, will feel its cogency but little. . . .

March 6. . . . Columbia College meeting at two. Rather more goodnatured than they have been of late. Bishop Jonathan missing, obliged to keep an Episcopal appointment. . . . Went into ballot to fill vacancy. First ballot, Gibbs 7; McCulloh 7; Schaeffer 1; Doremus 1. Second, third, and fourth the same; each Gibbs 9, McCulloh 9, so there was no election. Some other business done of no very special interest. Mr. Ruggles left for Albany immediately afterwards. What's to be done with the letter to Betts? Probably print it and keep all the copies close except one for each Justice. I don't think we should lose a single vote by so doing. It's not physically or abstractly impossible that we might thereby change one or two; for example, Spring, who has vigorous practical sense, if I rightly read his constitution, and Wainwright, whose selfishness and fears of public opinion are intense—delicately organized enough to sniff danger from afar. Of Fisher I know nothing. Berrian and Knox are impenetrably wrapt up in certain old traditional formulas, excellent both, but men who "remain unchanged in contact with logic" (chemical diction being appro-

priate here). Of Tom Wells and Gouverneur Ogden, it may be said that
their intellectual faculty "is not sensibly affected by any contact with any
known form of reasoning at the highest attainable temperature."

March 10. . . . The streets inexpressible. Snow gone, but every crossing ankle deep with confluent filth. Even the sidewalks reek with greasy,
slippery, semi-fluid nastiness. Ehninger dined here. After dinner Dorr
stumbled on Mr. Ruggles. Two good things said by Dorr: "An undertaker
called on Winthrop the other day to pay some rent and observed that
he understood Judge Edmonds was in communication with the spirit of
his wife, and that he thought she must have forgotten to remind him that
he had not yet paid the expenses of her interment." 'Tother was a quotation
from Soame Jenyns, that "a more keen sense of the ludicrous will probably
be among the sources of the happiness of the just made perfect.". . .

European news distinctly warlike. General war on a large scale seems
inevitable.

Mass-meeting came off Wednesday night. Sore throat and influenza
kept away Mrs. Gibbs, Mrs. Wright, and Tucker. Miss Lucretia Stevens
and the new tenor Safford (who did his work very well) were added unto
us. Performances were all Haydn's No. 2, and parts of his No. 1 and of
Mozart's 12th. Very satisfactorily done.

March 11.   *In re* Gibbs, I rather think Mr. Ruggles will print after
all. Last night he was dubious. And the question, as one of policy, is nice.

11 P.M. Mr. Ruggles has been here in the library discussing emendations to the Betts letter, supposing it addressed to Fish or Hoffman.

March 14.   Speck of war appearing wherein we may shortly be
involved with England and France allied against us. Question with Cuba
(or Spain) about liberties taken by the colonial government of that gem
of the sea with the steamer *Black Warrior*; threats of reprisal and letters
of marque and so forth. Anyway we shall be mixed up with the great
battle of Europe now opening, and identified with one or another of the
militant powers before many months are ended. One can't now foresee
exactly how we shall be involved, but somehow we will be, even should this
Cuban imbroglio come to naught.

March 24, FRIDAY.   The Nebraska bill, which went so swimmingly
through the Senate, has come to grief in the House, and is so referred as
to be shelved indefinitely. This was on motion of F. B. Cutting, who professes himself a friend of the bill, but has certainly stabbed it under the
fifth rib. Probably he feels, like many other northern politicians, that it is
one of those edged tools that it's dangerous to handle and better to shelve.

Although the Kansas-Nebraska bill passed the Senate on March 3 by the decisive majority of twenty-three, it had aroused a terrible storm of anger in the North and West, and the vote in the House was uncertain. Opposition there had become intense. On March 21 a sudden manoeuvre by Brockholst Cutting of New York sent it to Committee of the Whole; an unhappy fate, for debate in that body was unrestricted, and it might be delayed by talk on all kinds of subjects. The irate Southern Democrats made Cutting feel the weight of their wrath, and Strong's diary contains a record of the excitement in New York City when it seemed likely that the young Congressman might be pressed into a duel with John C. Breckinridge of Kentucky. Feeling between the slavery and anti-slavery forces was growing, and free-soilers of the North were rallying all their forces to prevent any further expansion of the institution they detested. At the same time, the international scene was becoming darker. The Crimean War was now fully begun. All efforts to bring Turkey and Russia to an agreement had failed, and France and Britain were resolved to permit no dismemberment of the Ottoman Empire. Dislike of the Czar and his tyranny was strong among all liberals of Western Europe; the French emperor was hopeful that he could strengthen his still-insecure regime by some glorious victories in the East; and the British government was anxious to safeguard its communications with India. By the end of March, 1854, forces were being gotten in readiness to defend Turkey against Russia, or if necessary to invade the Czar's domains. Nearer home, certain difficulties with the Spanish authorities in Cuba led many to fear a conflict with Madrid. The steamer Black Warrior, *voyaging between New Orleans and New York, touched at Havana. Because of some irregularities in her papers, she was seized by the Spanish port officials. Radical Southern leaders like John Slidell and John A. Quitman demanded drastic action, and for a few tense weeks war seemed a distinct possibility. Finally the steamer was released and the tension ended—but the Southern desire for the annexation of Cuba remained keen.*

The crisis in Columbia College affairs was now approaching its climax. All the principal newspapers had taken a hand. The Tribune *on February 3 had violently assailed the conservative trustees for their "illiberality" in "trampling on rights secured by the most solemn sanctions of the law" and trying "to establish a religious test as a condition of office." The* Evening Post *on February 2 had raised the question whether it was proper to place an institution of learning in the hands of men almost exclusively of one religious sect. The* Courier and Enquirer *printed a spirited expostulation. Senator Hamilton Fish was detained in Washington until the final vote was taken on the Kansas-Nebraska bill in the upper chamber; after that he was free to come to New York. Both parties plied him with letters; Ruggles urging him to take a stand for justice and law, while Gouverneur Ogden complained to him that the anti-Gibbs forces were being subjected to intimidation and outside pressure. But Fish sat stubbornly on the fence.*

March 27. At Albany Mr. Ruggles read some proof sheets of the Gibbs document to Hoffman, who of course bestowed some gas on Jonathan [Wainwright] the next time he encountered that venerable man. This led to a breakfast: Potter, Jonathan, Ruggles. Jonathan in perplexity. "If this thing can only be settled without trouble, there will never be any question of the same sort." "Haight and I can't take the back track so suddenly." "Do be sure that Fish and Hoffman attend the next meeting." "Don't let Gibbs resign if he's elected." "Tell him he may be sure of the most cordial support, laboratory, assistants, anything he wants." "Above all, don't let him be defeated." O, Jonathan, Jonathan! What must be the vital power of the church that lives in spite of such organs and ministers?

March 30, THURSDAY. Snowstorm nearly all day. . . . No [Cutting-Breckinridge] duel after all. People think now that there won't be any duel, and that all the talk is smoke and gas, or both. Miss Jenny Field (David Dudley Field, the codifier's daughter) took tea with Ellie and saintly Miss Ellen Rodgers, who goes to Lisbon Saturday with her diplomatic brother-in-law O'Sullivan.

The Gibbs manifesto printed at last. The conclusion of that job is a comfort. I've so read and reread drafts and copies, first proofs and second, of that document, that I'm disqualified to form any opinion as to its effect on others, or its merit and value. But it seems to me a very compact, clear, unanswerable paper. There can be no doubt that it is full of thought, and that there is in it much that will bear expansion and is capable of development, and that may perhaps need explanatory or rhetorical dilution to make it generally intelligible.

March 31. Very filthy drizzle all day. No prospect of any duel at Washington after all. With all its high moral sense, I think the public is disappointed, like a mob at an execution, balked by a reprieve. Gibbs manifesto sent out today among the trustees. Can't foresee its effect, can't name a single vote we shall gain by it, and do not think we shall lose any, but it's dubersome. . . . Mr. Ruggles went to Albany this afternoon and hopes to bring Hoffman down Monday, which hope is, I think, vanity. I don't know whether I wish Gibbs may be elected or not. It's a tolerably even balance of interest.

April 1. . . . Most pleased with Dr. Kane's volume of Arctic experiences.[11] It's far more attractive than any narrative of northern voyages and discovery that I've met. Franklin's first journey has a strong tragic interest, but this far surpasses it in clearness and picturesqueness of description and conveys a much more distinct image of the perils and marvels of the polar ice. . . .

Governor Seymour has vetoed the Maine Liquor Law. Whether he's right or wrong is a question on which an off-hand opinion is clearly presumptuous, for the questions involved are deep and dubious. I've no sort of sympathy with the temperance fanatics—rather a prejudice against them. But I am sure it would be better for mankind if alcohol were extinguished and annihilated. Has or has not society the right to make it contraband, as it forbids the sale or storage of gunpowder within certain limits, as it . . . assumes a right to confiscate and destroy a beauteous print brought into the custom-house from Paris? I don't know. If the popular voice demands this kind of legislation, we shall have it, and with the support of popular sentiment it will be enforced. Otherwise, the law will probably not be enacted, and if enacted will certainly not be enforced. The democratic despotism of a majority is a formidable element of injustice and oppression, but it is the power to which we are subject and which will determine this question.

Hamilton Fish is in town and will probably be present at the Columbia College meeting Monday afternoon. We are like to have a refreshing season there. Result uncommonly dubious. If Mr. Ruggles brings Hoffman down from Albany, and if Morris be absent, Gibbs will pretty surely be elected. Whether that be desirable or not desirable, I can't say. Should he be elected, we are only entering on the battle. Our fight has been thus far nothing but a preliminary skirmish. Should he be defeated, we may stand in a better position for the contest as to the strengthening or enlargement of our educational work, the conversion of the second-rate college into a university. And it may be well for us to gain this advantage by the loss of an individual agent clearly the best in his own department.

April 3, MONDAY.   All is lost save our honor. The trustees of Columbia

[11] Elisha Kent Kane's book, *Arctic Explorations: The Second Grinnell Expedition in Search of Sir John Franklin, in the Years 1853–1855,* published in two volumes, told an heroic story so ably that it reached almost every American home.

College met at two P.M. Present, beside the members usually attending, Governor Fish, Ogden Hoffman, and G. W. Morris. Absent, that sagacious man Jonathan the Bishop. Some interlocutory business done: question about the effect of John C. Stevens's thirty-foot excavation in an alleged bed of quicksand underlying the college; the possible tumbling into the gulf of McVickar's house and Charles Anthon's, not to speak of the whole college building up to Church Street being endangered should this traditional quicksand begin to run out. When that matter and some other affairs had been disposed of, the professorship came up. We went into ballot, and the result was as follows, to wit: (I put down names because each is certain and unmistakeable.)

For Wolcott Gibbs	*For one Richard McCulloh*
Charles King	Rev. Dr. Berrian
S. B. Ruggles	Rev. Dr. Haight
Ogden Hoffman	Rev. G. Spring
H. J. Anderson	Rev. John Knox
Edward Jones	Rev. G. H. Fisher
Robert Ray	William Betts
William H. Hobart	T. L. Wells
Clement C. Moore	G. G. Van Wagenen
G. T. Strong	G. M. Ogden
(9)	G. W. Morris
	Dr. Beadle
	(11)

Hamilton Fish voted for Professor Bache, virtually a blank, as Bache was not in nomination and would not take the place. His expectation no doubt was that the vote would be 10 to 10 and that by this inoperative vote he would keep the question open, retain the balance of power, and after moving for postponement (which he told me he meant to propose after the first ballot) dictate terms to both sides. But the defection of Beadle defeated this very politic purpose. Beadle has no doubt been converted by Knox and Fisher, in whose churches he is a deacon or a ruling elder or something else.

There was no fuss when the result was announced. Betts moved a resolution that McCulloh was elected, a piece of surplusage which he withdrew when Mr. Ruggles asked the ayes and noes on its passage. Spring proposed an inauguration and an inaugural address, but backed

out when King suggested that this business had better be hushed up and
that any parade of our choice might be impolitic.

We adjourned early. Had a long discourse with King, Hoffman,
Anderson, and Mr. Ruggles thereafter. O *Piscicule—Fecisti ridiculi—
Piscium minimiscule!* . . .

Beadle's defection may have been effected by the influence and exertions of Knox and Fisher, or perhaps by the very decided churchmanship
of the printed manifesto.

We're now just on the beginning of a shindy: legislative inquiry,
open controversy, war to the knife. King says that McCulloh will certainly accept the appointment. Seems to me not so certain. . . .

Fish says that when Colonel Benton is interrogated as to the probable fate of the Nebraska bill he replies: "Did you ever see a dog, sir, in
the month of July or August, which had been shot through the head
about a fortnight before? The condition of that animal, sir, after that
accident, is the condition of the bill you mention. Putrefaction, sir, and
decomposition, and tendency to annihilation, characterize alike the dead
dog and 'the dead bill.' "

*Strong's disgust and disappointment over the rejection of Wolcott Gibbs
were violently felt. "This Columbia College business half tempts me to turn
Roman Catholic," he wrote on April 4. "The clerical morality of that church
is certainly not below that of the Anglican Church, or of Protestantism generally. And its music is far better and higher." Feeling, like Ruggles, that a
good legislative inquiry was needed, he expressed fear that Fish was using his
strong influence at Albany to prevent one. Great excitement was felt among
the alumni, among whom the attorney Silas Weir Roosevelt (class of 1842;
an uncle of the future President Theodore Roosevelt) and George James
Cornell (class of 1839) headed a movement to censure the trustees. A pamphlet
war began to rage and attracted wide attention. Ruggles's well-written
manifesto, "The Duty of Columbia College to the Community, and its Right
to Exclude Unitarians from the Professorships of Physical Science," scattered
broadcast by the efforts of Moses H. Grinnell and others, evoked from Gouverneur Ogden a reply: "A Defence of Columbia College from the Attack of
Samuel B. Ruggles." An investigation by a committee of the state Senate in
due time took place. A dozen of the trustees declined to answer its inquiries;*

and it finally reported that while some of the individual members might have been guilty of a breach of trust, the college could not be said to have violated its charter.

April 14, GOOD FRIDAY.   To church at Trinity, where Hobart preached. Yesterday afternoon an April shower, this afternoon another, preceded by the deathliest cold chill wind and congealed before it reached us into a snowstorm which continues at the date of these presents, viz.: about midnight.

General war in Europe avowed at last; the Queen and Louis Napoleon have announced to England and France that they are at war with Russia. Probably we're entering on a historical period that will affect the map of Europe ten years hence.

Also, there is war in Columbia College, and all the signs of a coming shindy, far more bitter and vehement than anything yet. Mr. Ruggles's pamphlet is circulating far and wide, scattered by Moses H. Grinnell, backed by George Cornell and a batch of alumni. It excites attention and almost unanimous approval. The Harvard people (Mr. Ruggles is just back from Cambridge) are enthusiastic about its merits. Only Agassiz says he don't want this battle fought from within the Church. *I do.* If it's wholly without the Church, the field is not worth fighting for. From imperfect telegraphic despatches received last night, it would seem that the legislature has appointed a joint committee of inquiry, "with power to send for persons and papers," and has passed Cornell's bill giving the chairman of any such committee power to attach and imprison for contempt, or for refusal to answer a question. I anticipate a rumpus if this resolution has actually passed both houses, and it is clear that it has passed the Senate. Irreconcilable breach and "the rigor of the game" must follow. Bellows takes the same view with Agassiz, and objects to the "churchmanship" of the letter. Thank God he does. . . .

It is an immense fact that a *majority* of the churchmen in the board and H. J. Anderson (Roman Catholic) voted for Gibbs; that all the dissenters, Spring, Knox, Fisher, and Beadle, voted against him, in solid phalanx. . . .

April 15.   Easter eve. . . . At Columbia College from 1 to 2:30 with King, Knox, and Betts; meeting of our "Centennial" Committee, called at Knox's request, who thought the alumni meeting required some action by the committee, or some statement of facts to be laid before the adjourned meeting a week hence. Betts's self-complacency led him to think otherwise, and King and I saw no reason for any action. . . .

Our next meeting, first Monday of May, will be stormy, I think. McCulloh has accepted. Glad of it. But it don't raise my opinion of the man. Perhaps the Association for the Advancement of Science, about to meet at Washington, may so express itself as to change his views. . . .

April 17. . . . In the matter of Columbia College there is nothing new, except that the Senate has appointed a committee (Brooks, Hopkins, and Danforth) on its own account—the House non-concurring; and that the committee will probably act notwithstanding the non-concurrence. Unless there be much caution and circumspection, this will do far more harm than good. And I don't clearly see how it can do much real good in any way. . . .

News from across the Atlantic. The tocsin is clearly sounding for instant battle on the largest scale, with the most tremendous material agencies, and the most momentous interests depending on the issue. These months are important in the history of the century, perhaps of the age.

(Though Gurowski's vaticinations do not amount to a great deal, I used to hear him talk precisely the same talk which is written down and elaborated in *Russia As It Is*, hour after hour, and used to be bored thereby.)

But this is a serious controversy for the Old World, and for mankind, if it be vigorously prosecuted as it has begun. That the civilization of Western Europe, continental Europe, at least, is effete and worn out, like that of the Roman Empire, I can't doubt. Should the ultimate triumph of Russia introduce a new element, Cossack or Slavonic or whatever it may be, into the social life of the Old World, shattering and destroying all its present organizations, the disruption may well prove a blessing. And this seems to be what politicians hold up as the consequence of allowing Russia to go unopposed, and the reason for resisting her progress southward to the Dardanelles. As to the propriety of kicking Islamism out of Europe as it kicked itself in, four hundred years ago, I've no doubt.

The French and English forces at Malta or somewhere else have been exchanging musical compliments, the French regimental bands playing "God Save the Queen," the English, "Partant pour la Syrie." Very appropriate and significant in the latter, considering why, for what object, and in what spirit, "Dunois, the young and brave" departed thither. Alas for the old, undoubting, fraternal league of all the nation-alities of Christendom against pagans and misbelievers! Godfrey and Tancred and Saint Louis were indifferently posted up as to the balance of power.

John Bull goes joyously into the battle. But I think he will be tired before it is done (though I don't know but his rulers contemplate nothing more than a partition with their enemy of the spoils of their ally). Sup-pose he sinks or captures every Russian ship of war now afloat, drives the Czar across the Danube and out of the Principalities, bombards Odessa, Sebastopol, and Cronstadt, occupies St. Petersburg itself, how much nearer is he to victory and the conquest of peace? . . .

April 21. . . . European news vague, contradictory, and unreliable. Its utter uncertainty throws some light on the value of history in matters of detail. What the Russians have done since they crossed the Danube on the extreme left of their line and got into the notorious swamps of the Dobrudja, whether they've taken divers fortalices and strong places, Hirsova included, or have not, whether there is any demonstration against Kalifat or not, are questions no man can answer.

As was foreseen, the tempest of Saturday and Sunday was fruitful of disaster. More than one shipwreck on the Jersey shore, and sad destruc-tion of life. The *Powhatan,* stranded within three hundred feet of the beach, broke up slowly, and every one of her two or three hundred pas-sengers and crew perished in the surf.

As to Columbia College, I hear that the caucus of alumni that has been sitting from day to day through the week has adopted a scheme of action for the meeting tomorrow, and that a string of resolutions will be offered far from complimentary to the trustees. There is room for doubt whether this proposed action can be carried out, though a large majority of the older alumni incline to adopt it. The graduates of the last three or four years will probably be numerously represented, and will be generally in favor of cooperating with the trustees in a celebration. Ogden and Betts now say that they won't attend the meeting at all, from which I infer that their efforts to collect backers have failed and that they have found they will have no material to work with. Ogden has met with decided rebuffs from several persons to whom he has made application, as Dick Emmet and G. W. Wright, for instance. . . .

Have been looking into Maurice's *Theological Essays* tonight. Some things seem profoundly good and true, others (at the first glance) shallow and wrong. There seems to be much vigor and life in the "Broad Church" platform of F. D. Maurice, Charles Kingsley, and their backers. Am disposed to think their views more likely to *tell* on men and to be felt in the Church than those of either the High Church or the Evangelical party.

April 22, SATURDAY. . . . The alumni meeting was a great success. Very large and respectable, 125 present, thirty-four classes represented; Robert Kelly, Sedgwick, James A. Hamilton, John Jay, Russel, Cornell, Ike Fowler, Henry Nicoll, Rev. A. S. Leonard (converted and now adverse to the trustees), Dick Emmet, John Hamersley, Richard H. Ogden, W. T. Johnson, and so on, present and of one mind. They tried to gag Worthy Romaine, but couldn't. He declined the honorable appointment of associate secretary to take down the names of all present, and made a great speech, which the reporters tried to take down but abandoned at last, because it did not clearly appear on which side he was talking or what ideas he meant to convey. Then Weir Roosevelt took up his parable and made a speech which Anthon reports to have been clear and creditable, moving a long string of resolutions concocted in caucus during the week. Russel seconded them and made a long and vigorous talk, pitching energetically into the trustees. Leonard objected that what was done could not be undone and that it was entirely idle to pass resolutions about it (not so unreasonable a suggestion), but expressly declared himself hostile to the position taken by the trustees. Only a certain Rev. Coffee, who probably wants a D.D., and little lithping niminy-piminy Gillespie, who wants a professorship, took sides distinctly with the board. Jay offered substitutes for two of the resolutions and seems to have supported them very well, and the original resolutions thus modified were carried by about 90 votes to 30. It seems that the purport of the resolutions is to condemn and censure the policy of the board, to thank the minority, to recommend those members whose conscientious convictions interfere with the execution of their trust to resign their seats, to decline cooperation for the present with the board in any celebration, and to appoint a pretty strong committee of about thirty to ask the board about the programme of the celebration and the policy of its future administration, and report their answer to a future meeting of the alumni. On the whole, a very emphatic rebuke.

April 23. The alumni resolutions in this morning's *Herald* are better than I expected; appear to have been framed with care and accuracy and present no salient points for attack. And a list of the men who adopted them shews an array of very weighty and respectable names, Trinitarian and Unitarian. I think this is a shot that will tell a little. But it won't be as effective as Gould and Peirce and Lovering seem to suppose. . . . I hope for nothing from this demonstration, except a strong skirmish which may move all parties to increased energy and activity in moving uptown and enlarging the usefulness of the College. . . .

April 24, MONDAY. Meant to have been wildly energetic in business today, but it passed away somehow in confabulation with Mr. Ruggles, Cornell, Knox, and George Anthon over the Saturday's alumni meeting, which is conspicuous in this morning's papers, and was in fact an important demonstration. Mare's nest discovered; Betts, "Professor of Law," is also trustee. The Revised Statutes forbid any tutor or professor in an incorporated college to be a trustee of the same. Did Betts's acceptance of this professorship after Kent's death vacate his seat as trustee? If it did, Professor McCulloh is not elected. There was a tie on the ballot supposed to have resulted in his election, or rather no majority for any one candidate. It was Gibbs 9, McCulloh 10, Bache 1; eleven votes necessary for a choice. And was not Gibbs in fact elected on some of the earlier ballotings? I've not time to look back.

Rumor of an answer to Mr. Ruggles's pamphlet. Can't find out by whom, or where it can be seen. . . .

April 25. Combat thickening in Columbia College. People *vs.* Carrique in 2d Hill seems to make it clear that Betts's acceptance of the law professorship vacated his seat as trustee; *ipso facto*, that every vote he has given is a nullity. Very well for our professor of law. I hope the alumni committee which meets Saturday will suggest this little complication to the board. . . .

The pamphlet vehemently approved in all quarters. The college is like to be a "Bishop without a Church." Unless it is equal to self-sustainment in infinite absolute space, without support from its alumni or from any portion of the community, it would seem to be in a bad way.

April 26. News from Europe. No fighting yet in the Baltic; uncertain reports of Russian defeat in the Principalities and on the south side of the Danube.

May 1, MONDAY. Much complaint by the English press of delay in bringing troops into the seat of war and of inaction of the naval force in the Baltic and the Black Sea. John Bull thinks his screw-steamers and bomb-ketchers have only to bark once, and his enemies are scattered. He errs, I think; at least he is not entitled to expect so speedy and easy a victory. This looks like a grim fight. . . .

Columbia College meeting at 2 P.M. W.T.J. had written King a letter calling his attention to the fact that one if not two seats in the board are vacant by operation of law, which King read apropos of the question of approving the minutes. But King was borne down by Fisher and others and nothing came of it. . . .

May 4. Bilious. George Anthon dined here, and went with Ellie to the Crystal Palace, today "reinaugurated" under the auspices of Barnum.[12] Their report is claptrap, humbug, barrenness, and probable failure.

May 5. It seems that Gouverneur Ogden and some unknown confederates are meeting to devise an answer to Mr. Ruggles's letter, and Gouverneur considers it an outrage that that business should be thrown on him.

May 6, SATURDAY. Gouverneur Ogden has come out with a "defence" which reached me at dinner. It seems very feeble and flat, verbose, wooden, and stupid.

Went with Charlie to Century Club at eight. George Curtis, Marbury, Tracy, Durand, H. P. Gray, Bob LeRoy, Verplanck, Suydam, Ehninger, Cozzens, D. D. Field, O. S. Strong, Robert Kelly, Slosson, Schell, Van Winkle, and so on. Oysters and lobster salad and probable dyspepsia.

May 8. I think Gouverneur Ogden's pamphlet like to do no execution. Cornell, Dr. Hobart, and others pronounce it a failure; William Waddington (Gouverneur's friend) and Anderson express the same conviction; and their first impressions are significant.

May 9, TUESDAY. Got out of bed at six this sunshiny morning, breakfasted, and omnibussed down to the South Ferry, with a view to a Long Island Railroad train which the very timetable on the wall of the ferry office certified to start at 7:30. Found on crossing that it started at 7 and had gone. Also that the next train, announced in like manner for 9 A.M., had been recently postponed to 10 A.M. So I had two and a quarter hours before me to be killed in South Brooklyn. I improved the occasion by a walk to the Atlantic Dock, and took a first inspection of my "41 and 42" premises, unhappily under mortgage; on which mortgage I shan't pay off quite as much this spring as I meant to pay.

To Jamaica at last, and took a waggon to Rockaway; selected rooms,

[12] P. T. Barnum, who had a well-earned reputation for making money, had been induced by some of the stockholders to become a director of the languishing Crystal Palace enterprise. When he reluctantly consented, he was chosen president. It was already moribund, but he did what he could to arouse new interest. In his autobiography he remarks that "it was temporarily galvanized and gave several lifelike kicks."

loafed down to the beach, looked at the surf and sand hills and beach grass. Less stern and sad, I think, than the solemn cliffs of Nahant. May I not visit *that* place again! What followed so close on my last visit has colored my memories of our summer's sojourn there with tints of darkness and death, and has made that a place forbid. And, independently of all that, Nahant is full of stern and gloomy influences to which I don't want to be subjected. The glittering beach of Rockaway is cheerful compared with those austere ramparts of rock. The roll and break of the sea I watched this morning seemed inspiring and joyous when I remembered the sullen heave and subsidence of the sea on Pulpit Rock and East Point.

May 13. Looked at a *microscope* of Ross's, only $350, which I yearn to possess.

Went through the Astor Library yesterday for the first time. It is good and promises still better things.

May 15, MONDAY. Nebraska battle still raging at Washington with most dubious result. The meeting in the Park Saturday afternoon was a failure according to the *Herald* and the *Journal of Commerce*; a most stern, earnest, and unprecedented demonstration, according to the *Times*, the *Tribune*, and the *Courier*. Which is right, I don't know.

May 16. Fine weather. Dozed in the library chair till twelve, in a state of headache, then downtown and did some work, considering. Nebraska controversy still boisterous and bitter; the final, decisive explosion seems to be postponed to Saturday, when the bill will pass. Pierce seems to be trying to get up a war with Spain by way of diverting attention from this particular issue.

May 22. Long buttonholing talk with Professor Anderson today. He's more fully with the minority than I expected to find him—and condemns that murderous outlay on the Botanic Garden, and the consequent paralysis of the college for at least another generation, as heartily as I do.

Nebraska battle still undecided, but no one doubts the bill will pass the House. I'm resisting awful temptations to avow myself a Free-Soiler. Think I shall come out on the platform at last, a unit in the great Northern party the consummation of this swindle will call into being. I've never denied or doubted the wrong of slavery, assuming the fundamental dogmas of our polity to be right and true. I have denied that wrong because I could not affirm that all men were born free and equal. And I am no nearer the capacity to affirm that proposition. *Don't believe* all men so born. But if that be the conventional theory of our social institutions, we are entitled to enforce it and claim its benefits where its violation will do mischief. If North and South alike affirm the proposition, either may fairly insist on its consequences and corollaries; if that be our fundamental law, anyone may claim that it be consistently carried out, whatever he may think of its soundness.

May 23, TUESDAY.   Nebraska bill passed the House at two A.M. by a small majority. Senate will concur in the amendments. . . .

On May 30, while the free-soil press pealed its denunciation, President Pierce signed the ill-omened Kansas-Nebraska Act. By this heedless piece of legislation, Douglas had immensely deepened the chasm between the two sections and accelerated the march toward civil war. Already the forces of freedom in the North were preparing to assist in filling Kansas with anti-slavery settlers. Passage of the law was quickly followed by an explosion in Boston. The Negro Anthony Burns, a Virginia slave who had taken up residence in Massachusetts, was arrested, arraigned before a federal commissioner, and delivered over to the authorities for transportation to his former home. Rioting broke out; an attempt at rescue was frustrated; and the city, crowded with indignant men from half of New England, went into mourning. It required the united force of city police, state militia, and federal troops and sailors to carry the poor black man back into bondage. The Northern States, in their indignation over the Kansas-Nebraska Act, were soon framing Personal Liberty laws.

Strong was amusing himself this spring by scientific and literary studies. He had ordered a powerful microscope from England, with object-glasses and accessories. The cost was formidable. "But I take intense interest and delight in that sort of investigation," he wrote, "and I think it wholesome. One gets relaxation by this total change of work—and truer appreciation of the marvels around him. 'Increased Defining Power' is further insight into the marvels of God." He read John Henry Newman's University Education *with admiration: "Full of thought and truth, its reasoning and conclusions real, clear, and deep." If Newman had lost a little in polish of style by leaving Oriel College for Ireland, he had gained in other respects. Echoes of the Wolcott Gibbs case continued to rumble around the horizon. On June 5, the Columbia trustees held a meeting at which Betts, attorney, clerk of the board, and professor of law, announced that he had a painful statement to make. Referring to the communication from the alumni law committee respecting his status, he declared that although he believed their conclusions wrong, he had suffered "agony" since they had raised the question, and believed it his duty to resign both his law professorship and his post as trustee. Ruggles then wisely took the initiative, and moved that he be re-elected as trustee; which was done.*

June 10, SATURDAY. The order of *Know-Nothings* seems to have become a material fact. Late elections at Washington and Philadelphia shew it to be a potent agency. "Street-preaching" rows here and in Brooklyn prove it aggressive and bellicose and capable of using not only the ballot box but the carnal weapon. Every recent indication of Northern sentiment points to vigorous reaction against the Nebraska bill and the formation of a strong anti-slavery party at the North. Should the next move of the Administration be war with Spain, as predicted, there will be an energetic and immense minority dissenting.

June 18, SUNDAY. The conjunction of Barnum and Jullien at the so-called "Musical Congress with 1,500 performers" naturally produced one of the grandest humbugs on record. Went with Ellie, George Anthon, and Miss Tote. The last-named two dined here, as did Jack Ehninger, but after sitting down with them, I had to retire to the library for a headachy nap. The crowd was enormous. It is estimated at fifteen thousand by some and forty thousand by others. I've no opinion at all as to the accuracy of either estimate. But for some time after taking our seats I was seriously exercised about the possibilities of falling galleries and panic-stricken multitudes, and was tempted to evacuate the building at once.

The building is most defective, acoustically. Sound passes off into dome and transepts and is not reverberated by its flimsy walls of sheet iron and glass. Solos were inaudible; an occasional emphatic note or two, or a phrase from the orchestra, kept one *au courant*. To those who did not know *The Messiah* and so on, the solo pieces must have been a great mystery. Beside the unfitness of the building, there was the great mass of muslin and broadcloth behind the solo singers (the orchestra and chorus) which absorbed instead of reflecting their voices. And the incessant shuffling in and out of the vast crowd that was marching into and about the building was sufficient to drown the voice of any but Stentor or Boanerges. Four choruses from *The Messiah* (including the Hallelujah, which was encored!!!, and the first chorus, "All flesh shall see it together,") certainly gave to them all new power, and clearer expression of their meaning. That first chorus of *The Messiah*, it seems to me, may perhaps be the most awful embodiment of thought extant in music, with the possible exception of the "Hallelujah." The rest of the concert was mostly trash. Overture to *William Tell* was unheard except the sharply cut, martial finale. We watched Jullien leading its opening movement and wondered what he could be doing, till a familiar squeak or two very high up in the scale indicated that the orchestra was at work on this overture. Wagner's *Tannhäuser* Overture was rather better—audible, and seems nice. Of the Symphony in C minor only the third movement and part of the finale were played; the former half audibly, the latter very vilely.

As to the grand "Fireman's Quadrille," words can't express its clap-trap. It's a pleasure to see humbug so consistently, extensively, and cleverly applied: military bands beginning to play in the distance, drawing nearer and finally marching into the orchestra; red and blue fire visible through the windows of the dome; a clamorous chorus shouting "Go it, 20," "Play away, 49," "hay-hay," and so on. The audacity of the imposition reconciled one to its grossness. But Jullien is a genius after all. There were taking points, even in this atrocious production; e.g., a very clever appropriation of phrases from the second movement of Beethoven's *devilish* A Symphony, and some admirable pieces of instrumentation meant to imitate the thundering, quivering, shuddering rush and roar of falling walls. Friday and Saturday nights the performances have been less ambitious and the audiences much smaller, though the price was reduced. I doubt the success of the speculation. I doubt whether the stock ever struggles much above 21. I sympathize with those who bought at par and held on for a rise at 175. The building seems all but gutted. Its character has changed. It is now merely an extension of Barnum's Museum.

June 20. After the everlasting rains of the spring, we are entering on a period of drowth. The sun sets, a well-defined, coppery disk like a red-hot penny in a dark room, and all the western sky is curtained with dull, coppery haze. Cholera is in town, and pretty active—fifty-odd deaths last week. But many of these cases were doubtless aggravated diarrhœa and cholera morbus, and all are thus far confined to the lowest and filthiest classes, whose existence from one day to another in their atmosphere of morphic influences is a triumph of vital organization and illustrates the vigorous tenacity of life (under the deadliest conditions) bestowed on the human species. But we may well be destined to undergo an epidemic this summer. Coleridge's Cologne was not more fetid or mephitic than this metropolis. The stinks of Centre Street lift up their voices. Malarious aromata rampage invisible through every street, and in the second-rate regions of the city, such as Cherry Street, poor old Greenwich Street, and so on, atmospheric poison and pungent foetor and gaseous filth cry aloud and spare not, and the wayfaring man inhales at every breath a pair of lungs full of vaporized decomposing gutter mud and rottenness. Alas for our civic rulers, whose office it is to see that this be not so. . . .

Old Davenport's very promising young son, George, seems to have gone suddenly to the dogs. An only son, his father full of pride (ill-concealed under censures of his extravagance) in his appetite for books and music, married within the year, he seems to have taken all at once to drink and gambling, to borrowing from everybody, swindling his clients, and to reckless shortsightedness and dishonesty that looks like monomania. I'm sorry for his steady-going old Presbyterian father, and also for Charley Strong, though victimized to the extent of only $115, which he's not like to see again. I should have loaned the young gentle-man very readily anything my bank account would conveniently stand, had he come to me, for we all had the fullest confidence in him. His father has made himself penniless to meet a $2,500 embezzlement, monies advanced by some society, of which he was treasurer and master, George "Counsel," for an investment on mortgage, and fraudulently stopped *in transitu*. His wife, the daughter of a Connecticut parson, went home to her father. Poor little woman, how desolate she probably is this evening! She left today and I suppose is now in the midst of the eager, indignant home circle, feebly striving to palliate, and excuse, and suggest doubts, with all the weapons of her poor little loving woman's wit; or more probably, as it's past twelve, trying to go to sleep in her own little room of former times, and thinking of her dirty little swindling scamp of a husband, in the sure and certain hope that he'll yet put down calumny and shew himself the greatest and best of men.

July 6.   Wall Street all agog with the fraud on the New Haven Railroad Company by its President Robert Schuyler, whose failure was announced last week.[13] A swindle of near two millions, by no nameless money-making speculator, but by one of our "first" people in descent and social position and supposed wealth. . . . This swindle of Schuyler's is a great disaster and may well be the first crack that preludes general

[13] Robert Schuyler, president of the New York & New Haven Railroad, had signed hypothecated stock certificates to the value of about two millions. He absconded and efforts at pursuit failed.

APPLETON'S BOOKSTORE, 1853

BROADWAY, BETWEEN LEONARD STREET AND CATHERINE LANE

CHARLES KING
PRESIDENT OF COLUMBIA COLLEGE

crash and collapse. It has already, as its immediate consequence, weakened all confidence in a very large class of securities.

July 19. . . . Cholera has become somewhat threatening. The Board of Health makes daily reports. As yet, the cases are not very numerous, and the type of disease seems not specially malignant. Nineteen reported yesterday, I think, and two or three less today. . . .

July 26. Still fearfully and wonderfully hot. Cholera makes some progress, but less than one would expect, for this is said . . . to be the severest July since 1822. But many are a little out of order intestinally; cholic inflammation of the bowels and "cholerine" abound. . . .

We went to Rockaway Friday morning. Blistering heat. Waited at Jamaica some hours and dined there, then went to the Pavilion more comfortably. That evening did not promise much. Crowd, heat, bad fare, and mosquitoes, said to be exceptional and anomalous. Since then things have looked up a little, but the fare is indisputably villainous. Stayed over Saturday and Sunday. Saturday morning I took a long walk on the beach with my shoes and stockings off and pantaloons rolled up the knee. Result—pair of blistered legs that nearly deprived me of the power of locomotion the next day. Not only were they superficially *scalded*, but every now and then cramps came in the calf, so that I could not use the limb for a few minutes.

Came to town Monday; up Tuesday afternoon; down again this morning.

Saturday night the crowd was immense; lots of people were turned away without mercy. The Baxters came along with a large party, but three of them had to make their way back to Jamaica—the rest found accommodations on the floor somewhere. Mr. Ruggles slept on a sofa in Ogden Hoffman's cottage.

People at the Hotel: Carson Brevoort and wife, Mr. and Mrs. Cousinery, Mrs. Edward S. Gould and musical daughter, the Gerards, Le Barbiers, Mr. and Mrs. Meletta, *cum multis aliis*, mostly of a second and third rate type. . . .

Columbia College meeting Monday thinly attended. Van Wagenen read the proposed answer of the board to the queries of the Senate committee, which was ordered printed for examination. It denies categorically that any religious test has been imposed. Then Betts produced the long-expected result of his labors over the proposed remodeling of the college course. Long, prosy, and feeble, warm water at its tenth dilution. I thought Betts had more virility.

August 3, THURSDAY. . . . Judge Bronson is smashed financially by the fall of the Empire Stone Dressing Co. Gilbert Cobb & Johnson have stopped. Murder of Colonel Loring at the St. Nicholas last night by a Southerner, crazy drunk. In a healthy state of society, the murderer would be strangulated, drunk or sober, within twenty-four hours, instead of being given his "law" like a fox, with challenges to the jury and exceptions to evidence. The patent and notorious crime, even though perpetrated in voluntary mania, would be followed up by instant judgment and swift execution. . . .

August 9, WEDNESDAY. Walked uptown this afternoon and inspected a quite splendid little conflagration in Elizabeth Street near Spring; two or three wooden shanties blazing and disgorging an incredible number of cubic feet of Irish humanity and filthy feather beds. While I was there, another alarm and red glare to the south sent us on a trot down to Broome Street, west of Centre, where a certain old meeting-house was in vigorous combustion. Saw it burned out and walked home.

August 14, MONDAY. Went to Rockaway on the sultry afternoon of Saturday and found all there as it should be; Ellen and Johnny well and bright, and the two young ladies enjoying themselves. Saturday night was rather brilliant. People waltzed like mad, and they absolutely got up a German Cotillion. It was the culminating point of the season, I suspect, which is now just on the turn. Probably the departures will begin to outnumber the arrivals this week.

Sunday morning I took a long stroll westward on the beach and among the white sand hills and came back to hear Dr. Tyng read the service and preach a sermon in the very worst style of Low Churchism and pseudo-Evangelicalism. Full of anecdote it was, about suddenly converted Hindoos, and little Sabbath-school girls on their dying beds telling their pastors how they had dreamed about Heaven, and aged saints at New Haven expatiating after dinner on the blessedness and beauty of Earth, and the like nauseating twaddle; and underlying all this froth and trumpery was a stratum of the basest plausibilities and sophistries and bogus truisms and disguised falsehoods about the Love of God, and how all differences of creed vanish and are of no account where that exists.

August 30. Everything in Wall Street looks black. Some failure or other almost daily, and constant false reports of others, doing nearly as much harm as the reality could do. Erie Railroad is the index of the daily fluctuations of confidence. Since last April it has fallen fearfully; whether it will get up again at all or sink finally to zero and go into the

hands of mortgagees is a great question at present. My monetary condition harmonizes with that of the great financial system in which I am
a helpless and inoffensive unit, my bank account being at the lowest ebb,
while merciless creditors persist in reducing it still lower by bills that
come in thick and fast as mosquitoes into a Rockaway stage. Wonder
whether I'm on the verge of insolvency.

Rockaway is a barren place beyond question, but I was half sorry to
leave it as I stood on the piazza this morning waiting for the stage. The
sky was clear, the air like October, the sea still and blue, and long heavy
rollers raised by the wind of yesterday coming slowly in, not visible till
each rose gradually into a long ridge with its upper edge sharply defined
and then toppled over and came down in a cataract of sparkling white
foam. Were there a few resources there for times when it's too hot for
the beach, I could get on there very comfortably. . . .

Some good stories well told by Ogden Hoffman, Jr., last night. For
example, San Francisco judge in a bar-room looking perplexed, biting
his nails, scratching his head, and smoking a cigar with fitful puffs,
clearly much exercised about something. "I've got one of the worst
cases before me I ever knew, that great land claim of Smith *v.* Thompson,
very difficult to know what I ought to do. Jones and Brown have just
been arguing the law points before me for more'n six hours, and it's a
very difficult case, *for they're both on 'em friends of mine.*" Same functionary
charging a jury, states the law applicable to the case, in which plaintiff is
plainly entitled to a verdict, and winds up in this wise: "Well, gentlemen,
that's the law, but I don't really think it's God Almighty's justice, and
I guess you may just as well find for the defendant." Returned Californian
who has made his pile comes East to visit his home in New England,
but since his departure thence, a net-work of railroads has grown up
around it. He takes railroad No. 1 and brings up thirty miles to the south
of it; then tries railroad No. 2, which sets him down forty miles south-
southwest; then No. 3 and finds himself twenty miles too far northeast;
and after a week's indefatigable railroad traveling in every direction,
gives up the attempt in disgust: "If he had a mule, he could find his way
there, but there's no use trying to travel in this infernal country," and
goes straight back to California.

August 31, THURSDAY.   Nothing very noteworthy in Wall Street; no
relief in the stockmarket, and no alleviation of the drought. The very soil
seems to be in active combustion in some western regions; burning woods
have fired the substance of what were peaty bogs. Till noon today there

were signs of rain, but the clouds vanished, and the sun came out scalding
hot. Tonight sultry and still. Charles E. Strong dined here; afterwards
Mr. Ruggles, Jack, and George C. Anthon came in. Most of the evening
spent on the front door-steps. I walked down to Bond Street and called
on Miss Betty Rhinelander, and arranged about our intended journey to
West Point (Cozzens's, that is) tomorrow morning. . . .

Mr. Ruggles just returned from another sojourn among the Wise
Men of the East, *videlicet* at Cambridge, Boston, Nahant, and elsewhere.
Much impressed and exercised by Newman's *University* book, which I
lent him and which I want to read again. I was pretty sure the Rev. J. H.
Newman would harpoon him.

September 6, WEDNESDAY.   On Friday morning we went to Cozzens's
Hotel, West Point, in steamer *Armenia*. Miss Betty Rhinelander accompanied us, also Jack Ehninger. Pete [Strong] and wife on board, also
two of his sisters on way to Catskill. Sultry, muggy, and overcast, rain
manifestly close at hand. Found the hotel very full; got comfortable
rooms by good fortune. Lounged there the day. Saturday was just such
another, rain certain at last, indeed a few faltering drops did come down
while Ehninger and I were dawdling in the woods round the "Butter-
milk" millponds, but it was a failure, and Sunday morning the sun came
out blistering and to blister, and hasn't been "in" since.

People at West Point: Luther Bradish, urbane and Ciceronian at all
temperatures alike;[14] Judge Ulshoeffer and wife and two nice daughters;
Miss Jane Emmet; two Miss Irvings, pleasant but nowise handsome;
Miss Clark (Jem Ruggles's divinity), fresh and attractive looking but
not pretty, I think, even in that qualified sense in which alone I admit
brunettes capable of being pretty; Miss Rhinelander; Rev. Robert Howland; and so on. Also General Scott. . . .

Mario and Grisi don't seem to call out any special Lindesque furor.
Bad lookout for their enterprising importer.[15] Another Catholic *vs.*
Protestant row at Newark—Irish church gutted; those infatuated, pig-
headed Celts seemingly the aggressors, as usual. We may well have a

[14] Bradish (1783–1863), a prominent up-state Whig, had been a friend of John
Quincy Adams, Henry Clay, Daniel Webster, and other chieftains of his party, had
served as lieutenant-governor, and had unsuccessfully run for governor. At this time
he was president of the New-York Historical Society and the American Bible Society.

[15] James H. Hackett, the able character actor, who had managed various theatres,
had just brought Giulia Grisi and Matteo Mario to the newly opened Academy of
Music in Union Square. Their troupe gave *Norma, Lucrezia Borgia, I Puritani,* and
other operas.

memorable row here before the fall elections are over, and perhaps a religious war within the next decade, if this awful vague, mysterious, new element of Know-Nothingism is as potent as its friends and political wooers seem to think it. I'm sick of Celtism; it's nothing but imbecility, brag, and bad rhetoric. If the Know-Nothings were only political, not politico-religious, I'd join them. Stephen A. Douglas seems to have been badly beat and snubbed into silence on his own dunghill, to wit, Chicago. Foreign news down to August 23 unimportant. Bomarsund and the Aland Islands taken; no great exploit, fait, or geste, all things considered. Why don't Andrew Ross send out my compound achromatic microscope and its appurtenances, due weeks ago? But it's as well, for I don't know how I'd pay the duties just now, without negotiating a loan.

September 14, THURSDAY.   Went to Columbia College at two. Meeting of trustees in the President's new room of the library, the old room having been refitted for the department of physical science; the first material change within my memory in that temple of classical fogyism— for which thanks to the shindy of last winter. The meeting was brief and not important. The answer of the board to the Senate committee interrogatories was adopted after a brief discussion, and under a sort of protest from Mr. Ruggles, and we adjourned. . . . Haight surprised me by the information that Wainwright is seriously if not dangerously ill with bilious fever; and little Rogers, who rode up with me in the car, made it still worse, and said Hosack and Wilks had given him up—which I don't believe. To do Wainwright justice, he has worked indefatigably, and imprudently, in his episcopal office—periled if not sacrificed his health, without example and against earnest remonstrance.

September 19, TUESDAY.   Wainwright continues very ill. His case was reported nearly desperate this afternoon, and on sending to his house tonight the response is "no better." So a vacant episcopate before many days is not unlikely. This materially complicates my relations with G. H. Swords, Minturn, and C. M. Connolly. I'm depositary of $200, meant for purchase money of the Twenty-fifth Street lot, and belonging to somebody other than myself, to whom exactly may be debatable. I fear this case is a very bad one. Poor "poppy" Wainwright—would it were in my power to help you! Allopathy and homeopathy may have a battle over his remains, for he was attended in the first instance by Dr. Gray, who was displaced for Hosack and Wilks.

September 22.   Another expedition to Hyde Park by railroad Wednesday afternoon; agreeable ride enough, cool, clean, and free from dust.

Read a rather absurd book, *Peter Schlemihl in America,* which I got for the sake of George Anthon's "Eagle Lectern Correspondence," reprinted therein. Watched a gorgeous sunset. Strange that the splendors of our fall sunsets, so infinitely beyond all that art can dream of accomplishing, don't sometimes drive ambitious artists to suicide. Reached Hyde Park long after dark, and walked up with the indefatigable and ubiquitous Hall. . . .

Dr. Wainwright was reported better Wednesday morning, and I thought he had a fair chance of recovery. . . . But last evening's papers announced that his case was finally pronounced hopeless, and he died, it seems, at five yesterday afternoon. He will be deeply regretted. His pleasant manners made him pretty generally popular, and it was admitted by everybody that his administration thus far had been efficient and successful. . . .

Rumor that George Curtis's relations with Miss Eliza Winthrop are to be renewed. Not at all unlikely, and I dare say a very good thing for Curtis, though everybody is so *down* on the young lady for being intellectually unworthy that great man. I think a pretty, affectionate, healthy-minded girl good enough for any man, though he had written the *Nile Notes* of the "Howadji." Special force of character or intellect are dangerous things in a woman; unless combined with high religious principle, I believe they're apt to make her unhappy, and to be as scourges and scorpions unto that forlorn and woeful caitiff, her husband.

September 26, TUESDAY. Attended poor Dr. Wainwright's funeral at Trinity, Saturday, as one of the vestry. The coffin was in the room on the north side of the church; the face of its occupant peaceful and natural. Church was very densely crowded. Services well conducted; funeral sermon or address by Higby impressive, and unlike most productions of that class, in good taste.

The Bishop is deservedly regretted. I had supposed his administration would be one of indolence and white kid gloves, but it was laborious and earnest. His intercourse with the poor congregation and clergy of country parishes and semi-barbarous frontier missionary stations was such as to make him popular even with them. He was very anxious, by the by, that our litigation with St. George the Martyr should be avoided. Just before his illness set in, he sent for Minturn to tell him so, and that he was going to see Barclay and insist on some settlement, and if nothing could be done, to bring the matter before the Convention in a special message or some other manifesto.

Convention meets tomorrow. Many think it would be indelicate and unbecoming to go so promptly into an election and that the whole subject had better lie over. It don't so strike me. The longer it is postponed, the less chance is there that the election will be harmonious, the more likely that bitterness and party-feeling will grow rampant again. Haight is talked of by the Trinity Church clique; also Southgate by others, and Vinton. Taylor will probably receive the first vote of the Low-Church people. . . .

September 29, FRIDAY.   Senate committee in session, and some indications that their inquiry will be prosecuted with vigor. Mr. Ruggles and Gouverneur Ogden subpoenaed for next Monday; report that all the trustees are to be put on the stand. We may have a shindy yet, though the alumni committee seems to have backed out and disappeared. Probably it will be best to state, in answer to any enquiry about religious tests, that certain members, three or four at least of the board, declared that they could not vote for a Unitarian; that as to their names, many of them say that they consider whatever is said in the board as confidential; and that (though I think otherwise) respect for their views makes it proper that I ask to be excused answering that question. I'm half-ashamed of such an answer, however.

October 4.   The Senate committee sat yesterday and today. Mr. Ruggles yesterday answered the enquiry of the committee as to declarations of trustees at some length, and stated facts fully and clearly, without names. Strange I should have overlooked the considerations that enabled him to do so, without coming in conflict with Lord and Wood's opinion, and to illustrate his position by a reference to Gouverneur Ogden's viscid lucubrations. The objection to Gibbs was not "private or personal"; it was an objection to a *class* and to him as one of that class.

This morning at ten-thirty I found a summons and interrogatory on my desk, to be answered at eleven. Got to the college a little before twelve. Saw W. H. Hobart; found the committee had adjourned and that he had caved in and collapsed and *declined to answer* the enquiry addressed to each trustee whether he had voted in reference to the religious opinions of any candidate. Walked far uptown with him and down again, discussing the merits of the objection to answer, founded on the alleged "sanctity of the ballot," in which he had acquiesced and concurred, and which he was a little ashamed to have adopted. He is without backbone, unvertebrated.

Concocted a very brief answer for myself and handed it to Brooks at three. I think it will be found to hold water should it be criticised.

October 6. The *Arctic* considerably past due; some uneasiness about her. George F. Allen is on board. My microscope is in the *American Eagle,* which sailed September 15. News by the *Canada* that the allied expedition has effected a landing on the Crimea and is marching on Sebastopol. Two to one they take the place, but there will be, or more probably has been before this, some very stern and serious tragedy preliminary to its fall.

October 9. Weather very warm and summerlike of late, to the mighty encouragement of all mosquitodom. *Arctic* still missing; people who've friends on board begin to talk nervously about her. At the vestry meeting tonight, when the report of the evening gun (from the Navy Yard in Governor's Island) was heard, half a dozen men simultaneously interrupted a viscid oration of Dunscomb's about the Albany Street Committee, by exclaiming aloud: "There's the *Arctic* at last!" But it was a mistake. Trial of Graham for the murder of Colonel Loring at the St. Nicholas nearly concluded. Rumpus arising from the discovery that a cousin of the prisoner's wife was on the jury, and O'Conor's vehement, forcible, overbearing resistance of any action to cure that oversight, has probably injured the defendant a little, but he won't be convicted, although the juror in question is withdrawn by consent. There will be a disagreement, or a verdict of manslaughter. The *Know-Nothings* have been holding a convention and making themselves ridiculous by their nomination of Daniel Ullman for Governor.[16] Some say it's a mere ruse or trick, and that the real intent and design of this mysterious order, the very existence of which is not certainly known, will be revealed only by the result of the November election. Maybe so, but I rather think *Know-Nothingism* is a humbug that has seen its most prosperous days.

Went with Mr. Ruggles Saturday to the "Crystal Palace." Exhibition a little better than I'd expected to find it, but barren and naked compared with the splendors of a year ago. At Trinity Church yesterday,

---

[16] The campaign for the governorship was in full swing. The Whigs had nominated Myron H. Clark, a merchant and reformer who had pushed a prohibition law through the legislature only to see it vetoed by Governor Horatio Seymour. The Democrats split, the "Hards" nominating Greene C. Bronson and the "Softs" (most of whom detested the Kansas-Nebraska Act) renominating Seymour. The Native Americans, who suddenly displayed great strength, selected a New York attorney of pronounced appetite for office, Daniel Ullman. The ensuing contest was confused and exciting.

Sebastian Bach Hodges preached a decent sermon. His brother, Jubal Hodges, is understood to be an *Irvingite*. That sect has a synagogue or meeting-house of some kind in 16th Street.

Sophie has left us!, and was married at three today to one George Alger who works in a piano factory somewhere, at $12 a week. I hope he'll make her as good a husband as she deserves, for a nobler character than that dumpy little German girl's it would be hard to find. So perfectly simple-minded and single-minded and naïve and unselfish and full of unconscious generous impulse that she might pass for the Princess of one of Grimm's *Kinder-Mädchen* in her period of humiliation as *Gänse Mädchen* or *Kammer Magd*, waiting for the true prince to appear and dress her in pearls and diamonds. I remember one severe night winter before last when some old colored woman who'd been working here, scrubbing or some such thing, during the day, was going home, hearing that Sophie had given her money to enable her to ride, and cut her own shawl in two and given her half.

New York was suddenly stunned—the word is not too strong—by news of one of the greatest maritime disasters in history. The Arctic, one of the four crack liners of E. K. Collins's company (the others being the Atlantic, Pacific, and Baltic) had become overdue. Anxiety over its fate mounted. On the afternoon of the 11th October, intelligence came from Newfoundland that she had sunk after colliding with a screw-propelled steamship. Many in New York had friends and relatives among the nearly four hundred persons aboard. As details trickled in, little by little a terrible story was told. Running through a fog about fifty miles off Cape Race, the Arctic, about noon on September 27th, had crashed into the French vessel Vesta. Efforts were made to keep the liner afloat by manning the pumps. As she steadily filled with water, the undisciplined crew became panicky. When four lifeboats were lowered, Captain Luce tried to get them loaded with women and children; but the firemen rushed them and officers and men got most of the places. At 4:45 P.M., the Arctic went down with the captain aboard, holding his crippled child in his arms. As it happened, he was able to save his life by clinging to the paddle-box; but nearly all the passengers were drowned—among them the wife and two children of Collins himself, and the family of one of his chief financial backers, James Brown. A great outcry arose, for even if the six lifeboats had all been filled in proper fashion, they would have been utterly inadequate. The disaster lent impetus to the demand that all passenger ships be built with watertight compartments. It was by virtue of such compartments that the Vesta *was saved. Although the financial loss of the Collins line was largely covered by insurance, the calamity sapped public confidence in it and contributed to its early demise.*

The Anglo-French allies had effected a landing on the Crimean peninsula, and on September 20 won the battle of the River Alma there. Hopes ran high in London and Paris for the early capture of the Russian fortress Sebastopol and the ending of the war. Lack of adequate preparation and blundering leadership, however, caused protracted delays, during which inadequate food and bad sanitation cost tens of thousands of lives. The struggle was destined to drag into the year 1856 before Russia sued for peace.

October 11. Today will long be had in bitter remembrance by many. Those to whom its sad news announced no personal calamity and private grief will not soon forget the general mournful excitement and agitation that stopped all the workings of Wall Street this morning and kept brokers and lawyers and business men of all sorts around the newspaper offices and telegraphs all day long.

There was no serious feeling of uneasiness about the *Arctic* yesterday. It was taken for granted that she had put back in consequence of the breaking of a shaft or some such accident. I was at the Novelty Works yesterday afternoon (with Henry Youngs, about furnaces for Trinity Chapel) and talked of the missing steamer with Horatio Allen. He "wasn't anxious," there couldn't have been anything serious the matter, unless possibly fire, and that was not very likely. There would be news this morning by the Cunard steamer. I was waked this morning by the voices of the newsboys, something about "the *Arctic* and four hundred lives," and sent out at once for the extra.

What a chill that proclamation must have sent into scores of households! How many people sprang up at the sound of that half-inarticulate nasal cry, and hurried off to get the paper and refused to entertain the idea that they had heard the announcement aright, and paid their sixpences and unfolded their purchase in desperate haste, and saw the terrible truth in print! Allen, I. G. Pearson, Joseph Brown, Woodruff—to those households and many more it was the voice of death.

On Wednesday, the 27th September, the *Arctic*, being about 40 miles off Cape Race, in a dense fog, going at full speed, ran into, or was run into, by an iron-propeller steamer. What became of the propeller nobody pretends to say. It is generally supposed that she foundered with all on board. The *Arctic* floated for a time, probably about four hours, and then sank. Many of her crew are saved. Nearly all her two hundred passengers perished.

Three of E. K. Collins's family, wife, son, and daughter, my old tutor Abner Benedict and his wife, Woodruff (W. & Leonard) Lord's brother-in-law, Asaph Stone and his wife and young daughter, poor little George Pearson, young William Brown and his wife (daughter of Charles Moulton) and their child, his sister, George F. Allen, wife and child (Mrs. Allen another sister of Brown's), Edward Sandford, LeRoy Newbold, Captain Luce, Babcock in Twenty-second Street, George S. Howland the Brooklyn operator, and many others of whom I had more or less knowledge are lost. There is a faint possibility that some may have been saved in the boats, or picked up. Gilbert (G., Cobb, & Johnson), who was thought to have perished, has reached Halifax, with a nephew of Gibson's and two or three other passengers and a large detachment of the crew.

Captain Luce stuck to the ship with his only child, a boy of fourteen and a cripple. He refused to entrust the child to Bahlaam, the second officer. I understand from Gourlie (who had it from Dorian, the third officer) that Luce had no confidence in Bahlaam, and that Bahlaam showed sufficient reason for that want of confidence by leaving the ship with the boat in which he'd been ordered to keep astern or alongside and help construct the raft.

It is a sickening business; worse, I think, than the *Lexington* tragedy of fourteen years ago, worse even than the butchery on board the *Henry Clay*, at least in the number lost. There is a very unpleasant disproportion between the number of the crew and of the passengers known to have been saved. To be sure, self-preservation is the common instinct of waiter and fireman, Wall Street broker and Fifth Avenue millionaire, and the strong-armed sailors and engineers can't be blamed perhaps for acting on their earlier information of the extent of the peril and using their superior strength to fill the boats and save themselves. But it's hard to think of the scores of delicate women whose only chance of safety was thus destroyed, and who were left to perish without hope. It was the business of the officers to keep all hands under control and to provide what little help there was first for those who were least able to help themselves.

Captain Luce has given proof before this of decision and force such as the occasion required. But he was left with inadequate support; his first officer, Gourlie (brother of John H. Gourlie), had been sent off at once in quest of the propeller and could not be taken on board while the engines continued to work, and is not yet heard of. Bahlaam, the second officer, seems to have sneaked away. Dorian, the third, was engaged on the raft, so Luce must have been almost single-handed, dealing with a crowd of terrified passengers; and worse, with the firemen and coal-passers, men with whom the officers are ordinarily not much in contact, and who swarmed up from their murky depths below intent on availing themselves of any chance of escape. Never knew till today that Luce's wife was Eleanor's aunt, a sister of Charles and Dan Fearing. She is left a widow and childless.

Poor James Brown, two daughters, a son-in-law, a son and daughter-in-law, two grandchildren, all swept off together. William Brown's wife was Miss Clara Moulton, daughter of Charles Moulton. He lost his first wife in the spring of 1849 by malignant smallpox assailing her in her first confinement. How that household has been scourged by calamity!

October 12. The fatal propeller that encountered the *Arctic* is safe, it seems, and has brought into port some thirty or forty of the *Arctic's* crew; none of her passengers. Sad to think that had the two steamers remained together and not been hidden from each other by that disastrous fog, not a life of those on board the *Arctic* need have been lost. It will probably turn out that the crew and especially the engineers of the *Arctic* deserve the severest censure. Dorian tells Gourlie that the engineers abandoned their posts the moment the lower fires were put out by the advancing water, and looked out for themselves, and that had they remained at the engines, the upper fires would have amply sufficed to work the steam pumps, which were of capacity and power sufficient to have kept her afloat almost indefinitely with any amount of leakage.

James Brown was hardly expected to live through yesterday, so crushed and shattered was he by the terrible news of his bereavement. Isaac Greene Pearson stumbled on the intelligence that he had lost his only son as he turned over his morning paper before breakfast. There is a fearful element of tragedy in this, our human life; sorrow, bitterness, and agony that may break out upon any one of us, rending and devastating, at any moment.

October 14. We've passed through another stage of excitement about the *Arctic* today. At about ten-thirty a despatch arrived announcing that Captain Luce, George F. Allen, and one Smith of Edinburgh had been picked up by the barque *Cambria* and were at Montreal. Afterwards it appeared that three or four passengers, beside several of the crew, had been also saved, and Luce commenced sending on a statement, but the wires broke down, I suppose with this storm, and the despatch was left unfinished. Of course, I did little all the morning but rush about through the rain to newspaper offices, and Brown Brothers, and so on, and talk with people in sheltered doorways, picking up and imparting the contradictory stories that were afloat.

Luce went down with the sinking wreck, holding his poor crippled son in his arms, rose twice, the second time with one of the paddle boxes which had probably been started by the collision. It gave a lurch as he neared it, and the child's brains were dashed out. He gained it, nevertheless, with Allen, and the rest of this batch of survivors, and many more, who dropped off one by one before rescue came. . . .

I shouldn't like to be Gilbert, or any of those men whose strength or coolness enured to their own benefit in the scramble for life and who secured themselves places in the boats. Very possibly I should have done the same. I can't blame them for yielding to the strong instinct that makes every living creature cling to life, but I should hate to be in their shoes. I should quit this community, or die of nervous fever. And if Gilbert were in fact engaged to Miss Maria Brown and got into the boat, and beckoned to her, and she drew back or hesitated and her place was taken by the insurgent firemen and deck hands, and he "had to" push off without her? . . .

Poor George Pearson stands out in the shadowy crowd of frightened passengers and heartless crew, the one figure of a gentleman, the only individual known to have been occupied with thoughts of the helpless people about him, not wholly with care for himself. The husbands and brothers and fathers, of course, thought of those whom their instincts taught them to care for.

October 16. Nothing new about the *Arctic*. From people's talk I judge that opinion is setting strong against the survivors who took the boats, Gilbert particularly. His statement and Mitchell's in the morning papers don't look well. Gilbert recounts his exertions to save the ladies of the Brown party. They are the apologies of a man who had failed to get them seats in an omnibus as they came out of Wallack's with the crowd. Mitchell speaks of its being prudent to keep at "a respectful distance" from the sinking ship. A judiciously selected adjective certainly! Everybody almost speaks bitterly of the survivors. I'd rather be George Pearson than any of them.

October 19. Charley called on Luce this morning and spent a couple of hours with him. He regrets the fuss and laudation of which he is the subject and says that he did nothing but what was his plain duty, and that he deserves no special honor. I fear it is true that he was not equal to the emergency, and that Horatio Allen, and others competent to judge, are right in saying that a commander more energetic and thoughtful than Luce could have saved crew and passengers. In four hours and a half, much might have been done that for some reason or other was left undone. Even after the dastardly defection of the engineers and subordinate officers, there was an abundant force of able-bodied men left which a vigorous head and commander would have made efficiently available. But Luce is not to be condemned or censured because he was without extraordinary genius and capacity of command.

The passengers, abandoned for an hour and a half on the quarterdeck, after they were abandoned by those who had succeeded in saving the boats, behaved well, and met death with dignity. There were no outcries or lamentations. . . .

October 22. . . . This evening Miss Rosalie and her sister were here, and for a season W. Templeton J., George Anthon, and Theodore Winthrop, who has been in perils by land and by water on the Isthmus, in Nicaragua and California, and at the headwaters of various rivers unknown to the present writer; skirmishing with Indians, shooting jaguars, and doing and suffering other things incident to journeying in desert places and among pagan savages. But also this has not taken the stiffness out of his vertebral column, nor the solemnity of his face. He's a nice, intelligent fellow, I believe, but when with ladies always looks and behaves as if he were at a funeral.

News came yesterday of Sir John Franklin and his party, at last. How authentic the news may be remains a little uncertain, for it seems to come through two several sets of Esquimaux, unreliable links in any chain of evidence. It is that Sir John and his party died of starvation in 1850 after their ships had been crushed in the ice somewhere about Fox Channel, and that when they perished they were trying to make their way southward to the Hudson Bay settlements.[17] I think people generally will feel

[17] Sir John Franklin's Arctic expedition of 1845–1848 in the ships *Erebus* and *Terror* had for its main object the discovery of the Northwest Passage, which it substantially achieved; but he died on June 11, 1847, and his surviving men, forced to desert their ice-beset ships, all perished. The information here given was not authentic, and the truth about the expedition was not learned until in 1859 the British ship *Fox* found skeletons and a record in a cairn.

relieved by the intelligence, for there has been for some time past very little hope of his safety and this news, if reliable, sets the matter at rest.

Have subscribed to the Philharmonic, and went to the first rehearsal at three-thirty yesterday with Ellie at Niblo's Saloon. Heard the *Eroica* played, most of it twice. Beethoven was undeniably "some pumpkins." I'm still unable to hold the fourth movement of that symphony worthy of the other three. The first half of it is simply antic-grotesque, and means nothing to me.

October 24. A messenger from Wall Street with the news that James Foster (*Count* Foster, the leader of forlorn hopes for the endowment of opera) was very ill and wanted to see me.[18] Went forthwith to his house in Bond Street. The servant said he was very sick indeed, with the "diaree," and no better. Waited awhile in his gorgeously decorated drawing room, and was then shewn upstairs. Found him in bed; Francis and Clinton (relation of his first wife) in attendance. Very clear-headed and collected. Had been attacked with usual forewarning of cholera Saturday, had neglected it, had gone to E. K. Collins's place in Westchester Sunday, had been rather sick yesterday, and early this morning found his disorder taking a very formidable shape. . . .

Came home, drafted and copied the will, and was at Foster's again by a little after five. Waited an hour and a half before going upstairs. The news received from time to time shewed that he had been and was losing ground. And as I sat in the splendidly furnished suite of rooms, with the gilded and frescoed ceilings and paneled walls to which he'd given so much care, I heard now and then the groans from where their proprietor was agonizing with cramp. Went to him at last, and saw at once that his case was very bad and unpromising. Found the doctors (to whom was added Kissam, I think) had given him up; his hand was cold, face darkened, skin of the fingers corrugated, articulation thick. I read over the will very warily and distinctly, pausing at each material clause for a sign of assent, which I received. He said it was all right, but he wanted a codicil, about a $5,000 legacy. Sat down in the sick room to draw it, with the doctors, the wife, the weeping daughter, and all sorts of tragic elements all around me. Foster beckoned to Carter and told him that I'd omitted the affix of *Junior* to his name. Had to see his wife hanging over him, and to hear him say, "Well, Julia, this is the last night we shall be together"; had to watch his cool, deliberate effort to sign, with fingers stiffened by cramp; had to wait for a minute or two, I suppose, though it

[18] James Foster, Jr., was a wealthy gentleman residing in Bond Street.

seemed like half an hour, while Francis was rubbing the hand, and while the patient's blue, thin lips were retracted on his set teeth, till he could laboriously construct his signature. . . .

There is a strange flare-up of this [cholera] epidemic just now, among people of the more "respectable" class. Within a week have died Robert Smith, a certain young Mabbett, Edwin Williams, Dodd, the druggist, and others, all of cholera in a very obstinate and aggravated form.

October 25.   Foster died at four this morning. Cholera seems suddenly to have taken a fresh start. Mr. M. Davidson and John H. Cornell, cashier of the Mechanics' Banking Association, among the victims announced today. Oysters are charged with several cases, including those two of Foster and Robert Smith.[19]

October 26.   Luce was in Wall Street today, much distressed by the severe comments the papers have been making of late on his failure to do more to save his passengers of the *Arctic*. Fear that those comments are not at all unreasonable.

October 27.   There's an oyster panic in the city at present. Downing and George W. Brown are left desolate. The fall elections are at hand and never was their result more utterly uncertain. There is the Anti-Nebraska element, [and] the Maine law party; Seymour representing the party which opposes that law and sure to be earnestly supported by the large class whose pecuniary interest would suffer from its enactment here. Then there are the Know-Nothings, who will do a great deal, nobody can tell how much, but probably much less than they might have done.

October 28.   Attended sale at Merchants' Exchange, where the interests of the Seamen's Bank as a prior mortgagee wanted looking after.

October 31.   The oyster panic is subsiding a little, but Downing and George W. Brown are still like Rachel weeping for her customers. The former venerable Ethiop says: "If any gentleman can prove he died of the oysters I works in, I'll pay his expenses to Greenwood." There is no serious increase of cholera cases, and probably no foundation for distrust of oysters, raw, broiled, or roast.

November 2.   Ross microscope arrived this evening, after much bother in getting it through the Custom-House. It's a very superb instrument to look *at*; what it's worth to look *through* must be settled by further examination. George Anthon, Charley, Pike, and myself have been study-

---

[19] Reports that "poisonous" oysters had caused several deaths were quickly set at rest by chemists and physicians.

ing out its complications all this evening and knocking our heads together for looks through it.

November 5, SUNDAY.   Quite a levee here tonight in the library. Mr. Ruggles writing away at resolutions intended for the board of Columbia College tomorrow; Murray Hoffman and Jack Ehninger tumbling over books; Charley and John Weeks and I working away at the microscope.

November 6.   At two P.M., Columbia College Board held a stated meeting, full attendance, including Fish, who is neither dolphin, grampus, nor swordfish, striped bass, salmon, nor even brook trout, but a kitty-fish or minnow under the average size. His solemn demonstration, continued from the last meeting, against poor old McVickar's chaplaincy at Governor's Island, as a "professional employment" in violation of our statutes, was the flap and splash of a very small fish, indeed; if only because Mac in his glazed cap, giving everybody a semi-military, semi-clerical salute, is too ridiculous a subject to be gravely treated! A sort of nineteenth century Knight Templar. The calibre of this august board is really very small indeed. There was a debate about our answer to the civil enquiry of the Senate committee whether *we* want any change in our charter, in which Fish made it tolerably manifest that he was trimming his sails so as to keep on good terms with the alumni and tried to define his position, without success, for it was small and equivocal beyond mortal "defining power." The subtlety of Anderson and the object glasses of Ross would fail to define what he was at. On the other side, Gouverneur Ogden talked the most mucilaginous twaddle for some ten minutes. Van Wagenen's commonplaces seemed Websterian by contrast, and nothing came of it after all. Fish got exacerbated and called for the ayes and noes and couldn't get them. Last winter he entertained a very different view of the right to call for them and the expediency of their being recorded. . . .

Everybody exercised as to the result of tomorrow's election, and at a loss even to guess the probable result. I trust Fernando Wood mayn't be our next mayor, but it's by no means certain he won't. I predict that the "Reform" party in the city will fall off as compared with last year; that Maine Law and anti-Nebraska feeling will make Clark governor; that that man of uncertain birthplace, D. Ullman, won't get a large vote; and that everybody will be much surprised at many features of the results. . . .

The prominent candidate for the mayoralty, Wood, is charged in the papers with gross fraud and swindling in business transactions, and the charge is sustained by deposition and affidavits made in the due course of

legal proceedings and stating facts apparently quite incapable of explanation. Barker, one of his competitors, is accused of having set his store on
fire in 1845 or 1846 in order to cheat an insurance company (on evidence,
however, which is far less satisfactory than that against Wood). Holmes,
up for alderman in the First Ward, is in the Tombs on a charge of murder,
having stabbed a policeman a night or two since in an affray growing out
of his attempt to rescue some rowdy political friend of his from the ministers of the law. Pretty commentary, this, on republican institutions and
representative government as practically exhibited among us.

November 8, WEDNESDAY.   The election returns are as yet insufficient
to decide the result. It is clear that Ullman has run ahead of people's
expectations. So has Seymour. Clark has run far behind them. Bronson
is nowhere. The next governor will be either Seymour or Ullman.[20] The
Tribune is furious and charges the "disastrous" result to the machinations
of Know-Nothingism in suppressing and withholding Whig tickets in
Westchester County and elsewhere. The mayoralty lies between Barker
(Know-Nothing) and Wood; the latter has the better grounded hope,
according to tonight's papers, but I hope the city may be spared that disgrace. I'm surprised by the strength the Natives have shewn. The *Herald*
and *Tribune* speak of Know-Nothingism as a mere temporary perturba-
tion of our party system. Probably this secret organization will be short-
lived, but taking its late triumphs in connection with those of the Natives
ten years ago, it seems to me that its principle is likely to be an important
element in political calculations for some time to come. If I were now
entering on a political career and aimed at the Presidency, I should be
very careful to keep on good terms with the O.U.A., the Native Americans, the Know-Nothings, and all their friends. I should be wary about
saying a word that could be remembered against me by those who distrust the Roman Catholic and foreign voters. But for the Nebraska and
temperance questions, they would have controlled this election entirely,
and reduced the Whig and Democratic parties to insignificance.

We are so young a people that we feel the want of nationality, and
delight in whatever asserts our national "American" existence. We have
not, like England and France, centuries of achievements and calamities to

[20] Early returns were misleading. Bronson, identified with the unpopular Pierce
Administration, got only about 35,000 votes for governor. The Know-Nothings ran
up 122,000 for Ullman; and Clark and Seymour ran neck and neck with about 156,000
each. After several weeks of anxious vote-counting, Clark—who had the prohibitionists and the anti-Nebraska forces with him—was declared the victor. The outstanding
result of the election was the repudiation of Douglas's measure.

look back on; we have no *record* of Americanism and we feel its want. Hence the development, in every state of the Union, of "Historical Societies" that seize on and seal up every worthless reminiscence of our colonial and revolutionary times. We crave a history, instinctively, and being without the eras that belong to older nationalities—Anglo-Saxon, Carolingian, Hohenstauffen, Ghibelline, and so forth—we dwell on the details of our little all of historic life, and venerate every trivial fact about our first settlers and colonial governors and revolutionary heroes. A vivid narrative of the life and manners of New York fifty years ago would be received with enthusiasm here. London would take comparatively little interest in such a picture of the times of Pitt and Fox.

November 9. Seymour probably governor, and Wood mayor, but nothing is certainly known even yet. That jolly loafer, Alderman Brown of the First, was confident of Wood's triumph at three-thirty P.M., and I fear that calamity has befallen us after all. News from the Pacific tonight of an attempt by some squadron, British or Allied, to bombard Petropavlovsk (somewhere up in the Okhotsk, Kamchatska, and River Alma region), which squadron was repulsed with loss. Hope for the Czar even yet.

November 13. Met a prodigious Know-Nothing procession moving uptown, as I omnibussed down Broadway to the vestry meeting; not many banners and little parade of any kind, but a most emphatic and truculent demonstration. Solid column, eight or ten abreast, and numbering some two or three thousand, mostly young men of the butcher-boy and *prentice* type; many a Simon Tappertit among them, no doubt, and many a shoulder-hitter and shortboy beside; marching in quick time, and occasionally indulging in a very earnest kind of hurrah. They looked as if they might have designs on St. Patrick's Cathedral, and I think the Celts of Prince and Mott Streets would have found them ugly customers. We may well have a tremendous riot and carnage here at any moment.

November 15. The Know-Nothings have smitten Whig and Democrat hip and thigh in Massachusetts, and carried nearly everything throughout the state. The Pope will shake in his purple slippers. In this state the question between Clark and Seymour still undecided. General impression strong that Seymour is elected. . . .

Judge Edmonds more and more extravagant in his revelations of spiritual intercourse. Recently had a ghostly reunion in his parlor (visible to him) of Sandford and others, who perished in the *Arctic*. Isaac T. Hopper, Nat Blunt, and Dr. Wainwright were also present. The Bishop offered an "impressive" prayer. Sandford and others of the party came to the Judge for advice and assistance. Sandford said: "Good God, Edmonds, what is the meaning of this? Where am I? What am I to do?" and so on. He was delighted to be told that "Nat" was in the room, was "introduced" to him by the Judge, and they went off together to talk over matters. Edmonds gave them all a good deal of very sensible advice as to what they had better do in their new condition, which seems to have been thankfully received. It is very funny. There *is* something at least apparently new under the sun. Edmonds prints all this, and thousands of people, external to any lunatic asylum, believe it.

November 20.   Mr. Ruggles much impressed by his friend Fitz James O'Brien's poem in the last *Putnam's* about "The Three Gannets."[21] He was enthusiastic and cold-blooded, and we analyzed, criticized, and quoted parallel passages without conviction on either side.

November 26, SUNDAY. . . . Though there's no extra out today, it seems the *Baltic* has arrived with weighty news from the Crimea. Very large reinforcements have entered Sebastopol. There has been a sortie from the city, in great force, which stormed the French lines, spiking their guns and destroying the works. The French rallied and drove the Russians out again and back to the fortifications. Besiegers and besieged entered pell-mell together, and then the former, probably involved in the fire of masked batteries, were driven back with fearful loss: 5,000 men and upwards. Great sensation and depression in England, reinforcements urgently demanded, consols declining. Such is Ogden Hoffman's version of the news. If correct, the chance of Sebastopol being completely reduced grows less and less, and the partial success even of the Allies will be dearly bought. Hurrah for the Czar, whose partisan I am in this contest. But Englishmen are our brethren in race and speech and culture, after all. I wish they were fighting on the other side. It's hard to think of these brave young gentlemen, guardsmen and so forth, perishing in the trenches, or dying ignobly of cholera and camp fever, and of the grand old ancestral houses they shall never see again, the high-bred sisters and wives thrilling and agonizing with hope and fear as each post arrives, or kneeling in quiet country churches and feeling such new intensity of meaning in every supplication of the liturgy. Somehow the mishaps and casualties of

[21] O'Brien, a Dublin University man, had come to America about 1852 and was writing voluminously for New York newspapers and magazines and the stage. He was a leader in the Bohemian set that dined nightly at Pfaff's on Broadway. He is best remembered for his short story "The Diamond Lens."

Russian colonels and lieutenants appeal far less strongly to one's sympathies. France will begin to clamor for . . . Cavaignac before long, and grumble at Louis Napoleon and his military friends. Had the Allies prospered better, Louis Napoleon would never have come to such easy terms about that vagabond Soulé. On the other hand, if France and England get into a really tight place, our despicable government will begin bullying prematurely about Cuba or something else, and bring us to grief.

Tuesday night with Ellie to Eisfeld's quartette soirée No. 1.[22] Schubert's Quartette in A minor (Opus 29), very rich and abundant in beauties, especially first and second movements. Quintette, Beethoven, E-flat, (Opus 16), most delightful throughout. Not in the style of Haydn (commonly said to be that of Beethoven's earlier music), but in that of Mozart most emphatically. The first phrase of the andante "Batti, batti," verbatim. Haydn's Quartette in D major (Opus 63) very genial and Haydnish. . . .

Bancroft's speech before the Historical Society. Unitarianism savage and furious.[23] Speech does George Bancroft more credit than I ever expected to be able to give that gentleman. Rises into a far higher sphere than I thought he could attain. . . .

Thursday, I was at home nearly all day with a miserable sickening influenza that has not yet quite left me, and could not attend a special meeting of the trustees of Columbia College. There was no important action. Elements in the board seem rather tending toward harmony and peace. Bishop Potter will doubtless be elected to the vacancy, and will be an acquisition. As a new man he can be efficient in pacification. George F. Allen, Bidwell tells me, will certainly take his seat. We are therefore likely to gain rather than lose strength. Reading *Heartsease*, a novel by the author, or now probably authoress, of that lovely story, *The Heir of Redclyffe*.[24] Few fictions have such power as those two to make one loathe himself and long for higher and purer life; to shew the infinite good and infinite evil dependent on one's performance of "trivial" daily duties, the majesty and glory that are *potentially* (only potentially) present in everyone's daily routine of life.

November 30. A very bright, clear, cold Thanksgiving Day. . . . Further news from the Crimea (by the *Africa*) indicates no special change

[22] Theodore Eisfeld's "classical quartette" was beginning its fifth season at Dodworth's Academy, 806 Broadway.

[23] George Bancroft was now a resident of New York. His speech before the New-York Historical Society was on "The Necessity, the Reality, and the Promise of the Progress of the Human Race."

[24] Charlotte Yonge (1823–1901).

in affairs. The Allies are hurrying forward reinforcements and may yet accomplish something important. But should the reinforcements be tardy, their position is one of great peril, and the expedition may be disastrous. . . .

It was a refreshing sight today in the basement or cellar of Calvary Church; the crowd of little Irish and German emigrant children who had been picked up by Hawks and his associate [John] Towles from utter poverty and deprivation and reclaimed and humanized by the Industrial School connected with that parish. They were feasting on turkey and roast beef, a dinner provided them by a few of the congregation, and looked clean, well cared for, and most happy. Many were stowing away unwanted luxuries in their baskets for their brothers and sisters at home, if the word "home" can be applied to their wretched abiding-places. And among them, active, busy, sympathizing, and accustomed to such society, were a score of the young ladies of Calvary Church, in their costly furs and silks and wonderful little bonnets, ministering to the hungry crowd. Thank God for the impulse He has given the wealthier classes to seek out and aid the poor. It is a symptom of great good to be set off against manifold signs of social degeneracy and disease. Personal intercourse and contact and individual effort to benefit individuals is better than very many dollars subscribed to any charitable mechanism or organization. . . .

December 3, SUNDAY. Philharmonic concert last night. The glorious *Eroica;* Gade's "Reminiscences of Ossian," very grandiose, a little bombastic and tumefied, on the whole effective and good. Some of its phrases of melody very pungent. Lindpainter's "Overture to Abraham's Sacrifice" seemed to me commonplace and worthless. Mademoiselle Caroline Lehman, a prima donna from Copenhagen, just imported, sang: "Wie nahte mir das Schlummer," and "Casta Diva," effectively and well; the former especially. She's a well-looking young German or Danish blonde, not pretty, but with a good face and an honest, truthful eye. Also there was a concerto for clarinet and orchestra by *Eisfeld,* which was very creditable. The concert was well attended. Very few compositions can stand being played immediately after one of Beethoven's greater works. Even Mozart and Haydn suffer by the comparison. Handel, I suppose, might bear it. . . .

Friday morning, McCulloh's inauguration and "inaugural address" at Columbia College chapel. McCulloh is a feeble-looking, washed-out kind of man, but I did not think it possible he could deliver so deplorably commonplace, incoherently imbecile a piece of maundering as that which he bestowed on us. It was shameful to hear the man we have entrusted with the teaching of all that vast group of sciences, to whom we have committed the education of our students in knowledge of the material works of God, defiling his awful subject by the utterance of trivialities and platitudes so slovenly and contemptible.

December 7.   Worked pretty hard today, and tonight was visited by Professor Bache, Gould, and Dr. Hamel, a learned Kalmuck here on a scientific technological mission from the Czar. Very dry, funny, and erudite individual. Knows everything and has been twice to the top of Mt. Blanc. We adjourned to a session of the Florentine Academy, with whiskey toddy and oysters prepared by Bache à la chafing dish, to the infinite wonder of the Russian savant; from which séance I've just returned (half an hour past). . . . Before leaving for the aforesaid meeting of the bivalve, molluscous section of the said academy, we had a scientific conference here in the library over the big microscope, polarized light, and the portfolio of photographs, some of which (especially the glacier pictures) impressed Bache profoundly.

December 10.   Great shindy and internal convulsion in the New York Club, its immediate exciting cause certain performances of Mr. William Holly Hudson's. Rumor that Miss Ellen Rodgers is engaged to Rev. Morgan Dix, who must be eight or nine years her junior. The young lady is now at or near Lisbon, with her brother-in-law O'Sullivan. Thackeray's last Christmas story on the whole a failure, and apparently written in undue haste, but including some very funny things. Looking again into Longfellow's *Golden Legend*, which I rate higher than I did when it came out three years ago. . . .

Further news from the Crimea, quite indecisive. The battle of November 5 was evidently obstinate and bloody; four English generals killed. It's impossible to foresee the result of the campaign. The Allies are receiving reinforcements daily, but they are hard pressed, and their reinforcements do little more than make up the weekly deficiency by disease and casualty. I wish there might be speedy peace, for our financial condition is sadly impaired by the indirect consequences of European war. We are on the eve of very hard times indeed, I think.

December 13, WEDNESDAY.   Weather cold, but not unkindly, save to the hundreds or rather thousands of men with wives and children to be fed and kept warm, whom this cruel "pressure" has thrown out of work. They must see with dismay the indications of a severe winter coming on them. A week later news from the Crimea this morning by the *Pacific*. Nothing decisive; inaction on both sides since the last battle of Inkerman. The Allies and invaders hold the affirmative of the issue on trial under the walls of Sebastopol, and *inaction*, the absence of results, seems to tell against them rather than against the Czar. And winter, the natural ally of that potentate, is at hand. . . . Evidently this battle of Inkerman was a most grim and murderous struggle, in which the English were greatly out-numbered by an enemy resolved to drive them from their position at any cost of life. And the Russians seem to have shewn pluck worthy the sol-diers of Borodino. The English must have been helped by the nature of the ground, I think, otherwise not even their Anglo-Norman bulldog blood could have saved them. According to their accounts, exaggerated I trust, the Russians are fighting in a spirit of murderous barbarity, like Comanches rather than soldiers of a Christian and civilized power. A Russian major, prisoner in the hands of the Allies, is to be court-martialed and tried and perhaps hanged or shot for killing wounded English on the field. The practice seems, by English accounts, to be general among the Russians.

December 18. Have passed through an unusually long spell of pestilent sick headache, despite which I have worked a little, not a great deal. Philharmonic rehearsal Saturday afternoon. Mendelssohn's Symphony in A; brilliant and pretty, not much more, I think. There is some glow in the first movement, the finest of the four. The andante has a dreary suggestion of Presbyterian psalm-singing in its principal subject that spoils it alto-gether. It seems to me that the germ of almost every good thing of Men-delssohn's that I have heard exists in the Overture to the *Midsummer Night's Dream.* Weber's Overture to *Preciosa* also played. Don't think I've heard it before. Much lighter than his great overtures. Some passages seem as if they must have been written by Rossini; they suggest the Over-ture to the *Gazza Ladra*, not in structure or phrase, but in sentiment, or rather in the absence of sentiment, the substitution for it of *sense*, if that be a musical possibility. But it's a very agreeable composition. . . .

December 20. Tea fight has just terminated: Miss Emily and Miss "Tote" Anthon, Miss McIlvaine, Miss Jane Emmet, Miss Betty Rhine-lander, Miss Ulshoeffer, Jem, Jack Ehninger, George Anthon, Hall, Jemmy Otis, William Hoffman, very pleasant. The only drawback—a too crowded tea table, and perhaps that gave people something to be entertained with. Don't think the evening was dull and slow at any time. Miss Betty was funny, and broke out in a new place, new to me, that is. Miss Mary Ulshoeffer was gorgeous. She is physically among the most superb of the girls now extant, has a specially good, ringing, hearty, joyous laugh, and has not much beside that I can perceive. Miss "Tote" Anthon and

Miss Mary McIlvaine were as good and honest as usual. I prefer them to the most exquisitely elaborated damsels of "society." They *seem*, at least, to be more simple-minded and single-hearted. . . .

December 27, WEDNESDAY.   Weather all last week was detestable, cold and snowy; this week is worse still, with drizzle, fog, and sloppiness, or sliminess rather. Broadway is a long canal of mud syrup, all the sidewalks greasy with an abominable compound like melted black butter. After a sleety Sunday, Christmas introduced the thaw. It was a beautiful, mild, sunshiny day, "very good walking, overhead." At Trinity the music was uncommonly good and abundant; it was almost a "choral service." Higby preached very splendidly. Home after lunch at Delmonico's. . . .

Foreign news still very interesting, and very indecisive. All notion of taking Sebastopol this season is given up. The Allies are looking for reinforcements and supplies, and considering how they'll get through with a winter in the Crimea. No serious fighting since Inkerman, November 5th. The Allies are *de facto* the besieged party and are fortifying themselves to their best ability. If the Russians were the soldiers of Eylau and Borodino, they'd wipe out Canrobert and Lord Raglan. Terrible tempest has sunk some thirty transports and ships of war off Balaklava and Eupatoria, with a calamitous loss of winter munitions, clothing, and so on. It may well prove another Moscow campaign, but I think Anglo-Gallican pluck and power of endurance will prevail, though doubtless at fearful cost of life. And *cui bono?* To maintain the debilitated existence of Mahometanism and polygamy in Europe.

December 29. With Cutler this morning in the Albany Street matter. Bleecker's triumph in the Board of Councilmen a week ago (39 to 13 in favor of the minority report and repealing the ordinance for opening the street) was fruitless. When the question came up on the third reading, the vote was about three to one the other way. Some potent agency had been brought to bear on the 39 during the interval. I think it probable that Boorman exerted that influence. They say that the price of a councilman is from $10 to $25. This looks bad, but I don't think the street in question will ever be opened. There are some signs, however, of *Know-Nothingism* assaying itself against *all* wealthy ecclesiastical corporations.

Hard times the general subject of talk. No sign yet of any let-up on their hardness. Very few large parties thus far; Mrs. Walden Pell's last night the first within my knowledge. Brown (of Grace Church) admits the deficiency but says he'll "do his best to make the funeral as pleasant as possible." Project of a grand ballet [at] the Fourteenth Street Opera

House "for the relief of the poor in this city," originating with Haight, to which I'm "particularly requested" to be an accessory by note signed "Mrs. William H. Jones." It looks very dubious, questionable. To a poverty stricken demagogue, the plan of feasting the aristocracy on boned turkey and *pâté de foie gras* that the democracy may be supplied with pork and beans, and assembling the Upper Ten in brocade and valenciennes that the lower thousand may be helped to flannel and cotton shirting, would furnish a theme most facile and fertile.

December 30.　A clear bright day, rather sloppy and snowy under foot. To a Philharmonic rehearsal this afternoon with Ellie. Heard the Mendelssohn symphony and then came off. It seems a rather incoherent composition; there's no reason apparent on its face why its four movements are put together and called a symphony instead of being kept apart and called four "concert-overtures.". . .

But a symphony, like an epic poem, is either very great or worthless. Perhaps the same thing may be said of all orchestral compositions. Why should fifty violins, trombones, flutes, and so on, waste their time in laboriously rehearsing and studying out a production that is "exceedingly clever," "remarkable for its good taste and ingenious instrumentation," "full of striking effects," and "of higher merit than anything that has been produced for twenty years," when they might be so much more profitably employed on truly great and transcendent works, of which we all know far too little because we hear them so seldom? Why should the Philharmonic Society bother itself to produce correctly this beautiful production of Mendelssohn's (which would make the fortune and reputation of any composer) when so many of the Philharmonic subscribers have but the vaguest notion of Beethoven's symphonies in C minor, A or D, *Eroica* and *Pastorale*, Mozart's in E-flat and the *Jupiter*, Weber's and Mendelssohn's great overtures, and so forth? . . .

The *Atlantic* past due, and rather anxiously looked for. Did not go to Haight's tonight, to organize a "grand ball" for the suffering poor.

December 31, SUNDAY.　Cram dined here with Jem Ruggles and, as usual, made himself most agreeable. There is much vigor and weight of metal in him, and his marriage and consequent intimacy with the Sergeants and other high-bred people have given him a refinement of thought and manner which he used to want. Like Cornell, he has been burning his fingers in speculation. His special Delilah was an operation in some patent concern, whereby he cleared and pocketed about $40,000, and then lost it all and a little more in subsequent dealings with the ingenious inventor, his associate. He has now resumed the law, and formed a partnership with Cornell, and Townsend, who has just married Miss Bronson.

Clear moonlight night. Tomorrow promises to be a bright day; 1854 has now just fifty minutes more to live. I trust 1855 will be a better year. This has been fruitful of calamity; war in Europe, financial distress here, abundant disaster, everywhere. *Personally*, I have gained nothing, have rather retrograded toward evil. The tragedy and misery of November, 1853, unsettled me completely, broke up good habits, made the past a field of bitter memories, removed the old landmarks, and tore down slowly built buttresses of right and truth, and so left me to gravitate downward. I well know what I mean, though I've hardly made it intelligible.

This is a time for good resolutions. God grant that those I form may bear fruit, that they may not be barren like so many of their predecessors. Indeed it is time for me to bestir myself if I would be aught but a lump of carrion stinking on the surface of God's earth a certain number of years, and put under ground at last. I know that I'm very "respectable" and "estimable," like many a Pharisee before me, and that poor, dear Ellie's good fortune was quite remarkable when she secured a man of such "high position" for a husband. But the heart knoweth its own *rottenness*.

> O, what a glory *must* this world put on
> For him who with a fervent heart goes forth
> Under the bright and glorious sky, and looks
> On duties well performed and days well spent!

I substitute "must" for Longfellow's "doth," for I know not what the world "doth" to one who so plays his part in it. God enable me to know it yet, notwithstanding all the miserable past. Think of the life of a man who does, on the whole, always right, whose feet rest always on Eternal Truth! How secure he must feel against chance and change, how certain that calamity and bereavement will be but a more solemn joy, how glorious and perfect must be his sense of harmony with every happy landscape, every bright sunset, every true musical thought or phrase, every beautiful face, every one of the multitudinous forms of beauty that even this imperfect world of ours presents him. Such might be my estate this moment, through God's infinite Goodness which puts it within the reach of every man, but for evil passion and indolence, but for my own baseness and blindness.

There goes the clock, the old year is out, amid a fusillade from the distant German region, east of Tompkins Square, that sounds like the preliminary skirmish of a great battle. . . .

1855

———◦◦◦———

*I*n Europe the Crimean War dragged on, with no progress in the siege of
Sebastopol. Debates in Parliament revealed a rising discontent; while Lord
Aberdeen and Lord John Russell defended the policy of the government, it was
attacked in the House by Disraeli and in the Lords by Lord Derby. These
Opposition leaders praised the bravery of the British troops and commended
the alliance with France, but found much to criticize in the handling of men
and supplies. But the Russians were faring badly. At the battles of the Alma
and Inkerman their losses far exceeded those of the Allies. In the United States
the commercial and financial depression which had overtaken the country continued, and new failures were announced every day. By New Year's, however,
signs of better times were visible. National interest was centered upon Kansas,
where free-soilers and proslavery men were beginning a momentous contest
for control of the new territory. Already it was evident that this struggle
would be attended with violence. New York had a new governor in Myron H.
Clark, whose message at the beginning of the year denounced stock gambling and
railroad adventures, called for enlarged support of public education, and defended the justice and policy of prohibitory legislation. The metropolis had a
new mayor in Fernando Wood, of whom good citizens feared the worst.

On New Year's Day Strong, in the New York fashion of the time, paid
more than thirty calls. "I traveled from Dan to Beersheba—from Twenty-
ninth Street to Hudson Square," he writes. He was specially impressed by the
residence of the Douglas Crugers. "It's a most stately house, the finest I've
ever seen, with its grand hall and staircase and ample suite of rooms. Ampli-

[206]

tude and absence of ginger bread make it imposing, though I dare say (being built by Jemmy Renwick) it is bad enough in many particulars." The diarist rejoiced in his small son John R. Strong, who was becoming "a most lovable little creature." Busy as ever with the affairs of his law office, of Trinity Church, and of Columbia College, he found diversion in music, in a good deal of entertaining, and in his microscope. He records that his father-in-law Samuel B. Ruggles had become much interested in some of the foreign singers in the city. Early in the year the Strongs went to a large charity ball at the opera house.

January 8, MONDAY. Saturday evening at Century Club monthly meeting; supper with boar's head contributed by Verplanck. On the whole I thought it slow; got up no enthusiasm or excitement of any sort. Talked commonplaces with a few commonplace people, and came home at eleven through an ugly, malignant, chilly drizzle. . . . Woke with headache this morning and got downtown rather late. At Columbia College at two P.M. Encountered poor George F. Allen in Park Place on his way to the meeting, where he took his seat as trustee. Did not suppose he would recognize me, for it's very long since he's seen me, and I don't know that I ever spoke to him before, but he introduced himself, and we went in together. Poor soul, what a life of bitter memories his must be! There is no parade of grief about him. I should think from his manner that he was honestly striving to busy himself with present duties to keep his sorrows to himself and to interest himself in whatever work the present time has for him to do; but he looks old and careworn, and I thought I could see that the black shadow of the past came sweeping over him every now and then.[1] Little was done at the meeting, of course. We are a Board of Imbeciles. I never coveted any post in my life but a seat in that body, and now that I have my wish I'm perpetually longing to resign. Morris sent in his resignation today, and Bradford the Surrogate was nominated; a very good nomination in many respects, notwithstanding his connection with the *Protestant Churchman*. Mr. Ruggles named Daniel Lord in order to strengthen the fogy party (from whom Bradford's nomination came) in support of their nominee. . . . At the meeting a demonstration was made against King by Ogden on some sixpenny business of two days' holiday given the students. A proposition for a tutor in McVickar's overloaded department was

[1] Allen, it will be recalled, was one of the few survivors of the wreck of the *Arctic*.

killed by a reference, and we had other manifestations of density and inertia. . . .

January 10, WEDNESDAY.   Last night to our neighbor David Dudley Field's, where we were invited "sociably" to meet two hundred and fifty people; a soirée talkative, with a slight infusion of the saltatory element toward its finale. A chaos of ill-assorted people and a babel of clack— enough to unsettle one's intellects permanently. Got through it well enough myself. Tonight we took tea at the Lydigs' with the two tall Warner women, one of whom is author of *The Wide, Wide World* or *Queechy* or something else; respectable, prim, middle-aged damsels, one conversible and pleasant, the other conversationally costive.[2] Under my treatment, at least, she was obstinately so. Also the Rev. Mr. Weston (wish he'd marry one of the Miss L's) with whom Mrs. Strong had a very fervent talk about Trinity Chapel and parish schools and so forth. Thence we went to a sort of musical party at Mrs. Mills's. De Trobriand[3] sang, also Miss Randolph, and Miss Quincy of Boston did "Il va venir" from Halévy's *La Juive,* with the exaggerated contrasts of piano and forte, whisper and screech, whereby second-rate amateurs commonly eke out their performance of opera music. Such pieces belong to the stage, for which they were written. . . .

January 14, SUNDAY.   News from Europe tells of but little progress toward the overthrow of Sebastopol. The Allies, and especially the English, are suffering fearfully from disease and from deficient equipment and supplies. Bad management somewhere and want of system everywhere palpable; and the fourth estate of England, the London press, is loud-voiced in complaint and denunciation. The Ministry must expect to be rudely handled, and Lord Raglan may yet be recalled in disgrace, notwithstanding Inkerman and Balaklava.

January 21.   Further news from Europe shews no change; possibly the Allies are in rather better spirits. The London *Times,* now recognized as one of the great powers of the British Empire, is denunciatory and bitter about the blunders of the War Department and the non-feasance of Lord

---

[2] David Dudley Field (1805–1894) was one of the luminaries of the New York bar; his marriage to a wealthy widow had increased his worldly means. Susan Warner (1819–1885) had published *The Wide, Wide World* in 1850, and *Queechy* in 1852, these moral and religious romances attaining a huge popularity. Her sister Anna Bartlett Warner also wrote fiction.

[3] Regis D. De Trobriand (1816–1897), who had come to New York from France in 1841 and had married into the rich Jones family, was well known in the literary and journalistic circles of the city.

Raglan. It charges him with being unequal to his place and his duties. The
chances of peace seem to be rather improving. In this city financial pressure
continues. The unemployed workmen, chiefly Germans, are assembling
daily in the Park and listening to inflammatory speeches by demagogues
who should be "clapt up" for preaching sedition and marching in procession
through the streets. The large majority of the distressed multitude is
decently clad and looks well fed and comfortable. People anticipate riot and
disturbance; there have been two or three rumors of it in various quarters.
Friday night it was rumored that a Socialist mob was sacking the Schiff
mansion in the Fifth Avenue, where was a great ball and mass meeting
of the aristocracy. Certainly the destitute are a thankless set and deserve
little sympathy in their complaints. The efforts to provide employment
and relief, the activity of individuals and of benevolent organizations, the
readiness with which money is contributed do credit to the city. More could
be done and ought to be done, of course, but what is done is beyond precedent here, and more than our "unemployed" friends had a right to
count on.

There has been vast improvement during the last three or four years
in the dealings of our "upper class" with the poor; not merely in the comparative abundance of their bounty, but in the fact that it has become
fashionable and creditable and not unusual for people to busy themselves
in personal labors for the very poor and in personal intercourse with them.
It is a very significant thing and would have been held a marvel ten years
ago that women like Mrs. Eleanor Curtis, Mrs. Lewis Jones, Miss Field,
Mrs. Peters, Miss Gibbs, and others should be working hard in "ragged
schools"and the like. Perhaps it may be but a short-lived fashion, but it is
an indication most encouraging of progress toward social health. . . .

Thursday night at Mrs. Robert Gracie's third and (happily) last
reception. Such transactions are sheer lunacy. The house is small, and the
rooms were hot and crowded, so that one moved about like a fly in a glue
pot through a stifling, viscid, glutinous medium of perspiring humanity
and dilute carbonic acid gas. In the plenitude of their folly, people actually
cleared away a narrow space in the middle room, where half a dozen
idiotic couples polkaed and waltzed to a faintly audible piano-jingle,
increasing thereby the pressure on the house to one hundred atmospheres.
The crowd must have nearly burst out the walls. . . .

Yesterday . . . went with Ellie and her mother to the Philharmonic;
a very great crowd. Sat in the third gallery, where the orchestra is far more
intelligently to be heard than elsewhere in the house. The very elaborate and

involved instrumentation of the Mendelssohn symphony (the first and
fourth movements, particularly) I never heard before. . . . Mendelssohn
was clearly no melodist. Many of his phrases of melody are characterized
by something that I don't want to call *coarseness* or *grossness*. But contrast
them with the delicate, retiring, suggestive reserve with which Mozart
introduces and quickly withdraws his melodic thoughts of spiritual beauty
and purity. The overture to *Preciosa* went nicely. Miss Lehman sang
"O mon Fernan" and "Una voce" nicely.

January 27, SATURDAY.   Phil Kearny of the Trust Company is very
ill indeed. Erysipelas of an obstinate kind, with typhoid symptoms. Night
before last, when I sent to enquire about him, the answer was that he was
past hope. But he's still living, and has gained somewhat in the last forty-
eight hours. . . .

In the Crimea my friend the Czar still holds his own. Sebastopol has not
fallen yet. There have been certain sorties, repulsed, of course, but more
or less damaging to the besiegers. The British forces still suffer cruelly
from defective arrangements and want of system as to supplies and so
forth, and if the London *Times* speak truth, from want of generalship. . . .

We have been gadding of late extravagantly. It was refreshing to spend
this evening comfortably in the library with Ellie looking over books and
marking things for her to read. . . . Dickens's Christmas stories, "The
Seven Poor Travellers," respectable; Number 1 very good indeed, and
Number 2 fanciful and clever. The lawyer's story is perhaps the best of
the batch, for the first has too many melodramatic points in it.

J. G. Whittier is an American poet about whom I must learn more.
"Maud Muller" (cut out of the *Tribune* and pasted into a flyleaf of this
book, *vide post*) hits me very hard. It's a sign of real power to make familiar
and rather commonplace names and associations effective. I suspect that
only a poet would have dared to write "The *Judge* rode slowly down the
lane." (Not "the *Knight*.") And "The *tallow candle* an astral burned."

Not that I particularly admire the last line. But it's a good sign that a
man who can write with vigor and depth of true feeling ventures to deal with
matters of A.D. 1855 and tries to idealize realities of *our* daily life. Half
the poetry of the last hundred years is, in truth, worthless, because it deals
with Roman or Athenian or mediaeval institutions, not with the images,
objects, subjects, thoughts, manners, and events amid which its author
was living and which it was his office to illustrate and beautify if he were a
poet, and with which, if truly such, he could have worked so much more
effectively. Take perhaps the very strongest case that could be cited

against this notion. Walter Scott, in 1803 or 1804, surely felt and knew the lives and manners and rights and wrongs of Englishmen and Scotsmen then living and daily meeting him and dining with him even better and more deeply than the ways of his beloved Border moss-troopers and feudal barons. Why should he not have brought his great genius to bear on *them* rather than on institutions and ways of thinking that had perished three hundred years before? . . . The poet of A.D. 1855 will have his hands full with the men and women and things of 1855, and has no right to go back to other dead times, "revolutionary," mediaeval, classical, or patriarchal. His hand and his heart find enough to feel and to do at his own door. There is poetry enough latent in the South Street merchant and the Wall Street financier; in Stewart's snobby clerk chaffering over ribbons and laces; in the omnibus driver that conveys them all from the day's work to the night's relaxation and repose; in the brutified denizen of the Points and the Hook; in the sumptuous star courtesan of Mercer Street thinking sadly of her village home; in the Fifth Avenue ballroom; in the Grace Church contrast of eternal vanity and new bonnets; in the dancers at Lewis Jones's and Mr. Schiff's, and in the future of each and all.

February 11, SUNDAY.   In the Crimea things look bluer and more blue for the Allies; nothing said any more about that "assault next week at latest" promised so long. With the London *Times* the question is how to save the sickly, dispirited remnant of "our only army" from annihilation. Incapacity, ignorance, mismanagement, want of forethought, and caution are openly charged on the leaders in the Crimea and on the government. Lord John Russell has resigned his place on the ground that he could not resist the motion for a vote of censure on the Ministry, and left his colleagues to take care of themselves; probably the vote has been taken and the Ministry has resigned before this. It looks like another Moscow campaign. We hear less about Canrobert's army, but it has doubtless suffered severely, though so much better worked and more fully supplied with food, clothing, and the like than the English.

February 14.   Mayor Wood continues our Civic Hero—inquiring, reforming, redressing, laboring hard with ample result of good. If he goes on this way to the end of his term, he will be a public benefactor, recognized as such and honored with statues. His predecessors, reported of average honesty, did little or nothing to diminish the systematic profligacy of our city government. He is the first mayor, for thirty years at least, who has set himself seriously to the work of giving the civic administration a decent appearance of common honesty. He is a very strange phenomenon.

It is not a citizen of high repute for integrity, entitled to the respect of all classes, known to be a good and true man, not even one of whom little or nothing was known and who might very well be an undeveloped hero till he found himself in his proper sphere of action, that is doing all this good work. It is a man whose former career shews him a scoundrel of special magnitude.

February 18. This evening an unexpected gathering at tea: Jack W. Ehninger, Mr. Ruggles, Miss Rosalie [Ruggles], the Vestvali and her brother. . . .[4] The Amazonian Vestvali is certainly a very fine, frank, genial young woman; full of life and *Theilnehmung* and hearty faculty of enjoyment; intelligent, and a lady. She sang Arsace in *Semiramis* last night at the Metropolitan with brilliant success. . . . It is to be settled tomorrow whether she is to be engaged by the Fourteenth Street Academy or by Hackett's opposition.

That same confounded Superior Court case kept me from William Schermerhorn's private theatricals Thursday night—"*The Ladies' Battle*"; about sixty people invited and the performance very perfect. Everything the Schermerhorns undertake is carried out to the utmost perfection of detail. Mrs. William and little Mrs. Lewis Jones did their parts admirably, I hear.

February 25, SUNDAY. Mr. Ruggles has just returned from Washington where he has been colloguing with the President and the Cabinet and certain Senators, Gwin, Rusk, Seward, and Douglas particularly (think of Seward and Douglas being great friends in reality, enemies only professionally, while playing their respective parts in public!), about a grand celebration or banquet that is to be got up in May commemorating the completion of the Panama Railroad, an event in which the world of commerce and civilization is interested; a fact for universal history, and deserving commemoration and celebration. General Scott took the President's delay in sending in his name to the Senate for the new office of Lieutenant-General in high dudgeon, and went back to Baltimore on the 21st, not understanding that it was intended to pay him a sort of compliment by selecting the 22d as the date of his nomination. The General was good enough to speak well of me, and I'm vain enough to be tickled and flattered thereby, for I've a profound reverence for the General, with all his foibles. Were he in Lord Raglan's boots, affairs around Sebastopol would look very different. At least he would not suffer his army to perish lest some

[4] Felicita von Vestvali, German vocalist and actress, now performing in New York.

rule of office should be broken, or the privileged decencies of the quarter-
master's department be profaned. He'd find out what was needed and
order it done, and if official privilege demurred, he would hand the de-
murrant over to the Provost-Marshal, and do the needful himself. I
ought to go to bed, but after my day's dozing, I know I shall only toss
all night. The Vestvali engaged at the Academy of Music, partly brought
about by our meeting of last Sunday night. Her person and acting will
make her effective with the masses, but she won't satisfy the knowing
ones in vocalization.

February 28. Judge H. P. Edwards died last evening. He was thought
convalescent last week, but was reported *in extremis* Monday morning,
and though there was some improvement yesterday, it was not sufficient
to make his death a matter of surprise. He was a valuable man, and his
loss is justly regretted. An honest judge, of respectable learning and
ability, with dignified and courteous manners, is a serious loss to us in
A.D. 1855.[5]

March 2. Little news today except from England and the seat of
war. Sufferings of the British forces still murderous and horrible. But
there is again talk of an assault, the brunt of which will have to be borne
by the French, I think. The London *Times* continues to denounce the
predominant influence of the aristocracy as the cause of all this, with
vigor, plainness, and seemingly sufficient grounds. And I suspect it's
supported by the feeling and sympathy of a rapidly increasing class. This
war may well lead to a quiet, bloodless revolution in England.

Think of England undertaking this war as champion of the liberties
of Europe and the cause of civilization and so forth, and then condescending to strengthen her hands by a league with the despicable, cruel,
cowardly, profligate, barbaric tyranny of Naples, held up so lately to the
execration of the world by Gladstone himself! Suppose, by the way, that
the other great champion of the liberties of Europe, Louis Napoleon,
should find it advantageous in some new turn of the diplomatic cards to
pick a little quarrel with his beloved ally, and should use his steam navy
to land a few thousand Zouaves and chasseurs and so forth on the English
coast? Where's the British army now that would have stopped a march
on London? Doubtless the militia and yeomanry and brave gentlemen of
the island would do a great deal. But they'd have their hands full dealing
with French discipline and military spirit, and the exultation of the

---

[5] Henry Pierrepont Edwards (1808–1855) had become a judge of the State Supreme
Court in 1847, and of the Court of Appeals in 1853.

invaders at finding themselves actually avenging Waterloo on English soil.

March 4. Evening with Ellie and Mr. Ruggles to the Academy of Music concert, where our friend the Vestvali was announced to sing something of Naumann's; the great house scantily filled. The first part included most of Rossini's luscious *Stabat Mater*, not particularly well done, except Badiali's "Pro peccatis." The second part was chiefly *Le Prophète*, and the prayer from "Moïse" (not the Mose of the Bowery). The Vestvali did not appear at her proper place in the programme, and in answer to some hissing and clamor, Maretzek stated that the lady had not appeared at rehearsal, or at the concert, and that he could give no explanation.[6] So I suppose she has concluded to break her engagement. Probably Maretzek has not treated her well. His wife (little Bertucca), Patti, and most of the others form a kind of family party. The Vestvali complains she was compelled to sing in *La Favorita* an inconsiderable part, against her will; that Maretzek wilfully misplayed her part and tried to *put her out*, and so on.

March 5. Went to Columbia College meeting; pretty full—Bishop Potter in attendance. Principal matter the standing committee's report of their negotiation with W. G. Hunt & Co. for a lease of one of our best lots for $4,000; about two-thirds its value, probably. Considerable discussion and debate; the action of the committee at length reluctantly confirmed and its decree registered. I offered a resolution directing the committee to let at *auction*, in order that something like a protest might appear on the minutes. . . .

The Academy of Music has suspended operations. There is a fierce triangular duel between Maretzek, Ole Bull,[7] and Strakosch, and the orchestra and chorus war on all three and demand arrears of salary in vain. Vestvali seems to be all right, and to have been oppressively treated. . . .

March 13, TUESDAY. Sunday, Higby preached at Trinity one of the greatest sermons I ever heard from him or any one else. A vast "demonstration" at the funeral of our lamented fellow citizen, Bill Poole.[8] Two

[6] Max Maretzek (1821–1897), the impresario, was now in charge of a season of Italian opera at the Academy of Music.

[7] Ole Bull (1810–1880), Norwegian violinist; M. Strakosch (1825–1887), Moravian musician.

[8] William Poole, a pugilist and a leader of the Know-Nothings, had been murdered in cold blood by a gang of ruffians. He was given a funeral which surpassed the demonstrations at the deaths of Clay and Webster.

hundred thousand people, they say, were in Broadway; the street was crowded from Bleecker Street to the Ferry. Baker, who fired the shot that killed him, has got off, they say, in a ship bound to the Canary Islands, by connivance of some of the police. There is talk of sending a steamer in pursuit. Some say he is still in New Jersey. Should he be captured and brought here while the present feeling exists, I don't think he'd live to reach the Tombs. Sunday night divers people called, among them Vestvali and "the lobster." The lady stands the test of further acquaintance; she seems a genial, intelligent Titaness.

March 14. The *Pacific* arrived this morning. It was time; people were growing very anxious. Discontent in England still undiminished. Another "crisis," and Lord John Russell in office again.

March 15. Tonight with Ellie to the nuptials of George Jones and Miss Harriet Coster at 75 Fifth Avenue; a considerable crowd. Dr. Taylor officiated. The principal actors shewed self-possession, and the affair went off well. The bride is not pretty a bit, did not look well tonight, and a very bilious brunette is not an agreeable object to contemplate. Talked with Mrs. Charles Kuhn, the Rev. Mr. Chauncey, and others, ate no supper, and returned early to private life. Prosperity to George in his new estate, for he's an excellent fellow and deserves a good wife.

March 18, SUNDAY. Yesterday to Academy of Design with Charley [Strong] and George Anthon. The exhibition is at the old Düsseldorf Rooms on Broadway between Spring and Prince Streets; space smaller than usual and consequently the number of bad pictures less. Three of Jack Ehninger's, cabinet size. Alas, for poor Jack's high aspirations! He has mistaken his vocation. The discovery will be a bitter blow to him, but sooner or later it must come. He is without sense of color, though he draws well; his pictures are generally crude, cold, without sentiment, and perfectly unattractive. Huntington contributes a good Magdalen. Why do artists always represent that personage so dishevelled and décolletée in her penitence?—"hair loosely flowing, robes as free?" Her piety should be prudery. The beautiful sinner, reformed and regenerate, would rush into the opposite extreme of strict and grim propriety. St. Mary Magdalen should be pictured as a nun. Church's beautiful tropical landscapes, the result of his late visit to Ecuador, are the chief attraction. They are most lovely and beautiful: warm, rich, hazy air, copious masses of brilliant, many-colored equatorial foliage, with outlying festoons and draperies of tangled vine-growth and great pendant clusters of fruit and flowers. I think him our most promising artist. These pictures shew his versatility. His earlier landscapes have been marked most distinctly by northern character, a love of cold, stern New England seaside atmosphere, and have shewn special power in rendering it on canvas. He seems to deal quite as well with this new field of subjects; is as strong, real, and true in depicting the still sunny inland lake and the tropical wilderness as in the Mt. Desert region.

March 23. Went by myself last night to hear *Der Freischütz* at Niblo's. Agatha (Miss Caroline Lehman) was quite respectable; the other parts vilely filled; the orchestra weak and not very accurate. But it takes a great deal to spoil Weber's music and I enjoyed it. The *Spukereien* of the Wolf's Glen were on an extensive scale of mechanism and pyrotechnics, including an owl with fiery eyes, two bat-winged ghosts with pin wheels fizzing on their abdominal parts, several groups of moving pasteboard skeletons, crackers and blue lights behind the scenes, and a great dragon or crocodile that crawled about the stage with its nose on fire. But Samill's grand final entree through a trap door was an utter failure, and that demon and the carpenter had to exert considerable strength and activity to prevent the Bengal lights and red fire communicating with the scenery.

March 25, SUNDAY. Miss Rosalie here this evening; Ehninger, George Anthon, Lawrence, the artist, and others. A pleasant person is Lawrence. He knows Maurice, Kingsley, Carlyle, Ruskin, and others. Curious reason assigned for the last named gentleman's separation from his wife; I wonder if true? He, Lawrence, denounces Ruskin's books and theories without stint or qualification. I don't know which is right, but it's as natural artists should clamor against an iconoclast, an assailant of artistic conventionalisms, as that regular practitioners should abuse a medical reformer or innovator.

Yesterday afternoon with Ellie to Philharmonic rehearsal. The Seventh Symphony (A minor) was roughly but forcibly played. So many uncanny, unhealthy, bad associations and memories are connected with it in my mind that I went reluctantly, resolved to shut out old imaginings and to see the composition from a new point of view, to put a new construction on it. To retain the old interpretation is to debar myself of the privileges of ever recalling a single phrase of this all but most vigorous of compositions, for except the C minor, no orchestral work seems to me so full of life and power. . . .

Wagner's Overture to *Tannhäuser* also played, a composition on which I'd rather not commit myself till after a rehearing. Novel, most elaborate, and full of *talent*, clearly, but not altogether pleasing, and whether truly original and genial or merely outré and labored I can't say. . . .

March 29. Tea at the Lydigs' tonight, where were the Rev. Mr. Weston and Miss Arabella Griffith, of whom I've heard so much from the Lydigs; certainly the most brilliant, cultivated, easy, graceful, effective talker of womankind, and has read, thought, and observed much and well. Some of her stories of Frost, the reverend professor of Burlington, N. J., were funny enough. He is semi-Teutonic, partially cracked, thoroughly good and devoted to his duties, thinks aloud, centres his religious belief on the doctrine of the Apostolical Succession, and walks the streets of Burlington in a gown and an Oxford cap with a feather stuck in it (which he stated to Miss Griffith, confidentially, belonged to a rooster "dat crewed on the Island of Patmos"), and addresses the canine population *sotto voce*: "Little dog, little dog, you wag your tail in de presence of a servant of de Lord?" His conversation with a certain Miss Sally Brannan, a gaunt, middle-aged, notable heathen woman of the vicinage, who never went inside a church and defied all means of grace and all efforts to bring her to a better mind: "Wal now, it's no use talking to me, *I* never experienced religion; I don't know nothin' about your preachin's and prayin's and I don't see as I've any occasion"—"Well, but you hope to go to Heaven?"—"Wal, I don't know, 'spect I shall, think it's as like as not."—"But you believeth dat dere is such a place as Heaven?"—"Wal, I don't know, ya-as, like as not there is." Frost (with concentration), "But you believeth in de *Apostolical Succession*?"—"Wal, I don't know as I've anything agin' it."

March 31, SATURDAY. News by the *Asia* does not seem important. The battering of Sebastopol is resumed; the new Czar shews no pacific impulses as yet; Prussia has not got off her fence; little is expected from the conferences at Vienna.

Chief among the civic notabilia is the Mayor's foray or razzia among the unhappy fallen women who perambulate Broadway, the noctivagous strumpetocracy. Its legality is much debated, and Morris decided against it today on habeas corpus, rightly I think. What the Mayor seeks to abolish or abate is not the terrible evil of prostitution (for the great, notorious "ladies' boarding houses" of Leonard and Mercer Streets are left in peace), but simply the scandal and offence of the *peripatetic* whorearchy. He is right in assailing it and in trying to keep vice from proclaiming its allurements in the market place; for its conspicuousness and publicity are disgraceful and mischievous and inexpressibly bad. But are his *means* and *policy* legal and right, or lawless and wrong? Most people applaud him, naturally enough, for our civic affairs have sunk into such corruption that a public officer seeking to promote a good end is upheld though he overstep his authority. He becomes the more popular for his courage in taking the responsibility of action unsupported by precedent and statute. So rise dictators in degenerate commonwealths. I think his policy dangerous and bad. It enables any scoundrel of a policeman to lay hands on any woman whom he finds unattended in the street after dark, against whose husband or brother he may have a grudge, who may be hurrying home from church or from a day's work, or may have been separated by some accident from her escort, and to consign her for a night to a station house. Till morning no interference can liberate her; and if the policeman did make a mistake, the morning would find her disgraced for life, maddened perhaps by shame and mortification. The possibility of such remediless mischief and abuse cannot be authorized by law.

April 4. Columbia College meeting Monday afternoon. Nothing noteworthy, no important action. Some discussion and prosing, but only the babble characteristic of that imbecile board, the atmosphere of which paralyzes the faculties of every man who comes into it. Today was the first auction or allotment of pews in Trinity Chapel, confined to corporators and old pew-holders. About one hundred of the one hundred and forty-four were struck off at premiums unexpectedly high, very unequal, but in the aggregate near $3,000, upset prices being about $3,500. Got a good seat at an abominable price ($34.00+$80.00) *next* pew bringing $43 premium. It's number 69, one of the highest seats in the synagogue. I didn't care about the location, but Ellie wanted a seat where she could see the officiating clergyman in spite of nearsightedness. To-night at the Committee of Arrangements for consideration at John R. Livingston's. . . . Homer Wheaton, who came near election as assistant minister, is going to turn Roman Catholic!!!

April 9, MONDAY. Two important enactments from the legislative cloaca at Albany: the Maine Liquor Law and the Ecclesiastical Property Act. Much might be said about each and especially the former. I don't myself regret the passage of either. If the liquor prohibition can be enforced and alcohol be abolished by laws strictly executed, I'm not sure but it's best. To be sure, it's a novel stretch of law-making power, but social reforms can only be effected by new instruments. These Acts are not spontaneous with the legislature; both are forced through that Sanhedrim of rascality by pressure and clamor from without, which is much in their favor. The state was never cursed with such a gang for its captains and chief governors before. There may have been senates and assemblies as profligate, but never any before on whose faces the dirt was so palpable, never any so imbecile and contemptible. Their session ends soon, fortunately, and I hope it may end before the corrupt body has secreted any of the purulent legislation about this city with which we're threatened; for example, the Police bill and Broadway Railroad bill.

The state legislature had passed a prohibition law on the Maine model which was to become effective July 4, and which in the metropolis was regarded with considerable dread. Mayor Fernando Wood announced with a flourish that he would faithfully execute all statutes "even when fanaticism rules the hours." The general expectation was that, while rural districts would accept prohibition, the large cities would not. Another controversial enactment of the legislature was a law permitting religious congregations to own property in their own name and not that of the general sectarian organization. This was an outgrowth of the controversy in Buffalo which had brought the Papal agent Bedini to the United States; and while nominally passed to protect independent Catholics, it was really anti-Catholic. Erastus Brooks, a Know-Nothing leader, had delivered a fierce speech in the state Senate on March 6 in behalf of the Church Property bill, in which he charged that John Hughes, Catholic Archbishop of New York, held title to four or five millions of church property. When Hughes responded in a vigorous letter to the press, the controversy took on broad proportions. The trustees of St. Louis Church in New York came out in a blast against the "irresponsible clerical administration of temporalities"; and S. H. Hammond, editor of the Albany State Register, *assailed Hughes for meddling in politics—drawing from the archbishop another long letter. All this pother was beneficial to the Know-Nothing agitation. The legislature for a time seemed likely to pass a Broadway street railway bill which the New York* Times *denounced (April 9) as "a private speculation, started for personal profit, and carried through by intrigue and corruption." Fortunately it was stifled.*

Fierce and bloody fighting took place in the Crimea in March and April. In London a "Sebastopol Inquiry Committee" was bringing to light exposures of incompetency and neglect which shocked the British public. It also vindicated the remarkable work done in the Crimean hospitals by Florence Nightingale. Much attention was attracted by the visit, this spring, of Napoleon III and

Empress Eugénie to England, where they divided about a week between London and Windsor, with the usual entertainments and fêtes. Victor Hugo welcomed them with a vitriolic letter, and the British police had to keep a close watch on other French exiles.

April 17, TUESDAY. Trinity Chapel duly consecrated this morning. I didn't get into Wall Street till three o'clock. The services were well conducted and impressive; church packed full, of course. I was there at nine and found people assembling. Fussed about with Livingston and others for an hour and three-quarters between the chapel and the two houses opposite, where the clergy and others assembled—making arrangements and keenly sensible of my own importance. The entering procession was imposing; sextons of the church and chapels with very big staves gilded and colored in the early decorated style; the "parochial" church-wardens with lesser staves (like the pointers used by lecturers to indicate and demonstrate on their diagrams), which the committee had licensed them to "bear" on their solemn written request. I wanted to give them letters-patent authorizing cocked hats, also. Lots of clergy in surplices. Happily, it was a fine day and the distance walked by the procession very small, so they did not have to wear their hats and present the appearance of a holiday turnout of cartmen in clean frocks. The university cap or some ecclesiastical headpiece is wanted on such occasions. The string of fifty or sixty priests and deacons, and as many divinity students, passed into the chapel under my nose as "we" received them on the chapel porch, and I must say I was not favorably impressed by my review of their physiognomies. They don't contrast so very advantageously with the Roman Catholic clergy against whose outward appearance so much is said, except in point of cleanliness. If one must judge of their physiognomy, they are below the average trader, physician, attorney even, in expression, moral and intellectual. There were sensual pig-faces, white vacant sheep-faces, silly green gosling-faces, solemn donkey-faces; but the prevailing type was that of the commonplace fourth-rate snob, without any particular expression but mediocrity and grim professional Pharisaism. Here and there was a nice, manly, earnest face, now and then, among the elder clergy, one that shewed energy and cleanness. But they were mostly a sad set. Why does that profession attract so few men of mark, moral vigor, and commanding talent?

Bishop Potter preached the sermon. The music was tolerable. The multitude of voices gave much dignity to the chants and other pieces in which the congregation joined.

April 21, SATURDAY. Just in from the Philharmonic, with little time to write about it. At Niblo's; crowd excessive and most enthusiastic. Concert a great success. Beethoven's Symphony No. 7 greater than ever. Trio ("Lift up thine eyes"), and two choruses from Mendelssohn's *Elijah*. The trio beautiful, though feebly rendered; the choruses obscure, perhaps, because I heard them for the first time. Wagner's *Tannhäuser* Overture; Weber's "Konzertstück," nicely done; and the finale of the first act of Mendelssohn's posthumous *Lorelei*, of which neither Ellie nor I could comprehend much. Certainly the Overture is a great work as compared with the productions of the last twenty-five years. It's effective; it has unity and breadth with great elaboration in detail. . . .

April 22. There's an insurrection in that very venerable and somnolent institution, the New York Society Library.[9] An opposition ticket is printed, and my name is on it, with Russel, Cornell, Giraud Foster, Wolcott Gibbs, and others whom I don't remember. The present board consists, no doubt, of incurable fogies, and I've no objection to the insurgents succeeding to their hearts' desire. But I should decline serving, if elected, of which there is not much likelihood.

April 26. Election in Society Library Tuesday. Some ninety votes polled; whole new ticket elected!!! Some question about legality of election and possible litigation. Coit, Verplanck, Judge Inglis, and others horribly disgusted. Don't think I'll serve for many reasons. No time; no inclination to ally myself with Cornell, Russel, William H. Anthon, and others of the new set in hostility to or triumph over Dayton Hobart and others of the old. Besides, this coup d'état will be followed by others like it, now that a revolutionary precedent is established, and the new board will sooner or later share the fate of the old. The ground has been bought and contracts signed for the new building, wisely or unwisely, so the new trustees can hardly hope to establish any new course of policy.

April 29, SUNDAY. This morning to Trinity Chapel with Ellie and Miss Rosalie. . . . Some fine, vigorous thought in Higby's sermon today. For example, Christianity, the gospel, Revealed Truth (neither phrase quite suits, say rather, the Church), does not so much propound mystery and things hard to understand as clear them up and remove them. Before

---

[9] The New York Society Library had been founded in 1754 and reincorporated in 1772 under charter from George III. It was about to remove to its new home in University Place near Twelfth Street.

her voice was heard, there was the mystery of remediless evil, incurable sin, sorrow without hope, the grave without the resurrection.

May 4. News from Europe. Vienna Conference broken up and abandoned; no prospect now of peace. Bombardment of Sebastopol actively resumed, as yet with no decisive result. Austria understood to be winking at Russia and not very cordial with the Allies. Napoleon and his wife have made their call "over the way" and have been fêted and caressed and toadied and hurrahed-after by the British Empire from the Queen downward. There are mutations in this world.

Sad death of Charles King's son-in-law, the Rev. C. H. Halsey, who fell from an upper window of the unfinished Everett House at one P.M. Wednesday. People talk of suicide, and there are circumstances of strong suspicion. He had been for some time depressed and hypochondriacal.

Her Majesty has buckled the garter on the imperial leg of Louis Napoleon. That lady's pure hands might have found a more appropriate duty, for the leg she deigned to manipulate walked up and down Church Street and carried its proprietor into half the disreputable haunts of drinking and harlotry that New York could offer fifteen years ago. He was known in those days as a shabby, loafing "French Count," an un-shaven, dirty, penniless, *soi-disant* prince, whose estates were in the planet Jupiter. That respectable member of the legal profession, Nelson Chase, has a bill against him to this day, unpaid and never like to be paid, for services in a suit against some contemporaneous loafer for damages because some little bulldog belonging to the latter assailed the calf of the former. Ralph Lockwood was of counsel for the dog, Chase for the Emperor, and Eugénie's husband had a verdict against him.

May 6, SUNDAY. Hobart preached this morning at Trinity chapel, Weston this afternoon; Miss Arabella Griffith sat with us and came home and spent the evening. Mr. Ruggles here, much fascinated by the lady (men generally don't affect her a great deal, say she talks conversation and isn't natural). Also Murray Hoffman, Charley, and George Anthon. Dr. Hawks looked in and kept me in a tête-à-tête of two hours on all manner of subjects, so I didn't hear much of Miss Arabella's talk.

May 9. The controversy between Brooks and Archbishop Hughes much talked of. General opinion, wherein I concur, that the latter has damaged himself and his church inexpressibly. His published letters do him no credit and prove that an Archbishop may have a weak head and be without the instincts of a gentleman or the charity of a Christian; illogical, disingenuous, vituperative. A Prince of the Church should never descend to a newspaper controversy at all, but if compelled to do so, he should not write like a Celtic pettifogger in a passion. . . .

Old Spring's son-in-law, Johnson P. Lee, was killed this morning on the Hudson River Railroad; a coincidence, coming so close on the death of King's son-in-law, Halsey, and the two fathers-in-law being so prominently hostile in the board of Columbia College.

I shouldn't wonder if another grand fracas were approaching in that venerable body. I've given up all hope of any valuable result there, now or hereafter. All human organizations have a *quasi* life and character of their own. This has its individuality most intensely marked. It is the corporate embodiment of respectability and inertia. Each *new* trustee, as he is brought in, is digested and *assimilated* and paralyzed. Only Mr. Ruggles seems to be indigestible, and to exist as an obstruction and source of irritation. I feel the depressing effect of the corporate atmosphere, the hereditary carbonic acid, whenever I attend a meeting, and I see no reason to hope that the gradual substitution of new members can work any change in the general character of the board. . . .

May 21, MONDAY. Poor Phil Forbes of the Society Library, identified with the institution so long, its hereditary librarian and executive chief, has been requested to resign and has resigned. Cause, a deficit discovered by the new board of $1,000 which he could not make good. . . . His excision was an act of necessity, but I'm glad I was not in the board and compelled to vote upon it—especially as he'd been for years on a starvation salary.

May 24. Went up at three P.M. with Mr. Ruggles and Anderson to inspect the "Botanic Garden" premises of Columbia College.[10] They dined here and spent the evening. Digging, blasting, and excavating are furiously active in the Botanic Garden, which looks like the Allied lines around Sebastopol. It's a chaos, the elements whereof are piles of rock, great holes, vast puddles, crowbars, shanties, pigsties, and stramonium, a mile beyond civilization in any form that can aid the new street lots. The Fifth and Sixth Avenues are very slowly putting out feelers toward it. The calculation of Gouverneur Ogden & Co. is that we can get $100 a lot ground rent on a building lease. On that basis we are running up an aggregate debt of $180,000; spending $850 to dig out each lot, and paying therefor about $60 annual interest. A walk over the ground settles the question of the soundness of Gouverneur's financiering (*solvitur ambulando*); no sane man will pay $50 for the lots (one with another) for

10 The future site of Rockefeller Center.

six years to come. So much for that operation. Then we are to build at a cost certainly not below $150,000, and as certainly our removal to this suburban waste will lose us half our students and cut off half our income from tuition fees, at least. Let us look into the figures as worked out this evening and see where our academic speculation is going to land us.

Our old rental was	$14,000.00
Additional (Stevens and so forth, $2,500; $4,000 less $1,000 on account of grammar school)	5,500.00
Tuiton fees (say)	10,000.00
Making a total from that quarter of	29,500.00
Expenses: interest on the old debt, and taxes (say)	25,500.00
This left a surplus (cut down by an occasional assessment or extra expend.) of	4,000.00
But our removal uptown will surely reduce our tuition receipts by half and probably more, so instead of a surplus of $4,000, we have a minimum deficit (to be increased by accidental extras) of	1,000.00
Then comes the new rent from the south side of Park Place as extended, which, with decent management, would have been $20,000, but is (say)	14,000.00
against which may be set off interest on debt for grading and regulating Botanic Garden ($160,000+at least four years' interest on that time before the land is productive, viz., 40,000) $240,000:	14,000.00
Rents on north side of extended Park Place (the letting mismanaged according to usage) will not exceed	25,000.00

New college buildings (on the pig-sty premises) will cost $150,000.

Additions to library, apparatus, etc., to bring them up to the standard of passable respectability, certainly not below $50,000.

Interest on this outlay, for which additional debt is to be incurred	14,000.00
Surplus	11,000.00
But the reduction of tuition fees ($5,000) will cause this to be cut in upon to meet current expenses of our present organization	5,000.00
And the necessity of an allowance for house rent to President and three professors	6,000.00

(now accommodated downtown at $850 each), reduces this to $2,600, which sum seems the amount we gain by this risky financing with our princely landed endowment

downtown, supposing everything to go right, and that we
escape all dangers of debt.

Then in 1859 or 1860 we begin to receive the rent of 128
uptown lots (the Botanic Garden, less the portion reserved
for college buildings) at $100 each: 12,800.00

So $15,400 seems all the increased income we can hope to get for
twenty-one years to come by this borrowing and financiering and blind,
hazardous speculation, whereas we may be thereby made utterly bankrupt and annihilated, should a period of pressure and public calamity
intervene.

I think our policy is to urge a postponement of *building* on the Botanic
Garden property and the removal of the college to temporary accommodations hired *anywhere* almost. . . .

May 30, WEDNESDAY.   Summer at hand; one begins to seek the
shady side of the street and to think favorably of ice cream. European
news. Canrobert resigns (spontaneously or pursuant to particular request
don't appear). Pelissier reigns in his stead.[11] Nothing notable from
Sebastopol. Telegraph being wholly under government control, absence
of news doesn't indicate Allied progress.

June 4. . . . Meeting of Columbia College trustees, at which I *hope*
the Gibbs controversy appeared for the last time. (I'm so sick of the College and its concerns that I don't want to be mixed up with any more
squabbling about them. I want the old squabble to end, and shall take
care to identify myself with no new ones.) The Committee on the Senate
Investigation handed in a report sometime since, in which they referred
to Mr. Ruggles's evidence before the Senate committee as founded on
"misapprehension" and stated it to be "notorious" that no member of
the board had objected to Gibbs on the ground of his Unitarianism. The
report lay over to this meeting, and there was a manifest disposition to
shirk the subject and let it lie over indefinitely. But Mr. Ruggles called
for the reading of his protest, laid on the table at the last meeting; whereupon the Rev. William Berrian, D.D., remembered an engagement and
walked off as fast as possible. The Rev. Mr. Spring was absent. The pro-

[11] François C. Canrobert, commander-in-chief of the French forces before Sebastopol, handed over on May 16, 1855, to A. J. J. Pelissier. Canrobert, who had taken
part in the coup d'état which placed Napoleon III in power, had fought bravely and
been twice wounded at the battle of the Alma; but the delays of the siege and quarrels
with the English command cost him his post.

test was read; it objected to the report for that the testimony criticized was publicly given and was known to the board, and the board had abundant time to introduce evidence, contradictory or explanatory, had there been any to produce; also for that the censure of the committee was on an *ex parte* proceeding; also for that the testimony was true, and "the undersigned" (naming no names) was prepared to prove it true with divers hinted details of time, place, and circumstance. A grim pause of expectation followed its reading. The majority was a little puzzled. It wouldn't *do* to refuse to receive it or to deny it a place on the minutes. On the other hand, if put there, it would perpetuate the memory of things inconvenient, and by its precision and particularity of affirmation would altogether outweigh the general negative of the report. So Bradford, "as a new member," got up (I think at Anderson's suggestion) and moved that the report be sent back to the committee, taking it for granted that on that call Mr. Ruggles would withdraw his protest. This was done, Betts making some feeble objection about this being a "censure on the committee." . . .

My contempt for that board and indifference to its proceedings increase daily. No good result from our great endowment is to be hoped for in my lifetime, at least. . . .

The unanimous recommittment of the report was a triumph for Mr. Ruggles, or would be if he desired a triumph over anybody. The majority of the board swallowed their own words, and if that's not eating dirt, I don't know what is.

June 6, WEDNESDAY. Rumors this evening of a duel between two hopeful members of the Shakespeare Club, established in Mrs. Mary Jones's memorable Broadway house: Breckinridge and Leavenworth.[12] Their departure from the state with militant designs was ungenerously alluded to in a morning paper. The story tonight is that the latter is shot dead.

June 7. The duel was tragic but not fatal. Leavenworth (Charles King's nephew, Bob Strong's *Kleinmeister* and evil genius two years ago) very seriously hurt. Breckinridge, said to be rather a clever young man, also hit, but not dangerously. Poor little Jem Pendleton was Leavenworth's second, and is said to have made himself scarce; very prudently.

---

[12] The Shakespeare Club was not literary or dramatic, but a social organization. J. B. Breckinridge (of the well-known Southern family) was a lawyer with offices in Wall Street, and Frank Leavenworth a young man about town. They fought on the Canadian side of Niagara Falls with minor injuries.

It would be just as well for him to live in Paris and Italy and on the Rhine for two or three years, away from the suckers who feed on him here.

June 21.   Our first emphatic summer day; the sunshine is oppressive at last. Ellen went to Boston and Cambridge this morning with her father and mother and Mrs. D. C. Murray by New Haven train. Quite active at chambers and elsewhere till five-thirty, when I dined at Delmonico's, then came uptown, and, after a cup of coffee, took a long, hard walk down the Second Avenue and then down Grand Street even to the ferry, whence I looked in the twilight at the well-remembered outline of the Williamsburgh shores, and thought of the many pleasant Saturday afternoons that are now far away. . . .

June 25, MONDAY.   My father was taken ill last night, pretty seriously, I fear, with gout in the stomach.

June 26.   Anxious about my father, his condition not satisfactory. No return of pain, but he looks as if he'd been ill for a fortnight and is very weak.

June 27.   Sent for next door this morning at seven. My father had had a half-fainting fit, and fallen down. But when put on the sofa, he recovered himself very promptly, and during the day he has seemed no worse than yesterday.

July 10, TUESDAY.   My father died that same Wednesday night at about twenty minutes after ten, aged 72 years, five months, and seven days. He was buried Friday, the 29th, with my mother in Trinity Churchyard. . . .[13]

I don't yet realize it. I find myself every morning expecting to see him in his accustomed place at the desk where he worked honestly, wisely, and untiringly for fifty years. When I think of it as a fact that is indeed true, I feel like a child that has lost his way in the street. For while he was here, I felt safe in his advice and judgment and ready aid against all trouble, disaster, and perplexity, sure that there could be no embarrassment he could not set right, no difficulty from which he could not extricate me.

There is universal sincere regret, even in this thoughtless hurrying city, as for a public loss and general calamity; with good reason. Learning, judgment, candor, integrity, justice, charity and kindliness, courtesy to rich and poor, were all combined in him. How many have I heard of who spoke of him as the best man they ever knew!

[13] For an account of George Washington Strong and his legal career, see the introduction to this work.

Wonderful, untiring industry and fidelity in labor marked all his life. Not from love of money-making; that feeling was never manifest in him —did not exist in him. He repudiated all openings to wealth, and shrank from profit, except in the righteous and moderate wages of work. It was from higher than money-making motives that he toiled early and late, and denied himself relaxation and holiday. It was from the feeling that what work he had to do ought to be done thoroughly, promptly, and well. Truth, justice, and fidelity in every relation and every duty seemed part of his nature. I have not felt all their value, because I never could conceive of him as otherwise than perfect and spotless in integrity, because it was impossible he should do a wrong or fail to render to everyone around him more than the amplest measure of right. How he shrank from thanks for his quiet, spontaneous generosity! But his justice was stern and rigorous only against himself. For the faults and follies of others, he had silence and sincere pity, or (if the case could possibly bear it) a genial laugh. Never was there a laugh so hearty and so kindly as his, especially when some scape-grace was its subject.

The resounding event of the summer abroad was the capture of Sebastopol by the Allied forces; the great event at home was the emergence of the Republican Party as a powerful new political organization. On September 8, the Western troops made their grand assault on the Malakoff fortress, and the following day the Russians evacuated Sebastopol. Great rejoicings took place all over England and France. As the Russians had meanwhile been defeated by the Turks at Kars, hopes ran high for a speedy end of the war. "Russia," exclaimed the Czar, "never makes peace after a disaster!"—but it was expected that she would. As for the Republican Party—that had come into being the previous summer at various places, a meeting at Jackson, Michigan, on July 6, 1854, being usually regarded as the occasion of its birth. But it did not take on great vigor until the outrages of the proslavery "border ruffians" in Kansas during the spring and summer of 1855 aroused violent feeling in the North and West. The fraudulent election of a territorial legislature at the end of March had particularly incensed the free-soil elements. This legislature passed a series of laws of the most oppressive character. On September 26, the Whigs and Republicans of New York State met in convention at Syracuse. Reuben E. Fenton presided over the Republican gathering, and John A. King over that of the Whigs. A union was quickly effected, a strong free-soil plat-

form was drawn up, and a "Republican Ticket" was given to the state with
Preston King at its head as candidate for secretary of state, the most important
office to be filled that fall. In a chaotic campaign, with the Democrats again
divided between Softs and Hards, the Know-Nothings led the Republicans by
a narrow margin. The prestige of the Pierce Administration was gone.

July 15, SUNDAY.   Hobart preached at Trinity Chapel very effectively
and ably, better than I've ever known him to preach before. His new
position has spurred him to harder work, and if he keeps it up, he'll
justify all I've ever said of his talents. Charlie and George Anthon here
this evening, and we experimented on *maté*. Nauseous slop that makes
one feel a little ill.

In Wall Street, nothing new. Our regular clients seem to remain
with us. I can't help a feeling of surprise that any one should come to me
now. Daily expressions of the deepest sympathy and heartfelt regret
from people I thought incapable of either.

July 17.   Details of the Allied repulse on June 18th indicate murderous bungling.

July 18.   Another day of paralyzing heat. Awake nearly all night
in much discomfort; tried the library chair, and various other expedients,
in vain. . . . I see with surprise that Miss Florence Nightingale, the single
heroic personage who has come to light in this European war, is a Unitarian. Strange that she should be permitted to dispense liniments and
chicken broth in the hospitals of a Christian nation! Probably she will be
stopped when the great precedent set by Columbia College becomes
generally known in England.

July 26, THURSDAY. . . . European news: the besiegers of Sebastopol
seem to gain ground, but their progress is not rapid. They must triumph
sooner or later, but when the Malakoff towers and even the North Forts
are razed, when every Russian is kicked out of the Crimea, I think peace
will be more improbable than it is at present. Conquest of Russian territory and the prospect of its being permanently occupied by the enemy
will unite the whole empire in a patient but vigorous struggle, or in
sacrifice and passive resistance that all the energy of the Allies can't
overcome. Russia, I predict, will tire them both out, and may well end
by partitioning Turkey with France and England. That politic and ingenious person, Lord John Russell, has been over-reaching himself and
is in hot water; he has resigned or is about to do so.

July 31.   Report in the street of a defalcation. Edmonds of the

Mechanics' Bank is reported to have left town and to have left accounts behind him that don't balance; very bad, if true.

August 2. The trouble in the Mechanics' Bank proves to be some hitch between Edmonds and Burke, the clerk of the City Chamberlain's department. Edmonds has resigned and his resignation is accepted. It grows out of payments by some one to somebody, in the nature of secret service money to secure to the Bank the funds in court.[14]

August 15, WEDNESDAY. After a call on Mr. Ruggles this evening, I started on a walk downtown, my chief resource in the present derangement of my household gods, but was driven home by a sluggish, sultry rain. Marcotte's artists are in possession of the library at present. It is rank with the smell of paint, the bookcases are sealed up, the movables swept out or swathed in unsightly, paint-dabbled coverings. It's a piece of work to make one corner of this table available for my present amusement, the only one within my reach, for books are inaccessible, and it's too hot for making chords on the organ. There is a dearth of news. Before Sebastopol there is stagnation, even as here. People are beginning to worry themselves a good deal about yellow fever, without much reason as yet. It is raging at Norfolk and Portsmouth, to be sure, and there are cases at the quarantine. Robert Kelly is Chamberlain, vice Edmonds abdicated in a mystery; one of Wood's very best official acts is that appointment. Chief newspaper topics, the lamentable Louisville election riots and the question who began them (the weight of evidence rather against the Know-Nothings), and the Wheeler case in Philadelphia, Judge Kane's very queer decision, and Passmore Williamson's confessorship in jail for contempt of court. His passive resistance will trouble the Federal courts a little. If he lies there much longer, the prim, yellow-legged Quaker will be glorified into a hero and a martyr, his name will be a word of power north of Mason and Dixon's line, and an issue will be raised on which the fiercest Quattlebum must feel himself in the wrong. For Kane's decision is a monstrous stretch of judicial power abused to enforce conclusions equally monstrous.[15]

August 30. Weather cool and wholesome; this has been a mild sum-

[14] An investigation proved that the officers of the Mechanics' Bank had regularly paid funds for corrupt political purposes.

[15] A Southerner named John H. Wheeler had sued out a writ of habeas corpus against Passmore Williamson, a Pennsylvanian whom he alleged to be in control of certain freed or rescued slaves. Williamson denied any such control and refused to comply with the writ. He was then sentenced to prison for contempt of court by Federal District Judge John Kintzing Kane.

mer, and the city is said to be unusually healthy. People have stopped
prophesying yellow fever. Another destructive railroad "accident" at
Burlington, N.J.; the murder in this case chargeable to the directors, who
could not spare from their immense receipts the cost of a double track,
and to the conductor of the demolished train, who backed it at full speed
while the connecting signal from the rear car to the engine was out of
order.

September 9, SUNDAY.   Summer weather has returned upon us. . . .
Norfolk and Portsmouth fearfully plague-stricken; nearly depopulated by
yellow fever. Men and women die deserted and without aid; corpses rot
unburied in desolate houses. [Even the] wealthy have to strive to procure the interment of wife or child, in a pine box, carried off with others
on a cart and thrown into a common trench. Higby told me today that
the newspapers do scanty justice to the pestilence and its horrors.

September 13.   Went to Cozzens's [at West Point] Tuesday afternoon in the *Alida*, returned this morning by railroad. Left Ellie very
comfortable; hotel far from crowded. Some nice people there (as there
are in another place equally hot, where are no transient boarders): Mr.
Lewis Jones, General Scott, Colonel Scott and his wife, Luther Bradish,
and others. All yesterday I spent panting, with my tongue out, languidly
shifting my position in the vain quest of a cool spot. . . . Drove to parade
at five-thirty with Ellie and Johnny, Mrs. Lewis Jones, and her little
Sidney; had a pleasant time. The two children and little Winfield Scott
fraternized and rampaged over the plain, and I feared they would charge
the line of cadets and be made prisoners of war.

September 14.   Ate nothing till my five o'clock dinner with Anthon at
the new Chambers Street Delmonico's, where we fared rather sump-
tuously. Walked up and stopped at Greene Street synagogue. Israel does
not make a joyful noise. The monotonous solo ululations of the reader,
or rabbi, are sufficiently dismal, but the people vociferate their responses
in discord unspeakable, like eager bidders at a sale of stocks. It is
strange that the sentiment and expression of their worship should be so
utterly unlike that of any Christian culture I ever witnessed.

September 17.   *Waikna, or Adventures on the Mosquito Coast* is a clever
book. Vivid pictures of tropical nature and of consort with tapirs, spoon-
bills, wart hogs, and marine mollusca among palms, mangroves, man-
chineels, coral reefs, and the like; all seemingly truthful, except some
mystification about an Indian Pythoness, and an Indian Prince incognito
with a miraculous talisman. The new novels, a brace of stories by Reade

(author of *Peg Woffington*), flat. All the West Point men favor Russia, or rather are intensely anti-Anglican. Quiet reigns there; nearly all our old friends of 1849–52 are gone or going, except the professors. [Henry B.] Clitz and [Fitz-John] Porter are among the last; the former is ordered to stay, and Porter to the Sault Ste. Marie. Haight is out upon his new duties at Trinity Chapel with much energy. It is a most important missionary station, and I think he'll do his duty there. Ogilby is assigned him as lieutenant. Dix is at St. Paul's and Young at St. John's.

September 24, MONDAY. Much bunged up with an orgasm of cold in the head, producing what Tennyson probably refers to in *Maud* (just opened) where he speaks of "a sensitive nose," which left him "with the least little touch of spleen." Lucky fellow to get off so lightly. Tennyson is too recondite, elaborate, euphuistic, witty, and conceited for a durable immortality. *The Princess, In Memoriam,* and this volume are lycophrontic in their darkening of thought by remote allusion and obscure parabolic hintings—examples often of "reserve in communicating poetic truth," for Tennyson *can* produce the strongest effects by simple thoughts in simple words (for example, "Flow on, cold rivulet," or "Break, break, break, On thy cold gray stones, O Sea"). But he is fond, unhappily, of turning simple thoughts into elaborate puzzles; dressing them in queer diction and erudite illustration, as if he were getting up an acted charade, and the game was to devise something that could not be found out. It's a pity, for there are passages in *Maud* of rare sweetness and power. . . .

Plague in Norfolk and Portsmouth still most deadly and terrible. There is a vague presentiment about that it will be here next summer. Fanning C. Tucker is breaking up and coming to an end, and so I fear is George Curtis, the Howadji's father. Both (and the latter especially) will be missed in Wall Street for a few days; none are missed there long. . . .

September 28. The great news of the week comes from Europe. Sebastopol *fuit.* The Malakoff was stormed after a desperate contest (the English attack failed and the victory belongs to France), whereupon the mines of the south side were fired, the city was blown to pieces, and Russia marched grimly across a temporary bridge to the north side of the harbor, where her forts and field works are still intact, and where she may await another siege. But I predict the Crimea will be abandoned. What will happen then? . . .

On the whole, I don't think *Maud* will add to Tennyson's fame. Some things in it are worthy of Mother Goose—for example, "Blush it through the East Till the East is West And the West is East," and so forth.

Much is obscure. Much is bombastical bosh; much is disgraceful to a master of rhythmic melody like Tennyson, wooden, lame, rickety, and inharmonious.

October 1.   Went to a Columbia College meeting, where some small matters were disposed of. On Gouverneur Ogden's motion, a committee was appointed with plenary power to enquire into the state of the College, the causes of its alleged inefficiency in discipline and instruction, and into things in general. A good step if there were likelihood that the committee will ever do anything. Upjohn is to be architect of the new buildings. He shewed me some of his rough sketches a day or two since, which looked pretty well. He's going to attempt Venetian pointed, to which he's an utter stranger, so I dare say his work will be sufficiently bungling in detail, at least. Ruskin has inspired him with the notion. Also he's going to use brick of divers colors for external work. Mr. J. Wrey Mould set him the example in the Unitarian meeting-house, at the corner of Fourth Avenue and Twentieth Street. The contrasts of Caen stone and the reddest possible brick in that edifice are too glaring, but I'm glad the precedent is to be followed and improved on.

I've come to the conclusion that the college is hopelessly given over to coma, stupefaction, and probable poverty for the present generation. Some of these days it will be wealthy and efficient, but that will be after I've evolved lots of ammonia, deliquesced, and dried up into a pliable, pulverulent mass. So I take little interest in its proceedings.

October 8.   Have done an unusual amount of walking today, which I chronicle as a cheering sign of improvement. Started with Eloise after breakfast, as with a newly transported country cousin, marched her out to Fortieth Street on the Fifth Avenue, and thence downtown, and took a melancholy look at poor old shabby 108 Greenwich Street, and left her at the corner of Broadway and Rector Street to find her way back again. Had some locomotion to do in and about Wall Street. Walked uptown, and down again to a vestry meeting, and on my return, perceiving a promising fire somewhere to the northwest, I left the railroad car and went in pursuit on a dog-trot. My pyrotechnic tour was fruitless, the fire began to fade in the sky, and finding myself in an unknown region on the outskirts of the city, somewhere among the thirties or forties, where it was dark and vacant lots abounded, and there was a sparse and Celtic population, I turned about and walked back again. . . .

Ellie has heard Rachel tonight in *Les Horaces*. Unlike most people, she is able to retain some appearance, at least, of moderation and sense, in speaking of that artiste. For polite society generally the sound of her name is the signal for a display of mental alienation; persons generally discreet and accustomed to use language with ordinary accuracy babble the ecstatic exaggerations of very green school-girls and excited chamber-maids.

October 12, FRIDAY. Today's newspapers are interesting; they announce the return of Dr. Kane's Arctic Expedition, together with Lieutenant Hartstene's relieving party, luckily encountered by Kane on his way home.[16] The expedition did not find Sir John Franklin, of course, but seems to have made notable discoveries; the north face of Greenland, great berg-dripping glaciers, a *terra incognita*, and an open polar sea. Also we have copious details of the storm of the Malakoff, and how the English were badly beat trying to storm the Redan. General Simpson is censured for not having an adequate reserve or supporting party at hand; reasonably censured, one would think. And it is contrary to what I supposed the settled rule to let the stormers take cartridges with them. The men would not come up to the scratch but

> —with a hankering for existence,
> kept merely firing, at a foolish distance

and Muscovia, behind her breastworks and traverses and curtains, beat them at that game. The French newspapers and despatches are very civil and consolatory, but the invincibles of Inkerman and other places were indisputably forced out of the Redan, neck and heels.

October 17. At a Columbia College alumni meeting at four P.M. Seventeen present to make arrangements for the annual address, October 31st. Impossible, it seems, to put active life into alumni, trustees, or anything else connected with that somnolent seat of learning. It's an enchanted region; all who enter it doze and slumber and sleep. . . .

Anderson is to pronounce an address. I wonder if it will be like his late address before some convention of teachers at the "University" on

---

[16] The second American expedition in search of Sir John Franklin, fitted out largely by the merchant Henry Grinnell, and commanded by Elisha Kent Kane, had left New York May 31, 1853. It suffered heavily from scurvy and from inadequate equipment, but found open water north of Ellesmere Land and reported this as evidence of an open polar sea. In the spring of 1855, Kane was forced to abandon his vessel, the *Advance*, which had been frozen in, and he and his party finally reached Upernavik in South Greenland. At Disco he was found by a government relief expedition under Lieutenant H. J. Hartstene. The party had explored some unknown parts of the Greenland coast, had discovered Kennedy Channel beyond Ellesmere Land, and had found and named Grinnell Land.

physical science, which astounded the assembled Unitarians and Presbyterians and Negativersans by the doctrine that the state had no right to
teach science, nor the press, nor private teachers; that being the exclusive
duty and prerogative of the church. I believe, however, he made an exception in favor of "the family" considered as an institution, and was disposed
to wink at the presumption of a father shewing off phosphorus and potas-
sium and electrical machines to his children. And S. Weir Roosevelt, Esq.,
is to deliver a poem.

Looked in on Professor McCulloh in his room this afternoon. He was
unpacking nice new optical apparatus. There was certainly an air of life
about the place, at least as compared with the aspect of things *tempore*
Renwick.

The Rt. Rev. Doane in very hot water again. The charges this time
are said to be drunkenness and adultery.[17] Pamphlets and newspaper paragraphs are raging around him, but he's serene and comfortable. That such
charges should be openly made and that anybody should credit them is
bad enough, even after making all allowance for two facts: first, that the
Bishop has bitter personal enemies; and second, that his manners and
language are free from anything like Pharisaism or Puritanism. I fully
believe that if he was told he was wanted by a penitent in a house of ill-
fame, he would march into it at midday or midnight without any effort at
concealment or any precaution to preserve evidence of his object, or any
pause to consider whether the summons might not be a trap.

Apropos of that, much talk of the "Free Love League" of S. P. Andrews, Mr. Brisbane and others, of both sexes, lately invaded by the
police at 555 Broadway; "passional attraction" its watchword, fornication
and adultery its apparent object.[18] Further news from Europe yesterday
was unimportant. The Allies continue stationary, except that they seem
to be strengthening their force at Eupatoria.

October 21, SUNDAY.   George Anthon, who is not susceptible to his-
trionic impressions, is made captive by the Israelitish woman Rachel.[19]
She tasks his vocabulary to the utmost. Cram goes every night to hear

[17] Bishop George Washington Doane of New Jersey; the charges were baseless.
[18] A "free-love society," organized by Albert Brisbane, Stephen P. Andrews,
and other radical theorists, and laying claim to five hundred or six hundred members,
held bi-weekly meetings under the name of the Progressive Union Club at the address
here named. Its adherents attacked "compulsory morality" and extolled "passional
attraction"; but their movement, which provided a passing newspaper sensation,
soon died.
[19] Rachel or Elizabeth Rachel Felix (1821–1858), the great French actress.

and see her, and is in a worse spasm of enthusiasm than any since the
Kossuth hallucinations. Mrs. Eleanor also goes every night and experiences fevers and nervous flustrations, with ebullient and explosive hysterical tendencies. The moral repute of this Jewish sorceress is certainly
low, for though she's so prodigious a lion, she has been asked, I believe,
to meet ladies but once, viz., at Trobriand's. People whisper very black •
things of her.

October 26. Have been hard at work for the last four evenings till
after midnight with paste and hot iron, mounting the file of letters from
my father to John Lloyd, from 1820 till Lloyd's death in 1841, which was
found, rusty and forgotten, in a recess of my father's safe in Wall Street.
From the vast multitudes of letters addressed to my father and carefully
preserved by him, which I have examined, including hundreds from Lloyd,
it is evident that he was the man with whom my father kept up a regular
correspondence on other than business matters. . . .

Herrick, the first of our civic fathers indicted and tried for bribery and
corruption, has got off. The jury disagreed. The case against him was
strong, but perhaps there was room for honest doubt whether the main
witness for the prosecution was reliable. There are a dozen more indictments for the same offense yet to be tried. As this was the pioneer case,
chosen by the District Attorney, I fear it was the strongest. . . .

Columbia College meeting last Monday. Spring's Committee on the
Senate Investigation reported again (their former report having been re-
committed for Mr. Ruggles's protest) nearly to the same effect, only in
less distinct terms. Their fatuity and want of moral sense are portentous.
Action on the report postponed to December. I trust no farther shindy may
be necessary.

*The chief events of the fall were the return of Thackeray to the United
States; a brisk dispute between America and Britain over recruiting on
American soil for the British forces; and the before-mentioned victory of the
Know-Nothings in the New York elections.*

*"Who that saw Thackeray in this country in the fifties," asks James Grant
Wilson, "will ever forget that giant form, crowned with a stately and massive
head, covered with almost snow-white hair?" The great novelist came with
the partly completed manuscript of his lectures on "The Four Georges,"
finishing the last one after he reached America. Landing in Boston, he renewed his friendship with Longfellow, Ticknor, Dana, Lowell, Prescott, and*

others. In New York he stayed part of the time with his friends the Baxters, and in part at the Clarendon Hotel. One compliment particularly pleased him. Kane, the Arctic explorer, just returned from his most dangerous voyage, said that he had seen one of his seamen in the hold crouched hour after hour over Pendennis. *Bayard Taylor, George William Curtis, and others entertained Thackeray, and he was much at the Century Club. All the lectures were attended by overflowing and appreciative audiences. In January, 1856, the novelist went to Philadelphia to deliver them, and visited Baltimore, Washington, and Richmond. A southern tour then took him as far as Charleston, Savannah, Mobile, and New Orleans.*

It became evident during the spring and summer of 1855 that many men were being recruited for the British army in American cities and forwarded to Halifax for shipment abroad. Two British consuls, Mathew in Philadelphia and Barclay in New York, were engaged in this illegal proceeding. Early in the summer Secretary of State Marcy made formal complaint to the British government. Correspondence on the subject continued for some time, and culminated in a letter of December 28, 1855, in which Marcy asked that the British minister, Sir J. F. T. Crampton, be recalled, and that Consuls Barclay and Mathew, with the consul in Cincinnati, be removed from their posts.

Anti-slavery feeling was steadily rising in the North as inflammatory news continued to come in from Kansas. The star of the Know-Nothing party, too, was in the ascendent. The fall elections of 1855 saw the Democrats overwhelmed. In New York, Massachusetts, and Maryland the Know-Nothings won resounding victories. When Congress met in December, the Republicans counted 105 members, the Democrats 74, and the Native Americans 40.

October 28, SUNDAY. Went through Fulton market yesterday with Charles E. Strong and George Anthon and got some very special roast oysters for lunch at a stand there, famous for the quality of its bivalves rather than the refinement of its habitués. Inspected various tempting prodigies, ichthyological, crustacean, and so forth, and bought Johnny a pair of very lively and vicious grey squirrels with superb canopies of bushy tail. Scratch and Bite, I name them. Thereafter to the Philharmonic rehearsal with Ellie and George Anthon, Miss Tote, and the little McIlvaine. Heard the *Pastorale* and the *Tannhäuser* Overture. The latter is certainly a very noteworthy composition. As to the former, I doubt whether articulate language could express more intensely and distinctly than its opening movement the sense of joy and freedom with which one "long in populous city pent" finds himself some bright summer morning strolling through pleasant fields on his first day of liberty, after a good breakfast and with a healthy liver.

November 1.   My evenings still busy with the Lloyd letters, and I'm now near the end of the series. . . . Yesterday's cruel sick headache . . . kept me at home and in bed all day, and prevented my going to the Columbia College alumni meeting at "Hope Chapel" in the evening. The meeting was quite successful, I hear. Anderson's address seems to have been odd and a little absurd, but the indications of interest in the affairs of the college among alumni were encouraging, stronger than I expected, or the college deserves. . . .

The [George] Baxters gave a soirée to Thackeray last night, very pleasant and brilliant I am told.[20] They went on to Boston to meet their lion on his debarkation and so make sure of him. Went with Ellie tonight to hear his first lecture (George First) at the Rev. Mr. [Edwin Hubbell] Chapin's two-horned meetinghouse [the Fourth Universalist society] in Broadway.

It was good and pleasant to hear, but inferior to the lectures of his former course (The English Humorists), and quite vulnerable to unfriendly criticism. There were repetitions and diffuseness; much of it seemed incoherent, loose, rambling and slovenly, compared with what one expected of him, and he bungled in reading as if a stranger to his own manuscript. He dwelt rather too long on and returned rather too often to the left-handed wives, favorites, and concubines of the royal and noble personages of the period. To be sure, a picture in which that feature was not very prominent indeed would have been untrue. But there were strong points in the lecture. It set forth clearly, with a few vigorous touches of light and shade, the wretched social system of the continent when feudalism had finally given way to centralization; when there was nothing in Europe but ostentatious, frivolous, licentious, reckless courts, each with its profligate potentate and worshiping noblesse and degraded, enslaved, despised masses; when the splendid and wicked tyranny of Louis XIV was coarsely imitated and caricatured and exaggerated by every little German sovereign. . . .

Came home and had some roast oysters, a truly great institution.

November 2.   I finished the Lloyd letters, which terminated early in 1841, just before Mr. Lloyd's last visit to New York and his last illness

[20] The Baxters lived in Second Avenue, opposite the residence of Hamilton Fish.

of body and mind. If Johnny lives to manhood, I trust he'll prize these letters, and learn from them to value the blood he comes of. Types of character often skip one generation, it's said. If I'm without the noble traits of my father, I console myself with the hope that they will reappear in his grandson. . . .

And I have been this evening turning over some dusty, faded bundles of letters to him that Mary has disinterred from one of the vast chests in the garret of Number 70 that are filled with the old papers of years ago; old law papers, mostly. They are from 1803 to 1807, in the time of his college friendships and intimacies and when he was studying law. Some of them I must preserve with the Lloyd correspondence. It's like walking through a newly disinterred street of Pompeii to read them. There are the boyish brotherhoods of fifty years ago, brought again to the light of day, the forgotten college excitements, the new tutors, the appointments for the great day of Commencement, the change from the habits of New Haven to those of Poughkeepsie or Hartford or Albany, how this recent graduate is doing well and that one ill, how A. is studying law and B. going into the ministry and C. is in love with Miss X. Y., "with whom I spent last evening," and who will make such a "steady and virtuous" wife, and how the beautiful Miss Someone else is going to marry a mere "Haw-buck" (a Philister, in fact). Generally, the writers are beginning their labors in law or divinity, their good resolutions are definite and earnest, and their hopes of success confident. Their future has long been determined. It has ended in this world for most of them; the hopes have withered or borne fruit, the good resolutions have been kept or broken, as the case may be, and they are gone. "Doctor Dwight" was the first and best of men to this little set of friends, and fills a larger space in their vision than Napoleon.[21] Who thinks of Dr. Dwight now but a few old-fashioned New England clergymen? All is changed. These young gentlemen are anxious and unhappy about Colonel Burr and Jacobinism and French Politicks and spend two or three days voyaging by sloop from New York to New Haven College and get shipwrecked on the north beaches of Long Island, and their books are damaged by saltwater, and their light reading is Pope's *Essay on Man*. Now there are Seward and Atchison and Pierce and California and Nebraska and Dickens and Tennyson and the New Haven Railroad. George Bloom writes often and copi-

---

[21] Timothy Dwight (1752–1817), divine, president of Yale College while the elder Strong was a student, and author of what is sometimes called the first American epic poem, *The Conquest of Canaan*.

ously; seems to have been very amiable and lively and mercurial. Deplores his deficiencies in true piety, his falling off in a "sense" of various things since he left New Haven. Studies law very hard, attends court very punctually. Is much disgusted by the dissipated ways of Poughkeepsie, and Clinton is engaged to a "charming nymph" of Dutchess County.

November 4. Heard one of Higby's most pungent sermons today on Progress. Lawrence Williams, U.S.A., dined here and narrated divers marvels of Washington Territory and Puget's Sound. Murray Hoffman and Jem Ruggles here tonight. Jem was disputatious and bellicose, and we dogmatized and disputed and squabbled over the Russian war. His sympathies are with the Western Powers, mine with the Czar.

November 7, WEDNESDAY. Election returns today's prominent topic, of course. Result still uncertain. But it is manifest that Know-Nothingism has prospered beyond expectation, and that Fusionism has sustained a sore discomfiture. In this city the Know-Nothings are certainly triumphant, and Seward and Thurlow Weed run behind Hards and Softs and every other organization. Mr. S. B. Ruggles was in great glory this morning and pronounced the election a triumph of nationality over schism and faction—a great victory beyond all hope. Perhaps it is; certainly the Philo-Niggerites, who would sacrifice the Union to their own one idea, have done far less than they expected. But the returns from the western and southwestern counties tonight look dubious, and it won't surprise me to learn that Fusionism has carried the state by a small majority.

Erastus Brooks is triumphantly re-elected to the state Senate from the Sixth district, a cruel blow to Archbishop Hughes. I wonder if it be true that he received a large silent Irish Catholic vote?

The "Reform Committee" has failed signally. Wonderful to relate, Hagg is defeated. Vanderpoel tells me the committee will not allow itself to be discouraged, but will maintain its organization. Its candidate (F. E. Mather, a rather dubious person, I think, but for whom I voted on Vanderpoel's endorsement) in the Eighteenth Ward even is badly beat. So says Henry Day, Esq., Lord's son-in-law, commonly known as "The Lord's Day." There is a radical and fatal vice in the organization of that committee, which must prevent its ever accomplishing a great deal.

November 10. Saw Charles A. Peabody, who tells me that Cowles is probably defeated as Supreme Court Judge.[22] Unfortunate, for Cowles makes a good judge. But the Know-Nothings have carried nearly every-

---

[22] Cowles, the Republican and Know-Nothing candidate, was defeated by Whiting, the Democratic candidate.

thing and Fusionism is snubbed here, as in Massachusetts. The *Tribune* grieves, but looks through the clouds of the present distress to victories hereafter. Contrary to every one's first impressions, there is a chance for Hagg as city comptroller. He was reported to be safe this morning, but his prospects in the evening papers are less bright. . . .

I am glad this state declines uniting in a sectional Northern party.[23] Washington Hunt thinks Ruggles's letters and influence did much to keep the Old Whigs of the West from coalescing with Fusionism. The nigger question is vast and momentous; it is of infinite importance that this our republic sanction and abet no wrong or injustice against Cuff and Dinah. But our system includes other elements beside Cuff and Dinah, and we cannot sacrifice everything to them without wrong to others; and there is the great fundamental question beside whether Cuff and Dinah, who were born into certain social institutions, possess natural inherent rights in virtue whereof they are entitled to have those institutions revolutionized.

November 11. Know-Nothing majority in the state not much under 6,000. So "Sam" rules here as in Maryland and Massachusetts.[24] It's a resurrection from the dead. People thought "Sam" defunct or disorganized. Our antipathy to the Pope and to Paddy is a pretty deep-seated feeling. Were I about to enter political life, and selecting an available set of principles, I should be very apt to cast in my lot with the Natives. I could very honestly pronounce in favor of material change in the Naturalization laws.

November 14, WEDNESDAY. Saw the designs for the proposed Columbia College buildings at Upjohn's office. Somewhat original; will be respectable from their magnitude and effective from their independence of the stereotyped formulas and symmetries of our architects. But the groups want unity. . . . The cost will be formidable; added to the insane outlay on the Botanic Garden, it must paralyze us with debt for twenty years to come. But perhaps it's as well to put the college into permanent inaction and slumber, to suspend its growth for another generation. When it

[23] Actually the Republicans had done well. For the state ticket the Know-Nothings polled 146,001, the Republicans 135,962, the Democratic "Softs" 90,518, and the Democratic "Hards" 58,394. In the state assembly the Republicans would hold 44 seats, the Know-Nothings 39, and the "Hards" and "Softs" 45.

[24] The Know-Nothing vote in Massachusetts was in round numbers 52,000; the Republican vote 37,000; and the Democratic vote 35,000. In Maryland the Know-Nothing ticket led the Democratic ticket roughly 42,000 to 39,200. But the Know-Nothing victory was as much a result of the breakup of parties and especially of the Whig Party as of antagonism to foreigners and Catholics.

awakens, it may chance to have a wiser and more energetic board of trustees to use its abundance. . . . Talk of war with England growing earnest. Terrible times we shall have if it should come, and our Administration has every dishonorable motive to encourage its coming.

November 15. News from Europe by the *Pacific.* The British public seems in a terrible way about anticipated war with this country, a luxury the Mother Country can't well afford just now, and for which I see no decent apology anywhere. To do it would be a tremendous calamity, and for a year or two, a succession of ignominious defeats. But if it lasted long enough to accustom us to depression, insolvency, and blockade, and stir us up to obstinate, uncompromising warfare, England would fare badly. There would be no more dissensions about Kansas; North and South would be united. A great manufacturing interest would spring up and England's chief market would be lost, and I believe we should drive her flag from the seas, if war lasted long enough, and conquer Canada besides.

November 16. Minturn told me that there was to be a special meeting of the Chamber of Commerce this morning about my friend Barclay.[25] It's said that the war-panic in England is due to proceedings of his last month in reference to a certain vessel lying here, which he took to be intended for a Russian privateer with designs on the Cunard steamers. He attempted to lay hold of her, but became satisfied he was mistaken and gave it up. According to R. B. Minturn, there is to be a committee of investigation into Barclay's doings. Barclay is very unpopular with our merchants in his consular capacity, and is a very pragmatical, wrong-headed, absurd person, but I predict nothing will come of this move. R. B. Minturn detests him, of course; they've a bitter personal quarrel growing out of our St. Luke's Hospital matter. Minturn has been wanting in tact, but Barclay's share in that business has been most discreditable to him. . . .

November 17. Just from Eisfeld's quartette concert, where were Dick Willis and wife, old Schlesinger, Mr. D. C. Murray, Timm, Scharfenberg, and others, and *inter alia* Sam Ward, looking deteriorated and debased from the Sam Ward of fifteen years ago.[26] Concert was not bad. Mendelssohn Quartette, Opus 12, tolerably interesting. Chopin Trio, Opus 8, very good, some of it a little grandiose; two of the movements decidedly cor-

[25] The British consul in New York, Anthony Barclay.

[26] Samuel Ward (1814–1884), lobbyist and financier, had lost his money and gone to California as a forty-niner. He had also separated from his wife, a woman of Louisiana birth. The summer of 1855 found him in Europe, and the autumn back in New York, apparently in straitened circumstances.

rect and significant. Mozart Quintette for stringed instruments in G minor, delightful exceedingly, the adagio and finale very memorable indeed. Packing for the interspaces was furnished by Mrs. Clara Brincker-hoff, who "did" a song by one Kücken, and a cavatina from *Der Frei-schütz*. . . .

I value Mozart's music higher and higher every year, and am reluctantly conceding him place above Beethoven himself. Quiet strength is a nobler gift than vehement energy and restlessness. The highest art is not that which electrifies and intoxicates artist and audience alike. Self-control in the artist and repose in the work are better than "inspiration" and dithyrambics. But if the crown were in my hands, I should pause and ponder before awarding it. Neither Mozart nor any other mortal to my knowledge or belief has ever spoken to man as Beethoven in some of his orchestral works and Handel in his sublime choruses. Handel, Mozart, Beethoven— "these three" may abide in joint sovereignty. It's unprofitable and ungracious to consider which of them shall be called supreme.

November 18. As I came out of Trinity Chapel, a lady's veil went suddenly and swiftly straight up into the air and disappeared above the sacred edifice. She gazed about her in entire astonishment, and Dr. Hodges, who was with me, addressed her with solemnity: "Madam, your veil has gone to Heaven before you." It went up at such a rate that it must have reached the upper regions of the atmosphere before it stopped going, and I don't believe it'll ever come down. Higby preached this morning.

November 20. Looked at Longfellow's *Song of Hiawatha*. Regret I don't admire it. People call it the "Song of High Water, or Rejoicing of a Clam." They've begun summing up in Judge Stuart's case. His guilt is about as clearly proven as guilt can be in these cases where all must rest on the testimony of a *particeps criminis*, but he'll not be convicted. There are too many Know-Nothings about. From what they tell me at the Seamen's Bank I shouldn't wonder if Richard B. Connolly, the County Clerk, were a relative and ally of Mrs. Cosgrove, alias Connolly, alias Magistrate Duval, the respectable mainstay of the prosecution.[27]

November 23, FRIDAY. I must ascertain whether the mighty bug-destroyer Lyons has no modification of his cockroach powder that will exterminate organ-grinders. We suffer peculiarly here, for the street is

---

[27] Sidney H. Stuart, judge of General Sessions, had been indicted on the charge of accepting a $500 bribe in a criminal case. Mrs. Connolly was alleged to have paid the bribe. The jury acquitted Stuart, but unanimously censured him and recommended that he resign from the bench.

very quiet, and they play all round the square before they leave it and are more or less audible at each successive station. I have been undergoing the performances of one of the tribe for an hour and a half and have heard "Casta Diva," "Ah, Non Giunge," the first chorus of *Ernani*, and some platitude from the *Trovatore* languidly ground out six times each. It makes me feel homicidal. If Abel had gone about with hand organs, I shouldn't censure Cain so very harshly. There goes "Casta Diva" for the seventh time! . . .

France and England conquer the Crimea very slowly. Arrival today, no progress. Napoleon the First was a better man of business than the Allied generals and accomplished a good deal more in the same time. Professor Hare of Philadelphia lectures tonight at the Tabernacle on ghosts and their revelations! ! !28 Had half a mind to go and hear him but too busy and rather distrustful of the whole subject beside. A little afraid of it. Hare seems as mad as one of his quadrupedal namesakes in the month of March. He has published a thick octavo volume of the Edmonds and Dexter school all about the second sphere and the third sphere.

November 24. Am smoking the pipe of meditation over the fragrant memory of the Philharmonic concert just ended. Miss Mary McIlvaine dined here and went with us. Vast crowd; Niblo's filled full. Seats obtainable only in third gallery. N.B. It's the best part of the house for hearing the music. Part I was the *Pastoral Symphony*. Solo (bass) from St. Paul, very minor and very dreary. Concerto for two violins. The Mollenhauer brethren, composers and performers, trivial and tiresome. Part II, Overture to Glück's *Iphigenie*. Two German songs, one by Schubert (Morgenständchen) was very pretty and fresh. Sleight-of-hand violin solo. Mollenhauer (encored) and Wagner's *Tannhäuser* Overture. . . .

Glück's Overture was new to me. I know very little about his music. It was archaic, rather, in its structure, but clear and vigorous. The *Tannhäuser* is certainly very effective and strong and think it will last. I don't find in it the pungency and intensity of single phrases which seem to me the characteristic mark of the highest order of music, but as a whole, it is impressive and splendid.

November 26. Professor Hare's lecture last Friday night somewhat talked of. As reported it seemed sad stuff. . . . What would I have said six years ago to anybody who predicted that before the enlightened

28 Robert Hare (1781–1858), the noted chemist, inventor of the oxy-hydrogen blow-pipe and professor at the University of Pennsylvania, had just published a book on *Spirit Manifestations.*

nineteenth century was ended hundreds of thousands of people in this country would believe themselves able to communicate daily with the ghosts of their grandfathers?—that ex-judges of the Supreme Court, senators, clergymen, professors of physical sciences, should be lecturing and writing books on the new treasures of all this, and that others among the steadiest and most conservative of my acquaintance should acknowledge that they look on the subject with distrust and dread, as a visible manifestation of diabolic agency? I am surprised that some of my friends regard the prevalence of this delusion with so much indifference. It is surely one of the most startling events that have occurred for centuries and one of the most significant. A new Revelation, hostile to that of the Church and the Bible, finding acceptance on the authority of knocking ghosts and oscillating tables, is a momentous fact in history as throwing light on the intellectual calibre and moral tone of the age in which multitudes adopt it.

November 30, FRIDAY.   Prospect of farther rumpus in the matter of Columbia College growing out of the last report of the committee on the Senate Investigation (Spring, Betts, and Ray), which affirms that Mr. Ruggles's testimony before the Senate committee that the Unitarian objection was made in the board was not "uncontradicted" (that is, Gouverneur Ogden contradicted it by swearing that the statements of his pamphlet were true), and rather insinuates that that testimony was untrue and that Wolcott Gibbs was not defeated because he was a Unitarian. Ray is a cypher, and Betts a Miss Nancy and mere abstract formula of propriety and decorum, incapable of vision beyond the neat periphery of his own whiskers. But Spring is a man of sense and strength. Is it not wonderful that he should be so devoid of courage and honesty? . . .

What is the witness, Mr. Ruggles, to do for his own justification? How is he to get and preserve the evidence that what he stated and what is contradicted was true and is known to be true to everybody in the board? His first notion was a libel suit against Gouverneur Ogden founded on the allegations of that gentleman's pamphlet. But I think a suit against someone not a trustee will work better; for example, Raymond of the *Times,* who admitted one or two articles to the same effect. Such suit need never be brought to trial; the object is simply to get a judicial record of evidence proving the facts which Spring and others deny, and that can be done by depositions *de bene esse.*

December 2, SUNDAY.   Tonight with George Anthon, Hoffman, and Richard Grant White; also Mr. Ruggles, with whom I've spent two hours (it's now 12:30) in settling the form of a protest to be handed in at tomorrow's Columbia College meeting. I've condensed the paper, I think, and toned it down a little. It's a trenchant and pungent paper, but only because it states facts which this cowardly report tries to ignore and which Mr. Ruggles is obliged to state in self-defense against it. . . .

As to Columbia College, I'm very sick of its affairs generally and of this controversy in particular. And I don't know why I keep my seat in the board. It is discreditable to be connected with so mouldy a concern. There is no prospect of better times, but rather of worse. Nothing is before us but disgraceful paralysis for twenty years to come. I do no good there and can do none. I suppose I stay there mainly because it's an office of trust that gratifies one's vanity and from that great instinct of humanity that prompts a man to keep what he's got.

December 3. Nothing very notable in Wall Street. Went to Columbia College meeting at two. Rather full. Ogden, Hoffman, and Bishop Potter absent; most of the others present, including Bradford and Allen and for a wonder, old C. C. Moore. Dr. Hobart, by the by, sent in his resignation. After a little routine business, Mr. Ruggles offered his protest and proposed that it lie on the table with the report till next meeting, to give time for consideration; that some course might be agreed on which would spare irritation, and so on. This was objected to, however, and after a good deal of talk and questions of order, Mr. Ruggles read his protest, and there followed a succession of amendments and substitutes, and so on, not to be enumerated. Mr. Ruggles made a very forcible and pertinacious battle on point after point, almost unaided. King said a few words, but the members who did not, seem to have come there determined to vote down any disloyalty to the committee.

In the course of the jangle, it came out that Betts had entered the report on the rough minutes of the last meeting as "accepted," so that the report would appear on the minutes at length; though King had moved that the consideration of the report be postponed to this meeting expressly in order that it might not become a matter of record till Mr. Ruggles had an opportunity to examine it. At this procedure, Mr. Ruggles lost his temper a little and spoke of "sharp practice." Betts responded in a tone of urbane self-control, stating that but for sundry considerations he should notice the charge differently. This was got over by a motion from Bradford to reconsider the vote approving the minutes so that the report should not appear there. . . .

At last the series of motions resulted in a vote not to adopt the report, but to adopt the concluding resolution, and that the report be not entered on the minutes, but filed, which was carried. Mr. Ruggles, of course, moved that his protest be filed with it, which was lost. King, Jones, and myself, not forgetting Moore, were the minority. Anderson was in the chair, Knox having gone off to a funeral.

I guess this was positively the very last appearance of the celebrated Gibbs controversy. Mr. Ruggles thinks at present of publishing, to be sure, and of proving his allegations under some sort of suit to be commenced against Ogden or some one else. But I don't believe he will, or that there is occasion for either course. The personal slight to him is small, however stupid and malignant, and there is no hope of shaming Betts and Knox and so forth into anything by logical coercion or otherwise, or of bettering the condition of the college. My own feeling is to abandon it altogether and leave Sleepy Hollow in peace.

As to the fact in issue between the report and the protest, I think there are very few in the City of New York who doubt that Mr. Ruggles was right and that the defeat of Wolcott Gibbs was caused by his Unitarianism. . . .

December 18.   The House of Representatives is trying hard to get a Speaker and organize, but as yet in vain, and I don't perceive that the country suffers much. Kansas is in *statu quo*. The civil war there makes little progress. Probably the Missourian invaders will retire on becoming satisfied that there's a prospect of hard knocks and "Sharpe rifle" balls.

December 24.   Christmas eve. This has been a busy and a satisfactory day, though not remarkable for the kind of diligence that "maketh rich," and a pleasant day, though cold and cloudy, with a lowering gray sky such as precedes a snow storm. Most of the morning spent in the active pursuit of Christmas presents; after dinner, in arranging Johnny's for his astonishment, on the table in the middle parlor—Napoleon's Old Guard, the elephant with the moveable head, and so on, the railroad train ("long cars") being deposited on the floor. . . .

Reading the first two volumes of Prescott's *Philip the Second*, just out; an agreeable and solid book. Philip and Don Carlos remind me strongly of John Lloyd and his father. My father's correspondence with the latter (1833–36 or thereabouts) furnishes the outline of that tragedy, which is filled up by my vivid remembrance of what was said about it at the time. . . .

Why has no one yet given us an orchestral interpretation of Christmas, a Christmas Symphony? Probably Beethoven's C minor covers the ground, though not exactly. It might do for an expression of Milton's awful and glorious Christmas hymns, but not of the Christmas carol. Its sentiment is that of a transcendentally noble Christmas sermon, not of the Festival, half secular, half sacred.

December 27, THURSDAY.   Have been at work tonight, like the King who was "in the parlor counting up his money," making up a statement of assets, and income, and so on, which looks better than I deserve. When that incubus of an Atlantic Dock mortgage is paid off (if that time ever comes), I shall feel quite wealthy; provided California gold don't suddenly revolutionize values when peace returns to Christendom (as it soon will), and provided no other accident or catastrophe intervene. After all, this saving up tenpences and watching their accumulation is small business.

December 29.   News from Europe. Peace again talked of as probable. Kars has surrendered, so Mahound and Termagaunt don't have it quite all their own way in the present campaign. Re-read some of *Vanity Fair* tonight, certainly a most noteworthy book.

December 31.   The dawn of another year is traveling towards us round the earth, and 1856 will soon be with us in New York.

There is little more for me to say about poor 1855, now *in extremis*. It dies in a spasm of cold. The snow that fell on Saturday has not begun to thaw, except on one's boots after one has waded across Broadway ankle-deep in powdered frost. The city was splendid yesterday, in fresh linen garments, without pollution or rumple. Heard a very pungent sermon from Higby at Trinity Chapel. Sundry people came in to tea, among them Lieutenant Bent of the Japan expedition, who gave me astonishing accounts of the intelligence, culture, and education of his barbarian friends. He says they keep themselves posted up on European and American affairs, political and scientific. Tonight at St. Luke's Hospital meeting. Nothing special, except a glimmering hope of possible compromise with Burch and Barclay. Returning, find the Fourth Avenue blocked with engines and seamed with hose, fire in the basement of the Clarendon (under the barber's shop), which would have been a serious matter if postponed a few hours later. It was obstinate, but yielded at last. Came home with cold feet. Miss Rosalie [Ruggles] is staying with us. Sat with her and Ellie in the front parlor, reading Lewes's *Life of Goethe*, and modestly suggesting possible interpretations for some of Browning's enigmas over which the two were puzzling.

1856

TROUBLES IN KANSAS · PRESTON BROOKS ASSAULTS
SUMNER · THE BUCHANAN-FRÉMONT CAMPAIGN

———⟨∞⟩———

The new year was ushered in with the heaviest snowstorm in twenty years. Beginning on the forenoon of Saturday, January 5, it continued all night, and almost buried the city. For several days the inhabitants were busy digging themselves out. Trains from Albany came in almost twenty-four hours late—the first one down consisted of seven engines and four passenger cars— and the train which should have arrived from Boston about noon on Saturday reached the city at five o'clock on Sunday afternoon.

The principal topics of the day were the protracted speakership contest in Congress and the alarming civil strife in Kansas. The struggle in the House, which had disturbed business and disgusted the country, finally ended on February 2, after nearly two months of deadlock, with the election of the Republican candidate, Nathaniel P. Banks. This was hailed in the North as the first great victory for freedom over slavery. In Kansas two rival regimes confronted each other: one the regular government under Wilson Shannon, who had been sent out by Pierce as the second territorial governor, and who was supported by a legislature elected by fraudulent means; the other an irregular "government" chosen by the free-soil settlers, who had made Charles Robinson of Lawrence their "governor." Violence simmered in the territory, and something near open warfare was expected in the spring. John Brown had reached Kansas in the autumn of 1855, and was soon to place a bloody imprint on its history. Feeling in the North against the Pierce Administration continued to grow, even the Democrats having little use for the President. Already it was certain that the Republicans would make a strong bid for control of the govern-

[249]

ment. Discussion of the campaign began early; and on February 18–20, 1856, a national Know-Nothing convention nominated Millard Fillmore and A. J. Donelson. Opponents of the Know-Nothings declared that this premature action would give ample opportunity for exposing the dangerous nature of nativism.

At last the war in the Crimea was drawing to an end. The Russians, who had lost more than a hundred thousand men in the fruitless defense of Sebastopol, realized that victory was out of the question. Napoleon III was tired of the long and costly struggle, and the British were quite willing to see it end. In February, 1856, the Treaty of Paris was signed. By it the Allies gained just one clear result—Russian warships were to be excluded from the Black Sea. Even this agreement, as time showed, was to be respected only for fifteen years. But the integrity of the Ottoman Empire had been preserved, and Britain's sea route to India was safe.

January 5.   Today I enjoyed an hour of intercourse with the Rev. Eleazar Williams, believed by many three or four years ago to be the oppressed and suppressed successor of Louis XIV *de jure.* Wainwright came to me in the summer of 1854 about a deed conveying land to him and his successors in office, which was to be held on some vague trust, either for Eleazar personally or for a mission church he was organizing. The deed was waste paper, and so I advised the Bishop. The premises were thereupon given to him (Wainwright) absolutely, it seems, and it's now a question whether his heirs . . . shall transfer the premises to Eleazar individually or to some representative of the Church. . . . Bishop Potter has been called upon to direct what disposition shall be made of it, and he refers the question to Gouverneur Ogden and me as commissioners. Eleazar's manner impresses me favorably.

January 8, TUESDAY.   This is a stern winter. Saturday's snowstorm was the severest for many years past. The streets are like Jordan, "hard roads to travel." One has to walk warily over the slippery sidewalks and to plunge madly over crossings ankle-deep in snow, in order to get uptown and down, for the city railroads are still impracticable and walking (with all its discomforts) is not so bad as the great crowded sleigh-caravans that have taken the place of the omnibi. These insane vehicles carry each its hundred sufferers, of whom about half have to stand in the wet straw with their feet freezing and occasionally stamped on by their fellow travelers, their ears and noses tingling in the bitter wind, their hats always on the point of being blown off. When the chariot stops, they tumble forward, and when it starts again, they tumble backward, and when they arrive at the end of their ride, they commonly land up to their knees in a snowdrift, through which they flounder as best they may, to escape the little fast-trotting vehicles that are coming straight at them. Many of the cross streets are still untraveled by anything on wheels or runners, but in Broadway, the Bowery, and other great thoroughfares, there is an orgasm of locomotion. It's more than a carnival; it's a wintry dionysiaca.

January 14. The Philharmonic was a fair concert. Overture to *Euryanthe* good, of course, but there's very little of it. It's a flash of tropical light, over in a minute. Berlioz's *Frances Tufes* is ponderous. There were a couple of solos from Mercadente and Verdi, better rendered than they deserved, by Badish. Also a dismal, flatulent "concertino" for the horn—by Weber, but suggestive only of the murmurings and vocal cadences of one's alimentary canal after an indigestible dinner. . . .

People say that Miss Maria Lydig is engaged to Judge Daly![1] I doubt and disbelieve, but they are very much together, and it may be true, and would not be a bad arrangement, as it strikes me; provided, that is, the Judge won't preach and prose at his own fireside as he does elsewhere and desolate his own home circle as he lays waste foreign fields. Now if the Rev. Mr. Weston will make Miss Maggie an assistant ministress, two fine women will be saved from becoming rather detrimental members of society. No Speaker yet at Washington; so the wheels of government have been locked for six weeks. Not creditable to the democratic machine. They've now begun administering interrogatories to the several candidates for the speakership, and calling on them to define their position as to Nebraska, Know-Nothingism, slave labor in the southern dockyards and stations, and things in general. So there probably won't be any Speaker for a good while. Judge Roosevelt is making a special ass of himself in the matter of the Central Park.[2] He'll hardly be nominated for judicial office again. People have found him out. If they'd found him out three years sooner, there would have been no verdict against the Mason will.

January 19, SATURDAY.   Curtis is dead (Howadji's father); died at the

---

[1] Charles Patrick Daly (1816–1899), who after a successful career at the bar had been made judge of the Court of Common Pleas, did marry Maria Lydig, of the well-known banking family, this year.

[2] The report of the commissioners who had been empowered to lay out Central Park was being contested in the Supreme Court of the state, and Judge Roosevelt gave aid to the opposition; but on February 5 Judge Harris decided in favor of the report, enabling work on the park to go forward.

South, whither he had gone as a last resource, though without much hope.[3] He was a very valuable man. The two Lydigs dined here the other day, with Weston and Judge Daly. Shouldn't wonder if the reports about Miss Maria and the Judge were well founded. Court of Appeals has decided in favor of Judge Davies and against Judge Cowles. Talk of possible hostile complication with England grows rather more anxious. Received a pressing note late Tuesday evening from my unlucky quondam-student Fairbanks, dated at Eldridge Street jail, advising me of his arrest as a fraudulent debtor by his western client, whose money he had been losing at play. I have been twice to see him, have conferred with the people he thought might consent to bail him (but who wouldn't hear of it), with his wrathful partner, and with this creditor, who don't seem at all vindictive or inclined to oppress, and have corresponded somewhat with Mr. Fairbanks. I had to take a new tone in the letter I wrote him today and to tell him he ought to take a lower position. He has gambled away the money entrusted to him by a client, and before making confident demands on the charity of one who is almost a stranger to him, he ought to put his "self-respect" in his pocket and submit to the humiliation of addressing his own relatives and of allowing his name to be used against the keepers of the gaming houses where he played and lost. I fear he is altogether base metal. Eldridge Street jail is a dismal hole; my visits there were like scenes from Dickens. There is much in life that one don't commonly see. . . . Dickens's *Little Dorrit*, whereof I read No. 2 tonight, promises well.[4]

January 24. Tonight at Niblo's with Ellie and George Anthon; *Raoul.* The fun of pantomime is coarse and trivial, but very vigorous and not unwholesome. We had a very good time. Miss Maria Lydig's engagement to her Celtic lover is avowed and announced.

January 28. Eisfeld's concert last night. Haydn, Quartette No. 57, wonderfully fresh and genial; full of various and beautiful phrases of melody—the adagio and finale particularly good.

January 31. . . . Order made by Surrogate's Court appointing me trustee of Mrs. William H. Aspinwall's separate property.[5] The office

[3] George Curtis (1796–1856), a man of high integrity, best remembered as father of George William Curtis, had been first cashier and then president of the Bank of Commerce.

[4] Dickens's *Little Dorrit* was being published in instalments in the New York *Weekly Tribune.*

[5] William H. Aspinwall (1807–1875) was partner in the great mercantile and shipping house of Howland & Aspinwall and one of the founders of the Pacific Mail Steamship Company, of which he was now president.

brings neither pleasure nor profit, and I'm rather unwise to accept it. Wonder why I do so. It must be because William H. Aspinwall is a rich man and a merchant prince and one of our first citizens, and because I desire that men should say, "Yes, I know Aspinwall's wife had property in her own right, a man named Strong is her trustee." Such snobs are we, practically, with all our inward protestations against Snobbism. I asked Verplanck[6] yesterday if it were true that when in the legislature he had once quoted Cornelius Nepos, and that some honorable member on the other side had declared himself unwilling to be governed by that authority. He didn't doubt that Cornelius Nippers was a very respectable man, but Cornelius Nippers don't know anything about Cattaraugus County, where I come from. Verplanck said that was a fiction, but that after somebody had made a speech in which Marcus Curtius was conspicuous, a country member who was about to answer it came to him and said: "Verplanck, you know about them sort of things. Who was that Curtis that Dickinson spoke of— the man that jumped somewhere?" Verplanck expounded the story as well as he could, but not successfully; for as the enquirer was leaving him, he asked, "What did you say was the given name of that Curtis?"

February 1. News from Europe, very "important if true," viz.: that Russia consents to negotiate on the basis of the Allied propositions and peace is expected. It takes people here by surprise. Possibly a dodge to get time. But after all, why shouldn't the Czar agree to a compromise? He has fought a good fight and shewn himself a dangerous enemy. His antagonists have little to brag of.

February 5. William Jay's pamphlet *contra* Berrian is feeble and foolish. Philharmonic Society said to have bought Philip Hone's house (Broadway and Great Jones Street) and to propose the erection of a music hall. I'm exercised by the problem whether it be feasible (if we're alive and well and prosperous) this time next year to get up a Mass of Haydn's on these premises, with full orchestra and a chorus of fifteen or twenty and an audience of seventy-five or one hundred. It would be a charitable or missionary movement to proclaim to our music-loving friends who sit in darkness and the shadow of Donizetti a musical revelation beyond their dreams. I would make up the Mass thus-wise: Kyrie No. 3; Gloria and Credo No. 6, except the Et Vitam Venturi, which should be substituted from No. 16; Sanctus, etc., No. 6; Benedictus No. 4 (or No. 16); and Agnus Dei and Dona Pacem No. 6, or (if the keys of F and C

---

[6] Gulian C. Verplanck (1786–1870), writer, former Congressman, and civic leader.

major were not an objection) of No. 2. That would make a magnificent Mass, and the want of unity would not be much felt.

February 10, SUNDAY.   To old [Robert] Chesebrough's funeral. Quite a crowd of old New Yorkers in attendance, and two Dutch Reformed Improvisatori, clerical "Keeners," standing on the stairs, and one after the other hallooing and bawling the customary platitudes and semi-profanities of those who prefer addressing the Almighty off hand rather than after consideration. Vermilye informed the Lord explicitly, by way of preface, of the leading doctrines of Christianity, and then went on to report the special facts of this case: how that the deceased was ninety years old, had been much respected in this community, and had left a widow and a number of grandchildren; that very few of his contemporaries were living, that one generation succeeded another, and that the people now engaged in active life and business were mostly much younger men than old Chesebrough. He read Omniscience, in the corners of his prayer, a kind of lecture (or the heads of an essay) on the shortness of human life, the certainty of death, and the various considerations that should induce men to live aright while there is time. It was very horrid and shocking, this speaking to Bunkum— pretending to address Almighty God, but in fact, addressing Moses Taylor, Luther Bradish, old Coddington, and the rest. Interment was in vault in St. Mark's Churchyard.

February 13. . . . The Supreme Court gave the public some more matter of laughter this morning.[7] It has been evident for some time from the wit and humor embodied in the opinions of Roosevelt and Clerke that that august tribunal aims at supplying us with what *Punch* gives the London public; for as Judge Clerke facetiously observed in his judgment in a late case of Christy or somebody else, "Man does not live by bread alone, and if people would laugh more and eat less, the world would get on much better." The general term room was pretty well filled this morning, chiefly by the bar, in eager anticipation of a particularly good session. At five minutes before eleven, Peabody, Judge, was in his seat looking uncomfortable. At eleven Davies, Judge, entered blandly and took his seat beside him, trying to look nonchalant. A few minutes thereafter, Roosevelt and Clerke walked in together, looked astounded, took their seats, and the court was opened by Mr. Harry Bertholf, with great and special solemnity and a

---

[7] A dispute had arisen as to the title to one of the seats in the state Supreme Court, Henry E. Davies, Know-Nothing, asserting that he had been elected the previous November, while James J. Roosevelt, Thomas W. Clerke, and Charles A. Peabody denied him a place, holding that it belonged to Peabody. A prolonged struggle took place, but eventually Peabody gave way.

barely perceptible wink at his audience. Everybody watched the progress of affairs with keen enjoyment. The bar grinned as it has not grinned for years.

But Roosevelt didn't commit Davies, Judge; he began calling the calendar, called several cases twice, picked up papers, and turned them over incoherently, and showed himself disconcerted and unhappy. Evarts submitted one of the batch of Harper insurance camphene cases *pro forma*. Everybody hoped he'd hand up only three copies of his points and so bring matters to a crisis, but he was weak enough to furnish four. Then there was some more calendar-calling, without anybody ready, and then Roosevelt and Clerke walked out, and it was generally supposed that they'd come back with the power of the county at their heels and commit Davies to close custody; but they returned unattended, found a case that was ready and willing, and somebody began a dissertation on the law of life insurance, and I cleared out. It seems they went downstairs to frame an order that this court recognizes only Roosevelt, Clerke, and Peabody as justices, and that clerk and officers must act accordingly. Their spirited performance of the court's comic functions stimulated everybody's faculty of facetiousness. It was "a *very* general term"—"four judges out of three in attendance"— "Davies *amicus curiae* or *inimicus*"; "Peabody + Davies the binomial equivalent of one justice."

If Davies is entitled to sit, the order made by Roosevelt and Clerke is a nullity; if not, they should attack him for intruding on the bench and assuming judicial functions. Omitting to do this is a confession of weakness I did not expect from one so obstinate and self-willed as Roosevelt. Fear that Peabody has done himself much harm by his course in this matter. He's a nice person, I think, but has allowed himself to be made a tool of and has become rather ridiculous. Informed Cowles of the progress of affairs at the hall, which he enquired about with lively interest. I *guess* the plan is to get Davies out of the way, then for Peabody to resign, and Cowles to be appointed; a desirable result, but not so desirable as to justify the violation of law and the sacrifice of judicial dignity.

February 14. . . . To general term room of Supreme Court. Went early to secure a front seat. Davies planted himself firmly in his place at five minutes before eleven, took possession of one of the *three* chairs (Roosevelt had specially directed there should be *only* three, so priority of occupation was important), and affected to be deeply interested in a newspaper. The room filled and filled, with members of the bar chiefly. At least two-thirds of the lawyers of this city were there awaiting the advent of Roosevelt & Co.

as children watch for the rising of the curtain at a pantomime. Quarter past eleven, Davies still buried in the same paragraph of his paper, crowd growing denser and disposed to be riotous. Occasional outbursts of stamping, expressive of impatience for the commencement of performances, put down by vehement whishing in the interest of professional decorum.

Half-past eleven, the tergetto entered, Roosevelt at their head and Peabody at their tail; Davies regarding the procession with a bland look of gratification and welcome. Roosevelt observed, "This is Judge Peabody's seat, Mr. Davies," and Davies replied, "I believe the Court of Appeals has given me this seat, sir"; and another chair was handed up by Bertholf, and Davies good-naturedly edged up to make room for it, and the court was opened. Roosevelt said, "Adjourn to this day week," and proclamation was made, and the three left the bench as fast as possible, Davies following more deliberately. There was clamorous laughter and some cheering, which Bertholf tried to check and thereby made worse, and the crowd slowly dispersed. Peabody sent for me, and I had five minutes' talk with him. Asked me which way the general feeling was, to which query I gave the only possible answer, namely: that peoples' *personal* feeling was with him, but that the opinion of the bar on the legal question was almost unanimous for Davies. He began to argue the matter, but I could not stay to discuss it and didn't want to. I like him much, personally, and regret he's consented to a step that can hardly fail to do him great harm. John Van Buren says, "It don't amount to a great deal more than a *full* bench, after all."

February 15.　This evening with Charley [Strong] and George Anthon to a private lecture at Hope Chapel on the "Past, Present, and Future of the New York Society Library," before the shareholders thereof, by John McMullen, Esq., Librarian. Tolerably numerous assembly. None of the old board present, a significant fact. Lecture not far above commonplace, deformed by fearful exaggeration of the importance of its subject, and the merits of the donors it put forward for imitation. I don't believe, myself, that Miss Demilt's legacy of $5,000 could have carried that departed lady's soul so far up into Heaven as McMullen said it did. But I don't know. McMullen sinned against good taste sadly in his oration, but he retains the faculty of extemporaneous speech that used to command my admiration in the debates of the Philolexian so long ago. His meaning, be it more or less, is embodied in sentences that could be put on paper and are compact and colloquial at the same time. Thereafter a sort of meeting was organized. Kelly, Hugh Maxwell, W. H. Anthon, I. G. Pearson, and others discoursed a little and to little purpose.

February 21, THURSDAY.   With Cram to general term room. Pretty dense crowd. Davies took his seat. Then, to everybody's surprise and regret, Peabody came, and the other two followed. Court opened. Roosevelt gave some opinions, and a motion came on, in which that dirtiest and most impudent of dogs, Mr. Skeffington Sanxay, was concerned. Cram and I sat near him and urged him to take a high moral position, but he contented himself with asking who the court was. He saw the four gentlemen on the bench and would like to be informed who the judges were, in case they should not be unanimous. Roosevelt stammered and said that this was a general term and that there were three judges present. Mr. Sanxay might go on or not as he pleased, and Mr. Sanxay replied with more tact than I gave him credit for, "Then I will go on with my argument before the *three whom I consider to be judges*," and went on accordingly. Poor Roosevelt has not pluck even to assert Peabody's title, so low has that court fallen. Sanxay ought to have said that, on the whole, he had concluded to go on the bench and would aid his client by giving him a judgment instead of an argument. Peabody is much blamed, and justly. He is overriding his own most serious misgivings about his duty and his interest. Davies behaves pretty well, only he should not so cringe before Roosevelt and Clerke and smile on them so sweetly. But the law of his being is to creep on his belly. Lifting his head would make him sick.

February 24.   The *Atlantic* has arrived, and I hear the complexion of her news is warlike. England is sore at having played second fiddle in the Allied orchestra, and at being compelled by France to assent to a rather inglorious peace, and may well be inclined to vindicate her character by pitching into us. No news of the *Pacific*, and people begin to be very anxious. . . .

Eisfeld last night; a tolerable concert. Haydn's Quartette, No. 78, in B-flat (I think I've heard it before) and Beethoven's Quartette, No. 9, in C major were the features of the concert.

March 1.   People beginning to be much concerned about the *Pacific*, now thirty-seven days out. Some uneasiness about our relations with England; not a great deal—less, perhaps, than the position of things would justify. The opinion is universal that Clarendon is entirely wrong and wants to be overbearing, and that though the matter in question is very unimportant, Crampton ought to be recalled or dismissed and my friend Barclay's *exequatur* should be withdrawn. Barclay's troubles have had one good effect; they have awakened a sudden longing in that gentleman to settle his controversy with St. Luke's Hospital, and Swift is now conducting an informal negotiation on the subject with hopeful prospects of success. . . . To Gottschalk's concert Thursday night with Ellie, Miss Rosalie, and Cram and his wife; absurd crowd, idiotic excitement, infinite bother in getting seats for the ladies.[8] Any blacksmith excels this wretched, diminutive Jewish-looking coxcomb in strength of muscle; many mechanics could surpass his nicety and quickness of manipulation; and there was nothing in his performance, save his combination of a coalheaver's vigor with an artisan's dexterity. Music there was none. He pounded his piano and tickled his piano with wonderful energy and delicacy—and that was all. . . .

March 2, SUNDAY.   Murray Hoffman came in, and we had an evening of discussion over Heinrich Heine, whom English critics have lately discovered, and Ruskin's *Modern Painters*, volume III, just out. Ruskin is full of life and brilliancy. His books will surely exert vast influence for good or evil; on the whole, I think, for good. Paradoxes and extravagances and exaggerations and one-sided statements enough there about art and the works of artists, but his books deal with subjects weightier than art, and his keen knife seems to dissect out and lay bare the internal ulcers, tubercles, and "fatty degenerations" that make our life in the nineteenth century sick and sorrowful.

But we want a physician, not an anatomist. Carlyle has told us most truly that "self-consciousness" lies at the root of our faults of others. What good can come of the notification? It merely gives that consciousness another fact, and makes us yet more distrustful of the influences at work upon us; it suggests no remedy, invites us to look on nothing without ourselves. There is no help in philosophy. Each of us must come back to *Beati pauperes spiritu, beati misericordes, beati mites, beati pacifici*. There is our only materia medica, worth all the microscope can do in detecting morbid changes of structure and phenomena of disease.

Ruskin opens a question in this volume that has exercised me before now. How do you know that hillside and river and forest are entitled to awaken in you these emotions of joy and veneration? Homer and Dante, better and greater men than you, would have been unable to comprehend

[8] Louis Moreau Gottschalk (1829–1869), American musician, had studied abroad and made a brilliant New York debut in 1853, Barnum offering him $20,000 for a year's concert work—which he refused. Highly popular, he gave eighty concerts in New York this winter of 1855–56. A good pianist, he was also a busy composer.

your raptures over a mountain gorge or a woodland clearing. Till the last seventy years the feeling was unknown, or never expressed, at least. It is genuine with you, but is not its very reality a sign of sentimentalism, a badge of unfruitfulness and of incapacity to bear fruit, and does it not stamp your nature as unable to do works of righteousness, and as substituting for efficient action the aesthetic contemplation of the works of God?

March 3.   Went to a fogy Columbia College meeting, where I reposed through the afternoon. Much dreary talk, but nothing done or sought to be done. It's the Castle of Indolence, the College of Non-Feasance.

March 8.   Mr. Ruggles has got his "Performance on the Bones" finally printed, and is now modulating out of that theme into Peter Cooper's Polytechnique or "Union for the Advancement of Science," or whatever it may be that Cooper's crude notions will produce at last.[9] Cooper is very well meaning but very silly for a self-made millionaire. All his conceptions of his future university (now under roof) are amorphous, preposterous, and impractical. Unless he have wise counsel and consent to follow it, he will produce nothing but $500,000 worth of folly. Luckily Mr. Ruggles seems to have got somewhat of his confidence.

March 10, MONDAY. . . . Went to Trinity Church this afternoon to Society for Promoting Religion, etc. No quorum. Discoursed with the Rev. Dr. McVickar, who is strong on Ruskin. He talks to his classes about Ruskin, and does not hesitate to tell them that in "the combination of aesthetic and spiritual perception" and so on, "Ruskin is the greatest man since Plato."

This steamer brings news that poor Heinrich Heine is dead at last and buried in Père-Lachaise. Neither academic eulogy nor Christian rite accompanied the putting his body under ground, for "he desired there should be silence round his coffin." After all, what could one venture to say that would have been pertinent and true and not ungracious and inhuman?

March 16, SUNDAY.   People give up the *Pacific* as lost. There is an ugly story about fragments of wreck seen lying on drift ice. The only favorable indication is that the *Arctic*, which went in quest of the *Pacific*, is some thirty days out of Halifax, and if that steamer, built for northern exploration, is hampered in the ice fields, how much more difficulty would the *Pacific* have in working out of them!

March 17.   Weather grows rather milder. It is thawing copiously

[9] Cooper was maturing plans for his famous Union or Institute on Astor Place, which he began building in 1857 and which began its extremely valuable career in 1859.

tonight. Probably there may be a summer in A.D. 1856 after all. Busy day, vesicated and pustulated by several small acrid bothers. Saw E. K. Collins, who was quite exuberant in commendation of the fine weather. Wanted, but hadn't the heart, to ask him about the *Pacific*.[10] Apropos of that probable tragedy is one of E. A. Poe's hideous stories I've just read for the first time, "Adventures of Arthur Gordon Pym." There are "artists in hair," *vide* newspaper advertisements, and artists in dexterity and muscular strength, *vide* Gottschalk's concerts. So I suppose Poe may be called an artist in putrefaction (both moral and material), in charnel house effluvia. This story includes a scene worthy the author of "Facts in Relation to the Death of M. Valdemar," in which a ship laden with the corpses of her crew drifts slowly down on the waterlogged wreck to which the narrator and his companions are clinging.

March 19. . . . Tonight read Thackeray's *Miscellanies*, gave Miss Rosalie some instruction in chess, and rushed off at ten o'clock to look for a fire, which proved near at hand—certain manufacturing buildings on the northeast corner of Twenty-second Street and Second Avenue. The portion on the corner and that on the Avenue had been successfully defended up to the time I left, but all the long range of buildings on Twenty-second Street was blazing superbly. The crowd was dense and dirty; there was a pressure of ten loafers to the square inch, so I did not stay for the end of the performance.

Roosevelt and Clerke have collapsed at last. Peabody has written them a long letter withdrawing from his seat, in order to facilitate and expedite proceedings to determine his right to it, and saying several things he might better have left unsaid. Whereupon Clerke announced yesterday at special term that "Judge Davies would hear motions at chambers at twelve." The logical consistency of the announcement is hard to see. Unfortunately, it is coincident in time with certain legislative proceedings that look dangerous, a reference of the subject to the judiciary committee with power to send for persons and papers. This committee has cited Roosevelt, Clerke, and Connolly to appear before them tomorrow evening, the last-named being also called on to produce the *remittitur* from the Court of Appeals and sundry other papers in his official custody. I wish there might be a joint resolution to remove both Roosevelt and Clerke from their seats. They deserve removal, but I suppose nothing will be done. . . .

[10] The crack Collins liner *Pacific* had been the first vessel to reduce the Atlantic passage below ten days (1851).

March 21. . . . The *Arctic* reported herself at Sandy Hook yesterday, and went off again straight on her now all-but-hopeless quest. . . .[11]

March 22. . . . Went downtown, and on my way up visited the Academy of Design with George Anthon. Certainly a poor show of pictures, the shabbiest within my recollection. Tropical landscapes by Church good, but far below those of last year; New Testament picture by Huntington respectable, but it seems as if one had seen an engraving of it or something quite like it in some illustrated prayer book, or "Gems of Art." Capital portrait of old Colonel McKenney by Elliott.[12] Landscape by Durand, good, and remarkable as not in his beaten track; it is free from the Durand line of hills and the Durand tree in the foreground. Crayon portrait of Rosetta Post!!!—belonging to Haydock, one of her boarders. She looks older than when I was last at Whitestone, four or five years ago. Very careful drawing by Ruskin. Two pictures by Jack Ehninger, better than anything yet by far, but cold in color, uninteresting, unattractive.

Tonight with Ellie and Miss Rosalie to Eisfeld's concert; tolerably good. Concerto (Mendelssohn's) for piano and violin; Pychowski, composer and pianist, very bad. . . .

March 26. Easter was a splendid day. At Trinity Chapel the font and altar were decorated with flowers very prettily. The practice has prevailed for many successive Easters at Muhlenberg's Church,[13] and was quite general this year, I understand. Censured as papistical, of course. Nothing very novel for the last few days. Gerard has begun summing up in the Cox case and will probably get a verdict. His antagonist Chauncey Shaffer (the Thersites of the Know-Nothing camp) has outdone himself and hurt his client by the brutal blackguardism he has displayed. Spent last evening experimenting with a big magic lantern, with which I intend to astonish Johnny and some of his little friends. The troubles of the Nicaragua Transit Company are much talked of, especially by its unhappy

[11] The *Pacific* now had to be given up for lost, and the mystery of her disappearance was never solved. She had left Liverpool January 23, 1856; fortunately with only forty-five passengers, but with a normal crew. Possibly she had struck an iceberg. This blow, followed first by the reduction and then the abandonment of federal subsidies, brought the Collins Line to an end.

[12] Thomas L. McKenney (1785–1859), once head of the Bureau of Indian Affairs and expert on Indian life; Charles Loring Elliott (1812–1868), sometime pupil of John Trumbull, is reported to have painted over 700 portraits.

[13] William Augustus Muhlenberg (1796–1877), rector of the Church of the Holy Communion at Sixth Avenue and Twentieth Street, labored to reform the liturgy of the Episcopal Church.

stockholder, George Anthon, who maintains that Vanderbilt ought to organize an expedition, turn out Walker, take possession of the territory in the name of the company, and call it "Transition State."[14]

March 29. March certainly "came in like a lion," but it goes out like a rhinoceros or a polar bear rather than a lamb. Last two days cold and blustering, premonitory rather of snowstorm than spring flowers.

March 30, SUNDAY. . . . Looked once more into Thackeray's *Snob Papers.* Query, if that be not *the* great work of this century? His vision is as true and keen as Dante's, only exerted on a humbler field and on familiar objects. But its "penetrating" and defining powers are marvelous. He looks at the complex social relations and institutions as Dr. Quekett inspects a piece of suspected muscular tissue or a scrap of lung through one of Ross's objectives, indicates the diseased fibres and the "degenerate" cells with precision, and demonstrates the truth of his indications unanswerably.

It's a book to set one thinking of many things. First, it teaches its lesson with clearness and energy and emphasis far above anything this age has heard in the shape of indoctrination on kindred subjects. Second, its teaching impresses one with a sense of surprise and entire novelty. Third (with reverence be it spoken), its subject is that of the fundamentals of Christianity, of the Sermon on the Mount, no less—Charity, Humility, Purity of Heart, Contentment. In those words lies all its power. Their application to the "minor" social usages of this day is what the *Snob Papers* set forth and what makes the book so novel and original and full of life. But where has the Church been for the last hundred years??? The Church whose office it is to set forth these very truths, adapted to the varying forms of social life in successive ages, the Church to whom they were confided as an armory wherewith she should convict and crush the embodiments of pride and impurity and uncharitableness that should succeed each other till the end of time. In my day, alas, the Church has been discussing questions of Episcopal ordination, Baptismal regeneration, certain claims of the Bishop of Rome, predestination, the relative position of faith and of works in scientific theology. The subjects of which Thackeray treats she has almost ignored, and thus an outsider has come in to do her work and to weaken men's loyalty to her throne.

[14] William Walker, the filibuster, now briefly controlling the government of Nicaragua, had seized the ships and other property of the Accessory Transit Company in that republic. He thus incurred the enmity of Cornelius Vanderbilt, who promptly took steps to help organize a Central American coalition to overthrow Walker.

March 31. Have had an anxious and uncomfortable day, for Johnny was quite sick this morning, more seriously than I've seen him for two years and more, and I've been dwelling on measles, scarlet fever, "tubercular meningitis," and other perils of childhood. But Dr. Peters's ipecac seems to have been efficient, and he was quite bright this evening. Busy downtown with multiform botheration. Trinity Church vestry meeting at two. . . . This evening to St. Luke's Hospital meeting. Another $100,000 to be raised; it will be heavy work. Had the satisfaction of handing in our final report on the Barclay matter, and the board insisted on passing a vote of thanks, which I protested against as a bad precedent.

April 3. Johnny has a cold. . . . Apropos of babies, the Nursery makes about $6,000 net by its ball. Why not open St. Luke's Hospital with a ball (St. Vitus quadrille, tetanus polka, and so on) and so get $6,000 toward our $300,000?

Charley is very blue and desperate; talks of selling No. 38 East Twenty-second Street, and so on. Also my biliary ducts, or solar plexus, I don't know which, are in morbid preponderance over the rest of my system. Last night I had two hours of sleep, or rather of half-waking, dreamy cat-nap, and no more. Night before, the same. . . . Mrs. Bonaparte, Empress of France, has a baby, a man-child, and is doing well. May all mammas who look forward to like trial within the next two months pass their ordeal with like happy result!

April 5. Building committee meeting yesterday, about a school house for Trinity Chapel, and the proposed erection of a little gallery at the south end for Sunday scholars. This afternoon I went by particular request to Skidmore's office to help the Committee of Arrangements of the alumni of Columbia College (of which I didn't know I had the honor to be a member) to get a quorum. We settled on Gerard for orator and either McMullen or the Rev. Dr. Morgan Dix for poet for the next annual meeting.[15]

The Committee Advisory announces that John D. Wolfe and my distinguished self are in nomination for the Board of the New York Life Insurance & Trust Company. They must be hard up for trustees.

April 6, SUNDAY. Never so appreciated the dawn of spring as this year, though the season is backward and the air chill compared with what it should be. . . .

Mrs. Dubois has got a grant of $10,000 from the legislature for the

[15] James W. Gerard (1794–1874), distinguished New York attorney; Morgan Dix (1827–1908), son of John A. Dix, and already noted as a divine.

nursery by the application of her indomitable will to the legislators at
Albany, but only after a hard battle and a long debate. Had that lady
ordinary health and physical vigor instead of being, as she is, a mere
embodiment of "Neurology," a bundle of active diseases and morbid
changes of structure, unable to speak but in a whisper, and paralyzed
suddenly at intervals by disease of the heart, she'd found a dynasty and
die Imperatrix of the United States with a secured succession to her issue,
therein probably beating Louis Napoleon. I look with absolute awe on her.

April 8. Yesterday afternoon Columbia College trustees met. Much
solemn, stolid debate and viscid twaddle. Proposition (*ab extra*) that we
buy land in Westchester county and put the college there; referred to a
special committee, on which by an odd accident Mr. Ruggles and Ogden
Hoffman were put, with Van Wagenen, Gouverneur Ogden, and Bradford. There may be a fight on this question, and necessity for more talk
and fuss over the stale old academic cadaver. Hoffman has expressed himself in favor of making it a country college, and I for one have always
said it ought not to be removed from the city limits. I've not thought
much of the matter, but I may see reason to advocate this proposition. . . .

Jem Mason and Ring have quarreled,[16] and the client is hesitating
about a suit against his counsel and solicitor, which he'll probably pause
over until the latter has put the spoils out of the victim's reach. I always
said that if the Mason will were broken, Ring would get a magnificent
slice of Jem Mason's property, but I never thought he'd get more than
two-thirds of it. Yet it seems he has *all* the personality. Sixty lots of the
Fifth Avenue property (worth at least $90,000), and mortgages for
about $30,000 on the city property assigned to Mason by the Commis-
sion in partition, are now held by Mr. J. J. Ring, who declines producing
accounts or entering into explanations. But to this must be added that
since about 1844 he has lived with and on Mason, and (as I hear) has
lived luxuriously and imperiously, drawing the salary when Mason was

[16] Here the Mason will case appears again. John Mason, who had begun life as
a workman, had risen to be head of the Chemical Bank, a powerful force in other
banks and mercantile corporations, and an extensive holder of New York real estate.
At his death he left an estate valued at from $800,000 to $1,000,000, then a tremendous sum. Strong felt strongly that an injustice had been done "Jem" Mason
when O'Conor broke John Mason's will. The case now should be fought to the end,
he wrote. "It will shew that if old John Mason were indeed *non compos* when he
made his will, he acted under the pressure of inspiration, and knew how vulnerable
his sons were by vampyres, ovicide dogs, and other carnivorous and bloodsucking
mammalia." Had the will been upheld, "Jem" Mason's share would still have been
safe in the hands of trustees.

in the Custom-House; living better than Mason on Mason's income and acting as his committee. Furthermore, the "professional services" thus used to rob never did any good. The will was broken by O'Conor for Alston.

April 10, THURSDAY.　[H. A.] Cram has been here till long after midnight, discussing the frame of the complaint in Mason *vs.* Ring, which is a very promising controversy, for Ring will fight hard, and the facts will fight harder. His pugnacious self-conceit and the reputation of truth for right and ultimate prevalence make it a match sufficiently even to be interesting, like a contest between a bulldog and the jet from a hydrant. *You* know the bulldog must be beat, but *he* don't. I wish there were twenty-four hours more for polishing up the complaint; it'll be rather rough, but I guess it'll make out a pretty flagrant prima facie case.

Last night at Wallack's for *London Assurance,* a despicable production, but very well played. . . . I have often thought of this Ring and Mason controversy as a very probable event, but it seems I underestimated Ring's rapacity. Mason is left with a quantity of unproductive property, mortgaged, and nothing beside. Ring and Ring's father (the estimable Zebedee) and his mother and brothers and sisters-in-law have lived on Mason for some twelve years, and have been Mason's family and disbursed his income for him and paid his servants and his marketing bills, and Ring himself has absorbed $220,000 of his patrimony, and I suppose put it into circulation again at Mr. Patrick Hearne's establishment. I've re-drafted about one-third of Cram's "complaint" tonight and hope to do the same for the other two-thirds tomorrow. I'm more familiar than he with the facts and can do him service by resisting his pleadings, and it's a labor of love, for this controversy is the best justification of Mason's executors; it shews that their maintenance of the will was one long act of charity.

April 12.　Spent most of yesterday and a couple of hours today with H. A. Cram over poor James Mason's affairs, which Mason's helpless imbecility and ignorance of business and entire confidence for so many years in his blood-sucking parasite have converted into an obscure imbroglio, very hard to penetrate in a hurry. Luckily one or two great facts stand out unmistakeable and controlling. Ring has more audacity than sense; he is impudent, brazen, unscrupulous, pertinacious, energetic, but with talent for detail, shortsighted, rash—*very.* . . . Ring will certainly fight, but even should he back out and strike his flag (most unlikely, for it would be a confession of fraud), the facts recorded in the complaint are conclusive against the rhetoric of O'Conor and Ogden Hoffman on the trial of the issue in Alston *v.* Jones, January 7, 1853.

April 13, SUNDAY. Murray Hoffman here tonight. Richard Grant White (who is about to deliver certain lectures on various points of social ethics) and Charley and little Kate. Delighted that little woman with fashion-plates in the *Moniteur de la Mode*. Her infant appreciation of "scalloped flounces" is keen already, and she reveled in "skirts" and "corsages." White and Hoffman discussed some of the spasmodic phenomena of our present poetic school, from Peter Marié (poet and banker, the American Rogers) to Tennyson and the Browning couple. I recognize a prosaic power and subtlety in Robert Browning's crabbed, obscure, wooden rhymes, but Mrs. Elizabeth Barrett Browning's productions transcend my appreciative faculty. One need not spend much time over a book wherein one finds a *morceau* like this:

> Let us sit on the Thrones
> In a purple sublimity
> And grind down men's bones
> To a pale Unanimity.

But I have skimmed over her two volumes, nevertheless, "The Cry of the Human" and all, and I don't think it was worth while to go through so much for the sake of so little. There are signs of truth and simplicity and feeling in one or two things (for example, the "Rhyme of the Duchess May"), but all is smothered in affectation and artificiality.

Mr. Ring was served with process yesterday at the Union Club and observed that he "had expected something of the sort and was prepared for it." I guess that will be a less unequal fight than I thought at first. In the courts, Ring must be beat. He has spent and gambled away so much of his spoils that Mason will doubtless recover all that is left, the Fifth Avenue property, Ring's deed for which Ring will certainly be decreed to deliver up to be canceled. The balance, however large, is not worth fighting for. It's gone, like last January's snow, and Ring couldn't restore it even if penitent and anxious to make restitution. But public opinion? The decision of that enlightened forum is less certain. Many people have a notion that Ring's exertions and ability broke the will of Jem's father, and so on. I can't doubt, however, that facts so unmistakeable will conquer and convince.

April 17. It's raining now. Hope it won't rain tomorrow, for at two o'clock of that day I've engaged one Starr, a professional microscopist (oxy-hydrogen, not solar, fortunately), to come here with his apparatus and astonish a lot of little children, from little Florence Lydig of nine years down to little Sidney Jones of four. It seems they mean to bring their mammas and aunts, so it will be an unpremeditated scientific matinée. . . .

Pax in terra. The European war is ended, for the present at least, and preliminaries of peace were signed at Paris March 30th. Eugénie and her baby are doing well. Glad of it. Poor little Imperial mamma; if she have any sense, and if she has read any French history, she must have forebodings about the future when she looks at the gilded cradle. . . .

Last night to the opera house with Ellie and Miss Betty Rhinelander —and I'm sure Miss Betty had a nice time: *Ernani.* We sat in the balcony, just in the locale of my Astor Place seat in 1848; and at the end of the third act . . . I felt as if I were in Astor Place again, and Miss Ellen Ruggles was over there on my left on her papa's sofa, and old Peter Schermerhorn on the sofa in front, and Miss Mary Jones and Miss Emily in their box just behind me. I was walking down Broadway again in a kind of delirious whirl, with that music ringing in my ears, and thinking whether I should "call" tomorrow night.

April 19. Our *matinée optique* was charming, notwithstanding the state of my digestive system. The little people were delighted with the onisci and the water-tigers and the insectivorous larvae, but went into squealing ecstacies over the comic magic-lantern slides. They were a lovely little lot. It would be hard to get together twenty prettier or better-behaved babies, though three or four of them were old enough to spurn that designation. Optics gave them a glorious appetite, and they went vigorously into the ice cream and jellies afterwards. . . . Then George C. Anthon and I took a long walk on the Fifth Avenue past the desert places of the Botanic Garden, now nearly done, and out to St. Luke's Hospital.[17] That building will be all ready in the fall; they are vigorously at work on the whitecoat and carpentry. It is very respectable. . . .

Ring has retained Ogden Hoffman with Noyes, and means to fight hard. His engaging Noyes and Hoffman looks as if all the spoils of his late client were not yet spent. The late Attorney-General don't put on his armor without an ample consideration.

April 23, WEDNESDAY. Have just got through my first hearing of *William Tell* at the Fourteenth Street Opera House with Ellie and Miss Mary Ulshoeffer. The two ladies had a nice time, but this opera don't

---

[17] The building of St. Luke's Hospital was being erected on 54th Street just west of Fifth Avenue.

attract me much, and if I didn't know its high repute and take it for granted that it would develop its merits on further acquaintance, I should say it was very heavy, dreary, and dull—without a trace of Rossini's fluency and freshness, without a single sharp-cut, definite musical thought (except the familiar old hand-organ melody in the third act), without unity, breadth, or even effective contrasts.

Went to a party at Judge Hoffman's Monday night (in Thirty-seventh Street!!!—it seems but the other day that Thirty-seventh Street was an imaginary line running through a rural district and grazed over by cows). It was a rather slow kind of tea drinking.

April 24. Ellie went to Gottschalk's tonight with George Anthon. I couldn't well go, as I ought to have done, and I hate Gottschalk's profanations of music—dirty antics and dexterities that crowded audiences admire and applaud as if they were manifestations of musical art and not mere exhibitions of mechanical skill and muscular strength. They are to music what an acrostic (or "Peter Piper picked a peck of pickled peppers") is to poetry and eloquence.

April 29. Went tonight with Ellie to the Düsseldorf Gallery, which I've not looked at for three years at least. I fear I'm growing critical in art. If Boker went on his knees to me, I'm not sure he could persuade me into owning more than a dozen or so of his pictures, if I had to pledge myself to put them on my walls and see them daily. My choice would be (though not without misgivings) Steinbrück's "Adoration of the Magi"; his lovely little "Elves," I'm sure, would cloy and sicken me after a month or so. Camphausen's "Cavalier Stronghold Stormed by Roundheads," next, I think. Then, two marine pictures by Achenbach, and Gude's grand Norwegian ravine and mountain torrent. And after that progress in my selection, I should have to stop and ponder.[18]

May 1. Ogden Hoffman is dead![19] It seems incredible. I could not believe it when Snelling told me, as I was coming out of No. 70, that it was announced on the *Express* bulletin, and went out after dinner to

[18] Eduard Steinbrück (1803–1882), Wilhelm Camphausen (1818–1885), Oswald Achenbach (1827–1905), all German painters of the Düsseldorf school; Hans Gude (1825–1903), Swedish-German landscape painter. The Düsseldorf Gallery was still potent in introducing German art to Americans.

[19] The greatest criminal lawyer of his generation in New York, and one of the most popular figures in the city, Ogden Hoffman had lately exhausted himself in a contest over the will of Henry Parish. It was universally agreed that had he possessed more industry and concentration, he might have risen to the governorship or high Federal office. The city had no more graceful or eloquent orator. His sudden death left a great gap.

enquire. The news was confirmed, and it is a fact. After four or five days' illness, it's said, "congestion of the liver." Probably his illness became threatening very suddenly, for I'd not even heard of it.

Where will one look for anything like his genial courteous manner, his brilliant persuasive talk? I never had five minutes with him without being impressed by a feeling that he took *so* much interest in me and mine, and attached *so* much weight to what I thought. So it was with everyone who came within his sphere. Yet he was without affectation; his indolent disposition made it impossible for him to play a part. He was always sincere, always cordially sympathetic with and interested in and respectful to his companion of the hour. Faults enough there were: indolence and self-indulgence that I fear have left Mrs. Hoffman and poor "Tippy" at Harvard and the two little girls I used to watch at Rockaway paupers this minute. With all the splendid powers and talents their dead father possessed so long, I doubt if he has left behind him a month's subsistence for that poor, bereaved household. The two sons of his first marriage are provided for: Ogden by his California judgeship,[20] and Charles by the Wickham estate at Goshen devised him by an uncle. Neither has any great surplus.

I don't mean by the word "self-indulgence" anything more than slip-shod laziness—a way of basking in the sun all summer at Rockaway and lounging at the Union Club and strolling through the courts all the rest of the year, save when some special matter stirred up his faculties. He lived like the lilies of the field—took no thought for the morrow. Perhaps it was shiftlessness, perhaps a very different feeling, perhaps a blending of both. Who shall say?

May 3. Just from the Century, where I exchanged platitudes with the old set of people, ate oysters, and defended Trinity Parish against an unreasonable assault by John Jay. . . . Poor Hoffman's funeral this afternoon was very largely attended.

May 4, SUNDAY. Much talk of poor Hoffman. As Hamilton told me yesterday, the Bar Committee is to raise a fund for his family by subscription. It thinks it will be raised without difficulty, if they strike while the iron is hot. But will Mrs. Hoffman, with her pride and her strong practical energy and ability to stand alone, permit it to be done?[21]

[20] Ogden Hoffman, Columbia 1840, had been made Federal district judge in California; "Tippy," Samuel Southard Hoffman (Harvard 1859), rose to be a lieutenant-colonel in the Civil War.

[21] Mrs. Hoffman had been Miss Virginia E. Southard, daughter of Samuel L. Southard, Senator from Virginia and New Jersey and Secretary of the Navy.

May 8, THURSDAY.   Ogden Hoffman, it's now said, left assets insufficient to pay his undertaker's bill, and debts beside. . . .

The distinguished citizen, well known in financial circles and formerly
connected with the city government, to whom the newspapers are allud-
ing as in some mysterious scrape with a woman, is none less than old
Cornelius W. Lawrence.[22] It's a scrape of near twenty years' antiquity.
The woman was the mistress of one Brown, who also kept the Red House
at Harlem, a noted sporting place, and who afterwards married her. It
seems the gentleman and lady have been living on Lawrence ever since
he committed this indiscretion and bleeding him freely, cupping him by
atmospheric pressure of threatened exposure and so on.

May 14, WEDNESDAY.   Some uneasy feeling about possible complication with England in the matter of Nicaragua, Colonel Walker, and the
Padre Vijil whom Pierce is about to recognize as Walker's legate *a
latere*. J. J. Post badly beat in Superior Court in a suit growing out of
some indiscreet invasions of other people's freeholds by him and his
agents in the improvement of his own premises on Broadway. Columbia
College meeting this afternoon (special) over the report of Building Committee on plans for the new college uptown, and over a project of Dillon's
to open a new avenue between Fifth and Sixth from "Reservoir Square"
to "Central Park." No definite conclusion was reached on the subject,
and we were going to adjourn when Gouverneur Ogden rose solemnly
to lug in the twopenny business of the last meeting (the action of the
faculty on the offences of one Romeyn, a disorderly Sophomore, whose
father's petition for his reinstatement after dismissal by the faculty was
referred to the President at our regular May meeting). Gouverneur was
aggrieved because the President, who has been ill, was not prepared to
report any action and wanted a special meeting next Monday. Betts and
Tom Wells were ready to record his motion, or any other motion indirectly attacking King, but Bishop Potter came out very manfully and
distinctly in support of discipline, even Bradford was compelled to decline
supporting his friend's demonstration, and Gouverneur backed out. But
there may well be a serious shindy over that little matter. In the faculty
there certainly will be, for King is in vast wrath against Bull Anthon,
who has stimulated the disturbance to the utmost of his powers.

May 16, FRIDAY.   Yesterday spent in a state of virulent, outrageous,
unprovoked dyspepsia and headache, which I endured in Wall Street,

[22] Cornelius W. Lawrence had made a small fortune as partner in Hicks, Lawrence
& Co., an auctioneer firm, and had been mayor of New York 1834–35.

having promised Ellie to go with her and Johnny to see the Düsseldorf pictures again in the afternoon. She called for me, and we inspected those works of art. Hanslein was astonished, bewildered, and delighted. Hübner's picture of the "Wounded Poacher" fixed his attention especially.[23] Didn't dine; couldn't go and hear the Rev. John Lord's lecture on Gregory VII in the evening. Spent it in cutting the leaves of *Modern Painters*, volume IV. Went for Ellie to Mr. Ruggles's and brought her home at ten-thirty in a very bilious condition indeed. There are many fine, original, brilliant, suggestive things in this fourth volume, but I fear Ruskin is writing a little too fast. Many passages occur in it that are unlike anything in the first and second or in the *Seven Lamps*, passages of rhetoric and fine writing embodying commonplace thought, of vehement, ornate diction not justified by force or beauty in the meaning they convey, passages in which he seems conscious that he is reputed eloquent and must sustain his reputation. Looked over his pages tonight with Mr. Ruggles, whom I found here on my return from an expedition to Canavan's after chloroform. Mr. Ruggles's delight with Ruskin was unqualified by acquaintance with the better things he has done. . . .

Yellow fever abundant and malignant at Quarantine, according to Cyrus Curtiss; reminiscences of its last year's ravages at Norfolk; general uneasy anticipation of its planting itself here this summer; popular notion that it's working northward in a specially malignant form.

War with England, apprehension whereof has become prominent within the last forty-eight hours. Ruin, of course, to all New Yorkers.

This was a gloomy spring to thoughtful Americans, as Strong's diary suggests. Kansas was suffering under a veritable reign of terror; American filibusters under William Walker were engaged in lawless killing and property-destruction in Central America; the Administration had carried its quarrel with Great Britain to a point which made sober citizens fear war; and the Senate, where sectional passion had reached a new climax, witnessed the most disgraceful scene of its history in the assault of Preston Brooks of South Carolina upon Charles Sumner of Massachusetts.

Twisting the lion's tail, always a popular American amusement, was politically profitable to any party in power in a campaign year. The Democratic Administration had no reason to treat British infringements of American neutrality leniently, and the British representatives in America had put them-

[23] Rudolf J. B. Hübner (1806–1882), German painter.

selves sadly in the wrong in enlisting men for the Crimean campaign. All winter and spring rumors that Minister Crampton was to be recalled or dismissed were rife on both sides of the Atlantic. The request of Secretary Marcy that he be recalled, which was kept partially secret, was unpalatable to the British government. The foreign minister, Lord Clarendon, refused to call Crampton home, and declared to our Minister in London, Buchanan, that he must hear from the envoy and the three British consuls before replying to Marcy. Finally the Pierce Administration lost patience. Marcy, on May 27, sent a decisive note to Lord Clarendon. He would accept the British assurances that no disregard of American neutrality had ever been planned, but he must dismiss Crampton, and revoke the exequaturs of Consuls Barclay, Mathew, and Rowcroft. On May 28 the dismissals duly took place. For a few weeks men feared that Great Britain would send Minister Dallas home in retaliation (he had replaced Buchanan in London); but British opinion took a moderate stand, Gladstone made an able speech in criticism of Clarendon's policy, Dallas was kept at his post, and the risk of a breach between the two nations disappeared.

Meanwhile, horrifying events had taken place almost simultaneously in Kansas and the Senate. May 20 found a proslavery force under an irresponsible Federal marshal invading the town of Lawrence, headquarters of the free-soil element in Kansas. This large "posse," armed with five cannon, destroyed the printing office whence the free-soil newspaper was issued, fired the substantial stone hotel, and pillaged stores and residences. The outrage was intended to strike terror to the growing free-soil population—a population heavily reinforced this spring and summer by immigration from the East and Middle West. May 20 was also the day on which Senator Sumner concluded his abusive speech called "The Crime Against Kansas." Full of billingsgate and personal calumny, it aroused general indignation. Two days later Preston S. Brooks of South Carolina entered the nearly empty Senate chamber, approached Sumner busily writing at his desk, and rained heavy blows on his head with a guttapercha cane. This indefensible action seemed to many Northerners a fitting accompaniment to the partial destruction of Lawrence. All opposition to slavery, many said, was to be overborne by the use of violence.

May 18. Trinity Sunday. The separation of Paulding and his wife is avowed now. The lady and her two children stay with Wolcott Gibbs for the present at least. Paulding and his wife's brother, Jem Mauran, have had a rough and tumble fight in the New York Hotel, and Paulding was licked. Samuel Whitlock is dangerously ill at Staten Island with remittent fever. . . . War and yellow fever continue to be sources of alarm. I fear this is to be a dismal summer.

May 19. Fine weather, rather an active day. The war-chill (it's by no means a war-fever) has knocked stocks down to fearful depths, and Beardom rejoices with exceeding great joy. Jacob Little is of a cheerful countenance.[24] Ellie continues well, cramp her chief trouble. Went with her tonight to hear the Rev. John Lord's lecture on Innocent III (at the corner of Twenty-third Street and Fourth Avenue, the new medical college). Quite a clever lecture, though inferior I'm told to the others of his series on the papacy. Hearty recognition of some truths about medieval times that are unpopular with Protestants, mixed up with crude inconsistent ultra-Protestant commonplaces of censure and denunciation. Somewhat superficial, too, I think, though Mr. Ruggles ranks him so high. Denouncing St. Francis of Assisi and St. Dominic for the filthy corruptions and degeneracies of the mendicant orders is like describing the rise of Methodism and making Stigginses of Wesley and Whitefield. After the lecture, I went to the Century to announce that I could not attend the dinner in honor of Dr. Cogswell next Thursday. Found George Anthon here on my return, en route for a little sociable party of one hundred and fifty at Bob LeRoy's.

May 20. Samuel H. Whitlock is to be buried on Thursday, the first of that happy hopeful dozen of law students who took the world so easily and found my father's office so pleasant a rendezvous between 1838 (?) and 1843, that has finished his course on earth and gone forth to the silent world toward which we are all walking, toward which every pulsation is a step. Sad to think of Sam Whitlock's *past* nonchalant gaiety and good nature with Cram and Pete Strong and Post and George Anthon. Sadder to remember his enviable vigor and enterprise, walking, leaping and climbing years ago when we were together at Catskill.

May 22, THURSDAY. George Anthon dined here. After dinner little Lucy [Derby] and her mamma and Aunt Mary came in, and I performed on the magic lantern, to the delight of the two babies, Lucy and Johnny. News tonight that Charles Sumner of the Senate has been licked with a loaded cane by a certain honorable Carolinian Brooks for his recent rather sophomorical anti-slavery speech. I hold the anti-slavery agitators wrong

---

[24] The notorious stock market manipulator, whose *coups* with Morris Canal securities in 1835 and Erie Railroad stock in 1840 marked a new era in speculation.

in principle and mischievous in policy. But the reckless, insolent brutality of our Southern aristocrats may drive me into abolitionism yet.

May 23. Much angry feeling about the assault on Sumner at Washington. It will strengthen the Free-soilers and Abolitionists, and it's reasonable and right it should strengthen them, for it's an act of brutality and blackguardism that ought to tell against its authors and endorsers. Jay told me of it as we rode home from Whitlock's funeral Thursday.

May 26. Seven thirty P.M. I should be a graceless hound if I were not deeply thankful for today. It has been a nervous time, but Ellie has got through her troubles, thus far at least, very far better than I hoped. Last night I spent mostly in the library and got a brief, disturbed doze in the big chair and got no sleep but did not suffer severely till about four this morning, when I marched down to Fourteenth Street after Dr. Peters with awful misgivings. It was one of the loveliest spring mornings that ever dawned. Brought him back with me a little before five, and he soon began administering chloroform, pretty freely I thought, producing much alleviation, but nothing like insensibility nor even any apparent confusion of thought or difficulty of speech. From the time he came in, there was a very steady crescendo of suffering, and the last four or five paroxysms were piteous and terrible to see. Much worse agony I never witnessed. It ended a quarter before eight, when her nine-and-a-quarter-pound baby (George Templeton Strong, Jr.) came into the world, screeching an indignant protest against his change of domicile. . . .

The baby is a man-child, pronounced by all who've seen him to be a prodigy of infantine loveliness, in which decision I acquiesce, distrusting my own private judgment. He's certainly less flatulent, colicky, querulous, and quarrelsome than Johnny was at his age (twelve hours and a fraction), and has borne his honors meekly thus far, not puffed up with adulation or with wind. It's said he's going to look like the maternal side of the house. Well, may Heaven defend him and his mamma.

May 28. Never was the country in such a crazy state as just now. Civil war impending over Kansas; the Administration blundering us into the misery and ruin of war with England, in a quarrel about which no mortal feels interest enough to induce him to spend five dollars; North and South farther alienated than ever before. I believe civilization at the South is retrograde and that the Carolinas are decaying into barbarism. Brooks comes on Sumner at his desk unawares, stuns him with a cudgel, and belabors the prostrate orator till the cudgel breaks and splinters, and Southern editors and Congressmen talk about the "chivalry," "gallantry,"

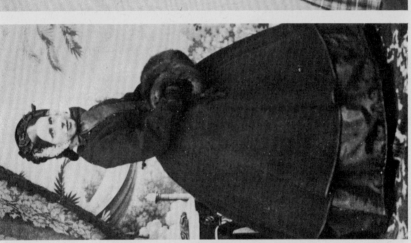

MR. AND MRS. CHARLES E. STRONG AND KATE (MISS PUSS)

THEODORE WINTHROP

WOLCOTT GIBBS

and manliness of the act, and they're getting up a testimonial for Brooks in Charleston. If Brooks belonged to the House of Commons, he'd be convicted and sentenced to a degrading imprisonment of two years, within six weeks from the date of his offence, if the blood of all the Howards and De Veres were in his veins. If Herbert, who shot the Irish waiter at breakfast the other day, were an English peer, he'd be hanged like Earl Ferrers.

The baby, thus far so quiet, seems disposed to discourse a little tonight.

Crampton is probably dismissed, and the glove thrown down. If England isn't wiser than we are, she will take it, and there will be a breach of the peace. Collision on the coast of Nicaragua may make it inevitable.

May 29, THURSDAY. No new vagaries from the wild men of the South since yesterday. The South is to the North nearly what the savage Gaelic race of the Highlands was to London *tempore* William and Mary, *vide* Macaulay's third volume; except that they've assumed to rule their civilized neighbors instead of being oppressed by them, and that the simple, barbaric virtues of their low social development have been thereby deteriorated.

A few fine specimens have given them a prestige the class don't deserve. We at the North are a busy money-making democracy, comparatively law-abiding and peace-loving, with the faults (among others) appropriate to traders and workers. A rich Southern aristocrat who happens to be of fine nature, with the self-reliance and high tone that life among an aristocracy favors, and culture and polish from books and travel, strikes us (not as Brooks struck Sumner but) as something different from ourselves, more ornamental and in some respects better. He has the polish of a highly civilized society, with the qualities that belong to a ruler of serfs. Thus a notion has got footing here that "Southern gentlemen" are a high-bred chivalric aristocracy, something like Louis XIV's noblesse, with grave faults, to be sure, but on the whole, very gallant and generous, regulating themselves by "codes of honor" (that are *wrong*, of course, but very grand); not rich, but surrounded by all the elements of real refinement. Whereas I believe they are, in fact, a race of lazy, ignorant, coarse, sensual, swaggering, sordid, beggarly barbarians, bullying white men and breeding little niggers for sale. The exceptions prove no more that's in favor of the class than Lochiel or "Fergus Mc-Ivor" can prove in favor of Highland civilization. Or a parallel might be drawn between the South Carolina statesman and fire-eater, and the Irish politician descended from Brian Boru, proud of his own beautiful Ireland, oppressed by Saxons, ready to give satisfaction to any political opponent, full of gas and brag and bosh. But it would be unfair to the Celtic gentleman.

May 30. Very busy day downtown. Charley came in after dinner with some papers that wanted attention, and I had to hurry down to Wall Street. On my way up at eight, I stopped at the Tabernacle, where the citizens of New York were summoned to meet and declare their sentiments about Sumner and the South. A vast crowd, earnest, unanimous, and made up of people who don't often attend political gatherings.[25] Significant that John A. Stevens called the meeting to order and old Griswold presided; men not given to fits of enthusiasm or generous sympathy, unlike to be prominent in anything wherein the general voice of the community does not sustain them. Evarts read the resolutions, which seemed discreetly framed and not intemperate. The meeting was prepared to swallow much stronger language. The roar of the great assemblage when Sumner's name occurred, and its spontaneous outburst of groaning and hissing at the sound of "Preston S. Brooks" impressed me. They seemed expressions of deep and strong feeling. I guess the North is roused at last. After the resolutions were read, Daniel Lord began a forcible-feeble speech, and I made my way out through the crowd as best I could.

Charley has just been here, and it seems the crowd multiplied after I left, and a separate meeting was organized outside with George W. Blunt for orator.

May 31, SATURDAY. The Sumner meeting last night is admitted by the *Herald* to have been an imposing demonstration. Mr. Ruggles made an emphatic speech after Lord finished; wish I'd known he was among the orators of the evening. Few dissenters from the action of the meeting, among them Cram, influenced, I guess, by his Southern connections (Henry A. Wise and others), and Mrs. ——, who's thinking of the nice Southern men she'll meet at Newport this summer and can't tolerate the idea of non-intercourse.

'June 1. Much discourse about Sumner and the South. Shall we pro-

[25] New York businessmen had long tended to sustain the South. Since the Kansas-Nebraska Act they had taken a different attitude, and now they felt outraged. S. B. Ruggles advised Southerners to think twice. "There are more free men within one mile of this platform than in the whole state of South Carolina."

claim non-intercourse with Southerners? Shall the New York Club, for example, blackball three gentlemen who belong to "the Chivalry" and are now in nomination, and shall I omit to call on Mr. Frank Hampton and Sally, his wife, when they come here? My present impulse answers both questions in the affirmative, but I see that it's a doubtful matter. Suppose we say: "Gentlemen, we can't get along with you, we had better separate into two confederacies and fight openly, for public war is better than private personal broils and assaults." But the idea of dissolution and division is intolerable. Union is a necessity. Schism is ruin to both fragments of the nation. Do not our preponderance in material wealth, intelligence, and every element of political power enable us to assert that union must and shall exist, that there shall be no decomposition, that we will maintain the Union against Southern folly?

June 3.   Long thundershower in progress, heavy and hot. Ellie has been sitting up half the day, so I hope she sleeps unconscious. . . . Nominating convention of the Democracy parturient at Cincinnati and in puerperal convulsion. It may bring forth Pierce, Douglas, Buchanan, or somebody else, as our Southern rulers shall determine, and I doubt if the North be even yet sufficiently irritated to unite in defeating their nominee. F. B. Cutting tells me, however, that he thinks the Sumner affair will decide the election against the Democracy. It will certainly weaken that party at the North, and it will be politic for them to promote Brooks's expulsion, and so pacify more or less the present strong feeling against the Administration.

June 6, FRIDAY.   Buchanan nominated at Cincinnati. It might have been much worse. Northern divisions will make him the next President. Pierce is served right. The South has used him sufficiently and thrown him away, enjoyed the fruits of his treason and kicked him out of doors. He'll find cold comfort at home when he goes there; his neighbors have just been hanging him and Brooks in effigy. Only one course is left for him, and that is to throw all the weight of executive power and patronage into the scale of the North during the ten months of power that remain to him; to strengthen the United States troops in Kansas and direct them to make war on Missouri, if it shew its grimy nose across the border, to adopt every measure of violence and extremity the most ultra Northern politician could suggest. So may he yet secure a few friends who will be willing to associate with him and recognize him in his approaching days of insignificance, and he cannot make himself more infamous than he is already by any new exhibition of baseness. . . .

Report that some officious friend has informed old Lydig that Judge Daly, his son-in-law elect, is subject to epilepsy (informed him by anonymous letter, it's said), and that Lydig and his whole house are urging Miss Maria to break off her engagement, which she stoutly refuses to do, and that there is "a time" about it. I don't believe the judge's epilepsy amounts to anything very serious, and I think Miss Maria had better maintain herself in her present position.

June 7. . . . Democratic ticket is Buchanan, and Breckinridge (F. B. Cutting's antagonist) for Vice-President.

June 8, SUNDAY. Extracts from Southern papers indicate that Mr. Brooks's brutality is endorsed and sanctioned by the South; that the feeling of the North on that subject and our strong, unanimous condemnation of Carolinian chivalry and Virginian ethics irritate and annoy and gall the gentlemen whose vocation is to breed niggers and flog them; and that they seek, therefore, to relieve their own minds and strengthen their own convictions by greater vehemence in assertion and bluster. In forming an opinion about the moral tone of the South as illustrated by its judgment on this matter, it ought to be remembered that slavery, which lies at the bottom of Southern institutions, society, and property, which enables the Southern gentleman to buy comforts for his wife and food for his children, on which Southern girls marry, and families depend, and which is interwoven with and supports the whole fabric of Southern life, is condemned as a wrong and a sin by the whole civilized world. Wrongly condemned, it seems to me, but still condemned and censured from London to Vienna. Our political theories of right and wrong are decisive that it is an iniquity; we start with the so-called self-evident truth that all men are born free and equal. The South has all the culture, civilization, intelligence, and progress of the nineteenth century against it, unanimous in declaring that it lives on oppression and robbery. Great allowance should be made for the soreness and bitterness that a consciousness of this fact must produce.

June 10. The Bank of New York is evacuated by Oothout and Halsey and their retinue of steady-going clerks and tellers and is to be pulled down. It's the last surviving monument of old Wall Street. The Union Bank, with its two squat doric columns, is leveled and won't be missed. In Broadway there is considerable demolition, including Masonic Hall, a very notable old landmark, and both corners of Pearl Street. . . .

Kansas meeting last night. Bleecker presided. Large and loud-mouthed committee to get money for Sharps's rifles and so on. Talk in the *Tribune* about invading Missouri. All rather resembling overt acts of treason. Perhaps the outrages in Kansas are in fact such as justify rebellion, but all accounts from that quarter are so discordant and unsatisfactory that no one has sufficient evidence of that fact, which is now, moreover, *sub judice*—under investigation by a congressional committee. So the right of insurrection is not yet established here; we at the East are not yet in a position that allows us to become revolutionary. If we proceed to organize civil war, we fight at infinite disadvantage, not merely because the whole militia of Kentucky, Tennessee, and Missouri can at once be brought to bear on the field of action, but because law and the Constitution are words of power which would make our opponents invincible. Reaction throughout the North would be instantaneous, and the Black Republican Party would become a byword like the Hartford Convention.

June 11. Rumor that Miss Maria Lydig has turned Roman Catholic, which I don't believe; also that the paternal Lydig distinctly and expressly forbids her alliance with Judge Daly, and that the young lady intends to have her own way and will be married this summer, which is not improbable.[26]

June 12. I'm full of sorrow and contrition tonight. A poor little mouse had been caught alive and unharmed, which I tended very carefully through the evening, and supplied with food and water. Its little eyes and whiskers were delightful, and I fully intended to set it at large in the street in front of somebody else's dwelling house after making it the subject of a slight scientific experiment, often heretofore tried on myself and rather pleasurable than otherwise—inebriation by chloroform. So he was "taken up tenderly, lifted with care" by the tail and lodged beneath a spacious bell-glass with a rag wet with a sufficient dose of that beneficent fluid. First he ran about vigorously, then his footing grew uncertain, then he tumbled down and kicked. Then I lifted the bell-glass and took him out, and he kicked more feebly and lay still and did not come to. I became alarmed. I exhausted the remedial agents within my reach, cold water, artificial respiration, and friction of the extremities. Ammonia and galvanism were not at hand. But it was unavailing. "The vital spark had fled." It makes me unhappy, for though mice are vermin, I hate to kill them. . . .

We shall have news from England in a day or two and shall know

[26] An unfounded story; New York generated many rumors.

what John Bull says about our insult in the Crampton matter.[27] Probably there will be a period of great depression and alarm thereupon.

June 13. Walked uptown with Mr. Ruggles. Looked in for five minutes at the convention (Free-Soil section of the Know-Nothings), busy making a President in the Apollo Room at Broadway. Heard some very sound and wholesome talk from a rather raw Connecticut Yankee named (I believe) Perkins.

Signs of the times: the Honorable Hannibal Hamlin, Senator and Democrat, announces to the Senate his defection from the Democratic party and hostility to the Cincinnati platform. The New York *Herald's* hose-pipe of dirty water begins to be directed uncertainly, and to splash not the North alone, but North and South impartially. It talks now of "nigger-drivers" as well as nigger worshipers. The trumpet of that respectable paper is giving forth an uncertain sound, and I guess Bennett and Hudson & Co. will be talking Billingsgate in support of the Northern candidate within two months.[28]

June 16, MONDAY. Another perfect summer day, of splendid sunshine and clear, bracing air. Stopped awhile on my way downtown to contemplate the ruins of the old "Peale's Museum" building in Broadway near Murray Street, which tumbled down spontaneously just before I arrived there. The house adjoining on the south side has just been demolished, and this edifice, being too weak to stand alone, began to settle and crack on Saturday evening. Proper precautions were taken, and Broadway was made no thoroughfare at that point, so nobody was hurt when the crash came. . . .

The "Vigilance Committee" has reappeared in San Francisco.[29] Dangerous and bad, but it might be worse. Not unlikely that within a few years this community will require a like organization, a "protoplasm" of new social agencies that will gradually take definite form and replace the old debilitated and inefficient instruments of law. But the transition process is fearfully critical and may lead straight to anarchy.

June 17. News from England looks bad, and we've yet to learn the

[27] That is, Secretary Marcy's rather abrupt dismissal of Minister Crampton, which was condemned by much of the press and many public men.

[28] Bennett's *Herald*, long sympathetic with the South, turned to support Frémont in the campaign.

[29] A new crisis had been produced in California by the murder of the trenchant reform journalist, James King of William, on May 14, 1856, by an ex-convict and cheap politician named James Casey. The "law and order" men of San Francisco tried Casey and his accomplice Cora and on May 22 put them to death.

effect of Crampton's dismissal. Dallas will receive a *vade in pace*, the two nations will cease to be on speaking terms, there will be an awful panic here, and that subtle mischief-maker, Louis Napoleon, may take advantage of our rift to intrigue us somehow into actual war.

The Philadelphia Convention nominates for President John C. Frémont, for Vice-President Dayton of New Jersey. *Hurrah for both.* I shall vote the Republican ticket, if alive and capable of locomotion to the polls next fall. Northern discords and splits will defeat that ticket beyond question, but I want it to have a respectable minority in its favor. I belong to the insurgent plebeians of the North arming against a two-penny South Carolina aristocracy—to the oppressed Saxons assailing our modern Front de Boeufs and De Bracys in their strongholds. . . .

It is said Miss Maria Lydig and Judge Daly are to be married next week; that papa is resolute in the most emphatic protest against the match, won't witness the ceremony himself, and won't allow any of his family to attend it.

June 21, SATURDAY.   Ellie has been making visits today. Called on Miss Maria Lydig, who's *not* at her father's, but at her aunt's, Mrs. William Remsen's, in Waverley Place. I'm sorry that lady's wedding takes place under a cloud, but lithotomy alone can get a crotchet out of her papa's system, when it has once established itself there.

June 23.   Frémont promises to run pretty well. Fillmore in town; nobody cares much.[30] Foreign news not warlike.

June 24.   Saw George Cornell, returned from his South American expedition, wherein he has made a good operation for himself, Cram, and Townsend, but not quite so good as he expected. The Park pretty well filled with loungers, loafers, policemen, awaiting the arrival of Fillmore's triumphal procession; not much sign of enthusiasm, though. The masses take both Frémont and Buchanan rather coolly. What little sign there is of life and excitement is for Frémont.

June 25.   Fillmore procession yesterday generally pronounced a failure and a "fizzle." The Frémont "ratification meeting" tonight at the Tabernacle will do better, I hope. Little chance of his success, it seems to me, though that sanguine man, Anthony Bleecker, declares Frémont will carry every Northern state by unheard-of majorities. There is a great hurrahing out of doors in the distance, which comes, I suppose, from some

[30] Ex-President Millard Fillmore returned from Europe to meet a reception from Know-Nothings (with many Whig allies), who had already nominated him for President.

enthusiastic band of peripatetic Frémonters in procession; "deluded souls that dream of" nice little places in the Custom House and jobs and pickings and stealings. Frémont won't be President, my dear, deceived, enthusiastic, short-sighted brothers. You are bellowing to no purpose, disquieting yourselves in vain. Better for you to go home and to bed, and husband your vital forces and bellow for Buchanan on the first opportunity. The *Aristocratuli* of the South still have power for a time and times. Their day is not yet come. Ten years hence there will be some Frémont who can make it worth one's while to hurrah for him, but *you*, my unknown vociferous friends and fellow-citizens, are premature. You don't perceive that "the Republican party" is a mere squirm and wriggle of the insulted North, a brief spasm of pain under pressure and nothing more.

June 26. Severely hot. Frémont meeting last night very imposing in character and numbers. The new Republican Party calls out many who have long eschewed politics. It will probably sweep this state and nearly all the Northern states. Reasonably efficient today. Decision of the Court of Appeals on the great case of Schuyler's over-issued stock of the New Haven Railroad Company, adverse to the spurious stockholders (or a large class of them), much discussed. Very acute, wise, and sound, I think. Generally approved, except by the Board of Brokers.

June 29. News from England: things in an uneasy state, with room for anxiety; but Bull is less obstreperous than was to have been expected. San Francisco is in anarchy to any government by established law. The "Vigilance Committee" has acquired the highest judicial office. It has solemnly hanged two notorious scoundrels and arrested several more, one of whom, the illustrious Yankee Sullivan, removed his case from the jurisdiction of the committee by severing an artery in his arm and bleeding himself to death. The committee treats habeas corpuses as a nullity, and the governor is trying to organize a hostile force. If it be true, as it is said, that a reaction is setting in, and that there will be a formidable resistance to this new development of Lynch Law, a civil war is unlikely. But the committee claims to represent all the respectability, property, and honesty of San Francisco, and if so, I hope its experiment may succeed. One like it will have to be tried in New York within ten years.

July 2. We went to the concert of the "Mendelssohn Union." Heard Mendelssohn's "Music to Athalie" and "Walpurgisnacht" by a large and capitally drilled chorus, with piano accompaniment. Solo parts well filled also; good voices, and evident careful study of the music, rare in these amateur performances. On the whole, the execution of the music was most unusually satisfactory and creditable. The Walpurgis affair did not impress me very much, but the Athalie must be a very splendid work—of that there can be no doubt even on a first hearing. I did not think Mendelssohn could sustain himself on a high level through so long a composition, nor that he could write anything so free from manner, and so full of beautiful melodic feeling. I hope I may hear it again.

Kansas battle beginning in the House. Indications that Douglas and others are scared by the storm their selfish folly has raised. Should things be compromised and smoothed over, the Northern party will accomplish little next November. I hope such may be the result; that is, that the mischief may be so far repaired as to make a sectional contest unnecessary.

News from England seems pacific, but can civil war between North and South be postponed twenty years longer? I fear we, or our children, have got to pass through a ruinous revolutionary period of conflict between two social systems before the policy of the U.S.A. is finally settled. The struggle will be fearful when it comes, as it must sooner or later, for an amicable disunion and partition of territory is an impossibility. In those days will the price of gunpowder rise suddenly? One thing seems clear; the North can hardly fail to have the moral support of England and the whole civilized world enlisted in its favor.

July 6.   The Washington statue, *"statua gentilissima del gran commendatore,"* unveiled on the morning of the Fourth.[31] I think the horse and his rider very creditable to their artist, particularly the former. They look raw and brassy now, but I'm told the weather will bronze them. . . .

July 8.   To meeting of [Columbia] trustees—barely a quorum. Resolution to buy the Deaf and Dumb building carried *nem. con.*, and without debate. It seems a prudent measure, and I hope we may abandon our present dormitory next fall.

Political matters unchanged. We're in a pretty uneasy and uncomfortable state, in which violent convulsion is possible at any moment; for example, there may well be some collision at Washington that would bring forward delegations from both North and South to support and uphold their respective representatives. The West is said to be decided that Kansas shall *not* be a slave state, if the physical power of the West can prevent it; so there may be civil war in these days. On good authority I hear that its possibility was urged in the Philadelphia Convention by

[31] This bronze monument in Union Square—one of the first equestrian statues in the United States—was by Henry Kirke Brown, with a base by J. Q. A. Ward.

Frémont's Western supporters as a reason for making him the candidate of the Northern party, his military experience and energy qualifying him above McLean to lead the North in civil war. This alienation of North and South is an unquestionable fact and a grave one. Straws shew how the wind blows. Here is Mrs. Hampton in the city, and I'm hesitating whether Ellie shall bestow a piece of pasteboard on the wife of a South Carolinian.

July 14, MONDAY. The Rev. Hawks, very limp and moist, loafed in after tea, and favored us with a Southside view of the present political issues; and a very clear, strong, and plain-spoken confession of faith it was. Don't dispute many of the Dean's propositions myself. It would be a rather strong measure to hang Sumner and Seward with Brooks and Douglas, but it might be expedient. . . .

Today cruelly hot. Tonight hotter, and but feebly mitigated by sea-breeze. Charley at Newport. Attended Hackley's examination of the Freshmen of Columbia College awhile this morning. Not so bad as I expected, though bad enough.

July 15. House of Representatives has disposed of the Brooks and Sumner case. The motion to expel Bully Brooks failed for want of a two-thirds vote, but the majority in favor of expulsion was considerable, so the *Cheval*, or *Hoss* (his nearest approach to a chivalric title) made an allocution to his Southern admirers and refractory Northern liegemen and indignantly resigned his seat. It's said that Butler is to leave the Senate and that this caitiff will be instantly promoted to Butler's seat.[32] Even South Carolina can hardly be so blind and drunken with insolence and folly. Reasonable men and gentlemen, North and South, must be unanimous as to Brooks's harangue, which has rarely been equaled for bad taste, self-importance, and brutality.

He said "even the North must allow that if he chose to strike a blow now, it would be followed by revolution"—and took credit for withholding his lightnings. He said almost *totidem verbis* that had Sumner resisted vigorously, he would have killed him, and admitted by implication that he went armed to his brutal work and prepared to be murderer as well as bully should occasion require. Yet it's said he was welcomed, as he left the House in his majesty, by the congratulations and embraces of Southern "gentlemen," and the kisses of Southern ladies, who crowded the galleries and rushed into his arms. Poor things, they are hero-worshipers by virtue of their sex, and if the true divinity is absent or under a

[32] This was not done; but Brooks was at once re-elected to the House.

cloud, they must be excused for bowing down before some braying Mumbo-Jumbo whose brag and finery eclipse all competitors.

Vivat Frémont—I fear I shall come out a "damned Abolitionist" after all.

July 16. George [William] Curtis is going about speechifying at political meetings in the cause of Frémont, and pretty effectively, it seems. Theodore Winthrop(!!!) active in the same work. It is clear that the "Black Republican" party commends itself much to educated and intelligent people at the North, particularly of the sort that commonly declines any concern in "mere" political matters. I don't think its principle has made its way down to the masses yet, or is taken hold of by them (unless in the New England states), though the working-class is deeply and directly interested in this controversy. Next fall will shew whether I am right. Perhaps some considerable part of the German vote may be cast for Frémont.

July 24. One of our civic scourges, an organ-grinder, is putting his broken-winded engine of torture through "St. Patrick's Day in the Morning," just so far off that I daren't shy anything at him for fear of stirring up the wrong man. . . .

Brooks *vs.* Burlingame of Massachusetts: Brooks challenged the Massachusetts man, who accepted and named Clifton House (Niagara) as the place of meeting. Bully Brooks instantly backs out. Publishes a statement putting his withdrawal on the ground that he'd be assassinated if he came North, but intimates that if Burlingame will challenge him (and give him choice of weapons) he may accept. General opinion is that Bully Brooks has shewn the white feather.

Anson Burlingame's stinging attack upon Preston Brooks in the House had resulted in a challenge. The Massachusetts Congressman, who had been reared on the Michigan frontier, accepted it; but he insisted that they should meet on the Canadian side of Niagara Falls, and Brooks feared that he could not pass through hostile Northern territory with safety. The duel was thus averted, both men laying claim to credit in the affair. Burlingame's course heightened his popularity in the North.

The campaign of 1856, remarkable for its fervor and its bitterness, was now reaching a climax of excitement. The Democrats had held their national convention in Cincinnati in June, with the civil conflict still raging in Kansas. Since the platform endorsed the Kansas-Nebraska Act, the logical nominee would have been its author, Stephen A. Douglas. But the popular condemnation of the law was so widespread in the North that he was an unacceptable candidate. The choice, therefore, fell upon James Buchanan, "available" because he had been safe in England while the Kansas quarrel was gaining heat. For Vice-President the Democrats nominated John C. Breckinridge of Kentucky, who was counted upon to carry his own state and neighboring Tennessee— neither of which the party had won since Jackson's day. The Republicans, meeting in an enthusiastic convention in Philadelphia on June 17, the anniversary of Bunker Hill, had drawn up a platform which called for exclusion of slavery from all territories, and for the construction of a Pacific Railroad. It included the Declaration of Independence, an appeal to radical sentiment at the North. For President the delegates had nominated the dashing explorer John C. Frémont, son-in-law of Thomas Hart Benton. It was evident that the battle between the two principal parties would be close. The Democrats rallied all their forces, Southern planters uniting with New York merchants and conservatives of New England and the Middle West. Douglas gave full support to Buchanan, and large sums of money were contributed by Northern businessmen fearful that a Republican triumph would spell secession and civil war. The Republicans, for their part, appealed to the idealism of the young men of the North and West and to popular resentment over the high-handed course of the proslavery men in Kansas and Washington. During the summer a group of Southern governors met at Raleigh, North Carolina, and proclaimed that their states would leave the Union if Frémont were elected. This and similar threats were denounced by the Republican press as an attempt to blackmail the electorate.

August 1. Spent most of the day in the Trust Company with Ludlow and Moses Taylor, as a Committee of Examination. All correct and prosperous as far as we could discover, but such an investigation is little more than a formality. Six months' hard work over ledgers and vouchers might enable us to report positively that Kearny and David Thompson had not cheated the company out of $100,000 or so, but no less amount of labor is of any real use.

August 4, MONDAY. Our brethren of the South are surely mad. Think of the Virginian Wise telling Mrs. Ritchie (Mowatt)[33] who told

[33] Henry A. Wise, governor of Virginia 1856–1860, and a man of fire-eating propensities; Anna Cora [Ogden] Mowatt, the noted actress, who in 1854 had married William F. Ritchie, editor of the Richmond *Enquirer*.

Mr. Ruggles, who told me, that "if Frémont were elected, he would never be permitted to reach Washington." Their brag and bluster can't well be paralleled, unless by a Chinese edict meant to intimidate the foreign barbarians. One thing is very clear and very important, that in Kentucky and Missouri and possibly in Virginia itself, there are germs of insurrection among the "poor trash," the plebeians who don't own niggers. Such a movement once formed and recognized must triumph sooner or later, and nigger emancipation and the downfall of the nigger-breeding (and mulatto-breeding) aristocracy of those states must follow.

Poor Edward Curtis is dead, after two years and a half of seclusion in the Flushing Asylum, during which there has never been any hope of his restoration or material improvement.

August 5. My old college friend, G. M. Hillyer, seems to be in trouble. He's a Natchez newspaper editor (I used to be confident that he and N. W. Chittenden would be rival candidates for the presidency as soon as they reached the constitutional age), and one of his "cotemporaries" publishes a card printed as a specimen of the courtesy of "The Chivalry" in this morning's *Times*, certifying Giles to be "a liar, a coward, a poltroon, and a scoundrel." Poor Giles! Long talk with Charles Kuhn this afternoon over the affairs of the nation. My platform is substantially this:

1. Slavery is not a wrong per se. If it were so, the states in which it exists ought to right it. We are not called on to interfere with it, supposing it a wrong, any more than we are bound to attack the serfdom of Russia or the iniquities of Naples. And there are so many practical difficulties in the way of righting it that the people who are in that case bound to act, the South, may be pardoned for pausing and hesitating and acting reluctantly. . . .

2. The practical working of the institution (whether it be in itself a wrong or not) includes iniquities that are probably curable by legislation, but are, perhaps, of its essence—inseparable: the selling asunder of families, remediless cruelty and oppression, enforced concubinage, incest, and so forth.

3. It practically demoralizes and degrades the whole community where it exists.

4. It operates against the material development and the progress in civilization and wealth of such community, and is guilty of the difference between Virginia and New York.

5. Any interference by Northern states or individuals with the legal

institutions of the Southern states, which is calculated to produce disaffection or disorder in their servile class, being not merely gratuitous, but most perilous to the insecure social system of those unhappy communities, ought to be repressed most sternly. The North would be merely acting in good faith if it made such interference a capital crime.

6. Congress has no power over any feature of the institution as it exists in a Southern state.

7. But it has power to legislate for the territories, and it may and should exclude from those territories while under its jurisdiction an institution which has thus far only done harm wherever it exists. When those territories have been set up in business for themselves, they may legislate as they please, and introduce slavery into their system if they are fools enough to do it.

Pity I'm not in the Senate of the United States!

Hydropathy was still one of the medical crazes of the period, though it had reached its apogee in the 1840's. Its founder was Vincent Priessnitz, a peasant of Austrian Silesia, who first healed himself and then many of his neighbors by copious use of the springs and streams abounding in his mountain region. Wealthy and fashionable people began to flock to him. He made his patients give up all stimulants, eat plain food, take plenty of exercise in the open air, and use large quantities of water both internally and externally. Naturally his regimen restored many debilitated people to health. He found an American apostle in Henry Gardiner Wright, an enthusiastic young man whom Bronson Alcott had brought back with him from England, and another in Dr. Joel Shew, who edited the Water Cure *Journal and Herald of Reform. The principal English exponents of the system were James M. Gully and Sir W. E. Wilson. Hydropathic establishments, modeled more or less on Priessnitz's original institution at Grafenberg in Silesia, sprang up in great numbers in Germany, France, and the United States. Many of them prospered, and they made a distinct contribution to medicine and sanitation. The cooling bath in fevers and the wet-sheet pack have become recognized implements of medical practice, while hydropathy did much to popularize the morning tub and the drinking of large quantities of water. Two of the principal establishments in the United States were the Brattleboro Water Cure House, and Dr. Shew's house at Lebanon Springs, N. Y.; Dr. Shew also founded the world's first urban water cure in New York City. As Brattleboro offered many cool charms*

*in addition to the hydropathic establishment, Strong had good reason to take
his family there for a summer visit. He left New York early in August, and
after suffering a minor train wreck, the same evening "was welcomed on the
piazza of Wesselhoeft's Hydropathic Asylum by Ellie and Miss Rosalie and
Mr. Ruggles."*

August 13, WEDNESDAY.   I tried all the various forms of the Aqua
Pumpi treatment: plunge bath, sitz bath, half bath, wave bath, douches
of every grade of intensity, and lastly "packing," not a pleasant way of
spending an hour. The packed patient . . . looks just like the pictures of the
gravid female white ant.

Brattleboro is a charming, thrifty New England town, set in a lovely
region of hills. "The country hunches up a good deal" in these parts.
Chesterfield Mountain on the other side of the Connecticut is a goodly
protuberance. The town has its town hall, academy, lots of meeting-
houses, an ambitious opposition water-cure wherein the Honorable
Bayard Clarke and that busted speculator Davison are somehow interested,
two hotels, nice shops, fine houses, droves of the ugliest curs, shoals of
women that ain't attractive, an undue percentage of elderly young ladies
in spectacles, several small thriving factories, plenty of sumptuous old
maples, and running water *ad libitum*. Our hospital or hotel—it's both—is
a queer, low, disjointed building, with ways unlike those of any hotel I've
known, combining usages appropriate to a German watering-place, an
insane asylum, and a penitentiary. Fare good of its kind and abundant. We
are mostly graminivorous. Walks, cold baths, and open air made me eat
as I have never eaten before; mountains of hominy and bowls of milk
vanished before me. I rose at six and turned in at ten, at which hour a
stern Teuton always came into the funny little parlors and silently put
out the lamps. Place agreed with dear little Ellie and the babies, too. . . .

Mr. Ruggles came up Thursday evening and left Saturday. Walter
Cutting also was added unto us. Mr. Ruggles varied the rather monotonous routine of the place by a row with that insufferable old hog, Count
Gurowski, who stays at the opposition "Lawrence Water Cure," and is,
of course, ubiquitous, all-seeing, malignant, mischievous, and abominated.
(I dropped the man's acquaintance, intelligent and instructive as he is,
years ago.) We went across the street to a "hop" at the other house, and
old Gurowski, after several unsuccessful attempts, caught Ruggles's eye
and came up with his usual obsequious Kalmuck purr. Mr. Ruggles told
him he would have no intercourse with him. The Count wanted to ex-

plain, but Mr. Ruggles waved him off in a majestic manner and told him he could do that "tomorrow." Next morning came a challenge in form— only the bearer was a little German waiter girl and a non-combatant. George C. Anthon took charge of the case, and the result was that the Count was very sorry for some things he had said and regretted them extremely, and so it was all satisfactorily settled.

August 14. Nothing new today but my own virtuous simplicity of manners. Yellow fever stock is falling like Nicaragua or Lucifer, son of the morning. None of it in town, and fewer cases at Quarantine. *Per contra,* the most astounding and terrific legends of its prevalence at Bath, New Utrecht, and Fort Hamilton; how everybody is running away, and no one lives there any more but people in the black vomit stage who are too much prostrated to run; how you can nose the poisoned deadly air of those villages a mile before you reach them; how all the dogs and cats are saffron colored, and so forth. But men are very susceptible of panic when the word epidemic is whispered to them. On the Battery tonight, the sudden recollection that the cool sea-breeze I was enjoying came from somewhere near the Quarantine, over nine miles of moonlit saltwater, quickened my walk for a moment.

August 30. Saw George [William] Curtis, wholly wrapt up in the Frémont campaign, wherein he does good and active service, speaking almost every night with great approval and with much more ability than I gave him credit for. Partly for money, I suppose (from some "Central Committee" or other), but somewhat for love of the cause, which commends itself to his Eastern proclivities, and of his pretty Miss Shaw, whose papa is a vehement Free-Soiler. Fillmore seems rather to lose ground. Frémont rather gains. His enemies help him by the bitter malignity of their personal attacks, which will surely decide some thousands to vote in his favor. Were I a moderate Know-Nothing or a mild Buchananier, any two numbers of the New York *Express* would drive me into Frémontism. . . . House and Senate still in extra session, at a deadlock over the Army appropriations. The House will be beat sooner or later.

September 1, MONDAY. I must record as matter of curiosity the results of my silly experiments with Hashish, or rather with the officinal extract of *Cannabis Indica.* I was incited thereto by Dillingham's story of his experiences, recounted at Brattleboro. Tried it very cautiously and warily in small successive doses, without very positive effect, without any effect that I was sure of, and made up my mind that the drug was inert or that I was insensible to it. Thursday night at twelve, just before retir-

ing, I treated myself to a larger bolus, as big as two peas perhaps, and
went to bed and to sleep as usual. At two A.M. I woke from a perturbed,
dreamy slumber that seemed to have been indefinitely long, and was
instantly aware that I was in an abnormal condition. The physical symptoms were dryness of mouth and tongue, slight sense of local pressure at
the pit of the stomach, occasional rapid fluttering action of the heart,
slow and weak pulse, and later coldness and slight numbness of the
extremities. I think, also, that my face was flushed. There was nothing
beside, and all this gave me no disagreeable sensation at all except the
leatheriness of my mouth, which was a little unpleasant.

But my mental gear was working strangely, so strangely that it
instantly occurred to me that my bolus must have been an overdose, and
the next step might be entire loss of self-control, insensibility, or perhaps
death. I felt very comfortable and easy, however, quite free from fright.
It seemed a grave matter, about which I ought to consider what was best
to be done, and the progress of which it was interesting to watch, but
which didn't concern me personally a great deal. The prominent feature
of my mental condition was that I was distinctly in a dual state. I was
two gentlemen in one night shirt: G. T. Strong No. 1 was in an agreeable, mild delirium, unable to control and hardly able to follow the swift
current of incoherent images that were passing through his head. G. T.
Strong No. 2, rather languid and lazy, looked on, noted the phenomena,
tried to remember them distinctly, and to devise some form of words
that would describe certain of his (or No. 1's) sensations which he rightly
thought could not be expressed in language.

This flow of images was wonderful and unprecedented, each distinct
and keen, but instantly giving place to a new one, equally vivid, all dis-
connected and hurrying on in swift succession. When I closed my eyes, a
phantasmagoria of living and moving forms kept pace with this current
of delirious thought. Louis XIV, with a splendid group of embroidered
coats and lace cravats in the background, stood with a lady holding his
arm in a long gallery, all pilasters and carving, and was evidently giving
a rebuke to a little footman who'd been caught in mischief. Gone like a
flash, and in their place I saw Schomberg's soldiers marching slowly over
a desolate withered moor, file after file of old-fashioned uniforms; I knew
they were Schomberg's, of course, intuitively. Then a flying crowd of
peasants, instantly recognized as Irish *keme* fleeing the Boyne (I'd been
turning over Macaulay's *History* just before going to bed); then like a
flash a Brattleboro landscape stood before me, so distinct I could have

counted the trees on the crest of the nearest hill, but it was gone, and in its place was Millais's "Huguenot" picture, not as picture but as reality, and so on. I could still catalogue the series by scores. All were tangible as if seen by the natural eye, but not strong in color; they were as if seen through smoked glass. The effect of the exhibition would have been delightful but for its hurrying succession, which wearied and bewildered me. A second set of impressions, the most intense of all, but which can't be described, occurred at intervals. I tried in vain to analyze and define them. Some object without form, color, or definability of any kind was present, some word without sound or syllable was spoken, and this unknown word or thing seemed long forgotten but perfectly familiar now it had come back and brought with it a whole world of associations, memories, influences, and I don't know what, shadowy but most weighty, unutterable, uncertain even whether they were good or evil, whether their intensity was of joy or sorrow, but most keen and searching. These were not pleasant by any means; there was something in them that seemed real and earnest and most uncanny. There seemed slowly to present itself something of this same class; the nearest approach to describing it, or rather suggesting what it seemed like, would be to say it was the sensible presence, embodied in something close at hand and drawing closer, of death, bodily death with its accessories. It was as if a corpse in its cerements was drawing near me, and I knew that with its first touch, I should be *It*. There was no illusion of sense, but a hideous horror of loathing and shrinking such as I never felt before.

September 9. We turned out to see the Grand Democratic Torchlight Procession. Large certainly, but rather straggling, and with a large infusion of youthful Democrats who'll hardly grow enough to vote next November! Not very joyous or enthusiastic and greeted by little outside hurrahing. The news from Maine hasn't helped to make them jolly. That rather doubtful state seems to have gone Republican with a rush. Frémont forever![34]

September 10. Three cheers for Maine! The election there is a great fact; it shews which way the cat is jumping and will make her jump farther. Doubtless it has already decided $x+y$ cautious gentlemen, waiters on Providence, uncat-like people to whom the *victoris causa* is always pleasing, to get down from their fence and go for Frémont, in-

---

[34] In the state election in Maine, with Hannibal Hamlin running for governor, the Republicans triumphed by a vote of roughly 67,000 to 42,500. They won by a still greater margin in Vermont, the vote being nearly three to one.

fluenced solely by a conscientious sense of duty. This x+y is a large figure; it may well be ten thousand in this state alone. Hamilton Fish is said to have seen a great light lately and to be trying the feel of the current with his toes before jumping in. I don't believe his accession will affect the fortunes of any party very essentially. It's said a Frémont electoral ticket will be run in several Southern states, including Missouri, North Carolina, and Virginia. Dubious. It probably won't be permitted by the oligarchy of little barbarous princes to which the white trash of the South is subject.

September 11. Long discourse with Walter Cutting, who's frightened at the Maine news; has a "betting opinion" still, but will give no odds on Frémont, and considers that the South will secede if Frémont's elected. Which the South *won't*, as long as Southern gentlemen can make a little money going to Congress.

September 16. Early train to Boston, breakfast, and then sat on a barrel for two hours reading Mrs. Stowe's *Dred*, for that the Nahant boat had privily changed its hour. . . . *Dred* is a strong and telling book. Ellie is now deep in the first volume, and much exercised thereby. Found all well at Nahant; hotel all but deserted; weather lovely. Small party that evening at Mrs. Paige's: Professor Felton, Agassiz and wife, and Longfellow (to whom I missed an introduction, not knowing he was there). Next day dined at Agassiz's with Felton—very pleasant; Agassiz and his wife most charming people. After dinner on the rocks at low tide (the "sunken ledge") with him for a couple of hours, and was presented to marine notabilia, chiefly of the zoöphyte family, many of which I've long sought to see.

September 21, SUNDAY. Committee of the Whole on the State of the Nation tonight. No talk but of politics as the momentous month of November draws near. Mr. Ruggles has been vice-presiding the Old Line Whig convention at Baltimore and drawing the platform resolutions of that sedate and venerable Witenagemot or Council of Notables, which has adopted Fillmore and Donelson as "Whig" candidates. It does look like a Historical Society or Congress of Antiquarian Associations, rather than a practical political assemblage, for the Whig party is dead, decomposed, and disintegrated. But Mr. Ruggles gives a pretty clear and plausible statement of its aims and policy, namely:

The pestilent little state of South Carolina, mad with metaphysics and self-conceit, gasconading itself day by day into greater wrath and keener sense of imaginary wrong, means to secede if the North elect Frémont.

It may by its legislature declare itself an independent nation, November 15th, or it may back out a little later, if it can secure Georgia or Virginia as allies, by refusing to go into ballot for President and Vice-President, and forming a Southern Confederacy. If it stand alone, it is easily dealt with; a couple of frigates can blockade its ports, and it will be starved into submission in about two weeks, being as poor and weak as it is insolent and irrational. But should it find aid and comfort from the sympathy of other slave states, *which is not an improbable thing*, if it put itself forward as champion of "Southern rights," the situation becomes a grave one and admits of but two probable solutions: a long and fierce civil war, or what's worse, dissolution of the Union. Now admitting Fillmore's chances to be none, that he will not get an electoral vote, which is likely to happen (though the Know-Nothings profess to have 186,000 registered voters in this state alone), it is desirable, when the South is considering about secession, to have *established* in both Northern and Southern states a party organization, under an old, familiar, national party name, ignoring the sectional questions at issue, opposing both sectional candidates, and proclaiming its cardinal principle to be hostility to all sectional parties. The existence of such a party South as well as North will (according to Mr. Ruggles) furnish a basis for compromise, a nucleus for moderate men, a remnant of political unity to connect New York and Virginia. There is much sense in all this. And this convention, though not great in numbers, seems to have been made up of strong and influential men from all parts. It may play an important part, as a brake on the train, and save us a bad collision.

September 22. With Ellie to see *The Rivals* at Wallack's tonight. Rather a satisfactory performance on the whole, in spite of a most un-Hibernian Sir Lucius O'Trigger and a very dreary Falkland and Julia. But for that dismal pain the author is mainly responsible. A "good comedy" well played is entertaining while it lasts, but after all, these productions, from Congreve & Co. down to Mr. Boucicault, seem to me as shallow, silly, frivolous, and unreal as any compositions I know of. One can imagine comedy that should be to *The Rivals* or *London Assurance* what *Pendennis* and *The Newcomes* are to the old novels of fashionable life.

September 25. Politics engross everybody's thoughts and talk, more and more daily. Hamilton Fish has pronounced at last for Frémont, and favors mankind with an analysis of his motives and reasons that fills two columns of the *Courier*, and is hard reading. Unimportant, except as shewing what an ambitious commonplace man, with some experience and opportunity of observation, thinks is for his own interest. It's significant like the diligence of spiders before rain, the movements of various animals in anticipation of an earthquake or a hurricane. . . .

As for our Southern friends, they're madder every day. *Vide* the Muscogee (Ga.) *Herald* on "Northern Society" as "made up of greasy mechanics and so on," not fit company for a Southern gentleman's body-servant. Also, somebody makes a grand allocution to the young men and braves assembled at a South Carolina militia muster, tells them that if somebody should "smite down the miscreant (John C. Frémont) beside the pillars of the Capitol, in case of his election, not a Southern regiment but would spring to the rescue" of the hypothetical Ravaillac.

Last night to Wallack's again with Ellie; *Old Heads and Young Hearts* one of the best comedies I've seen. Blake as Jessie Rural excellent.

Fought out in an atmosphere of public excitement over "bleeding Kansas," the three-cornered campaign of 1856 aroused the most impassioned feeling. Frémont and the Republican party attacked the repeal of the Missouri Compromise in vehement terms, and insisted that Congress must prohibit slavery in all the territories—Kansas entering the Union as a free state. Buchanan and the Democratic Party upheld the popular sovereignty doctrine embodied in the Kansas-Nebraska Act; the fate of Kansas was to be decided by her own voters. Fillmore, nominated first by the Know-Nothings and late in the summer by the remnants of the Whig Party, took a non-committal position on slavery, but denounced the sectional views and loyalties of the other two parties. A powerful and indignant uprising of Northern free-soilers gave the Republican Party tremendous strength. The pulpit and the religious press outside the slave states were generally for Frémont; so were the most important newspapers— Bryant's Evening Post, *Greeley's* Tribune, *Samuel Bowles's Springfield* Republican, *Bennett's* Herald, *Medill's Chicago* Tribune; *so were the famous authors—Longfellow, Irving, Emerson, Whittier, and Lowell. The* Independent *exhorted voters to remember that a Republican success would be a victory "for Christ, for the nation, and for the world." It added: "Vote as you pray! Pray as you vote!" Great meetings, marked by tumultuous enthusiasm, were held all over the North. The colleges, led by Harvard and Yale, were strongly on the Republican side. George William Curtis, who delivered a number of excellent campaign speeches, tried especially to rally young men in an address at Wesleyan University on "The Duty of the American Scholar."*

Indignant Southerners met this wave of free-soil feeling with threats of secession. Toombs of Georgia declared that Frémont's election would mean the end of the Union. The Republicans meant to dictate to the South: "I am content that they shall own us when they conquer us, but not before." Slidell of Louisiana asserted that if Frémont won, "the Union cannot and ought not to be preserved." Mason of Virginia avowed that "immediate, absolute, eternal separation" would be the result. But most Northerners, like Strong, scoffed at these utterances of the fire-eaters. They had heard such threats before, and did not believe they would be carried into execution. Southerners could not be kicked out of the Union, declared Senator Wilson of Massachusetts. It was only a minority who were trying to frighten the Northern voters. Said Curtis: "Twenty millions of a moral people are asking themselves whether their government shall be administered solely in the interest of three hundred and fifty thousand slaveholders."

The state contest was also embittered. The Republicans had nominated for governor John A. King, ex-Congressman and diplomat; the Democrats had named Amasa J. Parker, lawyer and judge; and the Know-Nothings, Erastus Brooks, an editor who had become prominent by insisting that Catholic property be taxed.

September 27, SATURDAY.   Nothing fresh in politics. George Cornell counts on 50,000 majority for Frémont in this state, allowing 10,000 majority the other way in this city. Dubious. . . . To *Star of the North* last night with Ellie and George C. Anthon. Opera admirably put on the stage and all the parts well filled. Music generally overworked and elaborated so as to obscure its not very brilliant ideas.

September 30. . . . Attended a ward meeting last night—the Eighteenth Ward Republican organization—and was duly enrolled; a respectable meeting in number and style of business. Fry of the *Tribune* office made a long speech, vehement, extravagant, and odd, but with some telling points. Judge Cowles presided. I don't count on success in this election, but I think it's time now for everybody at the North to aid, as far as he can, any decent party that aims at putting down the aggressions and assumptions of our Southern friends, and to try to bring them to reason.

Result of my political meditations as I lay awake last night. *Vide* Walter Scott:

SOUTHERN WAR-SONG
Tune, *Bonnets of Bonny Dundee.*

To the base churls in Congress 'twas Brooksy who spoke
"Ere the West shall be Free there are heads to be broke.
"So let each Southern Gent who loves Niggers and me,
"Come follow the bludgeon of Chevalier B."

Chorus:
Go finish your cocktail, go borrow a ten,
Go lock up your niggers and count up your men.
We'll pepper the Yankees for talking so free,
And it's room for the bludgeon of Chevalier B!

Bold Brooks is excited, he strides down the street,
The children drop senseless, the dogs they retreat.
But the Judge (well-bred man) says, "It isn't for me
To confine a real Gent like the Chevalier B."

As he marched by the office where Patents are kept
Each Yankee Mechanic turned livid and wept.
But the sly coffin-maker, he chuckled in glee
Saying, "Luck to thy bludgeon, bold Chevalier B."

With Free-Soil Canaille the Hotel steps were filled,
As if half of New York had come South to be killed.
There was buttoning of pockets and trembling of knees,
As they watched for that bludgeon of Chevalier B's.

These low "self-made" scrubs, they were full of their prate,
And had reasons and facts such as *gentlemen* hate.
But they fled to their rooms and the entry was free,
At the whisk of the bludgeon of Chevalier B.

He stalked to the bar, through saliva and smoke,
And with the wild Quattlebum gaily he spoke.
"Our District alone will raise regiments three,
"For the love of buck-niggers, big bludgeons and me."

The Quattlebum asks: "The Campaign? It is planned?"
"The spirit of Arnold our March shall command!
"You shall soon hear of Boston surrendering to me,
"Or that high swings the corpus of Chevalier B.

"There are streams besides Hudson, with towns at their mouth.
"If they've men in New England, we've Gents at the South.
"And loyal 'White Trash' (they can't read, don't you see?)
"Who will bite, scratch, and gouge for the Chevalier B.

"There are knives and revolvers that be about loose.
"There are Hounds in our Kennels we've trained up for use.
"The blood-hounds will bite and the pistols shoot free
"At the wave of the bludgeon of Chevalier B.

"Away to the Hills, to the swamps, to the Moon!
"Ere I recognize Frémont I'll couch with the Coon
"And tremble, false snobs, as you sit at your tea.
"You'll catch fits before long from my bludgeon and me."

He waved his proud hand and the toddies were brewed,
The glasses were clinked and the chieftains were "Stewed"
And in slight incoherence, chivalric and free,
Died away the wild war notes of Chevalier B.

> Go finish your cocktail, go borrow a ten,
> Go mortgage your niggers and muster your men.
> It's death to the North where the workies are free
> And hurrah for the bludgeon of Chevalier B. . . .

October 2. I have become a politician. I must immediately read the Constitution of the United States, also that of the State of New York, and make notes of those instruments respectively. Attended this evening a meeting to organize "The Young Men's Eighteenth Ward Frémont Vigilance Committee." About a dozen present—wire-pullers seemingly; men familiar with canvassing, who knew the best places to get posters printed, and were on intimate terms with stump-speakers and "central organizations." Mostly "middle-class people," but fair and intelligent, able to talk clearly and pertinently. Find myself on several committees and quite likely to be a great statesman some day.

Governor Floyd[35] made a speech in front of the Exchange this afternoon. Large assemblage at first, but far from enthusiastic; reason good therefor—at least half were Frémonters or Fillmoreites. A few claquers did the cheering in a perfunctory way. Saw only one man whose applause seemed genuine, and that was a soap-lock, about a block and a half from the orator, who said, "That old feller is making a *big* speech, now I tell yer." People generally listened with sad civility, and I was glad of the example of good breeding and fair play shewn to a secessionist from Virginia, where a free-soil Cicero would be lynched. To my surprise the speech was read from manuscript. What I heard was not impressive. It was spouted with great vehemence—deliberate animation. I hung around

[35] Ex-Governor John B. Floyd of Virginia, soon to become Secretary of War in Buchanan's cabinet.

for about an hour. People were then thinning off lamentably. The *Journal of Commerce* will lie loud tomorrow about the meeting.

Mr. Ruggles has come out in the *Commercial Advertiser* criticizing Banks's statistics delivered a week ago.[36] " 'Pears like" he pulled them to pieces. He's an ugly customer in a quarrel about facts and figures. Don't like altogether the form in which he puts his argument, namely, a reply to a formal request for his opinion from William B. Astor, Theodore Dehon, and "several others." " 'Pears like" being invoked as a sort of oracle. The *Evening Post* is very funny about it, though in a good-natured way. Shouldn't wonder if it were easier to laugh at than to confute. But I wish Mr. Ruggles were not on that side in the battle. Sent my doggerel (*vide supra*) to the *Evening Post*, which published it to my surprise. . . .

October 5, SUNDAY.   Mr. Ruggles has urged Hunt[37] strongly to propose the introduction into the liturgy of a prayer for the Union, but it's objected that this is not the proper time. South Carolina might think it personal. It's a weightier objection that prayers for the sick are only put up when the patient is past cure, and this would seem an admission that Toombs and Henry A. Wise are grave symptoms. A "Collect for Civilization" would do better, for civilization is clearly retrograde south of the Potomac. H. C. Dorr suggests a historical solution for the difference of manners North and South. New England and the Middle States were colonized by the middle class, commercial and laboring people. But Virginia, the mother of Southern society, boasts of her aristocratic settlers, and we know what were the manners and morals of that part of the English aristocracy which was likely to emigrate under the Stuarts and the Protectorate; the low-class Cavaliers, the race that produced the Mohocks and Lord Mohun and Colonel Blood, the raff of which Roger Wildrake (in *Woodstock*) has some of the faults with a great many extra virtues. Virginia took instantly to breeding horses; that's a significant fact. Now the Love-lock has degenerated into the Soap-lock. The words "Gentleman" and "Southern Gentleman" signify things different in genre. The two classes exist both North and South, but the latter class gives the tone to Southern society—ready to fight duels, slow to pay debts.

Signs of coalition and bargain between Democracy and the Fill-

[36] As a former Whig and a man of conservative tendencies, deeply alarmed by Southern threats of secession, Ruggles opposed Frémont.

[37] Ex-Governor Washington Hunt had similarly refused to ally himself with the Republicans.

moreites grow stronger. Probably they wait for the Philadelphia election a fortnight hence before deciding on their arrangements. It would be a desperate move, either killing Frémont or strengthening him immensely.

Bronson Alcott, now past his middle fifties, was resident for the time being in Walpole, N.H.; his family supported chiefly by the exertions of Mrs. Alcott and their daughter Louisa in sewing, teaching, and other work. His model co-operative community of "Fruitlands" had come to a swift failure more than a decade earlier. He was not an effective lecturer of the formal kind; but he devised a series of informal "conversations" or discussions, interesting if not particularly instructive, which he offered to select audiences in the East and the Northwest. Since he could be a brilliant though vague and indefinite talker, these lecture-discussions obtained much attention. It was at one of them that Theodore Parker asked Alcott to define his terms, and Alcott retorted: "Only God defines—man can but confine." Alcott's career as an educator of the young, the abrupt ending of which had been such a deep personal tragedy, was many years in the past; his "Concord School of Philosophy" was still before him. Strong was drawn to one of Alcott's meetings.

October 9. This evening at a meeting of our Frémont Executive Committee; thence to the Rev. Brother Bellows's, the parsonage of the Red and White Unitarian establishment in Fourth Avenue (which is a "pied variety" of the St. Sophia) where I spent two hours oddly enough. Some thirty people, generally notabilities, had been assembled to meet the illustrious Alcott, the father, I suppose, of Yankee-Platonism and hyperflutination, and to talk to Great Alcott and be talked to by him; the subject of tonight's discourse being announced in a sphinx of a printed card as "Descent," which left it uncertain whether we were to be enlightened about family history and pedigree from an aesthetic standpoint, the canons of art applicable to bathos, or the formulas expressing the law of gravitation. Bellows introduced Great Alcott in his usual pleasant conversation immediately, but everybody was afraid to begin. At last the Rev. Mr. Osgood plunged heroically into the dark profound of silence, and uttered certain dark sayings, and he and Alcott and Bellows had it all to themselves for an hour or so, belaboring each other with "representative men" and "cosmic men" and "whole men" (analogous, I suppose, to "entire horses"), "pre-existent souls," "ideal archetypes," "genial receptivity," and the "Handle of the Cosmos." The first ray of light I got came from the Rev. Mr. Osgood, who lifted up his voice after a pause that was becoming formidable, and affirmed the proposition:

"A Cat is an Individual. A Cat is not a Person."

Afterwards things began to lighten up a little, and I understood enough of Alcott's talk to see in it signs of genius, some power of illustration, and the expression of a kindly and hopeful temper. If he and the school he belongs to would spend three hours daily in trying to make themselves intelligible to plain people and would sign a pledge to use no word from their polysyllabic technical vocabulary, it would be a useful discipline to them. It would cut them off from a good deal and diminish the quantity of their talk, but make the residual balance easier to understand, and would possibly convert it into commonplace. Query: If the "Handle of the Cosmos" be any relation to the "Pan-handle" of Virginia?

Last night the first "mass-meeting" (under auspices of our polyonymous Republican Ward organization) at Demilt Dispensary; a decided success. Much concourse, room crowded till near eleven, many standing, and all classes represented. I *presided* (Heaven help me) with dignity and decorum; favored the audience with a prabblement of fifteen minutes on taking the chair, which was well received, and got through without making an utter ass of myself, to my own great astonishment. Oakey Hall failed us. Clarence Seward took his place (son of Senator Seward) and for so young a man did fairly, considering his manifest careful preparation. He was followed by one Joseph J. Couch of Brooklyn, not an educated man, but enviably fluent, and solid, substantial, and clear. The illustrious Chauncey Shaffer followed. I never knew what a stump-speech was before. It was not exactly like Demosthenes or the *Areopagitica*, being made up of slang, funny stories, and an occasional modulation into a high flight of Bowery theatre declamation, indignation, and "pathos and bathos delightful to see." But it was immensely effective, kept his audience in an uproar of cheers and genuine laughter, and shewed considerable tact in dealing with the ticklish ground of the orator's defection from Know-Nothingism. I was sick and sore with laughing when he finished.

Heard two acts of *Der Freischütz* Tuesday evening with Ellie at Niblo's; poorly sung, on the whole. It was sad to hear Agatha struggling and striving in vain to do justice to that freshet of strong joyous melody, her Allegro in the second act. She sang her notes, but the contrast between her visible toil and the free, spontaneous inspiration of her music was too manifest. The orchestral business was all admirable, the glorious overture could not have been played with more accuracy or truer feeling. Bergmann is a great leader. . . .

October 12, SUNDAY. Political news. The Connecticut state election has resulted in a Republican success, but the result is a little obscure and not quite satisfactory. Florida seems to have gone Fillmore; very "important if true" as a straw that shews how the wind is blowing south of Mason and Dixon's line. . . .[38]

Niggerism has got into the [Episcopal] General Convention at Philadelphia. Murray Hoffman was here this evening, full of the theme and of wrath at his father's defeat. The ex-assistant vestry counsel has been laboring long over a "proposed canon" for the church judiciary, establishing a general system for trial of malfeasant bishops, presbyters, and deacons in all the dioceses; very elaborate and judicious, and very possibly of no practical value, like many of the Honorable Murray Hoffman's most elaborate efforts. It was brought forward and was generally acceptable and was going to pass, when some Southern delegate suddenly discovered that it contained no provision whereby a nigger was precluded from giving evidence in proceedings in a Southern diocese. Every Southern delegation bristled up at once, vigilant against any attack on the peculiar institution, and stood to its arms. It was that Proteus of Abolitionism in a new disguise. Offers to amend by providing that the evidence in each case be governed by the law of the place of trial were respectfully declined. It was "unclean," it was to be distrusted, it was bad and dangerous, it had been tainted at best, and could never be made wholesome for the South, and so the South went against it in a body and squashed it. These are the gentry who call us Sectional.

Old Verplanck has pronounced for Buchanan! Talks like a filibuster, a South Carolinian, Brooks or Captain Rynders. Marvelous, but gratifying. I never knew old G. C. Verplanck to be on the winning side anywhere.

October 15. Another meeting last night, got up by our Vigilance Committee among the "roughs" in Fifteenth Street away down by the East River. The assemblage of freemen was tolerably large, and its quality would have been improved by a little soap and water. Honorable Abram Wakeman, our candidate for Congress, was chief speaker; his speech poor stuff, without even the merit of being limited to the capacity of the audience. . . .

Writing hard tonight, save an hour in a dresscoat at Mrs. Dubois'.

[38] Not true; the Democrats carried Florida by a safe majority.

Her "sociable party" was small and slow like a young mud turtle. Dirty little Erastus Brooks there, looking quiet, stealthy, and malignant. His "dog Noble" sobriquet is much too good for him, even judging from his outer man alone. If men are to develop into animal forms, each according to the law of his individual being, Erastus will be a very ugly, cunning, and vicious rat some of these days.

October 16. Fine weather. Excitement steady and increasing about election returns. Things look far brighter today. Morning papers announced that the Northern and Western counties had changed the result in Pennsylvania to a "Fusion" majority of 10,000. By noon this was changed to 4,000 and upwards the other way, and the next fluctuation was "no decisive result," and the contest so close "that we must wait for the official count." But I've just been to the *Tribune* office, where the bulletin says 3,000 majority against the Democrats pretty reliable.

So the result in that state may be considered as decisive against Buchanan. For even if there should be a couple of thousand for him now, the great reserved Quaker vote next month will be more than enough to sweep it away.[39] But the state seems in a queer kind of condition, and how much of this "opposition" vote belongs to Frémont and how much to Fillmore no man knoweth. The Republican leaders here whisper of a great "mine" that is to be sprung before November and to blow up everything; some intrigue with Know-Nothings, probably. They are a treacherous folk—veritable "Hindoos." I put no trust in any bargain to which they're parties.

Ohio seems all right, though there seem to be strange losses on the Congressional ticket. Indiana has probably given herself over to Democracy. . . .

October 19. Alas for Frémont! Woe is me on account of the prospects of the Republican ticket! Everything is out of joint. Seward and Thurlow Weed have got hold of the cosmos by the wrong handle, as the Great Alcott would express it. We are all exchanging despondencies and condolences and confident predictions of being *nowhere* next November. Perhaps we were unduly elated a fortnight ago, when everything looked

[39] Actually the Democrats carried Pennsylvania for their state ticket by a narrow majority, varying from 1,800 votes to less than 3,000 according to the candidates. But narrow as it was, it proved decisive. It chilled the hopes of Republicans for carrying that pivotal state for Frémont, and encouraged the Democrats to expect a victory for Buchanan. The state election in Indiana also went against the Republicans, and Buchanan was now expected to sweep the state (as he did) in November.

so bright and Frémont was so sure of every Northern state, and are immeasurably disgusted by discovering that he has more to do than to walk over the course at his leisure.

Pennsylvania is lost beyond all peradventure, though it may and probably will vote against Buchanan next month. Indiana is hopeless. And the Republican party loses fearfully in the House of Representatives. The "masses" of the North are very far from Abolitionism, whatever it may suit Southern politicians to say. They distrust any party that is hostile to the niggerocracy and can be misrepresented as Abolitionist. Though the Garrisons and Gerrit Smiths are clamorous in hostility to Frémont, people are apt to look on both as tending the same way, tainted with niggerophily (or philo-nigger-anthrophy), only in different degrees; and there is no doubt that such taint is most repulsive to the instincts of the American people.

For myself, party feeling has not changed my views about the abstract right and wrong of the institution of slavery. I still firmly believe that the relation of master and slave violates no moral law. I can imagine a state of society in South Carolina itself that should make the servile condition infinitely better for the black race than any other, especially if you leave out of view the doubtful possibility of higher development for that race in the future and look merely to their present welfare and happiness.

But slavery may exist in various forms and with various features. There is its Hebrew form, with all the privileges and safeguards with which the Gentile servant was surrounded; and the mediaeval form of serfdom which gave Gurth and Wamba their home in the forests of Rotheswood. It was no part of that system to legalize the selling of Gurth to a Northumbrian baron, Mrs. Gurth to a Squire of Kent. There was classical servitude, under which the slave might be a scholar or an artist and was expressly debarred from no kind of culture or development.

Our slavery system says to some three millions of people: You and your descendants are and shall be forever deprived of every privilege, right, and attribute of humanity which can be directly or indirectly reached by our legislation or our social system. Being slaves, you are, of course, not entitled to the fruit or benefits of your own labor. But in addition to that, you and your so-called wives and husbands and your offspring shall be separated by sale, and the disintegrated fragments of your pretended families shall be scattered from Maryland to Texas whenever we or our judgment creditors can make profit thereby. You shall be shut out from all that humanity has gained in past ages and is gaining still of food for the mind and the heart; you shall be denied any aid toward culture and improvement, moral or intellectual. We will imprison any person who shall give you the key to the outer vestibule of the great treasury of knowledge by teaching you to read. However trustworthy and true you may be, whatever trials your integrity may have stood, you shall in no case be believed under oath. Crimes may go unpunished, civil rights may be lost, but you are incapable of testifying to what you have seen and know as to either. Your owner is irresponsible to society for the exercise of his rights over you, and you must submit without redress to any form or amount of cruelty and oppression and wrong his caprice may dictate. Nothing of manhood or womanhood that man can take from man shall be left you. So far as we can effect it, we decree that 3,000,000 of men and women shall be three millions of *brutes*.

It strikes me that this institution—slavery as it *exists* at the South with all its "safe-guards" and "necessary legislation"—is the greatest crime on the largest scale known in modern history; taking into account the time it has occupied, the territory it covers, the number of its subjects, and the civilization of the criminals. It is deliberate legislation intended to extinguish and annihilate the moral being of men for profit; systematic murder, not of the physical, but of the moral and intellectual being; blasphemy, not in word, but in systematic action against the Spirit of God which dwells in the souls of men to elevate, purify, and ennoble them. So I feel now; perhaps it's partly the dominant election furor that colors my notions. Of course, slaveholders are infinitely better than their system. And we have nothing to say about this system where it is established, and we have no right to interfere with it, no responsibility for it. The question for the North is whether we shall help establish it elsewhere, in the "territories" our nation owns.

October 24. Tuesday night, I vice-presidented at a ratification meeting over the nomination of Mr. Wakeman; meeting very large and spirited. Republicanism has made strong adherents in the laboring-class, rugged, dirty-faced blackguards who listened attentively to the great Wakeman's dish-water oratory, and entered fully into his subject as it seemed. To be sure, it could hardly be otherwise. This is the workingman's party, emphatically the democratic party, resisting the spurious sham Democracy that subordinates labor socially and politically to capital. . . . My belief is that Frémont will carry Pennsylvania and New York, and be elected; if not, that it will go to the House. . . .

Another Alcott *conversazione* last night, or rather an Alcottian soliloquy with occasional stimulative interjections by the audience. It was *de omnibus rebus et quibusdam aliis;* nominally on "Health" moral and spiritual, sanity in the highest sense. The great Alcott is vegetarian, and I think attributes most of the sin and evil in the world to our carnivorous habits. "We are what we eat." "We make our flesh out of the substance of sheep and pigs, therefore, we make ourselves like to sheep and pigs," was the substance of his argument on that head. Generally, it was showy, insubstantial stuff; fanciful analogies, broad generalizations from single facts and doubtful facts, perversions of metaphor into logic. A certain rather literal and unplatonic Dr. Stone would burst in occasionally with medical statistics and physiological laws in conflict with Alcott's transcendental dietetics and therapeutics, but the great Alcott brushed them aside and slipped placidly over them with his eyes fixed on the clouds. According to him, the faculty of Pekin proceed on true philosophical principles when they prescribe pounded elephant bones for debility, that being the strongest of animals. . . .

October 27. After a chilly, wet day the city is steeping and stewing in a tepid mucilage of fog, such fog as prevails in cities, definable as the gaseous form of mud and civic filthiness; Fat Fog, lit up in every direction by the glare of tar-barrels and straw-bonfires that blaze before the multitudinous lager-beer saloons and pot-houses in which we, the people, congregate tonight, as we do every night now, and call ourselves ratification meetings, and the like.

October 28. "I rise, Mr. President, for the purpose merely of stating for the information of this meeting" that I am aweary of ward-meetings, and that my soul is sick of vigilance committees. I suppose it's one's duty in this country to mix in these matters and that like the majority of my friends, I've been criminally negligent all my life in omitting to exercise my sovereign functions otherwise than by voting and in letting the machinery that is practically so much more important than any single vote take care of itself. But it's a very dreary function. A ward-meeting is no Witenagemot. Gas, bad grammar, bad manners, bad taste, bad temper, unnecessary rhetoric, and excitement, and affected enthusiasm about "our" candidate for this or that twopenny office, agonizings and wrestlings over momentous points of order, conscientious misgivings whether we can "legally" take this question till we've taken that other question, dirty little substrata of intrigue and jealousy about chairmanships and the like. It doesn't raise one's estimate of humanity.

LEWIS BARTON STRONG

JOHN RUGGLES STRONG
GEORGE TEMPLETON STRONG, JR.

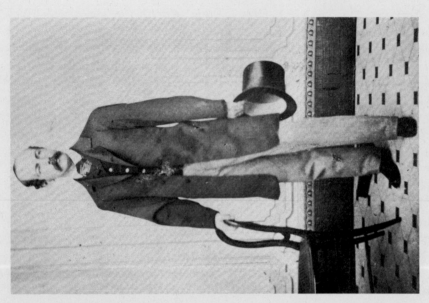

JAMES F. RUGGLES

GEORGE C. ANTHON

November 2, SUNDAY.   Walter Cutting here this evening, with Hoffman, George Anthon, and Mr. Ruggles, very full of his pamphleteering
against Mr. Speaker Banks's statistics. I fear Mr. Speaker Banks is considerably overmatched in this controversy. Last night at the last of our
"Vigilance Committee" series of mass-meetings; heard Joe Blunt deliver
a dull rambling argument on the Kansas matter, and our friend, Richard
J. Deming, like a Western prairie, a vast monotony of flowery flatness
about Webster and the shade of Clay, Scipio and the labyrinth of ages,
and the embodiment of ideas. Afterwards to Century Club, where I heard
the "memorial" strongly commended by sundry people who didn't know
its author.

I heard Benjamin, Bob Winthrop and Ned Bell pronounce a decided
opinion in favor of restoring the slave-trade—the next piece in the "Democratic" programme. Opinions develop fast in this age. Four years ago,
no Northerner would have dreamed such a thing possible.

The Frémont candle flickers up a little in the socket. People seem to
think his chance not so bad; certainly it will not be surprising if everybody
is surprised at his success. He may run far ahead of all inferences from
state politics. Many may vote for him who don't usually vote at all.

November 4, TUESDAY.   Four P. M. Voted after breakfast. Spent an hour
or two at the polls of my election district at the corner of Twenty-second
Street and Third Avenue. Went downtown to a Trust Company meeting,
and then spent two or three hours more in political service. In spite of the
foul weather, there is an immense vote; never larger in this city, I think.
People form in queues, and so far as I've seen, everything is orderly and
good natured; no crowding or confusion. Governor Fish told me he was
two hours in line before he could get his vote in. Peter Cooper and Dr.
Webster must have been still longer about it this afternoon. They were
half an hour off when I left them. There has been some fighting in the
First Ward and a couple of men killed; no other disturbance that I hear of.

Indications are not discouraging. The strength of the Frémont vote
went in early in the day. This afternoon Fillmore is gaining and Buchanan
still more. So it seems, but ordinary inferences from the appearance of
voters are not *perfectly* reliable this time. For example, a party of Irishmen came along this morning asking for Republican electoral tickets.
They were going to vote the Democratic ticket in the Fifth Ward where
they belonged, except for President, and they didn't like to ask for a
Republican ticket there. Frémont, I think, will run largely ahead of his
ticket, and I don't expect over 10,000 against him in this city. The signs

from Pennsylvania are good as far as they go, and the feeling this morning is that Frémont may well be elected. It's a momentous business; thank God, the responsibility of its decision doesn't rest wholly on me. Either way, fearful disaster may come of this election. . . .

11 P.M. Have been downtown exploring and enquiring; learned little that's new and less that's good. Nassau Street and the other streets round the great newspaper establishments (*Tribune*, *Times*, *Herald*, and *Sun*) pretty well crowded, in spite of sloppiness under foot and an occasional brisk shower. Bulletins put out from the windows as fast as returns came in and received with vociferations, the dissatisfied parties keeping silence as a general rule. The city is all one way. Buchanan gets hardly less than 20,000 majority, and the river counties will give him as much more, I suppose. So the western counties will have to come out very strong if Frémont is to get this state. Kings County reported Democratic by 6,000, which I don't believe. On the whole, I think Republicanism in a bad way. This storm (it's now blowing hard and the wind is coming round to the northwest) is inconvenient, for it will interfere with the telegraph and the community will have fits if it doesn't know about Pennsylvania and Indiana tomorrow at breakfast time.

November 5. Pennsylvania goes in for slavery extension and Buchanan by 20,000 majority. New Jersey the same way. New York Republican by an immense vote. Maryland probably gives her little all (eight votes) to Fillmore. So Buchanan is elected, unless Fillmore shall have got some Southern state besides Maryland. That would carry the election into the House, a thing rather undesirable. But I shan't be surprised to find that Indiana and Illinois are Democratic, in which case the Sage of Wheatland can afford to give the Snob of Buffalo a little small change in the shape of Louisiana and one or two second-class states in addition.

Consolatory fact that Beastly Brooks (as distinguished from Bully Brooks), the editor of that most filthy and libellous print, the *Express*, and Rat candidate for governor, has experienced a loud call to remain in private life, and that Oscar W. Sturtevant, actually Republican candidate for alderman of the Third Ward, is also allowed to continue by his own fireside. They may both abide, unless a more efficient and discriminating criminal code sends both to the State Prison. Washington Hunt was defeated at Lockport. Wood is doubtless mayor, the Democratic majority in this city being some 20,000. Whiting is nowhere; people think him a little crazy, and some of his performances seem to justify the belief.

Few observers were astonished by the results of the election. In October, as noted above, the Republicans had lost the hard-fought state of Pennsylvania, which was bound by a lucrative trade with the South and which had a conservative body of voters. By pouring large sums of money into Philadelphia, employing a small army of speakers, and making the most of the fact that Buchanan was a Pennsylvanian, the Democrats carried their state ticket by a majority of less than 3,000 in a total vote of 423,000. At the same time they won the less important vote of Indiana. In both states, many Know-Nothings and Whigs voted on the Democratic side. They feared that Frémont's election would mean civil war; they objected to placing a sectional party in control of the government. The November election added three more free states to Buchanan's column—New Jersey, Illinois, and California; while he carried the whole slave domain except Maryland, which stood alone for Fillmore. In all, Buchanan had 174 electoral votes, Frémont 114, and Fillmore 8.

Yet the Republicans, as Strong indicates, were left with solid grounds for optimism. They carried New York by a far more decisive vote than they had anticipated; Frémont's majority over Buchanan was 80,000, and John A. King's majority over Parker was 65,000. Moreover, Frémont had swept all New England and gained the day in most of the Middle West. Considering that the Republican Party had sprung up only since the Kansas-Nebraska Act of two years earlier, its showing was magnificent. "If months have wellnigh won the field," Whittier inquired, "What may not four years do?" It was clear that the Whig Party was dead, and that it would never again nominate a presidential candidate. It was clear, too, that Buchanan was a minority President; the combined popular vote of Frémont and Fillmore far out-topped that which he received.

The country could now turn its attention to other matters. One was another dreadful maritime disaster. The French iron steamer Le Lyonnais, *a new vessel, with thirty passengers and a crew of ninety-five, collided off Nantucket Shoals on the night of November 2 with the bark* Adriatic, *engaged in the coastwise trade. The Lyonnais stayed afloat for two days, while lifeboats and a raft were used to take off the passengers; but a heavy gale sprang up, the boats became separated, and several were lost. In all, only sixteen of those aboard were saved.*

Kansas continued to be a hot-bed of trouble, and sectional animosities did not abate.

November 8. Everybody, except a few Fillmoreans, is delighted with the election. The Democrats, because Buchanan is in—that's nearly beyond dispute now—and the Republicans because New York is with them actually by near 70,000, because the New England states stand unanimous on the same side, and because the Democracy has had such a bad scare that it will probably be cautious about affronting the North much farther.

November 15. A day of evil tidings for Charley [Strong]. His mother and his only sister, Mrs. Bailey, with her hypochondriacal husband, sailed for Havre on the first inst. on the French steamer *Le Lyonnais*. On the night of the second about sixty miles southeast of Nantucket, the steamer was run down by some sailing vessel unknown, and abandoned the following morning at eleven. There were six boats. Two of them are known to have been swamped soon after they were launched. A third was picked up after nine days of great danger, exposure, and suffering to its passengers. Two of them perished, and that any escaped is a marvel, for they were without sail, oars, or compass, and very scantily provisioned, and their boat had been damaged in the collision, was pronounced unseaworthy, and seems to have been resorted to only after the two others were lost. Charley has talked with the second mate and with a little Frenchwoman who went out as maid to certain Bossfords. It seems that when their boat drifted from the wreck, Mrs. Bailey was certainly in the best and largest boat, which had been reserved for the captain, first officers, and cabin passengers, and was secured to the wreck by a rope. There is every reason to suppose her husband and mother were also there. The captain with four seamen were on board the steamer, which being built with compartments, was sinking very slowly, and might float many days.

November 17. Columbia College meeting this afternoon. Torrey took his seat as trustee, a good appointment. Some little progress made toward better things. The Freshman class, entirely too large for a professor to deal with in a body, divided into sections.

November 18. Verplanck tells me that Dr. Ives tells him that Bishop Hughes is about beginning his grand *duomo* so long talked of, somewhere near Fiftieth Street on Fifth Avenue, and that its dimensions are to be most grandiose.[40] I forget the precise figures, but I think its alleged length is six hundred and eighty feet!!! "Iron is to enter largely into the structure" (as might be expected if this generation is to witness its completion on that scale), so it'll probably be a combination of Cologne

40 St. Patrick's Cathedral, designed by James Renwick_the younger, was begun in 1858 on Fifth Avenue between 50th and 51st Streets.

Cathedral and the Crystal Palace. Walter Cutting dined here, and we went to Thalberg's concert. Quite satisfactory; it's refreshing to observe the absence of affectation, pretension, and claptrap in all the man does. . . . Nothing more about *Le Lyonnais*, and it must be a couple of months at least before the fate of her passengers is absolutely decided and hope of their safety absolutely given up. Were I Charley, I should lose my reason.

November 22.   Just from Philharmonic. Miss Lucy Baxter and George Anthon went with us. Binney was to have joined us, but didn't come up to time. (He was here last evening, and has certainly improved. His admirable qualities have seemed to be impaired by a certain primness, priggishness, or indefinable something, which I think he's losing.) The concert was at the Academy of Music. Crowd unprecedented in the annals of that society. The building was packed full half an hour before Eisfeld rapped for his forces to come to order. We almost abandoned the quest of seats in despair; only the most indefatigable exertions obtained them at last. A great change from the old scene in the Apollo rooms, and not wholly for the better. Nine-tenths of this assemblage cared nothing for Beethoven's music and chattered and looked about and wished it was over. A smaller audience of appreciative people would have been far more agreeable, even to the orchestra, for it would have applauded with more sympathy and intelligence. However, it's well to bring masses of people into contact with the realities of music; it helps educate their sense of art, and Heaven knows they need it. Think of this vast congregation listening apathetically to the *Fifth Symphony*, and then exploding into a demand that Lagrange repeat her "Concert variations by Rode," a piece of inane vocalization; very difficult—"would to Heaven it were impossible," as Dr. Johnson said.

November 28.   Have been noctivagous this week. Monday night I took little Nelson Derby to Niblo's, where we saw *Pongo, or the Intelligent Ape*, and as the curtain fell on the dying tableau of that faithful and ill-treated animal at an early hour, we went to the Academy of Music and saw the last act of *Trovatore*. Nelson thought it not near as good as Pongo. Children often utter profound truths. I agreed with Master Nelson. Tuesday to Eisfeld's first "classical soirée" of this (the seventh) season. Mozart's Quartette C major, No. 6 (nice andante), Schubert's Trio B-flat, No. 1, and Beethoven's Quartette F major, Opus 18. Nothing very brilliant in any of them. . . . Last night with Ellie to Thalberg's[41] at Niblo's Saloon. First of a new series of concerts with an orchestra, and among

[41] Sigmund Thalberg (1812–1871), Swiss-German pianist and composer.

the most satisfactory performances (outside the Philharmonic Room) I've attended for a long while. Thalberg makes up his programmes very judiciously. I'm thankful to any man who gives us a chance to hear the Overture to *Oberon*, "Non piu andrai," and Beethoven's Concerto in C minor (in part), and even a good scrap from the *Barber of Seville* and the Overture to *William Tell*. Thalberg was superb, of course, but played nothing I much cared to hear save Beethoven's most lovely concerto. Thalberg is achieving a great success, and must be making lots of money out of us Gentiles (his features indicate him to be an Israelite).

December 1, MONDAY. Columbia College meeting today. Got there a little late, and found a resolution just passing, *sub silentio*, authorizing the Standing Committee *to sell* the whole premises on the north side of the new street; that is, the ground on which the college buildings now stand. I got Haight to move a reconsideration, and then the question was adjourned to a special meeting a fortnight hence. So much for the idiotic outlay in digging up the Botanic Garden property ten years too soon, a piece of financiering that will cost us at least one hundred thousand dollars in loss of interest. If the college endowment is to be frittered away by sales, and we are to be cut off from the hope of becoming a respectable institution twenty or thirty years hence, I will abdicate my seat in the board. This time I am in earnest. . . .

Then came a petition from McCulloh for a division of his chair, which was received in such a becoming way and so cordially referred to a committee with instructions to report at the next meeting, that I've no doubt the powers that be will grant his request and bring in Betts's friend, Schaeffer, to fill the new chair of chemistry and mineralogy. Schaeffer is a most diluted savant, and if he's put forward, I *will* resign and die and haunt them. . . .

December 6. Hurlbut[42] called here last night to "consult me" about certain matters connected with "the permanent organization of the Republican Party." A very transparent device, my opinion on any such subject being dear at twopence, and there being no man, woman, or child in the community who thinks it worth more. Mr. Hurlbut simply wants the entrée of this house, which he shan't have till I know more about him. He's very "thick" with sundry. of my friends and the place would be

---

[42] William Henry Hurlbert (born Hurlbut), 1827–1895, a native of Charleston, graduate of Harvard, 1847, and unordained graduate of the Harvard Divinity School, had been employed on *Putnam's Magazine* and the *Albion*, and was shortly to join the staff of the New York *Times*. He was brilliant, erratic, and unprincipled.

convenient. He has a vast social reputation just now, is considered very brilliant and fascinating, is an eminent litterateur in a small way, with political aspirings, has written some respectable little magazine articles for *Putnam* and a readable paper on American Politics in the last *Edinburgh*, and wishes to be considered intimate with the London *Times*. I suspect him of being an unprincipled adventurer, but perhaps I'm wrong.

December 11. Went to *La Traviata.* . . . *Traviata* is utter drivel. I could write as bad an opera myself. To call it bad is to do it more than justice; it has not strength enough to stand alone or to *be* anything. It is definable by the negation of every good quality.

December 18. Very great big party at William B. Astor's Monday night, and another last night at John C. Hamilton's. Both were favorable specimens of their bad class, particularly the former.

December 19. The Huntington trial (the Wall Street broker, indicted for forgery on a large scale) is still on. Evening papers set forth the opening of defendant's counsel (Bryan) who is down upon Charles Belden (the odious old fat uncle of Miss Julia and Miss Laura, brother and partner of their late papa) to a frightful extent. It is certain that Huntington was somehow tangled up with the tortuous dealings of those very wily old practitioners, in what precise way, I don't know. The defendant's counsel calls Charles Belden the most extensive and grasping usurer in the country, and charges distinctly that he was privy to all Huntington's frauds, and used him somehow in the usurious traffickings of the firm. It doesn't appear how this can be worked into any defence of the accused, and I guess Mr. Bryan has abused his professional privilege a good deal. But if he goes into proof of what he has opened, the trial will become interesting.[43]

A hideous story is current about Lorenzo B. Shepard, who died very suddenly, as people supposed, of apoplexy or epilepsy or some such thing some months ago, and was, at any rate, put into his coffin and buried in one of the "marble cemeteries." It's said the vault was opened this morning for another interment and that Shepard's corpse was found out

---

[43] Charles B. Huntington, a note-broker of about thirty-five charged with forgeries aggregating some $300,000, was being tried in General Sessions. His counsel were John A. Bryan and James T. Brady; the prosecution was being conducted by District Attorney A. Oakey Hall, who was assisted by William Curtis Noyes and Frederick A. Tallmadge. Huntington, who had lived in the most extravagant style, with a splendid mansion, rosewood furniture, ten or twelve servants, six or eight carriages, and a colossal tailor's bill, brought forward physicians who declared that he was deranged mentally.

of its coffin and half-leaning-half-lying against the door of the vault, and that he was buried alive. I trace the story to no authentic source, and am fortunate enough, as yet, to disbelieve it.

December 22, MONDAY. Huntington trial for today, William Curtis Noyes being of counsel for the people, on the retainer of the Belden concern (Tallmadge, who is to marry Miss Julia Belden, is Mrs. Noyes's brother). I find the public generally to be much delighted by the onslaught of Huntington's counsel on old Belden and his usury. . . .

At a special meeting of the Board of Columbia College this afternoon. Mr. Ruggles had to leave, *re infecta*, to attend the funeral at Noyes's. The special subject was the division of the chair of physical science— McCulloh's. The recommendation of the committee in charge of the subject was to divide that chair at once. . . .

It was determined to divide McVickar's, Hackley's, and McCulloh's professorships; a sound result, though not attained by the soundest reasoning.

December 25, THURSDAY. *Christmas*—always a day to be prized; one can't have very many of them, in the nature of things, and this one has been altogether good and genial and bright. First, special cause of gratulation and gratitude in little Babbins's convalescence, which seems established. Secondly, appropriate weather, frosty but kindly, and general good nature and good humor.

This Christmas began yesterday afternoon when I met Ellie at Trinity Church, where were some special services; the children got together, the church quite filled, a Christmas tree in the porch hung with lanterns and toys, distribution of presents, "Christmas Carol" sung, and an assemblage of clergy in the chancel, and marching with David Lyon at their head (his sextonical staff florid with a winter bouquet and streamers of ribbon) in stately procession down the middle aisle to inspect the Christmas tree; the little people, several hundred strong, coming after, very full of importance and delight, and much honored and caressed. Very right; this festival commemorates the consecration of childhood. Stopping at sundry places to complete the assortment of presents, we drove home and dined an hour late (but what's dinner to Christmas?). Then George Anthon came in; presents were coming in and going forth. Mr. John Strong returned, tired and happy, from a little juvenile party (!) at Mrs. Morgan's, where his dancing school meets, and had taken cousin Kate in to supper (!) and had a good time with Miss Emily Johnston and Mrs. Eda "Mavickar"(!) Then Mr. and Mrs. Charles E. Strong appeared, and we ate roast oysters vigorously.

December 31.   Huntington trial terminated yesterday with a verdict of *guilty* and a sentence to United States Prison. I expected the jury to disagree; but the moral insanity dodge was a little too steep. E. K. Collins says old Belden has lost $300,000 by Huntington. *Dubito.* If he has, eight per cent a minute will make it up very fast.

1857

THE CUNNINGHAM-BURDELL MURDER · POLICE TROUBLES · PANIC IN WALL STREET · COLUMBIA COLLEGE MOVES UPTOWN

---

*T*he year 1857 opened in prosperity and closed in gloom; for the terrible financial panic which began in New York and other eastern centers in August, gradually spreading through most of the country (though the South was less severely hit than the North) produced unemployment, poverty, and a discontent that found expression in angry public meetings and riots. Nevertheless, the year was fruitful in progressive enterprises in New York, some of which enlisted Strong's interest. During the early months Columbia College was preparing to remove from its original home on Park Place to a new site, the rather gaunt buildings of the Deaf and Dumb Asylum on Madison Avenue between Forty-ninth and Fiftieth Streets. The actual move was made in May. Early in the year preparations were also being made for commencing work on Central Park. Egbert L. Viele had drawn up a basic plan for its development. In 1857, Strong's future associate on the Sanitary Commission, Frederick Law Olmsted, joined with Calvert Vaux in submitting an elaborate design, and they were made architects in putting it into execution. The removal of Columbia and the development of the park showed how rapidly New York was growing northward. But as it grew, the problem of congested housing became acute. A legislative committee, appointed the previous year, was investigating the slums, and on March 9 it made a detailed report with valuable suggestions. This was the first great step toward housing reform in New York City.

But the chief sensation of the first weeks of 1857 was the famous Burdell murder. On the morning of Saturday, January 31, the dentist Dr. Harvey Burdell was found dead on the second floor of his home at 31 Bond Street,

[316]

stabbed by a knife or dirk in fifteen places, the walls, floor, and the stair rails
outside reddened with his blood. The other inmates of the house were Mrs.
Cunningham, her two daughters and two young sons, two men named Eckel
and Snodgrass, and the noted politician Daniel Ullman. Mrs. Cunningham,
widow of a distiller, had leased the house and kept it for boarders. As a coroner's
jury took up the case, public excitement mounted to a high pitch. The murder
almost crowded out of notice such events as the opening of a new season of
opera at the Academy of Music under Maurice Strakosch, with Teresa Parodi
and Mme. Cora de Wilhorst (a native of New York City) as stars.

> *Chronica de rebus gestis* G.T.S., *Legista, Anno Domini* mdccclvii.
> *Incipit feliciter.*

January 5, MONDAY.   Another year. God prosper the same and make
it more abundant in good works!

New Year's Day inaugurated 1857 pleasantly and with diligent work.
I achieved forty or fifty visits, every one more or less genial and satisfactory, between eleven-thirty A.M. and five-thirty P.M. Weather, at first
dubious and humid, with the reluctant ending of a snowstorm, gradually
resolved itself into sunshine and a cloudless sky. Dwight, Ehninger, Jem
Ruggles, Talboys, Miss Rosalie, and George Anthon dined here, and
sundry people came in upon us to spend the evening. Principal novelties,
a nice Miss Palfrey of Boston and a very rough-hewn and truculent General
Leslie Coombs[1] of Kentucky with a many-colored poncho of Mexican
wool. . . .

Mr. Ruggles came uptown with me, dined here and spent the evening,
and on our way up in the cold, damp railroad car made a significant remark
that shocked and depressed me. In substance, that he was convinced he
had disease of the heart and should not live long. All his brilliant, copious
talk this evening, mostly about himself and his past career (unusual subjects with him), had a testamentary twang, the thought that his career
was ending and the wish that he should be remembered aright were
evidently in his mind. I hope and believe his suspicions are mere hypochondriacal inferences from only little functional derangements, nervous
or dyspeptic.

January 6.   Have been honestly trying hard all the evening, and for
the tenth time, at least, to frame answers to the printed interrogatories

---

[1] Leslie Coombs (1793–1881), general, Whig leader, and close friend of Senator
John J. Crittenden. Miss Palfrey was probably Sarah Hammond Palfrey, daughter of
the historian and political leader John G. Palfrey.

as to improvements in Columbia College served on the trustees individually by the Omnibus Committee "On the Course." It's very difficult to do it satisfactorily or at all, and unless I give up the job in despair, it will cost me a month's work and probably never be read by anyone of the committee. Many of the questions are so badly drawn that they can be answered only by an essay on education. But I'll return to the work. Ellie is good for at least another hour at Moses H's, it being only half-past twelve. "A fool (that's Gouverneur Ogden) can ask more questions in a minute than a wise man (that's me) can answer in a day."

January 11, SUNDAY.   The Rev. Mr. Berrian held forth this morning, apropos of a collection for Mrs. Richmond's "House of Mercy." His sermon was rather out of the beaten road, and did him credit; handled a rather delicate subject plainly but without anything to offend propriety, real or conventional, and presented it in a more forcible way than is the Rector's wont. Startling announcement from the pulpit: "that during a ministry of more than fifty years I have not been in a house of ill-fame more than ten times!"

Seriously considered, it is not startling; one's first sensation *is* surprise at the avowal he had been there at all. But its significance lies in the fact that he has been so seldom, and in the surprise with which one hears of even one visit every five years on an average. Certainly the ideal of the clerical office and its practical working in this nineteenth century differ strangely. One would think the haunts of fallen women, friendless, desperate, and often persevering in profligacy they hate, shut out by public sentiment from all return to honest life, exactly the place for a clergyman to work. But I suppose fear of misconstruction, honest self-distrust sometimes, a thousand conventionalities and respectabilities always, keep the door closed tight. . . . But what can one do? Were I a clergyman (I don't know that my obligations would be much changed if I were) how should I begin? Should I begin at all? Now and then as one walks Broadway at night, the gaslight shines on faces so pretty, innocent, and suggestive of everything antipodal to profligacy and impurity that one is shocked at our indifference and inertness in regard to this calamity and scourge and feels as if the whole city should go into mourning over it, were there but one woman so fallen.

January 15, THURSDAY. . . . Tuesday afternoon I dined at John Astor's,[2]

---

[2] John Jacob Astor (1822–1890), son of William B. Astor, had married Charlotte Gibbes of South Carolina. His career was mainly devoted to administering the Astor estate, which came into his hands on the death of his father in 1875, and to the promotion of the Astor Library.

with D'Oremieulx, George Anthon, Cornell, Lord, Henry Day, Porter of Niagara, Edward Bell (the Great Bell of Moscow, where he was last winter), and Dick Emmet; very splendid and quite pleasant. The lady's elegance of manner was a little oppressive, but she improves on acquaintance. I had the honor to take her in and sit next her, and gradually warmed up to the conviction that she was amiable and agreeable.

January 19. Forgot to chronicle Miss Betty Rhinelander's engagement. The lucky man is William Edgar (Newbold Edgar's brother, the "Commodore" of the Yacht Club), old, forty-five at least, and not handsome, but very respectable, rich, honest, well-connected, and manly, and to his intimate friends genial and generous. A good step on both sides.

January 22. Tuesday night Eisfeld's third concert. The Quartette in F, Beethoven's Opus 19, was not intelligible to me, but admirable in the better informed judgment of others (for example, J. J. Post, who had heard it before). Eckart's trio, Opus 18—Hoffman at the piano, as extemporized substitute for the great Gottschalk, who was ill; clear, fluent, and pretty, particularly the scherzo, manifestly the germ of the old "Gaily the Troubadour" melody. Haydn's Quartette in G, No. 63, very familiar and genial. Last night a big, slow, splendid ball at Mrs. Peter Schermerhorn's in University Place.

January 24. Lieber came in this evening.[3] He wants a professorship in Columbia College, which I hope he may obtain, but I can't take a step or say a word to help him without doing harm and diminishing his chance of success. For a wonder, Gouverneur Ogden and one or two of his set beside are disposed to think favorably of Lieber. They've stumbled on a sensible thing by some lucky chance, and they must be permitted to meditate on it and develop the idea for themselves. If Charles King or Mr. Ruggles or I say a word in Lieber's favor, it will instantly drive them into opposition and hostility. After he went, I dressed and followed Ellie to Judge Daly's in Clinton Place, where was a little gathering of some thirty or forty people, very pleasant indeed. Welford and his wife, a showy Englishwoman with a magnificent physique and pounds of dark curls, not the most elegant of womankind but very splendid and very

[3] Francis Lieber, old-time friend of S. B. Ruggles, had resigned his professorship in South Carolina College and removed to New York (January, 1857). He was disappointed because he had not been elected president of the college in 1855. He was also disgusted with the course of events in the South, complaining of "the victory of Southern bullyism" in the election of 1856, and of the mad desire of Southerners to "extend slavery within the United States and into neighboring countries." His eminence in political science amply qualified him for a chair in Columbia College.

clever; Mrs. Mary Sherwood Murray, Lawrence, D'Oremieulx and his wife, Mr. and Mrs. S. B. Ruggles, Darley, Mrs. Hicks, Richard Willis, and others. Mrs. Daly is just what Miss Maria Lydig was, and appears very well as mistress of her own house.

"Garotting" and highway robbery, occurring often of late in frequented streets at an early hour of the night, have created a panic. . . .

January 29. . . . Columbia College premises sold today; net proceeds, $591,000.

February 1, SUNDAY.   An epidemic of crime this winter. "Garotting" stories abound, some true, some no doubt fictitious, devised to explain the absence of one's watch and pocketbook after a secret visit to some disreputable place, or to put a good face on some tipsy street fracas. But a tradesman was attacked the other afternoon in broad daylight at his own shop door in the Third Avenue near Thirteenth Street by a couple of men, one of whom was caught, and will probably get his deserts in the State Prison, for life—the doom of two of the fraternity already tried and sentenced. Most of my friends are investing in revolvers and carry them about at night, and if I expected to have to do a great deal of late street-walking off Broadway, I think I should make the like provision; though it's a very bad practice carrying concealed weapons. Moreover, there was an uncommonly shocking murder in Bond Street (No. 31) Friday night; one Burdell, a dentist, strangled and riddled with stabs in his own room by some person unknown who must have been concealed in the room. Motive unknown, evidently not plunder.

Berrian held forth at Trinity Chapel in a very minor key. Professor Lieber sat with us. He is very anxious for an appointment in Columbia College. Hope he may receive it, but I have fully explained to him why it would do more harm than good for me to come out in his favor. He overdoes the matter and makes himself a little of a bore; keeps cannonading me with notes, and if he take the same course with the rest, will cut his own throat.

February 4, WEDNESDAY NIGHT . . .

The chief subject of discourse, excluding all others nearly, is the Burdell murder, Mrs. Cunningham and Miss Cunningham, Eckel and Snodgrass, and the extravaganzas and indecencies of that ignorant blackguard the Coroner, Connery, who is conducting from day to day a broad farce called an inquest as afterpiece to the tragedy. When that is ended, I guess the audience will be dismissed. Probably no one will even be indicted. At present strong suspicion rests on Mrs. Cunningham and Eckel,

but no item of legal evidence is yet disclosed against them. The prevalent
theory is that Mrs. Cunningham and the doctor had certain love-passages
(she sued him for seduction and breach of promise, and the suits were
compromised); that Eckel and the lady also carried their mutual friendship to fanaticism; that they laid their heads together to get the doctor's
property; that they called on a certain Dutch Reformed Rev. Marvin,
Eckel personating the doctor, and a marriage was performed, the certificate whereof the lady holds, but which she says the doctor preferred
not to have disclosed till June; that the two thereupon murdered the man,
intending to use the cord alone and to throw the body into the street, so
that it might be taken for granted the case belonged to the prevailing
epidemic "garotting"—whereupon Mrs. Cunningham would come into a
very desirable slice of her victim's property; that their plans were deranged
by his proving a tougher subject than they expected; and that they were
obliged to use a knife and to cover the carpet and furniture with marks
that made it impossible to conceal the fact that the crime had been committed on the premises. This theory is consistent with the facts, and there
are considerable probabilities in its favor. But this investigation has been
so bungled that there is now little chance of the truth being reached and
sustained by proofs that will call for action even by the Grand Jury.

The excitement about the matter exceeds that produced by any crime
of violence committed here in my time, even the Colt and Helen Jewett
cases. Through all this miserable weather a crowd of several hundred
people of all classes is in permanent position in front of the house. Well-
dressed women occupy the doorsteps of houses on the opposite side of
Bond Street, and stare steadily at No. 31, and seem to derive relief from
protracted contemplation of its front door.

I had quite forgotten Burdell. He was frequently in the office a year
or fifteen months ago, and used to pay my father interest on a mortgage
held by the Lloyd estate, some transaction about which some shifting of
securities took place at that time.

The Senate committee has handed in a malignant report adverse to
Trinity Church, recommending no specific action, but full of misrepresen-
tation, unfair inference, and vague *ad captandum* insinuation. It is adroitly
drawn, not by any member of the committee; can it be Evarts? The investigation has been *ex parte*, Star-Chamber fashion, and no evidence has
been furnished on the part of the church nor have we yet seen the testimony. The committee has rather out-manoeuvred our committee (Dunscomb, Richard Ogden, Gouverneur Ogden, Verplanck, and Skidmore) by

leading them to believe that it was a mere formal matter and that the disposition of the investigators was altogether friendly to the church. This report, therefore, came on us as a surprise.

February 5. Thaw and slop omnipresent and omnipotent. Broadway is a "Grand Canal" of snow broth, and furnishes a splendid opportunity to naturalize the hippopotamus in this hemisphere, as the camel has been introduced into Texas. Nothing very novel today. The Coroner is still stupidly accumulating evidence utterly irrelevant and immaterial about the Burdell case.

February 9. The Burdell murder still the all-pervading subject of talk, and the Coroner still pursuing his blind and blundering investigation; but no light is shed on it by anything yet proven. The nature of Mrs. Cunningham's relations with the murdered man grows more suspicious. Her counsel has allowed himself to damage her case by evidence of privileged communications. It looks more and more as if the alleged marriage had been a fraud and had never been celebrated. This bears hard on the woman who sets it up and who consequently incurs suspicion of the crime for which such fraudulent marriage may have been the preliminary step. But then it seems as if the murder had been committed by some one person who left the house after it was perpetrated. I understand the physicians and microscopists to think that the stains found on towels and other articles in the upper story of the house could have been produced by the blood of the murdered man. The murderer's clothes must have been soaked in blood when he had finished his work. But there is no trace of them on the premises. Even the chimneys have been swept and their soot searched for traces of woolen filaments and the like that would occur there if the clothes had been burned up in one of the grates on the night of the murder. Charles E. Strong got into the house somehow yesterday and is very full of the subject. The chamber of death, by his account, is ensanguined like an old-established slaughter-house.

February 11. Very material evidence yesterday before the Coroner in the Burdell case; that of one *Farrell*, who identifies Eckel—for particulars *vide* newspapers. The man gives his testimony candidly and cautiously and seems to be a total stranger to all the parties implicated. First impressions as to its entire reliability are very decided. But looked at closely, it's a little queer, not quite consistent with other facts and very vulnerable, at any rate, to comment and criticism. . . .

Have finished my very voluminous answer to the Columbia College committee's interrogatories. Sorry for the committee if it undertakes to read and digest the document. It's a judgment on them; retributive justice for their own tedium and feebleness.

February 12. Opinions vary much as to the reliability of Farrell's evidence in the Burdell case. My confidence in it grows less. Its value depends wholly on the man's grade of intelligence and general reputation. His identification of Eckel is not conclusive in its favor. All the twenty or thirty people from among whom he selected his man knew what he was brought there for, and their glances at the one object of suspicion, even without any special sign of concern in Eckel himself, may have guided the witness.

February 14. . . . The Burdell inquest still unfinished. Its daily proceedings for the last fortnight have been and are the one subject of talk and interest. No abatement yet in the general curiosity and excitement. Crowds still watch the front door of 31 Bond Street from morning till night. People buy the newspapers for nothing but news of the murder. I don't hear a word said about the war with Persia, or the bombardment of Canton, or the proceedings of Congress, or the great disastrous freshet now subsiding; but everybody has some special view as to how *the* murder was committed, what were Eckel's relations with Mrs. Cunningham, who was the "English nobleman of the name of Thompson," what reliance should be placed on Mr. Farrell, and so forth. Today there are "new and important" developments. Some one from Alviset's cutlery shop identifies little Mr. Snodgrass as having bought a dirk there two or three days before the murder. That youth had previously denied any purchase of any like article. He stands committed. But how many thousand semi-loaferine young gents have been buying weapons of the sort since this garotte-fever broke out? As yet there is nothing like moral certainty, not to speak of legal proof. But circumstances of strong suspicion seem multiplying around the inmates of that rather questionable household and identifying them as principals or accessories; perhaps innocent and unconscious accessories, for if this dagger business amounts to anything, I guess it will prove that this poor little banjo-playing gent had been instigated to buy the weapon as a protection to himself in his nocturnal peregrinations, and that it was borrowed by someone else.

The Burdell case had grown more and more astonishing and sensational. Mrs. Cunningham and the boarder Eckel were both suspected of the murder. The coroner's inquest was sadly mishandled; but the jury finally brought in a verdict accusing these two, and declaring that Snodgrass and the daughters had possessed a guilty knowledge of the crime. Mrs. Cunningham vigorously protested her innocence. In addition, she produced a certificate of her marriage on October 28, 1856, to Dr. Burdell, and declared that she was pregnant with his child; she would be entitled to all of his property if the infant were proved his. Her claims came before the Surrogate's Court, presided over by Alexander W. Bradford, and were argued before crowds which filled the room and the street outside. Considerable evidence was offered that no such marriage had taken place; that somebody had impersonated Burdell in the ceremony, which was arranged as part of a plot to obtain his property. The surrogate decided against Mrs. Cunningham, and placed Burdell's estate in the control of the public administrator. To the gratification of most observers, the grand jury indicted Mrs. Cunningham and Eckel as murderers, and the weak-minded Snodgrass as an accessory before the fact. But evidence was lacking for a conviction, and on the trial all three were set free. The mystery of the murder has never been finally solved.

February 15, SUNDAY. Lieber sat with us at Trinity Chapel, and expressed great satisfaction at Hobart's sermon, so I introduced them after service. It won't hurt him with the Board of Columbia College to be known as a parishioner of Trinity.

Mr. Ruggles is rapturous about my Columbia College paper. He has vast power of admiring. It is free from gas, and it states a few prominent truths or truisms that have been heretofore overlooked or practically neglected, to our great damage, with tolerable plainness. Those are its only merits.

February 19. The Rev. Mr. Haight and Richard Grant White (retained by Trinity Church Committee) dined here. I wanted to get them together that White might be better posted up on matters of detail, and we had quite a satisfactory session. I have been studying the case since they left and have worked myself into a conviction that the church is absolutely impregnable. Sorely tempted to write a pamphlet; Ogilby and Vinton have done so, with tolerable effect, but they don't quite meet the case. Have seen proof sheets of another by General Dix, more to the purpose, and a fourth by Bishop Potter is coming.

Matters seem going on decently well at Albany, where we're putting in evidence before the Senate committee. I don't fear legislative action much, still less any practical harm from such action, while the Dartmouth

College case stands unreversed. But the pressure of public opinion is strong. Trinity Church is odious and stinks in the nostrils of all who have read Mark Spencer's malignant report. Even Coroner Connery is not more generally reviled. Of course, Spencer didn't write it, and it's a great question who did; some say Bradish and others Ketchum, but it's too clever, *ad captandum*, for either.

The wealth of Trinity Church Corporation had attracted widespread atten-tion and raised a question whether it was being properly administered. Having acquired a number of farms in the early days and held them while the city grew up around them, the Church had become one of the great landlords of New York. Its general policy was to refuse to sell but to offer leases for long periods. While the communicants were the real owners of the property, actually very few of them knew anything whatever about its management. Early in 1856 the church, in response to a legislative resolution, had submitted a report upon its corporate affairs. In doing so it had denied the right of the legislature to use any such document, stating that it was submitted as a mark of respect for the state government. The report showed that the value of the landed estate of Trinity Church, exclusive of accrued rents, was $1,446,371; that the church also held bonds, mortgages, and cash amounting to about $220,000; and that the entire productive estate came to some $1,665,000, minus a debt of almost $650,000. Trinity could thus be called a million-dollar church, and the value of its lands was rapidly increasing. On the other hand, the report showed that nearly all of the annual revenue of some $96,000 was being applied to the regular and necessary expenditures of the church. It also showed that the church, from its very inception, had followed a policy of great generosity. It had appropriated "for the spread of religion in all parts of the state, for the support of ministers of the gospel and the succor of their families, and for the aid and endowment of institutions of learning," a total of very nearly $1,300,000, together with so much valuable land that the property of the corporation had been diminished to one-third its regular extent.

But the clamor against Trinity continued. The demand for some form of regulation grew louder. On March 13, 1857, the Senate committee on the affairs of Trinity submitted a unanimous report and with it a bill. This pro-vided that the church must make an annual report upon its activities and its condition; while it offered certain amendments to the law of 1814, which had been designed to restore the ancient charter rights and privileges of Trinity which were abrogated or impaired during or just after the Revolution—particularly by the bad law of 1784. Altogether, the proposed bill struck a heavy blow to the church. Episcopalians, with other friends of Trinity, at once rallied to the defense. On March 25th a great many remonstrances from all parts of the state, numerously signed, were presented to the state Senate. They protested vehemently against the weakening or destruction of the favorable law of 1814; they denied that the state had any right to call for an annual report from the corporation. Bishop Potter took a determined stand and so did numerous laymen. No one threw himself more vigorously into the fight against the restrictive bill than Strong, and no one was more influential or effective than his father-in-law, S. B. Ruggles. One of the leading proponents of the legislation was Luther Bradish, Whig politician and former Speaker, who had been defeated for the governorship in 1842. But when the Episcopalians exerted themselves so defiantly and energetically, and when it became evident that the new Republican governor, John A. King, would not sign the bill, Bradish and others gave way. Before they did so, however, the vestrymen of Trinity had suffered a severe fright.

March 8, SUNDAY. Trinity Church (over the affairs of which I have been vainly drudging day and night, accomplishing nothing satisfactory till I am inexpressibly weary of the whole subject, and the mere thought of the controversy threatens to produce nausea) is in *statu quo*. Evidence before the Senate committee closed triumphantly, it is said, but not yet published and no final report made. Current of opinion strong against us still, but there are signs of reaction. It's a very anxious and delicate business.

In Columbia College there are signs of a breeze. McCulloh sends a communication to the trustees that he cannot teach certain branches of physics to the Juniors, because they are generally without the necessary acquaintance with mathematics. This compels us to do something about poor Hackley. I suppose he is, in fact, grossly unfit for his place, and it is a breach of trust to retain him there, but it's a disagreeable job to degrade or discharge him. Ned Renwick[4] called on me yesterday with his father, the emeritus professor, to secure me in his favor as a candidate for the pro-

[4] Edward Sabine Renwick (1823–1912), engineer and inventor, had been graduated from Columbia in 1839. After spending some years as superintendent of an iron works at Wilkes-Barre and patent expert in Washington, he had now opened an office in New York as consulting engineer and patent adviser. He had himself patented various devices of some importance.

fessorship of chemistry. He doesn't strike me as the right man; seems a slack-baked, green-gosling kind of raw youth, little changed from what he was in college. There is some quiet underhand kind of movement, by the by, on the part of Anderson, G. F. Allen, and others, to bring up Gibbs's name again. Not likely to succeed, and were he elected otherwise than unanimously, I've no idea he'd take the place, if he would do so under any circumstances. . . .

Bishop Potter's entirely spontaneous pastoral letter has done Trinity Church some service. It came out on the day selected for a meeting called to ratify and approve the Senate report, and upset the programme completely. The meeting did little but scold the Bishop. Taylor and Tyng[5] were most licentious in their speech. They called the letter "a lie and a libel," "extorted from the Bishop while under the influence of chloroform." He had "out-Hobarted Hobart and out-Onderdonked Onderdonk." Tyng wanted "to take the slanderer by the throat," and so on. I had a verbatim report that I wanted to publish, but on reflection it seemed too dirty a business. . . .

Great fuss lately about the great Hurlbut. Charges against him of various misdemeanors and particularly of habitually borrowing other people's raiment without permission. George William Curtis in the mess, also Messenger and one Carter, a former partner of H. E. Davies, all three in a semi-accusing capacity. Queer kind of "court of inquiry," mainly consisting of Charles Kuhn and David Murray, who held the charges against Hurlbut not proven and gave him a certificate of good character. Carter, chief accuser, threatens to "publish the correspondence." A very funny transaction.

March 11. Columbia College meeting Monday produced little result. The inquest on Hackley gave its verdict verbally, through Anderson, and not very clearly. McCulloh's averment seemed to be conceded substantially true, namely, that the Junior class knew so little mathematics that any proposition relating to or involving conditions of "time, space, quantity, or proportion would be considered by them equally mysterious, incomprehensible, and disgusting." It further appeared that that gentleman had called on the Juniors, after notice that he would test them in mathematics, to inform him "how much was the interest of $1,000 at seven per cent for sixty days"; "what was $\frac{3}{4}$ of $\frac{5}{8}$"; how they knew that "the square of the

[5] Stephen Higginson Tyng (1800–1885), Harvard 1817, was rector of St. George's Church in New York; Thomas House Taylor (South Carolina 1818) was rector of Grace Church; both were prominent in the Low Church party.

hypotenuse was equal to the sum"; and so on; and that none of them could tell him. It also appeared that Hackley had reported his classes to the Committee of Inquiry as in a very satisfactory state. On these facts, our action was not to kick Hackley out or call on him to shew cause why he be not kicked out, but to resolve on dividing his professorship, with the understanding that he occupy one of the two chairs. Bad. But there is certainly increase of life and vigor in the board. Van Wagenen, Bradford, Jones, and others are waking up.

March 13. Anderson took me yesterday to see the designs for the Roman Catholic Cathedral on Fifth Avenue. Very ambitious; scale very grand indeed—likely to be effective. Cheap ornamentation in iron; the mullions, mouldings, pillars, open work spires all iron. . . . Will surely rack itself to pieces by expansion and contraction of its incongruous materials within five years after it's finished.

March 17. At Columbia College a spirited meeting. Got the division of McVickar's chair made threefold instead of twofold, which gives an opening that Lieber will exactly fit.[6] All the elements seem harmoniously in his favor for the chair of history. That will be a great step forward. . . .

Sunday night, G. C. Verplanck and Richard Ogden with me in the library, drawing corporate remonstrances for Trinity Church vestry. Fifteen or twenty people here beside, among them Hall the state geologist, and McCulloh. Vestry meeting last night adopted the remonstrances. It's pretty well, but wants logical order and natural sequence of paragraphs.

The bill reported in Senate does much more than repeal the law of 1814. It affirms the construction claimed for that of 1784, and enacts that all Episcopalians shall vote. Grim fight coming; result doubtful. Mr. Ruggles retained and disposed to go into the battle heartily. Has just left here. A very valuable acquisition.

March 18. Tired to death nearly; fagged out with worry and with thinking on one subject. Most of the day with Mr. Ruggles, posting him up. He goes to Albany tomorrow and don't think badly of the case. I'm inclined to despond today, for the first time, as to the prospects in the legislature, though I believe we can rely on the Governor. Thurlow Weed is operating strongly against us. Remonstrances come in strongly; people generally glad to sign. We want an efficient central organization. I've

---

[6] The effort of Ruggles, Strong, and a few other progressive trustees to awaken Columbia College from its long slumber was at last gaining some successes. The Ruggles-Strong pamphlet or manifesto on "The Duty of Columbia College to the Community" had failed to bring about the election of Wolcott Gibbs to a chair, but it succeeded in convincing many readers that Columbia must turn a new page.

brought Haight in to superintend things at the Vestry office, for Dunscomb's indecision and sluggishness would ruin us.

March 20.   Trinity Church still the one engrossing subject, for the sake of which I'm neglecting everything else and fretting myself into a fever. . . . Things look about the same; that is, pretty black. Brooks still on the fence. Governor King said to be doubtful whether it's a case for exercise of veto power.

March 23.   Much to write were there time, but there isn't. Last night with Dr. Hawks and Mr. Ruggles in the library, making history perhaps, for Hawks was induced to sketch a bill and a recommendatory letter to the Honorable Erastus Brooks that may be most material in the progress of the Trinity Church campaign. More reasonable and proper, far, than Mark Spencer's scheme of agrarianism, but yet more flagrantly branded with unconstitutionality on its face. It is meant to distract the enemy, and I guess it'll do its office.

Today very busy. Columbia College meeting. Library and chapel dismantled. Met in the latter. Long, dreary debate about salaries, dubious question left undecided. Then a communication from Bull Anthon about the new site for the grammar school. Made a speech, and to my own amazement got the matter referred to a special committee: Haight, Anderson, and myself. Tonight had a brief visit from George Anthon. Drew a remonstrance from *Episc. Inhabi.* praying that the principle of the proposed bill may be extended to include St. Mark's, St. George's, and Grace. Don't see why it isn't logical and sound. Went to Mr. Ruggles's; Bishop Potter, Dr. Haight, Fearing, Mrs. Murray, Lieber, and others. A very busy and pleasant evening. Long indoctrination by Professor Davies, who wants the mathematical professorship in Columbia College, with his son-in-law Peck as adjunct. Very plausible, and somewhat dubious. Home and to work again hard at newspaper squibb No. 2. N.B. Mr. Ruggles's intervention at Albany has changed the aspect of things already (he came down Saturday night), but it's still a doubtful case.

April 7.   Journal sorely neglected of late, but I have been working night after night well into the small hours. The Senate passed Brooks's second substitute (not the Hawks plan) 19 to 12, at two this morning. Very bad. I hoped we should escape a vote against us by indefinite postponement, but Thurlow Weed is omnipotent. I can't see how we can prevent his forcing the bill straight through the legislature. However, Mr. Ruggles in his letter of yesterday predicted it could not get through the legislature.

April 10, GOOD FRIDAY.   I'm used up tonight, body and mind. A very depressed and penitential day, though I've seen the inside of no church. I was telegraphed for Wednesday, and started for Albany at once without a chance to bid poor Ellie goodbye. Left at 3:30, reached Albany and the Delavan House at about 9:30, and joined Mr. Ruggles, Gouverneur Ogden, Livingston, and Judge Parker at Congress Hall by a little after ten. Mr. Ruggles had been making that afternoon a pretty strong argument before the committee of the House (on charitable and religious societies). The general aspect of things very blue indeed; Thurlow Weed and a popular clamor are tremendous agencies to battle within the legislature of 1857. Next day in the lobby, and within the bar of the House on the Speaker's ticket. I saw the Governor, who talks firm, and whose veto I shall have to draw unless he fall away from his present conservative convictions; Daniel D. Barnard, a very dignified "party"; Senator Briggs and Senator Sickles (!!??).[7] Proposition made to De Zeng by one of our incorruptible legislators, and great debate as to whether it would do to make a row about it. Probably it won't, just now, especially as De Zeng is reluctant and timid. Another meeting of House committee in the afternoon, Judge Parker appearing for us and Porter for Belial. Left feeling sick, was miserable all the evening and never spent a more wretched night; a fevered, uncertain doze, with the Act of 1814, corporators, parishes, and so on flitting through it ghostly and vague and driving me nearly wild. Came off at eleven this morning. . . .

The bill *will go through the Assembly* like a dose of salts. That's a fixed fact. There will be two reports from its committee, for and against—which will be which was unsettled when I left; $1,000 in bribery would have secured us the majority report, and nine votes in the House. The prospects are very black indeed. But we could not possibly go before the courts on a better case than this bill gives us.

April 13. Mr. Ruggles, who left Albany last night, came here before I came downstairs this morning and sent Johnny up to say that "the church is safe." The trouble isn't quite over yet, but the chance of anything being done in the Assembly is diminishing. The Governor's veto is drawn, and he will interpose it or pocket the bill, as he shall think best. The legislature won't sit beyond Thursday. The House committee is divided, two and two, one of them (De Zeng's friend, I believe) having awakened to a sense of his

---

[7] Daniel D. Barnard (1796–1861), former Whig Congressman and one-time minister to Prussia, now practicing law in Albany—a great conservative; Daniel Sickles (1825–1914), one-time corporation counsel in New York, recently secretary of legation with Buchanan in London, now state Senator, and soon to be Congressman —a man of notoriously bad habits and associations.

situation and run away home. Very natural he should feel uneasy after putting himself into De Zeng's power so completely by so gross and ill-managed an offer. Perhaps it may die in the committee. If there be a report, however, I'm satisfied the bill will pass by party drill, the five minutes rule, the previous question, Thurlow Weed, and free corruption. . . .

Columbia College this afternoon. Came in late, supposing nothing would be done but read the weary testimonials of candidates for the chair of chemistry, the special object of this meeting; but found there was a breeze and a lively one. Fish had had the courage to do what many of the Board have talked about doing—bring forward resolutions looking to the removal of Hackley and McVickar for incompetency.[8] The matter lies over to next Monday. We shall have a very emphatic discussion about it, and unless Anderson's infernal ingenuity invent some formula of words that beats all his former achievements in the way of subtlety, I guess the proposition will be carried.

April 18, SATURDAY.   Heaven be praised for all its mercies. The legislature of the state of New York has adjourned. That gang disbanded itself at 10:30 this morning, and every honest man in the state breathed more freely when he heard the news. The Committee of the Assembly returned the bill, reporting that they could not agree upon it. Three several attempts were made to call it up out of its order and severally failed, each more signally than the preceding. Governor Seward has been secretly active for the last fortnight in our favor, and probably with important results. So it's a victory, but I've experienced no gleam of exultation. That conservative and intelligent men have consented to make this effort against us is a disaster. Success is better than defeat, but the whole subject is disheartening.

Mr. Senator Noxon made a most atrocious charge against the Vestry of Trinity Church in debate, vaguely and indefinitely, but distinctly enough to be calumnious—that as "he surmised" they or some of their connections made profit out of their trust property. Minturn's attention was called to this at Albany, and he was profuse in his declarations of surprise and regret that such a charge could have been insinuated. Now this speech of Noxon's,

[8] The Rev. Charles W. Hackley, professor of mathematics and astronomy, had been graduated from West Point in 1829; had taught at West Point and in New York University; and had written several textbooks. John McVickar had now been professor at Columbia almost forty years, having been invited in 1817 to a chair where he taught moral philosophy, rhetoric, belles lettres, the history of philosophy, and ancient history. In connection with moral philosophy he had expounded political economy, being one of the first to teach the subject in America. Primarily, as we have seen, he was a churchman.

retaining that paragraph, is printed at length in expensive form, and circulated, of course, by Minturn's committee. This decides my future personal relations with him, Bradish, John D. Wolfe, Dr. Webster of the Free Academy, Stewart Brown, and others, some of whom I know well and like, but with whom I shall have no further intercourse. Old Mark Spencer I've already enjoyed the luxury of cutting.

April 20. Columbia College at two P.M. Fish brought up his resolutions, as modified. As to Hackley, they merely revoke our action of a month or two since whereby he was assigned to one of the two chairs into which the present department of mathematics is divided, that of astronomy. This was discussed at great length, Anderson twining subtle webs of ingenious plausibilities against it, and was carried, Anderson alone dissenting. As to McVickar, the resolutions proposed to make him emeritus professor and would have been carried without a dissenting voice had not King interposed and asked delay that McVickar might have the option of resigning if he preferred not to have a censure recorded against him. It seems that Hackley and McVickar are unconscious each of his own peril, but each is satisfied that the other is very inefficient and ought to be removed.[9] We met in the chapel, half-dismantled, its doors off the hinges, utterly cold and dreary; our last meeting in the poor old college building. One of the landmarks of the New York of old times is falling and perishing.

April 25, SATURDAY. . . . Interesting Columbia College meeting at the Synod rooms of the Reformed Dutch Church, corner of Fourth Street and Lafayette Place, last Wednesday, lasting from two to past six P.M. Discussion on McVickar's case resulted in the "informal understanding" that certain of his friends would call on him with a view to some communication from him; a resignation, or a proposal that his present duties be changed. Then a motion for reconsideration in poor Hackley's case was carried; and a long and earnest discussion on Fish's resolution, Fish, Allen, and S. B. Ruggles severally vigorous in its support—ditto Spring. Anderson was jesuitical and Bradford rhetorical against it. Laid on the table at last by nine to eight. But the end is not yet.

April 28. Tuesday night, say rather Wednesday morning. Very busy day in Wall Street. Left a great mass of manuscript matter, finished last night, with Haight for examination. Meeting of legislation committee of Trinity Church vestry from three to five. . . .

[9] McVickar was actually dealt with more kindly than some of his critics had desired. His chair was split into three parts. He was kept on to teach the evidences of religion; Lieber was given the professorship of history and political science.

We had a long and interesting meeting of the Columbia College Board Monday afternoon; did not adjourn till near six P.M. McVickar sent in a communication asking for leave to withdraw from active duty in connection with the college and was shelved with a professorship of "the Evidences of Religion" and a salary of $2,000. Some further discussion on poor Hackley's case resulting in nothing, and then we went into committee of the whole and worked at details of a statute on the course.

April 30. Tonight is the first Thursday night that Mrs. Strong is "at home," with what results of comfort or of boredom time will tell. . . .

Half-past one next morning. The "reception" went off pleasantly; thirty or forty people—Judge Daly and wife, Albert Gallatin and wife, George Bancroft (who talked Trinitarianism to me with great pertinacity and expatiated on the significance and logical force of the Athanasian Creed), Miss Mary Ulshoeffer in full-blown splendor, the Anthons, Miss Jane Emmet, John Coster, Newbold Edgar, *cum aliis.*

May 5. . . . Eisfeld's last concert tonight with Ellie. . . .

Mrs. Cunningham's trial has commenced before Judge Davies. City Hall is crowded, of course, but the proceedings interest people comparatively little. Nobody supposes that Mrs. Cunningham can possibly be convicted. Very many hold her entirely innocent. . . .

May 6. Mr. Ruggles spent the evening in the library, talking over Trinity Church and Columbia College and sundry other matters. Present indications point to Schaeffer as professor of chemistry and Davies for mathematics; the latter probably not a very bad appointment, though there is certainly somewhat of sliminess and claminess about the man.

The Burdell trial seems to bring out no stronger evidence than was disclosed on the inquest. If the prosecution can prove nothing further, its case is one of strong suspicion and nothing more, and should never have been brought to trial.

May 10, SUNDAY. Friday night at opera with Murray Hoffman and Ellie, of course; *Lucrezia Borgia,* well sung. Perhaps from association, this is always pleasant to hear. A scene from *Columella* by Fioraventi, of whom I know nothing, but whom I suppose to be pretty profoundly debased, morally and artistically. This was a grotesque scene in a madhouse, a dance and chorus of lunatics; the music of an order more suitable had it been an asylum for idiots. Also an act of *Masaniello,* which was refreshing. . . .

Mrs. Burdell, alias Cunningham, was acquitted last night, and Eckel let off on his own recognizance. No other verdict was possible on the evidence, and I strongly doubt whether the woman had, in fact, any hand in the crime. . . .

The demolition of Columbia College has begun.[10] I inspected yesterday afternoon the progress already made by the invading forces. Hibernia is rampant and destructive in its very penetralia. *"Sic transit"*—*"Eheu fugaces,"* as McVickar used to observe with considerable research and singular power of illustration.

May 11. Nothing special in Wall Street. Columbia College meeting from two to six. Busied mostly with details of statute on the course; their settlement generally satisfactory. Some debate about the propriety of making French and German compulsory ended in postponing the question, which it's not easy to answer. As to one point, the division of McVickar's departments, we retraced our steps and merged "literature" and "philosophy" into one chair. . . .

I've the honor to be appointed a trustee or director or something of "Trinity School," at present a very debilitated institution, but seized of some thirty acres of land at or near Hell Gate, now productive only of taxes and assessments, but destined to constitute a most beneficent and glorious endowment for future generations if wisely managed.[11] I know little of the institution, its history or present condition, except that at some time it has been in a very paralytic state under the rectorship of the Reverend Mr. Morris. That gentleman has unhappily got involved in certain conjugal squabbles which have been brought before the civil courts in the shape of bills for divorce and have led, or are likely to lead, to his resignation or removal. With an efficient man in his place, a transfer of the school to a new locality farther uptown and more activity in the administration of its affairs, it may become a very great institution. Its income is already large. Trinity Church and the college take up all my spare time, but I can't refuse to go into this, especially since I've resigned off St. Luke's Hospital. I did so because I didn't want to meet Minturn, Webster and Cambreleng and wouldn't act with so questionable a person as Mark Spencer.

May 12. Attended the "inauguration" of the new Columbia College

[10] That is, the old building on Park Place.

[11] Founded 1709 by the Society for the Propagation of the Gospel. It long gave nearly all the free instruction for boys in the city.

this morning.[12] Six or eight of the trustees were present. Prayers by our chaplain, Duffie, and "Old Hundred" sung by the boys with much energy. The introduction of the little organ and of singing seems likely to work well. The president made a very brief address, and old Knox another— nasal trivialities. They're a nice-looking lot of boys we've got together there. Looked through the building and sat a little while in Anthon's lecture room, a session that brought vividly back the memory of many terrible hours twenty years ago. The lecture rooms are generally spacious and comfortable, a vast improvement on the old ones. The building has been very thoroughly overhauled, and is rapidly being got into decent order— "swept and garnished"; the old deaf and dumb spirit that possessed it so long being cast out. It remains to be seen whether seven other worse spirits, deafer and dumber, have not taken its place. All depends on the appointments we're on the eve of making. . . .

Met Professor Davies eating oysters at George W. Brown's; he tackled me, of course. Most eager he is for the mathematical chair, and I believe from fervent desire to promote science, for he will gain nothing in money or position by taking it. He's a very slimy kind of Uriah Heepish personage in manner, but that justice must be done him. He introduced me to another son-in-law, one Scudder, who has something to do with Trinity College, Hartford, and who spoke of Eliot in the most exalted way. I got Eliot's *History of Liberty* as I came uptown and have dipped into it. It seems very sound, thoughtful, and scholarlike.

A big reception tonight at Robert L. Cutting's on Fifth Avenue. I went with Ellie and Mrs. Ruggles. Very crowded; very musical—too much music, in fact, and out of place.

May 15.   Underwent yesterday one of the severest forms of classical tragedy, a grand state dinner at William B. Astor's[13] in honor of Mr. Secretary Marcy. Grand gold plate, costly wine, and sumptuous fare, on which we (Daniel Fearing, Charles H. Russell, Tom Ludlow, George Bancroft, and fifteen or twenty other "great oneyers," to be with whom was creditable) gorged ourselves comatose. Sat between John Astor and

[12] The move to the deaf and dumb asylum at Forty-ninth Street and Madison Avenue had been rather abrupt. It was proposed at first to use the rambling old structure only until suitable quarters could be erected on the Botanic Garden site, now Rockefeller Center. The building, however, was completely refitted, as Strong indicates.

[13] William Backhouse Astor (1792–1875), son and heir of the first John Jacob Astor.

Cogswell[14] of the library, and guess I had as good a time as anybody, for Cogswell is very conversible and instructive. But these solemn feasts are sore afflictions. Marcy, though he looks ponderous and stolid, has some fun in him. I came off at 9:30 and found reception No. 3 in full progress, despite the foul weather, and much pleasanter than the stately dinner table I left. (N.B. Not one word of disrespect meant to Mr. William B. Astor, who is always very kind and polite to me, and who is very liberal, unosten- tatious, and intelligent, were he tenfold a millionaire.) About fifty people were here; the evening went off pleasantly, and folks didn't seem to be bored. Ellie works hard to entertain her guests and does it with tact, ease, and great success. Mr. Ruggles is an invaluable ally, and George Anthon and Jack Ehninger both take great pains to help. There were Lewis Jones and his pretty little wife; the established binary system of Miss Berryman, looking her most gorgeous, and Jem Strong; Mr. and Mrs. Wickham Hoffman; Moses Taylor with his good-looking wife and pretty Miss Taylor; George Betts, Professor Davies, the Rev. Mr. Bellows, Lieber, Messengers, Brock Cutting, who seems a very attractive young fellow, Henry Brevoort . . . and others.

May 17, SUNDAY. Bradish sent for Mr. Ruggles yesterday afternoon to say how much he regretted to find that he was considered mainly instru- mental in getting up the late attack on Trinity Church. He deplored and disapproved it, and was disgusted; his motion was a remedy through the courts; the members of the vestry were his most valued friends, and so on. This looks a little uncandid. His name has been conspicuous from first to last. Probably he was willing to let it be conspicuous while it seemed to be on the winning side, and now that reaction has set in pretty strongly, remembers all at once that he didn't do a great deal of the work after all.

May 18. Columbia College meeting this afternoon at Lafayette Place (Dutch meetin' house; the "consistory room" in the cellar); twenty-one present. Election of professors the special order. Question of salaries brought up as a preliminary. Fight of an hour on a proposition to refer to a committee, or "await the action" of some existing committee; Anderson, Gouverneur Ogden, and Betts being strenuous in devising ways "how not to do it." Anderson's skilful sophistry was all put forth to induce delay. That man's motives and mental processes are a great mystery. I believe him perfectly sincere and absolutely blinded by his own intellectual dis- ingenuousness, but the board is beginning to see it, and he is fast losing

[14] Joseph Green Cogswell (1786–1871), since 1848 superintendent of the Astor Library, and chief builder of that invaluable institution.

his influence. He is distrusted and his web of plausibilities has lost its power of entangling and retarding. Bradford made a very straightforward, vigorous, and effective little speech in favor of action, and the effort to postpone failed by a decided vote.

Then the salaries were fixed at $4,000 ($1,000 being an allowance for house rent), and we went into ballot, first for professor of chemistry. It was thought best not to bring up Gibbs's name. I took it for granted Schaeffer would go in, and was agreeably surprised by the result: Joy of Schenectady[15] 11, Schaeffer 10. Then for history: Lieber 20, O. Harriman, Jr., 1. Then in mathematics: Davies[16] 14, Hedrick 1, Kemp 1, Docharty 2, blank 1, Green 1. Zabriskie didn't vote, being huffed because the ballot for that chair wasn't postponed for his accommodation, on his statement that he wasn't sure who ought to be elected. Zabriskie is a terrible donkey. The result is infinitely beyond my hopes.

After some discussion about postponing the election to the chair of literature and philosophy, it was postponed to next Monday; another step gained, for we are not prepared to go into that subject. Tappan and Eliot[17] seem the strong names, and the former is strong in the one department, the latter in the other. I gave notice of a motion to divide and retrace our steps, so as to have two professorships, which I guess we can carry. Should we be able to get both those men, we shall have a faculty to be proud of—though I confess to some misgivings about Tappan.

I sacrificed my dinner and went straight down to Cozzens's house, at the corner of Canal Street and Broadway, to gladden Lieber's heart with the news.

May 24, SUNDAY.   At and after tea we had George Anthon, Hoffman, Dorr, Professor Anderson, Mr. Ruggles, Lieber, and Wolcott Gibbs. Some two hours were comfortably spent round a very modest supper table. The reception Thursday night was quite "brilliant." Near one hundred present; Ellie's rooms almost full—some who had been here came again. Mrs. Little came, and Jacob, and Mrs. Dubois, Mrs. Robert

[15] Charles A. Joy, after studying in Germany, made a reputation as professor of chemistry at Union College. He had degrees from Union, Harvard, and Göttingen.

[16] Charles Davies, a graduate of West Point who had written good mathematical textbooks, but not a man of any real eminence, thus became professor of mathematics.

[17] Henry P. Tappan (1805–1881), since 1852 the president of the University of Michigan, which he was making in some respects the best of American universities. A graduate of Union College, he had published several philosophical books. Eliot was Samuel Eliot (1821–1898), at this time professor of history at Trinity College in Hartford; the author of several volumes on the history of liberty in ancient times and of translations from the Spanish poet José Zorilla.

Cutting, Mrs. William H. Jones and Mrs. De Trobriand, Miss Emmet and the Ulshoeffers, William Schermerhorn, Mrs. Bradish, H. H. Ward, the two pretty Lowndes girls, Mrs. Heckscher, Lieber . . . and so on.

Last evening Professor (or Chancellor) Tappan dined here with G. F. Allen and Mr. Ruggles, and we sat till near eleven in high discourse. Allen is a very agreeable person, and Tappan improves on acquaintance, though a little oracular. I'm uncommitted for or against him. His reputation here and abroad is high, and his great ambition is to be concerned in the foundation and organization of a university. That he's a clergyman, and a Presbyterian clergyman withal, is not in his favor, but he is a mild case of clericality. All our clerical colleagues have pronounced against him. Knox and Spring and Hutton, as loyal disciples of John Calvin and Jonathan Edwards, for Tappan has written with ability against Edwards on the will. Haight and the Bishop object to him as "New School," and, therefore, under strong suspicion of latitudinarian notions or tendencies. These considerations may be legitimate in regard to candidates for a chair of moral or intellectual philosophy. I should dislike to go against Bishop Potter's wishes in this matter, even if I disagreed with him, for on any question about the ethical teaching of the college his views are entitled to great respect. I suppose no definite plan can be adopted until we see who is brought forward on the other side. . . .

May 30. Luther Bradish came to see me yesterday to repeat in substance what he had said to Mr. Ruggles; that his share in the movement against Trinity Church had been only nominal, that he deeply deplored the form the controversy had taken, that he would have nothing to do with any renewal of the attack and did not believe it would be renewed, and so forth. He was very urbane, complimentary, mellifluous, and polysyllabic. I mentioned it to William Kent, whose comment was: "The time-serving old scamp was chairman of all their meetings. He'd have joined Catiline's conspiracy if they'd offered to make him chairman. Every man has his price, and that is Luther Bradish's." Of course, I treated Lothario with the utmost consideration and reciprocated his urbanity to the utmost of my power, only giving him to understand by the most delicate circumlocutions that the republication of the dirty insinuations in Noxon's speech was a thing for which somebody was responsible and that *prima facie* that burthen rested on his committee. . . .

Academy of Design unusually abundant in good pictures. Have spent but half an hour there, and that was enough to satisfy me it was worth ten of last year's exhibition. Magnificent, sultry-tropical landscape by Church, in the neighborhood of which I think a sensitive thermometer would rise rapidly. Ehninger and Mignot's partnership picture looks well, though ill hung.

June 1.   To Fiftieth Street for a Columbia College meeting on the premises. Our sub-graduates pursue knowledge under difficulties. Wading through mud from the Third Avenue where one leaves the railroad to the college is not pleasant. Sat from 2:30 to 5. Results not many, but several things foreshadowed or begun. Discussion on reduction of tuition fees from $90 to $50 or $25, or their abolition and making it a free college; question postponed. I go against their abolition, on some considerations that apply to the Free Church experiment. People at this day undervalue what they don't pay for. Better keep up fees, but reduce them to a minimum. Professor Joy is requested to commence his duties at once by organizing a laboratory. He is going to demand an expenditure ($15,000 at the lowest) that would have made our corporate hair stand on end three years ago. Zabriskie is venomous against his audacity. But our notions are far more liberal and our views far broader than of old. Zabriskie announced the figures in a whisper between his teeth, but there was no responsive shudder. I think we shall give the professor what he wants. Mr. Ruggles announced informally, without asking for action, that *Peter Cooper* is disposed to turn over his institute or "Union" to the college!!!! as the locale of its postgraduate university operations; an immense fact, should Peter's vague notions produce that definite result. Nothing done about the vacant professorships. But it seems that Spring has been calling on King to say that he considers the college to be founded on the basis of "solid Episcopacy" and "solid Presbyterianism," and to urge the claims of Tappan as a Presbyterian.[18] That *won't do at all.* . . .

The Bishop and Dr. Haight are severally in quite a state of mind about this question, and should they and Dr. Spring proceed to ventilate their respective views at our next meeting, we shall have a breezy and exhilarating session. I shall go heartily with the Bishop. Supporting Tappan as the strongest candidate though a Presbyterian would be one thing, but acquiescing in his election when he's put forward as a Presbyterian candidate and on the ground that dissent is entitled to be represented in the faculty is quite another.

June 8.   Columbia College at two. Haight read an abstract of testi-

---

[18] The Rev. Dr. Gardiner Spring, whose pastorate of the Brick Presbyterian Church was approaching its close, had long enjoyed a reputation as a stern Calvinist and a heresy-hunter.

monials of candidates for chair of literature. Some strong things said in favor of Eliot by the Bishop, Mr. Ruggles, Anderson, and others. I discharged my pop-gun on the same side. Betts, ever possessed by some petty formalism, thought we had gone too far in electing professors without regard to the "claims of alumni"; there was "a propriety" in our electing an alumnus and he should, therefore, support C. E. Anthon of the Free Academy. Then old Knox left the chair and made a canting speech of twenty minutes through his nose in support of his nephew, J. W. Mason, a young fellow of twenty-one; clever enough, I dare say, but wholly unknown and now a teacher in George C. Anthon's school. Quite an earnest and pathetic appeal it was meant to be; quite indecent it was as a piece of nepotism and in open disregard of his obligations as a trustee. He talked about the youth's *res angusta*, and the lovely character of his mother, and his descent from our old Provost Mason, and finally about the college not being Episcopalian, and our having elected so many Episcopalian professors. Beadle, who toadies Knox, said a word or two in support of the same individual. Result of ballot was Eliot 13, Mason 4 (!)—namely, Knox, Beadle, Hutton, Torrey—Anthon, 1. Bravo! Now comes the more difficult part of the job, getting Eliot to accept.

Then after some talk and a ballot begun, the election for the other chair was postponed for a fortnight. Tappan made little show. Fish repudiates him as a proslavery man. He had a squabble with Humboldt, it seems on that question, in Berlin. Bradford was absent and Spring silent. Had we gone on, I think Lord would probably have been elected, but I for one don't feel perfectly clear about his qualifications. Morgan Dix was nominated, to my amazement, and the more I think of the nomination the better I like it. Adjourned after doing a good deal of other work, expeditiously and judiciously. It's marvelous how the board's capacity for action has improved. We do in five minutes now what would have required at least three stated meetings and a report of two committees a year ago.

June 11.   At Columbia College from ten to twelve as Haight's substitute on the committee to attend examination. Heard McVickar's examination of Seniors in political economy and evidences. (Mack *is* the evidences of revealed religion.) Very creditable, though I suppose the *best* scholars were called up while the inspectors were present.

June 14, SUNDAY.   Today at church; Higby. Professor Agassiz dined here. Made himself fascinating, as I believe he always does, but he's much pulled down by hard work on his forthcoming *Opus Magnum*, Vol.

I, and depressed by the ill health of a daughter whom he's sending off to Europe.[19]

June 15. I dined downtown on six clams, and then went to College meeting. Met as usual in the subterranean crypt of the Lafayette Place Dutch Conventicle with a score of grim departed dominies looking down on us from the walls. . . . Tuition fees were reduced from $90 to $50. I expect no practical good, no increase of students from the reduction, but the board was nearly unanimous in its favor. Reference to the president, with the advice of the faculty, to settle practical details of the course of instruction; a very judicious move.

The problem of public order in New York City had become acute. The city had grown with tremendous rapidity, and with very little regulation. In the decade 1840–50, more than one and a half million immigrants arrived at the port of New York from Europe, and many remained to fill the congested areas of the East Side. The number of thieves, robbers, vagabonds, beggars, and generally dissolute people, foreign or native-born, was appalling. There were areas like the "Five Points" which were so lawless that it was dangerous for a well-dressed citizen to pass through them at noonday. Organized gangs— the Dead Rabbits, the Empire Club, Mike Walsh's Spartan Band, and others —fought in the streets, often with a number of fatalities. Brawls between rival companies of the volunteer firemen, or between rowdies and the firemen, were equally numerous. As both the gangs and the fire companies had powerful connections inside the political organizations of the city, and especially in Tammany Hall, it was almost impossible to deal with them. As for the thieves, prostitutes, and cutthroats who infested great areas of the city, they were plainly acting in collusion with the police and with important politicians.

By 1857 a drastic reform was plainly needed. London had shown the way by its creation of an improved metropolitan police. The legislature passed a number of bills to lessen the powers of Fernando Wood's disreputable administration in City Hall and its opportunities for graft. Chief among these measures was one creating the new metropolitan police, under a board of five commissioners whose authority extended over New York, Kings, Westchester, and Richmond Counties. Governor King appointed the first commissioners, with Simeon Draper of New York their most prominent figure. But at once trouble

[19] Louis Agassiz had projected a ten-volume work, *Contributions to the Natural History of the United States,* to which he had obtained subscriptions at twelve dollars a volume. Only four volumes were ever completed.

ensued. No sooner did the police commissioners attempt to act than they were openly defied by Mayor Wood. He had fought the new system tooth and nail in the legislature, and he now declared that it was unconstitutional. With the old municipal police force to support him, he refused to surrender the police offices or property to the metropolitan force. In this stand he had the eager encouragement of the worst classes of the population; for they hoped that some riotous clash would give them an opportunity for plunder. When Governor King appointed Daniel D. Conover as street commissioner, the fateful moment seemed to have arrived. Wood ejected Conover from the City Hall; the indignant street commissioner then swore out a warrant for Wood's arrest on two charges—for an assault on his person, and for inciting a riot; and with these warrants and fifty of the metropolitan police behind him, he boldly marched up to the locked doors of City Hall. As a battle might have had grave consequences, it was fortunate for New York that General Sandford's Seventh Regiment happened to be passing through the city. Strong tells us of these excited scenes.

June 17. Weather dark and drizzle, possibly the depressing cause of the incorrigible lethargy and stolidity wherewith I'm disgracefully paralyzed, even amid the excitement of the present civil war. It has been gradually growing up and taking definite form as a conflict of authorities ever since the last legislature passed the New Police Bill in order to take power out of the paws of Mayor Wood and get it into those of the other scoundrels at Albany. We have had two hostile bodies of police for some time and collision has been predicted, but I've concerned myself little, being quite indifferent as between the two gangs; waiting with perfect resignation for the Court of Appeals to decide which horde has the legal right to be supported by public plunder. The crisis was brought on by another step of Governor King's carrying out the line of policy that produced the Police Bill. He appointed a dirty politician Street Commissioner, on a vacancy being made by the lamented demise of the previous incumbent. Don Fernando Wood and his aldermen, denying the Governor's right to do so, appointed another to the same office. The two rival claimants contested the possession of the office and its books and furniture, and Wood's appointee, backed by Wood's drilled and organized myrmidons of the old police, hustled the Governor's appointee out, neck and heels, by "manifestations of physical force." Whereupon the latter instituted certain legal proceedings, civil and criminal, against the people who had caused him to be kicked. . . .

I lounged uptown as usual yesterday afternoon and observed signs that the flaneurs of Broadway were in expectation of something. "What was going to take place?" "The National Guard, the Seventh Regiment," was coming down Broadway to embark for Boston to take part in the Bunker Hill celebration. At Vesey or Barclay Street, I found that corps halted and at ease and stopped a moment to see it resume its march and observe its reputed perfection of discipline. Waddington joined me and said De Peyster Ogden had just told him that there was doubt whether the regiment would not be kept in the city, as conservators of the endangered public peace. Nobody seemed aware there had been any recent row, and we both thought the suggestion rather extravagant. Presently the band struck up, the files formed and dressed beautifully, and the column resumed its march down Broadway. I turned into the park to ask what the crowd of people round the wall was interested about, and was told there had been a very serious and physical fierce manifestation—a battle royal—but a few minutes before; and then the drums that were dying away began to grow louder and to draw nearer, and the National Guard reappeared defiling through the park gates and stationed themselves in hollow squares on the south front of the City Hall. I walked about with Richard Grant White, and after many enquiries and many false reports, ascertained that a detachment of the New or Metropolitan Police had just been trying to arrest Don Fernando at the suit of Conover (the Governor's Street Commissioner) and had been resisted by the Old Police under Wood's orders. The latter defended the north steps of the City Hall and successfully, of course, being aided by their position and in greatly superior numerical force, and being backed by a miscellaneous assortment of suckers, soap-locks, Irishmen, and plug-uglies, officiating in a guerrilla capacity. One of the coroners had also attempted to serve the writ, but had been repelled. . . . "A dozen of the New Police had been badly beaten"; that was true. "Several were killed"; "the Governor was at the head of the Seventh Regiment"; "the target companies were turning out to sustain the Mayor"; "Conover was so badly hurt that he was not expected to live"; "Captain Dilks (of the New Police) had been shot through the heart with a revolver"—these things and many other current statements of the most impressive and alarming character were not true. The excitement was considerable and interesting, but I had to come away, for I had asked Murray Hoffman and George Anthon to dine with me. . . .

All today the park has been occupied by a crowd of eager expectants.

Several hundred policemen ("Municipal," backers of Wood) on duty in the Hall. General anticipation of a row. But the process *was served* last night, and the Mayor seems to have caved in. General Sandford, who has behaved with discretion and decision, waited on him to say that the process must be served somehow, and would be served under the escort and protection of the militia of the county if necessary.

All day the City Hall has been occupied by from five hundred to a thousand policemen; Wood's *tappe-durs*—drilled desperadoes with their stout locust clubs or truncheons in their belts and protuberances about the breasts of their coats that indicated revolvers and sling shot within. Wood is sustained by a certain portion of the rabble and has the sympathy of a large class who feel strongly about "invasion of municipal rights," and "the Albany Regency," and centralization. But he has hurt himself irretrievably, I think, by forcible resistance of civil process, duly issued and sought to be regularly served; by using the *vis major* of his police corps to repel legal authority and defend him against the ordinary legal remedies for an alleged wrongful act. All the policemen (Metropolitan or New School) whose heads were broken in the battle of yesterday afternoon will sue him for damages. . . . Should one of them be public spirited enough to die of his wounds—and several are very seriously hurt—Fernando may be called on to plead to an indictment for murder. He is an egregious demagogue and scoundrel, and it's a great pity that his opponents are nearly as bad. I can't entirely except Governor King himself, for though a high-toned and most honorable man, utterly incorruptible and bent on doing his duty, he has allowed himself to fall into sad hands and is governed by evil counselors, as his appointments (of scamps like Simeon Draper) manifestly prove.

June 18. No material progress in the history of the coup d'état. Crowd in the park is much smaller today, and the uniform companies are understood to be no longer congregated in their drill rooms awaiting General Sandford's summons. Wood has been before his ally, Judge Russell, on habeas corpus. Dean, his counsel, claims that he is not liable to arrest for any wrongful act, being protected by his official character; a tolerably startling proposition, which Russell will very probably affirm. A score of suits commercial against him and an order made by Judge Hoffman against him for resisting service of the order of arrest. Returnable next Monday. From Murray Hoffman, Jr.'s, talk I infer that his judicial papa is not unwilling to give the Mayor his deserts. This may, therefore, be a very decisive move.

June 19. Our municipal civil war is suspended; decision of the Court of Appeals looked for next week. I predict they will affirm the validity of the New Police Bill, but it is a doubtful matter. Six of the eight judges are Democrats.

June 22. Today scalding hot. Columbia College meeting. When we went into ballot for professor of objectives and subjectives, but thirteen were present; four or five (including the Bishop!) having walked off on various pretexts. We took but one ballot, resulting thus: Nairne 2, J.H.M. Knox 2 (to wit his papa and Beadle, his papa's jackal), Lord 1 (King), Morgan Dix 5, Tappan 2, G. C. Verplanck(!) 1. Election thereupon postponed to fall. Little Knox was nominated by his father just before going into ballot. No testimonials produced in his favor, except a paternal eulogy. Old Knox's proceedings about this chair and that of literature have been indecent, and strangely shortsighted for a man reputed sensible. . . .

June 24. There are positive reports that Court of Appeals has made up its mind to affirm the judgment of the Supreme Court that declares the "New Police Bill" constitutional, but I suppose them to be lying rumors, for the members of that Court are generally close-mouthed. Such will be their decision, however, I've little doubt, and it will be a sore blow to that King of Scoundrels, Wood—the arch-knave of our civic structure (!). It seems an extravagant, impossible suggestion, but I'm not sure that Wood has not been indulging a little in some vague dream of a coup d'état, and a "free city" with himself Doge or Protector or some sort of tyrant for life. He is profligate, ambitious, and energetic enough to entertain such projects, and though they are preposterous, there could be a plausible statement made out to prove them feasible. We shall soon be ripe for a bold effort to accomplish some such result, though it may be a little premature just now.

June 25. . . . We've engaged a room at Round Hill (Northampton) for July 10. . . . My design is to stay at Mundé's till the sixth of July.

July 2. . . . We set forth by railroad Friday morning; dusty and hot, but not beyond endurance. Dined at Northampton, then drove three miles to "Florence," where we found good rooms and were received by the two Miss Anthons, and the burly hydraulic practitioner at the head of the establishment.

"Florence" lies in an uninteresting region of commonplace country, with hills on the horizon all around, so far off as to be impracticable. They are positive drawbacks, because their distant visibility aggravates the sojourner and inspires indignation at the stupidity of whoever it was that selected that spot for a summer resort instead of going five miles off in any direction. The village is a straggling nebula of little houses grouped round two or three raw, staring brick factories. Mundé's Aquarium is not notable for beauty of position. It's hedged in by an evergreen thicket which shuts off all possibility of any view, but this is the less important because there is nothing in particular to see. This leafy barrier is much prized by the mosquitoes generated in the adjacent millpond. The dwellers in the house are mostly invalids, in a state of depression from "packing," pumping, douches, and bread-and-water diet, beside the low spirits naturally induced by their respective diseases. . . .

Prospects for Monday being without improvement, I railroaded to Brattleboro in the morning with a vague hope that there might be truth in the story that the *Wesselhœft* was to be open. Found there was none. Met Alfred Schermerhorn, who insisted on my dining with him at the Lawrence, the opposition water-cure of last summer. Everything looked so much better than I expected that I conceived the idea of taking rooms there, returned to Florence that evening and took Mrs. Strong thither Tuesday, spent the day there, selected rooms, had a pleasant stroll through the woods and a good satisfying look at the lovely Connecticut and wooded slopes of Chesterfield Mountain, and came back.

July 4, SATURDAY. The customary din is raging without. The Chinese War has raised the price and diminished the supply of firecrackers, but our peace is not thereby promoted. The ingenious youth of the city adopt noisy pistols in their place. . . .

July 5. There was a riot yesterday afternoon in the Sixth Ward, and several persons killed. This afternoon and evening it has been renewed. The Seventh and other regiments are out with ball cartridge. Some of the downtown streets are made impassable by cordons of police, others, I am told, by barricades. A crowd is gathered round the hospital gates in Broadway; many cases of gunshot wounds have been passed in. We're in a "state of siege," and if half the stories one hears be true, in something like a state of anarchy. Rumors of hard fighting round Tompkins Square, in the Second Avenue, in Franklin Square, of houses sacked in the Fifth Avenue near Twenty-eighth Street. Probably lies and gross exaggerations. But the Old Police being disbanded and the New Police as yet inexperienced and imperfectly organized, we are in an insecure and unsettled state at present. I've just returned from prowling cautiously and at a very respectful distance round the seat of war; but I don't know what the disturbance is or has been about. It seems to have been a battle between Irish Blackguardism and Native Bowery Blackguardism, the belligerents afterwards making common cause against the police and uniting to resist their common enemy.

New York on July 4th witnessed its most disgraceful disturbances since the Astor Place riots of 1849. The trouble began about two o'clock in the morning when a party of Sixth Ward gangsters, members of the Dead Rabbit Club, attacked the public house at No. 40 in the Bowery with clubs and stones. They had burst in the windows and wounded several people when the police appeared from the Tenth and Thirteenth Wards and put them to flight. As the gangsters retreated to Bayard Street, they attacked a group of young men near the Five Points, and left one mortally injured. Fighting with the police was then resumed. At sunrise the rioters were driven to the tops of houses, whence they discharged their pistols and muskets and rained down brickbats and stones. The police were presently reinforced by the Bowery Boys, and a frightful scene of violence and bloodshed ensued. The gunfire became a fusillade; heavy missiles were thrown into the streets; and stretcher-bearers were kept busy carrying away the wounded, some of whom expired. Finally, the rival bodies of gangsters built barricades of carts, wagons, furniture, and lumber in Mulberry Street and Bayard Street, from behind which the Dead Rabbits and Bowery Boys continued firing at one another. Both sides were now defying the policemen. Large additional forces of officers were dispatched to the spot, and they finally succeeded, about seven in the evening, in tearing down the barricades and restoring partial order. Meanwhile, the Police Commissioners had asked General Sandford to use the militia, and three regiments were ordered out; but their services were not required.

On the following night (Sunday), the rioting was resumed. Again two rival gangs, the Dead Rabbits and Five Pointers, fought with firearms, clubs, and stones; again the authorities called upon the state militia for help; and again the police suppressed the outbreak, though not before half a dozen men had been shot. Nor was this the end. A dangerous spirit of violence had gotten abroad, and the debased slum population of the city was seething with unrest. On July 13th, for example, a mob of some five hundred, chiefly Irish immigrants with a sprinkling of Germans and others, attacked the metropolitan police with guns and pistols. Four or five hundred policemen were employed in suppressing this new outbreak, while the militia were again gotten under arms.

In all these disturbances the discharged members of Mayor Wood's old munic-
ipal police force were prominent. Strong voices the alarm and disgust which
were felt by all public-spirited New Yorkers.

July 7, TUESDAY.   Since Sunday night the city has been peaceable.
The "Dead Rabbits" and "Bowery Boys" repose on their respective
laurels. Wood and Wood's enemies both make a great handle of these
riots, drawing very diverse conclusions from them. On the whole they
are most effective in argument against Fernando. . . .

Yesterday morning I was spectator of a strange, weird, painful scene.
Certain houses of John Watts DePeyster are to be erected on the northwest corner of this street and Fourth Avenue, and the deep excavations
therefor are in progress. Seeing a crowd on the corner, I stopped and
made my way to a front place. The earth had caved in a few minutes
before and crushed the breath out of a pair of ill-starred Celtic laborers.
They had just been dragged, or dug, out, and lay white and stark on the
ground where they had been working, ten or twelve feet below the level
of the street. Around them were a few men who had got them out, I
suppose, and fifteen or twenty Irish women, wives, kinfolk or friends,
who had got down there in some inexplicable way. The men were listless
and inert enough, but not so the women. I suppose they were "keening";
all together were raising a wild, unearthly cry, half shriek and half song,
wailing as a score of daylight Banshees, clapping their hands and gesticu-
lating passionately. Now and then one of them would throw herself down
on one of the corpses, or wipe some trace of defilement from the face of
the dead man with her apron, slowly and carefully, and then resume her
lament. It was an uncanny sound to hear, quite new to me. Beethoven
would have interpreted it into music worse than the allegretto of the
Seventh Symphony. Our Celtic fellow citizens are almost as remote from
us in temperament and constitution as the Chinese.

Marcy's death (on the fourth, of disease of the heart) generally and
justly regretted.[20]

July 14.   Read an insane book by George Borrow, an autobiographical
romance, I believe, called *The Romany Rye,* poor stuff mostly, but with
an appendix that is readable from the liveliness and rampancy of its
malignity against several notions and things that are good and true *non*

[20] Ex-Governor William L. Marcy, who had just left the Secretaryship of State
after four years of able service, was found dead in his room at Ballston Spa at noon on
the Fourth, an open copy of Bacon in his hand.

obstante Mr. George Borrow. On my ride the other day I read what seems a very clever and funny treatise on *New York Boarding Houses*, one of the most genuine attempts at humor that I've lately seen. Borrow actually makes heroes of Thistlewood and Inge; *vide* the State Trials.

Stroll last night, far down on the east side looking for a mob and finding none. Walked through most of the dangerous regions past Tompkins Square. It appears from the morning papers that I ran some risk of being knocked on the head, of which danger I was wholly ignorant at the time. I saw nothing more alarming than sundry groups of sweaty Teutons jabbering gutturals with vehemence, and smelt no gunpowder, but the explosion of a park of artillery and the magazines would have been required to drown the overpowering, pungent stenches of that region. We're in a very perturbed state again. Riots yesterday and the day before, instigated, some say, by the old police if not by Wood himself. The new police seem very inefficient from want of organization, and a couple of regiments were under arms last night. Should there be occasion for their active intervention, I trust they will fire low and give the blackguardism of the city a sharp lesson. . . .

Stroll tonight and lounge round the station house at the corner of Third Street and the Bowery, the outpost or advanced guard of law and order. Police scarcely venture east of it. Meetings are being held in the region of Avenue A and near by, with bonfires and gunpowder orations, but I think it is generally known that the militia are under arms and sedition will confine itself to that district, omitting all hostile demonstrations. Shameful that it should be allowed undisputed rule there; that there should be a whole ward within which life and property have been notoriously unsafe for three days, which I cannot walk through tonight without serious risk—and that no vigorous effort is made to suppress the disorder. Some of the police with whom I talked seem dissatisfied with the timidity of their commanders.

July 16.   Stagnated at home in the evening till half-past ten, when an alarm of fire started me out and I chased the conflagration up Lexington beyond the bounds of civilization into desert places where Irish shanties began to prevail, and the region being lonely and suspicious and the fire still a dozen streets beyond and nearly out beside, I came back perspiring. It was a varnish factory in the latitude of Fifty-fifth Street.

Coroner's inquest in progress over the unlucky German, Miller or Muller, the "opfer" of the 17th Ward riot. Evidence hopelessly conflicting; impossible to form an opinion whether he was killed by the police or by one of his own party. Teutonia is watching the case with much interest, and some say that if the verdict be not against the police, there will be a grand insurrection and a provisional government proclaimed in Tompkins Square.

July 22. The only excitement is the police controversy and the Street Commissioner shindy, and one tires of them at last, though they, the latter particularly, are prosecuted with inexhaustible fertility of litigation, injunctions, attachments, and so forth. Every day has its new proceeding, or its hearing on some habeas corpus or order *nisi.* Wood has astonished everybody by taking his seat with the new police commission; the mayor of Brooklyn does the same. Draper has resigned (should never have been appointed), and filling the vacancy will be a delicate operation. It may lead to the very unexpected result of giving Wood and his friends the control which the Police Bill was expressly intended to take from them. Wood is a man of great energy, ambition, and perseverance, and most prolific in resource—pity he's a scoundrel.

John Hughes, archbishop of New York, has been lowering and injuring himself pitiably by a long newspaper article vituperating Raymond of the *Times*; a very undignified and rather scurrilous production, full of weakness and vanity. He writes like an Irish editor in a passion.

July 23. Jack Ehninger and Theodore Winthrop called. Winthrop is a good fellow, only he's subject to an offensive eruption of bad puns.

Strong's diary for August is largely filled with painful scandal affecting one of his closest associates, his cousin and partner, Charles E. Strong. This gentleman had married Miss Eleanor Fearing, a woman of wealth, with whom his relations were unhappy. They were vacationing at Newport. Now he came back early one morning, as the diarist writes, "the wretched bearer of a lamentable and disgraceful story." Looking for something in his wife's room, he had picked up a letter and noticed that while it was addressed to her in a female hand, it was "in the calligraphy of that treacherous scoundrel, his and her particular friend, the versatile and accomplished H." (That is, W. H. Hurlbut, journalist, dandy, and man about town; a figure noted in New York life of the day, whose portrait is partially painted in Theodore Winthrop's novel Cecil Dreeme.*) It was "such a letter as a foolish man would write to his mistress in the first week of concubinage." Though she denied that she was guilty of actual infidelity, the outraged husband declared that there must be an instant and final separation. This unhappy event imposed upon George Tem-*

pleton Strong the necessity of seeing and talking with all the parties to the triangle. "I have no doubt there will be an accommodation of the trouble," he wrote, "but it ought to be after a period of suspense and distress that the guilty party will remember—if it ought to be at all." Hurlbut came to the house for a talk. "The glass from which some water was given this dog when he was (unless he was shamming) overcome by agitation, I have smashed." The fellow for a time seemed to be trying to force the lady to accept his protection. "With her fortune they could live abroad, at least till he was tired of her; and he can always support himself by his wits and his pen." However, a recon-ciliation—of a sort—was effected between husband and wife. Early in August the diarist writes: "Telegraph informs me that affairs are in so satisfactory a condition at Newport that my unhappy friend there wants to get back to Wall Street. He'll probably return tomorrow, in which case I'll vacate the city tomorrow afternoon or the next day." Charley, in fact, returned to town in better spirits, reporting "contrition and good resolutions and the horizon far clearer." But the diarist had no confidence in his future marital happiness.

The diarist then betook himself to the sylvan delights of Brattleboro, where he enjoyed drives along the beautiful West River, listened to a lecture on Oxford University life, and enjoyed the companionship of his wife and children. Occa-sional trips to the Connecticut River town followed in September. An entry on September 27th indicates that photography was established in Brattleboro. "One morning spent with Howe, the Draperian artist," writes Strong. "Six or seven pictures taken, generally very good." These were ambrotypes. Strong invested this summer in an aquarium, which was a rich source of amusement in itself and contributed to his microscopic studies.

August 30.   Atlantic telegraph cable broken in the laying, to every-body's great disappointment, and probably to the serious loss and damage of Peter Cooper and the retardation of his schemes of an academic founda-tion. Mortimer Livingston dead after a brief illness, the last survivor of the old firm of Bolton, Fox & Livingston. . . . A financial crisis in Wall Street, which seems to have run its course and terminated in convalescence much sooner than the Bears predicted. It began with the failure of the New York branch or agency of the Ohio Trust Company,[21] and was fol-

[21] The panic, which had its origin in international wars and dislocations as well as in American over-investment and speculation, began with the smash of the Ohio Life Insurance & Trust Company of Cincinnati, which had a New York branch.

lowed by the suspension of De Launay, Iselin & Clarke, John Thompson, and one or two respectable concerns besides. Jacob Little stopped, but went on next day. The Surrogate has decided against Mrs. Cunningham's claim to the style and the rights of Mrs. Burdell in an elaborate opinion which seems conclusive as to the alleged marriage.

September 1. Very bright, beautiful weather, but clouds and thick darkness rule in "The Street." Financial crisis not over in the least; the panic very sore—and spreading. The Mechanics' Banking Association, not a large concern, but one long established and fully trusted, stopped short this morning, to everybody's consternation. Later in the day the story was current that it would resume in a day or two, that it is perfectly sound, but that a defalcation of some $80,000 had come to light, committed by a sinful teller, Van Blarcom by name, and that until its full and precise extent and all its particulars were discovered, it was thought right to do no business. But it's a rather grave step to close the doors of a Wall Street bank for five minutes during banking hours, and $80,000 or $100,000 is not so deadly a loss to a capital of $600,000—and people look dubious and whisper darkly. . . . There have been several pretty serious failures among the stock operators. This may be the beginning of terrible trouble, for the specie in our banks is a ridiculously minute percentage of their circulation.

September 4. Aquaria at a premium. Ever since I read Gosse's book[22] three summers ago, I've been predicting that they would become fashionable and trying to find a workman who would undertake to construct them. The obstacle has been the want of proper cement. Now they are announced on sale at several places and are destined to be the fashionable plaything of next season. I got a small tank yesterday and have stocked it with George Anthon's surplus that had been lying in jars since his return from Newport (soaking in putrescent sea water) and with a few fish from his aquarium. Results tonight are better than could have been hoped.

September 14. News in town not much, except the money panic, which is farther than ever from relief. Wall Street stocks panting and trembling under a pressure that reminds one of the financial tragedies of 1837. Prophets of evil say that if it last a week longer everything must go down in wreck, that this is but the beginning of trouble, and that a general smash is certainly close at hand. Things look very blue, un-

[22] Philip Henry Gosse (1810–1888), English naturalist, had published a book called *The Aquarium* (1854).

doubtedly. There have been several most startling apprehensions of old houses in the best credit; for example, G. H. Swords, and Allen of Providence, whose wealthy manufacturing concerns are brought down by the failure of one of the Swans (!) and will make a very bad show of assets, it is said.

September 18, FRIDAY. Columbia College meeting yesterday. To my surprise and disgust, a dispatch from Eliot to Mr. Ruggles declining, answered Wednesday. Next day brought letters. Bishop Brownell and Williams had addressed Eliot a joint mandate to stay in their diocese and this, coupled with a certain sentimentalism of standing by a weak institution, had determined his action. Unfortunate for the interests of the church, which he could have promoted so much more effectively in this wider field. He has not treated us well, in holding off so long and declining at last, but has doubtless acted on high motives and certainly with entire disregard of personal interests. Old Knox is lobbying busily for his son as professor of philosophy, and, of course, he will urge his nephew again for Eliot's chair. The old slyboots has been purring to King and Mr. Ruggles to "deprecate any sectarian objection," which is delightful after his course in the Gibbs matter. George F. Allen had sent in his resignation, because he thought his position affected by Stillman, Allen & Co.'s failure, and we had some trouble to get him to withdraw it. . . .

Loss of the *Central America* steamer, in the great gale ten days ago, the first of our treasure-ships that has perished. She foundered with several hundred passengers and a million and a half in California gold, sorely needed in Wall Street just now. The pressure there is still cruel, though perhaps less crushing than a week ago. East Indian news is watched with much interest. The Sepoy Mutiny threatens to swell into a great revolution, disastrous to England and to civilization. This Mahometan rebellion has been stimulated by exaggerated stories of English failure in Crimea, and looks like just retribution to England for backing up the empire of Mahound in Europe.

Widespread speculation, rising prices, rash investment in railroad construction and the expansion of mills and factories, a boastful though spotty prosperity, and general extravagance had marked the middle years of the 1850's. Much complaint was heard everywhere over the high cost of living, which it was fashionable to attribute to the steady flow of gold from California and Australia, and the consequent shrinkage in the purchasing power of money. The autumn of

1854 had witnessed a decided business recession, with much unemployment and hardship, accompanied by a brief panic in the money-market; but the country soon turned back to seeming prosperity, with over-investment, speculation, and extravagant living. Then in the last fortnight of August, 1857, came a series of crashes—a Boston sugar house, a Rochester bank, and most disastrous of all, on the 24th the Ohio Life Insurance & Trust Company of Cincinnati, which, with a branch in New York, closed its doors owing seven million dollars. Panic broke out in Wall Street and swiftly covered the whole East. Every day brought news of the failure of long lists of banks and brokerage houses. Railroads began to go under—in September the Fond du Lac and the Delaware, Lackawanna & Western; in October the Pittsburgh, Fort Wayne & Chicago, the Reading, the Erie, the Michigan Central, and the Illinois Central. Iron mills and other manufacturing establishments shut down. Hundreds of thousands of workingmen, skilled operatives, and clerks were thrown out of work—in New York City alone, as winter began, the unemployed were estimated at between 30,000 and 40,000. Angry public meetings were held by men whose families faced starvation, and resolutions were passed demanding measures of relief and reform. In cities with large masses of German and Irish immigrants, outbreaks of mob violence were feared.

Meanwhile, a melancholy disaster had taken place in the Atlantic. The steamer Central America had left Aspinwall on September 3rd for New York, carrying nearly 600 passengers and some $1,600,000 in California gold. She reached Havana with fair weather. But soon after leaving that city on the 8th she was overtaken by a terrible hurricane, and despite the heroic exertions of officers and crew, on the evening of the 12th she foundered off Cape Hatteras. More than four hundred of the passengers and crew and all of the treasure went down with the ship.

September 27, SUNDAY. Panic and pressure have made alarming progress during the last week. Philadelphia and Baltimore banks have suspended! Ours are still firm; "we" are sure they will stand; "we" rather crow over the tricky, drab-colored men of Philadelphia. Perhaps the crow may collapse and die away into a frightened squawk before long. Failures are many, and among them the Fosters, dry goods people with whom Dan Messenger is somehow concerned. Their fall is a disaster to him, no doubt, even if I am wrong in supposing him a partner. Probably it postpones his marriage indefinitely, and he and his very nice Miss

Nelson are unhappy tonight. Garner's house has stopped, a very suggestive and startling fact. Were I offered Aspinwall's paper tonight with
thirty days to run, or Grinnell's, or Moses Taylor's at fifty cents, I
would not take it. All confidence is lost, for the present, in the solvency
of our merchant princes—and with good reason. It is probable that every
one of them has been operating and gambling in stocks and railroad
bonds. Any given millionaire may have employed his million, and the
odds are he has employed it, in buying securities now all but absolutely
unmarketable and worthless.

September 28.   Panic is very dreadful in Wall Street. The banks will
probably stand, but failures are multiplying, and no one knows on whom
he can depend, or on what. Every security is distrusted.

Dialogue between two seedy street-operators at my barber's:

"How's money this morning?"

"I ain't seen any. Have you?"

"I saw a twenty shillin' piece this mornin' and I thought I'd try what
I could raise on it."

"Wal, I guess you can raise two dollars."

I am confirmed in my convictions on two points, namely: First, credit
systems and expanded paper currencies are mischievous and immoral.
Second, we should foster our own manufactures by protection instead of
running in debt to England, France, and Germany.

September 29.   O Posterity, Posterity, you can't think how bothered,
bedeviled, careworn, and weary were your enlightened ancestors in their
counting-rooms and offices and bank parlors during these bright days of
September, A.D. 1857. And I hope for your own sake you may find it
difficult to comprehend *why* they wasted this sunshine and balmy air,
and periled health of body and soul in a long, grim battle with endorse-
ments and due-bills and time-contracts, instead of living their lives in
freedom and peace and pure air with a competency and a cow.

They are fighting hard for the grand, ugly house in the Fifth Avenue;
for the gold and damask sofas and curtains that are ever shrouded in
dingy coverings, save on the one night of every third year when they are
unveiled to adorn the social martyrdom of five hundred perspiring friends.
They are agonizing with unavailable securities, and pleading vainly for
discount with stony-hearted directors and inflexible cashiers, lest they
forfeit the privilege of inviting Joe Kernochan and Dan Fearing to gorge
and prose and stupefy over the barbaric splendors of an unwholesome
dinner; that they may still yawn through *Trovatore* in their own opera

boxes; that they may be plagued with their own carriage horses and swindled by their own coachman instead of hiring a comfortable hack when they want a ride. . . .

Some say the "feeling" in the street was a little improved this morning. But it was bad enough. Joseph Lawrence of the United States Trust Company (who sent for me to suggest a candidate for the Columbia College chair of philosophy, the Rev. James H. Tyng of Morristown, N. J., brother of the Dragon of St. George's) says that confidence is more shaken than in 1838, but that the banks will stand and the storm will pass off, leaving things safe and healthy. It is devastating all the South and West, where the example of our yellow-legged Philadelphia friends is pretty generally followed. I believe the Rhode Island banks are going, too. The rest of New England is supposed to be steady.

September 30. . . . Lewis Jones sailed today. Heaven prosper his voyagings. I know few men of equal worth. He passes for an amiable, commonplace person, but he is somewhat more, and made of most reliable stuff. I've upheld him for ten years past to be among the strongest and finest-grained of our young men, and nothing but his own exceeding modesty has interfered with the general recognition of his pre-eminence. He has just been giving an instance of the force and weight of character he combines with so much kindliness and amiability. Charley gave him a hint two or three weeks ago of Hurlbut's unworthiness, without descending to particulars, and so Hurlbut was not admitted when he called in Sixteenth Street. Mrs. Jones sent down word she was acting on her husband's instructions. He called again, and demanded to see Lewis and insisted on knowing the "stories" on which he acted, and their author, to which demand Lewis replied with much urbanity that he had heard no stories and did not want to hear any, but chose to exercise the privilege of selecting his own and his wife's acquaintances according to his own discretion, and begged to wish Mr. Hurlbut good morning. Exit Hurlbut! Very good for Lewis, toward whom this loafer adopted a very different tone from that which he took with Charles Kuhn—doubtless inferring from Lewis's gentle manner that he was to be bullied.

October 4, SUNDAY. Nairne called.[23] He wants the intellectual and moral philosophy professorship in Columbia College, for which he seems

[23] Charles Murray Nairne (1808–1882), by birth a Scot and a man of reputed erudition, was now to become professor of philosophy and literature, thus taking the third chair into which McVickar's professorship had been divided. Nothing was more remarkable in the conduct of Columbia College at this period than the unabashed way in which applicants for chairs canvassed the trustees.

to have some points of adaptation. He don't look thoroughbred, or talk as if it were his vocation to guide the erratic, unruly thoughts of young men, but he is said to be original and vigorous. The Rev. Mr. Weston rates him very high. With George Anthon yesterday to Flushing Bay, at Mrs. James Strong's, where we spent the afternoon sweeping the eel-grass with scoopnets and bringing up "sparlings," synguathi ("billed eels"), common eels, tomcod, killies, toadfish, crabs, shrimp, and so forth for the aquarium; also looking in the outlet of the millpond (a tide-mill) for an elegant little anemone that blossoms on the oyster shells and which looks liker an Anthea than an Actinia. Very successful afternoon, though the weather was gloomy and unpleasant.

October 5.   Columbia College meeting at two P.M. First business the "course of study," hours of attendance, and so on. We tangled ourselves up with two or three schemes, either of which it would have required a week's hard labor to comprehend, and finally cut the knot by adopting the suggestions of the faculty in the lump, as we might better have done six months ago. Then we resolved to consolidate the chairs of philosophy and literature, and testimonials were read, and the election postponed to next Monday. Nairne stands the best chance, though old Knoxious is working hard for his reverend offspring, James H. M. Knox, and the name of Motley, author of *The Rise of the Dutch Republic*, was proposed today, with a strong letter from William H. Prescott.[24]

We are to have an instructor in drawing. I think the place suits Jack Ehninger's case exactly, and have written him to come to town at once to consider the matter and put himself in nomination.

October 8.   Bluer and darker every day; Monday's rally followed by collapse. Failures many and important, and among them that of Bowen & McNamee! They say their surplus is a million and upwards, but that there is no money to be got from their assets. The banks seem disposed to secure themselves and their stockholders from risk, as far as may be, at any cost, and they are quite right. Whether they can or cannot safely or profitably extend their line of discounts a trifle of ten millions is for them to judge. The merchants are clamorous for expansion and complain

[24] It must be remembered that Motley's great fame was in its dawn. He had issued his first historical work, *The Rise of the Dutch Republic*, at his own or rather his family's expense in London and New York early in 1856. Its success had been astonishing, the English edition selling some 17,000 copies in a little over a year and the American edition nearly as many. But Motley was not yet the great figure that he later became. If he were actually willing to come to Columbia, as Prescott thought, the college missed a great opportunity.

bitterly. They say that without it there must be universal insolvency. But it is better that the merchants sink than that banks and merchants go down together. Relief by voluntary suspension of specie payments by concerted action of the banks is out of the question. The State Constitution disposes of all doubt on that point, and makes it impossible for the legislature to sanction or legalize suspension directly or indirectly. . . .

Yesterday Miss Leavenworth and Murray Hoffman dined here and went to *Don Giovanni*; a satisfactory evening. Leporello and the Don were severally respectable or *decent*, at least. Lagrange executed Donna Anna's music honestly. . . .

October 9.   This has been the bluest day yet; distrust and despondency universal. The Harpers have suspended, but I suspect they have never been themselves since they were burnt out in December, 1853.[25] The Central Bank of Brooklyn is swamped, and within twenty-four hours after its failure to fulfil its promises, it was in the custody of the law. The banks of Wall Street will do well to contemplate the spectacle, and to bear in mind that the law will be as inexorable if they conclude to stop for the sake of the mercantile community. There was a run on the Park Bank this morning, which some people took to be the beginning of the end, and the crowd was great for a couple of hours in Beekman, Nassau, and Chatham Streets. But by two P.M., it had dispersed and the run was over. Certain concerns, which I won't name even here, are feeling the pressure cruelly, and though willing to submit to any shave, can get no money. Should they be driven to suspend, it will make matters worse, if possible.

October 10.   We seem foundering. Affairs are worse than ever today, and a period of general insolvency seems close upon us. People say "we must reach the bottom soon," but the bottom has certainly come out. Depression and depletion are going on without sign of any limit and promise to continue till we reach the zero point or universal suspension. This attack is far more sudden, acute, and prostrating than that of 1837. Will the banks stand it? I think *not*, and predict their downfall within ten days.

People's faces in Wall Street look fearfully gaunt and desperate. There are two or three millionaire friends of mine whose expression is enough to knock off three per cent a month extra from the market value

[25] This was not actually a suspension. Harper & Brothers had made a temporary assignment of their business to two sons, John W. and Joseph W. Harper; but business was conducted and accounts were paid as usual.

of their paper. I know of at least two "great houses" that are trembling
to their foundations. No merchant or banker, no man who has an obligation outstanding, can feel safe unless he has the needful gold in his own
custody. He may be worth any amount in stocks or bonds or land, and
yet be unable to raise five thousand dollars a week hence.

The Bowery Bank stopped yesterday. So did the little "East River
Bank," I believe. This afternoon as I came uptown there was a crowd
besieging the Bowery Savings Bank. I don't know how strong it may be,
but if it fall, there will be a run on the other savings banks.

Henry A. Coit suspended today!!! He has accepted drafts against his
usual consignments of sugar, and finds himself afraid to trust purchasers
or to sell for each, and unable to raise money on his securities. There are
other most significant failures, among them old Corlies. . . .[26]

The remedy for this crisis must be psychological rather than financial.
It is an epidemic of fear and distrust that every one admits to be without
real ground *except* the very sufficient ground that everyone else is known
to share them. I share the panic simply because I know the whole community feels it and because I know that a frightened community will not
buy property at its true value or give business men the credit to which
they are entitled. . . .

October 11, SUNDAY. This week may be epochal. If Tuesday morning's bank statements shew a large falling-off in deposits and specie,
there is no telling what progress in calamity will follow. If the banks
make a fair show, we may drag along till the expected reflux of specie
from the other side shall have had its tonic effect on our financial nerves. . . .

October 12. Aspect of this morning not encouraging, though Monday
is generally a day of reaction after the heavy work of Saturday. People
spent it mostly in lounging about Wall Street and standing in groups on
the corners, with their hands in their pockets, discoursing of trouble to
come, and wondering how long the banks would hold out. The Grocers'
Bank, a rather shaky concern, went down. It needed $50,000, but the
Clearing House was inexorable, and it closed its doors. Ten minutes
after, $100,000 in specie came up, the monetary sisterhood having re-
lented, but came too late. Possibly the excision of these unsound little
speculative banks may be no calamity. Run on the Bowery Savings Bank
has continued, and the Marine Bank in Wall Street has been attacked.

[26] Henry A. Coit was a prominent merchant, son of the distinguished merchant
Levi Coit. Joseph W. Corlies was a wealthy auctioneer and merchant, at one time
head of the firm of Corlies, Haydock & Co.

Both stand firm as yet. One of the Brooklyn savings banks is also in a state of siege, and the drafts on all of them largely exceed the deposits. Should this increase and become an energetic depletion, the banks proper will feel it most seriously. Peleg Hall's suspension announced today, and signs of general decomposition and disorganization multiplying. But tonight I hear that tomorrow's dreaded "bank statement" will be better than was expected; it is even said it will shew increased strength. If so, this may be the turning point, and the worst *may* be over, but I fear it is not so and that we have not yet got to the bottom. The utmost I hope is that six or eight of our strong banks may pass the ordeal; for example, the Manhattan, Commerce, New York, America, National, Phenix, and Merchants'.

Columbia College meeting. Motion to postpone election to the vacant professorship resisted. I held it my duty to state that a certain respectable person, who would not allow his name to be mentioned, had communicated to me very grave charges against one of the candidates whose name I would not mention and whom I would not indicate in any way; that I had not investigated those charges, but that they were of sufficient magnitude to make time for investigation necessary. Quite a little breeze followed. Bradford and the Rev. Mr. Spring and Van Wagenen thought I'd done wrong. Allen, Haight, King, Mr. Ruggles, and others thought I did right. I'm satisfied that my course was the true one. We postponed the election to next Monday. This may get me into a very nasty personal controversy, with no one to fall back upon as authority, but I could not have done otherwise. To sit still after the statements made to me would have been a criminal breach of trust. To go about among the trustees individually (as Van Wagenen thought I should have done) whispering discredit, would have been more injurious and less candid.

October 13. *"Tout le monde s'écria, Voilà L'Ouragan!"*

Here is the "crisis" at last. The community is at length actually enjoying the long-anticipated pleasure, perhaps questionable, of annihilating its own property as fast as possible. The chemical reaction of debtor and creditor has brought the financial crucible to a red heat and the elements are now finally deflagrating. The decisive process of decomposition has set in.

Morning was cloudy. Read the *Tribune* at breakfast and satisfied myself that the bank statement for the week was favorable beyond my hopes. Sent Ellie and her maid off in charge of Thomas for a visit to Mrs. Mary Wright at some place near Yaphank, L.I.; aerated the aquarium a little; had a visit from Jack Ehninger; started for downtown; got caught in a smart rain; spent a few minutes with George Anthon at his [Academy]; went to Wall Street; took a cup of coffee at Delmonico's; returned to the office; discoursed with Professor Bartlett of West Point about his forthcoming book on "Molecular Mechanics" and about the foreclosure of certain mortgages, and learned that there was a run on the American Exchange Bank. Went into the street and found it pretty densely crowded. Over a dozen banks (on the west side of the city mostly), including the North River, Merchants' Exchange, and Ocean had stopped. A steady stream was setting in toward the counter not merely of the American Exchange Bank, but of every other bank in the street, and not billholders alone but depositors were calling for gold. Old David Leavitt (of the American Exchange)[27] in his diaconal white cravat, addressed an allocution to the crowd, in substance that they might come on as fast as they pleased, that all the sound banks were acting in concert and would not suspend. The crowd cheered him with hysterical vehemence, but the influx and the drain of specie continued. From Hanover Street to Nassau, both sidewalks were densely packed with business men, capitalists, and operators. It was a most "respectable" mob, good-natured and cheerful in its outward aspects but quivering and tingling with excitement. They laughed nervously, and I saw more than one *crying*.

At a little after two the Bank of New York, Oothout's,[28] our oldest bank, had stopped. . . . Several second-class banks had succumbed. All closed at eight P.M. and a meeting was to be held at the Clearing House to decide whether any should pay specie tomorrow. The current talk of the street was that general suspension was inevitable, that Governor King would call a special session of the legislature instanter, and that the legislature would steer round the constitutional prohibition of legislation sanctioning suspension by some act affecting the remedy and not the right of the bank creditor; for example, altering the practice so as to require two years' notice of any motion for a receiver. A very honest and godly proposition.

The financial panic reached its crisis on October 13th–15th, when tremendous runs on nearly all the banks culminated in a suspension of specie payments. Great crowds filled the downtown streets, and long files of depositors stood in

---

[27] David Leavitt, a New Englander by birth who with two brothers had amassed a fortune in the dry goods business, was now president of the American Exchange Bank.

[28] John Oothout, director and president of the Bank of New York.

front of the banking houses. Scenes of intense excitement took place as successive reports of the failure of large mercantile houses and railroads came in. Banking officers of the city had applied to the Secretary of the Treasury for assistance, but without result. The worst of the panic might have been averted if all of the banks had agreed earlier on specie suspension; but each was reluctant to make the proposal. The great institutions in Wall Street held out until it was learned that some of their neighbors outside had suspended. Then, with their depositors more anxious than ever to obtain gold, they also decided to refuse payment in metallic currency. This suspension lasted until December 14th.

Under the State Constitution, banks were forbidden to suspend specie payments either directly or indirectly. By a rigid construction of this provision, the holder of a bank's notes might, when specie payment was refused, have applied to the Supreme Court for an order to show cause why an injunction should not be granted against the bank, and it be placed under the control of a receiver. General receivership would have been a terrible calamity, for nearly all the banks were perfectly solvent; they had ample long-term assets, but inadequate metallic reserves. The judges of the Supreme Court, therefore, met and agreed not to grant any injunction unless evidence was offered that the bank was insolvent or fraudulently managed. Contrary to the initial opinion expressed by Strong, this was wise. When one holder of notes of the venerable Bank of New York (founded by General Alexander MacDougall, Alexander Hamilton, and others) applied to the Supreme Court for an injunction and receivership, Judge Roosevelt decided against him on the ground that a genuinely solvent bank might refuse to redeem its circulating notes during a period of general insolvency.

October 14, WEDNESDAY.   We have burst. All the banks declined paying specie this morning, with the ridiculous exception of the Chemical, which is a little private shaving-shop of the Joneses with no depositors but its own stockholders.

Wall Street has been palpitating uneasily all day, but the first effect of the suspension is, of course, to make men breathe more freely. A special session is confidently expected, and the meeting of merchants at the Exchange at 3:30 P.M. appointed a committee that has gone to Albany to lay the case before Governor King. He ought to decline interference, but were I in his place I dare say my virtue would give way.

My great anxiety has been for the savings banks. Saw the officers of the two in which I feel a special interest (the Bleecker Street and Sea-

men's). Both were suicidally paying specie and thus inviting depositors
to come forward to get the gold they could get nowhere else and could
sell at a premium. The latter changes from specie to bills tomorrow; the
former did so this afternoon. All the savings banks are to do so tomorrow.
The run has been very formidable; some say not so severe as it was
yesterday, but bad enough. I think they will get through. . . .

O John A. Stevens, O George Newbold, how *could* you serve us so!

The Supreme Court Justices of this and the next district held a con-
clave today to consider what they should hold to be the law of banking
corporations when any application for a receiver should come before them.
They adopted certain views, not unreasonable, and gave the newspaper
reporters a semi-official report of their conclusions. They ought to be
impeached. Courts of Terminer sans Oyer, so prompt in despatch of
business as to dispose of the gravest questions before the litigants have
been heard or have had an opportunity to submit their papers, are novelties
that should be discouraged.

October 15.   Wall Street blue with collapse. Everything is limp and
flaccid like a defunct Actinia. Of course, suspension eases and relaxes the
dreadful spasm of the last sixty days, if only by making people think the
very worst has come and we can sink no deeper. This may be or may not.
But the banks as yet husband their resources none the less and shew no
signs of expansion, for they can't afford to lie long under water; they
must come to the surface pretty speedily, or asphyxiate. So the merchants
have gained little comfort beyond a vague notion that something or other
is going to turn up and that confidence will revive somehow. They find
some consolation in denouncing the banks, the late policy of which institutions is generally held to have been selfish, discordant, imbecile, and
suicidal. All this calamity is laid at their doors, and old John A. Stevens,
as president of the great ten-million-pounds Bank of Commerce, is
singled out as the representative man and concrete incarnation of their
system and is abused with great liberality. He's much cut up; cried a good
deal at the council that decided on suspension. He made a very poor show
there with his two hundred thousand in specie by the side of second- and
third-rate banks, like the National and the City, that were twice or thrice
as strong.

The run on the savings banks stopped short (thank Heaven) the
minute they came to their senses and began paying in bills. This is no
suspension, for their conditions of deposit expressly authorize them to pay
specie or current bills at their option. They have had a sore fright, and

one or two of the smaller concerns (Robert Dillon's, for example) are perhaps hardly yet out of danger.

Whether we've really reached the nadir, no one can tell. The old bank sagamores and great chieftains of Wall Street generally say "they hope so" and look very wise, not thereby seriously compromising their reputation for farsightedness and sagacity. The directors of the Bank of New York, some of whom I called on this morning, talk as if they thought themselves perfectly solvent and safe. Hope they are.

The extrajudicial decision of the judges of the Supreme Court in mass-meeting on the construction of the banking law and so on seems to find favor. It may be good law, though irregularly propounded. It certainly tends to quiet the public mind by removing the paralyzing fear everyone felt of a tremendous public calamity, to wit: the sudden impounding of all the assets of every bank in the city in the custody of receivers, and the consequent tying up of every man's balance. This would have made ruin universal and reduced us to barter. Perhaps the judges may have done right to overstep judicial usage in so grave and extraordinary a crisis, but the precedent is somewhat dangerous.

Under this decision an extra session isn't wanted and Governor King is said to decline calling one. He is right. Special legislation to protect insolvency and suspend legal remedies is a very demoralizing palliative. Probably His Excellency took also into account the risk of damaging the Republican party.

There are some signs of convalescence. The stock list has shot upward brilliantly, to come down again as fast, I fear. That the crops are beginning to move a little is a much more important fact. A famine next winter would be inconvenient. The wise men who write money-articles for the evening papers take an encouraging view of things.

October 18, SUNDAY. Mr. Ruggles has been visiting Albany, attending the governor with that great little man, Samuel Foot. They were sent up by the banks, who wanted an extra session at first, but, on reflection, and after the judicial *pronunciamento* of Roosevelt & Co., changed their minds and desired to retract and undo whatever conjurings and invocations they had uttered. King will *not* convene the legislature, but postpones announcing his decision till he shall have heard from the country, lest the rural districts should feel slighted. The decision is a wise one. The special session called in Pennsylvania is a warning. It has passed a general Stop Law giving private debtors twelve months' stay and the banks six.

Mr. Ruggles argued very plausibly that the banks were not insolvent. "Is Mr. Astor insolvent if he has not six cents in his pocket wherewith to pay his omnibus fare? Has your Excellency at this moment specie enough to make legal tender of payment to your Excellency's grocer and butcher and other current creditors, and is your Excellency therefore insolvent?" Ingenious but unsound. A bank is insolvent while it neglects to redeem its promises. That is true of every debtor and especially of a bank unwilling or unable to pay specie for its circulation and deposits. "Is not the truth the truth," though its admission may be inconvenient? . . .

October 19. Wall Street still prostrate and with little sign of convalescence. Ebb tide continues. Failures many, but there have been none of mark today.

Columbia College meeting this afternoon. The instructorship in drawing brought up. As much progress was made as we could expect; the question referred to Bradford, Anderson, and myself. We shall find it no easy job to secure that post for Jack W. Ehninger. Then King moved that Assistant Peck be promoted to a seat in the faculty, which move was properly denied, though I voted with the minority. The election for the vacant professorship followed.

First Ballot.		Second Ballot.	
Wilson	2	Wilson	2
Nairne	7	Nairne	10
Knox	4	Knox	3
Harwood	1	Lord	1
Lord	1		
Henry	1		

So Nairne was elected. I voted for him as a choice of evils, and before going into election stated that I had made enquiry as to the facts alleged against one of the candidates and referred to by me at the preceding meeting, and was satisfied that my informant had made the charge on insufficient evidence. Nairne is no commonplace man. He will be energetic for good or evil. Went with Mr. Ruggles to his house after the meeting to tell him of the result and to urge the importance of his entering on his duties without delay.

With the election of Charles Murray Nairne, an alumnus of St. Andrews and Edinburgh, and a ripe and efficient scholar, to be professor of moral and intellectual philosophy and literature, another step was taken toward giving Columbia College a vigorous instructing staff. The year 1857, as Strong's diary indicates, was a great landmark in the history of the institution. Not only did it remove uptown to a pleasanter and more commodious home at Forty-ninth Street, but it received a staff worthy of its place among American colleges. The professorship of ancient languages was divided into two parts: a chair of Greek occupied by Dr. Charles Anthon—old "Bull" Anthon, who had now served Columbia for many years—and a chair of Latin occupied by Henry Drisler of the class of 1839. The duties of the aging John McVickar (who was to retire in seven years) were similarly divided into three parts. He held a chair on the evidences of religion; Nairne received that already named; and Francis Lieber, a distinguished historian of philosophic qualities, was called to a chair of history and political science. By a division of the department of mathematics and astronomy, Professor Charles W. Hackley took the chair of astronomy, and Dr. Charles Davies, a graduate of West Point, that of mathematics. Following a separation of physics and chemistry, the German-educated Charles A. Joy became professor of chemistry, and Richard S. McCulloh, whom Strong always disliked, confined himself to physics.

As a result of the removal uptown and the expansion of the faculty and curriculum, Columbia experienced a remarkable boom. President Charles King was able to report to the trustees that fall that the record-breaking number of 154 students had matriculated. The alumni showed an increased interest in the College, and in various other ways it manifested a greater vitality.

October 22. Depression continues. Though there may be little side-eddies that some people look at with joy, the tide is still running out and everything is drifting down with it, or else stuck fast already on the black mud flats of insolvency and destined to rot there and perish long before the tide comes back again. It won't be dead low-water till the news of our general suspension and of the great railroad companies that have collapsed has reached England and reacted on us; that is, about three weeks hence. At our last advices, deluded souls on the other side, holders of "first-class" American securities, thought the panic had run its course.

The reaction upon us will be severe. This lamentable East Indian war is costly, and the hemorrhage of specie that it causes is already felt to be inconvenient and debilitating. When the British government and the Bank of England become aware that the Western influx of gold is stopped, that American debts won't be paid, and that Lancashire must buy the cotton which is its daily bread positively for hard cash only, they will instantly begin applying the tourniquet, and cauterizing if need be, to stop this new hemorrhage. They will raise the rate of discount, knock cotton down, and do their uttermost to keep an ounce of gold from coming here. Cotton princes and operatives will be thrown over without mercy, for India is worth ten Manchesters. The Hindoo combustion must be put out at any cost and with the least possible loss of time. If mills and factories are in the way, they must be blown up. If cotton can only be got by sending money out of England, cotton must be dispensed with. Such will be the policy of the financial powers on the other side, and a batch of failures among the great Anglo-American houses of London and Liverpool, a few tons of railroad bonds sent back for sale, and cotton falling thirty or fifty per cent, won't promote the return of cheerfulness to the sidewalks of Wall Street.

We are a very sick people just now. The outward and visible signs of disease, the cutaneous symptoms, are many. Walking down Broadway you pass great $200,000 buildings begun last spring or summer that have gone up two stories, and stopped, and may stand unfinished and desolate for years, or on which six Celts are working instead of sixty. Almost every shop has its placards (*written*, not *printed*) announcing a great sacrifice, vast reduction of prices, sales at less than cost. Many of them protrude their stock of goods into unusual positions outside the door, after the manner of Chatham Street, with tickets conspicuously announcing the price of each lot and interjection marks. Great dry-goods houses like Bowen & McNamee's condescend to implore mankind to come in and buy at retail and notify the universe that "this store will be kept open till 9 P.M." Traders who have notes out must sell or perish. In Wall Street every man carries Pressure, Anxiety, Loss, written on his forehead. This is far the worst period of public calamity and distress I've ever seen, and I fear it is but the beginning.

October 26. Lugubrious news from Europe. Like us, France and England have swelled up; like us they seem about to *bust.* There is pressure on the Bank of England and panic on the Bourse. Financial potentates are tightening the monetary screws. All the secondary commercial centres— Berlin, Hamburg, Vienna—are in sympathetic revulsion. The "Old Lady of Threadneedle Street" is flustered and anticipates a very bad attack, to judge from the promptitude and energy of her astringent, oppulative, constrictive, anti-diarrhoea treatment. She has thought it prudent to screw up the rate of discount relentlessly. Should people lose their self-possession and get frightened into a stampede, as we did, there may well be a very memorable smash in London and Paris before 1857 is ended.

The East Indian mutiny or rebellion don't seem to spread. Though Eastern news is said to be filtered and "doctored" for the Home Market, the press under censorship, and disagreeable truths more or less smothered, I think the indications are that this horrible outbreak of the Powers of Hell will be steadily repressed and put down. . . .

Mr. Ruggles here this evening, discoursing of the Erie Railroad. Ellie's indomitable grandmother has been somewhat indisposed of late. She is now comparatively well again, but any weakness or ailment affecting her is a startling novelty, and at her advanced age, significant.

October 28. Nairne's appointment seems to find favor. Several people have spoken of it to me as a good thing for the College. Davies (the professor, not the judge) has actually been glorifying and eulogizing Nairne to Weston!—forgetting his warning to me of Nairne's gross unfitness and his reluctant conviction that no calamity could befall the College much more disastrous than his election. I fear Davies is mean and slippery beyond precedent.

The financialities blue as ever. The little upward flickerings of the stock list have no real significance except so far as they may be attributed to foreign remittances for investment in American securities at their present prices. Wall Street is *dead* for the present, notwithstanding these traces of irritability still found in some muscles of the cadaver. If it don't come to life before long, decomposition will set in, and by the first of January next the legislature will be "hanging round"; two houses of carrion beetles will be in session over the defunct. As yet everybody despairs and everything is stagnant.

The three-days-later news by the *Persia* is not very important; the financial epidemic seems established throughout Europe, and pressure is severely felt from Glasgow to Trieste. We shall soon hear that something has given way under it, possibly the sceptre of Louis Napoleon.

November 2, MONDAY. The baby walked all alone today. Poor George Cornell's death is announced at last. He was a useful man, and his prominent fault, cynicism of speech, merely assumed. . . .

State election comes off tomorrow. Nobody cares. Twelve months and a crisis have toned down people's interest in politics wonderfully. John C. Frémont is a very insignificant person, and Kansas a very remote insignificant territory. The Democrats are likely to carry the state by default.

November 3. Voted, on my way downtown, in Twentieth Street. My contribution to the new glass ballot-boxes was a mosaic, little bits from all the tickets, and one or two John Smiths and William Browns derived from my imagination, for in some cases I knew nothing good of any candidate. It has been the quietest of elections. Voting was like going to daily service, a lonely thing to do. Even the ticket distributors in their little boxes seemed desolate and dreary as Simon Stylites (or Simon Stock, rather, in his hollow tree), and found it a delightful novelty to be asked whether this was a verdant voter's legal district, who was the other candidate for assemblyman or constable, and the like.

November 4.   What the people of the state of New York have done at this election no one yet certainly knows. The Democrats have either carried everything or come very near it. Last year's vast Republican majority is gone like last year's snow.[29] They have swept the city, of course. Winthrop Chanler goes to the Assembly, though honest and a gentleman!! Bradford is beat. There were but two candidates and West's election is a conclusive argument in a nutshell against the infallibility of democratic institutions. No man of average sense in the whole community doubts that Bradford is the fitter man for that office.

Very busy for several hours tonight reorganizing Aquarium No. 1. It has been for some time opalescent and semi-opaque like a strong glass of absinthe and water, whereas No. 2 is crystalline.

November 10. . . . This financial crisis has thrown thousands of the working class out of employment and made it a difficult matter enough to maintain peace and order in the city through the winter. But that arch-demagogue Wood, the appropriate punishment of property holders and respectable people generally for their years of fainéance, inertia, and neglect of the city government, has lately put forth an incendiary message recommending the Common Council to apply a few hundred thousand dollars in buying provisions for the poor and inviting attention to the difference between "the rich who produce nothing and have everything and the poor who produce everything and have nothing." Probably he has also used his talents for tortuous, subterranean operations to get up some movement among the "dangerous classes." His object has been either to gain votes among the unwashed by assuming to act as their patron, or to stimulate them to an outbreak on the eve of election, and to suppress it with a high hand, and gain votes among men of peace by

[29] Only minor state offices were filled this year. Interest in Kansas had abated, as Strong indicates, and the indignation over the Dred Scott decision could hardly express itself in a local contest. The Democrats, largely aided by the Know-Nothings, elected a secretary of state and other officers over the Republicans by a vote of about 194,000 to 175,000.

showing himself able to maintain order, and so forth. However this may be, his policy has produced sundry rather alarming demonstrations by the *canaille* of the city. They have been marching in procession—holding meetings in Wall Street—listening to seditious speeches—passing resolutions that they were entitled to work and the wages of work, and that if they were not provided with work they would take the means of subsistence *vi et armis.*

This morning the Hall was in a state of siege; all its front portico and a large space in the park occupied by a mob; some three hundred policemen on duty and ready for action inside. About one hundred and fifty United States soldiers from Governor's Island and marines were posted in the Custom-House and the adjoining Assay Office. General Scott was under orders from Washington to see that the treasure of the Federal Government be not violated. The mob in the park was mostly made up of blackguard boys under twenty-one, with some natural proclivity to a muss, Celts of the lower grade, loving whiskey rather than work, "yawping" about, too stolid to understand their own alleged grievances, and a few Germans. These last, the really dangerous class, were not fully represented. The Tompkins Square crowd did not come downtown. The orators were mostly fluent Hibernians. They spoke with ease and with some command of forcible and accurate language, and with great intensity of feeling, but I saw no sign of any deep earnest sentiment among the mob. They hurrahed and yelled, but I think the great majority of the vagabonds considered themselves merely on a lark. It seemed to me that there was no reason to apprehend serious disturbance, *at present.* The precautions that have been taken seem superfluous, but they can do no harm.

Wood is frightened. He has raised a spirit he can't control, a spirit that threatens to turn and rend him. The orators of this morning denounced him as a humbug, promising aid but unable to afford it. He will probably lose more votes than he gains by this dodge. . . .

Poor Haight is suddenly stricken with disease in one of its most dreaded forms. They call it congestion of the brain, a circumlocution, I fear, for insanity.

November 13. News from Europe of the fall of Delhi, for which all lovers of Christianity and civilization may be thankful. Financially, the effect of this steamer's budget will probably be good. Our disasters of October have produced less disaster and panic on the other side than was expected. The suspension of Wall Street on October 13 and the manifesto of our judicial synod meet the approval of English editors. . . .

November 17. If the stock market be a reliable index of our condition, we're reacting toward prosperous times. There are other signs, too, of returning confidence and ease. But this will be an anxious winter at best.

November 21. Nothing very new downtown, except that the large intelligent and spontaneous assemblage of my fellow citizens in front of the Merchants' Exchange yesterday gave the best evidence of their sagacity by putting *me* on their "Executive Committee." *A bas* Fernando! *Vive* Tiemann![30] I shall commence a series of philippics. "Strong's First Oration against Wood." "Second ditto." "How long, O Fernando Wood, wilt thou abuse our patience?" Walked down with Jack Ehninger and George Anthon. Didn't do much in Wall Street. Walked up again; went with Ellie to the Philharmonic concert. Crowd. Clack. At last an excited individual, Teutonic, rose up in the midst of a dreary adagio on the violoncello by one of these inevitable Mollenhauers, and exclaimed with much emphasis, as if in continuation of some fruitless private remonstrance: "Well, I can talk, too. So that everybody can hear me! Is it not possible for us to have some place where we can *hear?*" and then subsided with like abruptness. People were still as mice in that neighborhood for some time. This self-sacrificing champion of silence should receive some testimonial. At these concerts especially, the music is drowned, or at least one's capacity for enjoying it is paralyzed with vexation, by incessant, ill-bred, and obstreperous gabblings.

November 23. Evening papers tell of grave disaster in England. Discount raised to 10 per cent; banks falling, and several great houses with connections here—Dennistouns, Hoge, and Dutilh. Dennistoun, Wood & Co. of this city must follow at once; William Hoge and the Dutilhs must soon follow. After dinner to meeting of the Anti-Wood Executive Committee at 505 Broadway; fifty or sixty present, Cooley in the chair, Abram S. Hewitt prominent. No long speeches. Earnest, energetic, and business-like. But I anticipate defeat. Fernando Wood is strongly posted; the Devil has not deserted him yet. He is sustained by the Roughs, as a body, and many decent people who condemn the man as he deserves will vote for him by way of protest against last winter's alleged invasion of municipal rights by the legislature. His supporters met in a large and enthusiastic pow-wow at Tammany Hall tonight notwithstanding the foul weather.

Judge Cowles and one or two others want me to take the Republican nomination for Alderman of the Eighteenth Ward and assure me of success, the Democrats being hopelessly split, and the Americans ready

[30] Daniel F. Tiemann, soon to succeed Wood as mayor, 1858–1859.

to endorse any decent Republican nominee. Much obliged (and much gratified by Judge Cowles's good opinion), but I'd rather not. Misery and anxiety during my term of office would shorten my life. Whatever good name I have would be lost, for one can't touch the city government without being defiled, and my business income would disappear, for the office would demand every minute of my time. Our condition of degradation and misgovernment makes it a crime for any man to decline any municipal office in which he can promote reformation, if it be possible for him to accept it. But I fear I've not the force or capacity to do any real service against the sons of Belial, and should injure myself by taking the place without accomplishing any good whatever.

November 24. Cold. Wall Street stagnant and stupid, though stocks still fly upward. Buttonholed by James W. Otis, in pursuit of knowledge about Hurlbut, who frequents his house. Enlightened him in guarded language, giving him the driest facts, using no epithets, and withholding names. The picture is effective without color. Legislative Committee (Trinity Church) at three; passing of bills mostly. Bishop De Lancey has published a brief but valuable review of last winter's performances at Albany. Came uptown with Gouverneur Ogden, who thinks we cannot safely engage a corps of instructors at present. His obstructiveness is probably right for once. Increase of debt is not convenient. Bad for Ehninger and D'Oremieulx. William Hoppin dined here and we went with Ellie to the Broadway Theatre. Charles Mathews very admirable in *Bachelor of Arts*, and so forth. He is far the first of the actors I've seen, quite free from conventionality and stage manner. All his pieces, moreover, seem refined and wholesome.

The anti-Wood demonstration tonight at the Academy of Music looked imposing from afar. Prospect of that scoundrel's defeat improves somewhat.

November 25. . . . English news. Fearful panic, and what is called suspension of the Bank of England; incorrectly so called, it would seem. A restriction on the issue of notes is removed. The issue is authorized without regard to the amount of bullion on hand, but it doesn't appear that the Bank has ceased to redeem its circulation or is likely to do so.

November 27. Just returned from the Broadway Theatre; Ellie, Jem Ruggles, George Anthon, and I. Sheridan's *The Critic*, somewhat embellished with interpolated jokes and made a broader burlesque than it was intended to be. Funny almost beyond endurance. I am faint, sore, and weary with excessive cachinnation; had laughed myself before the play was over into a state of prostration, mental and physical, a permanent, feeble, hysterical giggle. Some of Mathews' points (as Puff) were equal to anything in the text.

On our way home we met a procession of the *demos* marching down from the Academy of Music, where Fernando Wood has been assembling his blackguard backers. The procession was strong in numbers; "Sons of Belial flushed with insolence" and bad liquor, but, considering that Fernando Wood is the regular Democratic nominee, perhaps not larger than was to be expected.

November 30.   Dined with Miss Josephine Strong and Murray Hoffman and went to the Academy of Music; the season opening with *Robert Le Diable* and Formes making his debut here as Bertram. There was the biggest operatic crowd ever got together in New York—no standing place was unoccupied. Deutschland thronged the galleries and endorsed Herr Formes with vociferous bellowings. The opera was well done. LaGrange admirable in the part of Alice, as she is in everything.

The panic had left terrible distress in its wake. One symptom of the depression and misery was the forced sales of goods at heavily deflated prices; even the largest wholesale houses in the dry-goods trade, as Strong noted, had to get rid of their stock at cut prices by retail sales. Another symptom lay in the repeated and clamorous demonstrations on the part of the unemployed, who met in Tompkins Square, listened to radical speakers, and organized impromptu parades. Mayor Wood's proposal to employ the workless and starving laborers of the city upon the improvement of Central Park was perfectly sound; but he accompanied it with appeals to the rabble that greatly alarmed most citizens. Graft obviously permeated many departments of the city government, while crime and disorder continued to stalk abroad at noonday. Sometimes within twenty-four hours half a dozen murders or murderous assaults would be recorded. On the occasion described above (November 10), the Dead Rabbits and other disorderly elements seized control of part of the City Hall and held it for an hour, meanwhile mauling their opponents in and about that building. It was plain to decent New Yorkers that Wood ought to be driven from control.

A reform party in Tammany Hall, headed by Samuel J. Tilden, John McKeon, and Isaac V. Fowler, nominated Daniel F. Tiemann for mayor, and the best citizens rallied behind him. Great public meetings were held in his support. The immense gathering at the Merchants' Exchange on November 20th brought out a long list of leading New Yorkers as sponsors and speakers, and as Strong notes, chose an able executive committee. When the election took place on December 1st, Tiemann triumphed over Wood by more than 2,200 votes. He made an honest and fairly efficient executive, but his political inexperience proved a sad handicap. Meanwhile, panic and depression had swept Britain and France; the charter of the Bank of England had been suspended; and international factors combined with domestic distress to make the winter of 1857–58 a dark season.

December 1. I believe the King of the Dead Rabbits is overthrown. But it is well to be sanguine about nothing in advance of election returns; 2,500 votes out of 80,000 may be erased out of existence yet.

Day opened wet, but became bright and warm by ten o'clock. Voted in Twentieth Street. Neither there nor elsewhere could I see any indication of a heavy vote such as was expected and seems to have been polled.

General hopefulness among the anti-Woodians, who are ninety-nine out of one hundred among the people I know. Rumors during the day of rows and riots, and a detailed story current of Alderman Blunt being shot in the arm near the elbow by a Celt whose vote he took the liberty of challenging. All fiction—never did election pass off more peaceably, notwithstanding the earnestness of the contest, and the inflammable elements lying about loose. The police deserve credit.

George Anthon dined here, and we left at eight P.M. to explore, first taking Ellie to the Beldens' to spend the evening. Bulletins in the shop windows appeared by the time we reached Waverley Place, announcing large Tiemann majorities in sundry wards, and the crowds that were pouring down Broadway on the same errand with ourselves stopped and gazed and took pencil-memoranda and seemed comforted. At Stuyvesant Institute and at 505 Broadway, the enthusiastic Tiemannites had assembled in force and were jubilant over a majority estimated at from two to five thousand. Before we reached Canal Street the newsboys were tearing madly uptown with the "Extry *Tribune,* got the defeat of Mayor Wood!" We went to the corner of Fulton and Nassau and found the street densely filled with people watching the returns placarded as they came in on a big canvas screen put forth from the second story of the *Sun* office. Here Wood's friends were largely represented, and the crowd was sulky and silent. Through a continuous swarm of people, mostly very democratic, we made our way to Tammany. The worshipers at that shrine had just made up their minds that their Divinity was like to be dethroned, and Dead Rabbits, roughs, shoulder-hitters, soap-locks, and dock-rats were tumbling out in a dense and dirty stream, making night hideous with obstreperous remarks, generally vulgar, not to say coarse, and occasionally profane. Stinkom also felt itself defeated, but was not cast down and sought to hide its spirits by demonstrations of jollity. Only here and there on the corners from little knots of disappointed blackguards was "the voice of cussing heard and loud lament." The excited newsboys, screeching out the revelation of their extras, came in for a hearty malediction from more than one disgusted Woodite and were adjured to be silent.

The most reliable statement is 2,345 majority for Tiemann. It seems certainly somewhere between 1,800 and 3,000. Nothing is known as to the complexion of the Common Council. Probably bad.

The defeat of the Father of Dock Rats is a thing to be thankful for, though it's lamentable enough that so notorious and certified a cheat and swindler could get some 40,000 votes. But Tiemann's election doesn't purify the city government or prevent yet more outrageous increases of taxes. It is one step gained, and it shews the decent part of our population that whenever they please to be in earnest and to disregard party politics, they can control the city government. If they will prosecute the campaign vigorously and harmoniously, they can restore tolerable decency to our municipal administration, but many battles must be fought and won before that is attained.

December 3. Official returns of election not yet forthcoming. Some say that Fernando Wood means to play the same game he tried before—to hold over on the ground that the legislature had no power to shorten his term of office. Pretty steep that would be, after accepting the issue and making so hard a fight on it. Should he try it, he's not unlikely to be sent out of the world with a rope round his neck. But though he's not only knave but fool he will not be so insane. . . .

William Schermerhorn discoursed with me today about a proposed new Medical College in which Dr. Peters and Dr. Carroll are to be engaged, and which is to be somewhat eclectic in its teaching. Suggested that it be organized under the charter of Columbia College and made part of our proposed university. Conference with De Zeng, who doesn't anticipate a renewal of hostilities against Trinity Church at this session of the legislature; the *next* session, I should have said.

December 8. Trustees of Columbia College met yesterday. That board is fast sinking back into its normal condition of chronic coma, stupor, and lethargy, after a brief period of unnatural liveliness, produced by stimulants. Another Gibbs controversy must be got up, or the College will doze off for another hundred years. . . .

Lamentable to relate, moreover, the faculty contemplate Peck's appointment as instructor in drawing, so Jack Ehninger's game is up. Probably he is ill-qualified for a large (if not the larger) portion of the course proposed, which is mathematical and industrial rather than aesthetic.

December 12. Banks resumed today, perhaps prematurely, but I think not. Money is plenty and business stagnant, the majority of the human race being "in liquidation." An easy-money market don't prevent the old "Cohoes Company" from being very sick—sick unto dissolution I fear, with an awful outlook for its stockholders under the stringent personal liability clauses of its charter, granted in 1826. I'm one of them, as trustee for Mrs. Bedell, and may have trouble. Under Peter Remsen's will, James Strong's children own some $65,000 of this property, which clings to them like the garment of Nessus. Mrs. James Strong holds as much more—so it's a serious affair to that family. Attended a meeting of stockholders at Brown Brothers' office on Thursday and another today. All parties in very solemn earnest; Pete especially much exercised. Result of all the accounts and reports and so forth is that somebody must somehow raise $400,000 to save the concern from total wreck. . . .

Other News. Things in General. Kansas "bleeding"again. Battle begun in the Senate. Douglas secedes from the Administration and the South, and the *Tribune* takes him to its bosom and forgives all the past. Nothing material from the Utah expedition, which will winter this side of Salt Lake, and is in peril. It is far from strong enough for the work it has to do. It may well be cut off by the overwhelming force Brigham Young's horde of brutalized fanatics can bring to bear upon it, and we may well have a pretty serious task before us to suppress this new Religion of Sensuality and its truculent champions. It is fortunate for mankind that the political aspect of Mormonism brings it into conflict with government and enables us to wage war upon it without stirring up a clamor about religious persecution. Left to grow unchecked, it might spread as Mahometanism did. The name Mohammed was probably as trivial and commonplace to the neighbors and countrymen of that prophet a thousand years ago and upwards as the name Joe Smith is to us, and that this most beggarly of delusions should prevail over half the world would not be a greater marvel than the progress it has already made—would be less astounding than the reception of "Spiritualism" by so many thousands as a new Gospel or a Commentary on the old one. The President has removed John McKeon, U. S. Attorney, for opposing Wood, the regular Democratic nominee, and the Administration party in New York will not gain strength by his removal on that ground. Theodore Sedgwick is said to succeed him. He has been quite out of the profession for several years, and is very unlike to sympathize with the orthodox theories about Kansas and slavery.

December 16. Walked up, stopped at Society Library in University Place, and read the reviews. Details of late performances in and about Delhi, Lucknow, and Cawnpore are novel and interesting. The blowing of a Sepoy from the muzzle of a twelve-pounder must be a curious process.

December 24. Christmas Eve has been duly celebrated. I was stunned and sore with headache through the day, but it has passed off. Presents came in and went out. Mine to Ellie were an ermine cape and an ugly staring three-quarter length "imperial photograph" of my own delectable person. Johnny gave her a little brooch I got at Tiffany's on my way uptown and laboriously printed the inscription on its case—"Mama from Johnny"—his first communication of a fact by written language. . . .

Poor Bob LeRoy[31] is in sad trouble. Providence punished Bob's sinful old semi-millionaire of a father some months ago for the scandal he has caused all respectable people, and the aid and comfort he has given sundry lewd women in their evil practices, for driving Mrs. Fanny W. up Broadway in his own flashy wagon, and for various other outbreaks against decorum and good order. Providence, I say, punished "Black Jake LeRoy" for all this by inspiring him with an insane desire to double his half-million by putting it into a newly established stock-jobbing firm in Wall Street and with a strong delusion that Bob, being constituted a partner therein, would in some mysterious way become "a man of business" and keep an eye on the doings of the firm. Bob performed his duties by keeping diligently away from Wall Street all summer, and tying himself up with gambling debts to sundry "professional gentlemen." The other partners had a glorious time operating with their delightfully large capital, and would doubtless have realized a magnificent profit only they got caught in the crisis. The result is that Bob's magnificent expectations are gone. His father's fortune is cut down from thirty thousand per annum to ten, out of which that venerable sinner and the families of his two children must be supported. Bob and his pretty wife want at least twelve to live at all. They

[31] Further misadventures of Robert LeRoy (Columbia 1841) and his father, Jacob Rutgers LeRoy (Columbia 1813), are recorded in 1860.

are obliged to retrench sharply and extensively. Their handsome house is conveyed to his father in consideration of an advance to pay Bob's pressing debts, and he's to spend the winter with his wife's relatives in Philadelphia, whom he hates, and will thereafter live in the country or go to Europe, at least until his father's shaky estate can be nursed into convalescence.

December 25, FRIDAY.   Christmas night. Higby preached (at Trinity Chapel) a very fresh, genial, and touching sermon on the suggestive text "The young child and his mother," the most eloquent and original thing I've heard from him for years.

December 28.   Tonight is a great anniversary. Ten years ago this minute I was in Mrs. John A. Stevens' house, in Bleecker Street, at a big party, in the crowded supper-room, where poor Johnny Parish had lodged himself in a very strong position at the supper table, and Walter Cutting was vainly trying to do likewise and telling me that he thought the true way was for men to "fire and fall back," and Frank Griffin (I can see him now) was urging me to go to Europe and descanting on his emotions when he entered Rome. And I was thinking about the young lady in blue silk (or blue something) I'd been talking with so pleasantly and sympathetically before supper. God bless her; she's now my dear wife and the mother of my little boys upstairs. I remember just where she stood, at the end of a dance, when I plucked up a sheepish courage (doubting much whether she'd recognize me), and accosted the young lady and the precise topography of the sofa in the back parlor where we discoursed somewhat at length. Just at this hour, about one A.M., I was no doubt walking fast down Broadway with Johnny Parish and the biggest of cigars. I remember his facetious enquiry whether I had fallen in love with Miss Ellen Ruggles. Next time I saw her was New Year's Day, 1848, ten years ago this coming January 1st. I'd been in the house once before, at a "Bee" the preceding spring, of which I remember little but that I thought the young lady wonderful and delightful to behold, and that I contrived to knock over a glass that stood on the little table just by the front parlor door (only a wine glass) with a rose bud or two in it, and to reduce the same to small fragments. Like most shy and awkward people, I was inexpressibly humiliated and crushed, and the graceful simple way in which Miss Ellen passed over the accident only made my anguish more poignant. I expatiated on it, I remember, to George Anthon, who tried to console me. The party of which tonight is the decenniversary was my first interview after that distressing contretemps.

December 30.   I've nothing very novel to record. The public interests itself in the arrest of the great Nicaraguan filibuster, General Walker, which disgusts our fellow-citizens at the South; in the progress of the Kansas controversy; and in the probability of a post office at the lower end of the park. Its erection will do more to change the aspect of old New York than any one novelty introduced in my time. The view of the park and the City Hall from Broadway below Park Place is and long has been the best-known and most characteristic feature of the city. A large public building covering that open space will modify all the aspect of downtown. . . .

Tonight with Ellie, Miss Anne Leavenworth, and George Anthon to hear *Fidelio*, my first introduction to that work. House scantily filled and not at all interested. All the parts badly filled but Ricco, in which Formes was very strong indeed. Leonora was lubberly, and sang false. The other women and Florestan were hardly respectable—languid, faint, and feeble. Pizarro was absurd; one of his ambitious failures was greeted with a loud derisive giggle by the whole house, and caused mortal agony and shame doubtless to the unhappy wretch. . . . The Rev. Dr. Bellows was there tonight, and I'd a pleasant talk with him.

1858

UNIVERSITY STIRRINGS AT COLUMBIA · BATTLE OVER
LECOMPTON · THE ATLANTIC CABLE · REPUBLICAN
GAINS · THE STATEN ISLAND QUARANTINE RIOTS

———————··◦∞◦··———————

The national scene, as the year 1858 opened, was stormy. Though Kansas had shown plainly enough that in any fair vote slavery would be over-whelmingly defeated, the proslavery politicians in Washington and in the territory were determined to try to bring her into the Union as a slave state. President Buchanan lent himself to this effort, and in an elaborate message to Congress early in the year supported the admission of Kansas under the swin-dling Lecompton Constitution. On the general issue Stephen A. Douglas, as Strong notes, had already broken with him and had attacked the whole spurious project with the utmost energy and courage. A fiery debate broke out in Congress, and more than once the members actually exchanged blows. Meanwhile, some-thing close to rebellion had raised its head in Utah. The Mormon hierarchy, supported by the inhabitants, had refused to accept any government but that fur-nished by themselves. It was necessary to make a strong show of Federal strength, and General Albert Sidney Johnston was sent westward with troops to reach Salt Lake City in April. This show of energy was refreshing. It was paralleled by the equally energetic action of a naval force which, under Commander Paul-ding, had sailed in December, 1857, to Greytown, Nicaragua, broken up a camp of American filibusters who meditated a new campaign of conquest in Central America, and brought their leader, William Walker, back a prisoner to the United States. The slavery question steadily grew more acute, and the breach between the Douglas Democrats and Buchanan Democrats constantly became deeper.

But in New York the year began placidly enough. The city was fast recover-

ing from the panic. Large numbers of workmen were employed on Central Park,
and Frederick Law Olmsted, in charge of operations, instituted a sick-fund
society that took care of all who fell ill. By the liberal gifts of William B. Astor,
the Astor Library, founded by his father, was doubled in size and made more
accessible to students. Peter Cooper's new institute or Union was rapidly being
completed at what is now Cooper Square. The New-York Historical Society this
winter furnished a number of lectures by Edward Everett, George William
Curtis, Rembrandt Peale, Francis L. Hawks, and others—which attracted
much attention. Mrs. Fanny Kemble reappeared in the city and read from
Shakespeare to large audiences. A large number of charitable entertainments
were held to succor the poor, and Mayor Tiemann took a prominent part in
relief measures. Among the events of the early weeks were a series of inaugural
addresses by the new professors at Columbia, and a fervent religious revival.

January 3, SUNDAY. . . . Higby preached a splendid sermon at Trinity
Chapel this morning, dwelling much on a very commonplace but impressive fact, the infinite multitude of the men and women who have lived and
loved and worked and achieved and died on earth, since earth began, and
the utter extinction and oblivion of all, save one or two out of a million.

Near a dozen people here at tea and supper tonight. Among them the
ugly and uncouth but very clever J. Wrey Mould, architect and universal
genius.[1] James W. Gerard here this afternoon to talk of Mr. G. G——'s
affairs. Mr. G—— sent for him yesterday to say that he had reason to fear
that some of his children contemplated a commission of lunacy. He appeared
to Gerard to possess all his faculties, except memory, quite unimpaired.
John C. Hamilton[2] had a long talk with me yesterday on the same business
and thinks otherwise. It's hard to tell where the truth is, and as matters
stand now, I shall be careful to take no sides and keep myself uncommitted
in the future inevitable controversy. . . .

Hamilton spoke to me yesterday about the great Hurlbut also. Asked
my opinion of that gentleman, and on receiving it, intimated that he should
be henceforth excluded from the Palazzo Hamilton. It is easy to see what
has stirred him up at this late day. The *Times* has been critizing Hamilton's

[1] Jacob Wrey Mould, English architect (1825–1886), had been brought to New
York by Moses H. Grinnell in 1853 to design and build All Souls' Church; he stayed
on to design the Terrace, bridges, and other architectural structures in Central Park.

[2] John Church Hamilton (1792–1882), son of Alexander Hamilton, lawyer, and
author of a six-volume documentary biography, *History of the Republic of the U. S. as
Traced in the Writings of Alexander Hamilton.*

life of his father, volume 1, pretty unduly, and treating with contempt the theory of that very filial biography that all we commonly attribute to Washington was in fact done and devised by his private secretary. Hurlbut didn't write the article, but Hamilton is determined to visit his wrath on somebody connected with the paper that published it.

January 4 . . . Sorry to learn that Dr. Haight has lost ground since Dr. Cammann gave us so hopeful an account of his condition. Dr. Knox tells me that my reverend cousin, Thomas M. Strong of Flatbush, is attacked in a similar way, only with more manifest signs of softening of the brain. . . . Mr. Ruggles dined here today, and I spent the evening in the library with Ellie, who's not quite well tonight—honestly meaning to do some urgent work, but dawdling over books instead.

January 5. That firebrand Kansas threatens incendiarism again, and I fear we're on the eve of a critical period. General Dix tells me that the fractious cabal of fire-eaters, which has so much more power than it deserves, has made up its mind to disunion or the Lecompton Constitution. I doubt if the North can submit to the latter. Will it have the pluck to repress and punish any movement toward the former? Doubtful. Our very remarkable executive head is a mere man of expediencies, I fear, without principle (moral or political) and devoid of all decision and courage, a jelly-fish, able to sting a refractory officeholder, but able to do no more.

January 8, FRIDAY. The Twelfth Night celebration, Wednesday, by the Century at the new building in Fifteenth Street was very original and successful.[3] Went with Ellie, Miss Leavenworth, and George Anthon. The drawbacks were crowd and heat.

January 11. Century Club Saturday night. Annual meeting, and a full assemblage. Schell (the Collector)[4] made himself absurd and got up quite a little breeze by attacking the committee on new members for omitting to report on Judge Davies and Judge Roosevelt whom he'd nominated, and whom the committee were disinclined to recommend for election. He made a hard fight, with points of order and appeals from the chair (Verplanck), but the Centurions (query, Centuriators?) voted him down and overwhelmingly. Before the meeting I looked in awhile at the crowded Philharmonic Concert, and heard the *Eighth Symphony* and the *Staffa* overture. The last two movements of the former are a little shallow, con-

---

[3] The Century Club had removed in the spring of 1857 from its old home at 24 Clinton Place to a house at 42 (now 109) East Fifteenth Street, where it was to remain until early in 1891.

[4] Augustus Schell (1812–1884), Democratic politician, now Collector of the Port.

sidering it's Beethoven, but the first is most glowing and magnificent, and the second, the memorable little allegretto, an absolute gem without flaw.

January 18. William Aspinwall's alleged Murillo is at Williams & Stevens'. I doubt its authenticity, and can't detect its $12,000 worth of merit. What do they mean by calling it an "Immaculate Conception," and are there any paintings so styled? I suppose it to be an Assumption, and am confirmed therein by Kosciusko Armstrong, who ought to know.

January 22, FRIDAY. Heard *The Barber of Seville* refreshingly sung Tuesday night; Formes[5] superb as Don Basilio. Visit with Jones Rogers at his mamma's in Fifth Avenue to inspect that lady's aquaria, the finest in stock and condition that I've seen; especially strong in Actiniae.

January 25. General Scott yields to the prayers of the Administration and has made up his mind to go to California, there to organize a campaign against Utah. So his daughter, Mrs. Colonel Scott, reports to Murray Hoffman. The General is a grand old fellow, too old for the fatigue and exposure of such an expedition. It's not likely he will ever return. We must get up a graven image of him on the other side of Union Square to balance Colonel Jem Lee's copper Washington.

Much delighted with a child's book by Charlotte Yonge, *Landmarks of History;* not so grand as the Prescotts and Macaulays, but looking at things more nearly as they are.

January 27. Yesterday there was abundant rain. I spent most of the evening with Ellie and Miss Rosalie at Lewis Rutherfurd's pleasantly enough.[6] It was a small tea-drinking. As the sky was cloudy, the planets didn't "receive" and we postponed our visit to the new observatory. The Columbia College instruments are there and Rutherfurd works with them very diligently.

January 28. Big party comes off tomorrow evening on these premises. Would 'twere well over.

January 30. Party unanimously adjudged a grand success. All the people came that were wanted, about 150. There was no crowd, and no contretemps, thanks to Mrs. Ellie's judicious generalship. Everybody seemed comfortable and everybody danced. Even I "stayed for the German." . . .

Made Belmont's acquaintance and found him quite disposed to be pleas-

[5] Karl Johannes Formes (1816–1889), German singer.
[6] Lewis M. Rutherfurd had built a small observatory at his premises on Second Avenue at Eleventh Street; launching his pioneer work in astronomical photography, he obtained his first photographs of the moon this year.

ant and free from any offensive millionaire-isms.[7] His wife is very beautiful. One of the very prettiest persons was poor Miss Caroline Strong. . . .
Miss Annie Leavenworth seemed to enjoy herself as heartily and unaf-
fectedly as when plunging about after mosses in woods last summer. Mrs.
Wright and Mrs. Schermerhorn and Mrs. Kuhn and Miss Serena Jones
and others were all very amiable, and the evening was in a high degree
satisfactory. It is understood to have been also "brilliant."

February 1, MONDAY.   Most imbecile Columbia College meeting this
afternoon; literally nothing done. We are anxious to teach French, and to
appoint a professor of that dirty dialect with duties and a salary. Thirty
or forty of our undergraduates want to be taught it. But we can't gratify
them. Ten or fifteen years ago, we gave the nominal appointment to a
man named Berteau who has emigrated to Chicago and set up a school
there. As he had never done any work for us or received any money, his
change of domicile was undiscovered and his appointment was never formally revoked, and it now stands as an insuperable obstacle in the way of
our employing any one else. We discussed the various ways of getting
around it for two hours this afternoon rather as Parliament debated over
James II after his change of domicile, but we could come to no result.
Could not decide how to get over the formalities, and we remain paralyzed
as respects the French language. Our venerable board is tied hand and foot
by the enchantments of a mythical Frenchman in Chicago. It's stated by
physiologists, I believe, that if you put a bird of the goose species on a
table and draw a charcoal line slowly and solemnly on the board before it,
the animal is powerless to cross the barrier and will stand still till it dies of
starvation and idiocy. But Heaven forbid I should compare Betts and Ogden
to a goose. Anderson was, of course, subtle, plausible, and earnest against
any action.

February 2.   Very busy day in Wall Street; Trust Company meeting.
Our losses by the late crisis seem wonderfully small. With millions invested
(and near a million and a half called in to pay off two deposits since
October), we've but $20,000 of suspended debt, of which one-quarter is
considered a liberal allowance for probable loss.

February 5.   At Mozart Hall last night was a scanty audience but

[7] August Belmont had returned from his service as minister at The Hague; all
accounts agree on his personal charm. He was influential in Democratic councils, and
a supporter of Douglas in the great schism developing in the party. His wife was a
daughter of Commodore Matthew Calbraith Perry.

rather larger than I expected.[8] Its name is rather suggestive of lager-beer saloons and lust-gartens, but it is a respectable room for concerts and meetings, in Broadway opposite Bond Street. The students were present in force and acted as *claqueurs*. William Betts, Esq., LL.D., opened the performances with a very genteel allocution or palaver of about an hour on the present position of the College and its contemplated improvements. Though utterly commonplace and trivial, it was an *infuriating* speech to hear, from the ineffable suavity and self-satisfaction with which the orator enunciated his truism and platitudes, the majestic consciousness of strength and wisdom and the serene condescending benevolence that irradiated his countenance and spoke in his modulations, and the beggarly feebleness and triviality of all he said. "In the Name of the Prophet, Figs!" Joy's inaugural address was a rather incoherent succession of notes on the history of chemistry, without much point or depth. But it was written and delivered in an unpretending modest way, and was quite cooling and delightful after Betts's grandiose twaddlings. Poor Betts! . . .

The Philistines at Albany are lifting up their horn once more. One Becker, an "American," of Ulster, has brought into the Assembly a bill to repeal the Act of 1814. We telegraphed up at once and got it referred to the Judiciary Committee. It was referred on Winthrop Chanler's motion. I hear he's all right on that question. What this movement means no one knoweth. Bleecker tells me he's confident there's a log-rolling coalition between the Broadway Railroad gang and our enemies and that the allied forces will prove formidable. Mark Spencer is at Albany on some job or other. Bishop Potter is confident that neither Muhlenberg nor Minturn know anything of Becker—so he told me last night. . . . Perhaps Becker is merely put up to it by the lobby, in order to get up a battle in which there will be work for the *condottieri*, or he may merely want to be bought off. I don't myself believe that Minturn is engaged in this, still less that Bradish has relapsed.

Went to the circus Wednesday afternoon with Johnny, Kate-lein (Catkins), Mr. Ruggles, Hoffman, and Ellie.

February 9. To Mozart Hall tonight for Professor Davies' inaugural. He drew a good house. Talked mostly about mathematical language and

---

[8] The new Columbia professors were now to deliver (after the English fashion) inaugural lectures in this hall usually given over to political conclaves. By this time the changed curriculum was in full force. To the end of the junior year students pursued much the same set of rigidly prescribed studies as formerly. In the senior year they had a choice of three departments—"Letters," "Science," and "Jurisprudence."

logic. That field being rather dry and chalky, he strove to relieve it by sundry parenthetical gushes of eloquence, ornate tropes, rhetorical artifices, and flights of fancy, not at all in the key of $x + y$, and generally calculated to excite a feeling of "gooseflesh." He turned on a tremendous head of elocutionary steam at his exordium, and kept increasing its pressure down to his peroration, and on the whole, piled up the agony beyond what was called for by any known function of x. But deducting the platitudes and the bad taste, it was a very respectable address. . . .

February 15, MONDAY.   Nairne delivered his inaugural Thursday night. It was very good as a sermon, though unconscionably long; near two hours. Included some very good things and much thought. Was quite glowing and a little wordy, and excellently well delivered.

With Ellie tonight to hear one of the Rev. Dr. Bellows's lectures on "Pauperism and Crime."[9] He blew well; his lecture was pleasant and instructive. But it is very curious to observe the un-practicality of all sermons, essays, and lectures by men of Bellows's school, Yankee-Arianism, when they undertake any practical subject. Channing, their great father, exhibits the peculiarity most distinctly. They are sensible, plausible, candid, subtle, and original in discussing any social evil or abuse. But somehow they don't get *at* it. You feel that you have heard or read a very clever and entertaining paper, embodying a good deal of clear and deep thought, and you ask *what shall I do?* and pause for a reply, and pause in vain. If you get a reply that seems definite, it is generally resolvable by analysis into some formula like "Lift yourself up by the waistband of your own breeches." "Move your limbs only once and your dead palsy will be cured." Convince your "dangerous classes" that honesty is the best policy, and they will become useful citizens. But Bellows is far sounder and wiser than the great majority of his school. Its defects are mitigated in him by his native masculine common sense, which is strong enough to neutralize a good deal of his Unitarianism.

February 17.   Lieber's address tonight (went with Ellie and George Anthon, who dined here) was the best of the four. Embodied much thought and clever illustration. Unlike the others, it was not delivered from manuscript.

February 21, SUNDAY.   Heard the Rev. Dr. Hobart this morning. Lieber and others here this evening. Lieber complains much of the Colum-

---

[9] Henry W. Bellows, the before-mentioned Unitarian minister of the Church of All Souls on Fourth Avenue, was soon to play a much larger role in Strong's life.

bia College faculty, which is settling a scheme of post-graduate instruction, or so-called "University" studies, to be submitted to the trustees. He thinks their plans hopelessly impractical, and he is probably right.

Apropos of individual folly, Charles Mathews has just married that showy little piece of harlotry Mrs. Lizzie Weston Davenport, with whom he's been playing at Burton's, and who's just divorced on her husband's suit.[10] He's quite betwattled and fascinated by her. The marriage is a mere nullity, but before it was solemnized, the lady had shewn her lover, as she had shewn many others, that she cared little for forms and ceremonies. It's a pity, but I suppose his first wife, Madame Vestris, was not much better.

February 25.   At Mr. Ruggles's awhile tonight to meet Governor Hunt and his wife. Their little boy was with them, now nine years old; a remarkably handsome, intelligent child. Discoursed with Mr. Ruggles of the post-graduate organization, which subject comes up at our next College meeting. I anticipate no result. We have to create the demand for higher education as well as the supply.

Professor Davies, just before marching in to deliver his inaugural, addresses the janitor: "Mr. Weeks, Mr. Weeks, did you light the two candles on the table where I stand? The play of the countenance is everything." (!!) To appreciate that observation one must be vividly conscious of Professor Davies's physiognomy, the ugliest mug extant, and capable of no expression but that of a shark. We have got to build our "University" out of queer, questionable material, and among our artificers and chief workmen are Gouverneur Ogden and Betts. It's an undertaking about which judicious men should not be sanguine.

March 2.   At yesterday's Columbia College meeting they elected old Spring chairman, and filled the two vacancies in the board with Rev. Mr. De Witt (as old Knox's successor), and Lewis Rutherfurd. Rutherfurd is not a bad appointment on the whole; very good in some respects, very dubious in some other respects. De Witt can't be a worse trustee than his departed brother dominie and may be better. . . .

Rutherfurd was elected by eight votes to John A. Dix's seven. Mr. Ruggles, King, and Bradford voted with the majority for the sole reason that Dix, having just signed a call for a pro-Lecompton meeting, is unfit to be a trustee of a college that teaches political ethics. I like Dix, and am

[10] Charles James Mathews (1803–1878), the popular English comedian, had first married his manageress, Lucia Elizabeth Vestris.

nowise excited about bleeding Kansas, but the reason doesn't lack plausi-
bility.[11]

March 3. . . . Mr. Ruggles is in labor with the post-graduate course. I
fear the result will be *null* for many years to come. If we had the institution
organized, fifty professors of the first force from Oxford or Boston in position with their lecture room swept and garnished, how many pupils would
matriculate? How many A.B.'s just set free from college would consent to
give two years more to "University" studies? We should produce less than
one Master of Arts per annum. This people is not yet ripe for higher education. The ingenuous youth of the Fifth Avenue wouldn't take it as a gift
without money and without price. Could we afford to lay out $10,000 per
annum in stipends to clever young men and hire a dozen post-graduate
students every year to stay in college and be pumped into, we might accomplish somewhat. Specimens of higher training thus produced would shew
people that something was to be gained by devoting an additional year or
two to study. But this outlay we cannot afford.

Therefore, I believe our only practicable road toward a "University"
is somewhat like this:

1. Establish a Law School and a School of Applied Science—on such a
scale and with such appliances that they will plainly produce thoroughly
trained lawyers, engineers, metallurgists, and so forth, and that young
men can acquire in them more knowledge of the sort that brings position
and profit than they can get anywhere else. Exhibit a seductive bait of
tangible material advantage, and you will catch students.

2. Having caught them, liberalize both schools by additional courses of
study, optional or imperative, gradually expanding and improving them,
and in effect saying: We will furnish you with all the armory of the mere
lawyer, on condition that you become also accomplished in kindred but
higher pursuits. We will qualify you to construct railroads and superintend
mines better than anyone else, if you will consent to go a little faster and
submit to a thorough education in liberal science.

But any tentative approach toward one object by indirection will find no
favor with the board. We must set about establishing at once, and *in vacuo*,
something like the skeleton of a complete "University" system, with all
its parts harmonious on paper; which will be about as sensible and hopeful
an undertaking as the attempt to produce an oak tree by constructing it

[11] This is evidence of the deep feeling excited even in conservative Northern
circles by the effort of the Buchanan Administration to ram the fraudulent proslavery
Lecompton Constitution down the throats of the Kansans.

instead of planting the acorn and letting it grow, and so bending and and pruning the young plant that it may grow according to our wants.

March 7, SUNDAY.   Spent half an hour last night at the Philharmonic concert, crowded and garrulous, like a square mile of tropical forest with its flocks of squalling paroquets and troops of chattering monkeys. Young America loves the Philharmonic. Acres of pretty little half-fledged girls frequent those solemnities for the sake of Mr. Timm or Mr. Eisfeld, who's teaching them music, and they are followed by cohorts of ill-bred juvenile males, whose gabble drowns the music. I heard part of a pretty symphony by Hiller, "Voi che sapete," and "Vedrai, Carino" (substituted when the former was encored), a dismal clarinet and orchestra concerto, and Beethoven's overture to *Coriolanus,* which I could not comprehend. Thereafter to the Century Club: Wolcott Gibbs, Van Wagenen, Rutherfurd, Cozzens, Verplanck, and others.

March 8.   At our Columbia College meeting at two P.M. there was barely a quorum, but the session was satisfactory and brought forth good fruit. All of us are of one mind about the outline and main features of the "university" experiment; all are tired of talking and committees of inquiry and "outlines of statutes" and want a beginning made without further delay. So the whole subject was referred to a good committee (the Bishop, Mr. S. B. Ruggles, Allen, Betts, Van Wagenen, and Torrey, I believe), with instructions to report a plan at next meeting that can be set a-going forthwith, if possible; at all events next October. Came up-town with King and Mr. Ruggles in a Third Avenue car with some four-score insiders, a Black-Hole atmosphere, and three stout gentlemen trampling on my feet, as oxen tread out corn. After dinner I sacrificed myself to the General Good and made my way downtown to Fulton Street and a Trinity Church vestry meeting, where I just made up a quorum. The meeting being so thin, we postponed electing a clerk for the comptroller. R. H. Ogden and Livingston are in great league over the claims of their candidate, one Dayton, who will probably be beat by the Standing Committee's candidate, one Duncan, a rather "ornary cuss," I suspect; but the other man would not suit our case. . . .

March 11.   No news except from England, where Palmerston is down, and Derby is up. But he won't hold office long. Armstrong (K.) and Murray Hoffman dined here yesterday, and we started thereafter on a demonological tour, and sought out a woman who hath a familiar spirit.

As during the spring of 1857, Strong was interested in spiritualism, and made occasional experiments with it. They convinced him that, as he writes, "these manifestations are made up of charlatanry and lies, with a small possible percentage of some uncanny physical and nervous agency." He adds: "It is only because this delusion is working on so large a scale and is so formidable a fact that I take any interest in it." His séances with a male medium named Redman in the spring of 1857, in which various friends participated, had furnished a good deal of evidence of telepathy or mind-reading. Now he, Armstrong, and Murray Hoffman went to the house of a Mrs. Brown. She was more intelligent than Redman, but the first sitting produced nothing of consequence. A later sitting (March 14) again produced evidence of mind-reading. "After one of the ghosts had distinctly committed itself to its identity and antecedents by a series of answers, the accuracy of which did it credit, I questioned it about an imaginary transaction, fixing my thoughts on an answer—and that answer was given with great precision."

March 14, SUNDAY. Joy is in a sort of squabble with the chemical committee of the board. Some criticism has been made on the catalogue of chemical materials he proposed to order, and he is affronted. Among the items was so many grammes of anaconda's feces from Paris, for the manufacture of uric acid, at quite a "high figure." Why not apply to the anaconda at Barnum's? Why should not the College keep its own anaconda and produce its own stercoration? Let domestic industry be encouraged. Is it certain that we could not get along with Gouverneur Ogden as a substitute?

March 15. The great Hurlbut, who has for some months been missing, has reappeared and is going to Europe, "probably never to return." So mote it be.

March 19. Walked to West Thirtieth Street at ten tonight to escort Ellie home from what I supposed was to be the smallest of aesthetic and family tea-drinkings at the Toppans'. (Mrs. Toppan is a first cousin of Mr. Ruggles.) Found some fifty people solemnizing "the lancers," and stayed till midnight, mostly in discourse with Mrs. John Sherwood, Mrs. Judge Ruggles, and Ellie's grandmamma, who seems well again and has renewed her youth. Mrs. Sherwood and the Judges were very gracious and agreeable, and nothing went wrong, but I've come home tired and bored and blue and in an evil temper. The Toppans' house is pleasant. They have filled it with nice pictures and engravings and other indicia of civilization; they have lived much abroad and seem uncommonly refined and amiable people.

March 24. People talk in these days mostly of:

1. "Lecompton." It has just scratched through the Senate, after a tough struggle, in a dilapidated and disreputable state. Opinions differ as to its fate in the lower house, but I predict that the Administration will triumph and the Senate will pass without material amendment. Maybe the world will come to an end in consequence, but I shall be surprised if it does, at least for some little time.

2. The "revival," which is spreading over the country and attracting more and more attention every day. One should think and speak cautiously of any thing which so many good men receive as a special manifestation of the Holy Spirit, but I confess that this movement does not commend itself to me. It is becoming daily more and more heated and morbid. Irreverence, presumption, indecency, and other symptoms of a mere epidemic religious fever multiply as the revival develops. I've visited one or two of its central points (John Street Church or meeting-house, and so on) for a few moments, and what I heard seemed to me no doubt well meant, but the profane and mischievous babblings of blind, foolish, shallow, vulgar Pharisaism, trying to hide its "I am holier than thou" under certain formulas of self-contempt; proud of its own admission that it is humble. The great object of the meeting seems to be to drug men up to a certain point of nervous excitement and keep them there. Was told today on good authority of an incredible hymn said to be popular among "revived" Methodists, of which this is one verse:

> Ye Saints rejoice, give cheerful thanks,
> For Awful Gardner's joined your ranks.
> And, while the lamp holds out to burn,
> There still is hope for *Patrick Hearne*.

Its author is said to be that most ferocious and vindictive personage, "Dr. Francis Bacon." More people will be harmed by the revival than benefited, I think.

Was at the Broadway Theatre this afternoon with Johnny and little Lucy Derby to see the grand *Relief of Lucknow* performance, with the real elephant and all the horses; not legitimate drama exactly, but the intensity of its commonplace and the extravagance of its clap-trap made it comical. Johnny was moved even to tears by the grand concluding scene where the "Demon of Cawnpore" (Nona Sahib, to wit), having ordered all the other English prisoners to be instantly put to death with frightful torments, invites Colonel Somebody to renounce the service of the English Dogs and enter his. "Do it, or your wife and daughter shall perish before your eyes." Colonel smites his forehead and undergoes a tremendous mental struggle. Wife bids him not hesitate. Colonel, encouraged and fortified, says: "Noblest of women, I will now shew myself worthy to be thy husband. Inhuman Monster, I defy thee." Inhuman Monster sends for elephant. "The child shall be the first." Child asks her mamma, with touching simplicity, "whether that man ever says his prayers." Enter elephant. The dumb slave in charge of that pachyderm, having been aided with cold water and human sympathy by the touchingly simple child while confined and pinioned as a spy (in Act 1), pleads in most moving pantomime for the preservation of that innocent. Demon of Cawnpore shrieks infuriated: "She shall die. I have said it. Bismillah." Elephant, subtly instigated by dumb slave, instead of trampling on interesting infant picks her up with his trunk, gives her a cockhorsical see-sawing ride in the air, and exits with her to a place of safety. Baffled miscreant says: "Ho! My guards!" Heroic wife of colonel becomes suddenly excited and listens and says "Dinna ye hear it?" and so forth. Demon in human form, with a vague presentiment of something wrong, strides uneasily about his musnud. Row and fusillade. Enter British soldiers with lavish expenditure of real powder; enter Sepoys on their side who tumble down and are prodded by victorious Britons. Single combat of gallant colonel with Demon of Cawnpore, and grand *final tableau.*

All this was to John R. Strong a new revelation of profound dramatic power. His face worked and his eyes filled, and he was ashamed, and got up an apocryphal story of sick headache. But the sick headache had vanished when we reached home, and he was full of chatter and enquiry about the marvels he had witnessed.

March 27.   Business is dismally stagnant (as our approaching quarterly office dividend will shew), and there is little sign of its revival. That fact has much to do with the existing "Revival of Religion." People miss their wonted excitement in Wall Street and seek a substitute in the sensations of a prayer meeting.

The Roman Catholics, however, attribute the movement to Aspinwall's importation of "The Immaculate Conception"—to the Madonna of Murillo, more or less authentic, working even upon heretics, graciously, though from the nature of the subject, imperfectly. I don't hear that the picture has yet winked at Williams & Stevens. "Spiritualists" say the revival is merely one among many features of the great manifestation vouchsafed to man in these days. "The Unseen World is drawing nearer, too, and acting on us more directly."

Hawks has disgusted sundry of his congregation by coquettings with Dissent, and has degraded the Lent Services of Calvary Church into a quasi-revival. At Tyng's (St. George's) there is revival *allegro con strepito*. "Many of the congregation both male and female" are said to be "enquiring." Enquiring! What has their rector been about so many years? They know full well what they ought "to do to be saved."

March 28, SUNDAY. I turned over the *Atlantic Monthly*, the much-praised flower of Boston intellect.[12] Except Holmes's "Autocrat of the Breakfast Table," its contents seem rather poor stuff. Also the last number of Thackeray's *Virginians*, which promises to win its author no new laurels and reads like the handiwork of a good imitator. . . . Have been turning over Croker's *Essays on the French Revolution*,[13] just received; very interesting by reason of the large extracts from obscure contemporary pamphlets and the like which their author produces. Very one-sided, but is there any other side? Written in the spirit of an old Red Sandstone Tory of 1800. But is not that the only spirit in which one can rightly treat of those devilish saturnalia? Were they not in truth the last great Avatar of Satan?

The "Great Revival," as the newspapers termed the religious excitement of 1858 (some comparing it to the Great Awakening of Colonial days), continued all spring. Its origins were probably connected with the great panic of 1857 and the ensuing depression. But in part it had been systematically worked up. A meeting of about two hundred ministers of various denominations, but chiefly Presbyterians, had been held in Pittsburgh late in 1857 and had made preparations for the movement. The revival created a fervent exaltation in city after city, from Portland and Boston to Philadelphia and Baltimore. In New York many churches were thrown open nightly; advertisements of sermons and prayer-meetings filled the shop-windows; and religious handbills were scattered in the omnibuses and ferries and on the streets. Tracts were distributed in huge editions. A plan of "Systematic Visitation" was adopted under which clergymen

[12] The first issue of the *Atlantic* had appeared late in October, 1857, dated November. With a list of contributors including Longfellow, Whittier, Emerson, Holmes, Hawthorne, Lowell (the first editor), Motley, and Mrs. Stowe, it at once out-distanced other American monthlies.

[13] By John Wilson Croker (1780–1857), the English Conservative politician and editor of Boswell's *Johnson*.

*prowled the streets, rang doorbells, inquired anxiously about the spiritual con-
dition of the inmates of each house, and exhorted them to attend church. Numerous
converts were made in unexpected quarters, and men of notoriously ungodly
habit, like the "Awful Gardner" named above, came to the altar-rails.*

*In Washington the efforts of the Buchanan Administration to push through
Congress a bill for the admission of Kansas under the proslavery Lecompton
Constitution had now raised the most passionate storm. Stephen A. Douglas put
the unanswerable argument in one sentence: "The Lecompton Constitution is
not the act of the people of Kansas, and does not embody their will." Buchanan
had used the executive patronage to force passage of the bill and to ruin Douglas's
influence. On March 23, the Senate accepted the measure by a vote of 33 to 25.
The measure then went to the House, where the Democrats had a decisive majority. One heated session followed another. Keitt of South Carolina attacked Grow
of Pennsylvania on the floor. During one night session a score of members
engaged in a general affray. On April 1, one of the Douglas Democrats offered
an amendment providing that the Lecompton Constitution should be submitted
to a vote of the people; and that if it were rejected, the people should then be
authorized to form a new Constitution and elect a state government under it.
Against this, the Buchanan Democrats rallied; but it was carried in the House,
120 to 112. The Senate thereupon refused to accept it. Ultimately the Administration majority in both houses carried the plan proposed by Representative
English, which offered Kansas a large grant of land, provided that the people
of Kansas should vote on the offer; and stipulated that if they accepted it, Kansas
should be admitted into the Union under the Lecompton Constitution, but if
they rejected it, the territory could not become a state until its population reached
the number required for a Representative (93,000). In effect, this offered the
Kansans a bribe to accept a proslavery Constitution.*

April 2.   Good Friday. Ellie being not yet at large, I went to St.
Paul's this morning instead of our usual Trinity Chapel. Much has
changed and gone since the last time I attended service there in May,
1846. From my earliest remembrance down to the consecration of Trinity
Church, I went to St. Paul's every Sunday with my mother and Aunt
Olivia and poor invalid Aunt Jane, who came sometimes, though seldom,
in the afternoon. But dwelling on those old memories is bad for one constituted as I am.

St. Paul's was crowded and what's very unusual (especially at a week day service) at least four-fifths were men—downtown clerks and business people. Vinton preached, tolerably. He and Morgan Dix have worked there to much purpose. When they began, that chapel was almost deserted. . . .

News from Washington important. The knell of our liberties is understood not to have tolled yet. We are all supposed to be rejoicing over a great crisis happily past. Perhaps we are. Executive dictation, pro-slavery propagandism, and so forth, by an uncorrupted and so forth. Infamous invasions of popular right, nigger-driving oligarchy, fraud, violence, and the border ruffians of Missouri are put down, rebuked, driven home to the obscene dens from which they emerged, and so on, by and so on rising in its majesty. Hoo-ray! By 120 to 112 the House has so amended the Senate Lecompton bill as to provide for submission of the Lecompton Constitution to the people of bleeding Kansas. May that hemorrhagic territory rest in peace! But I fear it won't, and that old Buchanan & Co. won't give it up without further contest. And the chances are in favor of Buchanan's success after all. Three or four dirty little Representatives can surely be bought off by executive patronage.

April 7, WEDNESDAY. Columbia College meeting (Monday), busied mostly with university-building. We founded our Oxford. The recommendations of Mr. Ruggles's committee were adopted with entire unanimity and referred back to that committee with power. Our programme with its three schools is far too elaborate. The full-grown plant we are sticking into the ungenial soil of New York will take no root. The utmost I hope is that when it withers and perishes it may leave some nucleus or germ surviving whence there may be natural development and expansion hereafter. Our experiment will begin failing at the commencement of the next term, October at latest.

Lewis Rutherfurd took his seat, and Knox's successor, the Rev. Mr. De Witt, a Dutch dominie of high caste and real merit. He looked fat and wise and good and sour (*acetic* not *ascetic*). He is not lovely to behold, for the sanctity and solemnity of his aspect might easily be mistaken for sea-sickness, but I suspect he'll be found an improvement on his predecessor. The Rev. Mr. Spring, our new chairman, is a great gain. . . .

We must set up a new debt for our university, of $4,000 or $5,000 per annum, till the Botanic Garden lots come into the market. And I fear they will produce less than we count on. Perhaps the Fifth Avenue above Forty-second Street will command lower prices, and cease to be the special line of costly improvement. The Reservoir will make a most manifest

solution of continuity in its lines of brown stone, and by the time buildings have reached that latitude I think the frontage on the Central Park
will be more coveted by millionaires. . . .

Revival less talked of. Lecompton in *statu quo.* Significant that the
Herald recommends the Senate to concur with the House "and thus secure
the Administration its triumph!"[14]

April 10. I could not refuse the invitation of today's sunshine. I
strolled out with George Anthon on some frivolous pretext or other,
walked farther than I intended, and roamed far away, at last, among the
remote regions of Southern Brooklyn, near Gowanus and the place where
was of old the Penny Bridge. The growth of that region is marvelous. A
great city has been built there within my memory. The compact miles of
monotonous, ephemeral houses which one overlooks from the Greenwood
Cemetery ridge impress me as does some great reef half bare at low tide
and dense with barnacles. Each is a *home,* each is throwing out its pre-
hensile cilii into the great sea, with better fortune or worse, good investments or bad, credit or disrepute, progress up or down. Each has (or
had) its children, its young girls, its boys hopeful or otherwise, its own
domestic history and prospects, its memories of joy and sorrow, each is
an epitome of human life within each shabby domicile. . . .

Thomas H. Benton is dead.

April 15. Last night I went to one of the Rev. Dr. Bellows's recep-
tions, pleasant enough, having first spent an hour at the Academy of
Design with Hoffman, Anthon, and others. Stopped there again on my
way uptown this afternoon; saw Mignot, Bob Messenger, and others,
and confirmed my first impression that the exhibition compares very
favorably with those of former years. The number of inoffensive and
respectable pictures is quite large. They are too many to enumerate. We
went through the rooms critically and discussed the relative merits and
respective weak points of clever Niminy and talented Pimini. There exist
problems more momentous perhaps. Have we any artists, or are they all
picture-wrights more or less dexterous? A question not to be asked! Jack
Ehninger's large picture is his best work yet in technical merit, among
the very best in the collection. But there are so many not near so good
that interest one so much more. One doesn't care for his personages,
they are unreal and phantasmagorial. The group is an opera tableau
dexterously transferred to canvas. The artistic lover is manifestly doing
an impassioned tenor air, which the old gentleman (basso) doesn't hear.

[14] James Gordon Bennett's *Herald* was espousing the Buchanan Administration.

It's a scene from the *Barber*, substituting painter for music teacher. Jack receives many compliments on it, for which substance he has intense elective affinity.

April 17, SATURDAY. On my way up stopped at Estey's factory to hear a first-class organ just completed and destined for some Presbyterian conventicle at San Francisco. . . .[15] Our big party is to be Monday night, and I fear it will prove dreary.

April 21. Monday night's grand soirée was brilliant and delightful; that's an instance of discomfort skillfully mitigated. I don't think our one hundred and twenty or one hundred and fifty guests suffered beyond the inevitable doom they brought on themselves by coming. Rooms were too hot, but not overcrowded. Supper was good. Under Mrs. Ellie's generalship everybody was provided with somebody to talk to all the time. So the maximum of human felicity which a talking party aims at producing was fully attained. What the talk thus facilitated was reasonably worth is an independent branch of the enquiry on which I don't propose entering at present. The elder respectabilities honored us; that is, His Eminent Respectability Luther Bradish, Esq., George Folsom and wife, that venerable man Gerard the Elder, old Leavenworth, the Lycurgic D. D. Field, the Rev. Mr. Weston, Irreverent or *Soi-disant* Reverend Bellows, Charles King, Professor Lieber, ancient Professor Jem Renwick, Bidwell, distinguished Bancroft and his wife, General Dix, and others whom to receive and feed is creditable. By coming, they practically called me Rabbi, Rabbi, with respectful emphasis. To be so addressed is soothing and grateful now, as it was 1,800 years ago. Rossiter, Kensett, Mignot, Darley, and other artists assisted, whom it's not only creditable but aesthetic and refined to have at one's parties.

Also, there were superb Mrs. Jacob Little, Miss Lyman, Professor Joy and wife, the Rev. Mr. Edward Anthon and wife, old Mrs. Anthon, Miss Annie Leavenworth, the poetic Tuckerman, Mr. and Mrs. Isaac Wright, the Kuhns, the Schermerhorns, Pete Strong and his beautiful wife, Judge Daly and Mrs. Maria Daly, and Miss Maggie Lydig and her mamma, and others.

April 23. Warm and wet. George Anthon has been dining here. Jem came in afterwards. . . . Last night at the "Bachelor's Ball" at Niblo's, where was "everybody" that "anybody" knows, blooming freely in an atmosphere of 110° Fahrenheit, containing fifty per cent of carbonic acid

---

[15] Jacob Estey (1814–1890), after creating a successful organ factory at Brattleboro, had placed a branch agency in New York.

and vaporized perspiration, with an orchestra at least threefold too power-ful, tooting, bellowing, and braying Lydian measures, and stunning the crowd into stupefied bewilderment. No wonder the Wedding Guest "beat his breast" when he "heard the loud bassoon." How many hours could a man of average power of physical endurance and free from latent disease survive under this terrible combination of nervous irritants and stimulants, the crash of brassy music, glare of gas, and a shifting, fluc-tuating, high-colored crowd? Not many, even without the terrible drain on the vital forces produced by a constant agonized, fruitless effort to evolve commonplaces and secrete small-talk. . . . The grand saloon, though sultry, mephitic, and crowded, was brilliant and pretty to behold, and there were tons of pretty young girls in fresh, gauzy, spring-suggest-ing toilettes, enjoying themselves very heartily. Ellie had a particularly nice time.

Grand demonstration last night by the exiled Polish, French, German, and Italian patriots now domiciled in the city in honor of the pious memory of Orsini and his colleague, who killed a dozen inoffensive people by hurling explosive projectiles into a crowd for the chance of killing Louis Napoleon and his pretty Empress, and who were, there-for, most justly guillotined. It was a great scandal and disgrace, but I suppose nobody had the right to suppress it. I saw a little of the per-formance in Union Square, and the glaring torches and the great black "catafalque" made it quite imposing to look at. But the Reds were not numerically strong, hardly two thousand, I guess. Lookers-on generally expressed contempt and disgust. Continental liberalism is a specimen of evil as nearly free from adulteration of good as is to be found anywhere. Chartists are saints beside Carbonari.

As I expect accessions to the aquarium population, I here record the present condition of the tanks. Water clear. Killies healthy and hungry, except one which seems damaged as to the fauces, perhaps from single combat with a crab. Crabs vigorous and growing; they have cast their shells more than ever (I refer to the swimmers) and are very tame, com-ing to the top of the water whenever I put in a finger. The mud-crabs are quiet, stealthy, and ravenous as ever. To my great surprise, there appeared in No. 2 a month or six weeks since an eel which I supposed dead and devoured long before; he had been invisible during the winter and was slowly emerging from the sand. He went back again, but has since mani-fested himself for an hour or two at a time more than once.

April 24. Philharmonic concert tonight with Ellie: Mendelssohn's

A-minor Symphony, a "scherzo and finale" in E by Schumann, and Wagner's *Tannhäuser* Overture. This last gains on better acquaintance. . . .

April 27. . . . Nothing particularly new. "Lecompton" has rallied, is coming up again in the House a little modified, and will pass. There is a "Revival Newspaper." The little total depravity newsboys of Wall Street tender one *The Way of Life*—"on'y three cents," with the "*Express* an' *Post*." Walked to 109th Street Sunday afternoon with George Anthon. The cutting on Fourth Avenue at Fiftieth Street through the old Potters Field is a disgrace and scandal. It exposes a fossiliferous stratum some three feet thick of close-packed coffins or shells, and debris of dead paupers. Ribs, clavicles, and vertebra abound all along the railroad tracks, and one might easily construct a perfect skeleton from these stray fragments without resorting to the remains *in situ*, were not many of the specimens imperfect, having been gnawed and crunched by the gaunt swine that are co-tenants with Hibernian humanity of the adjoining shanties. This is within a hundred yards of a dense population.

May 3, MONDAY. Trinity School meeting today at one o'clock at Trinity Church. Signs of trouble brewing. Left, *re infecta*, for Columbia College stated meeting at the Dutch Church Consistory rooms, Fulton and William Streets. Omnibussed up thereafter with Mr. Ruggles and inspected the lecture room in the new Historical Society building ("Herodotus Hall"?) in Second Avenue,[16] which is suggested as suitable locale for such post-graduate lecturing and teaching as can't be administered with advantage in the high latitude of Forty-ninth Street; the Law School, for instance. "The cabin is convenient" and can be had cheap. Looked through the premises. The New York Gallery of the Fine Arts is deposited in the cock-loft. Old Luman Reed's collection is its nucleus. Vanderlyn's very gorgeous "Ariadne" is there, splendid in color. . . .

Lecompton has triumphed in Congress! But it will probably be squashed and squelched in Kansas.[17]

Our Columbia College meeting this afternoon was animated. Gouverneur Ogden, unconsciously influenced by disgust at being off the University

---

[16] The New-York Historical Society, founded in 1804 as the second oldest organization of the kind in the country, now had its home at the corner of Second Avenue and Eleventh Street. Its "Egyptian Museum" was counted specially exciting.

[17] The English Bill, or more properly English Amendment to the Lecompton Bill, had passed Congress. As it submitted the odious Lecompton Constitution to a vote in which it was certain to be crushed—the original object of the Lecompton men having been to avoid a popular vote—it was rather a defeat than a victory for the Lecompton scheme.

Committee (though I hate to attribute such motives to anyone), moved that that committee be instructed to take no steps toward the engagement of additional teachers or the hiring of additional accommodation, and supported his motion by an elaborate speech on the danger of debt; $5,000 per annum beyond our income being probably wanted. Zabriskie backed him in his usual tone; the Poor Richard of the board, he owns one idea, the evil of debt, and that a penny saved is a penny earned. It's his Gospel, and he preaches it in the tune of a St. Dominic. Anderson was on the same side, though "entirely agreeing" with the other, and propounded an incomprehensible bit of subtleties as his reasons for suppressing development and progress. He is wonderfully ingenious in devising reasons why anything should not be done. After some sharp-shooting and a very vigorous little speech from Mr. Ruggles, the whole subject was laid over to a special meeting a fortnight hence. It will never do to rescind our action and organize our University at the College exclusively and with our sub-graduate teachers alone, and thus certify that we don't intend or expect it to succeed, and that our parturient brag and cackle in Betts's speech last winter and on other occasions meant nothing.

May 8. With Ellie and George Anthon this afternoon at Academy of Design. Careful survey. Mignot's ambitious Cordilleras and Kensett's two marine pictures (especially the Newport; in the other the cliffs are conventional and unreal) are the cleverest things in the collection.[18] Inoffensive mediocrity—amiable, diligent, commonplace—the prominent characteristic of the rest. . . .

William Schermerhorn goes to Brattleboro this summer. So do Alfred Schermerhorn and the Hones. They will all be in boarding-houses —not at the hotels. Saw George Anthon tonight, full of an insane proposition from George F. Jones that we take his Newport cottage!! carriage, horses, and furniture!!! for the summer.

May 9. My intellects must be failing. I find myself considering the propriety of undertaking a serious investigation of the financial feasibility of the Newport scheme!!! I know I'm a fool and can't afford the luxury. George Anthon urges it strenuously. Ellie would be delighted. It's close to the Rutherfurds. "Smash-traps" would save Ellie all trouble in organizing the menage. Opportunities for studying marine zoology unlimited. But the *Monish*!!!

May 10. Have been sour and grim, much exercised and exacerbated

[18] Louis Remy Mignot (1831–1870) and J. F. Kensett (1818–1872), American artists.

by the Newport question about which George F. Jones came to see me this morning. Am to make my answer to his proposition tomorrow, and I shall give up so tempting an offer with some reluctance. But I fear the *Diva Pecunia* looks unpropitiously on the project. At breakfast Ellie was, on the whole, decided against it. At dinner (with George Anthon) she was unshaken. I went off to Trinity Church vestry meeting, and on my return found George Anthon and Jack Ehninger here and a general revulsion of feeling. I don't clearly foresee what I shall say to Jones, but I know what a sensible man in my shoes would tell him.

May 11.   Called on G. F. Jones this morning at his new house in Twenty-third Street. . . . I reluctantly declined the equine bargain and the Newport cottage, and Jones and I condoled with each other over the frequent failure of projects the most hopeful, and exchanged assurances of distinguished consideration. . . .

With Ellie tonight at Academy of Music. Heard *The Messiah* excellently well rendered.

May 17, MONDAY.   Thursday morning was cloudless. Set forth at eight o'clock with Ellie, an umbrella, a valise and a basket of sandwiches on the New Haven Railroad. Journey a record of incidents. The wondrous horse of brass and iron rushed squealing into Springfield early enough for us to stroll for half an hour through the town before the Vermont steam pony started. At 2:40 we resumed our northward career along the Connecticut Valley, by Holyoke and Hadley, with its great pulsating dam, Northampton and the Deerfield Hills. . . . Established ourselves at the Brattleboro House and did full justice to an early and munificent tea, and then walked a couple of hours through the cheerful village, enquiring at divers places about rumored rooms to let and houses reported (untruly) to be hirable with their furniture. Sauntered awhile on the Common, looking north over the velvety alluvial grounds of the State Lunatic Asylum to the West River hills, no less beautiful in May than in midsummer. Saw pretty, blonde Miss Laura Pell in deep black for her poor little sister, Sophie; also, George Folsom, the erudite, and his wife, and Mrs. Chanler, who were at our hotel. . . . Left Friday afternoon, stopping at Greenfield. . . .

Summer prospects wholly vague. . . . Rooms at Brattleboro in the house of one White, on High Street near Samson's, where William Schermerhorn is to go, would be very economical but are not at all promising. . . .

Columbia College trustees accomplished something at this afternoon's meeting. Gouverneur Ogden, whose paralyzing resolution was the special business before us, kept away. His resolution was squelched. Zabriskie "let" a vote in its favor, but he was sole representative of narcotism and paralysis. Anderson fidgeted a little. Probably he had a budget of sophistry in reserve, but felt that he could do nothing to retard and embarrass and thought it best to bide his time and hold his mellifluous tongue. The prospects of an efficient law school are very promising.

May 20. . . . Suicide of Herbert ("Frank Forester"), an ancient sporting pal of Tom Griffing and Fred Anthon, whose brother Phil all but witnessed the act. Herbert was an uncommonly poor devil but a man of very scholarly culture, and there are elements of profoundest tragedy in the transaction.[19]

The ambrosial Hurlbut has gone to Europe at last.

May 23, SUNDAY.   I think we've *lit* for the summer at Great Barrington in the classical county of Berkshire and State of Massachusetts. Our Friday morning railroad ride, by the New Haven road, to Bridgeport and thence north by the Housatonic railroad through the quiet valley made glad by that beautiful small river brought us to the Berkshire House in Great Barrington at 2:30 P.M. The substantial, well-ordered hotel and its lovely surroundings were at first highly afflictive and aggravating, for we were told no rooms could be had. We dined debating Whither Next? But Ellie undertook a closer enquiry into the resources of the place after we did justice to its abundant dinner and careered through the house upstairs and down, indefatigable and resolute, till she had planned and combined and arranged and bargained her way to a very satisfactory settlement. Thereafter we had a walk and a long, cool evening drive. Barrington beats Brattleboro, even now, when the distant hills look as if clad in mere dead, bristly brushwood tinged here and there with faint traces of greenish moldiness; when they are garmented with their summer glory and the stately elms and maples ranked along the village street are in full leaf, Barrington must be a magnificent place. . . .

A very funny paragraph in a Boston paper has been copied by the *Evening Post* about the "Rev. W. H. Hurlbut," and his departure for Europe, "Christian Socialism," and Rev. Hurlbut's object in crossing the Atlantic, namely, to publish a volume of "hymns" and a novel describing his experiences while propagating his peculiar doctrines in New York

---

[19] Henry William Herbert (1807–1858), prolific and talented English-born writer, now best remembered for his books on field sports and horses, had made an unhappy marriage, and been deserted by his wife.

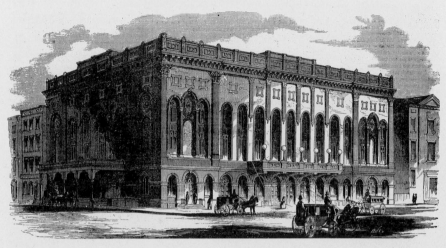

ACADEMY OF MUSIC
IRVING PLACE AND FOURTEENTH STREET

SLEIGHING IN BROADWAY

SPRING IN THE CITY

DRAWING BY WINSLOW HOMER

Society. Carter, the lawyer, or Thayer of the *Evening Post* must have written it.

May 28. Yesterday dined here his honor Judge Murray Hoffman, Bidwell, G. F. Allen, Professor Guyot of Princeton,[20] and Mr. Ruggles. Guyot talks like a man of learning and original thought; rather disposed, perhaps, to strain his analogies too far, to stretch his grand generalizations on the universe till they become mere all-pervading floods of moonshine. He's our possible post-graduate lecturer on geology, and I don't know that we can do better than take him.

May 31. Have just heard *Favorita* tolerably rendered by Gazzaniga, Brignoli, Amodio & Co.; Miss Leavenworth and George Anthon with us. The opera is certainly among Donizetti's best, poor and thin as it is. . . .

Death of W. A. Duer, ex-President of Columbia College, at seventy-eight, in this afternoon's papers.[21] Regret to say that my first thought on reading the announcement was of his life annuity or retiring pension ($1,200 or $1,500) saved to the College, and of what the College could do with that money.

Much talk of possible war with England, the right of search, outrages on the American flag in the Gulf of Mexico, arrogance of British cruisers, and so forth. Bunkum speeches at Washington breathe only battle and murder and sudden death. Things look a little squally. Collisions may occur and breed inevitable disaster. But barring accident, I think our grievances will be adjusted without breach of the peace.[22]

June 5. A vigilance committee has just been triumphantly superseding the legal authorities of New Orleans. Very bad, for the transaction doesn't seem to have been (like the memorable movement at San Francisco, which probably forms its precedent) a unanimous up-rising of the conservative men and property holders of the community, compelled in self-defense to put down rampant scoundrelism, even at the expense of violated formalities and legalities. It has been rather a struggle for power

[20] Arnold Henry Guyot (1807–1884), the Swiss-born geographer, had been invited to America by Agassiz, and in 1854 had accepted the chair of physical geography and geology at Princeton—where he is commemorated by Guyot Hall.

[21] Judge William A. Duer, who had served as midshipman along with Decatur and had practised law with Edward Livingston, had been president of Columbia College when Strong was a student, retiring because of ill health in 1842. He had since written several books.

[22] British officers trying to stop the illicit slave trade had shown an excess of zeal, and Southern tempers had taken fire; as Strong expected, the blaze was brief.

between armed political factions, a party insurrection and revolution, of evil omen to democratic institutions.

We shall very soon be ripe for a similar outbreak. Had Fernando Wood been reëlected mayor last year, it might well have occurred in this city before now. People are fast coming to the conclusion that democracy and universal suffrage will not work in crowded cities.

June 10, THURSDAY. Monday's College meeting was harmonious and brief. The University committee reported progress and nominated Guyot, Dana, and Marsh of Burlington, on whom panegyrics were pronounced by Dr. Torrey and Mr. S. B. Ruggles, Betts purring acquiescence. Theodore Dwight, now of Hamilton College, was nominated, or suggested rather, for the Law School. Edward Jones was put on the committee, vice Van Wagenen, too busy to attend, a good exchange, and we adjourned to the twenty-first instant, then to elect professors. The university begins to look more hopeful; it may come to something after all, but as yet my faith is very weak, and I behold the post-graduate classes of the future as through a glass darkly.

June 24. Burrill Curtis has just taken a First-Class at Cambridge. His brother, George, the Howadji, is getting deplorably mixed up with the Lucy Stones and Mrs. Roses and A. J. Davises and other he and she philosophers, and has just united with the craziest of them in signing a call for a grand convention at Rutland, Vt., to look after the interests of progress and humanity. It's a great pity, for George is a nice fellow. . . .

Satisfactory session of Columbia College Board Monday. Mr. Ruggles reported his eight resolutions organizing the Post-graduate Course, appointing Guyot, Dana, and Marsh, and referring it back to his committee to appoint Dwight or some other suitable person (!!) law professor; and the eight passed, *nemine contradicente.*[23] Only Gouverneur Ogden grunted a timid enquiry, and Anderson suggested some inscrutable

[23] A distinguished list of names. James Dwight Dana (1813–1895) had been assistant to Silliman at Yale and was now professor of natural history there; destined to remain in New Haven for his entire career. He agreed to deliver lectures in Columbia, but ill health prevented him from fulfilling the engagement. Theodore W. Dwight (1822–1892), already distinguished as professor of law at Hamilton, now became head of the Columbia Law School, the second in the city, beginning his lectures in November, 1858. His brilliant success is one of the brightest pages in Columbia history. George P. Marsh (1801–1882), a talented linguistic scholar as well as lawyer, had been minister to Turkey and was now railroad commissioner in Vermont. His lectures at Columbia on philology and etymology fixed his position as an authority on these subjects. But Strong was right in believing the establishment of a post-graduate school premature. Only in law did the new departure prove a success.

subtlety of dissent which he did not venture to back by his vote. Very marvelous revolution. *Tempora mutantur*, and the temper of the board has undergone the strangest mutation since 1854, when stagnation and the standing committee reigned and Mr. Ruggles was the Catiline of our Senate.

Health, prosperity, and development to
  The "U-
   -niversity" we've got in Town
   -niversity we've got in Town.—A very weakly baby, but
perhaps we may raise it. If it survive three years, it will grow to something. The elements celebrated its foundation by a grand thundershower and tornado that caught me on my way home from the meeting and drenched me through and thoroughly between the corner of Twenty-first Street and Fourth Avenue, where I emerged from the car, and the shelter of my own house. The storm blew down trees in Gramercy Park and Union Square, chimneys, telegraph poles, a factory, and a church—the Rev. Ralph Hoyt's to wit—and was the severest to which the city has been exposed for many years.

June 29.   I went up at six to President King's at Forty-ninth Street to a feast of fat things. We were Charles King, his jolly daughters Miss Mary and Miss Henrietta, Miss Fanny King of Highwood, Miss Annie Leavenworth, Mr. Ruggles and Jem Ruggles, Mr. William King, *Egomet Ipse*, Lord Frederick Cavendish,[24] and the Hon. Mr. Evelyn Ashley. Our session was pleasant, for "College Hill" is a comparatively cool place. I like the young Englishers. These two, with the third of their party, Lord Richard Grosvenor (younger son of the Marquis of Westminster), spent Sunday evening here. Cavendish, a younger son of the Duke of Devonshire, is a boy of twenty or thereabouts, blonde and boyish, promising to be a handsome man. Grosvenor is not very stylish in appearance but jolly and clever. Ashley, son of Exeter Hall Ashley, and late private secretary to his grandfather, Palmerston, the eldest of the trio, is lively, fluent, and well-informed. They are fresh from Cambridge, whereof they talk lovingly, and very well-bred, unpretending pleasant fellows, seemingly anxious to please and delighted with what they see and with the attentions they receive. The two younger are strangely unlike young America. Though perfectly at ease in the society of ladies and gentlemen, they are boys and affect to be nothing more.

[24] Lord Frederick Charles Cavendish (1836–1882) was to become chief secretary for Ireland, and lose his life in the famous Phoenix Park murders in Dublin.

Columbia College Commencement today. Wyllie Baxter graduated with distinguished honor. King made formal proclamation that the trustees had just been confined of a "University" and were doing well. Bull Anthon declines all share in its duties unless he is paid an extra $100; "*point d'argent, point de Bull.*" He admits his salary is large enough, but complains that his colleagues do less work for the same money and will retire to his tents like Achilles unless that wrong and inequality be rectified. Not very logical. He won't get his extra pay, and we can get along without him, but when he discovers that fact the difficulty will be to keep him out. Hope we may, for he is as fit to lecture on anything above ancient geography as a deaf and dumb man on the genius of Beethoven. He is utterly incapable of perceiving anything in antiquity but an aggregation of dates and names, and of words to be scanned and parsed. One might as reasonably give an intelligent monkey a printed case in the Court of Appeals as ask Bull Anthon to attempt the discussion of anything within the range of higher scholarship, to indicate the differences between classical and romantic poetry, the art of Sophocles and the art of Shakespeare, the democracy of Athens and the democracy of New York. Even his familiar spirit of scissors and paste would fall barren. He would not know what to steal, for he has no sense or faculty that would enable him to deal with a subject of that class. . . .

Stifling and choky beyond expression, no breeze.

I wish I was a Walrus adrifting on a floe,
I wish I was an Arctic fox a-trotting through the snow.

I wish I were a Toad-fish, that I might swim away,
To pleasant Waters round the Bergs that float in Baffin's Bay.

I'd gladly be a Polar Bear or Puffin or an Auk,
If I might live where they're at home, and far from hot New York.

I wish it was mid-winter, the Croton pipes hard-froze,
The mercury at zero, and a frost bite on my nose:
Broadway blocked up with snow drifts I'd just been wading through,
And James just answering the bell, with features pinched and blue—
Saying "Furnace won't give no heat, sir, all that I can do."

July 1. No news yet of Atlantic Telegraph squadron. Much betting on the result; odds that it will be failure.

July 8, THURSDAY. Tomorrow to fresh fields and pastures new—

Great Barrington, to wit. We are all ready to decamp; trunks are packed and the house wears an unsettled look like Great Salt Lake City pending the latest Mormon hegira. Whatever good thing we find at Great Barrington will be so much clear gain, for my anticipations are at zero. I shall do well enough, but I'm very dubious about Ellie's prospects.

July 14, WEDNESDAY. Home again, having left Great Barrington 10:34 this A.M. and reached here at 4:30. Ellie seems bright and well, thank God, and the young barbarians were both at play and prosperous. . . .

The surroundings of Barrington are Brattleboroid and very promising. There are miles of woody hillside crying aloud for exploration. Three summers would not exhaust the locality. Our hotel wants a piazza badly and is close upon the road, but the cabin is convenient and the people who administer its internal economy seem kindly and obliging. The fare is not to be beat. So testifies that stern critic of dinner-tables, George Anthon, out of the fullness of his heart (and stomach), for he gorged himself like an Anthonaconda. Our fellow-boarders are certain Worths (the family of the defunct General Worth) and Drapers who look like rich snobs. Their talk is mostly of horses. Ellie's little private parlor, though in the third story, makes her very independent. . . .

July 21, WEDNESDAY. Atlantic telegraph squadron has failed again and worse than last summer. Disastrous for Peter Cooper and Cyrus Field. . . .

Last evening at Mr. Ruggles's, with Curtis Noyes, discussing the canal-commissionership. Mr. Ruggles wanted to decline; Noyes wanted him to accept. Noyes urged it very strongly on many grounds, personal and political, and he is probably right. It is only for five months, the residue of the late incumbent's term. Mr. Ruggles is preëminently qualified for it; he would come in at a critical period and connect himself with the consummation of what he planned in 1838, and with the fulfilment of the predictions for which he was then reviled and derided. Noyes thought, moreover, that the Griffin slanders of 1851 still survive in certain quarters, and will be finally squelched by this signal mark of confidence from the government and by the distinction Mr. Ruggles is likely to win in fulfilling his duties. There were many pros and cons, but Mr. Ruggles accepted today, wisely, I think.

August 5. All Wall Street stirred up into excitement this morning, in spite of the sultry weather, by the screeching newsboys with their extras. The *Niagara* has arrived at Trinity Bay with her end of the telegraph cable in perfect working order. But the *Agamemnon* has not yet linked her end at Valentia, and in this enterprise nothing whatever has been done while enough remains to do. The transmission of a single message from shore to shore will be memorable in the world's history, for though I dare say this cable will give out before long, it will be the first successful experiment in binding the two continents together, and the communication will soon be permanently established. It seems to me that gutta percha must undergo some change under the vast pressure of superincumbent water, and that the wire will soon cease to be insulated.

Ever since 1854, when Cyrus W. Field, Peter Cooper, Moses Taylor, and other New Yorkers had formed a company, the city had taken a keen interest in plans for an Atlantic cable. Two and a half years had been required to build a telegraph line across Newfoundland, and to connect this with the Canadian shore by cable. An English company was organized, and more capital raised in Britain than in America; a route across the Atlantic was surveyed, the great oceanographer Matthew F. Maury lending his talents; and the British and American governments were persuaded to assign a frigate apiece to help lay the cable. In 1857 the work was begun by vessels steaming westward from Ireland; but the projectors knew little about the best method of procedure, and after several hundred miles had been laid, the strand broke and disappeared into the Atlantic. Half a million dollars had been lost. Now in 1858 a new plan was tried. Two cable-bearing ships met in mid-ocean, spliced their cable ends, and steamed in opposite directions for Ireland and Newfoundland. Thrice the cable broke. The discouraged backers of the enterprise talked of giving up their undertaking. But it was resolved to try again—and the fourth attempt, in July and August, 1858, was to prove successful. Strong chronicles the effort that ended in triumph. When success was finally achieved (August 5, 1858), with a copper strand nearly two thousand miles long, much of it two miles under water, uniting the Old World and the New, the wildest enthusiasm reigned in America and Britain. Queen Victoria and President Buchanan on August 17th exchanged messages amid jubilant celebrations; so many fireworks were let off in New York that the City Hall caught fire; and a grand civic ceremony was held, as Strong records below, at Trinity Church. But the rejoicings proved short-lived.

August 10.   Everybody all agog about the Atlantic Cable. Telegraph offices in Wall Street decorated with the flags of all nations and sundry fancy pennons beside, suspended across the street. Newspapers full of the theme, and of the demonstrations the event has produced from New Orleans to Portland. The *Agamemnon* has brought her end safe to Valentia, so the whole cable is now in position. Newspapers vie with each other in gas and grandiloquence. Yesterday's *Herald* said that the cable (or perhaps Cyrus W. Field, uncertain which) is undoubtedly the Angel in the Book of Revelation with one foot on sea and one foot on land, proclaiming that Time shall be no longer. Moderate people merely say that this is the greatest human achievement in history. Possibly not the very greatest; some few things have surely been done in the old time before us that run the cable rather hard. Morse's first forty miles of telegraph wire included this, and much more that shall be hereafter (perhaps), and the first message between Washington and Baltimore was a grander event than this. Laying this wire rope unbroken across the abysses of the Atlantic was no light undertaking, but success, with all the armories of modern science in the service, is not so much to brag of. Is it success after all? No message has yet been transmitted, and we are not told the reason why.

If no great revolution or cataclysm throw mankind off the track they've been traveling for the last half-century, if the earth doesn't blow up or get foul of a comet and be not rebarbarized by Brigham Young or Red Republicanism, it will be a strange place in 1958, most unlike what it is now. The diverse races of men certainly seem tending toward development into a living organic unit with railroads and steam-packets for a circulating system, telegraph wires for nerves, and the London *Times* and New York *Herald* for a brain.

August 12.   Hasket Derby has sailed for Europe in search of knowledge. I expect to take Miss Leavenworth to Barrington tomorrow.

August 24.   There were few things very memorable during this long holiday. Mrs. Ruggles left on Tuesday (17th) in a state of influenza, with Miss Mary Bostwick. That day came news of the Queen's message over the telegraph cable. Church bells rang their loudest all the morning, and when we returned that evening late, after a long drive to Tyringham (a lovely valley, east of Stockbridge, with a Shaker settlement), the one street of Barrington was illuminated with multitudinous tallow candles in every shop window, and a big bonfire that reduced the blessed moon to insignificance. The Grand Army of Barrington, with one fife and a drum, followed by a string of citizens at large carrying torches, marched perseveringly up and down, attaining the dignity of a prolonged procession by executing manoeuvres in Indian file, and finished the performances by a grand fusillade in front of the Berkshire House. Then one Emerson, the village jurist, delivered an allocution to the assembled multitude, and told them that war, revulsions, and other calamities were henceforth impossible, that the millennium had been manufactured by electro-galvanism, gutta-percha, copper wire, and Cyrus Field, that "tomorrow the whisper of the Kremlin and the song of the Persian dancing girl would be heard in the hills of Berkshire," that "the homesteads of good old Mother England" were now situated in Massachusetts, and other like startling propositions.

It's almost alarming to consider the amount of impious brag which this cable has generated all over the country. Has so extensive, simultaneous, vociferous and insolent a bray been emitted by puffed-up humanity on any previous occasion? Here in New York the triumphant pyrotechnics with which our city fathers celebrated this final and complete subjugation by man of all the powers of nature—space and time included—set the City Hall on fire, burned up its cupola and half its roof, and came near destroying the County Clerk's office and unsettling the titles to half the property in the city. The Hall presents a most draggled and crestfallen appearance, all singed and reeky and shorn of its headpiece.

August 27. First news came over the Atlantic cable yesterday. Peace with China. Another despatch followed. This looks like successful reality.

The city is utterly dismal. I'm thinking of a course of lager-beer saloons and low theatres.

The periodical alarm about yellow fever is setting in. It seems to have got some foothold at Staten Island, round about the Quarantine. There has been a fatal case at 16 Greenwich Street and another at Hoboken.

August 29, SUNDAY. It's down in the programme of next Wednesday's grand celebration, it seems, that the mayor, and the civic *Di Majores* generally, attend service at Trinity Church. Hodges tells me he has got together a choir of thirty. The music is mostly his own. A sort of temporary rood-screen has been erected under the chancel arch, which is to be covered with flowers.

August 31. The streets tonight are crowded with people manifestly imported to see the sights of tomorrow. Probably it will be quite a brilliant show. Have been besieged for orders of admission to Trinity Church. Spent some time there watching the labors of Reid the florist and his men on the temporary rood-screen they were beautifying. The effect of the rich floral coloring on the tracery, the legend (Glory be to God on high, and so forth), and the cross surmounting the whole, is very splendid.

The stained glass of the west window doesn't quench the bright lines of the gladioli and tiger lilies and fuchsias as I feared it would. The church was fragrant this morning, its atmosphere heavy with exhalations from the cartloads of fresh flowers that lay about everywhere. The workmen, mostly English and Scotch, worked with a will, evidently pleased with their task. All the flags of the *Niagara* are to be hoisted on the church spire. I wanted to have the British and American flags inside, too, but it seems there are people who object and consider such things improper and wrong in a church. Very queer and unaccountable; why should the symbols of two great Christian nations be secular and profane? Probably the feeling that prompts the objection is that which says "religion has nothing to do with politics," an aphorism generally received in these days, and embodying as much practical atheism as can well be expressed in seven words.

A militia company from Montreal is parading tonight and loudly cheered by groups of spectators. It's long since British soldiers have marched through the streets of New York. The newspaper organs of our Celtic fellow-citizens will probably do a little frenzy on the subject. Fresh cases of yellow fever are said to occur, and I'm sorry to find that Dr. Peters thinks we shall have a serious visitation from that uncomfortable disease. He says these "sporadic" cases have been remarkably well-defined and virulent.

September 11, SATURDAY.   Yesterday was scalding. Left Great Barrington with Miss Rosalie and Miss Annie Leavenworth and brought them to town, hot and dusty. But the two young ladies endured the trials with angelic patience. We came through the tunnel with horses, for the first time. Locomotives are now suppressed below Forty-second Street, and travelers at that point execrate the owners of real estate on Murray Hill, who have effected this questionable reformation after a long struggle. . . .

The telegraph cable celebration on the 1st seems to have been a grand affair. The services in Trinity Church were impressive, they say. The Fields are very puffy with the adulation they've swallowed, and no wonder. But people begin to tire of hearing Cyrus called the Great, and of parallels between him and Galileo generally to the disadvantage of the latter. We are a little disgusted, moreover, with the humors of the wondrous cord itself, which has remained obstinately silent for the last ten days. Its managers assure the public that it's all right, but descend to no explanation. Should it be permanently paralyzed, it will be curious to see the general reaction from our late orgasm of glorification. Possibly Cyrus will be lynched.

The great excitement of the last week though has been the Quarantine War, [with] destruction of the hospitals by a mob on two successive nights, [and] supineness of the authorities, including Governor King, who was in town all the time junketing with the blackguards of the city government, and who came out after this infamy was consummated with a wordy proclamation declaring Richmond County in insurrection. An army of occupation is now on the ground, enjoying the view and the sea breeze, but with nothing in particular to do. This is the worst villainy that has been perpetrated in my day; indeed, the *demos* of Staten Island may claim the credit of having exceeded by this act all achievements of cowardice, inhumanity, and baseness by anarchs of every place and period. The mobs of Paris did their carnage in a hysterical delirium of exaltation. They were drunk with certain shallow notions which Frenchmen might easily mistake for grand regenerative truths. They were executing what they took for justice, with its forms, on traitors and public enemies. These mean ruffians of Richmond County were impelled, according to their own account, by pusillanimous fears for their own safety. But the danger was a pretext, and had it been substantial and serious, they elected to abide it when they settled round the Quarantine, and have no right to set it up as an excuse for their crime. This riot, robbery, and arson, and murder, this outrageous assault on men and women struggling against smallpox and yellow fever, was in fact a mere operation in real estate, a movement which Staten Islanders consider justifiable for the sake of ten per cent increase in the market value of building sites and village lots.

A mob of screeching blackguards breaking into a hospital by night, dragging out men and women labouring under most formidable disease, and dropping them about the grounds while they proceeded to burn and destroy, is a sorry sight, especially when "Peace on Earth and Good Will towards Men" is so recently inaugurated on earth. I fear that this millennium over which we've been braying is made of gutta-percha and copper wire and is not the real thing after all.

For many years, and particularly since the yellow-fever excitement in 1856, the people of Staten Island had regarded the Quarantine Station on their shores as a menace to health and an impediment to the growth of their borough. Grave charges were brought against the establishment—that it was a political institu-

tion giving the Health Officer $100,000 in patronage, that it treated the merchants and citizens of the island arrogantly, and that the patients were not properly cared for. When yellow fever reappeared in 1858, the antagonism mounted to new heights. A number of men (the New York Tribune called them "a large and powerful confederation") resolved to make use of the night of the great cable celebration in New York to destroy the station. On the evening of September 1st a mob marched up to the Quarantine, broke down the wall about it, and began applying the torch to the buildings. Under the head, Dr. Bissell, the hospital force set to work and extinguished the flames almost as fast as they were set. They were holding the situation in check when the local firemen arrived. This body hustled the doctor and his aides out of the station, formed a cordon around the burning buildings, and effectively did nothing—saying that the mob had cut their hose. A dozen structures, including the smallpox hospital and the disinfecting building, were soon ablaze. It was only by heroic exertions on the part of the nurses that some of the smallpox patients were saved from being burned alive. While this was going on, Governor King and the police commissioners of the metropolitan district were feasting at the great cable dinner at the Metropolitan Hotel. But Dr. Bissell's residence and the principal hospital building survived. The leaders of the mob, therefore, resolved upon a second attack, which was carried out on the night of September 2d. Headed by some leading citizens—Ray Tompkins, captain of the fire police, police-justice Charles De Forest, and one William Muller with a crowd of Germans at his back—the mob this time made a clean sweep. The central hospital, one of the largest and best equipped in the country, poured up flames which lighted up the island and bay for miles around. The patients, many delirious and some dying, were carried out and laid on the grass; and there they remained the rest of that night and most of the following day. "One thousand infuriated devils were more than we could manage," wrote Dr. Bissell, who had lost his house. The more respectable people of the island condemned the affair, but not too vehemently, and though arrests were made, not much was expected from them. A boatload of marines and the Eighth Regiment of state militia arrived after it was all over.

September 15, WEDNESDAY.   The Oracle of the cable is still dumb, and we begin to revile our Fetish. The grand Cyrus is making little sales of stock. At Quarantine the hosts of New York are still camped in grim repose. The Columbia College meeting Tuesday failed for lack of a quorum. Van Wagenen is moribund with internal cancer. Ellie writes in the best of spirits, notwithstanding a bad cold. Jem Ruggles is at Lenox, guest of that truculent Amazon, Mrs. Fanny Kemble Butler.

George R. Ives of Great Barrington keeps a Ghost!

Sadducismus Debellatus – being a True Account of the Dinner Table
Devil of Great Barrington. By G. T. Strong, Gentleman.

At the south end of the village, close to the railroad depot, stands the Ives mansion, or "smug, white-painted villa of gentility," with a pert turret and a comfortable piazza and a smooth-shaven lawn. Its aspect is not in the least suggestive of spooks. On the contrary, one would not be more surprised to learn that it was infested by duck-billed platypi. It is all very modern except the dining room and certain rooms above that apartment, which were part of the old Barrington parsonage of fifty years ago, where St. James's Church stood somewhere near "Mount Peter." These have been modernized, and the whole structure looks homogeneous.

In this dining room there have been for years past unaccountable and uncanny noises at night, especially about Christmas time, loud enough to disturb the whole house. During the last two years they have been less frequent, but before that they seem to have caused serious annoyance. Servants would not occupy that part of the house, and people were kept awake by the clatter. It was as if a heavy trunk were dragged about the floor. Sometimes a large party seemed to be pushing back their chairs as they rose from the dinner table, or people seemed to be walking about clattering plates and setting the table. (Were the old rectors of Barrington notable for high feeding and conviviality?) Ives tells me he got up one specially noisy night and marched downstairs in a dressing gown to investigate, but that when he reached the door the racket within was so loud that he concluded to go straight back to bed again. He and his son clearly think the house is haunted, though they won't quite say so.

Ives's daughter, Mrs. Seymour, a stout young woman of twenty-five, wife of an Episcopal clergyman, was passing through the dining room one winter night four years ago when she saw indistinctly someone standing by a window through which the moon was shining, or rather she saw two eyes and the outline of a face. She thought it was her brother and spoke, but got no answer. Some lady who was with her also saw it; they satisfied themselves there was no one there, and ran off in a fright. Since then, on the 24th of February of each year, Mrs. Seymour sees this same pair of eyes looking at her for some short time, wherever she is. They are hazel eyes. Their expression is not malignant. She does not seek or avoid them on the anniversary, for she fears that if she did so, they would appear to her when she was not expecting them. She has painful recollections associated with that day.

Mrs. Seymour is a rather nervous, fanciful person, is evidently profoundly impressed by this experience and told the story very well, frightening Ellie and her other auditors most successfully.

September 24, FRIDAY.   Agricultural Fair commenced Wednesday, and the quiet village has been in unwonted bustle and excitement. All Berkshire County comes up to this great annual solemnity. Bulls and sheep and oxen were magnificent. They satisfied their biped exhibitors. . . .

Jem Ruggles came very near furnishing the newspapers with a lamentable paragraph last week. A two days' expedition to "Mt. Everett" and its circumjacent notabilia was organized by Mrs. Fanny Butler, or (as she prefers to call herself), Kemble.[25] There were that lady and her pretty daughters, Professor Agassiz and wife, Miss Lizzy Clark, David Dudley Field and his sister Miss Jenny, Jem, and sundry high well-born Bostonians. After visiting "the Dome" they proceeded to explore "Sage's Ravine," a picturesque, spookerish locality somewhere on the skirts of the Taconic Hills. The younger folks undertook some kind of scramble, probably to reach the top of a water fall, leaving the elders below, and in the course of this proceeding Jem missed his footing. He fell about fifteen feet into the water course where it was too swift for him to recover his footing and went down some thirty feet farther—with the picturesque cascade into its deep pool. Thence he extricated himself unaided and instantly hailed his horror-stricken friends with the assurance that he was "all right." He seems to have shewn very good pluck. Agassiz and some of the other men took him into the woods and rubbed him down with brandy. He returned to Mrs. Butler's at Lenox, and suffered no harm from his perilous adventure. Ellie drove off to Lenox to look after him, spent a night there, made Mrs. Butler's acquaintance, and had a very pleasant time.

September 29.   The Atlantic cable speechless still. Its high priests talk of defective insulation at some point probably not less than two hundred miles west of Valentia, and are quite confident the interruption is only temporary. Hard to conceive of a remedy! People begin to turn up their noses at the house of Field and at the grand Cyrus in particular. What can the precise difficulty be? Perhaps some weak point in the gutta-percha

[25] Fanny Kemble (1809–1893), the famous actress, who had been divorced from Pierce Butler of Georgia in 1848, lived in America 1849–1868.

casing has been infiltrated under the pressure of a thousand fathoms of water. Perhaps some huge sting ray grubbing in the oozy bed of ocean for bivalve mollusca has closed his massive grinding dental plates on the cable, mistaking it for an overgrown scrupula, and given it a fatal crunch.

October 5, TUESDAY.   Home again. Left Great Barrington at ten-thirty and brought Ellie and her babies and her Abigails and Miss Josephine safe to town by five. It was an auspicious day for railroad travelers; recent rains had laid the dust, and the air was cool. There was an alarm of fire as we emerged from the tunnel at Thirty-first Street, and a majestic column of smoke was marching southeastwardly across the blue sky, and men said the "Crystal Palace" was on fire. So when we reached the Twenty-seventh Street depot, I put the party in charge of James (the waiter, known as Pam from the likeness he bears the portraits of a British statesman), who met us there, and then "fled fast through sun and shade" up Murray Hill in pursuit of the picturesque *magna comitante caterva.* Up every avenue a miscellaneous aggregate of humanity was racing on the same errand. So scampers a wide area of yellow-fallen leaves down the street of Barrington when smitten suddenly by a strong wind from the north-west. Over our heads was rising and wreathing and flowing onward this grand and ominous torrent of vapor, glowing with golden and coppery tints imparted by the setting sun. My run was hard. I panted and perspired before reaching the scene of action. It was the "Crystal Palace." But before I got there, the dome, roof, and walls had gone down. Only a few iron turrets were standing and some fragments of wall that looked like the wreck of a Brobdignagian aviary. The debris was still flaming and blazing furiously. I contemplated the bonfire awhile and then came off, being tired and wanting my dinner.

So bursts a bubble rather noteworthy in the annals of New York. To be more accurate, the bubble burst some years ago, and this catastrophe merely annihilates the apparatus that generated it. Don't know how the fire broke out. The building must have burned up like a pile of shavings. They said in the crowd that many lives had been lost, the swiftness of the fire having cut off egress from the building in a few moments. But I don't believe it. Anyone thus headed off could have kicked his way out through the walls anywhere.

Found Mr. Ruggles here when I got home, and he dined with us. Much exercised inwardly, he is, about canal boards and Cayuga Marshes, but Columbia College is not quite forgot. Board met yesterday. Betts's quarrel with Gouverneur Ogden about the custody of the money-box remains undecided. Election was postponed to November. Miss Josephine Strong also dined with us. Barrington has done her good. George C. Anthon looked in, and has just gone. . . .

The Crystal Palace, which had been erected in 1853 by an association of public-spirited men in partial imitation of the great London structure, and which had cost all told about $750,000, had taken a great place in the hearts of New Yorkers. It had been opened with pomp and parade; it had shown millions of visitors more of the wonders of art, science, and mechanics than they had ever seen before; it had again and again been the scene of brilliantly colorful gatherings. But it had fallen upon evil days. The receipts never reached the expected level. In 1854 the association which built it went into bankruptcy, no bondholder having ever received a penny of interest. The property passed in the spring of 1858 into the hands of the American Institute, which soon opened an interesting exhibition there. On the afternoon of October 5th the cry of fire was raised, and within fifteen minutes the handsome structure was a heap of ashes, bent ironwork, and glass fragments. Some people had foolishly talked of it as fireproof. But the floor and exhibits were highly inflammable; they no sooner caught fire than the heat began to warp the iron and glass framework, and within a few minutes the dome came crashing down into the center of the structure.

Meanwhile, the Atlantic cable had completely broken down. From Newfoundland there came daily the cheerless word that the station there heard nothing from Ireland, and that the cable was devoid of electricity. The experts employed announced that their experiments showed that the water had reached the conducting wire in at least one spot not less than 220 miles from the shore. It seemed plain that the wrapping of the copper conductor was defective, and that this conductor had been too small. Newspapers which had hailed the cable as the greatest feat of the age now blamed the company for pursuing haphazard and unscientific methods. It was generally assumed that a new effort would be made—but the Civil War was to intervene before success was attained.

October 12. George Allen was here and others, including John Sherwood. . . . Allen has a story (apropos of the beneficial effect of exhibitions of art like that at the defunct Crystal Palace upon the masses and the middling classes) of his overhearing a man explaining Thorwaldsen's group of the Apostles to his wife. "Them's the Presidents of the United States; that's Jefferson, and that chap with the sword—that's General Jackson." . . .

October 18.   People begin to forget the Atlantic cable, now generally conceded a failure. This is Cyrus's Katabasis. The frantic orgasm of only fifty days ago seems a strange, remote, historical fact. *Punch* is very funny over our extravagancies of that date. Other English periodicals rebuke them more gravely. We made fools of ourselves beyond all question, but these Anglican criticisms are ungracious. What we exulted over so absurdly was the prospect of closer communication and hourly intercourse with England. The general spontaneous rejoicing of that time (Charles King says every half-fledged village on the upper Mississippi had its bonfire and its speechifications) is among the healthiest and most hopeful symptoms of this people in my day.

October 20.   Murray Hoffman had got a seat for me at the Academy of Music and would take no excuses, so I went with him to the Piccolomini's[26] debut in *Traviata*; seats in parquette. House jammed. Opera put on the stage far better than it deserves. There was the superfluous imbecility of a ballet (*pas seul* by some strapping black-eyed Spanish woman, a bullfighter's bride). Orchestra and chorus well drilled and strong. Opening chorus of whores and whoremongers quite effective. The Piccolomini's reception was uproarious. She was called out over and over again, and bombarded with bouquets. Nice-looking little body, acts with archness and spirit in a fresh, unconventional way and sings quite well enough for Verdi's music and grins at the audience rather too much. She will make no profound impression, unless she confine herself to lighter roles, like Zerlina or Rosina in *The Barber*, or the heroine of *Don Pasquale*, or of the *Elisir d'Amore*. She would do such work delightfully, I think. She is said to be a very respectable little lady.

The baritone (name forgotten) was very effective. Tenor (Steffani) was vociferous beyond what was written, though Verdi wrote it.

October 21, THURSDAY.   Principal news the issue of the much-talked-of prize fight. Morrissey prevailed against "The Benicia Boy."[27]

October 23.   People begin to be a little excited about the next election, a many-sided fight. Gerrit Smith running on his own account will get a heavy Western vote, some say 50,000. Republicans run [E. D.] Morgan for governor; Americans, [Lorenzo] Burrows; but the two parties are fused at many points on local candidates. The Democrats are in mutiny

---

26 Marietta Piccolomini (1834–1899), Italian singer and actress.

27 John Morrissey and John C. Heenan, two pugilistic Irish-Americans, had fought at Long Point Island in Lake Erie, about eighty miles from Buffalo; Heenan was knocked out in twenty-one minutes.

and ill organized, and the Administration will lose congressmen where it is met by a hearty, well-cemented fusion of the opposition. But I think Judge [Amasa J.] Parker will be governor, unless he kill himself by stump oratory, wherein his cunning is small. It's significant, however, that the *Herald* has suddenly changed its note and predicts that the Democracy will be routed. One can tell something about the wind by the direction a stench takes.

October 28. The Columbia College post-graduate experiment is about commencing. We are still in labor with our unborn treasurer. Tomaso Wells is very cantankerous about Betts's claims—Tomaso *furioso*—and has injured Betts's prospects, I fear, by his bitterness against Gouverneur. Gouverneur has brought into action every bit of interest he can command and used outside influence without scruple, forgetting his lofty moral position in the Wolcott Gibbs controversy. . . .

Morgan's prospects improve from day to day. The Republicans will probably carry the state. They say that will be a great point won in Seward's game, and will secure his nomination in 1860.

November 1. . . . Went tonight to the Historical Society building at the corner of Second Avenue and Eleventh Street, where we committed our [Columbia] first post-graduate Overt Act. Dwight delivered his introductory lecture on law, successful beyond my hopes. Dwight looks a little uncouth, but his lecture or address was scholar-like, vigorous, sound, and genial. I think he will prove a great acquisition. The audience was respectable and many names were put down for the course at $75. Noyes was delighted; so were Davies, Pierrepont, Bosworth, Daly, and others of our judicial lights. I can see that Lieber is jealous of Dwight already.

Prospects of the Lecompton-Democracy for tomorrow don't improve.

November 2. Our new Law Professor Dwight dined here with Mr. Ruggles and Jem [Ruggles] and Bully Betts (!). Favorable impression of Dwight confirmed. Prospects of the Law School brightening. Betts made himself solemnly agreeable and was warmed into a dignified approach to urbane jocosity by his Romanee. I was politic, for the first time in my dinner-giving career, when I asked Betts to come today. He has fallen out with his brother-fogies in the Columbia College Board, and I wanted to smooth his way to other and wiser alliances; to bring him nearer, in his bereavement, to active, progressive men like Mr. Ruggles and our jurist.

November 6, SATURDAY. Result of the election is the success of Morgan and the Republican state ticket by about 20,000. Democrats carry their county ticket in this city; Horace F. Clark (rebellious Democrat) sent back to Congress; Daniel Sickles elected over Williamson (Republican) by a small vote. The latter means to claim the seat, and is like to succeed in a Republican House. The contest between Haskin and Kemble in the Westchester District is very close—the former probably elected. Moncrieff is Judge of the Superior Court, vice John Duer, deceased!!!!

Douglas seems to have beaten the Administration in Illinois after a hard struggle. If so, he will be Democratic candidate for the presidency in 1860.

Strong had made no mention in his diary of the great series of joint debates held in Illinois by Lincoln and Douglas. But quite apart from the Illinois contest, the elections this year were of unusual interest. In the "October States" of Iowa, Indiana, Ohio, and Pennsylvania the tide had run strongly against the Buchanan Administration. The defeat of the Democrats in Pennsylvania, Buchanan's own state, by a coalition of Republicans, Know-Nothings, and Free-soil Democrats, was particularly striking; for out of twenty-five seats in Congress for the state, the Democrats were left with only three. November now brought a still more emphatic verdict against the Administration. In all New England, in New York, and in most of the Northwest the Democratic Party went down in utter defeat. Beyond question a host of voters had been alienated by the effort to make Kansas a slave state under the Lecompton Constitution.

In New York State the four-cornered campaign had developed great heat. The Republicans, their choice controlled by the astute Thurlow Weed, nominated for governor an able merchant of New York City, E. D. Morgan; the Democrats named Amasa J. Parker, who stood for Buchanan and the Lecompton idea. It was during this campaign that Seward made his "irrepressible conflict" speech, asserting that the United States must "sooner or later become either entirely a slaveholding nation, or entirely a free labor nation." On election day the Republicans won decisively, placing Morgan in the governor's chair by a majority of nearly 17,500, and obtaining twenty-nine of the Congressional seats.

November 9. Much engaged of late with Bidwell and William Curtis Noyes, trying to secure them as lecturers in our Columbia College Law School. Effort not desperate but rather promising, though Noyes is a director or trustee of the New York University on Washington Square, which has started a law school of its own with Judge Clerke and Peter Y. Cutler for its teachers.

Lord says: "Clerke is equally ignorant on every subject, but if Cutler be more ignorant of any one branch of legal science than of any other, his weak point is undoubtedly the law of real estate," his specialty in this precious course of the New York University.

November 11. Notified by James DePeyster Ogden this morning that I was elected trustee or director of the Bank for Savings, the Bleecker Street bank (formerly of Chambers Street) of which my father was many years a prominent officer. It is the oldest and the most important of our institutions of that class, holds many millions of deposits, and is controlled by a very highly "respectable" board—Ogden, Lord, Bidwell, Najah Taylor, Suydam, Kennedy, and others. The appointment titillates my Pharisaism so agreeably that I am disposed to accept it, though acceptance involves much time and work and anxiety in times like those of a year ago and cuts me off from a share in the profits of our professional business for the bank, heretofore divided between Charles E. Strong and myself, Bidwell having been a trustee for a long time past. But Rabbi Strong is such a self-sacrificing, philanthropic Rabbi! If I accept, I shall try to do the work according to my capacity, such as it is, but what folly to select me for this responsible place! I could name forty men of my age and standing who would fill it better. . . .

Last night Ellie and I, with Miss Rosalie and Mignot, heard *Don Giovanni* at the Academy of Music. Zerlina taken by Piccolomini, Donna Anna by Gazzaniga, Elvira (forgotten), very respectable. Don Ottavio's music decently rendered by one Tamais and Don Giovanni by Gassier. . . . *Don Giovanni* in concert room or parlor is always more and more noble and transcendent; it is a little disappointing on the stage, I think, because its music is too exalted for the barbaric foolery wherein we think we delight and which we honor and applaud as opera or "lyric drama." Its glorious melodies are degraded and their effect impaired by their accompaniment of idiotic puppet-show behind the foot-lights. I don't refer to this production in particular, but to opera *per se*. What we call "good" acting only makes the mesalliance more conspicuous. If the swine be a fine large fat specimen of his dirty kind, you are only the more offended by the jewel of gold in his snout, and the less disposed to admire it. Donizetti's and Verdi's music being mostly poor and shallow, its depravation is less disgusting, but Mozart's celestial melodies, condemned to the office of illustrating the conventional absurdities and imbecilities that make up a representation of this or any other opera, are somewhat lamentable to hear, like a choir of angels diligently harping and hymning the accompaniment to a Chinese comedy or to a troupe of trained monkeys and dancing bears.

November 15. Bidwell and Curtis Noyes, Bully Betts, and Professor Dwight partook of gratuitous refreshment. I've singular hopes of Bidwell and Noyes; expect them to ally themselves with the Law School, which thrives beyond expectation. Lieber and others were here last night. Proposed revision of state constitution is squelched by a small but decisive vote. Sorry the opportunity is lost for reforming our disastrous and deplorable judiciary. The result seems at first to indicate an unexpected and unprecedented conservatism and aversion to change. But its one solution is that while nobody in particular made any exertion to sustain the measure, the Democrats issued a secret circular against it (because they would have been unable to control the revising convention) and some of our very politic judges also operated privily to defeat it.

The Abbé Hurlbut has returned!

November 20, SATURDAY. Last Wednesday evening, went with Mrs. Strong, also with George Anthon and Murray Hoffman, to the playhouse known as Laura Keene's, to see *Our Cousin from America.*[28] (Whereof the title I have thus transposed for metre's sake.) The play is very good; and it was acted well. One Jefferson was admirable as the Yankee hero. The fair and sinful Laura, though less fresh and dashing than she was some five years back, is fascinating still. I've seldom had a more satisfactory time at any theatre. . . .

Some scoundrel, not yet hung, had advertised a dole of bread and meat to all the poor folk who should attend at noon in Union Square Thanksgiving morning. Several thousand came, worn sewing-women, hungry children, Celts insolvent and solvent, all the poor of every type, and there they sat and waited hour after hour in vain, and went away, reluctantly at last, with empty baskets, weary and cold and sad and disappointed.

What would one like to do with this facetious practical joker? Putting him to death by a slow crescendo of elaborate torture, keeping his vital forces and his sense of pain up to the last by stimulants, would be appropriate. But I'd rather starve him for seven long days, then tie him hand and foot and take him to some jolly dinner party, some feast of fat things with a dozen courses, at Astor's or Grinnell's or Daniel Fearing's, and stick him in the corner there to witness four hours of luxury and deglutition.

George Anthon called here this morning, and I walked with him to

---

[28] Tom Taylor's *Our American Cousin* was first played this year. Joseph Jefferson appeared in the New York production.

the foot of Tenth Street, crossed to Greenpoint, and we walked through
that new suburb and through Williamsburgh, and through the very unfinished district that lies behind the Wallabout and then through Brooklyn
to the Fulton Ferry and so to Wall Street, having traversed what seemed
an infinite region of monotonous shabby streets and small cheap houses.
From Greenpoint to Gowanus there is now a continuous city, except for
the partial solution of continuity at the Wallabout.

November 26. Benjamin F. Butler died at Paris of a sudden acute
attack of diabetes.[29] "Bible Butler" was a good lawyer, and I suppose a
valuable man, but I never had great faith in him.

Heard *Nozze di Figaro* for first time Wednesday night. With us Mrs.
S. B. Ruggles and Mignot. Formes as Figaro and Florenza as the erratic
Count were excellent. Piccolomini sang Susanna's music nicely enough
and was saucy, pert, petite, piquant, and "Aggravating." . . . Music beyond my expectations, which were high. That it's of the same exalted
order with the music of *Don Giovanni* is manifest even on a first hearing.
But it's useless to platitudinize about it. Grammar must be enriched with
a new double extra super-superlative degree of comparison before I can
do justice to Mozart—on the whole, the greatest of composers. Admitting
that Handel's sublimities of choral effect, the inspirations of *Israel in
Egypt* and *The Messiah*, cannot be matched in his works, that he had no
faculty for the uncanny depths and intensities of Beethoven's greater
orchestral compositions, he outdoes both in every other kind of creative
power, and in the exuberance and the loveliness of his creations. Amen.

The accomplished Hurlbut is "about." He has enjoyed great social
"success" and lionization in London as an intelligent and cultivated
American, being, in truth, a very fluent, clever, plausible, and cultivated
man. Professes himself disgusted with the "petty gossip" of New York,
and anxious to return speedily to a field where his talents can have freer
scope and where there will be no gossip about his past career, which is
not surprising. I hope he'll soon be enabled to do so. . . .

Trinity School trustees met Tuesday night, and did nothing of the
least importance. After an inoffensive childhood, meritorious and beneficent on a small scale, that has lasted a century and upwards, that corpo-

[29] Benjamin F. Butler (1795–1858) had studied and practiced law in Kinderhook
with Martin Van Buren, had been one of the revisers of the New York Statutes of 1828,
attorney general in the cabinet of Jackson and Van Buren, and United States district
attorney for the southern district of New York; in 1857 he had organized the law
school at New York University.

ration is just entering on the critical period of transition to puberty. The "Baker Farm" begins to produce assessments for paving and grading and severing Seventy-ninth Street and the thoroughfares adjacent, swindling assessments that must be paid or resisted. If paid, there must be mortgages to raise the money or the sale of a lamentably large slice of our endowment. . . .

December 1. We went to hear *Nozze di Figaro*, from which I've just returned, and I'm still tingling and nervous from undergoing that most intense and exquisite music. It's not so potent merely, but the dose is of such heroic magnitude! Donizetti could dilute any ten bars of it into two grand operas. . . .

This lovely *Nozze di Figaro*, though so famous, and so brilliant, melodic and popular, has been unheard and unknown in New York till 1858, except in a mutilated and mangled English version twenty-five years ago. It may sleep now for another generation, or until another performer turn up with special qualifications for one of the parts, like little Piccolomini's for that of Susanna. . . .

Every author of symphony or opera should produce his work with a rope round his neck. If the work be merely creditable and clever, not truly great and genial, he should be hanged. For by bringing it into the world he has helped to lessen the few opportunities accorded to mankind of hearing the great masterpieces of music that are to most of us as if they had never been. Why should Gade and Wagner write symphonies and overtures? If they devoted themselves to sawing wood instead, my chance of knowing Beethoven and Mozart would be better.

December 6, MONDAY. College trustees met at two o'clock. . . . I brought up the proposition to hire a house and buy a library for the Law School, which went unfortunately to the standing committee instead of the committee on the post-graduate course. The standing committee was instructed to report a plan for bringing the Botanic Garden lots into market. Drisler got a year's leave of absence. He's threatened with amaurosis.

On the whole, I think the College made considerable leeway this afternoon. . . .

The day Sunday was made memorable by a youthful Levite at Trinity Chapel who preached at us a flood of sophomorical conceits, shallow truisms, and shallower sophism, complacent slip-slop, and grandiose gibberings, seldom equaled in that or any other pulpit. Evacuating so enormous an accumulation of pestiferous fluid, imbecility, and bosh must have relieved the man's system inexpressibly, but I wonder somebody didn't

shy a prayer book at him. Higby must mean to coerce us into paying the
money he wants by subjecting us to a course of green deacons and wild
missionaries. We must emulate the fortitude of the early Christians under
analogous cruelty of persecution and stand firm in our duty as vestrymen. A gander like this should be silenced by ecclesiastical authority. His
cacklings do mischief. There is legitimate work for him in abundance out
of the pulpit and every sermon he preaches is a calamity to the church. . . .

The signs of the times are naturally and necessarily as blue for the
state as for the church. Our imminent pressing peril is neither foreign
influence nor humanism nor the "slave power," but simple barbarism.
For twenty years at least have we been gravitating that way. Life and
property grow less and less secure. Law, legislature, and judiciary are
less respected; skepticism spreads as to the existence anywhere of anybody who will not steal if he have official opportunity. Our civilization is
decaying. We are in our decadence. An explosion and crash must be at
hand. With which cheerful ratiocinations I close the journal and go to bed.

December 10.   Jem Ruggles dined here and spent the evening reading
music, *Martha* and *Nozze di Figaro*, with Ellie. Looked into the third
volume of Prescott's *Philip the Second*, mainly devoted to the Moresco
Insurrection, Don John, the Escurial, and Lepanto. Better than the first
two volumes, I think; less wordy and more picturesque.

December 13. . . . Another contemptible mess in the Gulf of Mexico:
British aggression, right of search, Nicaragua filibusters, Monroe Doctrine, possible collision, and so forth. May it breed no mischief!

I'm very sick and weary of the perpetually recurring newspaper
announcements under the telegraphic head or in the truculent editorials
of the New York *Herald* that the President and Cabinet have at length
"concluded to take a decided stand" or to "forbid all further French or
English intervention or interference in Central America."[30] As if either
France or England couldn't silence our brag at any moment by sending
half a dozen of their spare war steamers to the Gulf, and drive us out with

[30] With civil war raging in Mexico, European governments were irritated by the
losses suffered by their nationals. Some Spanish naval movements had been interpreted by rumor-mongers as threatening war, and the Spanish minister in Washington had to announce late in November that his government intended no hostilities.
The British and French ministers, Lord Napier and Count Sartiges, made similarly
pacific statements. Early in December Buchanan, in his annual message, proposed the
military occupation of northern Chihuahua and Sonora by American forces, and made
threats of violent action in Central America. Many thought that the bankrupt Buchanan Administration was looking for an excuse to go to war.

the naval tail between the national legs. Were I an Englishman or Frenchman I should long to give this braggart republic a wholesome lesson, a
good vigorous pounding, without the gloves, that should teach it humility
and decorum. We have our good points, but we are no match for the naval
powers of Europe.

December 16. Downtown very late, of course, near two o'clock.
Walked up with George Anthon and Charley Strong, talking of the possibility and the charming consequences of war with France or England,
which some day that old runagate Buchanan means to get up by means of
the anticipated if not inevitable collision between the foreign cruisers in
the Gulf and the shipload of unhanged filibustering pirates which our
government made a pretence of trying to stop and allowed to slip through
its fingers. It has declared that they have no right to the American flag,
but is understood to be ready to make it a *casus belli* if any other power try
to promote public order and peace by stopping them while they carry that
flag. If old Buchanan is in fact so utterly depraved and God-forsaken as to
be capable of attempting to save or strengthen his party by a war (which
word means the slaughter of thousands and the destitution of hundreds of
thousands) on so scandalous a pretext, then is he a proper subject for
private tyrannicide, if there be any case conceivable that justifies the
assassination of a wicked ruler.

December 18.   Last night with Ellie to call on the Wolcott Gibbses
in Twenty-ninth Street; a pleasant visit. Made Gibbs talk chemistry and
polarization. He told me a piece of scandal about aluminium. Ball & Black,
the jewelers, had sundry scraps of that new and interesting acquisition of
metallic society fused in a crucible, with intent to run it into bars, when it
exploded with violence and without apparent excuse, knocking crucible
and furnace into pi. Strange that so placid, quiet-mannered, inert a substance should so disgrace itself before company.

December 20.   We called for Miss Josephine Strong and went to
Wallack's Theater: *Merchant of Venice.* Old Wallack embodies Shylock
perfectly; it's a most intense, vivid, truthful impersonation. Portia was
respectable, and in the trial scene something more. Women of genius would
do well to study Portia—the noblest recorded specimen of the intellectual
woman (I say *recorded*, because she is, relatively to us, quite as real as any
of the Margaret Fullers and other strong-minded women who were once
actual flesh and blood and lived on earth, and died, severally to the great
relief of some man or set of men). She shews how lovely intellect makes a
woman while it is subordinated to heart and womanly impulse.

December 22.   William Betts wants to put me on Columbia College Standing Committee, a manifest absurdity while Mr. Ruggles is in the board, and especially just now when the critical work of leasing the Botanic Garden lots is about to begin.

December 23.   People talk somewhat of Thorndike's[31] will, the malignant old Boston millionaire, whose son Steuart Thorndike married Miss Henrietta Delprat. He cuts off one of his daughters, who married without his approval, giving her only a $400 annuity and providing most elaborately for the forfeiture of all he gives his other children in case they assist her directly or indirectly. Mrs. Henrietta's husband takes a larger provision, but she is specially excluded from anything more than a nominal annuity, in case she survives him, and this is justified by a long recital (in substance) that she and her mother had entrapped him when young and inexperienced "by deception" for the sake of his anticipated inheritance. This post-mortem libel is going the rounds of the papers. Somebody should be indicted for the publication of so infamous a falsehood. The testator is no longer within the jurisdiction of any earthly court. His executors are bound, I suppose, to offer his will for probate and publish its wicked slanders. It seems a *casus omissus* for which the law gives no remedy. The truth is the Delprat family opposed the match strenuously, holding Miss Henrietta too good for little Thorndike, and his old Jink of a father used all his influence to bring it about till just before the marriage, when he suddenly changed his mind. . . . Old Thorndike's name is likely to be long remembered. It will be one of the received regular commonplaces of counsel for disinherited heirs; the recognized symbol of testamentary malignity, of morbid impotent effort to make one's evil passions operative and mischievous by forms of law for a whole generation after their sinful subject has died and relieved the world of his personal presence. This effort must surely prove impotent. No court in Christendom could enforce these forfeitures, and as the prominent object of the whole will seems to be the discouragement of charity and natural affection, the whole instrument must surely be void as against public policy. I would like to be retained against it!

December 24, FRIDAY.   Christmas Eve. The day has been one of sunshine, moral and meteorological; everything has looked Christmas-like, or Christmatoid, Christmatic, or Christmal. Shops are full of business,

---

[31] Augustus Thorndike (Harvard 1816), a wealthy Bostonian, was one of the first Americans to study at Göttingen; he was a man of vigorous intellect and very conservative. Strong frequently encountered his son James Steuart Thorndike (Harvard 1848), a New York lawyer.

streets are thronged; every other pedestrian carries a parcel or two, or escorts one or more eager, expectant children with big eyes fixed on the gorgeous succession of shop windows. Everyone looked good-natured this afternoon. . . .

Early part of the evening spent in hard work unpacking and arranging presents and sending them out. Much is in store for Johnny and Babbins tomorrow morning. Well for them that their weak minds cannot take in at once the multitude and magnitude of their new possessions—the shock would be too serious. The Cavalry Regiment, and the cow with a movable head, and the steamboat that runs about the floor, and that stupendous village (Mrs. Eleanor's kind contribution) with its cottages and its *stadthaus* and its rustics and its cattle, and Johnny's military equipment (from mamma), and Babbins's big drum (from Miss Annie Leavenworth), will make them a pair of millionaires.

My present to Ellie is a silver soup-tureen, and a pair of gilt and glass brackets to be hung against the wall and hold flowers. Mignot surprised her with a lovely tropical landscape sketch, full of color and feeling. Mary sends me the *Encyclopaedia Britannica*.

December 25. Christmas. Most satisfactory day. Higby preached at Trinity Chapel.

1859

THE SICKLES-KEY MURDER · VICTORIES OF NAPOLEON III
AND GARIBALDI · CENTRAL PARK TAKES SHAPE ·
JOHN BROWN'S RAID AND EXECUTION

The year 1859 opened under gloomy auspices. After some delusive tokens of commercial and financial revival, the country had relapsed again into depression. Many factories remained closed; a great part of the country's shipping was idle; few railroads were earning dividends; stock prices were almost at panic levels. Immigration had fallen off heavily, for industrial centers were afflicted with unemployment and want. Wages, rents, and profits were all greatly reduced. In political affairs, the Buchanan Administration had steadily fallen in prestige and was now held in general contempt. Its effort to bring Kansas into the Union under the proslavery Lecompton Constitution had broken down, for when that instrument was submitted to the voters of the territory, they rejected it with contempt and indignation. Having failed in this endeavor, the Administration seemed to turn its back on Kansas. Violence still abounded in the territory, where slavery men and free-soil men were fighting out the issue for themselves—with victory now certain to perch on the free-soil banner. But the reports of murder and outrage which came over the telegraph were sickening. Nor had the Buchanan Administration fared any better in the international sphere. Relations with Great Britain were still disturbed, chiefly because Secretary of State Cass objected vehemently to the course taken by British warships in visiting a number of supposed slave-carrying vessels in West Indian and especially Cuban waters. That American and Cuban ships maintained a prosperous slave trade was well known, but Cass denied that the British had any right of visit and search. As 1859 opened, the subject remained open as a source of future controversy; for the United States failed to suggest any effective

alternative for determining the nationality and the innocence of suspected vessels. Much anger and mortification had been produced in the North by the flagrantly open landing of a large cargo of African slaves on the shores of Georgia, imported by Southern citizens. In Central America, meanwhile, filibustering operations continued, the American government seeming powerless to stop them.

Worst of all was the deepening animosity of the sectional conflict. As the people of New York during January read that civil war was raging with fresh violence in Kansas, and that Slidell of Louisiana had introduced a bill in the Senate to purchase Cuba for the erection of two or more new slave states, feeling ran high. The tariff and the Homestead Bill emerged this month as more distinct issues than ever, with North and South definitely opposed upon them.

January 3, MONDAY. First of all, God watch over and defend my three through this coming year, as hitherto. Amen. . . . Record of New Year's. . . . There were no special incidents. Mrs. Serena Fearing and Mrs. Julia Talmage, each "receiving" for the first time in her own house, were severally very grand and happy and pleasant to behold. At John Sherwood's I had a pleasant talk with his handsome and buxom sister-in-law, Miss Charlotte Wilson, and at Mrs. William B. Astor's with her very intelligent granddaughter, Miss Ward (Sam Ward's daughter).[1] Henry Cram's wife, who has always spent the holidays heretofore in Philadelphia, was at home this New Year's Day—very nice. Mrs. D'Oremieulx trotted out her little Leon to be admired, and I admired him most cordially. He's in Babbins's style, but more mature by a couple of years, and if possible, handsomer. Scarce a house among the forty-odd, the atmosphere of which did not seem kindly and cordial—and which I did not feel glad to have visited and rather reluctant to leave.

Of course, a very large percentage of this aggregate of radiance and hospitality is social sham. But there is still left a certain very valuable residuum or balance of sincere good feeling which is brought out by this much reviled institution of New Year's Day. And this kind of *sham* hurts no one; social usage that requires everybody to receive everybody else with the shew of kindness and cordiality one day in the year does no harm. Perhaps we should be the gainers if the anniversary came *twice* a year.

Home a little before seven, when we dined; Miss Rosalie, Miss Leaven-

[1] Sam Ward had married Emily Astor in 1837; she died in giving birth to their daughter, Margaret Ward, who married John Winthrop Chanler (Columbia 1847).

worth, Miss Josephine Strong, George Anthon, Murray Hoffman, Thorndike, Mignot and R. M. Hunt, and a very jolly session we had—decidedly
a roystering evening. . . .

Actively engaged today in Wall Street till two o'clock. Then to Columbia College meeting. Mr. Ruggles not yet back from Albany. We sat long,
but not without results. King, on behalf of the faculty, applied for tutors,
and further subdivision of classes; motion refused. Most desirable—if we
can afford it.

Standing Committee applied for leave to go on and lease the Botanic
Garden lots, reporting a scale of valuations and rents that astounded me
(an aggregate of $41,000 rental on three blocks). Bradford opposed stren-
uously, insisting that a year's postponement would bring *higher* prices—
but he stood alone and the committee was authorized to proceed. They
will try to negotiate the leases, lot by lot, and it will be long enough before
all are disposed of. I shall rejoice greatly if they come within twenty-five
per cent of what they propose to ask at present, and they will, of course,
take advantage of any rise. We need an increased income, for we run
behindhand $6,000 or $7,000. . . .

Standing Committee reported in favor of hiring a house for the Law
School, and with some difficulty I got a vote referring it back to them with
power to do so. As to the purchase of a library they await a further communication from Professor Dwight. I suppose this was our most important
action this afternoon. . . .

Walked up from Columbia College meeting with Lewis Rutherfurd,
who shewed me a lunar stereoscope picture of his own production.

January 4. Snow kept falling till noon. Now it is warm and thawing,
with a cloudy sky, southwest wind, and a falling barometer. Rain tomorrow,
therefore, and people who may come to Ellie's experimental party will have
to come in boats. The impending party is on a novel plan. Invitations for
five P.M. People are expected anywhere from six to eight and to stay till
twelve, instead of coming at ten and leaving at three. The people invited
are mostly of the dancing class—Young America and his beloved object.
It is a sensible arrangement, but will probably result in failure.

January 6. . . . Last evening was pleasant and satisfactory, with general
good humor and seeming enjoyment. Ellie's innovation on the usages of
late hours was much applauded and succeeded beyond my hopes. I supposed
it impossible to bring together a dozen people before half-past eight. De
Trobriand (that "hungry Frenchman"—*vide* Ullman) and his wife (of all
people) and Walter Cutting appeared at half-past six, and their advent was

followed by a pause, which Helmsmüller's musical corps enlivened with little gratuitous adagios, the violoncello very prominent and very larmoyant. But the whistle of the illustrious Brown was soon heard with unceasing frequency; by half-past seven there were people enough to begin dancing, and by eight the rooms were quite full. The meeting danced vigorously till a little after twelve and then adjourned. . . .

Among our one hundred and twenty guests were Mrs. Augustus Schermerhorn and her nice daughter, Miss Ellen; little Southard Hoffman (Ogden Hoffman's son "Tippy") and his sister Miss Mary, just "out," a lovely blonde, Mrs. Thomas E. Davis, Jr.; pretty Miss Abby Stevens; Peter Strong and his wife; Lord Frederick Cavendish and Mr. Ashley, unscalped by the Sioux; Henry Fearing and his nice Mrs. Serena; Miss Charlotte Wilson; a daughter of (Boston) Robert C. Winthrop's; Miss Rosa Macarty; and so on. . . .

Spent an hour tonight with Ellie and Miss Rosalie at the Century Club Twelfth Night celebration; a great crowd. Not so elaborate a performance as that of last year, but it seemed to go off pleasantly, old Verplanck masquerading as King and a Miss Titus Queen. Old G. C. Verplanck in his coronet and other trappings was fearful and wonderful to behold. His colleagues in the Life and Trust and in Trinity Church vestry would have gazed on him with respectful astonishment. The celebrated Hurlbut was missing; so was that insufferable old Gurowski—both usually invited heretofore.

Trinity Church Committee on Legislative Proceedings met this afternoon; agreed to retain W. M. Evarts with Judge Parker in the suit brought against us in the name of the people.

January 7. Drizzle and liquefaction all day. In the lowest depths of laziness, inertia, and nullity. Murray Hoffman dined here, and we went together to hear *Nozze di Figaro*, Ellie and Miss Rosalie protesting that after two nights of dissipation they must retire early. Very beggarly house. Mozart is repulsive, of course, to lovers of Verdi.

January 13. Poor Hanslein has had a dreadful struggle with subtraction. The educational hour before dinner today was tragic and tearful. He grasps new notions slowly and hardly, and the instant he gets wrong, loses his self-possession and becomes hopelessly muddled. But he is a brick and his future promises none the worse for his developing slowly. . . .

January 15, SATURDAY. Went with Ellie last night to Dodworth's rooms and heard Mrs. Kemble read *The Tempest*. She is fat, but not comely. Very admirable performance. Vocal resources wonderful. She has half a dozen voices in her; drew a separate stop for each character; produced a deep, sullen, brute roar and snarl for Caliban that seemed an impossibility from any feminine windpipe. Prospero's tone was grand, and nothing could be more tender and gentle than her Miranda. Her tipsy Stefano was transcendent; equal to Burton in *The Toodles*, and all her comedy was rendered with a spirit of fun I did not in the least expect. No stage performance could be more satisfactory or bring out the beauties of the play (poem rather) more vividly. And what a glorious poem it is!

January 16. Both Lieber and Joy are astounded by the report of the Columbia College Committee of Inquiry, a copy of which has been sent to each of the faculty. Its printing (which, however nominally confidential, is virtual publication) was a singular indiscretion. The essence of Anthon's evidence is his denunciation of McVickar's pet methods of instruction. McCulloh's evidence amounts to little else than a strongly-worded certificate of Hackley's inefficiency and worthlessness. It was hardly worth while to print this. Still more amazing is the publication of extract from minutes of the faculty on this subject of discipline, giving the names of students charged with various boyish crimes and misdemeanors, and perpetuating the memory of things that ought to be forgotten as soon as possible. I shall not be surprised if it raises a breeze. Gouverneur Ogden has had the principal charge of the matter, and no one need wonder at his obtuseness on any question of delicacy and propriety. But it's marvelous that a man of Anderson's refinement of feeling, and Betts, with his reverence for the proprieties and urbanities of life, should have signed the report and concurred in the printing of this rubbish.

January 20. According to the newspapers, there are symptoms premonitory of a European muss. The majesty of France has personally snubbed the Austrian Ambassador, and the pent-up elements of trouble in Padua and Milan and Italy in general seem simmering with special energy.[2] Poor Italy! God will guide the storm when it comes, and no one can foresee what weather will follow it—but one thing is certain, that no insurrectionary triumph of liberal institutions will "regenerate" that land of faded glories, or do much for any people that has been given up for centuries to humbug, dilettantism, and the Papa of Fibs. (I don't mean by Papa the Pope, but the Devil.) It is true that they have been oppressed for centuries. So

[2] Napoleon III and Cavour had agreed in July, 1858, that France would help Sardinia eject the Austrians from Lombardy and Venetia, with the object of creating a unified North Italian state; France to be rewarded with the duchy of Savoy and city of Nice. Military preparations to attack Austria were openly begun, and the insult to the Austrian minister heralded an imminent war.

was Kaspar Hauser, for the reason that he had been locked up all his life. What would have become of him if he had been turned into the street in full enjoyment of his invaluable right of free agency and the pursuit of happiness?

January 25. Long and peaceful [Trinity] vestry meeting tonight on the resolutions recommended by Dix's retrenchment committee. Have just got home at 11:15 and am waiting for Ellie, who has gone with Jem's escort to Mrs. Gerry's party. The resolutions were opposed by Bleecker and Livingston in a rather reckless spendthrift way, by Anderson (Abel T.) more soberly, and by old McDonald with senile, muddled, incoherent prolixity, painful to hear. Poor old boy; I don't believe his wits amounted to much in their best estate, and they are nearly worn out now. He seemed very infirm and shaky tonight. Result satisfactory, though perhaps hard on some of our beneficiaries. Possibly our action was too spasmodic and reactionary, closing up and drawing in abruptly like a frightened Actinia. But with a minimum deficit of $50,000 ($80,000 last year), it is best to err on the safe side. I called for ayes and noes and recorded a conservative vote. On the cutting-off of old Barrow's $1,000 allowance, Bleecker stood alone. On the list of allowances to churches as recommended by the committee—greatly reduced in number, and putting the churches not wholly cut off on short allowance—there was a series of sharp contests. Economy prevailed in [nearly] every case. . . .

Very probable our action of tonight will raise a breeze, but I am content to abide by my share in it. It's hard to stint on scanty dole to a score of struggling parishes, but if we have no money to give them, it's our duty to lock the strong box and be flinty-hearted. Liberality would be a criminal breach of trust till we can pay our own expenses and the interest on our debt without encroachment on our capital, or enlarging our debt at the rate of $50,000 a year. . . . With Dunscomb for financial manager, and a half-million debt, we may go to protest any day.

Abolish and destroy the prevalent superstition about Trinity Church that it is an inexhaustible fountain of pecuniary aid to every good work, a church-propagating Hercules bound to *put through* every newly organized parish, an ecclesiastical Atlas with the diocese on its shoulders, and individual liberality will at once become two-fold more abundant. "Why don't you go to Trinity Church?" has been the excuse for an infinite amount of inaction and lethargy.

January 27. Walked uptown yesterday afternoon, stopping at Bleecker Street Savings Bank to meet my venerable colleague DePeyster

CRYSTAL PALACE

ATLANTIC CABLE CELEBRATION IN CRYSTAL PALACE

THE GREAT EASTERN

THE ATLANTIC CABLE PROJECTORS
PETER COOPER, D. D. FIELD, CHANDLER WHITE, MARSHALL O. ROBERTS,
SAMUEL F. B. MORSE, DANIEL HUNTINGTON (THE ARTIST),
MOSES TAYLOR, CYRUS W. FIELD, WILSON G. HUNT

Ogden and the Legislative Committee (Opdyke of the Fifth Avenue and his two pals) now here on a marauding expedition dirtier and meaner, I think, than was ever before organized under the banner of any state or sovereign, Robber Barons included. Their office is to see whether there be not old inactive accounts in the city savings banks to such an aggregate as to make it worth the while of the people of the State of New York to confiscate them "for the pressing of the canals"! This pious project will amount to nothing. . . . Wolcott Gibbs came in a while to-night, also Mr. Ruggles, who says he's having done with the canals. He is indignant they should be named in disgraceful connection with this delectable legislative scheme for appropriating the sixpences of servant girls, and apprentices, nurses, and old women.

January 28. Mr. Ruggles came in this evening delighted with the effect his final report as Commissioner is producing among the anti-canal enlargement people—The Constipation Party.[3] Finding its facts and logic troublesome, they are attacking it as coming in too late, that is, after the expiration of his official term (the only period for a final report, one would think), and because he had thoughtlessly put "Canal Commissioner" after his signature, though describing himself as "late Commissioner" in the body of the report.

January 31. The illustrious Prescott died suddenly at Boston. I shall not miss the highly respectable volumes of *Philip the Second* that perish unborn. I am tired of history in dress coat and patent-leather pumps, Clio in hoops and powder.

February 1. Newspapers still busy with predictions of European war; France and Austria to fight for Italy. Doubtful. Neither can afford the luxury.

February 2. Hoffman tells me K. Armstrong is investigating spiritual-ism again with Peter Porter, and that the lady who is now working the telegraphic lines to the invisible world for their benefit (one Mrs. Hayden) produces sundry marvelous phenomena. I query whether society was in a *more* or *less* enlightened and healthy state of morals and intelligence a couple of hundred years ago when this wonder-working female would have been whipped at the cart's tail, or yet more severely dealt with.

[3] Since his appointment to the Erie Canal Board in the summer of 1858, Ruggles, who was chosen president, had been active in promoting the interests of the great artery. The report here mentioned was the Annual Report of the Board for the year 1858; a document which argued the immense value of the canal in spite of the growing traffic of the railroads. The use of the canal was indeed soon to increase tremendously.

February 7. People wonder why a couple of overdue steamers don't arrive, and whether their detention hasn't something to do with the expected outbreak of war on the plains of Lombardy. Columbia College trustees met at two o'clock; barely a quorum. Professor Dwight reported progress in a clear and creditable paper, and that we need $2,000 for a law library. Rutherfurd from the Committee on Observatory recommended that we suspend our movements on that question for the present. Under the auspices of Marshall of Cincinnati (who has been lecturing to crowded houses at the Academy of Music), W. H. Aspinwall and other outsiders are organizing themselves into a committee and talking of raising funds for an observatory. Rutherfurd thinks that if they succeed, we shall be asked to cooperate and perhaps to take charge of their hypothetical institution. We determined to meet hereafter at the College; evening meetings, the second Monday instead of the first. A good resolution, but we shan't keep it. The College territories are too remote and unsettled as yet to be frequented at night by elderly respectable gentlemen like Berrian and Dominie DeWitt.

February 9. Did little downtown. Savings Bank trustees met at half-past four in the afternoon. Recommendations of the Examining Committee adopted, one of them on a close vote. Every board of trustees, directors, managers, and so on that I've had to do with keeps a donkey—one donkey, at least. It is a great physiological law of corporate existence; an asinine element is essential to corporate life. It seems represented in this body by one Benjamin H. Field, who makes it a point to be vehemently garrulous on the wrong side of every question that comes before it.

February 13, SUNDAY. Heard Professor Guyot's introductory (post-graduate) lecture Thursday night; very earnest and effective, but spoiled by scanty vocabulary and foreign accent. . . . Murray Hoffman talked of spiritualism. Has heard a lecture by one Van Kleeck or Van Vleeck, a converted medium, who professes to reveal the tricks of his order. The lecturer was frequently interrupted by "spiritualists" in his audience, and (according to Hoffman) with a remarkable intensity of feeling—a personal bitterness, such as one would expect from a Roman Catholic listening to a Protestant harangue by a renegade priest. This is a badge of sincerity in delusion; it seems to show that this miserable humbug has made a lodgment in the moral nature of its believers and has allied itself with their affections and their religious instinct; has become the outlet of their faculty for worship and reverence. Several "mediums" have publicly renounced their idols of late. From newspaper reports I perceive that they agree in assigning say seventy-five per cent of the spiritualistic phenomena to mere trick, twenty per cent to psychometry or thought-reading (whatever that may be), and a residuum of five per cent more or less to something they cannot explain.

February 17. Last night with Ellie at Mrs. Wolcott Gibbs's in Twenty-ninth Street, the first of certain little informal musical gatherings that promise to be very agreeable. . . .

The Rev. T. H. Taylor of Grace Church fights a good fight, not only of faith (in the way of his profession), but also pugilistically. Young Banks (Ellery Anderson's partner) wrote him a lawyer's letter about a certain protested note, the back of which that Levite had perhaps thoughtlessly embellished with his autograph, and he called at Banks's office to *settle*. They differed about the amount due. (Banks's practice was in fact rather sharp, I believe; he wanted to extract from the reverend endorser of the note the costs of a judgment he had obtained against the maker.) The difference developed into a squabble. The presbyter forgot the lesson of meekness and lowliness he inculcates on Sundays, like a love of a man, as he is. He let his angry passions rise and called the attorney a pettifogger and a swindler. The attorney replied by an averment that the presbyter lied, whereupon the latter proceeded to a laying on of hands—uncanonical, but worthy the best days of Ecclesiastical Discipline—and gave Mr. [Francis Saltus] Banks an emphatic shaking and cuffing.

February 20. From what John Sherwood tells me, his chance of success in his great Nicaraguan Transit Company suit against old Vanderbilt seems good.[4] That energetic old scoundrel, the general trustee and manager of the company, has somehow about three millions of corporate assets, for which equity should compel him to account. Possibly George C. Anthon's stock may yet be worth something.

February 22. Thorndike, George Anthon, and Murray Hoffman here this evening. Strolled with George Anthon to Forty-second Street and back, discoursing of old times—college days—when our walks above Tenth Street took us into the fields, when the "House of Refuge" stood where Madison Square begins, and the Fifth Avenue was a mere tentative group of houses from Washington Square to Tenth Street and the new

---

[4] The directors of the Pacific Mail were giving battle to Commodore Vanderbilt for control of the trans-Isthmian traffic. A year of fierce competition between Vanderbilt's Atlantic & Pacific Steamship Company and the Pacific Mail Company, accompanied by legal warfare, opened. Various New York interests participated in the struggle, which was still continuing when the Civil War began.

Ascension Church. "Thinking on the days that are long enough gone" is always sad work.

February 23. European news rather indicative of coming war, France and Sardinia *vs.* Austria. May England, Russia, and all the German Powers side against France and lick her into due appreciation of what she is, a mere element of mischief in Christendom since the days of Louis XIV.

February 27, SUNDAY. Mr. Ruggles thinks Louis Napoleon means mischief and that there will be war in Europe. Mary Johnson's funeral was at half-past one. The pall-bearers were Dayton Hobart, Henry Pierrepont, Joshua Coit, Stephen Williams, Campbell (who married one of Dr. J. Augustine Smith's daughters), Henry Winthrop, Theodore Winthrop, and Rufus Delafield. Binney, Templeton, and I were together her only near male relatives or connections. Services at the Church of the Holy Communion, Dr. Muhlenberg, Dr. Berrian, Hobart, and young Lawrence officiating. Thence to Trinity Church, where the black old Brownjohn vault was yawning once more and received her. Many poor persons attended the service, followed her all the way to Trinity Churchyard, and cried a great deal. Such, perhaps, is "the rain" referred to in the old proverb about weddings and funerals. She gave most of her income and far the larger portion of her time to the charities or to the church; was abundant in labor and self-denial, visiting, relieving, and tending the sick, destitute, and ignorant—energetically doing good by systematic personal effort.

February 28. The news of the day is that the Honorable Dan Sickles has attained the dignity of homicide. Having ascertained that Mr. Philip Barton Key, district attorney of the District of Columbia, has been too intimate with his pretty young wife (daughter of old Bagioli, the music teacher), he put three pistols in his pocket and shot Key in the street yesterday morning at Washington. Probably he will not be even indicted. Were he not an unmitigated blackguard and profligate, one could pardon any act of violence committed on such provocation. But Sickles is not the man to take the law into his own hands and constitute himself the avenger of sin.

Butterworth of this city is in a yet worse position. He had no wrong to avenge and no passion to cloud his sense of right and wrong, but he seems to have gone forth at Sickles's request and engaged Key in conversation till Sickles could get his pistols and come up and use them. He clearly deserves hanging.

Daniel E. Sickles of New York City, after a decidedly disreputable career in municipal and state politics, had been elected to Congress in 1856, and held his seat there until 1861. He had married Theresa Bagioli, seventeen-year-old daughter of an Italian musician, several years before coming to Washington. One of the foremost figures in Washington society, Philip Barton Key, son of the author of "The Star-Spangled Banner," frequented the Sickles house. The story of the sequel is well known; how Sickles suspected his wife and Key of guilty relations, how he laid a trap for Key and shot him down on a peaceful Sunday morning in Lafayette Square, within hailing distance of the White House, and how Sickles successfully withstood trial. President Buchanan knew Dan Sickles well, for the young man had been secretary of legation while Buchanan was minister to Great Britain. The President ostentatiously showed his sympathy with the murderer, and it was generally assumed that the public prosecutor, District Attorney Ould, who was later prominent in the Confederate service, would not displease the President by too rigorous activity. Sickles employed for his defense Edwin M. Stanton, then known chiefly as an attorney in patent and land cases. For the first time in American jurisprudence, the defense set up the plea of a brain-storm or temporary aberration of mind, and Sickles was acquitted. He was given a courtroom ovation and a round of dinner parties by his coarse-grained friends; and he forgave his wife—who had much to forgive him.

In Europe a new war was about to begin. Napoleon III and Cavour had agreed on their program and booty, and the bargain was duly carried out. The early weeks of 1859 found Sardinia making obvious preparations for war, and in April the alarmed Austrian Government delivered an ultimatum. When this was rejected, fighting began and lasted until July. Most Americans had equally little use for Napoleon III and for Austria, and felt like Strong that both ought to be defeated. But the French and Sardinian victories at Magenta and Solferino advanced Italian liberation and unity by a long step.

Meanwhile, Strong had passed some weeks of acute anxiety over the illness of his small son, George Templeton Strong, Jr., or "Babbins." And he had to fling himself into another public cause when certain interested persons at Albany delivered a vigorous attack upon the endowment of the Trinity School, of which he was now a leading trustee.

March 2.   Went for Ellie tonight to Mrs. Wright's, where the little Musical Club met to rehearse. Wolcott Gibbs there, much delighted with the results of his investigation into the group of platinum metals and their ammonia compounds. He is following it up earnestly—and thinks himself just about grabbing a new metal!!!—first cousin to ruthenium, osmium, iridium, and the rest of their tribe that look so imposing in the catalogue of elements, each saying to oxygen and carbon and hydrogen and iron and the other aristocratic independent entities of science, "I, too, am an element and brother—obscure and friendless, but just as good an element as you, and with rights you can't invade"; like a high-spirited bootblack asserting the dignity of manhood against William B. Astor.[5]

Gibbs charged me to say nothing about his hopes lest they should prove unfounded after all, and his two nitrates should turn out mere delusive double-faced isomeric salts of the same metal. But I think it very likely he is going to make the first addition the New World has yet furnished to our list of primal elements. I suggest he should call it Buchananium after our revered Chief Magistrate.

March 5, SATURDAY. The diverse views men take of the relative positions and duties of Mr. Sickles, Mrs. Sickles, Mr. Key, and Mr. Butterworth in the late "tragedy" at Washington are amusing. Walter Cutting says, "By gracious, you may depend upon it, poor Key's great mistake was mixing himself with a low set like the Sickleses." The distinguished Bancroft feels for Mrs. Sickles: "Poor child, what a cruel thing to deprive her of her sole stay and support. Key was the only man she could look to for sympathy and protection. Under the circumstances, it was too bad for Dan Sickles to take his life." Mr. S. B. Ruggles, always disposed to err on the side of sympathy with anyone in trouble, no matter what his antecedents, is half inclined to think it would be a good thing for some of the friends of Trinity Church to remember now the good fight Dan Sickles fought for the church in the legislative battle of 1857, and to write him some expression of condolence and good will. But the whole case is so very fishy, and Sickles's career has been so disgraceful, that I can hardly think we are called upon to do so.

There is some reaction against Sickles. People say the confession extorted from his wife and put on paper before witnesses was the dodge of a Tombs lawyer, and shows the homicide to have been premeditated from the first. Butterworth's course is condemned, and the worst inference against him adopted. That Sickles seduced his mother-in-law and silenced her husband by telling him there was another Mrs. Bagioli in

---

[5] Gibbs's work on the platinum metals was of great value to science, for he did more than any previous investigator to establish the nature of their complex compounds. But he did not discover a new element.

Italy, and also seduced the daughter before their tardy marriage, appears granted. The story had long been generally received. Buchanan's calling on Sickles in jail is rather exasperating. The decision in Sickles's case would ultimately devolve on that disgraceful old Chief Magistrate in the most improbable event of Dan's conviction. Some people talk of relations between the lady and old Buck, of which Dan had full notice and in which he acquiesced, and which put that venerable sinner in Dan's power. Some say other things as bad. There is hardly a kind or degree of baseness that somebody is not quite ready to vouch for.

March 10, THURSDAY.   Columbia College meeting (special) Tuesday afternoon. Did nothing very memorable. Thomas Wells resigned, having become a citizen of New Jersey. . . . For the two vacancies there were nominated John Astor, the Rev. Morgan Dix, Carson Brevoort, and John C. Jay, all good names but the last. The Jays of this generation are generally devoid of common sense. Brevoort would make a capital professor of comparative anatomy, ichthyology, and many other ologies; but I am not quite clear as to his fitness to be a trustee. So I shall support Astor and Dix. To be sure, we have a surplus of clergymen already, but Haight is practically shelved, I fear, and the Bishop and Berrian seldom come near us. Hutton and Spring attend, on the whole, with perverse schismatic punctuality, but that only makes it desirable to have some young and energetic churchmen like Dix to meet them in the event of any subtle attempt to Dutch-Reform the College. As I expected, we concluded it was impossible to hold future meetings at the College, and the resolution to meet there was rescinded. No great harm done. Our new Law School building (one of the Colonnade houses in Lafayette Place,[6] formerly occupied by John Astor) will be in our possession May 1st. It will be a convenient place for our meetings, and we can then bid farewell to the "Prayer Meeting Rooms" in Fulton Street, with their disgusting placards, "Prayers and exhortations not to exceed five minutes in order to give all an opportunity."

March 12.   News from Europe looks more and more pugnacious. My belief is that Louis Napoleon intends to fight. I would bet on France in the coming fray, but I *hope* she may be thrashed and humiliated.

March 15.   Very busy day without notable events. Conference with Gouverneur Ogden about the expediency of appointing a "rector's

[6] Rather on Lafayette Street just south of Astor Place; the eight colonnaded houses (four of which survived in 1952) were a fine manifestation of the Greek Revival style.

assistant" (of Trinity Church), an office provided for by the church, but long vacant. This mythical functionary could act in case of the rector's disability. The assistant ministers could not. Should Dr. Berrian be visited with some sudden apoplexy or paralysis, a loss of power for months or years, incapable of duty and without the volition necessary to give legal efficacy to any act, without power to execute even a valid resignation (no extravagant improbability; not impossible at least), Trinity Church would continue in like paralysis while his life lasted. There could be no meeting of the vestry, no appropriation of money, no corporate act. The corporation would perish unless helped out of this deadlock by special legislation, which the powers at Albany would probably refuse. So the appointment of a rector's assistant seems a wise precaution, the plain dictates of common prudence.

March 20, SUNDAY.   Conferred with Mr. Ruggles and Cyrus Curtiss about the Trinity School bill.[7] With characteristic tact and energy, Mr. Ruggles had rushed it nearly through the Senate, when that brute Noxon suddenly intervened and objected. "There was more in this plausible little bill than appeared on its face. There was an immense estate on New York island to be affected by it, which had probably *escheated* to the state, and about which the Attorney General had already been called upon to act." This stayed all progress, of course. On inquiry it turns out that Hogg, our tenant on about one-third the land, has been lobbying and intriguing with Noxon and with the Land Office and the Attorney General to get up some attack on our title by the state—assuming, no doubt, that if we were got rid of, his rights as tenant in possession would be gently dealt with and he would be allowed to buy out the state at a bargain.

March 28.   Have been rushing about town tonight, seeking affidavits to be used before the Senate Judiciary Committee, showing that "Trinity School" notoriously existed before it was incorporated, and in 1796, the date of Baker's will. Hunted up old Samuel Gilford at last, whose ancient recollections serve my purpose. He remembers the Rev. Mr. Inglis, the last of the loyal rectors of Trinity Church, preaching his farewell sermon in St. George's Chapel prior to his evacuation of the city along with the royal forces.

April 2.   Energized in Wall Street. Tonight through the rain to the

[7] Dr. John Baker had left some valuable real estate to Trinity School, which fell to it on the death of nine prior beneficiaries. Six of these had died and the other three had surrendered their claims. The school wished to sell enough land to meet some special tax-assessments for improvements, and a bill for that purpose was presented at Albany. Ruggles was employed to push the bill in the legislature.

Century Club: Verplanck, Dr. Bellows, William Hoppin, David Dudley
Field, Lewis Rutherfurd, Egbert Viele, and others. Pleasant evening.
Mrs. Rutherfurd has just set up another baby, a small boy, and is doing
well. To Albany Tuesday afternoon, just at the finale of a heavy rain
that had prevailed all day. My railroad ride was not disagreeable. . . .
Reached Albany at eleven P.M.; Delavan House and Mr. Ruggles. Crowd.
Every man looked at each newcomer as he entered with his overcoat and
his carpetbag, distrustfully and uneasily, as who should say: "Who are
you and what brings *you* here? Have you come to interfere with that little
bill of mine?" Next morning early at the Capitol. Trinity School bill
referred to Judiciary Committee of Senate, namely, James Noxon, Willard
of Troy, Lamont of Lockport, Diven, and Scott. Meeting fell through;
Willard, a respectable, formal old gentleman, had to go home and look
after a sick son, and Diven and Scott were missing. Struck up an intimacy
with Noxon, the arch-enemy of Trinity Church in the campaign of 1857,
and found him a better fellow than I supposed. Trinity Church is still his
bug-bear. As soon as he found that Hogg had been lying, after his swinish
nature, and that this bill was not intended to "enrich the coffers of Trinity
Church," he began to look into it with candor and intelligence. Till then
he was girded up for resolute opposition. Waited and waited, a suitor to
the sovereign Demos, most of the morning session for opportunity to
make another appointment. The Senate, on the whole, impressed me
favorably. Though "Drunken Doherty" was factious and disorderly in
his own impudent incoherent way, he was steadily and gently put down
and kept down, without excitement and in strict conformity to rules.
Went into the Court of Appeals; Judge A. S. Johnson, very civil—for the
sake of microscopy, I suppose. Into the House, just in time for the vote on
old Boorman's bill for digging up Trinity Churchyard, the everlasting
old Protean Albany Street business transferred from the Common Council
to the legislature. To my surprise and delight, it was summarily squelched
by a huge majority (Opdyke among its few supporters). We have done
little or no lobbying against it—nothing compared with Boorman's
energetic efforts; so the result is the more satisfactory. It shews that the
general instinct is with us. Before the Senate Committee at four. Mr.
Ruggles supported the bill very ably for about an hour and a half, and
wound up with a most ferocious onslaught on Hogg as coming forward
to interfere without any status in Court and seeking to embarrass the
operations of a most meritorious charity without the slightest interest—
as a mere common informer and with no motive but to blackmail.

Hogg got up when Mr. Ruggles sat down (Reynolds, his counsel, was not in attendance) and let off a little sneaking, malignant, pettifogging speech, full of the dirtiest personal slanders, some of which Mr. Ruggles at once denounced as infamous falsehoods. He intimated that he knew of heirs of Baker, but would not say who they were; seemed to suggest that he was himself an heir; said Baker was an alien, and they can't prove he was ever naturalized; the Baker farm belonged to the heirs; it belonged to the state; Baker gave it to the school to be kept forever and not to be sold—with other equally consistent suggestions. Thereafter we adjourned.

Hogg's performance did him more harm than Mr. Ruggles's clear and forcible argument did us good. The committee seemed to understand him and came at once to a realizing sense of the motive and merits of his opposition. When he finished, Diven, who had seemed captious and dubious, remarked, very quietly: "Well, if this devise be void, and if the property *has* escheated, I think the state had better release its claim *right off.*" . . .

From noon till midnight (Thursday) drawing a report for the committee, which I don't believe will be signed, and redrawing the same. It's a rather plausible paper, considering who drew it, and it's a pity it should be lost. But the session is drawing to an end; both houses are crowded with work; every legislator is worn and weary with buttonholing by anxious outsiders; everyone of them, however well disposed, hears the talk of applicants listlessly and with an expression of the dreariest boredom—at best with polite endurance. I can't hope that members of the Judiciary Committee will be induced to read, consider, and sign this long, dreary paper.

Friday morning another session of committee. Bill virtually agreed to; authorizes sale under direction of Supreme Court. Hogg opposing and snarling, but rather ignored and passed over. Today's papers announce its third reading. . . . Had a couple of interviews with the Governor, Morgan.[8] Discoursed with him at much length about the larcenous designs of Opdyke and Diven on the Savings Banks. Both bills are like to pass, especially Diven's ("to enlarge the powers of public administra-

[8] Edwin D. Morgan, long a successful merchant, banker, and broker in New York, was now displaying unexpected qualities of grasp, vision, and independence as governor. George Opdyke (1805–1880), also a merchant and a Republican, was now briefly in the Assembly, and about to become mayor. An independent reformer, he lacked Morgan's steadiness of judgment.

tors"), and it seemed to me that I made some impression on His Excellency. I dare say he is a humbug, like most politicians, but he listened to the talk of my insignificant self with very flattering courtesy and attention—made me feel influential and important.

I hardly hope we can get our Trinity School bill through, but things look far brighter than they did Wednesday morning. Anyhow, Mr. Ruggles has fought a good fight, and I certify and declare that I worked like a dog while at Albany. Whatever the result, we have done our best.

Last night at Mrs. Gibbs's in Twenty-ninth Street; another of our musical gatherings. Talked to Scharfenberg, Miss Mary Hamilton (Mount Vernon's "Regent") and Mrs. Schuyler, George Bancroft, and others, and had a rather good time.

April 3, SUNDAY.   Mr. Ruggles dined here and we took a Third Avenue car to Seventy-ninth Street and waded about through the abysmal mud of divers newly opened and nominally "regulated" streets and avenues, inspecting the Baker Farm. Some souvenirs of faded rurality and respectability still survive in the old mansion, with its lawn sweeping down to the East River—formerly called "Sans Souci," but now "Baker's Retreat," as the testator described it in 1796; the Delafield country seat for the succeeding half-century. All the rest is shabby and seedy and dilapidated; horrid with shanties and newly excavated trenches (that will be streets hereafter), with unwholesome, water-soaked fields between; pigs and stramonium and mouldy old tottering fences. Country in the first stage of morbid organic change of structure, ossifying into city, a process that is purulent and gangrenous and most unlovely while it lasts, but which will result in city lots and leases and a rent-roll, if we can but hold the property long enough and are not rooted up by our Hogg. It's going to be a very anxious and arduous business, in which I shall have responsibility more than enough.

April 7, THURSDAY.   At Columbia College Monday we elected John Astor a trustee. Tried to elect Morgan Dix to the other vacant seat, but gave it up after four fruitless ballots. Gouverneur Ogden and I hold consultations about Dix now, and about the affairs of Trinity Church. We are allies and intimate. . . .

Dan Sickles's trial is commencing at Washington.

April 8.   Murray Hoffman dined here, and I went with him to the little dingy, sour-smelling Bowery "State Theatre" to hear Wagner's *Tannhäuser*. A great crowd, Teutonic and generally frowzy. Lieber was there and Willy Marsh, and Dan Messenger, being earnest enquirers after good music. . . . Lager beer and cakes handed round between acts. Audience grimly attentive to the music, which is grim likewise.

First impressions: The well-known overture is to the opera as potable soup to beef; nearly all the nutriment and strength of the opera condensed and concentrated therein. Repetition of the overture phrases incessantly recurring throughout the three long acts. Lack of fluent melody. The attempt to give each several word its proper musical expression makes free-flowing song impossible. Very bold instrumental effects, original rather than beautiful, and too continuously kept up. But the opera, on the whole, decidedly impressive. Something of this due to libretto and plot—most unusually good, consistent, clear, and significant. Dramatically considered, it's the best opera I know; the only one, rather, that's not beneath contempt. Performance was not to be found fault with, though the principal "artistes" would have been sniffed at by the Academy of Music habitués. Orchestra unimpeachable. Chorus the best I ever heard in opera. *Mise en scène* most careful and elaborate. It was a very satisfactory evening and did Deutschland credit.

April 10. Special meeting of trustees of Trinity School yesterday in the organ loft of Trinity Church. Dr. Seabury in the chair. Appropriate *locale.* The school was first organized one hundred and fifty years ago in the belfry of the *first* Trinity Church, on the same point of the earth's surface. Action of the meeting satisfactory. Have not heard from Mr. Ruggles since Friday, but from letters received by Mrs. Ruggles, I infer that the opposition in the Assembly is not insuperable and that the bill is being pushed vigorously and with prospect of success.

Theodore Eisfeld has returned from Fayal in good bodily preservation, considering the perils he has passed, but with a battered and weather-beaten exchequer. So a "Welcome Concert" was got up for him last night at the Academy of Music by the Philharmonic people. George Anthon dined here and we went together. Sinfonia *Eroica* and "Jubel" overture; blessed be the memories of Beethoven and Weber.

April 14. Savings Bank meeting yesterday afternoon. Charles R. Swords is full of wrath about the dismissal of his Freshman brother-in-law (Willis) from Columbia College; dismissed along with a son of limping Augustus H. Ward's, for peppering Professor Schmidt with sugar plums, and their petition for restoration denied. Our first act of resolute earnest discipline for many a year. Swords's furious. Talked of *going to law*!! I wish he would. That ass, Benjamin H. Field (who has a son among the undergraduates), put in his oar and talked sense for once. Said that many

merchants of his acquaintance would give a clerkship to no boy who had
been through Columbia College, because necessarily without habits of
order, punctuality, and subordination. Very likely he was "gassing," for
I don't believe many merchants of New York have sagacity enough to
draw that inference, or know or care anything about our poor little College and its administration. But our discipline has long been a scandalous
farce, beyond all question. My jolly old friend, King, is inexcusably
slack, unsystematic and worthless.[9] Probably the College and its endowment do more mischief than good to the community. Very lamentable
and disgusting. Query: Might it not be wise to concentrate our resources
on post-graduate courses of study—the Law School and the like—and make
the College a secondary matter, a subordinate training school for the
University?

April 19. Our School bill got through the Assembly (69 ayes)
Saturday morning; an immense result even for Mr. Ruggles's energy
and talent. Signed by Governor Morgan the same day. Our petition was
printed and ready, and copies are now "out" for service on the life-
tenants—the Hogg family. My personal apprehension is that we shall be
unable to effect personal service on all of them. If we can, I think we shall
put a ring in their snouts.

Sickles's trial still in progress. Evidence of Mrs. Sickles's criminality
let in, though her written confession was (properly enough) ruled out.
The prosecution should not have objected to that paper's being read. It
is manifestly Dan Sickles's work, copied by his wife, and tells damagingly
against him.

War not yet pronounced in Europe, but probably at hand. The pacific
rumors of congresses and concessions are dying away, and the armaments
of France, Austria, and Sardinia are not reduced. Any casual outbreak of
"liberal" lunacy against its keepers, in any hamlet of Italy, would bring
on collision and general crash at any moment.

April 22. Sickles's trial near its close. Some people think there's
a chance of the jury disagreeing, but I predict they will acquit without
leaving the box. It was a deliberate, premeditated murder; no doubt the
skillfully-drawn and certified confession proves that. But it has become

---

[9] King, handsome, courtly, and eloquent, was seventy this spring; as editor of the
New York *American* he had failed for want of enterprise, and in other fields he had
never shown iron qualities. He was no disciplinarian—but the students loved him
for his kindliness and interest. Francis Willis got himself readmitted and was graduated
with his class in 1862; Edmund Augustus Ward took the LL.B. degree in 1867.

part of our Common Law as interpreted by jurors that the seducing of a wife or near kinswoman (or even the erroneous belief in such seduction) justifies homicide. Or, in other words, that the seducer or adulterer has forfeited his life, and the injured party is authorized by law to take it. In this case, Sickles was simply acting as the minister or deputy sheriff of this higher law when he shot Mr. Key, and is to be protected, just as Jack Ketch would be against an indictment for taking the life of the next man who shall be "run up" in the courtyard of the Tombs.

This right of assassination is now practically so well settled that legislation has become necessary to regulate and define it and prevent its abuse. As the law now stands, Othello can shoot Michael Cassio at sight and be sure of acquittal, because he did so on his best information and belief derived from Iago. But Cassio should be presumed innocent like other people till he is proved guilty. He should not be condemned *ex parte* and executed without a hearing. So far the law is plainly defective. Moreover, none can avail themselves of this right at present without a certain amount, more or less, of address in the use of the knife or revolver. It is practically denied to a very large class of the community. And what is to be done if Cassio be forewarned, if Othello's first shot chance to miss, and Cassio respond with another that does execution? How are we to dispose of his plea of "*Se defendendo*"?

April 23, SATURDAY.   Tonight at Wrey Mould's funny little house in Twenty-sixth Street, hearing his little musical club. I think they out-do us. Organ and piano accompaniments, eight-handed—and difficult music clearly rendered at sight. Cherubini's Fourth Mass, a couple of movements from Mozart's Seventh (far the finest of his shorter Masses, I think—certainly most lovely from credo to finale), parts of the Lobgesang, and so on. Performers not generally "in society," I think; some of them semi-professional. My old grammar school teacher Dr. Quin is among them.

April 24.   Cisco says his friend Butterworth tells him he advised Sickles to challenge Key or else to give him notice and kill him in a street "collision," but that Sickles avowed his preference for an *ex parte* assassination. Also, that the fair and frail Theresa says with great naïveté: "It was too bad of Dan to *publish* that paper I wrote for him. I'll *never have anything more to do with Dan* if he behaves that way."

Ellie with her papa tonight at the Rev. Mr. Lord's lecture on Oliver

Cromwell, and much delighted.[10] Tackled Rev. Lord afterwards and told him that he had not done full justice to Charles I.

April 26. Sickles acquitted, of course. Ellie at the Beldens' this evening. Everyone says the next steamer must bring news of war in Europe.

May 2, MONDAY. Columbia College meeting at two; Potter, Berrian, Haight, and Billy Harison attending to back Morgan Dix, thereby driving Ray, Jones, Rutherfurd, Zabriskie, and others into more earnest recalcitrations against any accession to the clerical element in the board. There were three ballots, Dix always nine, and nine divided between Carson Brevoort, and John C. Jay. No election. Zabriskie made an ass of himself by an oration eulogizing Jay, very unnecessarily. Dwight's suggestions about the Law School (prizes, additional lecturers, division of proceeds of School) were carried *nem. con.*, and Gouverneur Ogden and I were added to the Committee to select assistants and settle details. . . .

Some months ago we (that is, the College trustees) voted $500 per annum to pay an amanuensis, clerk, or private secretary to the president, who said he must have help to do the entries and computations required by the new system of daily marks for merit and demerit. He has actually made his two nice daughters (Miss H. and Miss M.) the registrars of the college, and they sit in his room, hear the excuses of the students, and giggle with them when his back is turned. Was ever a good old soul like King so obtuse and blind? so inconsiderate and absurd? I've the greatest respect and regard for him and his house, but if I did not know him and them as I do, I should move that the president be censured or displaced. He does scandalous wrong, in his thoughtlessness, not only to the college, but to the young ladies.

The Misses Henrietta Low King and Mary Alsop King (then 26 and 20), daughters of President Charles King by his second wife Henrietta Liston Low, were the first of the many thousands of women employed by Columbia University. Miss Henrietta grew fat and remained a spinster. Miss Mary became the wife (in 1874) of William Henry Waddington, a Frenchman educated at Trinity College, Cambridge, who was Senator, Minister of Foreign Affairs, Pleni-

[10] The Rev. John Lord (1810–1894), who made a great success as historical lecturer delivering some six thousand discourses on many topics. His eight-volume *Beacon Lights of History* was long a popular subscription set.

*potentiary to the Congress of Berlin, French representative at the Coronation
of Alexander III at Moscow, and for the last decade of his life Ambassador
to the Court of St. James's. Madame Waddington, a handsome, vivacious woman,
even in her youth a grande dame, published four volumes of her memoirs, and
lived until the summer of 1923.*

May 5.   Spent this evening in Lewis Rutherfurd's observatory. He
was watching the movements of a miserable little loafing comet, like a
detective policeman, and poor Hackley was recording them. It looked
like a distant street lamp dimly seen through the fog by a near-sighted
man, a small, amorphous, hazy blotch of faint light. The inscrutable
decrees of Creative Power deny it the dignity of a tail. When this work
was finished, Rutherfurd proceeded to reveal to me, through his equatorial, something of the Glory that belongs to celestial bodies. Very
unlike terrestrial. Never knew before *how much* one star differs from
another in glory. Splendid purples and blues. . . .

J. Phillips Phoenix dead; a very influential pecuniary citizen, politician, and real estate holder. . . .[11]

Theodore Winthrop has been writing the most polysyllabic pamphlets
about Church's picture, like the ravings of Ruskin in delirium tremens.[12]
Winthrop has undergone a "fatty degeneration" of late and become a
lump of grim conceit. Seems to consider himself a sort of Vivian Grey
modified by a percentage of Voltaire, and shocks and offends women (for
example, Mrs. Rutherfurd) by letting off gas about atheism, and pro-
pounding horrible paradoxes. He takes every opportunity of giving
judgment on heaven and earth and all things visible and invisible, and
generally puts their alleged Creator out of court in a summary way.
Perhaps he's in some stage of development, but at present he seems a bad
specimen of Yankeeism in its worst form.

May 7.   To Wall Street, where Dayton Hobart called to talk of
Dick Ogden's family, left absolutely destitute, without five dollars in

[11] Jonas Phillips Phoenix (1788–1859), long a prominent Whig leader in New
York City, had served in Congress 1843–1845 and 1849–1851. He was a well-known
merchant.

[12] Theodore Winthrop was a close friend of Frederick E. Church, having traveled
in the Adirondacks and the Maine woods with him. At this time Winthrop, after
vigorous electioneering for Frémont in 1856 and a venture in the law in St. Louis,
was busy as a free-lance writer in New York. The work of which Strong speaks was
his detailed and flowery description of one of Church's pictures: *A Companion to the
Heart of the Andes.*

money, property, or credit; with literally *nothing* but what change there may have been in poor Mrs. Ogden's *porte-monnaie* and her husband's pocketbook.

Walked up with George Anthon. Church's "Heart of the Andes" is at the Tenth Street Studio Building. Very splendid picture; it beats any landscape I ever saw. But I don't believe it merits all people say about it. Pete Strong commenced a fine cackling about it this evening, but I silenced him by saying that I thought it was "very pretty and did Mr. Church a great deal of credit." . . .

European news: General arming, concentrations and preparations in France and Austria and little Sardinia. Austria either has or has not crossed the Ticino in great force at three points. London *Times* asserts that she has, others say she has given Sardinia fourteen days' further time for reflection. Probably she has *not*. Alliance between France and Russia announced, to the amazement and consternation of England. Italy seems in ferment. Ruction and revolution in Tuscany. That is enough of itself to bring on a general shindy. . . .

Mr. Ruggles's souvenirs of Aaron Burr are rather good. *Inter alia*, on his suggestion to Aaron to make petition to the legislature about something or other, Aaron responds: "Sir, I petition God. Women sometimes. Men never." Man complaining of his trials, errors and anxieties, about his wife's tedious illness, winds up: "I do wish she'd get well, *or something!*" (That has nothing to do with Burr.)

May 16. Opera tonight with Ellie and Charley Strong and wife. *Puritani*; Mrs. Cora de Wilhorst, Brignoli, and Amodio. That smallest of prima donnas sings and acts very respectably. The opera is poor stuff —its so-called "great" melodies seem to me specimens of a faint, sickish, nasty sweetness like that of a rotten pear or a damaged banana. . . . Further European news today. Austria had entered Piedmont with force and arms but had done no fighting yet; seemed losing hours, each of which may be many hundred thousand florins to the imperial finance-chamber.[13] She ought to have smashed Sardinia before France could come to the rescue. The Duke of Tuscany and Duchess of Parma have severally cut and run, their respective peoples rising in the cause of Italian nationality.

[13] The Austrian government had demanded that Sardinia cease her preparations for war; and the rejection of this ultimatum brought an outbreak of hostilities. While the Austrian troops moved tardily, French forces under Napoleon III and Marshal MacMahon hastened to invade Piedmont and join the Sardinian troops under Victor Emmanuel II.

May 18. Further European news, imperfectly telegraphed from Halifax, to the seventh instant. Humboldt dead. Austrians repulsed with loss trying to cross the Po at Trapinol, a place I can't find on the map. My prognosis of Kaiser Franz's case is unfavorable. Though without the gift of prophesying, I see, moreover, that all Italy will be in arms within a month. The poor dear Pope has probably packed his carpet bag already and ordered the signor chamberlain of the robes to get out his holy overshoes and surtout. Whither will he flee from the fury of the people? . . .

May 22, SUNDAY. At the French Theatre Thursday night with Ellie, William Schermerhorn and wife, Mrs. Georgey Peters, and Murray Hoffman. Highly satisfactory. They tell me it's second- or third-rate French acting, but it is far above our standard, in good taste, simplicity, attention to detail, and naturalness or reality. Met with the Law School Committee of Columbia College and agreed to invite as lecturers Bidwell, Lord, Evarts, Sedgwick, Noyes, and Bradford. Mr. Ruggles knocked up with quite serious rheumatism in right shoulder.

May 24. Have seen Lord, Noyes, Bidwell, Evarts, and Sedgwick about their Law School appointments. Bradford is probably secured, and. Bidwell and Sedgwick are in a hopeful state. Evarts and Noyes noncommittal, but favorably disposed. Lord is coy, being too much overwhelmed with work already.[14] But I forgot to mention to him that the *locale* of the school is what was John Astor's dwelling. That would be a word of power with Lord. How could I have been so thoughtless? And John Jacob Astor is a trustee! Dolt that I am! Never was seducer so oblivious of his own resources. Lord will "listen as a three-years child" when I tell him an Astor actually stands in a position of constructive supplication to him for aid and comfort. After all, we want nothing of these gentlemen but the prestige of their names.

May 26. Law School Committee of Columbia College met at Mr. Ruggles's office with Professor Dwight. We are doing pretty well. We shall probably secure all our lecturers but Lord. He is high and mighty and Daniel Lordish, and evidently expects us to go down on our knees to him and beg him the privilege of using his name.

Yesterday, Mrs. Perkins of Boston (née Miss Lily Chadwick) dined here with Jem, and we attended the opera. Very full house. They said it

---

[14] Daniel Lord (1795–1868), the distinguished attorney, had been at the New York bar since 1817. Devoted to his profession, he conducted a long list of important civil cases with great success. He was an alumnus of Yale, and one of the leading members of the Brick Presbyterian Church.

was also a "brilliant" house. Donizetti's *Poliuto*, or, *I Martiri*; Piccolomini, Brignole, and Amodio. Music Verdesque rather than Donizettioid, and a somewhat favorable and mitigated form of its bad type. There are grand brass-band movements (suggestive of the Seventh Regiment executing a strategic movement up Broadway) and several lively high-peppered duets and scraps of concerted music. The newspaper critics seem to have been profoundly impressed with the grandeur and genius of the work and write of it as sensible people might of a newly discovered symphony of Beethoven. I should say it was not Burgundy, but a tolerable article of small-beer. . . .

That noble and patriotic Son of Erin, Smith O'Brien, took himself off Saturday, in a blaze of glory, with escort of militia companies, cannonadings, banners, orations, presentations, shamrocks, spread-eagle, and all sorts of gammon. Union Square and Broadway were densely thronged, as I walked down, with specimens of every Celtic type, male and female, all waiting wearily but patiently to hurrah for O'Brien and the other expatriated wind-bag, Tommy Meagher, who was to accompany him. "Meagher of the Sword" they call that commonplace decent attorney-at-law. " 'Tis he will sheathe that battle axe in Saxon gore."[15]

June 3. European news: No battle yet. Austria slowly backing toward the Ticino unmolested. Perhaps Louis Napoleon begins to feel misgivings about his capacity for handling masses of 100,000 men.

June 6. Went to Columbia College meeting at two o'clock. . . . Application from the old fossil Medical College for some kind of affiliation or alliance referred to a committee of conference.[16] I do not specially admire Delafield and his staff of Heroic Phlebotomizers, the extreme right of conservative orthodoxy, but I incline to favor the proposed liaison, if it can be consolidated on advantageous terms. It may enable us to keep Professor Guyot and others going another year by providing them lecture rooms in a good and accessible place (at the corner of Twenty-third Street and Fourth Avenue) without expense to us, and bring them in contact with a set of young men whose professional pursuits would

[15] William Smith O'Brien (1803–1864), Irish politician and revolutionary; Thomas Meagher (1823–1867), Irish-American politician, later brigadier-general in the Civil War.

[16] The College of Physicians and Surgeons, which was as bad as other American medical colleges, had removed to Fourth Avenue and Twenty-third Street in 1856. It had wretched facilities and a few well-trained men. The connection it was now about to form with Columbia was to be purely nominal until Seth Low took the subject in hand in 1891.

interest them in post-graduate courses of physical science. Botanic Garden lots begin to be called for. Twenty or thirty applications for leases received since our last meeting. Old Spring resigned his chairmanship.

June 10.   Garibaldi makes progress in Northern Lombardy; he has reached Como, and is lighting up what may prove a formidable insurrection in the Austrian rear.[17] I predict Milan will be abandoned before July, though the operations of the Allies seem neither vigorous nor enterprising. This invasion of Garibaldi's is the only bold and brilliant move yet made in the campaign.

June 11.   Improved the day by leaving Wall Street early and set off with George Anthon and Johnny to explore the Central Park, which will be a feature of the city within five years and a lovely place in A.D. 1900, when its trees will have acquired dignity and appreciable diameters. Perhaps the city itself will perish before then, by growing too big to live under faulty institutions corruptly administered. Reached the park a little before four, just as the red flag was hoisted—the signal for the blasts of the day. They were all around us for some twenty minutes, now booming far off to the north, now quite near, now distant again, like a desultory "affair" between advanced posts of two great armies. We entered the park at Seventy-first Street, on its east side, and made for "The Ramble," a patch just below the upper reservoir. Its footpaths and plantations are finished, more or less, and it is the first section of the ground that has been polished off and made presentable. It promises very well. So does all the lower park, though now in most ragged condition: long lines of incomplete macadamization, "lakes" without water, mounds of compost, piles of blasted stone, acres of what may be greensward hereafter but is now mere brown earth; groves of slender young transplanted maples and locusts, undecided between life and death, with here and there an arboricultural experiment that has failed utterly and is a mere broomstick with ramifications. Celts, caravans of dirt carts, derricks, steam engines, are the elements out of which our future Pleasaunce is rapidly developing. The work seems pushed with vigor and system, and as far as it has gone, looks thorough and substantial. A small army of Hibernians is distributed over the ground. Narrowness is its chief drawback. One sees quite across this *Rus in Urbe* at many points. This will be less felt as the trees grow. The tract seems to have been judiciously laid out. Roads and paths twist

[17] After his failure in 1848–49, Garibaldi had lived and prospered in the United States. Now in Italy again, he was ready to make the most of the spirit of Italian nationalism kindled by the successes of Cavour and Napoleon III.

about in curves of artistic tortuosity. A broad avenue, exceptionally straight (at the lower end of the park) with a quadruple row of elms, will look Versailles-y by A.D. 1950. On the Fifth Avenue side, the hideous State Arsenal building stares at students of the picturesque, an eyesore that no landscape gardening can alleviate. Let us hope it will soon be destroyed by an accidental fire. From the summit of the rock mount in which "The Ramble" culminates, and from the little wooden framework of an observatory or signal flag tower thereon erected, the upper reservoir (lying on the north) is an agreeable object, notwithstanding the formalism of its straight lines. Johnny was delighted with his walk. . . .

We inspected the site of Bishop Hughes's *duomo* on Fifth Avenue near Fiftieth Street. Little doing there; a derrick and half a dozen Celts dawdling around it, with their dudeens.

June 15.   Dined with Ellie yesterday at Mrs. Georgey Peters's and went with her and Dr. Carroll to the Academy of Music for *I Puritani*; prima donna, the very distinguished amateur, Mme. de Ferussac (Colonel Thorne's daughter). We expected a crowd and a grand excitement, but on entering our box—very late—twenty minutes behind time, we found two-thirds of the front boxes empty, and the parquette sparsely sprinkled with people, *rari nantes in gurgite vasto.*

June 20.   Great news. Great battle of two days at Bukalovia and Turbigo, and at Magenta (on the Austrian side of the Ticino); a battle on the scale of Wagram. France claims a great victory, Austria a drawn game.[18] Hard to tell which is right from these telegraphic hints. But Louis Napoleon announces three guns and one standard as the trophies of battle, and concedes a set-off of one French gun taken by the Austrians. His uncle was the more efficient man of business. This is not the bulletin of a decisive victory. But triumphs like Marengo and Jena and Austerlitz and Friedland are not won every day—nor every century. The Allies have doubtless forced poor Austria a step farther back, and I guess they have twisted her armies round into a position at right angles to her original line of battle, so that the road to Milan is open to the hosts of France and Sardinia. Milan is said to be in insurrection and to have proclaimed Victor Emmanuel King of the Milanese.

June 22.   Columbia College meeting two P.M. at the Dutch Reformed Prayer Meeting Rooms in Fulton Street. Sat till five and compelled Mr. Ruggles to dine with me at Delmonico's. The Columbia College trustees

---

[18] By the battle of Magenta—an unquestionable victory—the Franco-Sardinian forces gained the city of Milan.

met not wholly in vain. The proposed confederation with that mouldy
but reverend old College of Physicians and Surgeons was agreed to,
though not without a little bafflement. The question came up on the
favorable report of the committee of conference. Zabriskie (the College
Remora) objected, and made a speech—his stereotype speech on the
advantage of doing nothing. He was not prepared to vote; he had not
heard of the proposition because he had omitted to attend the last meeting, so he wanted us to stand still till October that he might give the
subject meditation and consideration and examine it in all its bearings,
and so catch up with his colleagues who had attended to their duties and
made up their minds. He is a most dense and pig-headed wiseacre. Rutherfurd also demurred, because this is a "sectarian school" of medicine; it's
a plausible objection and (abstractly considered) fatal. But no catholic or
eclectic school exists in New York or, so far as I know, in *rerum natura*.
In the present state of the profession and of medical science, it is a dream
which cannot be realized. Only these two dissented. Bradford and Anderson supported the alliance with ability. Betts and I blew a penny-trumpet
apiece on the same side, and the subject went comfortably to the same
committee to settle details. There was a good deal of discussion about
the question of continuing the post-graduate experiment next winter.
Guyot and Dana were finally appointed.

July 7. There has been another battle on the largest scale and
Austria beat again. Poor Austria!—"*Bella gerant alii*" indeed. Only a brief
telegram had reached London. It was on the banks of the Mincio. Two
hundred and eighty thousand Austrians (it's said) concentrated on that
line (but this must include the garrisons of the four strongholds there); a
complete victory after sixteen hours of fighting and immense carnage.
There will be another *Te Deum* in Notre Dame, and, I think, a *Te Diabolum*
down below.

July 9. The great battle was of "Solferino," June 24th. No particulars yet. Allies won, but at heavy cost. Austria recrossed the Mincio
without molestation, it would seem. But this Austrian retreat is growing
monotonous and wearisome. I fear Italy is doomed to become a French
satrapy again. Its people will, of course, be consulted, and 100,000 French
bayonets will guarantee them a free choice and free expression of their
views, without fear of compulsion.

July 20. The last and most surprising phase of Dan Sickles's domestic
difficulties much talked of. He publishes a well-written manifesto in
today's *Herald*. Probably the lovely Theresa had a hold upon him and

knew of matters he did not desire to be revealed. Some say he had promoted her intrigue with Key; others that our disreputable old Buchanan's interest in his welfare was due to relations with her which her husband had encouraged. He must have been in her power somehow, or he would not have taken this step and sacrificed all his hopes of political advancement and all his political friends and allies. He can hardly shew himself at Washington again. . . .

Insurrection in Perugia, repressed by the secular arm, doubtless with severity, but probably without some of the atrocities and brutalities recorded in the newspapers. This complicates matters. Louis Napoleon is too wary a practitioner to alienate the papal militia of France and all Europe if he can help it.[19] But a philanthropic crusade against bad government in Milan and Venice that is blind to the woes of Rome and Bologna and to the alleged atrocities of papal tyranny in Perugia—a movement to regenerate Italy according to the ideas of the epoch that leaves Pio Nono and his monsignorini Switzers unmolested—is too palpable a humbug.

July 25. Peace. Rather vaguely reported, but it would seem that Sardinia is to have Lombardy, Austria to keep Venice and her dependencies and the four strongholds, Italy to be some sort of "Confederation" with the Pope for President!!! A "regenerated" Italy with Uncle Pius for Chief Magistrate!!! Mazzini and the Reds will denounce it as a base and vile concluded peace, and there will be hard swearing in various dialects. But it was a politic move, no doubt, for Louis Napoleon is a smart man. Proposing an armistice and then granting easy terms to the defeated Kaiser will get him credit for moderation and magnanimity, and secure him another recruit for the continental league against England in which, I think, he intends his career to culminate, and for which Russia and Piedmont are already secured. He is generating history very fast.

August 12, FRIDAY.   Poor little Louis Napoleon has lost credit by the compromise he cobbled up over his breakfast table at Villafranca, which the *Evening Post* calls a "peace that passeth all understanding." The liberals and reds denounce it and him. Middle Italy, Piedmont, and Lombardy are disappointed, sulky, and perturbed; Garibaldi still under

[19] Napoleon was indeed taken aback by the fierce wave of Italian nationalism, which threatened to overwhelm the Papal States. French Catholics became angry. At the same time, the Emperor was worried by a Prussian mobilization, and disturbed by the costs of his war. As Strong forecasts, he brought his campaign up short. This very month, leaving his Italian friends in the lurch, he signed an armistice at Villafranca with the Austrian Government. Cavour was so enraged that he resigned.

arms. Nothing is settled by Magenta and Solferino, except that his Imperial Majesty. is a smarter scoundrel than anybody thought him. Last news is that France is to disarm—and English newspapers draw a long breath and exchange congratulations with mankind.

August 30, TUESDAY.   Graham had an effective story of a haunted house at Astoria, obtained directly from its terrified tenants. He says I know them or of them, but would not give their names. Sounds of some-one tramping upstairs and down, all night. Ceasing whenever people looked out into the entry. Two big ugly, indomitable bull dogs were turned loose on the stairs at night. The steps were heard again, and the moment the bedroom door was opened, the dogs rushed in with their tails between their legs and hid under the bed and fled the house next day and could not be wheedled back. The tenants could not stand this and fled after them. Very remarkable if true, but nowise supernatural, unless the Sunday night aurora was supernatural because we cannot explain it, define its laws, or guess at its use in the system of the world.

September 2.   Busy day uptown with Murray Hoffman, and explored Central Park from the reservoir southward. Great progress since last May. The ragged desert of out-blasted rock, cat briars, and stone heaps begins to blossom like the rose. Many beautiful oases of path and garden culture have sprung up, with neat paths, fine greensward, and hopeful young trees. The system and order and energy of the work are very creditable, considering especially the scale on which it's conducted. Some three thousand men are employed, and there are no idlers. Everybody is earning his pay. Number of visitors quite large. Several bridges are completed and look well. Most of the larger transplanted trees (elms mostly) have perished.

September 5.   Had to leave Wall Street early for a College meeting at two—our first summons to the new Law School, in John Astor's former residence in Lafayette Place. It looks well; books and desks, and so on are in their places and one janitor. . . . There was no quorum. Spent a little while with Mr. Ruggles and Dr. Torrey in the Astor Library, just reopened, after the completion of the new building and the rearrangement of the books, which makes the shelves look thinly populated. George C. Anthon called this evening. There is a mysterious movement for the restoration of the Rt. Rev. but suspended Mr. Benjamin T. Onderdonk to the office and functions and jurisdictions of the Episcopate. Hawks seems to have originated it, and Tyng and Anthon and others of the Bishop's bitterest unfriends take it very quietly. The House of Bishops (or else both Houses of the General Convention that is to assemble at Richmond next month) is expected to legislate the Bishop back into the position he occupied before his disasters of 1844 and 1845. I don't believe the plan will work. It is part of the old scheme for a division of the diocese, Potter to take Albany and its dependencies, and our resuscitated prelate New York.

Benjamin T. Onderdonk, like Dr. Muhlenberg, Dr. Francis L. Hawks, and Bishop Doane, had been a prominent figure in the so-called renascence of the Episcopal Church between 1830 (the year in which he was consecrated Bishop of New York) and 1845. He had carried on a great pamphlet war with the Presbyterians upon the divine right of Episcopacy; he and Dr. Muhlenberg had taken the lead in editing a new collection of hymns; and he had shown himself a stern, vigorous, aggressive High-Church leader, striving to make religion a living force and to expand the influence of the church. A native of New York and a graduate of Columbia College, he exercised great influence in the city. When in the fall of 1844 he was presented for trial upon charges of "immorality and impurity," brought by three fellow-bishops, the whole church was shaken. This was the most sensational episode in American church history, in fact, prior to the famous Beecher trial. Much feeling was aroused between the two principal groups in the Episcopal Church; The Churchman as organ of the High-Church party asserting that the trial had grown out of a Low-Church conspiracy against the bishop. He was suspended; but the trustees of the General Theological Seminary declined to dismiss him from his chair in that institution, and many people remained convinced that he was innocent. Now, as Strong records, Dr. Francis Vinton offered a resolution in the New York diocesan convention requesting the House of Bishops to terminate the suspension—arguing that an indefinite suspension was unjust, and that the General Convention had itself recognized this fact by providing that all further suspensions should have a time limit. The diocesan convention passed the resolution, as noted below, by very heavy majorities—the clerical vote being more than seven to one. Onderdonk himself petitioned the General Convention for the removal of his sentence, admitting that parts of his conduct had "betrayed indiscretion," but declaring himself innocent of some of the offenses charged against him. The wrangle in the church over the affair aroused intense interest, as the length of Strong's entries on the subject indicates. It may be stated here that before final action on the case was taken by the General Convention, Onderdonk died (1861).

September 16. To the newly opened exhibition of French and English paintings, which I inspected hastily. There are several good things there, and several amazing Pre-Raphaelite pictures. On the whole, I incline to favor Pre-Raphaelitism. These pictures are hideously ugly, but new, unconventional, laborious, and faithful. Then to Bishop Potter's, who wanted to see me. He talks very cautiously and objects to the B. T. Onderdonk plan mainly because it leaves the question of jurisdiction unsettled, and makes controversy and heartburnings inevitable if it be carried out. I don't like it, and I don't like the mystifying formula of words in which Bishop Onderdonk envelops what they call his confession of the justice of his sentence. . . .

I have always held his conviction to be erroneous, because unsustained by sufficient evidence—and the outside rumors that were not made evidence, I ignore altogether. In other words, I assume him *innocent* of everything but perhaps certain ill-bred familiarities and caressings that meant nothing. But there stands the recorded judgment, and after a good deal of grumbling and pamphleteering it is acquiesced in by nine-tenths of the community. The church convicted him capitally and executed the sentence, and he has been hanging in chains for fourteen years. The church works miracles no longer; it cannot restore him to life, and if he is cut down and galvanized, he will only be a scandal and an offence.

September 19. Berrian has signed the Onderdonk restoration testimonial. So have all the city clergy, I am told, except Taylor of Grace, who still holds out. As yet the movement goes onward smoothly and swiftly. But Hamilton Fish, Bradford, Bradish, and other prominent laymen are hostile. General Dix and Gouverneur Ogden and Robert Hyslop and others of the Trinity Church set are bitterly hostile.

If Bishop B. T. Onderdonk means to confess himself guilty of the charges he denied in 1844 and has continued to deny for fifteen years, his confession should be explicit and unequivocal. If that be his intention, he has been maintaining a lie all this time, and a slanderous lie. And the lying slander has been against the purity of women. His defense was mainly founded on the proposition that Mrs. Beare and Mrs. Butler and the two Rudderow girls misrepresented his attentions under partisan hostility, or misconstrued them because themselves impure. Newspaper articles and pamphlets, put forth in the Bishop's interest, asserted this theory of the case most earnestly and explicitly. It is said, I don't know how truly, that Mrs. Beare died one day and one of the Rudderows was sent to a lunatic asylum because they severally felt themselves disgraced and degraded by the cloud under which the Bishop's assertion of his innocence placed them. However this may be, much of the mortification they suffered, and many of the hard things said of them, resulted from their own discreditable weakness in courting the attentions of a bishop who had, by their own account, insulted them so grossly. But making all due allowance for this, if their stories were substantially true each of them has been shamefully and cruelly maligned and injured by our suspended diocesan and his advocates.

September 24. The Rt. Rev. Dr. Onderdonk's affairs are in a bad way; far less hopeful than ten days ago, when I thought his restoration very probable. The two meetings at Tyng's house (Wednesday and Friday of last week) were inharmonious. Hawks, Anthon, and Tyng brought each some six or eight prominent laymen to consult and advise. Reverend Anthon withdrew his signature and notified the public of his withdrawal, by a newspaper card, which has exposed him to attack and especially to a most savage assault in this afternoon's *Express*. On the other hand, Judge Murray Hoffman speaks strongly of the candor and moderation of Anthon's course. Bradish, Bradford, Fish and others opposed the whole movement. A letter from Bishop Potter was read, suggesting doubts and difficulties and throwing cold water on it. This seems to have staggered Hawks and Tyng. The meeting finally adjourned after doing nothing, and the story today is that the project is abandoned, all the papers called in, and the Bishop's anticipatory letter dated next October destroyed and returned to him. It's a fortunate disposition of what threatened to be an ugly question. But I am sorry for poor Bishop B. T. Onderdonk.

A row in Trinity Church is to be anticipated. After a good deal of discussion and whispering about the question of a "Rector's Assistant," Gouverneur Ogden had the good sense and courage to advise the Rector that unless he took the initiative in the matter, some of the vestry were prepared to memorialize him in form and call on him to nominate under the charter. Thus cornered, the old gentleman, after a slight struggle, consented to act, and though he thought at first that he must be governed in his nomination by the seniority of the assistants, concluded to nominate Morgan Dix. A special meeting is called for tomorrow night. Dunscomb wanted delay, but was overborne by representations of the mischief and discord that would follow if it were known that the appointment was contemplated, and each of our half-score clerical gentlemen and their respective friends, male and female, commenced intriguing and lobbying about it. . . .

Dix's appointment will be judicious and proper. He has both intellect and business talent. . . .

September 30. Mr. Ruggles came in. He is a delegate from Calvary Church. Tells me the Convention finally adopted a resolution recommending Bishop B. T. Onderdonk's restoration, but not without conditions. There has been stormy discussion of that painful business for the last two days. Hawks, Tyng, and Anthon abandoned the case as hopeless, at least for the present. Vinton took it up and pushed it triumphantly through this stage, thus gaining half the battle. Bishop Potter was (according to Mr. Ruggles) somewhat wavering and uncertain in his position. A clear expression of disapproval from him would have squashed the movement, but he seems to have hesitated and dubitated, shifted his ground, and lacked the courage to take a stand on either side.

Mr. Ruggles is elected a delegate to the General Convention at Richmond, and *Egomet Ipse* a substitute. Very marvelous.

October 6. All day spent on the Shedden case with Bidwell. All my days are devoted to that ancient embroilment now. Archibald, Her Majesty's Consul, is the best examiner, referee, or commissioner I ever attended. Nicoll's examination wanders off into abysses of irrelevancy and the commissioner holds that he can only note objections without passing on them. But Nicoll is not to blame; he and his colleague Jesup make private apologies for loading the record with the bosh they've introduced. Their mad client insists on it, and they know nothing of the rules of evidence that will be adopted by this new-fangled Matrimonial Causes Court, and cannot take the responsibility of checking her. I am sorry for the poor young lady. She is not bad looking, has nice wavy brown hair, is very bright, full of indomitable spirit, and has been brought up, no doubt, on traditions of this ancient family quarrel. It's a rather rich and picturesque case, too, is the plaintiff's, and full of stimulating matter for any one who believes in it, as this lady does most omnipotently. Old William Shedden is a grand merchant who marries a young wife. They have children, one of whom, the elder Miss Shedden (aunt of Miss Annabella), produces reminiscences of her childish years (high-colored, if not wholly fictitious), vague memories of a fine town house and grand dinner parties, with Judge Pendleton and Dr. Hosack and Dr. Bard and Mrs. Hamilton and other magnates of seventy years since for guests, and a lovely young mamma and an affectionate father, and the country house at Fort Washington and the big dog and the little carriage, and so on. Then the affectionate father dies, commending his babes to the protection of John Patrick, the nephew and next heir, who falsely and cruelly suppresses all evidence of their legitimacy, talks of binding out the daughter, who'd been nursed in the lap of luxury, as apprentice to a dressmaker, carries off the son to Scotland, keeps both in ignorance of their rights, and bags all the property by some collusive law-suit or other proceeding in Scotland. But then there is the fact that the papa married the mamma on his death-bed in 1798, and wrote to his friends in Scotland to say that he had married her in order to legitimate their offspring according to the law of Scotland, and the fact that during their connection, the mamma was grantee of real estate not as Mrs. Shedden, but as Ann Wilson, spinster. Thus far the proof has done the defense but little damage. . . .

The Rev. Mr. Dix accepts, though reluctantly (*teste* Berrian); the assistants said to be cooling down.

October 15.   Entered George Anthon with a telegram from Richmond to his reverend papa. "Unconditional restoration" (of Bishop Onderdonk) "voted down in the House of Bishops by twenty-six against eight." Very right and wise, I think. But won't they agree on some compromise between restoration pure and simple and restoration with jurisdiction? This looks unlike it, to be sure. . . .

October 16, SUNDAY.   Expected Mr. Ruggles here today from the Council of Richmond, but he hasn't come. And Jem is still lingering among the Adirondacks. Bishop B. T. Onderdonk's friends feel discouraged and discomfited by the action of the House of Bishops against the restoration project. Perhaps their despondency is premature. But he is losing ground now. The adverse movement throughout the diocese grows stronger every day, letters and memorials to the House and to individual bishops are pouring in, and I fear poor Onderdonk's chances are growing less and less. Restoration on condition of his resigning jurisdiction is very possible, but that I suppose he neither asks nor wants.

October 18.   Walked out this evening with intent to have myself "registered" under the new law, but I could not find the officials, so I dare say my valuable vote will be lost at the fall elections. Our catistocrats have nullified that law by appointing their own creatures to administer it. Isaac Bell, Jr., who professes to be a gentleman and consorts with reputable people, ought to be expelled from decent society for the conspicuous part he took in the dirty intrigue by which the community lost this chance of ridding itself from the domination of blackguards and shoulder-hitters and political bloodsuckers. . . .

News from Harper's Ferry of a strange transaction. Some sort of insurrection, an armed gang getting possession of the United States Armory: railroad trains stopped, x+y hundred fugitive slaves under arms, government troops, marines, and other forces sent on. Seems to have been a fight this morning (and the rebellion quashed, of course), but the whole transaction is as yet most obscure, and our reports probably much exaggerated.

On Sunday night, October 16, John Brown—who had been staying with his followers in two farmhouses rented on the Maryland side of the Potomac— armed his little band of eighteen men, seized the Baltimore & Ohio Railroad bridge across the river, and invading Virginia, captured the United States armory, arsenal, and rifle-works at Harper's Ferry. Making himself master of the town, he cut the telegraph wires and began seizing masters and liberating slaves in the country around. At break of dawn the citizens gathered with their weapons, and militia companies soon joined them. Hot fighting commenced. Brown and a surviving remnant of his force were hemmed in at the engine house in the armory grounds, where they withstood a siege all afternoon. During the evening Colonel Robert E. Lee and a company of United States marines reached the town. As morning broke on Tuesday, they battered their way into the engine house, disarmed the little garrison, and took Brown prisoner. In this criminal attempt to begin a slave insurrection, Brown had lost ten men killed; four, with himself, were seized, and four more escaped—two only temporarily. The whole country was thrown into hot excitement, which in parts of the South amounted to frenzy.

October 24, MONDAY.　Mr. Ruggles not yet returned from Richmond. The House of Bishops has given poor Bishop B. T. Onderdonk leave to withdraw his memorial. Some deny it, but I've good reason to believe they have so decided. Their action is probably final, for the case is not likely to be stirred again. His friends are savage against Potter, and also against Hawks, who, they say, misled them by representations that a majority of the bishops could be relied on to favor restoration. Sorry for B. T. Onderdonk, but I don't regret the result. Notwithstanding the strong vote in the Diocesan Convention, the laity are generally opposed to the Bishop's restoration, and it would have bred mischief. The assistant

ministers of Trinity Church continue to scold about Morgan Dix's appointment, and incredible as it seems, that truculent Mrs. Higby has broken
off her handsome daughter's engagement with Abel T. Anderson's son,
who looks like a nice fellow, because she can't let her daughter marry the
son of a man who has been guilty of acquiescing in so outrageous a procedure. So I hear from half a dozen sources.

The Harper's Ferry insurrection (seventeen white men and five niggers) is suppressed (after conquering a town of two thousand inhabitants)
by a combined movement of state and federal troops. State of Virginia
was awfully frightened. The leader, old Ossowatamie John Brown of
Kansas, seems cracked; a free-soil Balfour of Burley. Insanity won't save
him from the gallows. He will undoubtedly be hanged. Were I his jury,
I could not acquit him, and twelve terrified Virginians will have little
difficulty about a verdict. This insane transaction may possibly lead to
grave results. If Gerrit Smith and other fanatics of the extreme left are
compromised by the papers found upon Brown, they may be indicted, and
a requisition for them from the governor of Virginia would embarrass
the governor of New York a little.

October 25, TUESDAY.   Mr. Ruggles here tonight. Returned from
Richmond this afternoon. Bishop B. T. Onderdonk's case before the House
of Bishops seems, by his account, to have been nearly hopeless from the
beginning. Not more than one-third disposed to favor even restoration
without jurisdiction. It's the best result for the interests of the church. A
bishop under a cloud, charitably tolerated because penitent for past mis-
deeds, would not do in these days of laxity. This age needs precedents
not of mercy, but of rigor. Clemency and lazy, good-natured acquiescence
in acquittals and pardons have long been vulgar and cheap. I'm very glad
that Mr. Ruggles went to Richmond (he took pains to interfere on neither
side of the Bishop's case). He has been prominent there and useful. He
has been put at the head of an important committee of thirty-three laymen
to systematize, develop, and bring out the financial resources of the church.
I tell him he is the Lay-Patriarch of the Protestant Episcopal Church in
America.

October 29.   Trial of Brown and the other Harper's Ferry conspira-
tors on indictments for treason and murder is pushed vigorously, and it
will result in a speedy verdict of prompt execution. The conduct of the
prosecution is rigorous, or seems so in these days of rose-water criminal
practice. We are accustomed to see defendants in a capital case treated
with a hyper-delicacy of double-refined tenderness and consideration,

favored with every unreasonable delay and encouraged to insist on every frivolous or fraudulent quibble. The rigor of this Virginia court is right enough, but eminently inexpedient. The court should give Brown the maximum of indulgence and vigilantly shut out his prospective claim to the honors of martyrdom. It should be astute in protecting him by subtlety of quibbling or by inventing pleas of insanity for his benefit. If the slaveholding interest were wise, it would exert itself to secure his conviction on some minor offense, inciting to a riot, or the like, and his punishment by flogging, imprisonment, and the pillory. I'm not sure the South can afford to hang him, though he plainly deserves it.

Sent in my resignation as trustee of Trinity School today.

November 2, WEDNESDAY.   Opera Monday night with Charley Strong and Mrs. Eleanor, who dined here. Donizetti's *Maria de Rohan*; thinnest small beer, but less objectionable than Verdi's rotgut and not much worse than Meyerbeer's staple article of stale champagne. It is marvelous that people who think they appreciate Mozart and Beethoven can sit out three hours and a half of the paltry commonplaces that make up this opera. Music is a wonderful thing in every point of view. Gazzaniga sang, and a very nice tenor, Stigelli, and a good baritone, Terri (facetiously called Fulltone Terry). Ullman's force seems strong, but the "season" is a failure, thus far. Speranza, who was imported for the purpose of raising a furore, is an utter failure, and "Lasciate ogni speranza" is written on the portals of the Academy, according to Murray Hoffman. They talk of producing the *Zauberflöte*, and I hope they may, but it will only mire the management deeper. Its music will be thrown away on audiences that tolerate Verdi.

November 4.   Just from opera, with Ellie and Mrs. Georgey Peters; *Lucrezia Borgia*, [with] Gazzaniga, Beaucardé, a new tenor, whom I like, though his voice has lost its freshness, and that fattest bull of Bashan, Amodio. I left the ladies in their box, in the second act, and went down to the footlights, where it was rather pleasant to watch Gazzaniga's expressive face in the "Madre mia" terzetto. Rarely heard that very clever little bit of trumpery better done.

November 8.   This evening with Ellie to Mrs. Wickham Hoffman's, Nineteenth Street, a small party, chiefly Lenoxions. Mr. and Mrs. Ellery Sedgwick, whom I like, and a few more, including a lively Miss Mary Edgar, Murray Hoffman's latest divinity. Also Pierre Kane and Robert Cutting, bringing news of the election and bewailing Democratic defeat, that is, less than twenty thousand Democratic majority in this city. It may be an important fact if the state has gone decisively for the Black Republicans or (as the South would prefer to designate them) the John Brown Republicans.[20]

November 9. Ellie and I have just returned from a concert (at the City Assembly Room in Broadway above Grand Street), one of the performances commemorating the centennial anniversary of Schiller's birth. It was a great success. It gave me a new sensation, or rather, recalled the sensations of 1843, when each successive Philharmonic marked an era by its new revelations. There was a great, silent, appreciative crowd of Teutons in a good room, listening to an admirable orchestra and a passable chorus doing a programme of the first order. Began with the Overture to *Tannhäuser*. I never heard it as well rendered. Its magnificent lights and shadows were fully brought out. It is something more than a mere prodigy of elaborate construction. I admit it at last to rank among works of the highest order. Ellie said its first movement (the grand "Pilgrim-chant") seems hewn out of granite, a felicitous criticism.

Part Second was Beethoven's *Symphony No. 9*, the Choral Symphony —all but absolutely new to me. I heard it some twelve or more years ago, vilely done at Castle Garden, and afterwards by Satter and Timm on two pianos, but retained not a single phrase. My impressions of it were that it was long, *outré*, and dull, and I was surprised tonight to find that I was able to follow it throughout, and, in some moderate degree, to appreciate it. Beethoven meant it to be his greatest work. The first three parts certainly on the grandest scale; they seem to contain as much thought as any two of his earlier symphonies. But they are not inspired in the same sense with the *Eroica* and C minor. The scherzo, however, is full of fire, and the slow movement that follows it of lovely melodic feeling. The fourth part, with its chorus, seems like an afterthought. It's built on a fine and sharp-cut melody and worked up into striking effects. But Beethoven is not at home with a chorus.

November 13, SUNDAY.   Tonight . . . Tom Appleton of Boston, Mignot, Mould, Stone, who brought Leutze, Murray Hoffman, and Henry Dorr. Story of Mr. and Mrs. Sturgis of Boston—the lady, a niece of Dr. Parkman's. Appleton saw them one morning just after Dr. Parkman's disap-

[20] The Republicans achieved a signal victory in the state election this fall, though only minor officers were to be chosen. They gained heavy majorities in both branches of the legislature, and chose six out of the nine state officers; though the Democrats and Americans had in general united against them. The election proved that the American or Know-Nothing Party was dying fast, and that its free-soil members were all going into the Republican ranks.

pearance, while he and everyone else supposed the doctor had wandered off in a state of insanity, before any suspicion had attached to Dr. Webster. The lady looked wan and weary, and after some pressing for its cause (she and Appleton had had mesmeric confidence and she was an impressible subject, though not clairvoyant), she said: "I have had such a restless and miserable night. I seemed to be seeking and searching for Dr. Parkman all over Boston, and feel as tired and worn out as if it had been a real search. I hunted through the whole city. I found him at last. He was dead, and cut up into little pieces."

November 14. After dinner to Trinity Church vestry meeting. We sat late. Proposition to change our clerical appointments and transfer Vinton from St. Paul's to Trinity, and "associate" Morgan Dix and poor incapacitated Haight (who has been at Trinity) in the charge of St. Paul's. Dunscomb opposed it strenuously and at great length, in usual style of opacity, but he stood alone. Then (against my advice) Cisco moved that Dix's pay allowances be raised to the full assistant grade. This also carried, though Skidmore and Sands and others were reluctant, and wished a postponement. They urged delay, lest we should still further offend the other assistant clergy. I should have preferred to let it lie over for Dix's sake. I fear he will be damaged if he get the reputation of being a pet of the vestry. . . .

The rector and others were pleased to be distressed this evening about my resignation from the Board of Trinity School. That board passed a series of flaming resolutions on the subject, of which it should have been ashamed; it carried civility to fanaticism. Don't know whether I can adhere to my intention after such a battery of compliment, but I do desire we may be better strangers. It seems the school proposes celebrating its 150th anniversary—in the usual way, I suppose—by boring an assemblage with gab and speechification.

November 18, FRIDAY. Last night there was a sound of revelry on these premises; a little dancing party of fifty-odd, partly "for" the Lenox set, partly "for" Miss Grace Coles, Mrs. Edward Snelling that shall be hereafter (I don't clearly understand, by the by, the force of the preposition "for" used in the connection). Being engineered by Mrs. Ellie, it went off pleasantly, of course. Helmsmüller pianized. George Anthon, and the Kings, and Miss Annie Leavenworth being (conventionally) under deep domestic affliction, couldn't come. There were Miss Ellen Schermerhorn and little Miss Helen Lane, Ulshoeffer, Mrs. John Kernochan, little Miss Gerry, Mrs. Peters . . . , William and Edmund Schermerhorn,

Wickham and Murray Hoffman, Dr. Peters and Dr. Carroll, Cutting, Mignot and Stone, Dick Hunt and his brother Leavitt, Ellery Sedgwick, Tip Hoffman, Hazeltine, and so forth. . . . There was a prolonged German, but it was over by one.

John Brown, captured on October 18, was immediately indicted, and on October 26 arraigned for trial before the Virginia circuit court. He was slowly recovering from his wounds, and so weak that he had to lie on a mattress in the courtroom. The trial was concluded within five days, and on October 31, after deliberating less than an hour, the jury rendered its verdict: "Guilty of treason, and conspiring and advising with slaves and others to rebel, and murder in the first degree." This was entirely just; no other verdict was really possible. In a speech when sentence was passed, Brown declared: "I deny everything but what I have all along admitted, of a design on my part to free slaves." He had rejected the plea of insanity which his counsel wished to make for him. Court at once sentenced Brown to be publicly hanged on December 2. Meanwhile, the South was filled with anger, and much public alarm over the possibility of slave insurrections existed in Virginia. John Brown's letters, conversations, and public statements, given to the public by all the Northern newspapers, had telling eloquence. As Emerson remarked, some of his champions made a dubious impression on people; "but as soon as they read his own speeches and letters, they are heartily contented—such is the singleness of purpose which justifies him to the head and heart of all." Brown summed up his final utterances in one sentence. "It is a great comfort to feel assured that I am permitted to die for a cause." At noon on the appointed day, in the presence of fifteen hundred Virginia troops, he was hanged on the scaffold. Strong's attitude toward the man, his crime, and his punishment was probably typical of that of most Northerners; it was quite as sympathetic as Lincoln's attitude, rather coldly defined in the Cooper Union address.

November 20, sunday. Reading *inter alia* the record of our New York Negro Plot trial of 1741, to see whether our little community of a century ago was driven as wild by panic about a servile insurrection as the Sovereign State of Virginia has been by the insane raid of John Brown and his company. Not much to choose between the two cases. The overt acts in New York were far less clear and the panic seems to have been as shameful. The evidence that anything deserving to be called a conspiracy existed is imperfect and suspicious. The "plot" may very well have been a mere phantom called up by the fright of those who punished the alleged plotters. Virginia certainly has facts more tangible to scare her from her propriety. . . .

There is no doubt that old St. John Brown will be hanged. Virginia is too badly scared to think of clemency, and why should she think of it? Hanging is the logical consequence of unlawful homicide, and it's at least doubtful whether a flagrant, deliberate case like his can be justly or rightfully made an exception for the sole reason that a pardon would be good policy and raise the credit of the community. That he undertook his mad, mischievous enterprise under a wild impulse of mistaken duty, and so forth, is assuredly no reason for pardoning him, or remitting any part of the penalty he has incurred—though I suppose most people have a vague notion that it *is* and that no man should be hanged for doing what he thought at the time to be right. . . .

However that may be, I fear this savage old wrong-headed Fifth-Monarchy-man has done us a mischief that will be memorable. The South is frightened into frenzy, utterly without reason, but that makes no difference. Fanatics and sedition-mongers at the North are doing all they can to exasperate and irritate—and Virginia is giving them a batch of martyrs to stimulate their sentimentalism and flavor their vaporings on platform and pulpit. This next Congress and the Charleston Democratic Convention and the next presidential election are full of peril. God grant the Union may survive them!

The change in the arrangements of the House of Representatives— the removal of the desks—though in itself a change for the better, is unfortunate at this time. We shall have real debates at the next session instead of prosy speeches to Bunkum and essays for the newspapers delivered to Mr. Speaker and an inattentive, letter-writing house—and honorable gentlemen are going to meet next month in a temper that will make earnest *debate* dangerous.

November 21. Murray Hoffman dined here, and we marched to the Opera House through unexpected pelting rain to hear the *Zauberflöte*, from which I've just returned.

House very full considering the foul weather, and inclined to be amiable and patronize Mozart. It was funny to hear people talking during the entre-acte, comparing this with the *Sicilian Vespers* and pointing out their respective merits and demerits; one was more *this* and the other more *that*, and so on, as if one should undertake an analysis of the relative position in art of *The Tempest* and Sylvanus Cobb, Jr.'s last sensation story for the *New York Ledger*.

It was very fairly done. . . . Scenic effects and properties as contemptible as their silliness deserved. As to the plot, the dramatic element of the opera, human language is unable duly to express its idiocy. Let us hope that to the fashionable public of seventy years ago, for which it was written, it conveyed some gleam of a notion about Truth and Virtue (always with a big T. or V.), Illuminatism, Initiation, *Frei Männerei*, or something else. But it is a question whether real music be not heard at less disadvantage when allied with a mere absurd, incoherent series of stage effects like those of the *Zauberflöte*, with the representation of something that can hardly pretend to be real or historical or in any way connected with the movements and doings of human beings at any era of this planet's existence than when it illustrates and accompanies something unreal that claims to be a sort of caricature of real human passion and action.

November 24. To the *Magic Flute* again last night with Ellie and Mr. and Mrs. D'Oremieulx, who dined here. Ellie was delighted. It finds far more favor with opera-goers than I thought possible. Our oracles of the lobby say that it is "very pretty," and others proceed to distinguish Mozart's music from Verdi's as *undramatic* and *unimpassioned!*

People of Virginia are still making themselves ridiculous by panic and bluster. Charlestown thrown into consternation by the mistake of a sentinel in taking a cow for an invading Abolitionist contemplating a rescue. Cow didn't stand when challenged, was fired upon, and the community got under arms. All this and a great deal more of the same sort would be great fun were it not likely to prove disastrous.

November 25. Threatening snow all day; very raw, chilly, rueful weather, and as we left the Opera House just now, it was beginning to come down. We were Ellie and I, Mrs. Georgey Peters and Sus (who married a sister of Dr. Peters's and seems to be a nice person; lives at Staten Island), and we heard the *Zauberflöte*. Mrs. Professor Joy was on one side of us, and as the box on the other side was vacant, Walter Cutting and his brother Robert, Hazeltine, Mignot, and Jack Ehninger took possession of it, and the ladies had a nice time. *Zauberflöte* is delicious, and Mozart the King of Melody, *jure divino*. His work is so simple and *true* that it seems easy, and one must know something of other composers to appreciate it. But how far below him are even Handel, Beethoven, and Haydn in fertility of deep and various melody; how much *more* has he given us of pure, bright musical thought than any other composer! More than Beethoven himself, though I fully admit Beethoven's C minor, *Eroica*, and A major symphonies to be intense beyond, and far beyond, all other music. . . . People call Mozart's work undramatic. "He's a great composer, no doubt, but he could not write *dramatic* music like Verdi's and Donizetti's." I suppose dramatic music to be music that expresses passion or emotion capable of dramatic representation. And no one has ever done that like Mozart, to my knowledge, unless it may be Weber in the "Leise, leise, fromme Weise," Agatha's scene in the *Freischütz*. Look at "Batti, batti," for example. Never mind its melodic beauty, attend only to its narrative power, to the story it tells. Could words express more clearly the serio-comic, solemn-sham penitence and apology of the flirtatious little Zerlina, perfectly conscious of her power over her clown of a lover, than its first movement, or the triumph of the little coquette, dancing round him and reiterating her "batti, batti" when she has teased and wheedled him into reconciliation and submission, than its final allegro? Is not this unequalled as dramatic music?

November 28. I went downtown, encountering at Eighth Street half the scoundrelism of New York marching in procession with colored lights, Roman candles, torches, and hideous howls to a Fernando Wood ratification mass-meeting at Cooper Institute. I greatly fear the city is about to be disgraced by the reëlection of that knave and demagogue to the mayoralty. Party division will put him in. As a friend of the railroad conductor remarked this evening: "Wood's crowd's bound to win, the other fellers ain't got no *spunk* like what Wood's men's got."

Mr. Philo T. Ruggles (Ellie's uncle) has just gone to smash in a kerosene oil manufacturing company speculation, and has dissipated what I suppose was a snug little fortune acquired as master and referee.

November 30. Washington Irving died suddenly night before last. Peters has been visiting him twice or thrice a week for a long time. He has had asthma and some nervous disorder that made his night wakeful, and was suspected of hypertrophy of the heart. But his death was most sudden and without a minute's warning. He leaves a fragrant memory, personal and literary.

What's to be done about the mayoralty election next Tuesday? There are four candidates, viz:

1. Havemeyer—set up by Tammany Hall
2. George Opdyke—Republican

3. My venerable foolish friend, DePeyster Ogden, nominated by a little knot of people who call themselves Old Line Whigs, the fossil remains of an extinct party.

4. The King of the Dead Rabbits, that indomitable knave and demagogue, Fernando Wood. How shall Wood be kept out? is the question with all decent people. Shall we vote for Havemeyer or Opdyke? If we only knew which would poll the stronger vote, the question could be readily answered. But these miserable party differences will divide the vote of those who want a decent man for mayor, and the *canaille* will carry in their champion. Two to one on Wood. I have been advocating Havemeyer thus far. I prefer him because Opdyke's career in the last legislature was discreditable (witness his abortive move against savings banks), and I have thought Havemeyer the more available candidate. But I may be wrong, and my vote will be reluctantly given for Opdyke if he shall appear to be the stronger man. Reluctantly, not only because I prefer Havemeyer, but because my "Republicanism" has waxed cold of late. The *Tribune* and other Republican papers treat the John Brown case, the Harper's Ferry insurrection, too sympathetically; they disapprove in words, and do all they can to elevate that fanatical law-breaker and homicide into a martyr. If the Republican party endorses murder and every crime of violence and lawlessness that may be perpetrated against the institutions of the South, I shall withdraw therefrom. The *Post* and *Tribune* and our Brownists generally put their sympathy on the ground of their martyr's insanity (or they try to do so), and talk of its being shameful to hang an insane man, but laud and magnify him at the same time as sacrificing himself for a principle as a heroic redemptorist, giving his life for his brethren in captivity: Cuff and Sambo, to wit. But why make this fuss about him, if his raid were a mere freak of lunacy? Well, he'll probably be hanged day after tomorrow, and I only trust and hope his crime and his punishment may not lead to the gravest disaster.

December 2. . . . Old John Brown was hanged this morning; justly, say I, but his name may be a word of power for the next half-century. It was unwise to give fanaticism a martyr. Why could not Virginia have condescended to lock him up for life in a madhouse? Had Edward Oxford been hanged for shooting at Queen Victoria in 1840, his death would have stirred up scores of silly shopboys to regicide (or reginicide), merely from the inscrutable passion for notoriety; for being thought about and talked about—that has much power over man's vanity. This man Brown's elements of popular available heroism and martyrdom are unhappily numerous.

December 4, SUNDAY. George Anthon looked in just before tea in great excitement. The corpus of old John Brown is in the city at No. something in the Bowery. Carpenter, the sexton of St. Mark's, had told George of the fact, confidentially. Carpenter had been employed in his undertaking capacity to attend to putting the relics of that sainted redemptorist on ice, and George Anthon could probably be admitted to a sight of the remains, as a great favor, and wanted me to go, which I didn't. . . .

Old Brown's demeanor has undoubtedly made a great impression. Many heroes of the Newgate Calendar have died game, as he did; but his simplicity and consistency, the absence of fuss, parade and bravado, the strength and clearness of his letters, all indicate a depth of conviction that one does not expect in an Abolitionist (who is apt to be a mere talker and sophist), and that tends to dignify and to ennoble in popular repute the very questionable church of which he is protomartyr. Slavery has received no such blow in my time as his strangulation. There must be a revolution in feeling even in the terrified State of Virginia, unless fresh fuel be added to the flame, as it well may be, within the month. The supporters of any institution are apt to be staggered and startled when they find that any one man, wise or foolish, is so convicted of its wrong and injustices as to acquiesce in being hanged by way of protest against it. So did the first Christian martyrs wake up senators and landed gentlemen and patrician ladies, *tempore* Nero and Diocletian, and so on. One's faith in anything is terribly shaken by anybody who is ready to go to the gallows condemning and denouncing it.

December 5. Drizzle, and what's worse, I think it means to go on drizzling tomorrow. That will make Wood—F. Wood, the king of the Dead Rabbits—inevitable. The clouds in their courses fight against Opdyke and Havemeyer. I shall vote for the latter, though with hesitation.

DePeyster Ogden has withdrawn, but the little squad that calls itself the Old Line Whig Party (refusing to die and take refuge in history, where that party belongs) instantly nominated Havemeyer, and if the weather be fine, will help him with perhaps a score of votes. Notwithstanding that accession to Havemeyer, I should prefer to bet on Wood.

Talked with W. T. J. this morning. He's rabidly Republican, and can see nothing in the present situation but the insolence and folly of Virginia and South Carolina. Also with Charles Augustus Davis, who's insane on the other side, and inclines to throw away his vote and help that scoundrel Wood into position once more because even Havemeyer is not quite free from some taint of free-soilism. . . .

The indomitable Fernando Wood had quickly rallied his following after his defeat in 1857. Unable to regain control of Tammany Hall, he, with the aid of his brother Benjamin, had organized a new group called from its meeting-place the Mozart Hall faction. He had also curried favor with the national leaders of Democracy, taking pains to ingratiate himself with President Buchanan, and in 1858 lending the Stephen A. Douglas organization a large sum to finance the Douglas campaign against Lincoln in Illinois. Mayor Tiemann's administration, though honest and efficient, displeased many businessmen as well as the lower orders of the city. A general union of Democrats, immigrant groups, and the disreputable classes made it easy for Fernando to defeat the opposition, which was divided between Tammany Democrats and Republicans, and to capture the mayoralty for the third time in 1859. He thus became a minor power in national politics, and was able to appear at the Charleston Democratic Convention in 1860 at the head of a contesting delegation of pro-Southern views; while his brother Benjamin, purchasing the Daily News *in 1860, made that a pro-Southern organ.*

December 6. "Fernandy" Wood has won. The day has been wet and bad, but when I voted the decent part of the community seemed out in full force, and Havemeyer certainly ahead. Many Republicans were voting for him as the most available candidate, though preferring Opdyke, and everybody ready to bet two to one on his election. Downtown the talk of the street was to the same effect. The *Evening Post* and *Express*, however, talked of a heavy vote for Wood in sundry districts, and I omnibussed downtown through the drizzle at eight o'clock with some misgivings. Found a vast crowd around the great newspaper offices of Nassau and Beekman Streets, mostly rough and in high jubilation. Returns in from all but four wards, and Wood 1,600 ahead. So *vivat F. Wood, diaboli gratia* mayor of New York. . . .

A grand meeting is to be called to protest against Northern sympathy with John Brown. Like nine-tenths of the community, I am free from such sympathy and strongly disapprove of the way the *Tribune* and other papers are glorifying his memory and purring encouragement to treason and homicide. But I'm tired of Southern brag, and of seeing the North on its knees, declaring it is a good boy, and begging the South not to commit the treason and violence it is forever threatening.

December 9. Have been attending with Ellie and Jem and Murray Hoffman (who dined here) one of Sam Cowell's Drawing Room Concerts (so-called) that are given on the off nights of the French Theatre; "Lord Lovell," "The Cork Leg," and other specimens of genuine British song, the Muse of the Cider-Cellar, Pothouse "Free and Easy's" or Easies. It was intolerably funny. In costume. Not elegant, but decidedly low comedy; buffoonery, in fact. I'm weak enough to enjoy buffoonery when there is any true comic *vis* in it, and when it's free from essential coarseness and hints of dirt. This was excellent of its kind, and thoroughly enjoyed by a full house. As an actor of broad comedy, this man rivals Burton. . . . No speaker yet in the House of Representatives; but the want of an organization does not seem felt at Washington. One branch of the legislature is making buncombe speeches about John Brown and his supposed secret instigators; in the other, Southern members are denouncing a book against slavery by one Helper, and thereby advertising it with all their might. Whoever owns the copyright should be very grateful to them. There is no breach of the peace as yet. Our national gift of the gab has its drawbacks, but it is invaluable as a safety-valve. Heaven grant it or anything may save us from disruption. They say Northern members shew more backbone than heretofore. Perhaps so, but they certainly let themselves be catechized and put on their purgation by fire-eaters and disunionists in a way that seems humiliating.

The whole South seems bewildered with fright and fury. It seems an incredible infamy, but the *Richmond Enquirer* endorses the suggestion of a correspondent that the South secede from the Union and put itself under the protection of Louis Napoleon! England would be the preferable ally, but then Her Majesty is shrewdly suspected of free-soil tendencies. This transcends any atrocity I've heard attributed to Garrison or Wendell Phillips. But the ultraism of either section is enough to sicken one into renouncing our model republic for Naples or Vienna.

George Anthon is happy in the possession of a lock of John Brown's hair, and a small section of his halter; relics of S. Giovanni Bruno, obtained through the sexton of St. Mark's.

No party had a majority in the House, which was composed of 109 Republicans, 88 Buchanan Democrats, 13 Douglas Democrats, and 27 Know-Nothings. A spirited contest for the Speakership at once began. It was rendered more acrimonious and dangerous by a fierce accompanying debate on Hinton Rowan Helper's controversial book, The Impending Crisis of the South: How to Meet It, *which had been published in 1857, and which had been endorsed and promoted by many Republican members. Helper, a North Carolinian, had argued that slavery was a terrible evil to the non-slaveholding majority in the South—and had offered many facts and statistics to support his view. The abolition of slavery, in his opinion, would greatly benefit all but a small aristocratic oligarchy in the South. Many slavery leaders, comprehending how dangerous the book was, declared that they would never permit any Representative who had recommended it to become Speaker. As the debate grew angry, violence ensued. The removal of the old desks, as Strong had foreseen, made for closer contact and for more spirited and intimate discussion. Members were soon indulging in fist-fights. As practically all the Representatives were armed with knives or revolvers, many observers feared a bloody battle. Throughout December and most of January the deadlock over the Speakership continued. John Sherman of Ohio, the Republican favorite, once came within three votes of obtaining the honor. As the contest went on, tempers became badly frayed in Washington, and sectional antagonisms in the country at large increased. Numerous Southern Representatives, supported by newspapers in their part of the country, were threatening secession. Helper's book meanwhile was, of course, selling like hot cakes.*

December 15.   Cutting told me that the meeting of the John Brown sympathizers at Cooper Institute tonight, at which Wendell Phillips and others were to spout, would probably be interfered with and broken up. I'm not sure that I've much objection. Lawless disturbance and violence are always bad, of course. And I'm still Northern enough to prize freedom of speech and discussion, if only as a comparatively harmless evacuation of peccant humors, a safety-valve for mischievous impulses. Fanatics— especially mere *talking* fanatics, like Garrison and Phillips—are most effectually neutralized by being severely let alone. And in a free community people of every stamp ought, as a general rule, to have the privilege of meeting and discussing any subject undisturbed, under the protection of the law. Abuses of that privilege should be redressed by legal process, not by a mob. But there may be a practical limit to this right, in the best regulated and most law-loving society. The free-love meetings of two or three years ago would have been broken up had they not been prudently discontinued. Their ostentatious advertisement was an outrage on the general sense of right and decency. This Brown meeting is called to endorse and encourage attempts to stir up servile insurrection, with all its horrors, on our own soil—to sanction what the law of the land calls robbery and murder. If the roughs attended and howled, I cannot harshly censure them.

December 16. There was a row at the sympathetic Brunonian meeting last night, but the police kept it under control. Sundry arrests were made. Jerry Larocque spent the night in a station house.

December 19. About one hundred ornaments of our liberal and enlightened profession—one hundred "gentlemen of the bar"—were congregated in the Special Term room this morning. I scrutinized the crowd, to determine how many there were whom I would be willing to receive as visitors at this house, or rather whom I would not be annoyed and disgusted to receive. There were really not more than *three* who were not stamped by appearance, diction, or manner as belonging to a low social station, and as having no claims to the conventional title of "gentlemen." It was manifestly a mob of low-bred, illiterate, tenth-rate attorneys, though it included many successful and conspicuous practitioners. Such is the bar of New York. May our Columbia College Law School do something to elevate it.

After dinner I went to the Union Saving meeting at the Academy of Music. Crowd most dense and formidable. Happy to extricate myself without broken limbs, for the crush and pressure were serious. Whole house packed full. Even the lobbies and stairways crowded. Bonfires and ancillary meeting outside, and cannon in Union Square. Virginia should be appeased by our act of submission and apology; if she be a magnanimous commonwealth, she will hear our deprecations of her wrath and our cheers for Governor Wise will be a sweet-smelling sacrifice. But I detected little sign of spontaneous enthusiasm or hearty feeling in the plaudits of this vast assembly. It seemed a business meeting, and the points of the orators awakened a response not from the concourse itself, but from a minority of claqueurs.

When I had forced my way within the doors, somebody seemed to be making a speech. It proved to be some clerical gentleman (old Spring?) making a prayer. Then our dear friend James Brooks moved the resolutions and pitched into clerical agitators—the Cheevers, the Beechers, and others —less effectively than their demerits deserve.

Him followed Charles O'Conor with an elaborate argumentation that fully adopted the extremist south-side view of the blessings to the North that are embodied in the Southern institution. He went the furthest length in endorsing slavery as right, necessary, and beneficent. Half his speech

must have grated on the perceptions of two-thirds his audience. His want
of tact is marvelous; for example, he maintained that every Northerner
is a slave till he attains twenty-one years—there is only this difference,
that the right to his services cannot be sold in market overt here as in
South Carolina. I longed to be John Jay or Horace Greeley or Wendell
Phillips that I might take his speech and rasp it to rags. Were I an Abolitionist I would so crush O'Conor that he should never shew his head among
civilized Northerners again. But I'm not an Abolitionist—and O'Conor
was half right.[21]

When he took his seat, I was nearly flattened out between an obese
German and a long Irish gent. The compression was growing more intense
every minute, and I made my way to the door after an arduous struggle,
with ribs unbroken.

December 20. After dinner to a primary election in Nineteenth
Street—the Eighteenth Ward Republican Association. My Republicanism
is not ardent just now, and I only went at the urgent request of D. D. Field
and Judge Cowles, and because it's of great importance to get the ward out
of "bad hands," namely, the faction of one Manierre whom I take for a
very Pecksniffian personage, and into "good hands"; I don't know exactly
whose, but I am in that crowd, it seems, for my name is on the opposition
ticket as delegate to some convention or committee. There was a large
attendance. Roughs preponderated, and I heard frequent denunciations
of "my" ticket as having "too much kid glove on it, by God!" So, I rather
suspect I'm defeated, which I shall not in the least regret.

Called at Mrs. Ruggles's for Ellie and saw Governor Hunt, who spoke
at the Union meeting last night.

December 21. . . . J. A. Stevens, Jr., called to say that "our ticket"
succeeded last night by a large majority. So the country is probably safe.
I'm elected to something, but don't know what and don't much care. I must
see more clearly what the Republican Party means to do before I consecrate
my vast energy and influence to its service.

The medical students of Philadelphia belonging to the Southern states
have held a meeting and resolved to evacuate that city as Northern and
unclean and to investigate nosology and the materia medica at Southern
institutions. They are to be received with military honors by the silly

[21] At this Union-saving meeting Mayor Tiemann, ex-Governor Washington Hunt,
and John A. Dix also spoke, and letters were read from ex-Presidents Fillmore and
Pierce. But as Strong indicates, public sentiment in the North was hardening against
the proslavery men and the men who refused to recognize that slavery had a moral
aspect.

citizens of Richmond and carried gratis over Southern railroads. Probably their prescriptions and prognoses will not be more sagacious and beneficent in consequence of this step. They will know less about calomel and quinine, and vital statistics at the South may be affected ten years hence by their exodus. But the proceeding is rather significant. . . .

Lieber in deep affliction because our Columbia College Law School committee decided that examination on the subjects of his lectures should not be conditions of a degree. So I learn from Mr. S. B. Ruggles. Lieber says his chair is degraded, and so on. Mr. Ruggles sympathizes with him and asks whether we want the Law School to turn out mere attorneys. Of course, high and liberal culture is most desirable, but we are not yet in a position to insist upon it. We cannot yet, in the infancy of the school, require young attorneys and lawyer's clerks to sacrifice a couple of hours daily to political science and legal philosophy. It is a great point gained that so many (upwards of sixty) consent to come in to be taught the practicabilities of their profession.

Pity Mr. Ruggles seems inclined to withdraw himself from the College Board and its committees. So strong a man could afford to overlook the little slight of Fish's election to the presidency of the board.

December 22. After dinner with Ellie, Mrs. Georgey Peters, and Walter Cutting to Wallack's. *Everybody's Friend*, a three-act comedy, by Brougham[22] (I believe), very clever and well-acted by Brougham, Lester and Wallack. . . .

No material change in the state of the nation. It's a sick nation, and I fear it must be worse before it's better. The growing, vigorous North must sooner or later assert its right to equality with the stagnant, semi-barbarous South, and that assertion must bring on a struggle and convulsion. It must come. Pity it could not be postponed some twenty years, when Northern preponderance would be overwhelming. If Northern Abolitionism precipitate the crisis and force the battle on us *now*, it will be a fearful and doubtful contest.

I cannot find out why it is against the law of God for one man to own another. But I am better satisfied every day that slavery demoralizes and degrades the slave-owners. For example, when John Brown's gang was finally defeated and captured, one of them was carried wounded and dying into a certain house at Harper's Ferry. The victors proposed to kill him there and then. A young woman (Miss Christina Foulkes or Fowkes, sister-in-law of the proprietor of the house) threw herself between the

[22] John Brougham (1814–1880), Irish actor and dramatist.

wounded prisoner and the muskets of his captors and implored them to spare him—to let the law dispose of him, and said and did all that the kind, merciful instincts of a good girl would naturally suggest. Whereupon these chevalier gentlemen dragged him out and killed him in the street. Northern newspapers noticed this fact, and there was talk of getting up a service of plate for this humane young woman. So she is compelled by stress of popular feeling (no one can doubt that *something* compelled her to deny the generous impulses of her womanhood) to write and publish a letter certifying that she was actuated by no regard for the life of an Abolitionist, but only and exclusively by an apprehension that her sister's carpet might be stained and damaged by an Abolitionist's blood.

December 23.   Fine day. Cold. Diligent in Wall Street, though wasted an hour attending a meeting called at Trinity Church to see about raising funds to put Lamson's Church for Americans in Paris on a permanent foundation. . . .

We went to Cowell's again. He is wonderfully clever and funny, but this is my third attendance. It will suffice for the present. The house was full and there were people there we knew. People have begun to find him out and he will become popular. Though he deals in the very lowest of comedy, there is not even a whisper or a look of aught uncleanly in his performance, wherein he has the advantage of our theatrical people generally. For although the stage has greatly improved in that particular, one seldom hears a farce or comedy in which there is not some *double entendre* or questionable joke that would not be tolerated in the presence of ladies elsewhere.

December 25, SUNDAY.   Weather appropriate, clear and cold. Yesterday afternoon at three, I attended the "Children's Festival" at Trinity Church, which was crowded. Choral service: carol by the children, with accompaniment of the organ and of the chimes in the steeple, was very pretty. Uptown I worked hard to send off presents and harder at unpacking and arranging those that kept coming in. Ellie rejoiced greatly over mine to her—certain glass and silver dinner-table decorations that I knew she coveted. She had got for me a very carefully finished and colored cabinet picture of herself (a photograph elaborated into a miniature). Considered as a likeness, it is a libel, I regret to say. All the treasures for the children were duly marshalled on the piano and tables as usual, and a grand display they made.

Also, there is a big Christmas tree in the hall, surmounted by the flag of our country, on which Mrs. Ellie has with great care and labor inscribed "THE UNION FOREVER"! . . .

The first business of this morning was, of course, the introduction of the two little men to the treasures set forth in the music room. The spectacle was overpowering. Both were driven nearly wild with ecstasy and wonder. Then to church; music rather good and Higby's sermon very respectable. Dined at Mr. Ruggles's, taking the two boys with us—both of whom did credit to their bringing up. After dinner, Mr. and Mrs. D. C. Murray and John Sherwood and his very agreeable wife came in. . . .

This has been a happy and sunshiny Christmas. Would that the good and genial influences of the day might make themselves felt in soothing the acrimonies of our national family quarrel—that He Who "maketh men to be of one mind in a house," Whose "Name shall be called Wonderful, Counselor, the Prince of Peace," and Whose advent on earth Christendom celebrates today with traditional usages of reconciliation between parted friends and of re-affirmance of all social and family ties by words and tokens of kindliness, could be heard in our discordant Councils: that the government might now (as surely hereafter) "be upon His shoulders" and no longer administered by contending sectional factions, each inspired by hate, ambition, and selfishness, or, in other words, by the Devil. . . .

This present political crisis promises to divide the Republican party of 1856. Its radicalism will become avowed Abolitionism. Conservative Republicans will have to organize independently. Bob LeRoy identifies himself with the extreme Republican Lefts and went on the platform with a revolver in his pocket when George William Curtis lectured in Philadelphia.

December 28. Lieber came to see me Monday morning in great sorrow and soreness. Perhaps it may be worth while to reconsider our action about his Law School lectures.

December 30. Worked with decent efficiency in Wall Street. Dined on roast oysters at Downing's, and spent the afternoon on duty at Bank for Savings, which I visited this morning also, taking down with me to the Manhattan Bank a carriage-load of specie and bills accumulated during the week.

This was the Women's afternoon, no he-depositors being admitted. The crowd was dense, garrulous, and mephitic. Biddy generally brings a young baby with her, if she has one, thinking that she will be "attended to" the sooner. There must have been thirty babies, at least, when we began, and the aggregate of their howlings was something grand and terrible. But I retained my presence of mind and executed my high office with dignified composure, tempering the rigor with which I enforced the rules by a certain suavity of manner peculiar to myself. I presented, no doubt, a sublime spectacle. . . .

Store in Pearl Street just above Wall (west side) is threatening to tumble down. The front wall has separated from the side wall, the solution of continuity being manifested by an ugly crack that extends from the roof downward through one or two stories. Police have stretched ropes across the street, and a crowd was watching patiently this morning in the cold for the crash. Another storehouse on Broad Street crumbled down from its own weight, and that of its contents, a week ago and killed one or two innocent outsiders who happened to be in its neighborhood.

House of Representatives not yet organized.

December 31. This year and this decade will soon be among the shadows of past times. It seems scarce possible ten years have passed since we went out of the forties. They have been ten years of change. Two more have been given to me—the two little men whose portraits Ellie and I have just been admiring: God protect them both—and two more have been taken away, my mother and my father, since December 31, 1849.

INDEX